methods
of
Research
in
sport
sciences

Dedications

This book is dedicated to:
Ravid—The analytical mind
Noam—The creative mind
Sharon—The critical mind
Malibu and Sierra—The minds humans only dream of having
Hony—The incomparable mind, and the devoted
wife and mother who unites and navigates us all.

Gershon Tenenbaum

Robin, whose trust and encouragement made it all happen

Marcy P. Driscoll

Methods

of

Research

in

Sport
Sciences

quantitative and
qualitative Approaches

**Gershon
Tenenbaum
Marcy P.
Driscoll**

Meyer & Meyer Sport

British Library Cataloguing in Publication Data
A catalogue record for this book is available from the British Library

Methods of Research in Sport Sciences
Gershon Tenenbaum / Marcy P. Driscoll
Oxford: Meyer & Meyer Sport (UK) Ltd., 2005
ISBN-10: 1-84126-133-5
ISBN-13: 978-1-84126-133-1

© 2005 by Meyer & Meyer Sport (UK) Ltd.
Aachen, Adelaide, Auckland, Budapest, Graz, Johannesburg,
New York, Olten (CH), Oxford, Singapore, Toronto
Member of the World
Sports Publishers' Association (WSPA)
www.w-s-p-a.org
Printed and bound by: Finidr s. r. o., Český Těšín
ISBN-10: 1-84126-133-5
ISBN-13: 978-1-84126-133-1
E-Mail: verlag@m-m-sports.com

CONTENTS

CONTENTS

PREFACE

This book is aimed at teaching students and experienced researchers to theorize, conduct, analyze, and critically reflect on their research intentions and projects. Our view takes a somewhat different approach to the study of sport and exercise behaviors in that it encourages the researcher to integrate data of various sources and different nature, be aware of the limitations of one single method, and learn to take advantage of all the information available in the research environment. Science, we believe, is not just asking questions, designing a study, carrying it out, analyzing data, and writing discussion and conclusions; it is much more than that. *Science*, we believe, is a term that entails a sound theoretical and conceptual framework, that may be challenged, investigated, and altered by research methods that best fit this aim.

It is our aim to educate students and young researchers to become scholars with *wide horizons, critical thinking*, and *integration of thoughts and concepts* to enable them to become professionals with a wide research experience. Throughout the various chapters in the book, we introduce both the *concepts* and the *techniques* that operationalize them. In several cases we show how *qualitative and quantitative* concepts can be integrated to provide a greater meaning than each one of them alone. We also introduce critical views on the inferential statistical techniques, and encourage researchers to further elaborate on the best methods for studying questions.

Our aim is to teach the *principles of research methodology* and to introduce *alternative methods*, to enable the learner to apply and integrate them, and to develop an *integrated approach* towards research. This approach is not deterministic in its essence. We teach the learner to think and not to imitate what is recommended in this book, but rather clarify the research questions first. When one feels that questionnaires are biased, why shouldn't an alternative approach be adapted, or shown how one approach of inquiry is limited in its scope as compared to another? We urge the readers of this book to seek different methods, to examine their questions, to use alternative or mixed methods to better account for the phenomena they look for, and to find *various explanations* to their results. In an era of computer domination, let the computer do the calculations and computations and the human mind create and think.

In sport and exercise sciences, just like in other academic domains, the quality of the research is as good as the techniques of data collection. Once these tools are not sufficiently reliable and valid, it is almost impossible to rely on them in any study. In addition to the *quantitative research methods* we introduce *qualitative methods*, which enable the researcher to make meaning of verbal expressions, and at the same time give freedom to interpretations.

Many of the techniques of data collection, data treatment (screening), and data analyses that we introduce in this book are identical to techniques that are used in almost all the other domains of inquiry. However, due to the uniqueness of the sport and exercise sciences domain in which physiology and psychology, history and sociology, learning of skills and information processing are studied simultaneously, one should apply the method or triangulate methods that best represent and examine the questions of intention.

The dualism and holism of the body-mind concept, the coupling of perception and action, the combination of biological, physical, psychological, educational, sociological, historical, and philosophical domains into one *integrated concept*—called *sport and exercise sciences*—is undoubtedly a *unique* one that needs a comprehensive research methodology to supplement it.

The environment in which exercisers and athletes operate and are studied can be divided into three categories: *natural environment, semi-natural environment, and artificial and fully controlled environment. Natural environment* is constrained-free, and can vary from being task specific (e.g., the game of tennis) to being general (playing in the school yard during a break).

Semi-natural (manipulated) environment is established by letting people function in a natural manner, but manipulating it intentionally (e.g., new play equipment in the school yard) and observing how they behave. *Artificial*, fully controlled, environment is one we use in the laboratory. The environmental components are under control and we know precisely what the experimental conditions are. We observe and measure the behaviors in a manner that gives no doubt as to its reliability and objectivity. Each of these environments has its merit in sport and exercise sciences research. The *questions* that are associated with them are illustrated as follows:

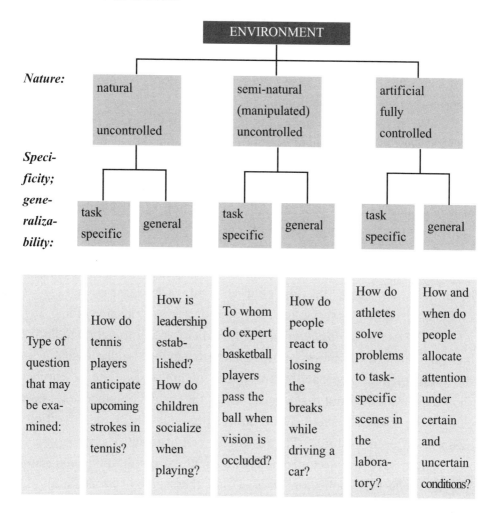

The study of exercise and sport integrate both objective and expressive (i.e., perceived) measures. Heart rate, lactate level, and hormones are important indicators of physical effort, but they are insufficient indicators for the variations among people's perceptions of effort, pain, and discomfort. To study effort perception one should also question the degree of commitment, determination, and efficacy associated with the intentions to complete the task. Such an approach means to triangulate the resources of information in order to better account for variations in human behaviors.

This book was written with the intention of initiating *balanced* methodological strategies used to answer questions in a research process. The research approach we advocate here consists of asking the correct questions in the domain of sport, exercise, and physical activity. This approach states that *questions of interest* can be derived from the relevant theories, but also from the domain itself.

We strive to study *behaviors* that occur in the sport, exercise, and physical activity environment. Sometimes the explanations given to these behaviors are not adequately sufficient. In other cases, the same behaviors are not defined in the context that they occur. For example, the motivation to adhere in a physical task and tolerate exertion is not identical to the motivation to achieve high scores in school. Thus, asking questions relies on defining and categorizing the behaviors that occurs in the environment we wish to study. Then, the questions we ask should be related to behaviors that occur in this context. Only when these stages are established, can we observe, measure, and/or assess (interpret) them.

The use of *multiple methods* of *data collection* to get quantitative and qualitative information on designated behaviors is also essential in the multi-method approach to research methodology. The researcher should always ask about the consistency of the results obtained, e.g., how can one be sure about replicating the results under the same conditions again in different cultures? The researcher ought to investigate *how* and *why* people vary when confronted with identical conditions (*inter*) and *how* and *why* their behaviors vary within themselves (*intra*). Studying human beings is not identical to studying objects. The laws that govern the universe are somewhat different from the laws which govern human behavior. We are more susceptible to change. We do not respond to environmental conditions in the same manner every time. We vary among ourselves and within ourselves. The *models* and *theories* that account for human behaviors should therefore be comprehensive and flexible in nature. Each theory is limited in the extent it can generalize its explanations and predictions across conditions and situations. The researcher should be aware of the conditions under which the participants exhibit the behavior derived from the theory. Traditional methodologists term it *external validity* of the experiment. We define a multi-method approach within research methodology as one that takes into account the *theory* and the *environment* using multiple sources of judgment and measurement that allow *critical views* and *alternative argumentations* to be made. We introduce in this book a research methodology for sport and exercise sciences that meets these requirements.

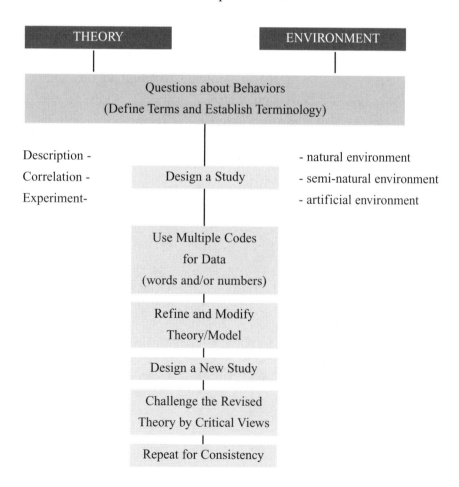

This handbook describes the various processes of gaining scientific knowledge. The multi-method approach offers a wide variety of insights, ideas, and proposals in regard to realizing research in the wide range of sport and exercise sciences. Only if the available methods are known, the researcher is able to choose the appropriate research approach for a given research question.

CHAPTER 1: RESEARCH PLAN AND DESIGN

Science starts with problems, problems associated with the explanation of the behaviour of some aspects of the world or universe. Scientists propose falsifiable hypotheses as solutions to the problem. The conjectured hypotheses are then criticized, evaluated and tested. Some will be quickly eliminated. Others might prove more successful. These must be subjected to even more stringent criticism and testing. When a hypothesis that has successfully withstood a wide range of rigorous tests is eventually falsified, a new problem, hopefully far removed from the original solved problem, has emerged. This new problem calls for the invention of new hypotheses, followed by renewed criticism and testing. And so the process continues indefinitely. It can never be said of a theory that it is true, however while it has withstood rigorous tests, but it can hopefully be said that a current theory is superior to its predecessors in the sense that it is able to withstand tests that falsified those predecessors or theories (Chalmers, 1982, p.45).

1.1   FIRST STEPS FOR CONSIDERATION

Chapter 1 introduces the first stages of theory and hypotheses construction. The logical steps involved in this construction development of theories and hypotheses are outlined in detail: from curiosity and personal reflections of a topic in question to a systematic literature search.

Any systematic search for information can be considered research. Today, electronic resources enable the researcher to rapidly review the literature fully or partially. The technological advances change how science and research is conducted. We claim that this introduction of advanced technologies has increased the demands on researchers in that it shapes the theoretical concepts, which are based on the literature.

This chapter is aimed at describing both the technologies and the methods of integrating research outcomes with personal intentions when designing a research project. The chapter is structured as follows:

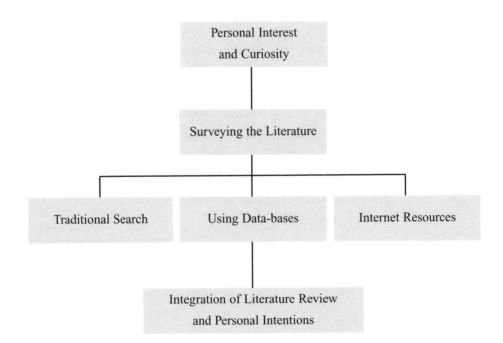

Contents

(1) Showing Interest and Curiosity

Every scientific inquiry begins with a question or a series of questions, which result from curiosity. Curiosity is a consequence of the interest people develop while interacting with various objects and aspects of their environment.

For example, athletes who are interested in improving their personal achievements show curiosity, which leads them to ask questions such as, "which erogenic aids can I use to help me to enhance my performance?" A question such as this leads to inquiry and investigation. The typical sequence of events, which leads to an answer to a question (illustrated in figure 1), originates from curiosity.

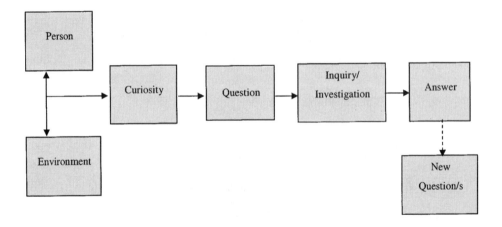

Figure 1.1   The process resulting in scientific inquiry.

The first initiative a person generally takes when aspiring to learn more about a topic or field is typically to contact knowledgeable people (experts) in the domain of interest. Since humans are limited in their ability to memorize all of the details on a given subject, the first step in the inquiry process is to conduct a literature review in order to become familiar with relevant information in the domain. The technological advancements in recent years have facilitated the review of literature by the use of computers with direct access to databases. The most efficient means for proficiently reviewing the literature is discussed next.

(2)   Surveying and Reviewing the Literature

The first things to remember when beginning to survey and review the literature is to keep in mind that:

The literature is wide, detailed, and can be categorized into various levels.
Choose the level which satisfies your needs.

Despite the fact that we often think our new ideas are original and innovative, generally our curiosity has also been of interest to others in the past. While surveying the literature, we may often find that others have previously, in part addressed our question or some aspect of the topic, although perhaps they arrived at the question through a different reasoning process. In most cases, the survey of the literature takes us back several years to the landmark articles that first attempted to address the topic of interest. It is necessary to decide what to SELECT from the plethora of informational materials. At this point in the process, we should use several criteria to assist in the decision process.

The first criterion is:

THE ACADEMIC LEVEL OF THE INFORMATIONAL RESOURCES
SHOULD BE APPROPRIATE FOR OUR INTEREST LEVEL.

Scientists often rely on the most complex sources such as empirical studies which performed under controlled conditions, used reliable and valid tools, and boast high external validity. However, coaches, teachers, and students who have more practical or applied concerns may find that coaching periodicals and popular magazines supply them with necessary information they seek to answer their questions. It is important to recognize that this type of resources may not meet the robust and scientific criteria of a systematic inquiry, but provide very useful and relevant information.
The second criterion is:

DETERMINE HOW CURRENT AND RELIABLE THE RESOURCES ARE.

When the literature consists of several informational resources with differing publication dates, there is a tendency to prefer and select the most up to date sources. A common assumption is that the most recent sources are better than the older resources, however, this is not always true. the case. Many "dated" sources are classic; seminal investigations can and should be used as evidence for argumentation at any time. Begin by first read the abstracts of the articles, or even solicit an expert opinion before making a selection decision. Remember, in many instances "an old wine is a good wine".

The third criterion concerns:

THE APPROPRIATE TERMS THAT RELATE TO THE DOMAIN OF INTEREST.

This is an important criterion because several informational resources assist us in finding the best terms to locate the literature that was published on the subject matter under investigation. However, too many terms and descriptors for searching literature in data bases may result in an "information explosion". How to effectively use keywords and terms to search the literature will be discussed later.

The fourth principal requires us to:

BE FOCUSED, PAY ATTENTION TO RELATED VIEWS, CONCERNS, CONSTRUCTS, AND CONCEPTS.

Once a decision is made as to which resources to use, it is common for attention to shift to other views and concepts, which have not been considered in the initial investigation stage. Diverting interest is often a more common problem for the young researcher, but also happens to the experienced researcher. Preserving a balance between maintaining focus on the original ideas versus new ideas found in the literature is difficult yet critical.

Unfortunately, the exact balance cannot be precisely defined as it depends on many factors pertaining to both the researcher's wishes and the domain of investigation, however this skill (like all others) is developed through practice.

It should be noted that surveying and reviewing the literature may result in asking more questions, modifying the original questions, or even finding answers and consequently becoming satisfied, or alternatively come up with new questions. These possibilities are graphically presented in Figure 1.2.

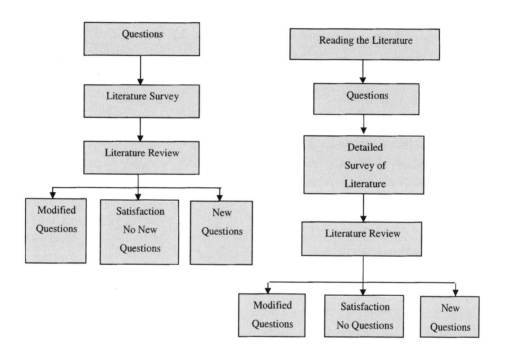

Figure 1.2   Possible relations between asking Questions, surveying the literature, and reviewing the literature.

Library Research in the Age of Information Technology and the Web
by Gretchen Ghent

2.1   Introduction

Over the past two decades the research process and methodologies used in college and university libraries have changed dramatically. Access to library resources through the card catalogue and printed indexing services has been replaced by the multi-point and convenient access of online public access catalogues (OPACs) and online periodical article databases. Computer hardware and software developments have had a profound effect on the life of the researcher, for now most researchers have access to automated libraries and have personal computers to compose, store and transmit research. Graphics programs enhance and edify research work. Publishing can now be done on desktop, and websites can easily be established.

While information technology has played a great part in enhancing research methods and strategies, this technology is a still just a tool to be used to its limit. The researcher, however, has the important responsibility of learning how to effectively and efficiently use the computer-based systems. This requires a more thorough awareness of the procedures to access information and a more indepth knowledge of database structures and features. The decision-making processes involved in determining what sources are appropriate for the particular research problem or term paper are a critical skill. Consultation of colleagues and academic experts in the field also remain an important part of the traditional research procedure. In addition, the fundamental skills of competently synthesizing readings and research, and clear writing are expected of the undergraduate and graduate researcher.

This chapter will take the sports sciences researcher through the steps necessary to find a topic, discover appropriate sources and learn how to use key online databases.

2.2   Starting Points

When attempting a complex search, the organized researcher keeps good notes on where, when and what was searched. A standby of many researchers has been the 4x6 card where sources are listed, notes made as to usefulness or what was searched. For the contemporary researcher use of a laptop computer or PC with the usual word processing package can be augmented by the addition of bibliographic software. *Reference Manager, ProCite* and *Endnote* are three bibliographic software packages used by many academic researchers to download results of searches, store and produce bibliographies.

In the more modest price range is *Endnote* that has a strong bibliographic database program where the researcher can download citations from most databases or create a personal list (the system calls it a library) of bibliographic references. The data elements in your personal "library" of bibliographic references can be manipulated to conform to a particular periodical publisher's bibliographic style (has over 16 styles). *Endnote* supports the ISO (International Standards Organization) computer communication standard of Z39.50. Many libraries have the databases mounted on server hardware (ERL) that support version 3 of the Z39.50 protocol. The result is that records from databases, including SPORTDiscus, ERIC, Sociofile, can be downloaded easily into *Endnote, ProCite* and *Reference Manager*.

These three citation software packages, available in Windows or Mac versions, can be found at the ISI ResearchSoft website:

http://thomsonisiresearchsoft.com/

For the undergraduate sports sciences researcher, a course professor or instructor usually assigns a term paper topic as part of the course requirements. For the graduate student, a research topic for a Master's or PhD thesis usually results from many discussions with academic colleagues and advisors and the investigation of the literature in a very specialized field. This type of research project requires an original investigation of a problem.

Prior to beginning an original piece of graduate student research, there should be an extensive search of the extant literature. This includes searching indexing/abstracting services and databases for other master's and PhD theses and dissertations. These latter databases (e.g. Dissertation Abstracts or ProQuest Digital Dissertations), Kinesiology Abstracts (formerly University of Oregon, International Institute for Sport & Human Performance, Microform Publications of Human Movement Studies, http://kinpubs.uoregon.edu/KinAbs.html) assure the graduate researcher that the proposed original research has not been done before. (Note: all KinAbs theses citations appear in SPORTDiscus)

2.3   Your Library and The Library's Online Catalogue (OPAC)

For those researchers who have not utilized a college or university library, the first problem is to decipher the organizational intricacy of the library. In academic libraries, most libraries maintain a reference or information services desk. Professional librarians and knowledgeable assistants who can be consulted about the literature of a subject area staff this service.

One of the reference librarians may also have subject specialties in the sport sciences field and are variously called the kinesiology librarian, the human kinetics and exercise science librarian or physical education librarian. This professionally trained person can be invaluable in recommending the best sources for a particular topic, has in-depth knowledge of particular resources and should be used as a consultant on search strategies.

If the researcher is not familiar with the library's online public access catalogue (OPAC) the staff in many libraries offer instruction sessions in the use of the library's OPAC or, on how to use the databases available in the library (the OPAC is a database of the home library's holdings of books, serials, audiovisual and other materials). Most integrated OPACs also show the circulation status (whether the book is signed out to a borrower) and location of each volume.

The enterprising, computer literate researcher, with the appropriate computer and internet access, can discover much about the library's online database offerings (the OPAC and periodical databases) by experimentation, reading the help screens and the introductory sections in the home library's "how to use the OPAC."

Prior to commencing the search of the OPAC, the *Library of Congress List of Subject Headings,* should be consulted for the suitable subject headings. In some libraries, especially the public libraries that use the Dewey Decimal Classification, the *Sears List of Subject Headings*, (17th ed, NY: Wilson, 2000) is the key to this numerical subject classification system. After determination of the appropriate subject headings, a comprehensive search can take place. In those libraries which have implemented a second generation OPAC, the researcher has more access points and flexibility in finding needed sources, e.g. Boolean searching, book contents notes.

2.4   Reference Sources, Annual Review Publications, Manuals and Handbooks

As mentioned previously most libraries maintain a reference collection or a place where dictionaries, indexes, manuals, and encyclopaedias are available for consultation.

2.4.1   Specialized Encyclopaedias and Dictionaries

Most disciplines have a long heritage of specialized encyclopaedias and dictionaries that serve the researcher with definitions, background information, and overviews of specific topics. Sport and physical education has older well-known titles that provide a good historical foundation (*The Oxford Companion to Sports & Games*, London, Oxford University Press, 1975). These are partially supplanted by more in-depth and up-to-date sources including:

Encyclopaedia of Sports Science

Edited by John Zumerchik

NY: Macmillan Library Reference, 1997. 2 vols.

This two-part encyclopaedia examines the physics of a wide-range of individual sports and, in Part Two, the physiology of sport. This latter section is entitled: The Body. Each section deals with certain aspects including aging, ankle & foot, body composition, energy & metabolism, female athletes, heart & circulatory system, nutrition and many other aspects.

Encyclopaedia of World Sport: from Ancient Times to the Present.

Edited by David Levinson and Karen Christensen

Santa Barbara, CA: ABC-CLIO, 1996. 3 vols.

This encyclopaedia covers nearly 300 sports as distinguished from games and other leisure activities. Each article presents a history of the sport, its basic rules and goals, its relationship to society and culture, and the nature of the competition. The authors, from many countries, draw on the scholarly literature of each sport. Although there is less emphasis on sporting facts, nevertheless some of the articles include significant statistical information.

Oxford Dictionary of Sports Science and Medicine, 2nd ed.

Edited by Michael Kent

NY: Oxford University Press, 1998

An up-to-date dictionary of terminology in the sports sciences field.

2.4.2   *Other Resources to Consult*

Most subject bibliographies with the exception of those which survey the historical literature or literature not covered by the online database, are out of date by the time they are published. The indexing and abstracting services, in print form or online, all have a subject approach, usually have a wide coverage and should be utilized, in most cases, to search for current research and citations.

One type of publication that may be of assistance in finding ideas or reviewing the latest information for research topic is the "annual review" publication. In most instances these publications present a yearly overview of current research topics. The authors selected for these publications are usually well known and respected in their specific fields.

An important source sponsored by the American College of Sports Medicine covers behavioral, biochemical, biomechanical, clinical, physiological and rehabilitation topics in exercise science. It is:

> *Exercise and Sport Sciences Reviews*
> 1973 to date (1973-1999 as an annual, 2000+ quarterly)
> Hagerstown, Md: Lippincott, Williams & Wilkins

Other sources of overview articles appear in many disciplines. These annual reviews may or may not have applied sport review articles per se but do reflect the important topics within the discipline which may have applications to sport. The following two are representative of the many disciplines:

> *Annual Review of Medicine*
> Palo Alto, CA: Annual Reviews, 1950 to date
> *Annual Review of Psychology*
> Palo Alto, CA: Annual Reviews, 1950 to date
> Website: http://www.annualreviews.org/

In addition, one other type of "annual review" is the *Year Book of Sports Medicine* (Chicago: Year Book Medical Publishers & St. Louis: Mosby, 1979 to date), which surveys a wide range of journals of proven value and selects periodical articles from these journals that represent significant advances or statements of advanced clinical principles. Each periodical article citation includes an abstract and commentary by a knowledgeable researcher.

As part of the research project, especially at the advanced level, the researcher may want to include tests or testing as part of the original research. To find the most appropriate tests, consultation of test bibliographies is useful. In the field of educational psychology there are many directories to including the well-known *Mental Measurements Yearbook, 14th ed.* (Lincoln, Neb: Buros Institute of Mental Measurements & University of Nebraska Press, 2001, Website: http://www.unl.edu/buros/). This source does include some relevant tests for the physical education/sport sciences field and should be consulted along with the more specialized directories which include:

> *Directory of Psychological Tests in the Sport and Exercise Sciences, 2nd ed.* Edited by Andrew C. Ostrow
> Morgantown, WV: Fitness Information Technology, 1996
> Website: http://www.fitinfotech.com/
> Note: Individual tests also available online for a small fee.
> *Kirby's Guide to Fitness and Motor Performance Tests*
> Edited by Ronald F. Kirby
> Cape Girardeau, MO: BenOak Publishing Co., 1991

To augment these convenient tools, the databases (*SPORTDiscus, PsycINFO, Medline*) should also be searched. In some cases the name of a test is used as an official descriptor or subject heading but it is also important to search databases in a free text mode. Frequently the name of the test or its abbreviation is mentioned in the abstract (for details on these techniques consult section 2.6 following).

For a guide and list of tests found in SPORTDiscus, consult http://www.ucalgary.ca/library/ssportsite/sguide.html and look for the *Search Guide For Finding Test/Testing Information in SPORTDiscus.*

2.5 Online Indexing/Abstracting Services: How to Find Periodical Articles and Current Research

Searching indexing and abstracting services has come full circle in past decade. Prior to the availability of computerized, online database services, the researcher performed a literature search for periodical articles in the printed indexing services. This task required a dedicated searcher, for there were usually fewer access points to each periodical article and many hours were spent going from the subject index to the "main entry" or periodical article citation. Cumulative subject and author indexes were published in the more indepth indexing services that tended to decrease research time. These sources are still needed and are utilized when the subject matter warrants a historical search or the researcher needs earlier literature where research methods or topics have stood the test of time. Most online database services began in the late 1960s so topics which dictate searches prior to the 1960s need to be conducted manually.

Many researchers in the 1960s and 1970s, when using some academic libraries, could not search the online databases but required intermediaries, the librarian skilled in online searching. In the 1980s and 1990s with improved computer storage and software, and advent of the CD ROM, the researcher, once again, has control of the research task. Along with this control, however, is a most important responsibility for the researcher. The researcher now must learn the key elements of the database in order that efficient, effective and competent searches are performed. To accomplish this, the researcher should acquire a good working knowledge of the database structure and its basic conventions. This information can be found online in the "Help" section of the online database, or in the introductory sections of the printed thesauri. The printed thesauri are usually located in the library's reference area or are available online with the database.

To illustrate the important features of a simple and advanced search, a sample search of the international sport database, *SPORTDiscus* and *Medline* will be used. The scope of these two databases is described below.

SPORTDiscus

Ottawa, Ontario: Sport Information Resource Centre

1975 to date, Updated monthly

Thesaurus: *SIRCThesaurus, 2002 edition* (on CD ROM or as part of the online database Website: http://www.sirc.ca/products/sportdiscus.cfm)

A database of over 650,000 records to periodical articles, books, book chapters and essays, conference papers, reports, and videotapes on all aspects of sports sciences, psychology, administration, sociology, coaching, training, physical education, physical fitness, and recreation. The bulk of the University of Oregon's Kinesiology Publications collection (formerly *Health, Physical Education and Microforms Collection)* from 1949 to date is also included as is the discontinued SIRLS database (sociology of sport). The database is available on CD ROM and from online search vendors, Silverplatter,

Ebscohost and OVID. *Heracles*, the French database produced by the INSEP in Paris; *Atlantes*, the Spanish language sport database; the *Catalogue du Musée Olympique*, Lausanne, Switzerland; and the catalogue of the Amateur Athletic Foundation of Los Angeles are now incorporated into SPORTDiscus.

> *Medline (Medlars onLINE)*
> Bethesda, Maryland: National Library of Medicine
> 1966 to date, Updated weekly
> Thesaurus: *Medical Subject Headings* (MeSH Descriptors), Annual
> Print edition: Medline corresponds to three print indexes: *Index Medicus, Index to Dental Literature, International Nursing Index*
> PubMed Web Access: http://www.ncbi.nlm.nih.gov/PubMed/
> A database of biomedical periodical articles, indexed from over 3,700 international periodicals in all languages and covers clinical and experimental medicine, pharmacology, and, for the sport researcher, sports medicine, physiology, exercise science, doping and drugs. The PubMed database, available free for personal use only, has access to 14 million records in the Medline and PreMedline databases. A MeSH browser is available at this NLM website also.

2.5.1 *Performing Searches in a Key Database*

Most online databases have a similar structure and each contain units of information called **records** or similarly known as a reference or citation. Within each record there are a number of **fields** where specific information is placed. For instance a typical record structure for a periodical article found in the *SPORTDiscus* shows the short field name along with the long name.

	Shown are the most important fields:
TI	Title of article
AU	Author of article
JN	Journal title
IS	International Standard Serial Number
PY	Publication Year
LA	Language of article

DT	Document type (Includes serial, monograph, book analytic, microform, videotape, URL)
LE	Level of difficulty (includes basic, intermediate level or advanced)
DE	Descriptors (subject headings from the *SIRCThesaurus* applied by the indexer)
AB	Abstract of article (sometimes written by the indexer or written by author of the article
CP	Country of publication (A UNESCO number which designates a country, e.g. 840=United States, 124=Canada)
SX	SportExpress document delivery number (same as Accessions No.)
AN	Accessions Number (a unique number for this record only)

The AU, TI, JN, PY, DE and LA fields are very common among databases. Some databases do not assign a level of difficulty (LE) because their database indexes only in the research-type articles (*Medline, Biosis, Sociological Abstracts*). *SPORTDiscus* serves a wider and more varied clientele.

The Use of Boolean Operators

Boolean logic originates from mathematics and is used in manipulating sets in a precise and logical fashion. Boolean logic supports three ways in which sets can be combined using the operators: **and, or, not**. Databases use these Boolean operators and, to a limited extent, so do many search engines used to find websites.

A Sample Search in SPORTDiscus

To illustrate a typical search, an example comes from a particular course professor who suggested a term paper on the topic: "To examine the tension and mood states of swimmers prior to or during competitions."

The first step is to interpret the request and identify key words and synonyms. In this case, to get one started, the words **mood, tension, swimmer, competitive** can be considered. Thus a searcher can begin by:

Step 1. After signing on to the SPORTDiscus database, check the descriptor terminology in the *SIRCThesaurus* which is available online with the searching software or consult the CD ROM edition.

Step 2. The researcher discovers from the thesaurus that:

a) **mood** is not used as a descriptor but **emotion** is

b) **tension** is not used either but **anxiety** and **stress** are used

c) **swimmer** is not used but looking down the list, **swimming** is used

d) **competitive** is not used but **competition** or **competitive behaviour** is.

The thorough researcher should also look up the most specific terms. In this case, the researcher looks up **anxiety** and finds under the narrower terms (NT) specific names of tests, the broader term (BT) **emotion** and related terms (RT) that include stress and three other terms which are deemed not suitable for this search problem.

Step 3. After looking at the RTs, BTs, NTs (narrow terms) for all of the above, it is decided which terms are most specific and elemental. It seems that the most succinct terms are **anxiety** and **stress** and **swimming** and the search is set up in this way:

Search 1) anxiety or stress

Search 2) swimming

Search 3) "and" the results of Searches 1 and 2

This search uses the two boolean operators "or" and "and" to perform the search. The boolean operator "or" is used for similar terms, and where it is the intention of the searcher to extract a record where any one of the "or" terms appears in a record. Thus the record will be retrieved when, in Search 3, the "and" operator is used on the results of Searches 1 and 2.

For instance the combinations can be; swimming and anxiety, swimming and stress appearing in each record.

Depending on the software the researcher is using, it is important that for the initial search the descriptor field is designated, otherwise the system will search "free text" meaning anywhere in the record. Most web-based software allows the researcher to specify the field to be searched.

Or a search expression can also be stated as:

anxiety in de or **stress** in de

The results of the search may look like this:

Results	Search Term(s)
#3 173 Items	(#1 and #2) in de
#2 13221 Items	(swimming) in de
#1 5683 Items	(anxiety or stress) in de

Limiting a Search

This search can be further refined by **limiting** the results to particular years, languages, level of difficulty and country of origin of the publication. On the Advanced Search screen, boxes for these limiting factors are available. For instance if the researcher wants to see only English language records, then the following search expression could be used in the WebSPIRS software:

English in la (or click on Change in Search Limit box)

or

EBSCOhost, type in English in second column

Language	English

Thus, the system acts upon the previous results or as part of the original search and will then eliminate all of the non-English language records (the short field tag for language is **la**).

In addition, as this is a research paper, the basic level material of practical, easily understood sources could be eliminated as well. The following search expression can be used:

not basic in le

or

EBSCOhost, highlight one of the following in column 2

Level of Difficulty	*Advanced*
	Intermediate
	Basic

LE is the field tag for level. The remaining records are the intermediate and advanced level records only. If the number of records is still too large (hundreds of records), the researcher can further refine the search limiting the year of publication. For example:

	1990-2003
or	**EBSCOhost**

Year Published	*1990* to *2003*

The final result below is one record pulled from the SPORTDiscus search and is shown in the basic citation.

	Brief Record (citation plus abstract) retrieved from this search:
TI	Mood states as an indication of staleness and recovery.
AU	Hooper,-S.-L; MacKinnon,-L.-T.; Hanrahan,-S.
JN	International journal of sport psychology (Rome) 28(1), Jan/Mar 1997, 1-12 Refs: 19.
PY	1997
DE	Australia-; elite-athlete; **swimming-**; emotion-; burnout-; **stress-**; recovery-; overtraining-
AB	Elite athletes repeatedly completed the Profile of Mood States (POMS) during a six-month training season to determine whether athletes who are stale show different values from those who are intensely trained but not stale. Nineteen elite male and female swimmers were studied at five time points: three times during training (early-, mid- and late-season), during tapering prior to, and then shortly after, major competition. Of the 14 subjects who completed the entire monitoring program, three were classified as stale based on several criteria....
AN	416583

Other Searching Techniques

Additional search strategies that can be employed by the savvy searcher include:

Truncation

Most systems use the asterisk (*) as the truncation symbol. When searching free text (anywhere in the record), the asterisk can be placed on the end of the root word;

e.g. comput*

will search for computer, computers, computing, computed

Proximity searching

A very advanced technique used in many databases includes proximity searching. The two most common are:

adj (abbreviation for adjacent and requires that two words must stand next to each other e.g. playing adj hurt)

near (two terms must be present and adjacent to each other in any order, e.g. playing near hurt will retrieve "athlete was hurt playing volleyball" which has an entirely different meaning than the example used in **adj** but will also retrieve "playing hurt"

Database conventions

Other conventions to watch for include:

Singular form or plural form of descriptors

To specify a particular population of persons *SPORTDiscus* uses man, woman, boy, girl, adolescent, infant, while *PSYCInfo* uses the singular sometimes and the plural form for others.

Sample Search in Medline

The number of MeSH Subject Headings and sub-headings applied to each periodical article are quite numerous in the Medline database and this greatly assists in the retrieval of periodical articles to satisfy the specific search questions. For instance, if the researcher is seeking articles on hockey, the sub-headings applied to each article are very important to include in a search in order to limit the search in this very large and powerful database. A complete list of these sub-headings and form subject headings can be found in the Medline thesaurus, *Medical Subject Headings*. Some examples include:

Epidemiology

Etiology

Injuries

Physiology

Psychology

Rehabilitation

Statistics and numerical data

Standards

By selecting one or more of the above, the researcher can further limit the search of the major MeSH subject heading "hockey." Other MeSH subject headings further define a topic and a few include:

Human

Linear Models

Male

Female

Reviews

Prospective study

Follow-Up Studies

In addition, the searching software to Medline has a limiting factor called **Focus**. Click on the **Focus** box to limit your search to documents in which your subject heading is a major focus of the article. Articles that refer to the concept peripherally will be eliminated from the articles you retrieved in your search.

With the search on the subject "hockey" and limiting the search to Injuries and Standards, the researcher can retrieve:

Unique Identifier	96160653
Authors	Roberts WO. Brust JD. Leonard B. Hebert BJ.
Institution	MinnHealth SportsCare Consultants
Title	Fair-play rules and injury reduction in ice hockey.
Source	Archives of Pediatrics & Adolescent Medicine. 150(2): 140-5, 1996 Feb.
MeSH Subj Headings:	Athletic Injuries/ ep [Epidemiology]
	Athletic Injuries/ et [Etiology]
	Hockey/ in [Injuries]
	Hockey/ st [Standards]
	Human
	Incidence
	Male
	Minnesota /ep [Epidemiology]

Prospective Studies

Abstract: Objective: To determine the rate, type and severity of injuries incurred and penalties assessed during the qualifying fair-play (points for playing without excessive penalties) and championship "regular" rules (winner advances) portions of a 1994 Junior Gold ice hockey tournament. Design:...Setting:...Participants:...Measurements/Main Results:...Conclusion..

2.5.2   *Other Important Abstracting/Indexing Services*

In order to be thorough in conducting research, there are many other powerful databases that can be searched, depending on whether the search topic is in sport psychology, sociology, management, or sport sciences. It is suggested the researcher begins the research process with the most specific and continues with the databases that are broadly-based in their own disciplines.

Below are some of the additional databases consulted by the sport sciences, kinesiology and physical education community:

PsycINFO

> Washington, D.C. American Psychological Association
>
> 1967 to date, Updated monthly
>
> Thesaurus: *Thesaurus of Psychological Index Terms*, 9th ed., 2001.
>
> Print edition: *Psychological Abstracts*, 1927 to date

Provides access to the international literature in psychology and related behavioral and social sciences literature including psychiatry, anthropology, education and pharmacology, sport psychology and leisure. The major emphasis of the database is on original research, while case studies, reviews, surveys and discussions are also covered. Approximately, 36,000 periodical citations are added in a year along with 12,000 dissertations, books and chapter citations.

SPOLIT (Sportwissenschaft)

> Hamburg, Germany: Bundesinstitut for Sportwissenschaft (BISp)
>
> (Federal Institute of Sport Science)
>
> 1970 to date, Updated bimonthly
>
> Thesaurus: SPOLIT Descriptors (in German) Schorndorf: Verlag Karl Hofmann
>
> Subscription: freely available on BISp website
>
> Web: http://www.bisp-datenbanken.de/index.html

SPOLIT database contains over 130,000 records of which 55% of the records are in German, the rest being in English and other languages. The Institute surveys 500 periodicals and includes books and conference proceedings.

ERIC

> Washington, D.C.: Educational Resources Information Center, sponsored by the US Department of Education
> 1969 to date, Updated monthly
> Thesaurus: *Thesaurus of ERIC Descriptors*, 14th ed, 2001.
> Printed indexes:
> *Current Index to Journals in Education* (CIJE) EJ numbers
> *Resources in Education* (RIE) ED numbering system
> Website:http://www.askeric.org/Eric

This database contains over 950,000 periodical articles (CIJE) and educational reports (RIE) on all aspects of education including physical education/intramural sport from K-12 and college/university. Many libraries also subscribe to the RIE reports that are available on microfiche or can be purchased from the ERIC Document Reproduction Service (EDRS). This database is available gratis at the web address above or through the library system.

Sociofile

> Bethesda: Cambridge Scientific Abstracts
> 1963 to date, Updated quarterly
> Thesaurus: *Thesaurus of Sociological Indexing Terms*, 6th ed, 2003.
> Print index: *Sociological Abstracts*, 1963 to date
> Website: http://www.csa.com/csa/factsheets/socioabs.shmtl

Contains abstracts of the world's periodical literature in sociology and related disciplines and citations to relevant dissertations. Over 1,900 periodical and other serial publications are scanned each year. Approximately 30% of the 510,000 records are from sources outside the US.

BIOSIS

> Philadelphia: BioSciences Information Service
> 1976 to date, Updated monthly

Thesaurus: *BIOSIS Search Guide,* Updated annually

Printed index: *Biological Abstracts*, 1926 to date

Website: http://www.biosis.org/

Contains over 10.5 million citations from major biology and biomedical periodicals along with books, meeting abstracts, reviews, letters, selected institutional and government reports, research communications and patents.

ABI/INFORM Global

Ann Arbor, Michigan: ProQuest Information & Learning Co.

1971 to date, Updated weekly

Thesaurus: Included in the CD ROM version (ABI/Inform) and the ProQuest Direct version

Indexes over 1,000 business periodicals, and includes abstracts for most articles. Database has over 1.4 million citations. Many libraries also subscribe to the fulltext article service where over 70% of the articles cited are available. This is an excellent source for sports administration and finance, especially professional sports.

ProQuest Digital Dissertations

Ann Arbor, Michigan: ProQuest Information & Learning Co.

1861 to date, Updated semi-annually

Thesaurus: none (key words are used for subject searching)

Printed index: *Dissertation Abstracts International*, 1861 to date

Website: http://www.umi.com/

Includes citations for over 1.6 million theses and dissertations ranging from 1861 to date from mainly U.S./Canadian universities and colleges, with coverage of some European universities. From 1980 to date each record includes an abstract. Master's theses from 1988 to date are also included. Many recent theses and dissertations are available in fulltext format.

Kinesiology Publications (formerly Microform Publications of Human Movement Studies)

Eugene, Oregon: University of Oregon, International Institute of Human Development and Performance.

1949 to date

Index to the Collection: Kinesiology Abstracts (formerly Microforms Publications Bulletin), 1949-

Website: http://kinpubs.uoregon.edu/KinAbs.html

This microfiche collection consists of master's theses in all fields of physical education, sport psychology, and sport sciences from U.S./Canadian colleges and universities. Some libraries catalogue each title individually and apply subject headings and others keep microfiche together in one numerical collection and use the *Kinesiology Abstracts* publication (formerly *Microform Publications Bulletin)* as the author, title and subject approach to this collection. The *SPORTDiscus* database has indexed each thesis from 1949 to date.

Current Contents Connect

Philadelphia, PA: Institute for Scientific Information

1995 to date, Updated weekly

Thesaurus: None

Printed Indexes: Publishes many series in major disciplines including: Social and Behavioral Sciences, Life Sciences.

Website: http://www.isinet.com/

Is a current awareness tool and index where the table of contents for currently received periodical issues are recorded. Searching is done on key word in title, by author or title of periodical. Covers over 5,000 academic and scholarly journals from the sciences, humanities and social sciences.

Ingenta (formerly UnCover)

Website: http://www.ingenta.com/

Another service which many institutions have access to is *Ingenta*, a current awareness service of over 22,000 periodical titles. This service has greatly improved searching software and does include the more general periodicals along with a strong base of scholarly periodical titles in the sciences, humanities and social sciences. Searches can be done by keyword in the title, by author and periodical title name.

2.6   Resources in Other Libraries

In addition to searching for books and theses, the researcher can query the OPAC for the periodical titles of each citation retrieved from *SPORTDiscus, Medline, ERIC* and other databases. The determination of what the home library holds is the last important step in the research process.

If a periodical title, conference proceedings or other research materials are not held by the home library, the library will have a document delivery service (DDS) or Interlibrary Loan department. For the researcher, access to a college or university interlibrary loan or document delivery service has become more important in the past decade as most library budgets are not large enough to purchase all the material necessary to support fully all college or university programs.

In some institutions, only the graduate and faculty researcher is able to utilize the DDS service, but this restriction is changing in many institutions as more of the time-consuming document delivery tasks are automated. Scanning technology and improved software (*Ariel* and *Relais* from the National Library of Medicine), and the automation of the home library's online document delivery request form have all assisted in speeding the process. However, the astute researcher allows enough time in the whole research process for the DDS service to deliver the requisite periodical articles, books or other materials. In many cases, a few weeks are needed to locate a library that holds the requested periodical title. When DDS applies for a particular periodical article from another library, the busy staff in the holding library has to retrieve the volume from the shelves, scan or photocopy it, and send it to the requesting library.

On many college and university library's web home pages, the dedicated researcher can also find links to other university library OPACs. Most university library OPACs can be freely accessible and the library will supply the linkages necessary. Included usually are links to the national library OPACs:

    Library of Congress Catalog
        http://catalog.loc.gov/
    National Library of Canada (ResAnet)
        http://www.amicus.nlc-bnc.ca/wapp/resanet/searche.htm
    National Library of Australia
        http://www.nla.gov.au/catalogue/

One of the finest resources to find library OPACs worldwide is *Libweb: Library Servers via WWW,* (http://sunsite.berkeley.edu/Libweb/) and also *The WWW Library Directory*, (http://www.webpan.com/msauers/libdir/). Through these directories, the researcher can find libraries in any worldwide geographical region.

2.6.1   *Union Catalogues*

Instead of searching one large library at a time, research libraries subscribe to large union catalogues where many libraries report their holdings. Two important sources are *RLIN* (Research Libraries Information Network) and OCLC's *FirstSearch* services which include the large bibliographic database, ***WorldCat***, and many other databases and current awareness services (http://www.oclc.org/). The Library of Congress, National Library of Canada and the British Library are a few of the major libraries that send their records to WorldCat. Look for access to these services on your own library's home page or ask a reference librarian about access.

2.7   Internet Resources

Usage of the Internet is growing exponentially every year. Originally, electronic mail was the main Internet traffic. Within the last five years, visits to websites have gained on electronic mail. Up to this point, sports information on the Internet has been dominated by the general sports sites for the professional and university sports of football, soccer, baseball, basketball and hockey. Sports associations and professional sport organizations are making inroads and providing the needed balance. Finding the more academic and scholarly websites is a difficult task at best, but more sport biomechanics, exercise physiology and psychology, sports history and sociology websites are becoming prominent. A recently developed website called *Scholarly Sport Sites: A Subject Directory* contains links to scholarly and expert associations, databases/directories, national sport structures, et al. to aid the serious sport researcher (http://www.ucalgary.ca/library/ssportsite/).

The Internet is a very democratic medium, which is changing so rapidly and where anyone with the right equipment can develop their own website. This results in websites that may have dependable information, dubious information and "disinformation" e.g. gossip, offensive, deliberate untruths as well. To distinguish which is which among the many sites can be a daunting task. However, there are directories to the Internet produced by reliable universities or companies with good reputations.

The Internet can be used as a research tool for many topics. A few guidelines can assist the researcher in evaluating websites and determining whether information from the site has validity, relevance and authority.

a) The first criterion is that of authoritativeness of the site. Can it be determined whether a person or organization with credentials and credibility has created or is responsible for the editorial content of the site? Does the site have full address and contact information? Anonymous sites should be approached with extreme caution.

b) Is the site updated on a regular basis? Usually on the home page of the site, at the bottom of the page, appears a date when last updated. Sites that are specifically for "archived" material should be labelled as such.

c) Is the format of the site well organized? On the home page is it evident what the major sections on the site are? Is the information arranged well, are the navigational paths easy and clear? Pleasing graphics, up-to-date links and a speedy downloading process all assist in making the website a satisfying place to investigate and visit

2.8   Search Engines

With the criteria in mind, the researcher can set to the difficult task of finding sites to meet the research need. Recently, an excellent meta search engine, Google (www.google.com) has actively sought out academic websites, allowing educational institutions the use of its search engine in order to provide more in-depth access to this important source of information.

Single search engine companies were the first to be established with *Lycos*, *Alta Vista* and *Yahoo* leading the pack for a number of years. So many single search engine companies have come upon the scene that other companies or institutions have established multi-search or meta search engines to find and organize the results of searches.

Other multi-search engines include:

Google	http://www.google.com
Metacrawler	http://www.webcrawler.com
Teoma	http://www.teoma.com

Other single search engines available at present include:

AltaVista	http://www.altavista.com
Excite	http://www.excite.com
Lycos	http://www.lycos.com

2.9   Website Directories and Portals

Some websites catalogue or organize websites by subject, type, or location. The Sport Information Resource Centre's *SPORTQuest* website maintains over 14,000 links to other, mainly sport-specific sites, listing sites by topic, organization and sport (http://www.sportquest.com).

Some sport specific directories include:

SPORTQuest	http://www.sportquest.com/
Google Directory: Sports	http://www.google.com/Top/Sports/
Infosport.org (France)	http://www.infosport.org/
iSportsDigest.com	http://isportsdigest.tripod.com/directory.html
Lycos Directory: Sports	http://dir.lycos.com/Sports/
Open Directory Project: Sports	http://dmoz.org/Sports/
Search the Outdoors	http://www.searchtheoutdoors.com/
Virtual Library of Sport	http://sportsvl.com/
Yahoo Directory: Sports	http://dir.yahoo.com/recreation/sports/index.html

For the large discipline of biomechanics, the *Biomechanics World Wide* website (http://www.per.ualberta.ca/biomechanics/) has a comprehensive directory to other biomechanics sites. Each link is organized under 18 sub-topics of biomechanics, including: biomechanics journals, societies, computer simulation, orthopaedics, ergonomics, biomedical engineering, gait & locomotion, motor control.

The current development for organizing the various services on the web is the development of web portals. Web portals bring together many web features including news sources, business information, chat rooms, games, search engines, finding people, addresses and many other services.

Other scholarly website directories to investigate include:

INFOMINE: Scholarly Internet Resource Collections
http://infomine.ucr.edu/

Librarians' Index to the Internet
http://lii.org/

2.10   Key Academic and Association Websites

In the past few years, significant changes have taken place in the information base for associations and societies. Websites are starting to offer far more up-to-date information on professional associations than the standard yet still important print reference sources (e.g. *Encyclopaedia of Associations, Yearbook of International Organizations*). In the case of *PE Central: the Ultimate Web Site for Health and Physical Education Teachers* (http://www.pecentral.org/) originating from Virginia Tech, a website can offer a wide range of resources. This site has the latest information about contemporary developmentally-appropriate physical education programs for children and youth plus lesson plans, assessment ideas, adapted information, books, clothing, companies/products, other top websites and has many fulltext documents and references (on the especially important topic, that of defending the physical education program in schools).

Association sites include information about the organization's goals, mission, Codes of Ethics, publications, bibliographies of scholarly articles, fulltext publications or tables of contents of their periodicals, membership information, conferences, links to similar organizations, and sometimes provide listservs for members. See the website, Scholarly Sport Sites for a fairly comprehensive listing of scholarly and expert sport sciences, recreation, leisure, coaching, and physical education associations (http://www.ucalgary.ca/library/ssportsite/assoc.html).

2.11   Listservs

Listservs, chat rooms, and Usenet news groups have blossomed with the advent of individual email, and in the case of the academic sports researcher, a number of listservs are utilized by professors and, in some cases, graduate student researchers are granted access. Instructions for subscribing to listservs can be found on online directories including: TILE.NET (http://www.tile.net).

Some of the most active listservs include:

H-Arete (Sport Literature Association)

BIOMCH-L (Biomechanics and Movement Science listserv)

COSIDA-L (Sports Information Directors Discussion Group)

ISCPES (International Society for Comparative Physical Education & Sport

NASSServ (North American Society for the Sociology of Sport)

Sport-Able (discussion group for and about sports for the disabled)

SPORTHIST (ISPHES - Sport History Scholars List)

SPORTPC (Use of Computers in Sport)

SPORTPSY (Exercise and Sport Psychology)

SPORTMGT (Sport Management)

Sportsmedicine

Sportscience (for researchers in sport science and exercise performance)

USPE-L (Teaching Physical Education)

WISHPERD (for Women in sport, health, physical education, recreation and dance)

2.11   The Future

Library services are evolving and developing rapidly with professional librarians and computer specialists looking at issues of further connectivity and accessibility. The goal is to deliver articles and other resources to desktop on demand through a seamless interface to the end user (the researcher). Issues of copyright will probably be the most important discussion point among publishers, libraries and the researcher in the next five years. Compensation to creators for use of their print or online versions of fulltext papers will complicate delivery issues, but are not insurmountable. These issues are very important to the livelihood of the publishers and database producers.

Enhanced connectivity is in the experimental phase and some library consortia have established union lists of serials that are part of the online database system. Searchers click on the icon for library holdings to view the periodical titles within the consortia of libraries. This abbreviates one step in the searchers quest to find the specific periodical title.

Libraries have also chosen to subscribe to core collections of periodicals where all articles are available in fulltext (*InfoTrac, ProQuest Research Library, EBSCO*) The Ingenta service offers 1 hour delivery of frequently requested articles for those libraries or researchers with deposit accounts or handy credit cards.

In this and many other ways the library user will find research more convenient, and, in the past few years, great strides have been made by libraries to provide a large number of periodicals online. True document delivery is in the throes of experimentation and constant change.

2.13   Notes and Bibliographic References

2.13.1   Style Manuals

In most universities and college departments and schools, the faculty have selected a style manual that students use for all the research papers and other written assignments. Many departments recommend the *Publication Manual of the American Psychological Association* and encourage students to purchase a copy for personal use that can be used throughout undergraduate or graduate programs. Many of the physical education and sport sciences periodical publishers also require usage of this manual when submitting papers for publication.

Publication Manual of the American Psychological Association

5th ed. Washington, D.C., APA, 2001

2.13.2   For background information and earlier methods of using library resources consult:

Shoebridge, M. ed. (1992) *Information Sources in Sport and Leisure.* London: Bowker-Saur.

Thomas, J. R. & Nelson, (1996) *Research methods in physical activity.* 3rd ed. Champaign, Ill: Human Kinetics Publishers.

2.13.3   General sports resources of the Internet

Weaver, B. (1997) Reference on the Internet: Sports. *Reference Librarian*, (57) 187-190. (This is part of a special issue entitled: Reference Sources on the Internet: Off the Shelf and Onto the Web)

2.13.4   Explanation of Search Engines

Web Searching Tips (SearchEngineWatch.com)

http://www.searachenginewatch.com/facts/index.php

Internet Searching Strategies (Fondren Library, Rice University)

http://www.rice.edu/fondren/tmp/neetguides/strategies.html

2.13.5   Academic Research and the Internet

Cox, R. W. & Salter, M. A. (1998) The IT Revolution and the Practice of Sport History: an Overview and Reflection on Internet Research and Teaching Resources, *Journal of Sport History*, 25(2), 283-302.

Delpy, L. (1998) Sport Management and Marketing via the World Wide Web, *Sport Marketing Quarterly*, 7(1), 21-28.

(3)   Integration of Literature Review and Personal Intentions

Once the researcher has selected the appropriate information and scientific resources, the next stage in the research process is to summarize and integrate this information with personal intentions. As mentioned before, reading the literature will often result in new ideas and/or directions to be investigated. An efficient reading of the literature consists of noting key elements such as the theories discussed. At this early stage "clustering" the notes according to general topic areas is useful. In the next stage, the clusters of information (including findings of the various studies) will be critical in the integration of ideas. Critical thinking skills are essential throughout this entire process. Always consider:

WHETHER THE RESULTS OF THE STUDY CAN BE EXPLAINED BY AN ALTERNATIVE THEORY THAN THE ONE SUGGESTED.

When integrating the literature notes with the personal intentions and ideas, one should be CRITICAL, CREATIVE, INNOVATIVE, and LOGICAL in order to successfully INTEGRATE all of the ideas and information into a HOLISTIC perspective. This holistic view should later be used for formulating basic assumptions and/or hypotheses and methodology, which guides the RESEARCH PLAN. The following principles should be remembered when the researcher integrates the literature review and his/her personal intentions in formulating the theoretical foundation of a study:

(1)   **A GUIDING MODEL can be established through the summary of theories, methodologies, and findings in a simple and clear manner.**

(2)   **Scientific argumentations can be logically organized to form a holistic view of the research area.**

(3)   **In the first stages of the writing, explain the purpose of the current investigation, present the problems and alternative explanations.**

(4)   **Progressively develop the argument so that hypotheses and methodology derivation are a direct and logical consequence of the holistic view.**

An example from: Dlin, R., Tenenbaum, G., Furst, D., and Weingarten, G. (1987). Type A personality components and the blood pressure response to dynamic exercise. *International Journal of Sport Medicine, 8*, 35-40.

> *Research has indicated that a relationship exists between psychological, physiologic, and health variables. This was documented in relations between personality type and coronary artery disease (18,21), blood pressure and personality (15,16,37), vascular reaction and personality traits (41), and state and trait anxiety and injury proneness (28)*
>
> *The type A behavior pattern has been established as an independent cluster of behaviors and attitudes (called an action-emotion complex) that relates to the risk of developing coronary heart disease (36). Type A individuals are said to be hard driving and competitive, feel pressured by time, aggressive, impatient, and hostile (22).*
>
> *Physiologic responses to similar physical stress may vary among individuals. A notable example is the systolic blood pressure (SBP) response to an exercise task. Several authors have shown that the BP response to exercise may be useful in prediction of future hypertension (6,19,43).*
>
> *Weingarten et al. (42) examined the relationship between SBP response to exercise and state and trait anxiety in elite water polo players. They found a significantly higher resting SBP in the group scoring higher on state anxiety, with a trend (not significant) to higher SBP during exercise.*
>
> *Competitive athletes have been shown to have a higher SBP response to exercise than non-trained individuals in the same age range. This was true for adolescents (4,7) as well as for adults (5). Due to the various components of the type A personality, it could be assumed that competitive athletes have more tendencies towards type A personality. This, however, was not measured in the above studies.*

> *Whether this holds true for specific sports groups is unknown. There is some evidence that certain psychological characteristics are common to successful sportsmen participating in a specific sport (33,34). This gives rise to the question of whether a relationship exists between the psychological make-up and the SBP response to exercise.*
>
> *While some data are available on the influence of psychological status (anxiety, extroversion, motivation) on performance (9), there are no studies examining the relations between type A personality and objective physiologic parameters during exercise and more specifically SBP response to exercise.*
>
> *This paper attempts to examine some of the relationship between type A personality traits and SBP response to an exercise task.*

An efficient method, which helps the scientists to synthesize and integrate the information and personal intentions, is to establish a SYNTHESIS PLAN. Such a plan is displayed in Table 1.1.

Table 1.1

"SYNTHESIS PLAN" for the Integration of Informational Resources and Personal Intentions

Study	Main Concerns	Sample	Method	Main Findings	Personal Comments and Intentions
Festinger (1992)	Heart-rate during imagery.	20 Female athletes. Age 22-32.	Using computerized equipment. Silent Room (10 sessions)	No changes in excitation. Changes in relaxation.	Short imagery sessions. No voluntary sessions.
Allen & Graham (1996)	GSR during imagery.	15 high-school students. Age 15-17.	Using computerized equipment in the gymnasium. (15 sessions)	Dramatic changes.	No control over changes. No report on effect sizes.
Bar-Eli (1997)	Alpha waves during imagery.	10 Olympic athletes. Age 19-25.	Using computerized equipment in laboratory. (20 sessions)	Non-significant changes.	Use of imagery is part of the training.
Blumen-stein (1998)	Physiological responses during imagery.	17 wrestlers. Age 22-28.	Using computerized equipment before competition. (10 sessions)	Dramatic changes.	Very efficient method before competitions which evoke arousal

Every scientific investigation begins with curiosity and reflective thinking. Once a theory is established, hypotheses can be developed and statement of expectations and predictions or theories can be postulated. A theory thus consists of "ELEMENTS" which are often referred to or considered as "VARIABLES." These variables are interrelated with other variables and are thought to PREDICT (i.e., account for) each other. A group of variables constructs a PATTERN, GROUPS OR CLUSTERS. The LINKS among the clusters create MAPS or CONCEPTUAL MAPS. The conceptual maps are the essence of the THEORY. A THEORY is illustrated in Figure 1.3

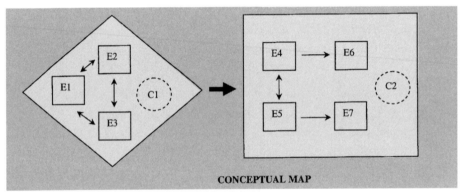

CONCEPTUAL MAP

Figure 1.3 A Theory which consists of elements (i.e., E- variables), constitutes clusters (c), and concept maps.

In Figure 1.3 there are 7 elements/variables. Three elements (E1, E2, E3) are interrelated withto each other and together establish the first cluster. This cluster effect s (accounts for), another cluster of variables in which elements 4 and 5 are related to each other. However, each element of them, separately, predicts elements 6 and 7. To illustrate these relations by example, let's assume that the first cluster is dispositional anxiety, which has 3 dimensions: perceived somatic (e1), cognitive (e2), and physiological (e3) arousal. According to the theory, disposition anxiety (c1) effects cluster 2 (c2; state anxiety). Within cluster 2, there are two predictors (e4 and e5), state emotionally and state worry (i.e., state = task and situational specific), and two predicted elements, e6 and e7, which are performance variables, gross motor and fine motor skill tasks respectively.

Theories vary in complexity, depending on the number of elements and clusters they contain. Today, new computerized technologies allow us to conduct investigations, which consist of many elements and clusters. The multi-level and multi-variable techniques will be introduced later in the book. At this stage, one should keep in mind that the more complexity of a complex is the theory will effect, the more questions that will develop and that can be asked, and the more complex intricacy of the will be the RESEARCH PLAN.

The theory is the basis from which hypotheses are derived. In the case illustrated in Figure 1.3, the researcher may be interested in many questions along the lines of those listed here:

- The strength of the relations among the elements/variables within each of the two clusters separately.
- The strength of the relationship between the two clusters.
- To what degree does the combination of the first cluster (dispositional anxiety) and state emotionality account for a variety of gross motor skills, and alternatively, what percentage of fine motor skills can be explained by c1 and state cognitive (worry) anxiety?
- Are there other variables that can predict or account for the variance of fine ($e7$) and gross ($e6$) motor skills?

This last question may cause the researcher to seek additional variables and/or a more comprehensive theory. The eagerness and curiosity to understand, predict, and account for all what happens in the universe is a positive phenomena, though it makes the theories and the research plans much more complex. The theory guides the RESEARCH PLAN. The abstract elements ($e1$, $e2$ ....e_n) should be operationalized, and if possible become measurable. The implementation of a RESEARCH PLAN is the topic of the next chapter. The theory and its subsequent hypotheses are the corner stones of this plan.

Summary

Researchers, in particular the young researchers, are known to be very enthusiastic about their ideas. This enthusiasm should be accompanied with systematic review of the literature, so that the best research product will result. Literature review usually results in modifications of the basic assumptions and/or hypotheses the researcher initially started with. This process is fruitful as long as the scope of the study is not too large broad and unfocused. The direction and clarity of the integrated product should be sound. It is this product which will later guide the whole research process.

1.2 THEORETICAL AND PRACTICAL PLANNING

In this chapter, we will discuss the formation of the basic assumptions and how the formulation of the hypothesis dictates the research plan. We will begin by exploring the theoretical framework that drives the research and continue to the operational definitions of the variables in the study. We will then explain how to choose the most suitable research methods and research design to appropriately answer the questions of interest. We will also explain how, during the planning phase, the researcher can become aware of any threats which may jeopardize the research findings. The control over possible errors and alternative explanations to the research finding are described in detail. Finally, general aspects of data collection techniques, data analysis techniques, and the importance of running a pilot study prior to conducting the research are described. How to prepare a research proposal by a grant allocation is introduced at the end of this chapter. The logical construction of this chapter is as follows:

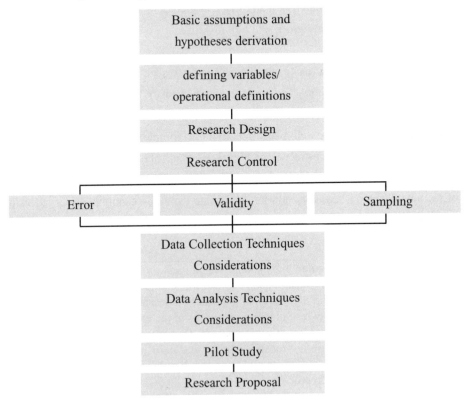

Contents

(1) Formulation of Basic Assumptions and/or Hypotheses

The questions and concerns and questions which led to the literature review and consequently redefining or modifying of the research questions, are aimed at formulating basic assumptions and/or hypotheses which are used later for establishing a final RESEARCH PLAN. The BASIC ASSUMPTIONS and/or HYPOTHESES are based on sound theory, or in some other instances, on discrepancies between two or more theories. Thus, the strength of our basic assumptions and/or hypotheses depends on "how sound is the theory " upon which we are relying. Kerlinger (1972), argued that in essence every general scientific argumentation could be considered a theory. A theory therefore consists of TERMS, DEFINITIONS, and ARGUMENTS, which are logically related to each other interrelated in a CONCEPTUAL manner. A sound theory is one, which sufficiently meets the following criteria:

- **Contains logical arguments, which are related to each other and establish an integrated concept from which behaviors and events can be inferred.**
- **Holds assumptions, which are used for the establishment of the concept.**
- **Incorporates arguments and concepts from which a research plan can be derived, examined, and verified or rejected.**

Scientists believe that a scientific theory is one, which enables us to CONTROL, UNDERSTAND, and PREDICT events and behaviors in the world around us. It is assumed that some laws, which the scientists will hopefully uncover, govern all events and behaviors in the universe. These laws are deterministic in nature (e.g., $F = mg$). However, in the behavioral and social sciences (which are targeted towards human and social issues), the differences among individuals, groups, cultures, educational backgrounds, etc. have led researchers to understand, control, and predict events and behaviors with some degree of CERTAINTY (i.e., PROBABILITY). Under certain conditions the probability that a given behavior will occur is in the range of 0-1. Recent, post-modernist, feminist, and constructionist approaches allow for more personal interpretation, less robustness, and more freedom in the definition and nature of understanding the human, social and cultural natures. In the cultural sciences (e.g. sport history, sport philosophy), it is necessary to use non-deterministic theories as a basis for research and planning.

Any theory is only as good as its assumptions are valid. For example, we assume that the resting heart rate of most humans ranges between 40-80 beats/min. We assume that most people who experience life-threat will be anxious and attempt to improve their condition. We may assume that under high arousal states, the heart rate, galvanic skin response, breathing rate, and depth all increase. Based on these assumptions, one may develop a theory which postulates the relations among the psychological and biological component, which are influenced by people, who sense, feel, think, and interact with their environment. Once a theory is established, basic assumptions and/or hypotheses can be postulated. The research plan is aimed at the examination, verification or rejection of the basic assumptions and/or hypotheses (i.e., questions and expectations that are derived from the theory and personal-logical cognitions). A RESEARCH PLAN is based on a logical process, which is illustrated in Figure 1.4.

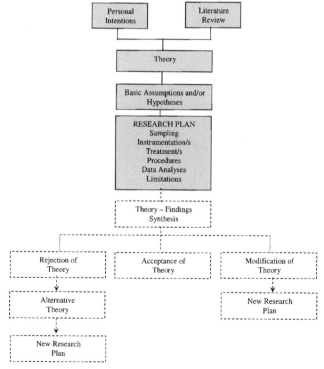

Figure 1.4   Establishing a research plan based on theory and subsequent processes.

1.1   Formulation of Hypotheses

HYPOTHESIS is a scientific statement, which is derived from a theory. Hypotheses infer information based on statistical quantity (i.e., a parameter) about the population of interest (i.e., athletes, coaches, exercisers, etc). This information is termed hypothesis because there is only "some" certainty that this statement may be true. Usually, scientists use a representative sample from the population to then later make inferences about the entire population.

A statistical hypothesis is usually notated as H. In the process of statistical inferences, there are at least two hypotheses. One is a statement which infers EQUALITY between groups or lack of relations among variables, (H_0 - null hypothesis), while the other infers INEQUALITY (i.e., differences) between the groups or some relations among the variables (i.e., H_1—alternative hypothesis). H_0 and H_1 complement each other so that both statements contain all the possibilities, which exist about the variables or their relations. For example:

H_0: Athletes and non-athletes have similar basic metabolic heart rate.

H_1: Athletes have lower basic metabolic heart-rate than non-athletes.

In the above example, the researcher, based on a sound theory, postulated that extensive practice results in larger heart stroke volumes and consequently lower heart rate in athletes compared to non-athletes (H_1). The null hypothesis (H_0) statement infers that the basic metabolic heart beat of athletes and non-athlete is equal. This is however, one very rare possibility that non-athletes have a lower basic metabolic heart rate than do athletes. This possibility, despite its low probability, still exists and therefore should be included in as one of the hypotheses. Usually in such a case, the possibility that non-athletes have lower metabolic heart rates becomes part of the null hypothesis. The two complementary hypotheses will be thus:

H_0: Non-athletes have similar or lower basic metabolic heart rate than athletes.

H_1: Athletes have lower basic metabolic heart rate than non-athletes do.

Let us assume at this stage, that the MEAN heart rate is the best representational ESTIMATION of the two samples' heart rate. If μ represents the mean, i represents non-athletes, and j represents athletes, thean the two hypotheses will be represented as the following:

$$H_o: \ \mu_i \leq \mu_j$$
$$H_1: \ \mu_i > \mu_j$$

Since H_o is usually the hypothesis that the researcher strives to reject, the equality sign (=) remains always with H_o.

In some cases a certain value, which is derived from other experiments or theories, may be used in postulating hypotheses. For example, let us assume that previous findings indicated that the basic metabolic heart rate of long-distance runners averaged 38 b/min and the highest of them was 44 b/min. If we are interested in comparing long-distance runners to weight lifters, we may, and based on a sound theory, use the hypothesis that long-distance runners (i) will have a substantial lower heart rate than their weight-lifter (j) counterparts. The hypotheses, which will later guide the research plan, are:

$$H_o: \ \mu_i \geq \mu_j$$
$$H_1: \ \mu_i < \mu_j$$

In this case we desire to use the mean and the highest long-distance heart rate reported in the literature as a criterion, so we may state the hypotheses as follows:

$$H_o: \ \mu_j \geq 38 \text{ b/min}$$
$$H_o: \ \mu_j \leq 44 / \text{bmin}$$
$$H_1: \ \mu_j > 44 \text{ b/min}$$

In keeping with this line of reasoning, H_o can <u>never</u> be stated as:

$$H_o : m > 38 \text{ b/min}$$

or

$$H_o : m < 38 / \text{bmin}$$

or

$$H_o : m \ \pi \neq 38 \text{ b/min}$$

It should be kept in mind that hypotheses refer only to one PARAMETER, which the investigator intends to examine. The illustrated cases contain more variables of interest and more parameters which ought to be examined; in a true research investigation, more hypotheses should be included.

Hypotheses can also be inferred based on relationships between two or more variables. Relations are usually represented by the letter r. In accordance with the previous procedure, we may state that:

$$H_0 : r_{ab} = 0$$
$$H_1 : r_{ab} \pi \, 0$$

which infers no relations between variables "a" and "b" (H_0) and "some relation" (positive or negative) between variables "a" and "b" (H_1). Due to other theories, the researcher may infer that:

$$Ho : r_{ab} \text{\pounds } 0$$
$$Ho : r_{ab} > 0$$

or in an other case:

$$Ho : r_{ab} \geq 0$$
$$Ho : r_{ab} < 0$$

or

$$Ho : r_{ab} \geq 0.50$$
$$Ho : r_{ab} < 0.50$$

This kind of reasoning (i.e., stating hypotheses and later examining them by using null hypothesis testing; NHT) has recently undergone substantial criticism. However, we shall introduce this debate more in detail later in this book. At this early stage, which precedes the research plan and examination of the hypotheses, we prefer to introduce the traditional methods of Null Hypotheses Tests. We feel obligated, however, to say that the statements, which are termed HYPOTHESES, should rely more heavily on values, which derive from previous observations and theories.

We would prefer young less experienced scientists to state hypotheses, which follow the simple example: Research has shown that the mean heart rate of athletes in rest is 38 b/min with a range of 32-44 b/min. Non-athletes (regular population) mean is 72 b/min with a range of 62-95. If a researcher desires to combine heart rate of athletes with non-athletes in his/her study, thus the hypotheses should be stated as follows (note: i are athletes, j are non-athletes, HR is heart rate, h and l are "high" and "low" values of HR, respectively).

The possible "range of differences" between athletes and non-athletes is:

$$(HR_{jl}—HR_{il})—(HR_{jh}—HR_{ih})$$

or

$$(62—32)—(95—44) = 30 - 51 \text{ b/min}$$

In this case the hypotheses will be stated as follows:

$$H_0 : m_j - m_i = 30 - 51$$
$$H_1 : m_j - m_i \ \pi \ 30 - 51$$

These hypotheses are much more sound than the previous ones. In this case, to reject the null hypothesis one should rely on samples, which do not represent the population. There may be other reasons, which should be accounted for and addressed.

Hypotheses may be simple or complex. A simple hypothesis relates to a sample within the population, which meets the assumption of normality with known parameters. For example: The mean oxygen uptake of the population in the 20-40 years range is 48.5 m/ min/ kg and standard deviation of 5.24. A complex hypothesis is postulated in cases where the researcher is not acquainted or does not have any information about the distribution of the population in the variables he/she is investigating. In most cases researchers postulate complex hypotheses and assume that the distributions they will obtain will approximate normality. Later, we will discuss what to do in the event that normality is not met.

Hypotheses can also be precise or imprecise. A precise hypothesis is stated when the scientist knows much about the populations' parameters in the area of investigation. An imprecise hypothesis is stated when a range of values should be given but the scientist does not have sufficient information to generate precise hypothesis.

Precise Hypothesis:	$m = 52.5 \pm 3.4$
Imprecise Hypotheses:	$m > 52.5$
	or $m < 52.5$
	or $m \ \pi \ 52.5$
	or $m - 30 - 80$

Hypotheses can also be UNIDIRECTIONAL or BIDIRECTIONAL. The scientist may hypothesize, that the mean of one sample of a population is greater or smaller than that of another population's mean. The alternative hypothesis will be postulated as UNIDIRECTIONAL, meaning that the mean of the sample, derived from a population, is equal to the mean of the sample. In cases where there is NO EVIDENCE (whether experimental or logical) for existing differences between the populations, then the alternative hypothesis is postulated as bi-directional. A bi-directional hypothesis is one that states that the two samples' means are not equal.

In the following unidirectional example, a researcher desires to examine gender differences in the exertion tolerance of long distance runners. Below, male runners are notated as i, female runners as j, and the mean is represented by m. If there is previous evidence, for example, that female runners can tolerate exertion for a longer time than their male counterparts, the ALTERNATIVE hypothesis will be stated as:

$$H_1 : m_j > m_i \text{ (unidirectional)}$$

However, if such evidence does not exist, and there is no logical reason to assume gender differences, than the ALTERNATIVE hypothesis will be:

$$H_1 : m_i \, \pi \, m_j$$

These hypotheses are usually stated in words (i.e., "female long distance runners will tolerate high levels of exertion for a longer period of time than male long distance runners" or "female and male runners will tolerate equally high levels of exertion").

Hypothesis can relate to any parameter, which is of interest and will be measured. It can be the MEAN, VARIANCE, PROPORTION, and CORRELATION of one or more samples of populations. The research methods used to verify and reject hypotheses will be discussed in details in part V, chapters 15 and 16.

At this early stage we would like to note that prior to analyzing the data, there are several assumptions that should be met. We shall elaborate on them later and illustrate many examples.

(2)   Selecting and Defining Variables

When scientists wish to conduct a study, they are required to select and define the variables, which operationalize their theory. More specifically, researchers operationally define the variable of interest in the study by using tools such as questionnaires, observations, and any other measurement tools. Empirically oriented researchers need operational definitions in order to construct the instrumentation necessary for measuring the variables. Also, hermeneutically (using words and sentences as a measurement unit) oriented researchers rely on definitions of terms to enable concepts to be established. Variables are also used as keys for collection, treatment, and analysis of word-based data.

In line with the theoretical consideration mentioned earlier, a theory consists of integrated terms, which form one or more concepts. A theory is then used to exert terms, which are THEORETICALLY DEFINED, and variables, which can be MEASURED (or ESTIMATED) (i.e., FUNCTIONAL DEFINITION). This conceptualization is presented in Figure 1.5.

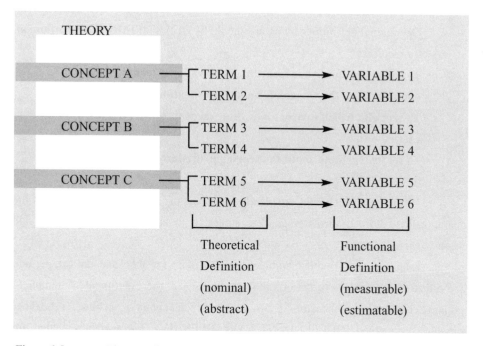

Figure 1.5   Theory relies on concepts that consist of terms, and measured (manifest) or estimated variables.

Terms such as oxygen uptake, competitive anxiety, heart rate, goal orientation, group dynamics, and the like can be defined theoretically. For example, "motivation is an inner drive, impulse, etc. that causes one to act" (Webster Dictionary, 1990). Theoretical definitions (i.e., usually termed "dictionary definitions") are not sufficient for direct observations. To enable the researcher to observe directly (measure and/or estimate) the theoretical terms, they should become variables, which have functional definitions. Next, variables are explained in the context of an empirical study. The functional definitions of the theoretical terms are used as a bridge between the theoretical and the applied consideration of any scientific inquiry. A functional definition is for example:

A	**Motivation is the score of the testee on the "motivation for exercising scale".**
B	**Anticipation in fast ball games is the precision with which one can predict upcoming events when the available information presented to him/her is occluded in early stages (say 100 ms after action onset).**

Operational definitions by nature should be QUANTIFIABLE. The definition of variables requires:

- **To construct or use a measurable/observational technique to operationalize the variable/s under investigations.**
- **To set rules which instruct how these measures/observations will be carried out.**
- **To set instructions about the scoring procedures.**

When these procedures are clearly stated, the precision (i.e., reliability) of the operationally—defined variables are less subjected to any type of fluctuations and inconsistencies.

In any logical scientific argument, one or more variables account for, predict, and affect other variables or set of variables. In science, the experimenter attempts to explain behaviors by other factors. The variables, which explain or account for the other variables are termed INDEPENDENT VARIABLES (IV). The variables, which are dependent on or are explained by other variables, are termed DEPENDENT VARIABLES (DV). The most simplistic example is shown in Figure 1.6.

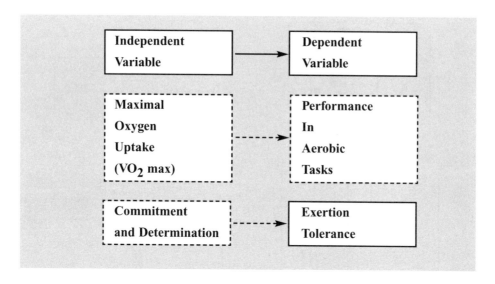

Figure 1.6   Illustration of theory construction—independent variable predicts/accounts for the dependent variable.

In Figure 1.6 two examples are introduced. People with higher VO_2 max can run longer and faster than their counterparts with low VO2 max. People who are more committed and determined can sustain physical exertion for a longer period of time than people who lack these traits.

Usually, a theory consists of more than one DEPENDENT VARIABLE and one INDEPENDENT VARIABLE. Some of the independent variables can be related to each other while others are not. The researcher can decide the scope of his/her research. Some researchers prefer to concentrate on a smaller number of IV and DV, but investigate the variables more in-depth while other researchers prefer to "better understand" the whole, and expand the VARIABLES' NETWORK.

More complex relations between DVs and IVs are illustrated in Figure 1.7.

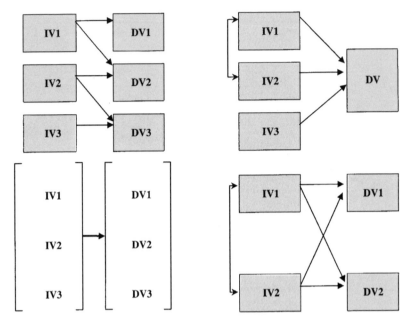

Figure 1.7   Illustration of 4 out of an endless number of possible combinations of IV-DV relationships.

The IV-DV relations are not as simple as one may think. In many cases, it is impossible, both theoretically and experimentally, to determine which variables are the IV and the DV. There are often MUTUAL RELATIONSHIPS between two or more variables, where both variables directly affect each other. In other cases MUTUAL RELATIONSHIPS may also affect additional variables. Furthermore, in many cases, IVs do not directly influence the DVs. For example, people with high VO_2 max may poorly run long distance courses because they lack motivation. Motivation is then viewed as an INTERVENING VARIABLE, or a variable which MEDIATES between the physiological capability (VO_2 max) and running long distance. In Figure 1.8 some examples are illustrated:

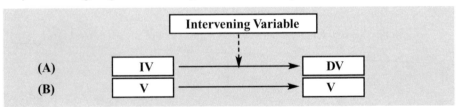

Figure 1.8   Illustration of (A) relations between IV and DV through an intervening variable, and (B) mutual relations between two variables.

(3)   Choosing Appropriate Hermeneutic and/or Measurement Concepts as well as Operational Definitions

To operationalize a variable the researcher must choose the appropriate METHOD of measurement of the theoretical terms. Method of Measurement pertains to any SYSTEMATIC, RELIABLE (i.e., PRECISE, contain as MINIMAL ERROR as possible, CONSISTENT), and VALID (i.e., measure the trait or state that ought to be measured) way of operationalizing the variables (i.e, collecting data). Though the terms RELIABILITY and VALIDITY are viewed by several recent schools of scientific methodologies differently than the traditional scientific views, here they are presented in their original form.

In the processes of research development, the METHODS OF MEASUREMENT and the OPERATIONAL EXPERIMENTAL DEFINITIONS (i.e., TREATMENT MANIPULATION) are usually two separate entities. In our concept these procedures are perceived as complementary because both need an operational definition. The OPERATIONAL EXPERIMENTAL DEFINITION outlines the MANIPULATION OF CONDITIONS, which take place in the experiment.

For example, let's assume that the researcher is interested in establishing conditions under which perceived physical exertion will be examined. The definition of the term perceived physical exertion is:

> **The subjective intensity (i.e. detecting and interpreting sensations arising from the body) of effort, strain, discomfort, and/or fatigue that is experienced during exercise (Noble & Robertson, 1996).**

To establish conditions under which participants in the study will EXPERIENCE and PERCEIVE exertion, an OPERATIONAL EXPERIMENTAL DEFINITION should be established. In the current example, the researcher can measure in the first session the Maximal Oxygen Uptake (VO_2 max) of each participant. In a second session, about 2-3 days later, the participants may be asked to run on a treadmill, at 90% of their individual VO_2 max level identified by using a heart-monitor and oxygen analyzers. Every 30 seconds the runner will be shown the Rate of Perceived Exertion Scale (RPE; Borg, 1982) and be asked to point out with his/her finger his/her feelings of exertion on the RPE which ranges from "1" (not at all) to "10" (very, very hard). This

OPERATIONAL EXPERIMENTAL DEFINTION can be expanded if the researcher is interested in examining the effect of any internal mental technique or external technique (for example, various types of music) on exertion tolerance. In this case, the techniques should be planned and described in detail so that the same, or other, researchers can identically REPEAT them when replicating the study.

The INSTRUMENTS which OPERATIONALLY DEFINE the variables in the study should be RELIABLE, VALID, and OBJECTIVE (i.e., independent of who scores or provides it). Also, the MANIPULATION/TREATMENT should be carried out in a manner which does not leave room for fluctuations and inconsistencies. It is critical to remember that the sounder the psychometric properties of the instruments, the equipment used, and the manipulation/treatment, the more generalizable and sound the results of the study will be.

OPERATIONAL DEFINITIONS OF A VARIABLE and their MEASURE-MENT have various forms. Each form has various techniques. MEASUREMENT can be operationalized via:

INTROSPECTION	-	how participants perceive different experiences, traits, states, etc (questionnaire)
INTERVIEW	-	responses, statements, and individuals' facial expressions, when someone interviews them (coding).
DISCUSSIONS	-	responses, statements, facial expressions and other individual behaviors that occur when discussion takes place (codings).
OBSERVATION	-	what behaviors of individuals occur in natural, semi-natural, and artificial environments (coding).
ANALYSIS	-	what patterns of movements, responses, and other behaviors occur during performance.

Introspective measures have different response formats. Achievement tests for example, are usually scored dichotomously (correct/error) or in a "partial-credit" format (when solutions have several stages, and for each stage a "weight" is assigned). Interviews, discussions, and observations share different formats, dependent on the environmental conditions and the purpose of the study. Analysis is usually applied when the researchers use equipment which enables them to monitor biological or behavioral responses such as heart rate, EEG, EMG, forces, powers etc. Scientists in the fields of biomechanics and motor-control rely on movement analyzers and forceplates to provide them with the necessary operational definitions of the variables. Sport physicians and exercise physiologists rely on various computerized ergometers, gaze analyzers, and other equipment which output online data related to the variables of interest in a study.

(4) Research Design

The combination of curiosity, reading, and motivation often lead to the establishment of a knowledge base. The questions and concerns encountered by the researcher are very rarely completely answered, but rather are stated as basic assumptions and/or hypotheses to be investigated. To examine (i.e., verify, reject, or partially verify) the hypotheses a RESEARCH PLAN/DESIGN is necessary. The research design should be planned very carefully so that alternative explanations of the findings will be minimal or will not exist at all.

Research design relates to the description of past or present day situations (DESCRIPTIVE RESEARCH). Furthermore, research design primarily pertains to RELATIONSHIPS between two or more variables or to EFFECTS that certain treatment/intervention/manipulation have on some defined variable/s. The research designs, which are designed to investigate relationships, are termed CORRELATIONAL RESEARCH DESIGNS while the research designs aimed at "EFFECTS" are termed EXPERIMENTAL DESIGN. The design, which best fits the purpose of the study, and the variables of interest, should be used for basic assumptions and/or hypotheses examination or for theory development.

Correlational studies are designed to infer relationships among several variables; they do not deal with causation. Therefore, when one finds a strong and positive relationship between oxygen uptake (VO_2 max) and a 5000m run, it is not correct to infer that VO_2 max CAUSES the runner to run faster. In order to infer CAUSABLITY another research design is necessary- experimental design. One can take a group of runners, train them with methods which increase their VO_2 max, and then examine them prior and again immediately after the manipulation/method of training ended. Of course, another CONTROL group with similar "intervention time", but without VO_2 max increase, should be similarly examined to verify that other variables have not been

INTERVENING in the process. If differences between the two groups are evident, then causality between VO_2 max and a 5000m run is evident.

In recent years, this "causality assumption" has come under scrutiny. Many researchers believe that causality can be inferred by logical induction and, therefore, when relationships among variables are established, the researcher can infer causality, i.e., one or more variables have an influence on other variable or groups of variables. RELATIONSHIPS in correlational studies are not necessarily determined by the APPROPRIATE RESEARCH DESIGN, but rather by logic inferences.

Experimental designs consist mainly of the MANIPULATION of the INDEPENDENT VARIABLE and measurement of the DEPENDENT VARIABLE. In correlational designs the relations among the ASSIGNED (UNMANIPULATED) VARIABLES are the primary interest of the researcher. When a researcher is interested in examining differences between two or more groups on any given variable (i.e., DV) without conducting any manipulation, this research is categorized within the correlational designs. In cases where the researcher is interested in investigating how an intervention of any kind affects the relationship between variables, this research is classified as an experimental design (see Figure 1.9).

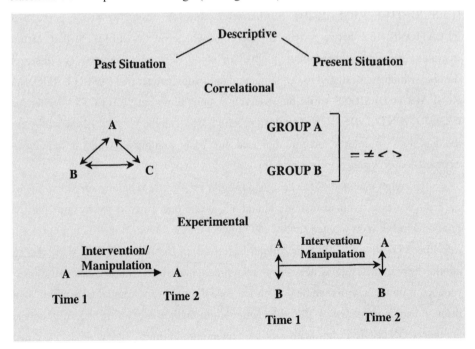

Figure 1.9   Illustrations of correlational and experimental research designs.

In both the correlational and experimental research designs the researcher should choose a sample of people from a given population who VARY on the DEPENDENT VARIABLE (DV). Correlations cannot be computed if the assumption of normality (i.e., variability) is not met (this assumption and others are presented in detail in part IV, chapter 11). Experimental studies are not only intended to examine the averaged changes of the sample on a given DV, but also investigate the variability changes among the participants. It is possible that on average, participants have not changed on the DV, but they became more homogeneous (look similar) or heterogeneous (look different) with respect to the DV. Several such possibilities are illustrated in Figure 6.4.2.

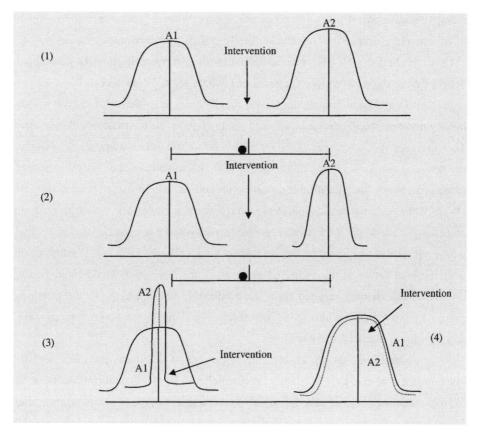

Figure 1.10   Four possibilities of experimental designs: (1) DV, A, increases on the average. (2) DV, A, increases and variability Decreases, (3) DV, A, remains consistent, variability decreases, and (4) neither A nor variability changes.

**(5)   Research Control: Elimination of Alternative Explanations
         and Speculations**

The essence of any research—if not descriptive—is the CONTROL over its
DEPENDENT and INDEPENDENT (manipulation) variables. The control over the DV
is achieved mainly through the PSYCHOMETRIC PROPERTIES (I.E., RELIABILITY,
VALIDITY, AND OBJECTIVITY) of the RESEARCH INSTRUMENTS and the
procedures under which the study is conducted. The control over the IV (i.e.,
manipulation) is determined by the MANIPULATION INTENSITY, NUMBER OF
REPETITIONS, NATURE OF THE MANIPULATION, and most importantly, by
assigning a CONTROL GROUP and/or a PLACEBO which is exposed to some other
manipulation, equal in many instances to the experimental group, but differing in its
main features. Additional control over the IV can be practiced through a design of a
"MANIUPLATION CHECK", i.e., asking, measuring, or observing how the participants
behave during the intervention/manipulations, what they do, think and feel.

Rosenfeld and Tenenbaum (1989) for example, were interested in investigating
how 15 minutes of daily exercises affected productivity in the pharmaceutical industries.
They designed an exercise plan for 48 weeks, 6 days each week, and randomly assigned
the workers into two groups, the experimental (exercisers) or the "social attention"
(controls) groups. The industrial engineering unit objectively measured productivity, the
DV. A better designed replication of this study would include two control groups: one
consisting of workers which would receive attention but not exercise, and one which
would not receive any attention but would rest for 15 minutes each day. Because of the
well designed nature of this proposed experiment, the researchers could avoid finding
differences which only resulted from the additional attention given to the treatment
group. In this case, the results of the study would not leave room for any other
speculations or alternative explanations.

Control over the IV enables the researcher to determine the cause and the
outcome. Control over the DV enables the researcher to be precise and confident that the
instruments indeed measure the intended variables, and the type of sampling procedure
(discussed later in this chapter) enables generalizations to be made beyond the sampled
participants in the current study. Random assignments of participants to groups ensure
that the various groups are equal in all the other variables, which were not measured in
the study.

The control over the variables' nominal and operational definitions (i.e., measurement), the sampling procedure, and the manipulation (DV) involves 4 main concerns:

a) EXCLUSIVENESS
b) SENSITIVITY AND MAGNITUDE
c) SYSTEMATIC REPLICATION
d) CAUSALITY

EXCLUSIVENESS is achieved by precisely defining the IV, and by assigning a control or several control groups, which differ from the experimental group only in this definition and its operationalization. Control over the IV means that the manipulation/intervention really works, i.e., participants experienced the feelings and thoughts intended to be delivered to them by the researcher. It is important to remember that the stronger the manipulation, the more sound the results and the conclusions of the study, and the stronger CAUSALITY can be inferred. In behavioral and social sciences as well as in life sciences, this may raise some ETHICAL CONSIDERATION because of the invasive nature of some treatments.

The researcher(s) must decide on the MAGNITUDE, the NUMBER OF REPETITIONS, and the DURATION of time the participants will be exposed or involved in the intervention. Each experimental research design involves manipulation to some extent. Some manipulations are carried out in the field (natural or semi-natural conditions) while others are performed under more controlled and structured conditions such as in the laboratory. Both environments have benefits unique to the setting. Natural environments permit more freedom for INTERVENING VARIABLES to "interfere" with the CAUSE-EFFECT conclusions, while they are closer to the reality, i.e., the real complexity of life. Structured laboratory environment allows for more control over the CAUSE-EFFECT interaction because more control is exercised over the manipulation and various intervening variables than what is possible in semi-natural environments. However, such structural and controlled conditions are rarely present the real world.

Recently, there has been an increased advocacy for the importance of REPLICATIONS (over significance level) in reaching sound and reliable results, and in the establishment of sound theories (Cohen, 1994; Loftus, 1996). If the manipulation is well controlled, it is possible for researchers to REPLICATE IDENTICAL

CONDITIONS under which the study was conducted. Systematic replications are of utmost importance in research because they allow for the addition or modification of conditions, which were not present in the previous research. By doing so, the findings of additional studies may shed more light on how people behave in a complex environment when conditions are systematically changing but are ACCOUNTED FOR and controlled.

Control over the IV and DV enables the researcher(s) to infer CAUSALITY. When one or more control groups are used to falsify any alternative explanations, the inferred causality becomes undisputable. The effect of intervening variables can be controlled by taking into account the individual differences among the participants. For example, in a study by Rosenfeld and Tenenbaum (1989), the results could be attributed to the fact that productivity of pharmaceutical workers may be influenced by their every-day habits of exercising. To control this possible explanation, participants were asked to report on their exercise habits, its frequency and duration. Once these reports have been collected, it enabled the researchers to examine whether every-day exercise habits are associated with work productivity and whether this variable INTERACTS with the manipulation (DV). This possible interaction will be discussed later in more detail. This concept of control over the DV, Intervening variables (IV) and DV in Rosenfeld and Tenenbaum's study is illustrated in Figure 1.11.

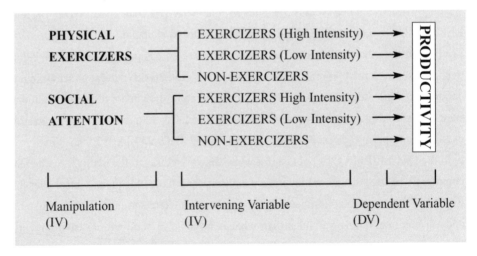

| Manipulation (IV) | Intervening Variable (IV) | Dependent Variable (DV) |

Figure 1.11   Illustration of controlling the IV, intervening V and DV in a study where the manipulation involved physical exercising or social attention. The DV was work productivity, and the intervening variable was the rate of every-day exercising by the participants.

To arrive at sound results, the researcher is required to ensure that the participants in both the control and experimental groups are equal in all the possible variables (e.g., demographics, behavioral, personality, fitness, and others).

The experimental and control participants should be exposed to the different conditions at the same time and (if possible) be under identical environmental conditions. They should be similar in all conditions, except the one which constitutes the DV. All the procedures and instructions before and during the experimentation period ought to be also identical.

Another control that should be practiced and implemented relates to the VARIABILITY (i.e., differences among the participants), which exists among the participants of the experimental and control groups. In cases where no variability among the participants on a RELEVANT VARIABLE exists, then any differences between the two groups are a TRUE DIFFERENCE. In this case, the VALIDITY of the experiment is questioned because there are INITIAL DIFFERENCES among the two or more groups of participants. Such a difference is very much UNDESIRABLE and should be carefully controlled prior to exercising the manipulation (IV). Differences among the groups are termed SYSTEMATIC VARIANCE or BETWEEN GROUPS VARIANCE, and the differences within the members of each group are termed ERROR VARIANCE or WITHIN GROUP VARIANCE. It can be exerted at this stage that at the outset of each study, it is desirable that the ERROR and SYSTEMTIC VARIANCES will be equal between the groups while at the end of the study, the differences among the group (i.e., SYSTEMATIC VARIANCE) will substantially exceed the within group variance (ERROR VARIANCE). Only then the researcher may conclude that there are CAUSAL RELATIONSHIPS between the IV and the DV. How to control the two types of variances? Figure 1.12 demonstrates the sources of variance (i.e., ERROR) that a researcher should be aware of.

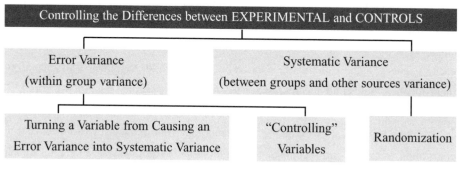

Figure 1.12   Sources of variance (i.e., errors) in an experimental research design.

5.1 Systematic Variance

SYSTEMATIC VARIANCE is a variance, which biases the estimates of the dependent variable (DV) in a systematic manner. For example, if a yardstick or any other measurement device is not appropriately calibrated, then ALL the participants' measures will contain some given systematic error in the DV value. Systematic variance can also result from environmental or procedural consequences such as testing the participants in different conditions (climatic, environmental, psychological, etc) by different examiners/researchers/assistants, or during different periods (days, weeks, months, etc). Also the attitude and personal or social climate, set up by the examiner, are causes, which may affect the scores of the DV, and therefore, are considered to be sources of systematic variance. To eliminate such errors, complete RANDOMIZATION (random assignment) of participants into the experimental and control groups should be implemented.

By randomizing the assignment of participants into experimental and control groups, the researcher assumes that on any variable, which was not controlled in the study, participants are distributed equally within each of the studied groups. Thus, randomization ensures that a BETWEEN GROUPS differences (i.e., variance) becomes a WITHIN GROUP variance.

To control the systematic variance, which results from the various conditions (examiners, periods or measurement, environment, etc.) the researcher should plan the study in a manner that participants are exposed to IDENTICAL CONDITIONS/. Otherwise the differences, which may occur between the groups, can be attributed to systematic variance rather than to TRUE DIFFERENCES.

5.2 Error Variance

Error variance refers to differences among the participants in a variety of traits and states. These differences (i.e., integration of all possible causes) are assumed to be equal across all conditions. It is almost impossible, especially in the behavioral and social sciences, but also in the life sciences, to control all the variables or to keep all of them identical across all the research sessions. The probability that such errors will occur is equal across all the testing conditions.

There are at least two ways the researcher may control the error variance: first by controlling variables, and second by turning a variable from causing an error variance into a systematic variance (see Figure 1.13). Controlling variables is a relatively easy procedure, but may require an increase in the number of participants in the study if meaningful results are desired. Let's assume that gender is a variable, which cause an error variance, and the researcher desires to control it experimentally. In Figure 1.13 we demonstrate how such a control can be established.

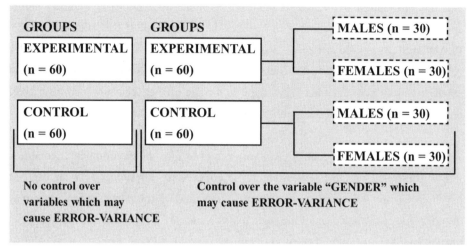

Figure 1.13 Ignoring and controlling "gender" as a possible source of error variance.

As we can see, by controlling "gender" as a possible cause of error variance, four groups instead of two were established. Rather than 60 participants in each, we now have only 30 participants in each of the four groups. If a control for age is desired, then the plan (Figure 1.14) will be as follows:

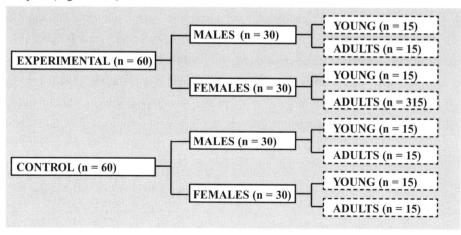

Figure 1.14 Controlling error variance may result from differences in "Age" and "Gender".

In this case, each of the groups are broken-down by both "gender" and "age category". Eight (2x2x2) groups consisting of 15 participants in each have resulted. If the researcher desires to control more variables, which may cause error variance in the study, more participants should be recruited. At this early stage, we should keep in mind that the assumption of NORMALITY (i.e., normal distribution) is required before applying any statistical technique to the data. Thus the smallest CELL in the STUDY PLAN/DESIGN (in the last case—8 cells with 15 participants in each) MUST MEET NORMAL DISTRIBUTION. To reach such a requirement, at least 30 participants in the smallest cell is recommended. Thus there is a trade-off between how many variables ought to be controlled and the number of participants, which are required.

Another way to control error-variance is to turn the environmental condition into a controlled variable. For example, if an exercise physiologist or an exercise psychologist are interested in investigating how people tolerate exertion, they may design a study in which each of the participants is measured for his/her maximal oxygen uptake, and then ask each of them to run on a treadmill, 90% of their maximal value as long as possible until a state where they can not go any longer, and hold the front bar of the treadmill until it comes to a full stop. One may question whether 80%, 70%, or any other value of the maximal oxygen uptake may end up with identical results? Or alternatively, if another ergometer was used, say a cycle ergometer, will identical results be evident? Furthermore, some participants may be better able to tolerate an aerobic type of exertion, but not the exertion required of a strength-endurance task such as squeezing a dynamometer. In all these examples, error-variance may be controlled. The same or similar participants may be asked to run 50%, 60%, 70%, 80% and 90% of their maximal value on two or more ergometers, and perform different tasks. Once these are controlled, the results obtained contain less error (less "noise") and can be GENERALIZED to a larger population of people, conditions, devices, etc. To enable GENERALIZATION, a repeated experiment that recruits the same samples, and shares the same procedures, conditions, and instrumentation is required.

One method used to account for error variance is to change a variable that may cause error variance into a defined variable which may cause a systematic error. Let's assume that in the "exertion-tolerance" experiment, people with longer familiarity with aerobic-type experiences (runners, joggers, cyclists, etc.) may tolerate an aerobic-type of exertion for longer periods of time than people who do not engage in physical practice. In this case, within each of the experimental and control groups (if necessary) "exertion familiarized" and "exertion unfamiliarized" participants can be distinguished and their DV (i.e., "time in exertion") be estimated separately and be compared. Using the "exertion-tolerance" study as an illustration for controlling error-variance, Figure 1.15 summarizes this concept.

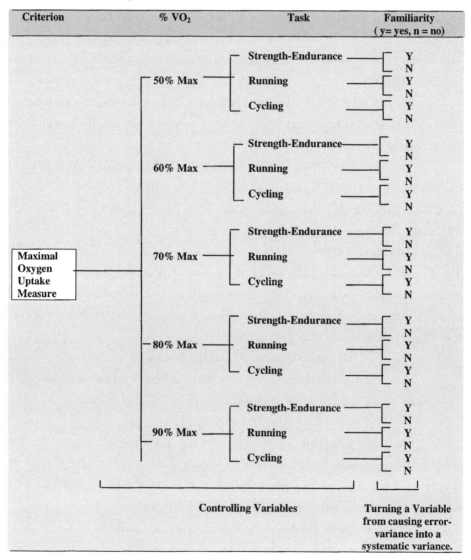

Figure 1.15   Turning a variable from causing an error variance into a controlled variable which causes a systematic error.

(6)   Validity and Plausibility of Research Findings

Previously, the aspect of GENERALIZABILITY of the research findings was discussed. However, to limit the possibility of alternative explanations to the research findings, there are additional matters that should be taken into consideration. According to Cook and Campbell (1976) these considerations relate to the generalizability of the research findings across populations and conditions (i.e., external validity), and across the operational definitions of the DVs and IVs (CONSTRUCT VALIDITY). We refer here to the validity of the RESEARCH FINDINGS and not to the validity of the INSTRUMENTATION.

The four validity types discussed here apply to any research which is aimed at verifying a hypothesis (question) which refers to causality, i.e., any IV which causes alteration to any DV.

These are: (a) CONCLUSION VALIDITY, (b) INTERNAL VALIDITY, (c) CONSTRUCT VALIDITY, (d) EXTERNAL VALIDITY, and (e) LOGICAL PLAUSIBILITY. We shall refer to each of this five in more detail next.

6.1   Conclusion Validity

When a researcher finds a relationship (i.e., correlation) between two or more variables, causality cannot be easily inferred unless there is sufficient logical and empirical evidence. In experimental studies, however, causality can be inferred when the following 3 conditions are met:

a)   A relation between the IV and DV exists,

b)   DV changes were noted only after the IV was manipulated, and

c)   Lack of alternative explanations to the DV alterations.

Cook and Campbell (1976) stated several causes which account for the possibility that causality is not inferred despite the confirmatory findings, and the possibility of inferring causality when findings were not confirmed. Statisticians refer to these possibilities as type I and type II errors. Briefly, these are:

Statistical Power: Relates to the number of participants who took part in the study. To infer generalizability, one expects that an expected difference or relations will be true only if a sufficient number of subjects participated in the study. Statistical power is also related to the statistical tests, which are applied to the data and the type of hypotheses (unidirectional or bi-directional) that are examined. The relationships between power, and the type I and II errors are discussed in more detail later in this book.

Error Rate: The more groups or conditions the researcher introduces in the research plan, the higher the probability of getting a significant difference by chance and the more conservative he/she should be about acceptance or rejection of the null hypothesis (i.e, no differences or relations between the IV and DV exist). It is common to use the 0.05 probability value (a value which became "sacred" during the 20th century), as a criterion for verification or rejection of the null hypothesis. When two comparisons are made, the probability adjustment should be 0.10 (0.05 + 0.05), three (0.15), four (0.20) and so on. The exact equations for probability adjustment is $1—(1-p)^c$ where p is the probability for committing a type I error and c is the number of paired comparisons in the study. In studies with multiple variables, the probability of rejecting the null hypothesis is reduced by p/k in which p is the significance level for rejecting the null hypothesis, usually 0.05, and k is the number of DVs in the study. Thus, to reject the null hypothesis when many DVs exist, is much harder than rejecting the same hypothesis with one or two DVs. Logically this approach makes sense. These procedures ensure that chance findings will be minimized as much as possible. However, there are many other problems with the Null Hypothesis Significance Testing (NHST) and these will be dealt with later.

Reliability of Measurement: When the measurement is not reliable due to external factors, (instability over time periods and conditions), or internal factors (items of a scale do not share reliably the underlying variable they ought to construct), the DV is subjected to error in both the experimental and control groups participants. Increasing the measurement reliability and decreasing the time intervals between the subsequent measures in the study are optimal solutions to overcome this kind of error-problem.

Reliability of DV (intervention/manipulation): The method of delivering the treatment or manipulation (DV), if not appropriately applied, may result in an error variance. Instructions and procedures should be delivered identically to all the participants in order to eliminate undesirable explanations of the research findings.

Irrelevant Factors: Various factors, which were not designed and are unexpected, such as noises, climate, experimenters, etc., may have, to some extent, an effect on the DV. Sound manipulations and precautions that should be taken prior to the study commencement reduce these sources of "noise".

Unexpected Heterogeneity of Participants: Participants can vary in their susceptibility to the treatment/manipulation. Some, because of this tendency, can accept it favorably while others can be annoyed or lack motivation. Controlling such possible variables is recommended in order to minimize error variances.

6.2   Internal Validity

Internal validity refers to the question of whether the intervention/manipulation was the cause for the DV being altered or if there is an additional, external possibility to the findings. Campbell and Stanley (1966) stated that there are several threats, which can be considered as artifacts to the internal validity of the research findings. These are: (a) history, (b) maturation, (c) instrumentation, (d) mortality, (e) statistical regression, (f) selection, (g) morality, and (h) statistical interaction with selection. Additional threats include: (i) resentful demoralization of control group subjects, (j) local history, (k) diffusion of treatment to the central group, (l) compensating equalization of treatment, and (m) compensatory rivalry. We will briefly discuss each of the threats next.

History: Refers to all the events which take place during the treatment manipulation.

Some events, which are unrelated to the intervention, may account for the differences or lack of differences between the experimental and control participants, or among the same participants across the experimental period.

Maturation: In cases where the treatment is very long, participants mature naturally regardless of the intervention to which they are exposed. In such cases, many variables should be controlled and in some cases more than one control group is required. Additionally, measures of maturation in the relevant variables are required to partial out alternative explanations.

Instrumentation: When the instruments are not identically calibrated on each occasion, the results of the study may be invalidated. Also, the length of a measurement instrument may result in a threat to internal validity. For example, participants responding to a very long questionnaire may become fatigued or frustrated, and therefore provide inaccurate information.

Testing: When instruments are used for measurement in several consecutive periods, the results in the late occasions may be due to "learning" or "adjustment" effects.

Statistical Regression: It is a common belief that measures of participants on various traits regress towards the mean, i.e., participants who obtained high scores on the first test may gain somewhat lower scores in the second test, and similarly, low scorers will gain higher scores in subsequent test. This "regression towards the mean" results from some lack of reliability of the instruments used and from the internal characteristics of the participants. Using high reliable measures and replications of results are required to minimize the threats on the internal validity of the findings.

Selection: Relates to the sampling procedures. There is a strong threat to the internal validity of a study when participants are not appropriately assigned to the experimental and control groups. However, in some cases there is a specific reason why random assignment is not used and therefore, different sampling procedures are preferable.

Mortality: Subjects can drop out from one group more than from another one due to poor selection or some exceptional physical, emotional, or social demands. In such a case, the final findings cannot be attributed to the DV manipulation.

Statistical Interaction with Selection: Some of the threats (maturation, testing or regression) can interact with the selection threat and together threaten the internal validity. For example, in cases where participants in one of the groups mature earlier than others, the findings of the study may be attributed in part to the "selection by maturation" interaction (i.e., combination).

Resentful Demoralization of Control Group Participants: If participants in the control group realize that the experimental group participants get "more" or "less" attention, they may develop resentment and bias their responses. Social comparisons and verbal or physical interactions among the participants of the research groups should be avoided.

Local History: Some events, which are usually unexpected, may occur to one of the groups but not to the other, which could not be expected. It is suggested therefore to randomize the research conditions so that the probability of such events to occur is equal in both groups. If conditions are counterbalanced, they should be equally counterbalanced in the control and experimental groups.

Diffusion of Treatment to the Control Group: If the participants of the experimental groups communicate with the participants of the control groups, the last may use the information given to them and apply it. In this case, the expected differences among the groups due to the IV manipulation will not emerge.

Compensating Equalization of Treatment: In some cases, manipulations and interventions cost money. In instances where the control condition consists of equal compensation, the expected results may not emerge due to equal allocations of resources given to the control. In some cases, equal compensation is required and the nature of the intervention may play a major role in the study. In such cases, this threat is not applicable.

Compensatory Rivalry: When subjects in the experimental and control groups know to which intervention they belong, a competition may evoke. In such cases, the motivation "to do better than the others" may mask the real relationship between the IV and DV.

Other threats to the internal validity include: (n) the experimenter expectations, (o) guessing the research intentions, and (p) desire to gain recognition from the experimenter. The experimenters can control these three last threats by behaving in a manner that should not cause any of the personal threats to occur.

6.3 Construct Validity

Construct validity of the research findings refers to the generalizations one can make as to whether the findings can be clearly associated with the operational definition of the variables in the study. In behavioral and social studies in particular, researchers define the variables in the study by different definitions. The operationalization of these variables also differs. In many cases, when "other" variables can account for the research findings, the researcher concludes that there is a CONFOUNDING EFFECT.

Threat to the construct validity may occur because of (a) uncomprehensive definitions of the variables in the study, and alternatively, (b) over-conclusive definitions, i.e., definitions that consist of more than one clear variable.

Lack of Classification of Theoretical Definitions: In cases where more than one acceptable definition exists, the research findings cannot be confidently generalized. If for example, "aerobic capacity" is defined differently by various exercise physiologists and coaches, then its impact on physical activities, which depend on it, may in some cases not emerge.

Mismatch between Theoretical and Operational Definitions: When the theoretical definition of the IV is complex or multidimensional, it may cause difficulties in its operationalization. It is recommended that each of the dimensions be separately operationalized in various combinations. In such cases, the number of participants and therefore the costs of the study will substantially increase. Similarly, in cases where the DV is also complex and/or multi-dimensional, all the various dimensions should be operationalized (i.e., measured) to ensure the validity of the study.

6.4   External Validity

External validity refers to the degree to which generalization of the research findings can be made across populations, periods of time, and conditions. Cook and Campbell (1976) pointed out the following "interactions" which may threaten the external validity of the experiment. These are:

Interaction between the Measurement and the IV: In experiments which require participants to respond to any stimulus or stimuli, read and answer questions, etc., be exposed to an intervention, and again respond to the same studies, stimuli, or question, the participants behaviors in the second session may be affected by their exposure to the stimulus or questions in the first session rather than the intervention. To overcome this threat, the researcher may choose an additional group of participants, who will not be exposed to the stimulus prior to the intervention. These participants' responses will be compared later to participants who were exposed to both the measurement and intervention and those who were exposed only to the two measurements without being exposed to the intervention. Such a threat may not be applicable in many of the studies in the life sciences.

Selection by Treatment Interaction: In some cases, mainly in a survey, a possibility exists that some participants do not wish to be treated or respond to some types of questionnaires. In such cases, the findings are limited only to these participants who share some common traits. The generalizability of findings is therefore limited. To overcome such potential threats it is recommended that one should choose participants using a random procedure; otherwise the findings will be limited to the current sample or other samples that share the same traits (which sometimes are not clear or known to the researcher). It is recommended that one should choose samples which vary in several characteristics (may be cultural, demographic, educational, physical activity, etc.) and repeat the study on each of them separately. By applying such a procedure, the random variable is treated as a systematic variable, which is controlled.

Setting or History by Treatment Interaction: In field studies, the environment (mainly the natural or semi-natural) usually changes and thus the treatment, which is applied, may result in different effects on the DV. In such cases, a careful description of the unique characteristics of each environment is desired; use the descriptions as an IV, and conduct several experiments in each environment.

When appropriately taken care of, all the threats can be controlled whether statistically or by experimental control (i.e., procedures). The threats to the internal validity of the findings are the crucial ones and should be dealt with in the appropriate means. However, generalizability of the best controlled study may also be questioned, even on theoretical grounds only.

(7)   Sampling Procedures

Sampling, i.e., choosing subjects who represent a population of interest, is one of the most important procedures in research. If the sample does not represent the population from which it was derived, the findings CANNOT BE GENERALIZED. A sample from a population can be large or small depending on the questions the researcher intends to answer. There are domains (in medicine for example) in which N=1 and the findings are of the utmost importance and can be generalized. This can happen in cases where there is sound evidence to believe that the population is very homogeneous on the variable or variables under study. Both sampling and replications are necessary for generalization. However, how many n (participants) from N (population) or how many repetitions (k) are needed is and will always remain a matter in dispute.

A sample from a population is drawn because in many cases, particularly in experimental studies in which intervention/manipulation takes place, it is logistically and financially impossible to sample all the population. The statistical procedures, which are performed to examine the hypotheses of the study, are aimed at verifying whether the findings can be generalized or not. In cases where ALL THE POPULATION of interest is studied, statistical tests are not required, because any differences among groups or relations among variables are "TRUE".

A NON-REPRESENTATIVE sample is one which consists of participants who do not share the same opinions, attitudes, traits, and other characteristics of the population of which they are a part. For example, an exercise physiologist is interested in recruiting participants for a study in which he or she is interested in determining the anaerobic threshold value and its relation to the ability to exercise and sustain the workload in conditions of high humidity and temperature. To recruit sufficient number of participants to conduct the research, the physiologist may advertise the details of the study. The participants who agreed to take part in the study may have been long-distance runners or cyclists who were more interested in verifying their anaerobic threshold rather than participating in the study. In such an extreme case, the findings cannot be generalized to the whole population because the selection of the sample was inappropriately conducted.

A non-representative sample can also be a consequence of CONDITION ALTERATION. If a survey is conducted to determine election of politicians or opinions about an important issue, unexpected and uncontrolled events may cause people to change their opinions. In this case, it is not necessarily the sample that was NOT representative, but rather the conditions were the main attribute of the change.

The degree of SAMPLING REPRESENTATIVENESS is a function of the SAMPLING method the researcher applied in the study. In general, there are two methods of SAMPLING: PROBABILITY SAMPLING, and NON-PROBABILITY SAMPLING.

In probability sampling, four conditions should be met:
a)   Each person or item in the population has a given probability to be chosen for the sample,
b)   None of the persons or items have certain probability to be selected,
c)   None of the persons or items have any chance to be selected, and
d)   The selection of one person or items is independent of the other selection (note: this is not a requirement in all the probability sampling methods).

Each person thus has a probability (P_i) to be selected where $0 < P_i < 1$ and P_i is known in advance. In non-probability sampling, at least one of the first three conditions is not met, i.e., the probability is unknown. There are persons or items, which certainly will be selected, or some persons or items will certainly be not selected. SAMPLING ERROR can be estimated only in probability sampling. This sampling method is also the most common and is being used in the majority of the studies in both life and behavioral/social sciences.

As previously noted, the SAMPLING PROCEDURE depends on the POPULATION CHARACTERISTICS and on the SELECTIVE VARIABLES the researcher desired to measure. In the previous example, if the exercise physiologist was interested in studying how aerobic athletes with oxygen uptake above 70 ml/min/ kg tolerate very humid and high temperature conditions, then the sample of such a small and homogeneous population may consist of a relatively small number of participants. In this case, the population characteristics (certain level of oxygen uptake) substantially limit the population size and the question relates to those with 70 ml/min/ kg (a "selective variable"). The majority of the questions that researchers ask pertain to the whole population or to the population, which is more heterogeneous on many variables. In such cases, a larger sample is required to enable generalization.

7.1 Non-Probability (Purposive) Sampling

A non-probability sampling method is used in cases where probability methods cannot be applied or in cases where it is necessary to investigate the research question/hypotheses. In some cases, a non-probability sampling is attributed to causes, which may arise during the participants' selection, communication, interviewing or observations of them.

In cases where the population of interest consists of participants who are involved in illegal activities (e.g., drugs, import/export of forbidden indices, etc.) or have some kind of disabilities (e.g., emotional, mental, or physical), it is often hard or even impossible to recruit such participants to the study. People who are engaged with such a population may help the researcher to gather information, which enables them to recruit such participants to a study in which confidentiality is secured. In cases, such as the ones pointed out above, communication problems are common. Sensitive issues and an excessive number of questions may cause substantial dropout. A compromise is to sample a "quota", a sufficient number of participants from the population who were not selected randomly, but are identical in all the characteristics to the population of interest.

7.2 Sampling Framework

SAMPLING FRAMEWORK refers to the characteristics of the population from which a sample of persons or items should be drawn. The random sampling method is aimed at the best representation of the population. Too many inconsistencies exist which relate to the mismatch between the characteristics of the population and the sample used in the study. CONVENIENCE sampling is often prevalent in psychology departments. However, it is important to remember that the sample of students does not necessarily represent the population. In such cases, it is impossible to translate the research findings to the "general population". This concept is represented in Figure 1.16.

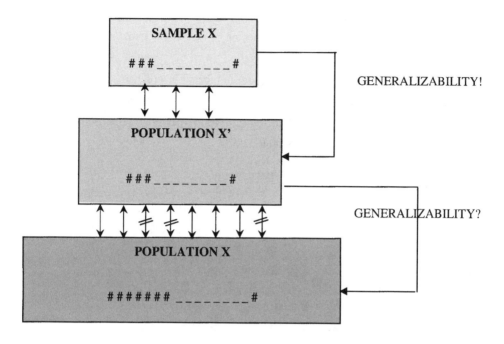

Figure 1.16   A Sample of Elements (# #....#) of Sample X Matches Perfectly ( ) the same elements in population X,' and therefore generalizability from X to X' is inferred. Elements of population X' and X (general population) are not completely matched ( )), and therefore generalizability from X' to population X cannot be inferred.

7.3   Probability Sampling Methods in Regards to Number-Based Data

Probability sampling methods are divided into seven categories:

a)   Simple random sampling,

b)   Systematic random sampling,

c)   Stratified random sampling, and

d)   Cluster sampling.

e)   Randomized controlled trials,

f)   Cohort studies,

g)   Case-control studies

We shall briefly elaborate on each of them:

Simple Random Sampling:

In simple random sampling each person or item in the population has an equal chance to be selected to the sample. If a detailed list of the population is known, it is a common practice to use the "table of random numbers" in order to select the random sample. Each person or item is assigned one of the random numbers (there are random tables for 2,3,4,5 …n digits) and then the number of persons or items required are selected from the list, which matches their names.

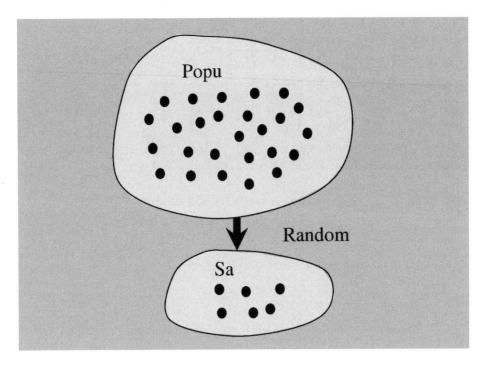

Figure 1.17   Illustration of deriving at a random sample.

Systematic Random Sampling

Systematic random sampling is used when the population consists of too many persons or items, and simple randomization procedures may consume too much time and resources. Instead of using the "table of random numbers", the persons or items are ordered and then the first one is chosen. From here on, each person/item, k, in the list is selected. For example, we are interested in a sample of 30 athletes of a population of 2700 athletes in our town. In this case, 2700/30 = 90, i.e., each 90th athlete in the list will be selected to the sample. As we can see, there are 90 groups, which contain 30 athletes each (90 x 30 = 2800). Of the 30 athletes in Group 1 we randomly chose one, assume number 23, then we could go to select the second athlete, which is 113 and so on, 23,113,203, 293.. The ratio of sample/population, in our example, 30/2700 or 1/90, is termed SAMPLE FRACTION.

The systematic random sampling is efficient when the sampling framework is randomly ordered with respect to the desired variables. In cases where some kind of systematic order exists within each of the sample fraction, the final estimates of the sample will be biased.

To avoid such situations, one should carefully ensure that a systematic ordering, whether intentional or not, does not exist. Once that is established, the simple random sampling method should be applied for the selection process.

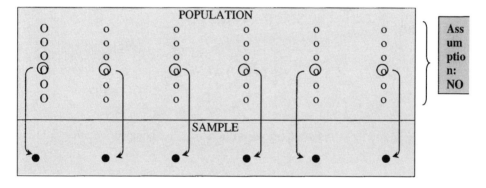

Figure 1.18   An Illustration of Devising a Random Sample.

Stratified Random Sampling

Stratified random sampling is used similarly to the complete randomized method, but to each STRADA (section) of the sample separately. Let's assume that the population of athletes from which we are interested in selecting a random sample consists of 30 athletes (24 females and 6 males), and we are interested in selecting 10 of those for the sample. In this case, there is a strong chance that a completely random selection method will result in none of the males being selected. To avoid such a situation, females (n_1 = 24) and males (n_2 = 6) will be randomly selected separately using the 10/30 = 1/3 sampling fraction. Thus 8 females and 2 males will be included in the final sample.

Let's assume that a sport sociologist is interested in a sample of 500 athletes out of 5000 to examine their attitudes towards aggression and violence in sport as a function of their age. The researcher believes that age is an important component in determining the severity of such acts, and therefore the sample of athletes should take this component into account. To appropriately select the sample, the sport sociologist should first investigate the proportion of age-distribution in various sport types, breakdown the sample to such sections, and within each section randomly choose the appropriate number of athletes. To illustrate this method, let's assume that sport-type will be broken down as follows:

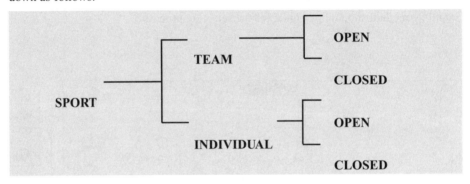

and the population age categories (in years) in active and competitive athletes are as follows:

10-12	:	30%
12.1-14	:	25%
14.1-16	:	20%
16.1-18	:	15%
>18	:	10%
TOTAL	:	100%

We also assume that a ratio of 1:2 between the number of athletes in individual and team sport is known and remains consistent in both open and closed skills within each category (see Table 1.2).

Table 1.2   *Stratification of 1000 Athletes with Respect to Sport Type and Age.*

SPORT		Age Category				
		10-12	12.1-14	14.1-16	16.1-18	>18
% in Population:		**30%**	**25%**	**20%**	**15%**	**10%**
TEAM **(n=3334)**	**OPEN** **(n=1667)**	500	417	333	250	167
	CLOSED **(n=1667)**	500	417	333	250	167
INDIVIDUAL **(n=1666)**	**OPEN** **(n=833)**	250	208	167	125	83
	CLOSED **(n=833)**	250	208	167	125	83
n = 5000						

From the stratified population, presented in Table 6.1, we chose the sample, taking into account the sample fraction of 500/5000 = 1/10. In this case from each of the 20 cells in Table 6.7.1, 10% of the athletes should be randomly selected. The final number of athletes in the sample will be then (see Table 1.3).

Table 1.3   *Stratification (500/5000) with Respect to Sport-Type and Age.*

		Age Category				
SPORT		10-12	12.1-14	14.1-16	16.1-18	>18
TEAM	**OPEN**	50	42	33	25	167
	CLOSED	50	42	33	25	167
INDIVIDUAL	**OPEN**	25	21	17	13	8
	CLOSED	25	21	17	13	8
n = 500						

If the proportions of open-closed skills were different, or additional stratifying factors were added, then the stratification of the population would be different. It is of the utmost importance to consider all the possible STRATIFYING FACTORS, which may account for the questions investigated. Once these are determined, the sampling procedure should follow their presence in the population. Lack of considering the stratifying factor may bias the findings of the sport sociologist on violence and aggression of athletes.

In the example presented in Tables 1.2 and 1.3 the stratification was proportional, i.e., proportional numbers of persons or items that exist in the population were assigned to the designated sample. This procedure is termed PROPORTIONAL STRATIFIED SAMPLING. In cases where the researcher decides for any reason not to follow the population stratifications, the procedure is termed DISPROPORTIONAL STRATIFIED SAMPLING. This last procedure has several advantages, depending on the research questions, which ought to be investigated.

Stratifying factors are determined according to their RELEVANCE to the RESEARCH QUESTION.

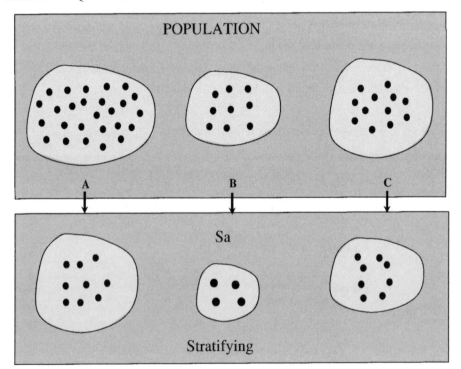

Figure 1.19   Illustration of Stratified Random Sample.

Cluster Sampling

When the population of people or items is very large and is spread over a very wide geographical area, it is difficult to apply any of the random sampling procedures described so far. It is of particular difficulty when the records of remote areas do not exist and the access to the people or items is problematic. In such cases, the population can be divided into CLUSTERS. A random selection of clusters takes place and ALL of the people or items within the selected clusters can be sampled. The number of people or items under such a procedure cannot be determined. Also the findings may be biased in cases where the clusters include people or items, which vary as a consequence of their location or any other cause. In stratified sampling, we sample people or subjects from each section and therefore the sampling error results from the variance, which exists among the people/items within each stratifying factor of the population. In the cluster sampling, all the people/items within each cluster are sampled. Therefore the sampling error stems from the VARIANCE AMONG THE CLUSTERS.

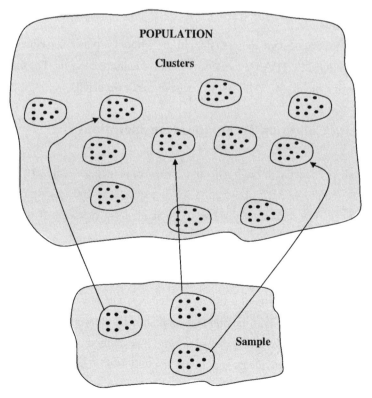

Figure 1.20   Illustration of Cluster Sampling.

Randomized Controlled Trials

The sample of participants from a particular population is RANDOMLY allocated to different groups, which undergo some treatments. When non-randomized controlled clinical trials are selected, none of the groups have inherent self-selected differences before the interventions/treatments were applied. This causes a SYSTEMATIC BIAS in the study's outcome.

Cohort Sample

The selection of "comparable controls" to a group of participants, which were chosen for the study, is a difficult task, sometimes even impossible. Equality in age, gender, socio-economic status, and presence of coexisting illness are often difficult to obtain. But the treatment/intervention is hard to achieve. Only through the STATISTICAL ADJUSTMENT can such differences be accounted for and/or controlled.

Case-control Sample

The experiences of individuals with or without a particular behavior/trait are analyzed RETROSPECTIVELY to identify putative causative events. The main concern here is to define the exact TIME that the behavior/trait occurred.

(8)   Data Collection Techniques Considerations

Data is collected through objective measures (e.g., gaze analyzers, force-plates, biofeedback monitors, etc.), observation, asking questions and relying on written or other resources. We shall briefly relate to each of these methods of data collection separately.

8.1   Observation

Observation consists of a variety of methods. The most often used include:

Field Research: This method is used mainly by anthropologists who stay with a given group of people for a long period of time. The method consists of recording any observed behaviors of individuals and groups, as well as written impressions, which the observer experiences. Field research methods vary according to the questions and aims of the study. There are cases in which the observer arrives periodically to the environment of objects or subjects, observes only a given number of behaviors and completely ignores others. Field research is also termed ETHNOGRAPHIC RESEARCH and this will be introduced more in detail in Part III, Chapters 8 and 9.

Laboratory Research: This method consists of assigning a task to individuals or groups in a fixed laboratory condition. The researcher is either part of the group or an external observer who codes all or selected behaviors using a coding format, film, camera, tape-recorder or any other device, dependant on the aim, task, and the extent of the desired reliability (precision) of the observation.

8.2 Questioning

Asking questions is a method of collecting data, which relies on the participant's responses to items or questions asked by the researcher using written, vocal, or videotaped means. This method is applied to gain insight (i.e., impressions and reflections) of the observed participants, which cannot be visually observed.

AN IN DEPTH (i.e., clinical) INTERVIEW often lasts a long time and follows guided outlines. The interviewee responds and in some cases, even asks questions and/or seeks clarifications. Studies which use in-depth interviews do not contain many subjects. There is a large amount of raw-data that is collected and used for making inferences.

A SURVEY is another means for asking questions. Usually the surveys contain structured items, which were designed in advance, and frequently the respondent has several choices without the freedom to choose a unique response. Sometimes the participants do not have time limits to respond to the interviewer's questions.

The most common method of asking questions are QUESTIONNAIRES which are designed to measure variables such as personality, psychological traits and states, attitudes, abilities, and achievements.

8.3 Written or other Resources

Written or other resources such as historical documents, paintings, and recordings are sources which are used to answer research concerns, frequently asked by social scientists. The main aim here is to make sense of financial reports of firms, minutes and protocols from meetings, letters, diaries, or any other documents which may shed light on the nature and policies of individuals and organizations. Researchers who use their findings for complementing their resources use results of surveys and other statistical information.

8.4 Objective Data Collection

Data collection, which consists of high-tech equipment, has become more and more popular in recent years. Even questionnaires are designed in a manner that answers can be collected by the computer and be immediately scored and profiled if necessary. However, in the life sciences, physiologists, biomechanics, physicians, and biochemists are using manual or computerized devices to collect or analyze samples of blood, urine, and other liquids, and/or tissues, and later use these as quantifiable values for further analysis. Usually these types of data are independent of the researcher's intentions and therefore are very reliable.

(9) Data Analysis

Data analysis pertains to the techniques that researchers use to make sense of the collected data. Data analysis is aimed at the questions asked, basic assumptions, and/or hypotheses postulated.

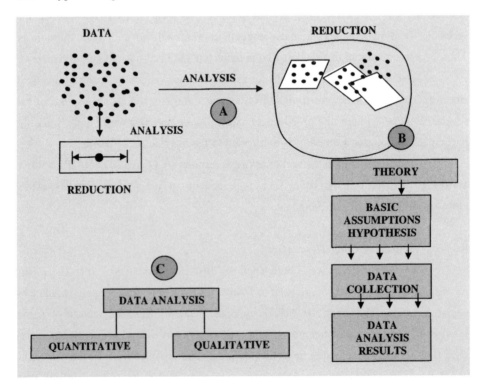

Figure 1.21   The Nature of data analysis in research.

There are various techniques of data analysis, which take into account the TYPE OF DATA which was collected. Quantitative data analysis consists of estimation of parameters (i.e., population estimates) from the sample statistics. Qualitative data analysis consists of techniques which make sense of words, sentences, documents, and observations. Data analysis is the REDUCTION of MASSIVE and DETAILED INFORMATION into several statistics, parameters, structures, and models, which capture the essence of the data.

The majority of this book centers on techniques of data analysis. Data analysis can also be viewed as the link between basic assumption and/or hypotheses postulation as well as research planning and finding meaning. The nature of data analysis is displayed in Figure 1.21.

(10) Conducting a Pilot Study

Once a research plan is ready and all the necessary procedures have be taken into consideration (preparing the equipment, questionnaires, laboratories, consent form, assistant recruitment, etc.) it is of importance to conduct a study which is identical to the intended study but with a limited number of participants. This procedure is aimed at refining the tools and devices needed for the study and making FINAL ALTERATIONS in the study procedures (protocols) prior to collecting data for the study.

In more complex studies in which several researchers collaborate at the same time, practice sessions are required to synchronize the various actions which are taking place. For example, while running on a treadmill, one observes the progression of the test on the computer screen, one monitors the procedures next to the runner and gives instructions, one shows the rate of perceived exertion every 30 seconds, one takes blood samples, and another administers questionnaires and interviews the participant immediately after the termination of the run. There are many other examples where training is needed to avoid any confusion among the researchers. If such behaviors take place during the study, the internal validity of the study is jeopardized.

In a technological era, the role of the pilot study should not be minimized. Extra care and skill should be taken in the calibration of the electronic devices, their operation, as well as their data storage and format. These features are displayed graphically in Figure 1.22.

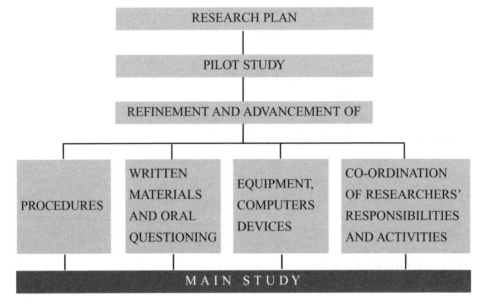

Figure 1.22   The role of a pilot study.

In addition to the roles of the pilot study mentioned above, the researcher may conclude that some of the study procedures result in over load and burden on the participants and therefore should be modified, released, omitted, or scheduled. Such changes may lead to a "smoother run" of the study and to more valid findings. If serious modifications were made, an additional pilot study with few participants should be carried out to ensure that the modifications made are working as expected.

(11)   Preparing a Proposal

Basic Procedures

When a good idea and a comprehensive review of the literature are integrated into a holistic view, basic assumptions and/or hypotheses are formulated, and appropriate methodologies are postulated, it is the stage to prepare a research proposal. A research proposal is a document that consists of both theoretical/academic and practical matters. Once a researcher desires to conduct a study that requires equipment, instrumentation, questionnaires, administrative support, payment to participants, assistants and other expected and/or unexpected costs, a RESEARCH BUDGET accompanies the theoretical and methodological parts of the research proposal. Financial support is usually given by governments, private grants, trusts, donations, and academic institutions. In most cases allocation of financial resources is decided by committee members who read the research proposals and then decide if assistance will be granted. To increase the chances of successfully obtaining a research grant, the researcher has to follow the following guidelines:

- Create an *innovative* and *attractive* proposal (usually studies which have immediate practical implementations are preferred by research committee members).

- Write in a simple, elegant, and logical style and emphasize the *potential contribution* of the study in *solving the problem* at which it is aimed.

- Succinctly, state the basic assumptions and or hypotheses and the research plan, that is designed to give answers to these questions (i.e., participants, instrumentation, intervention/s, procedures, and data analysis).

- Outline in detail the necessary equipment, assistance, and travel costs, and other items, which are required to carry out the research. For each of these describe the exact costs.

- Prepare a timetable, particularly when you plan a longitudinal study. In each of the time periods, justify the costs of items and human capital.

- Include in the proposal all the appendices which are needed such as: questionnaires, consent form to participants, extra-detailed budget, details about intervention, recommendations from "head" or "directors", letters of support, and any other relevant information that the different research grants require.

Summary

This chapter is of the utmost importance. As we stated before, when the selection of variables, study's design, sampling procedure, data collection, and data analyses are sound, the generalizability of the findings cannot easily be disputed. Furthermore, when the researcher is aware of all the possible methodological limitations of the study plan, sound alternative explanations to the findings can be exerted, whether the findings match with the basic assumptions and/or hypotheses or not. The understanding of research control and design is the cornerstone of any scientific enquiry.

1.3   SUMMARY AND PRESENTATION

In this chapter, we introduce the logical principles which guide the researcher when he/she is confronted with the theory on one hand, and the research findings on the other hand. How to integrate, interpret, and make sense of the findings which confirm, partially confirm, or contradict the research's basic assumptions and/or hypotheses is a main concern of researchers in all the scientific disciplines. We conclude by introducing the principles that guide the summation of research procedures, and the preparation of it for written or oral presentation.

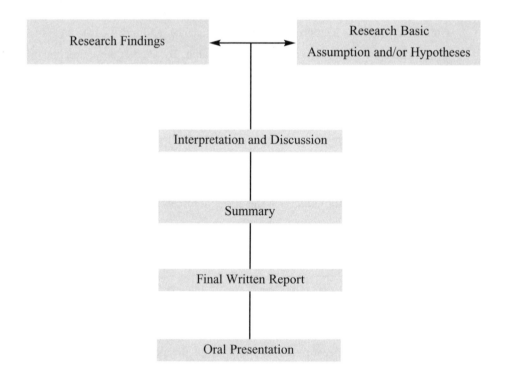

Summary and Presentation

(1) Relating Results to Basic Assumptions and/or Hypotheses
(2) Interpretation of the Research Findings (i.e., "Discussion")
(3) A Short Summary (Abstract)
(4) Submitting a Final Report
(5) Preparing a Research Report for Oral Presentation
(6) Examples of Studies Which Used Holistic Methodology

(1)   Relating Results to Basic Assumptions and/or Hypotheses

The THEORY and the derivation of BASIC ASSUMPTIONS and/or HYPOTHESES determine the RESEARCH PLAN. The research plan consists of participants, instrumentation/materials, intervention/manipulation, procedures, and DATA COLLECTION/ANALYSES. After the data is analyzed, the critical stage comes in which the researcher carefully examines whether or not the results of the study confirmed the basic assumptions and/or hypotheses (i.e., expectations). It is a stage of critical thinking and creativity. When the results confirm the basic assumptions and/or hypotheses, the theory seems to be "working" to predict behaviours or desired outcomes. Even if this happens, the investigator must examine whether an ALTERNATIVE THEORY or another EXPLANATION may account for the results. The main concern is when the results do not confirm the theoretical foundation and the basic assumptions and/or hypotheses which constituted the research plan. In such a case, there are several logical measures that can be taken in order to establish a NEW THEORETICAL FRAMEWORK (i.e., DISCUSSION). The new theoretical framework consists of all the possible arguments which led to the theory-results mismatch. These arguments come from several directions, which are illustrated in Figure 1.23.

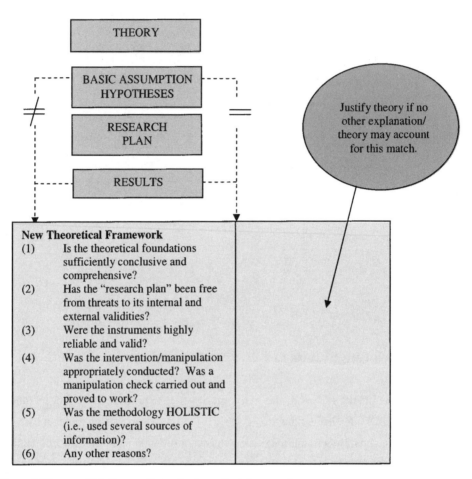

Figure 1.23   Relating results to the theoretical framework.

The bottom box in Figure 1.23 presents ideas as to how the research findings should be interpreted. Additional ideas and directions for "discussion" are presented next.

(2)   Interpretation of the Research Findings (i.e., "Discussion")

It is assumed that the theory, used as a foundation for the basic assumptions and/or hypotheses derivation and the research plan, has already been challenged by other researchers. New theories are born from older theories, which were found to be invalid or lacked to account for the findings of studies which derived their basic assumptions and/or hypotheses from them. In many instances, this is also the case with the current study's findings, which the researcher attempts to interpret. We claim that some researchers are so fanatical in their beliefs about one theory that any findings, even those which do not match the basic assumptions and/or hypotheses, are interpreted in line with this one theory. Rival or ALTERNATIVE THEORIES should always play an important role in the interpretation of research findings. At this stage, we claim, it is too late to consider an alternative theory to account for the study's findings! One should always keep in mind the possibility that there is no one theory that can account for all the possible outcome behaviors! Unfortunately many researchers rely on one theory when writing the "discussion section".

For a comprehensive interpretation of the research findings we suggest taking the following measures prior to logically developing the argument:

- Be aware of several theories which may account for the behaviors examined in the study.
- Be aware of old and recent studies in the field of the research you conduct.
- Be critical of the "research plans" which were carried out in previous studies.
- Be critical about the interpretations given by the researchers to their findings.
- Establish your own thoughts and research plan, which you believe will improve, enhance, and better account for the behaviors you study.

One may claim that these important issues should precede any research plan. We really agree with this argument and claim that in many cases a single or even a team of researchers can not comprehend all the possible theoretical alternatives which may better account for the research findings. Nor can they question all the previous methods and research plans. The CURRENT FINDINGS stimulate the researchers to seek ALTERNATIVE EXPLANATIONS to the findings, in particular when the findings do not conform to the basic assumptions and/or hypotheses which they have postulated. Such BASIC ASSUMPTIONS and/or HYPOTHESES-FINDINGS MISMATCH cause many researchers to wonder WHETHER THEY WHERE HOLISTIC ENOUGH IN THEIR THEORETICAL AND PRACTICAL VIEWS. Thus, the interpretation of the findings follows the logic presented in Figure 1.24.

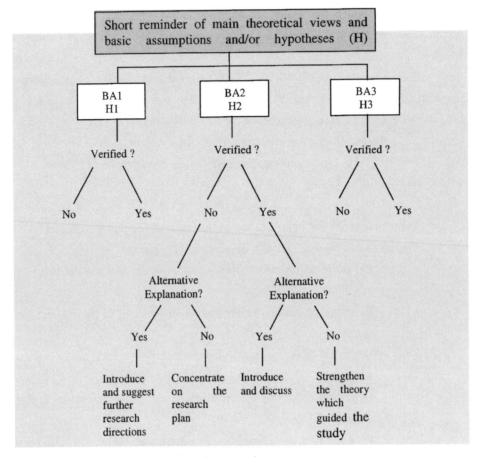

Figure 1.24 Logical steps in findings interpretation.

In Figure 1.24 the researcher postulated three basic assumptions and/or hypotheses. A short theoretical review and the three basic assumptions and/or hypotheses can be introduced first to remind the reader the reasons behind the study and its direction. Each of the basic assumptions and/or hypotheses should then be discussed separately, as it is believed that each of the hypotheses relates to different aspects of the theory. When a basic assumption and/or hypothesis is verified, it is believed that the theory is sound, the research plan was appropriately executed, and the findings are used as an evidence for the soundness of the theory. Also in such ideal cases, we recommend the researcher consider alternative explanations to the findings. Only elimination of such explanations, even on theoretical grounds, gives support and validates the arguments of an ideal "findings-theory match".

In cases when basic assumptions and/or hypothesis are not verified, then explanations can be centered on the theory itself, but also on the research plan (i.e., methodology). In regard to experimental studies, the hypotheses we make when we plan manipulations and interventions are not met in practice. In other cases our methodologies are not "sensitive" enough to depict the behavioral changes we are expecting to occur. In other cases the instrumentation contains too much "measurement error". Yet in other cases, all the above integrate to yield a poor research design and plan. Finally, we may be completely wrong in the way we were thinking from the outset.

Indeed "clean research" where findings match the driving theory, have better chances to be published in journals and it is easier to comprehend. However, we strongly believe that science has advanced and keeps advancing as a result of disputes and mismatches between findings and theories. Only a mismatch leads to a better CRITICAL THINKING. We completely disagree that such research has lower chances of being published. In many cases—the opposite is true. However, the quality of a discussion in cases of mismatches should be such that it acknowledges all the possibilities for this outcome to occur. And most importantly, that it suggests NEW and INNOVATIVE VIEWS and RESEARCH PLANS which are believed to be more appropriate to account for the behaviors we study and give rise to more sophisticated research in the future.

Interpretation of research findings should always end with integration of the explanations, verifications, and falsifications to all the research's basic assumptions and/or hypotheses. An INTEGRATED HOLISTIC VIEW, which postulates the summary of the findings and the future directions that should be taken, ends this section (see Figure 1.25).

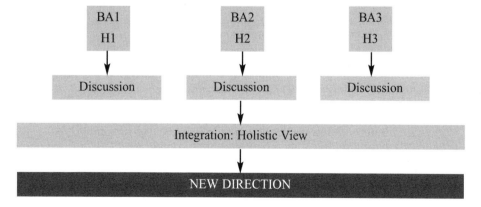

Figure 1.25   Integration of Interpretations and New Directions.

(3)   A Short Summary (Abstract)

A summary, which contains 250-500 words, is written when the study ends. It consists of the following logical sequence: The purpose of the study, short methodology (research plan: sample, instrumentation, and interventions/manipulations when necessary) main results, and conclusion/implication. Usually it is of value to add a reference or two when a sound theory was used as a foundation for the study. It is also important to state whether the findings verified the basic assumption and/or hypotheses, and if not, add a sentence or two of implications/future directions.

In a completely theoretical paper in which qualitative or quantitative data were coded in words and/or numbers, the summary consists of the basic ideas which were challenged, the main argumentations for or against certain views, and conclusions. A summary of a theoretical, basic, or applied research appear first, so that researchers may choose if the study is of interest to them, and if so, what they should expect to find in more detail. Two examples of an abstract, one experimental and one descriptive, are introduced below.

This study examined the consistency of Weiner's three-dimensional attributional model using subjects who differed in situational variables (outcome, group vs. individual), psychological characteristics (perceived ability, expectations for success) and gender. A total of 138 subjects participating in competitive sport were asked to rate their own perceived ability and expectations for success prior to competition. Following competition, the subjects listed a maximum of three reasons for the outcome. A separate two-way factorial analysis on each dimension and category revealed that in each grouping variable (gender, situational or psychological) perceived locus, stability and control were inconsistent. Results generally confirmed previous research, which used the first attribution. However, the second and third attributions consistently changed, and in some cases were reversed. Further, attributional research using more than the first attribution is recommended. From: Tenenbaum and Furst, 1986.

In this article a motivational perspective to exercise and sport are reviewed. The review emphasizes the social-cognitive approach that has recently been utilized extensively in sport psychology literature. The review concentrates on the goal perspective approach to achievement motivation, the concept of competitiveness in sport, and the psychological constructs of perceived competence, efficacy, and control in association with the environmental conditions under which performance is evaluated. An integrated model of motivation is postulated to better account for motor/physical performance. The model is used later to show how performance can be examined in emotionally (i.e., frustration) and physically (work hard) demanding situations that can be manipulated and standardized. Experimental Support for the model is provided. From: Tenenbaum, 1996

(4)   Submitting a Final Report

A final report is usually sent to the committee members who granted the study. It is also distributed to various people who supported it and showed interest in its execution and results. The first page contains the title of the study, the researchers' names, titles and affiliation (the order should be agreed much before the conductance of the study), and the grant sources details (usually the full name and the grant number). An example of the first page is as follows:

Exertion and Discomfort in Athletes

and Non-Athletes Undergoing and Strength Tasks

Steven Ten[1]

Harvey H. Lentop[1]

Gerry L. Sten[2]

1. The University of S.A., Dept. of Physical Education

2. The Gehenem Institute of Behavioral Studies

This study was supported by grant number 759353D
The South Pacific Research Council.

The second page is devoted to all the people who helped in any capacity to carry out the study and is not included in the list of authors. Usually, researchers express their thanks to the participants, technical stuff, heads and directors of programs, departments, faculties and institutes. We recommend keeping a list of supporters from the first stages. There are always supporters who are forgotten, not mentioned, and feel bad when they realize that they have not been thanked.

The first 3-5 pages, sometimes, are devoted to a "foreword". In the "foreword" section, the researchers express their ideas and thoughts which pertain to the questions they address, why these questions are important, how they address them in a way that others omitted, what the reasons are which caused them to try a new approach/methodology, and so on. It gives the reader a more personal view about the motives and reasons for conducting the study.

The next page is devoted to the short summary and then to the theory, basic assumption and/or hypotheses, research plan, results (findings), discussion, and conclusions and recommendations. Immediately after the conclusion and recommendations, a list of references follows which consists of all the references, which were used throughout the whole study. There are several methods of quoting references in the text and in the reference list such as the American Psychological Association (there are several versions which change with times), the Harvard method and others. Usually, research grants and journals point out clearly the rules in the "instructions to authors" section. The two most popular methods used are those, which ask the surnames of the authors to appear in the text and full details which include the names, publication source, year of publication, and pages in the "reference list" in alphabetic order. The second one requires using numbers for each author/s in a sequential manner and these numbers appear in the reference list with all the details mentioned in the first method.

Following the reference list are the appendices which were referred to in the text. Appendices contain the original questionnaires, instructions to participants, descriptions of intervention, manipulation, consent form, photographs of documents, photographs of the equipment, and any other materials that are important for the readers who are interested in all the details, and to researchers who show interest in the application of the study.

Research reports are usually shortened and prepared for journal or book publication. The most important principle in converting a research report into a refereed publication is TO KEEP ITS ESSENCE with LESS WORDS. In cases where the original report contains many analyses, tables, figures, interviews, quotations, and observations, it is recommended to prepare two or three publications with similar titles but adding I, II, and III to signify that the two or three studies share identical sequence. The shorter publication follows the same sections of the larger research report, but only the MAIN THEORETICAL ARGUMENTS, BASIC ASSUMPTIONS and/or HYPOTHESES, RESEARCH PLAN (METHODOLOGY), FINDINGS (RESULTS), DISCUSSION, AND REFERENCE LIST should be included. Only when it is essential for understanding the study should an instrument, a document, or a procedure be included. When a study is aimed at developing a new instrument or methodology, it is required to add them as appendices.

(5)   Preparing a Research Report for Oral Presentation

Some years ago oral presentation of research and/or theory consisted of reading from notes or of formal lecturing. With technological advancements, the methods of presentation have been changed. Today one may choose an overhead, a slide projector, a computer, or a combination of delivery methods. Frequently, a computer or a laptop is offered as options. Computer presentations have become dominant in the last years because of the development of user friendly softwares such as Power Point, Harvard Graphics, and others.

With the development of multi-media software, it is possible to film segments of the experiment and show it to the audience during the presentation. Preparing a filmed video-cassette or a computer multimedia film adds very much to the presentation. Instead of describing the treatment/manipulation and procedures, the presenter may choose to present the film and freely comment on other aspects which are not seen in the movie. The computer and the video/slides enable us to introduce much more information during the presentation.

Usually oral presentations are limited in time. The time given to presenters varies from 15-45 minutes depending on the conference type, the status of the presenter, and other components. It is always important to prepare the presentation in accordance with these requirements. General guideline for the preparation of overheads, slides, videos, or computer simulations are:

(1)   One slide which includes the title of the study, the authors, and their affiliation.

(2)   2-5 slides, which summarize the fundamental theoretical issues and basic assumption and/or hypothesis. Each slide should contain a minimal number of words. Overload of information is detrimental to the presentation.

(3)   4-6 slides which describe the research plan, preferably in graphical mode: e.g. sampling participants, instrumentation, manipulation, research design.

(4)   4-6 slides for the results (findings) section. Each slide contains only one figure or table (prefer figures over tables). Figures are clearer and more meaningful, particularly when the analysis is complex and contains many "interaction effects".

(5)   2-3 slides for discussion/interpretation.

(6)   1-2 slides for conclusions and recommendations.

Again, choose the terms and sentences which guide your oral presentation. Whenever possible, avoid reading from a paper. It does not excite the audience and gives the impression that the presenter is not competent and confident. Change the tone of your voice to avoid sounding monotonous. Be convinced that your study and findings are sound, and show enthusiasm. Rehearse before your friends or practice in front of a mirror and ask for honest feedback. Always keep in mind: we learn from our own mistakes before we learn from other's mistakes. It is only a presentation and those who listen to you do not desire to harm you. Just like everyone, they are curious to know what you have to tell them.

Here is an example of an oral presentation prepared for a conference in the form of slides or, a computer using the Power-Point software.

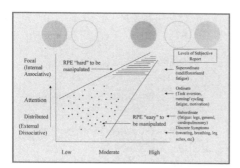

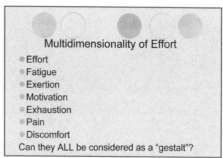

Multidimensionality of Effort

- Effort
- Fatigue
- Exertion
- Motivation
- Exhaustion
- Pain
- Discomfort

Can they ALL be considered as a "gestalt"?

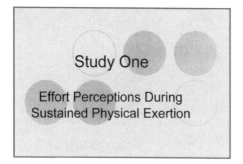

Study One

Effort Perceptions During Sustained Physical Exertion

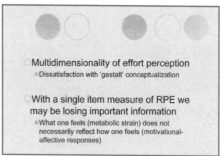

- Multidimensionality of effort perception
  - Dissatisfaction with 'gestalt' conceptualization

- With a single item measure of RPE we may be losing important information
  - What one feels (metabolic strain) does not necessarily reflect how one feels (motivational-affective responses)

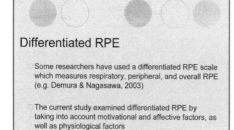

Differentiated RPE

Some researchers have used a differentiated RPE scale which measures respiratory, peripheral, and overall RPE (e.g. Demura & Nagasawa, 2003)

The current study examined differentiated RPE by taking into account motivational and affective factors, as well as physiological factors

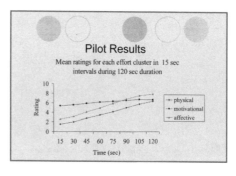

Pilot Results

Mean ratings for each effort cluster in 15 sec intervals during 120 sec duration

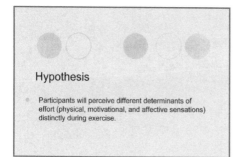

Hypothesis

Participants will perceive different determinants of effort (physical, motivational, and affective sensations) distinctly during exercise.

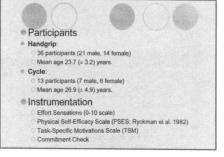

- Participants
  - Handgrip:
    - 36 participants (21 male, 14 female)
    - Mean age 23.7 (± 3.2) years.
  - Cycle:
    - 13 participants (7 male, 6 female)
    - Mean age 26.9 (± 4.9) years.
- Instrumentation
  - Effort Sensations (0-10 scale)
  - Physical Self-Efficacy Scale (PSES; Ryckman et al. 1982)
  - Task-Specific Motivations Scale (TSM)
  - Commitment Check

Handgrip Task

- Three hand-strength squeezing tasks at 25% of previously established maximum grip to fatigue

- During each task participants rated their current perception of each sensation on a 10-point scale at 15 second intervals

Cycle Task

- The cycle task required participants to cycle at 50% VO_2 max for 5 minutes, 70% VO_2 max for 5 minutes and 90% VO_2 max to volitional fatigue (based on HR plot)

- During each task participants rated their current perception of each sensation on a 10-point scale at 30 second intervals

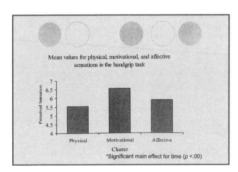

Mean values for physical, motivational, and affective sensations in the handgrip task

*Significant main effect for time ($p < .00$)

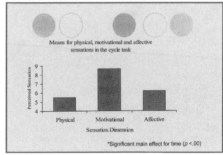

Means for physical, motivational and affective sensations in the cycle task

*Significant main effect for time ($p < .00$)

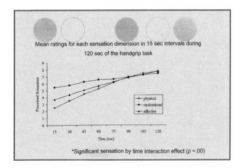

Mean ratings for each sensation dimension in 15 sec intervals during 120 sec of the handgrip task

*Significant sensation by time interaction effect ($p < .00$)

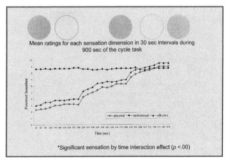

Mean ratings for each sensation dimension in 30 sec intervals during 900 sec of the cycle task

*Significant sensation by time interaction effect ($p < .00$)

Discussion

- Results indicate that perceived effort comprises several distinct inputs that are perceived differently across the duration of an exertive task

- Conclude that exertion is only one of many sensations that are felt during exercise engagement

- Questions the efficacy of a single-item measure of effort (e.g. Borg scale)

(6)   Examples of Studies Which Used a Holistic Methodology

Kirker (1997) investigated how aggression and violence develop in basketball and ice-hockey. He assumed that aggression is most likely a result of a combination of factors, and therefore the more causal factors that are present, the greater the likelihood that an aggressive act will occur. Also the severity of the aggressive acts is believed to be a function of the number and intensity of actors present. The sequence or combination of causal variables is not easily specified, and factors may operate simultaneously. Thus multivariate causal traces should be considered.

Kirker believed that self-report and introspective measures alone have limited value in understanding sport aggression in real competitive settings. Such tools are best applied in conjunction with more ecologically valid and objective measures (i.e., naturalistic observation). The observation of behavior in a natural setting provides opportunities for researchers to better understand the complex dynamics of aggressive behavior in sport. Aggression is best studied in real time and in the context it occurs. Practical constraints, such as the need for extensive training of observers, expense, and lengthy data analysis have traditionally been the main barriers to observational research. Today, through the use of the computer and video technology, these logistic difficulties can be overcome, and observational analysis can be used in a more sophisticated manner.

In Kirker's study, questionnaires were constructed to assess the attitudes of players and officials towards aggression, to determine relevant aspects of histories of aggression, and generally to gain some insight into the factors found to be related to aggression in sport but not directly observable, and thus not able to be analyzed through observational coding.

With observational analysis, intentionality can only be inferred. In this study, such inferences were made under rigorous conditions by experts through repeated replays of sport-specific behavioral typologies, incorporating hypothesized typical intention and severity of actions. This approach has advantages over the use of single measures such as officials' ratings of penalized behaviors made without the aid of video replays and without supplementary data from the athletes themselves. In the determination of causality, the use of observational analysis, questionnaire data, as well as players' and officials' comments on a video replay of behaviors of interest, advances on previous methodologies.

Experts have been used previously to assess the nature of aggressive-like behaviors. In these previous studies, the experts used were not directly involved in the behaviors under investigation. They were using their personal experience to infer intention behind acts committed in general. Here, experts involved in the observed behaviors of interest were used. Furthermore, the role of the experts was expanded so that they became involved in the categorization of behaviors (taxonomies for coding), questionnaire development, observation of behaviors, and inferences of causation.

To carry out the study the following measures were taken:

- The histories of games between the teams involved were reviewed and recorded.

- Four experts, two in each sport, were recruited to develop two taxonomies of violations and aggressive acts based on the literature, their experiences, and the official game regulations. Taxonomies consisted of several dimensions and classifications of severity.

- Attitudes Toward Aggression Questionnaires and single items were provided to players and officials at training sessions prior to filming games.

- Four games, two ice-hockey and two basketball, were filmed. A CAMERA (Computer Acquisition of Multiple Ethnological Records and Analysis) video coding equipment was used for observational analysis. The CAMERA system contains PC-compatible computer software which records the sequence of distinct behavioral events occurring in real time, each with start and stop times. Complex interactions were broken down to manageable segments and sessions. For each game, two cameras were used: one directed to the play, the other to the court-rinkside behavior of coaches and substitutes. Also, microphones were placed on officials and on the sidelines to pick-up comments from the bench and crowd.

- Classification, considerations of causation, and rating-like behaviors were recorded by the experts individually on the computer while watching the games on video. The taxonomies were used as references.

- The players exhibiting the aggressive behaviors were invited to observe their acts on video and reflect on the reasons behind these acts.

- The most severe aggressive acts were selected and referenced as "Zero" point. Up to four minutes of footage before and after each act from each game was analyzed. Details of players exhibiting these behaviors and recipients of the behaviors were recorded on the computer output, along with game score, time phases, and any other relevant information. The single analysis for each aggressive act enabled Kirker to integrate the information collected and generalize the findings across the two games in each of the two sports. When such procedures are adopted, more meaningful conclusions can be made as to how aggressive acts are developed and subsequently how we can modify or minimize their occurrence. The use of multiple measures was instrumental in achieving the aims of this particular study.

Another way of improving the reliability of research projects involves the use of measures that are ecologically valid. One of the most frustrating experiences that social and behavioral scientists undergo is the low amount of dependent variable variance accounted for by the independent variables. This can be improved by the use of more ecological paradigms in which performance is measured according to some objective criteria in addition to the self-ratings that seem to form the bases of so many studies in sport psychology. We argue that when the dependent variable is measured under conditions which completely mimic the real world, more variance of this dependent variable will be accounted for by other psychological variables. Again, this is easier to demonstrate by referring to another research project in our laboratory.

In exercise physiology, measures such as oxygen uptake and anaerobic threshold account for the majority of the variance of long-distance running times. The non-accounting variance is sometimes attributed to psychological variables. Recent psychological theories have postulated that goal-orientation interacts with environmental conditions to influence effort and adherence in exertive-type tasks. Perceived ability, self-efficacy, self-control, and determination are also believed to be important mediators of behavioral outcomes. Two studies have examined this theory using real-life exertive conditions to measure consistency and adherence under such conditions. Calcagnini (1996) asked non-active participants and anaerobic and aerobic athletes to squeeze the handlebar of a dynamometer at 50% of their maximal squeezing strength for as long as they could until there was a decrease of 10% of their designated value. Freeman (1999) asked his participants to run on a treadmill for as long as they could for 90% of their maximal oxygen uptake. Measures of the psychological variables were taken prior to and after the completion of the tasks. The dependent variable was the amount of time participants could sustain in the zone of exertive tolerance. In each study, the "time in the zone of exertive tolerance" was the dependent variable while physical activity, goal-orientation, coping strategies, and determination were the predicting clusters in a hierarchical regression procedure.

As expected, the results in both studies revealed that psychological variables play an important role in determining how one can tolerate exertive conditions. Though the participants' activity type determined 11% of the exertion tolerance variance, goal orientation added 20%, and 21% of the additional variance was accounted for by coping strategies. Determination added 16% of accounted variance. These values are far above those that are common in social and behavioral research. We use these studies to illustrate our point that this line of research should be encouraged and applied.

Summary

The end product of a research study is the integration of the results (i.e., findings) and the basic assumptions and/or hypotheses which guided the research plan. This chapter's aim was to introduce the main principles which guide this integration and its end-product: Short summary, final report, and oral presentations. These skills are important as many readers do not have the time and motivation to read extensive, large reports. Research, as long as it is, should be presented elegantly, precisely, and in clear terms.

References

Borg, G. (1982). Psychophysical bases of perceived exertion. *Medicine and Science in Sport and Exercise, 14,* 377-381.

Campbell, D.T., and Stanley, J. (1966). *Experimental and Quasi-Experimental Designs for Research.* Chicago, IL: Rand Mc Nally.

Chalmers, A.F. (1982*). What Is This Thing Called Science? (2nd edition).* Brisbane, Australia: University of Queensland.

Cook, T.D., and Campbell, D.T. (1976). The design and conduct of quasi-experiments and true experiments in field settings. In M. Dunnette (Ed.), *Handbook of Industrial and Organizational Psychology.* Skokie, IL: Rand Mc Nally.

Noble, B.J. and Robertson, R.J. (1996). *Perceived Exertion.* Champain, IL: Human Kinetics.

Rosenfeld, O., and Tenenbaum, G. (1989). The effect of physical activity on objective and subjective measures of productivity and efficiency in industry. *Ergonomics, 32,* 1019-1028.

Tenenbaum, G.T. (1996). Theoretical and practical considerations in investigating motivation and discomfort during prolonged exercise. *Journal of Sports Medicine and Physical Fitness, 36,* 145-154.

Tenenbaum, G., and Furst, D. (1986). Consistency of attributional responses by individuals and groups differing in gender, perceived ability, and expectations for success. *British Journal of Social Psychology, 25,* 315-321.

Recommended Literature:

Whitley, B.W. (1996). *Principles of Research in BehaviourBehavioral Science.* London: Mayfield.

2.1 NUMERICAL STRATEGIES

In this chapter we teach the reader to REDUCE and MAKE MEANING of a large data set. We also teach how to INTRODUCE the data summation in tabulated and/or graphical modes.

The chapter begins with introducing the different "levels" that data can be collected. Then, the basic and common procedures of data summation are described. The different techniques used for estimation of central and dispersion tendencies in data follow, and finally the normal curve and its use for making comparisons, profiles, and exertion of probable events is postulated. This logical sequence is introduced graphically as follows:

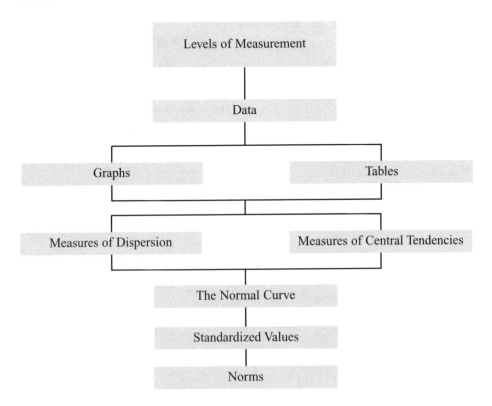

Contents

(1)　Levels of Measurement

An operational definition of a variable allows EACH CASE to be assigned to ONE and ONLY ONE CATEGORY of the variable. Thus there are two principles, which should be remembered when a SAMPLE of the POPULATION of interest is measured. The first principle is that of EXCLUSIVENESS, each case should have one value for a specific variable, i.e., one case is a male or female with respect to gender. The second principle is that of EXHAUSTIVENESS, i.e., every case should be classified into a category. For example, if the sample is classified into ACTIVITY TYPES, then all possible activity types should be possible so that a case will not be left without a category.

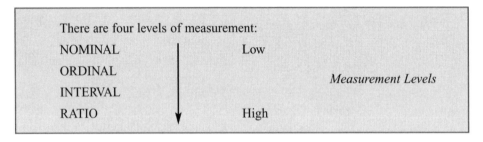

There are four levels of measurement:

NOMINAL　　　　　　　　　Low

ORDINAL

INTERVAL　　　　　　　　　　　　　　*Measurement Levels*

RATIO　　　　　　　　　High

The higher the LEVEL of MEASUREMENT the more OPERATIONS and MANIPULATIONS we can apply to it. Next, a definition of each measurement level is given followed by an example.

NOMINAL level of measurement indicates a CATEGORY that a case belongs with regard to a variable.

Examples: Type of activities/fitness components:

	(1) Aerobic
	(2) Anaerobic
Or	(3) Power
	(4) Endurance
	(5) Strength
	(6) Flexibility
	(7) Agility

The number assigned to each activity does not have any meaning beyond that of IDENTIFICATION of ACTIVITY-TYPE.

> **ORDINAL level** of measurement allows classifying, ranking, and ordering cases by some assigned "degree" or "extent".

In ordinal level of measurement ranking is performed by assigning values to ORDER or RANK.

Examples: Physical fitness can be classified in an order fashion like that

(1)	(2)	(3)	(4)	(5)
Very low	Low	Moderate	High	Very high

100 m running times can be ranked as follows:

(1)	(2)	(3)	(4)	(5)	(6)	(7)	(8)
12.1	13.2	13.3	13.7	14.0	14.5	14.7	14.8

As one can see the 100 m times are ordered from "fastest" (12.1 seconds) to slowest (14.8 seconds) and the differences among the subsequent five values vary. However, the RANKING DIFFERENCES remain IDENTICAL throughout the whole range of the variable values. Once it is crucial or necessary to rank the values of a variable, a limitation exists with respect to the ANALYSIS of these values. The running times supply a better platform for the subsequent analysis.

> **INTERVAL level** of measurement consists of units of measurement that allow any mathematical manipulations on them.

Examples: 100 m times in seconds
12.1, 13.2, 13.3, 13.7, 14.0, 14.5, 14.7, 14.8
VO_2 max in ml/min/kg
42.7, 44.3, 54.7, 55.6, 59.1, 62.8, 63.7

In the first examples the 3rd runner is running faster than the 5th runner by 0.7 of a second (14.0-13.3) and the VO_2 max of the 6th person is higher of that of the third person by 8.1 (62.8-54.7) ml/min/kg. Averages and other important values can be also calculated.

> **RATIO level** of measurement consists of interval scale with definite origin (i.e., zero point).

A ratio scale exists when a certain value indicates an ABSENCE of the entity that is measured.

For example: HEIGHT that is measured by a yardstick, AGE by years, INCOME by any currency, and number of children in the family.

In the case of height, one should note that "zero" is used to represent the point of origin. However, it is impossible for an individual to have a height of zero. In contrast, a "zero" in degrees Celsius means "freezing point", a cold temperature, but not absence of its entity. In many cases we treat interval scales as a ratio scale, and conduct similar mathematical operations. However some caution should be given to the interpretation of the results when such operations are performed. When a point of origin does not exist, and the variable we measure is not conceptualized on a linear continuum with equal units of measurement, one should be careful not to make the assumption that "the difference between 100 and 90 on a scale is equal to the difference between 50 and 40". This is a MISTAKE that is common among researchers, teachers, and even book authors.

Each of the above levels of measurement can accept either DISCRETE or CONTINUOUS values.

> **DISCRETE** values are numbers, which signify an amount and cannot be divided.

In team handball there are 7 players, in basketball—5, soccer—11, volleyball—6, etc.

> **CONTINUOUS** values signify units that can be divided infinitely because any numerical value can be obtained.

Running times, jumping distances, fat measures, length of throws, values of oxygen uptake, scores on attitude scales are all considered to be continuous variables.

As one can notice, nominal types of data provide less information that can be further analysed using higher levels of measurement. However, one should keep in mind that DATA are good as long as they MAKE SENSE and ANSWER THE RELEVANT QUESTIONS raised by the researcher.

(2)   Descriptive Statistics and Techniques

A summary of a large data set allows the researcher to make meaning of this data. When one observes a table, which contains hundreds or thousands of single numbers, unless presented via a graph or a table, they cannot be understood. Tables and figures, which contain SUMMARY information about the data and consist of simple mathematical concepts, allow a simple DATA DESCRIPTION. Thus, DESCRIPTIVE STATISTICS are viewed as NUMERICAL, GRAPHICAL, and TABULATION TECHNIQUES for ORGANIZING, PRESENTING, and ANALYZING DATA (Argyrous, 1996).

In general, each set of data has a MATHEMATICAL AVERAGE (i.e. MEAN), around which the rest of the data is distributed. This DISTRIBUTION is also termed DISPERSION. Descriptive statistics consist of both MEASURES OF CENTRAL TENDENCY and MEASURES OF DISPERSION. There are also MEASURES OF ASSOCIATION, which indicate how two or more variables relate to each other. We shall relate to each of these descriptive statistics later in this book. In Figure 2.1 we demonstrate what questions we asked and what we attempt to do in order to answer these questions.

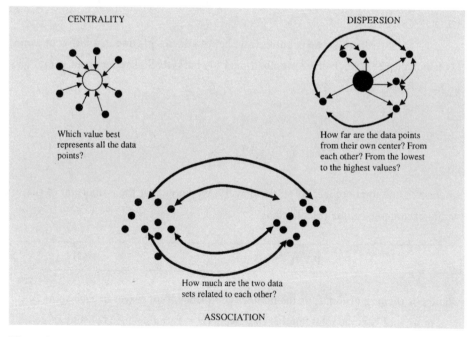

Figure 2.1   Graphical presentation of questions which pertain to measures of centrality, dispersion, and association.

The measures of centrality, dispersion, and association are used to capture the essential features of the data set but at the same time some information is lost. For example, in a study where thousands of observations are collected, a few EXCEPTIONAL values may not be noticed if we rely merely on the central and dispersion values. Again it is a matter of judgement as to how much attention should be given to such exceptional values (i.e., OUTLIERS). In some cases such attention is useless, in others it is of vital importance.

(3)   Describing Data in Tables

3.1   Proportions and Percentages

Proportions are useful when we desire to describe observations, which are categorized by some nominal scale (level). For example, 25 males and 42 females or 54 team athletes and 48 individual athletes. In such cases, the size of the GROUP OF OBSERVATION is used to calculate PROPORTIONS. In calculating proportions it is assumed that the GROUPS of interest are MUTUALLY EXCLUSIVE and EXHAUSTIVE. In other words, each subject belongs to ONLY ONE GROUP/CATEGORY.

Let's assume that we count the number of athletes playing in 4 different games: (1) handball, (2) volleyball, (3) football, and (4) basketball. The numbers within each group is f_1, f_2, f_3 and f_4.

Thus

$$f_1 + f_2 + f_3 + f_4 = N$$

where N is the total number of all the players. We know that the proportion of players within each game can be calculated as

$$p = f_k/N \qquad (1)$$

where p is the proportion, f_k is the number (frequency, f) of player in each sport (k = 1, 2, 3, or 4), and N is the total number of players (N = $f_1 + f_2 + f_3 + f_4$), and

$$f_1/N + f_2/N + f_3/N + f_4/N = 1 \qquad (2)$$

Let's assume that $f_1 = 20$, $f_2 = 25$, $f_3 = 34$, and $f_4 = 21$ then:

$N = 20 + 25 + 34 + 21 = 100$, and

$p_1 = f_1/N = 20/100 = 0.20$

$p_2 = f_2/N = 25/100 = 0.25$

$p_3 = f_3/N = 34/100 = 0.34$

$p_4 = f_4/N = 21/100 = 0.21$, and

$p_1 + p_2 + p_3 + p_4 = 0.20 + 0.25 + 0.34 + 0.21 = 1.0$.

PERCENTAGES, like proportions, are statistics that standardize the total number of cases to a base of 100 rather than 1.0 (in proportion), thus

$$P\% = (f/N)100 \tag{3}$$

In the previous example, the percentages of the 4 ball game players are

$p_1\% = (f_1/N)100 = (20/100)100 = 20\%$

$p_2\% = (f_2/N)100 = (25/100)100 = 25\%$

$p_3\% = (f_3/N)100 = (34/100)100 = 34\%$

$p_4\% = (f_4/N)100 = (21/100)100 = 21\%$

and $\quad p_1\% + p_2\% + p_3\% + p_4\% = 20\% + 25\% + 34\% + 21\% = 100\%$.

This information can be presented as such:

Table 2.1

Frequencies, Proportions, and Percentages of Athletes belonging to 4 Team Sports

Team Sport	Frequency (f)	Proportion (f/N)	Percentage (f/N)100
(1) handball	20	.20	20%
(2) volleyball	25	.25	25%
(3) football	34	.34	34%
(4) basketball	21	.21	21%
Total	*100*	*1.0*	*100%*

Another example with an additional nominal scale is presented next. Let's assume that we had a sample of team and individual athletes at which some were young and some adults as follows:

Sport Type	Age	
	Young	Adult
Team	35	25
Individual	40	55

In this case, several proportions and percentages can be calculated, depending on what TOTALS we use as a CRITERION. There are 3 major totals in this example:

(1) total team: 35 + 25 = 60

total individual: 40 + 55 = 95

(2) total young: 35 + 40 = 75

total adults: 25 + 55 = 80

(3) Grand total: 35 + 40 + 25 + 55 = 155.

Now, if the question is, what is the proportion/percentage of teams and individual athletes within each age category? Then

total young: 35 + 40 = 75

total adults: 25 + 55 = 80

and therefore within the younger age

35/75 = .47 or 47% team players

40/75 = .53 or 53% individual players

and within the older age

25/80 = .31 or 31% team players

55/80 = .69 or 69% individual players.

If the question was: "what is the proportion/percentage of young and adults among the team and individual players, the calculation will be:

total team: 35 + 25 = 60

total individual: 40 + 55 = 95

And subsequently,

within the team sport

$$35/60 = 0.58 \text{ or } 58\% \text{ were young}$$
$$25/60 = 0.42 \text{ or } 42\% \text{ were adults}$$

and within the individual sport,

$$40/95 = 0.42 \text{ or } 42\% \text{ were young}$$
$$55/95 = 0.58 \text{ or } 58\% \text{ were adults.}$$

We may also ask, what is the proportion/percentage of young team players, adult team players, young individual players, and adult individual players of the total sample (N = 155). In this case,

young team:	$35/155 = 0.225$ or 22.5%
adult team:	$25/155 = 0.162$ or 16.2%
young individual:	$40/155 = 0.258$ or 25.8%
adult individual:	$55/155 = \underline{0.355}$ or $\underline{35.5\%}$
Total	***1.000 100.0%***

Additional questions can be asked, such as: "what is the proportion/percentage of young (f = 35 + 40) and adults (25 + 55) of the total number?" In this case:

$$(35 + 40)/155 = 75/155 = 0.484 \text{ or } 48.4\% \text{ young}$$
$$(25 + 55)/155 = 80/155 = 0.416 \text{ or } 51.6\% \text{ adults}$$

or what is the proportion/percentage of team (35 + 25) and individual (40 + 55) athletes of the total number of players? In this case:

$$(35 + 25)/155 = 60/155 = 0.387 \text{ or } 38.7\% \text{ team}$$
$$(40 + 55)/155 = 95/155 = 0.613 \text{ or } 61.3\% \text{ individual.}$$

These and the previous proportions and percentages are presented in Table 2.2. Charts and figures are often the most elegant way to present this type of information. We will elaborate on this later in this chapter.

CHAPTER TWO

Table 2.2

A Summary of Proportions and Percentages of Young/Adults and Team/Individual athletes within a sample of Athletes

	Frequency (f)	Proportion (f/N)	Percentage (f/N)100
Total Number of Athletes	155	1.00	100%
team	60	0.387	38.7%
individual	95	0.613	61.3%
Total Number of Athletes	155	1.00	100%
young	75	0.484	48.4%
adults	80	0.516	51.6%
Within Young Age	75	1.00	100%
team	35	0.47	47%
individual	40	0.53	53%
Within Adult Age	80	1.00	100%
team	25	0.31	31%
individual	55	0.69	69%
Within Team Sport	60	1.00	100%
young	35	0.58	58%
adults	25	0.42	42%
Within Individual Sport	95	1.00	100%
young	40	0.42	42%
adults	55	0.58	58%
Total Number of Athletes	155	1.00	100%
young team	35	0.225	22.5%
adult team	25	0.162	16.2%
young individual	40	0.258	25.8%
adult individual	55	0.355	35.5%

3.2   Ratios

The division of A by B defines the ratio of value A to value B. For example, let's assume that we have sampled 395 recreational athletes, 94 professional team sport athletes, and 60 professional individual athletes. The ratio of recreational and team is 395/94; but of recreational and individual 395/60; of team and individual 94/60. The ratio of recreation AND individuals to team athletes is (395 + 60)/94. In contrast to proportion estimation the RATIO MAY BE GREATER THAN 1.00. The RATIO COEFFICIENT reduces to the simplest presentation of the nominator/denominator ratio. Very frequently the ratio is presented as 1:X. In the above example, the recreational/team athletes of 395/94 can be expressed as 4.2:1, which means 4.2 recreational athletes in the sample for each professional team player. And similarly, the ratio of team to individual athletes, 94/60 can be represented as 1.57:1.

When PROPORTIONS are estimated, the ratio is the portion of a sub sample of the total sample. The RATIO is the proportion of the sub samples, where each sub sample represents an entity. The more subgroups or subsamples that exist, the more ratio coefficients can be calculated. When such a case occurs, it is more convenient to use proportions or percentages. It is possible to directly calculate proportions from the ratio. For example, if we know that the ratio of male to female athletes is 3:2 then we also know that of 5 (3 + 2) athletes, 3 are males and 2 are females. Then the proportion (percentage) of male athletes is 3/5 = 0.60 (60%) and female athletes 2/5 = 0.40 (40%).

A ratio is determined with respect to some CRITERION. The BASIC VALUE is the MAGNITUDE of the DENOMINATOR. For example, the gender ratio is represented in terms of the number of males to 100 females. A ratio of 65 means that there are less males than females, while a ratio of 125 means that there are more males than females. BASES such as 1,000, 10,000, or greater are useful when the proportions are very small. For example, the ratio of athletes who use anabolic steroids can be expressed in the number of users to 1,000 athletes.

RATE OF INCREASE is another type of ratio. Usually such ratios are calculated when a given variable is measured a number of times within a period of time. The increase rate is related usually to the BASELINE value. For example, let's assume that the number of competitive athletes increased from 20,000 to 30,000 between the years 1990-1999, the increase rate was: *(30,000 - 20,000)/20,000 = 0.50 or 50%.*

The percentage increase can be greater than 100%. In the case of a minus sign, a decreased rate is expected.

3.3 Frequency Distributions and Grouping (Interval Scales)

A FREQUENCY DISTRIBUTION consists of reporting for each VALUE or CATEGORY of VALUES, the NUMBER of CASES that has this value or category, their PERCENTAGE, and CUMULATIVE FREQUENCIES and/ or PERCENTAGES.

Let's take as an example a hypothetical data set of 30 students who underwent 100 m run (in seconds) and high-jump (in meters). We shall show here how a CLASS INTERVAL can present the data set of these two variables. The hypothetical data set is presented in Table 11.3.3.

Table 2.3

A Hypothetical Data Set of 30 Students, which Were Examined in 100 m Run and High jump

	Id	run100	h.jump
1	1.00	15.60	1.23
2	2.00	13.20	1.69
3	3.00	12.50	1.65
4	4.00	17.50	1.12
5	5.00	13.20	1.54
6	6.00	13.00	1.64
7	7.00	17.20	1.10
8	8.00	12.30	1.09
9	9.00	14.50	1.46
10	10.00	15.40	1.29
11	11.00	16.80	1.25
12	12.00	15.70	1.28
13	13.00	11.60	1.87
14	14.00	13.50	1.47
15	15.00	13.90	1.48
16	16.00	11.90	1.78
17	17.00	13.90	1.57
18	18.00	16.80	1.11
19	19.00	13.60	1.55
20	20.00	18.90	1.00
21	21.00	14.80	1.28
22	22.00	15.60	1.27
23	23.00	15.20	1.47
24	24.00	12.60	1.87
25	25.00	16.50	1.34
26	26.00	16.40	1.21
27	27.00	14.60	1.36
28	28.00	13.90	1.35
29	29.00	15.30	1.59
30	30.00	16.50	1.25

Raw data commonly share small differences among its values. We can reduce the number of values by a CLASSIFICATION PROCEDURE. To do so, the NUMBER OF CLASS INTERVALS should be determined by the researcher. One should keep in mind that the more class intervals are chosen, the more accurate the information kept and vice-versa. However, too many class intervals make it difficult to capture the MAIN FEATURES of the DATA.

The more class intervals we choose, the smaller the CLASS LIMITS (i.e., difference between the upper and lower bounds of each class interval) will be. The common procedure to start producing class intervals is to estimate the differences between the largest (X_{max}) and lowest (X_{min}) values in the distributions. This difference is termed RANGE.

$$\text{RANGE} = X_{max} - X_{min}. \qquad (4)$$

Let's say that we decided to divide this range into k intervals. Then, the class (interval) limits will be

$$L = (X_{max} - X_{min})/k \qquad \text{or} \qquad \text{Range}/k \qquad (5)$$

The principle of establishing a table of class interval is very simple and is demonstrated as follows:

Class #	Low Class Limit	High Class Limit
1	X_{min}	$X_{min} + L$
2	$X_{min} + L$	$X_{min} + 2L$
3	$X_{min} + 2L$	$X_{min} + 3L$
:	:	:
k	$X_{min} + (k-1)L$	$X_{min} + kL$

For example, the best high jump in our data set was 1.87 m and the lowest 1.00 m. We make now an arbitrary decision to produce 3 class intervals (k = 3). Thus

RANGE = 1.87 - 1.00 = 0.87

and therefore the class limits will be

L = RANGE/k = 0.87/3 = 0.29 m.

Following the procedure just introduced the 3 class intervals will be as follows:

| Class # | Class Limits | | Frequency | Percentage | Cumulative |
	Lower	Upper	(f)	(%)	Percentage (C%)
1	1.00	1.289	12	40.00	40.00
2	1.290	1.579	11	36.67	76.67
3	1.580	1.870	7	23.33	100.00
Total			30	100%	

Once the class limits (intervals) were established, each of the RAW VALUES is counted and classified into each of the 3 classes. In the high-jump data, 12 values were within the 1.00-1.289 m range, 11 were within the 1.290-1.579 m range, and 7 within the 1.580-1.870 m range. Thus 12 of 30 pertains to 40%, 11 of 30 to 36.67%, and 7 of 30 to 23.33%. The cumulative percentage indicates that 40% of the students jumped up to 1.289 m. 76.67% jumped with the range of 1.00-1.579 m, and 100% within the range of 1.00-1.870 m.

As previously mentioned, the more class intervals we decide to establish, the lower their interval limits will be. If for example, we wished to have 4 instead of 3 class intervals, then the class limit will be

$$L = (1.87 - 1.00)/4 = 0.217 \text{ m}$$

And the table of class intervals will be:

| Class # | Class Limits | | Frequency | Percentage | Cumulative |
	Lower	Upper	(f)	(%)	Percentage (C%)
1	1.000	1.217	6	20	20.00
2	1.218	1.434	10	33.3	53.33
3	1.435	1.652	10	33.3	86.67
4	1.653	1.870	4	13.3	100.00
Total			30	100%	

As expected, the class limit with 3 class intervals was larger than with 4 class intervals (0.29 vs. 0.217, respectively). In each subsequent lower limit of the class interval we added 1/1000 m to avoid identical values in two subsequent classes. The interpretation of the 4-class intervals distribution is identical to this with 3 class intervals, but with more detailed information.

We have performed similar analysis for the 100 m results, once with 3 class intervals and once with 4.

With 3 class intervals, the class limits are

L = (18.9 - 11.6)/3 = 2.433

and with 4 class intervals

L = (18.9 - 11.6)/4 = 1.825.

Thus:

Class #	Class Limits		Frequency	Percentage	Cumulative
	Lower	Upper	(f)	(%)	Percentage (C%)
1	11.600	14.032	13	43.73	43.33
2	14.033	14.466	11	36.67	80.00
3	14.467	18.900	6	20.00	100.00
Total			30	100.00%	

and

Class #	Class Limits		Frequency	Percentage	Cumulative
	Lower	Upper	(f)	(%)	Percentage (C%)
1	11.600	13.424	8	26.67	26.67
2	13.425	15.249	9	30.00	56.67
3	15.250	17.074	10	33.33	90.00
4	17.075	18.900	3	10.00	100.00
Total			30	100.00%	

Once we prefer to choose the class limit as the main criterion for class intervals, so that a round value will result, the procedure is reversed since

$$RANGE = k \bullet L$$

thus $\quad k = RANGE/L$

In this case, L is determined by the researcher or surveyor. The Range is $X_{max} - X_{min}$, and finally we divide the Range by L to determine the number of class intervals. For example, say we have a data distribution which ranges between 40-100 and the class limit we are interested is L = 10. Thus

k = Range/L = (100-40)/10 = 6 class intervals
and the intervals will be
40.00-49.99
50.00-59.99
60.00-69.99
70.00-79.99
80.00-89.99
90.00-99.99

and once this process is completed, each raw data is classified into the class intervals, and frequencies, percentages and cumulative frequencies are counted and added to the final table.

In all the examples the upper limits of one class interval and the lower limit of the subsequent class interval were not identical. This is intended to prevent an arbitrary decision when a value is identical to the "border line" in case it is identical to both class intervals. However, these very small differences are practically not a threat to the presentation of information. Instead we can present data such as the following:

6-10
11-14
16-20.

The real class limits in this case are
5.5-10.5
10.5-15.5
15.5-20.5.

The class interval shares 5 units as follows:

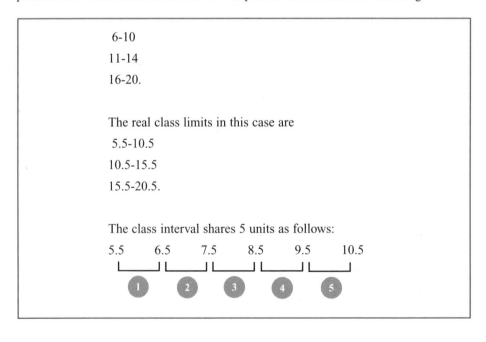

However, just for mathematical reasons, it may be presented as:

5.5-10.499

10.5-15.499

15.5-20.499

Judge for yourself how relevant the differences among the class intervals are and what precision level is desired and logical.

3.4   Frequency Distributions and Grouping (Nominal Scales)

Frequency distributions can be constructed also for nominal-type scales. We shall demonstrate it by using data collected on 20 athletes divided by GENDER (1—males, 2—females) and 5 sport-types (1—soccer, 2—handball, 3—volleyball, 4—rugby, 5—basketball). This data are shown in Table 2.4.

Table 2.4

A Hypothetical Data Set of 20 Male and Female Athletes of 5 Sport Types in Maximal Oxygen-uptake and Long Run

	Name	VO$_2$max	Run	Group	Sport
1	1.00	56.00	540.00	1.00	1.00
2	2.00	35.00	670.00	2.00	1.00
3	3.00	58.00	523.00	1.00	1.00
4	4.00	34.00	682.00	2.00	1.00
5	5.00	72.00	470.00	1.00	2.00
6	6.00	54.00	510.00	2.00	2.00
7	7.00	65.00	497.00	1.00	2.00
8	8.00	35.00	712.00	2.00	2.00
9	9.00	36.00	693.00	1.00	2.00
10	10.00	61.00	488.00	2.00	2.00
11	11.00	45.00	667.00	1.00	3.00
12	12.00	36.00	652.00	2.00	3.00
13	13.00	47.00	653.00	1.00	4.00
14	14.00	52.00	512.00	2.00	4.00
15	15.00	41.00	623.00	1.00	4.00
16	16.00	39.00	672.00	2.00	4.00
17	17.00	54.00	513.00	1.00	4.00
18	18.00	37.00	679.00	2.00	5.00
19	19.00	36.00	691.00	1.00	5.00
20	20.00	46.00	645.00	2.00	5.00

We can express the number of males and females as well as the number of athletes from each sport (f_i) in proportion (p) to the total number of subjects in the sample (n = 20) using

	$p = f_i/n$
and	$p\% = (f_i/n)100$

It is common to use also cumulative percentages in order to estimate relatively how many athletes are added to each subsequent sport type. The Table for sport-type looks as follows:

	Frequency	Percent	Valid Percent	Cumulative Percent
1.00	4	20.0	20.0	20.0
2.00	6	30.0	30.0	50.0
3.00	2	10.0	10.0	60.0
4.00	5	25.0	25.0	85.0
5.00	3	15.0	15.0	100.0
Total	*20*	*100.0*	*100.0*	

We can show the same data by using a BAR CHART as follows:

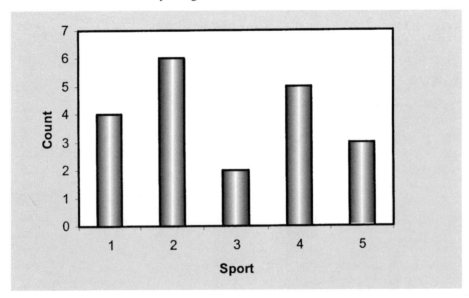

or a pie chart

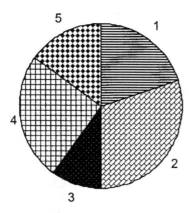

In a percentage or a cumulative percentage, the same figure with frequencies expressed in percent values look as follows:

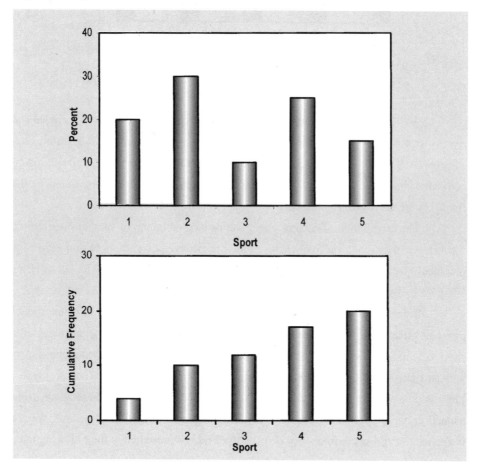

and for each sport-type by gender group (1—males, 2—females), the frequency distribution as a bar-graph looks as follows:

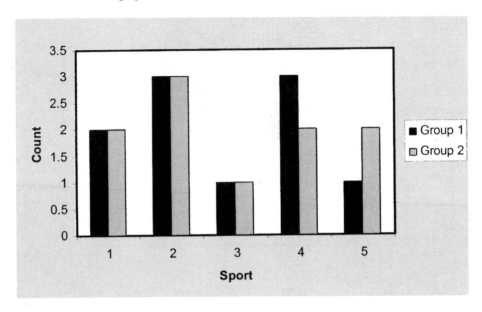

A PIE GRAPH presents the distribution of cases in the form of a circle. The relative size of each slice of the circle is equal to the proportion of cases within each category. A BAR GRAPH presents the frequency of each category as a rectangle rising vertically above each category label, with the height of the bar proportional to the frequency of the respective category.

The distribution of each category can be layered on top of another distribution. These layers may represent frequencies of their respective percentages or proportions. A graphical presentation of this kind is termed COMPONENT BAR GRAPH or STACKED BAR GRAPH.

These types of graphs are useful to compare the distribution of categories of different groups and sectors, as well as changes which occur in these frequencies over short to long periods of time. The principle here is that each bar is divided into layers with an area proportional to the category's frequency. In our case we had five sport types. Let's assume that we have asked our 20 subjects to express their attitude about using banned drugs in sport. The responses could be negative, positive, and neutral. We are interested to express the frequency distribution which is presented in the following table in a stacked bar graph.

Sport	Attitude Towards Banned Drugs			Total
	positive	neutral	negative	
Soccer	1 (25%)	2 (50%)	1 (25%)	4
Handball	0 (0%)	2 (33%)	4 (67%)	6
Volleyball	0 (0%)	2 (100%)	0 (0%)	2
Rugby	5 (100%)	0 (0%)	0 (0%)	5
Basketball	2 (67%)	1 (33%)	0 (0%)	3
Total	*8*	*7*	*5*	*n = 20*

The stacked bar of the frequencies of each attitude within each sport is presented as follows:

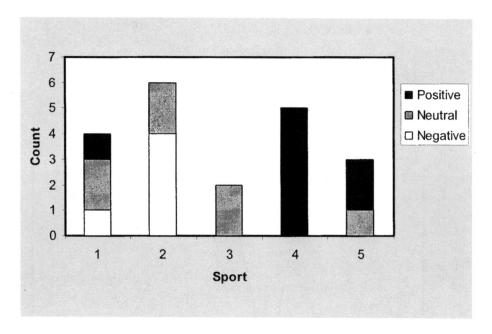

3.5 Case-Values/Charts

In studies where the number of participants is relatively small (up to 30), each of the participants' values can be presented in a LINE CHART with or without a sign that signifies his/her value. Here are the individual values of 20 participants in their RUN and VO_2 max values and similarly with individual "signs", and sport type (1, 2, 3, 4, 5) the individual values in RUN and VO_2 max look as follows:

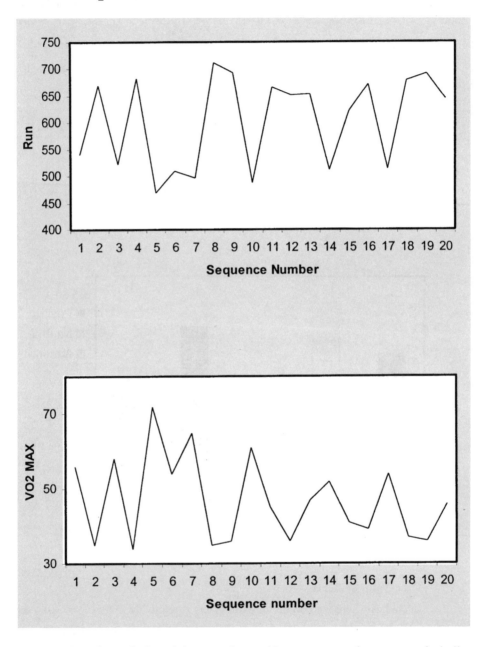

In cases where instead of participants, other entities are surveyed or measured, similar approaches can be adapted, however "years", nations, etc. can replace the participants.

For example,

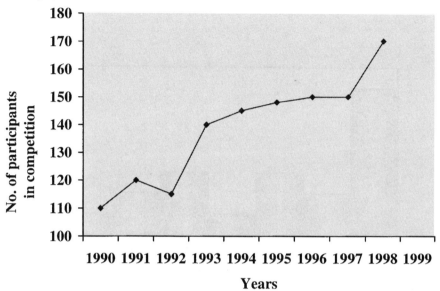

Similarly, such charts can include different nominal categories such as gender (males and females), nations, or any other nominal variable by using different types of lines to designate the different categories.

3.6   Histograms, Polygons (Frequencies and Shapes), Ogives

BAR graphs are useful in presenting nominal or ordinal data. The bars are in a given distance each from the other, because there was no logical sequence between the various categories: sport-types, gender, etc. However, once a CONTINUOUS VARIABLE is graphically presented, CLASS INTERVALS should be established, and then a HISTOGRAM (a bar chart for continuous/interval scales) should be drawn.

The bars are united so that a CONTINUUM can be established, i.e., any value in the distribution of values falls within this continuum which is broken-down by CLASS INTERVALS. A histogram contains CLASS LIMITS and each bar's area presents proportionally the frequency of the class in the whole distribution. Some time ago, the class limits (see previous tables) were also presented in the figures. Today, with computation development, the MID-POINT of each CLASS INTERVAL is presented instead. The following two histograms, one for "VO_2max" and one for "run" present clearly this idea. The "VO_2max" continuum was broken-down to 8 intervals and the "RUN" into 10 intervals.

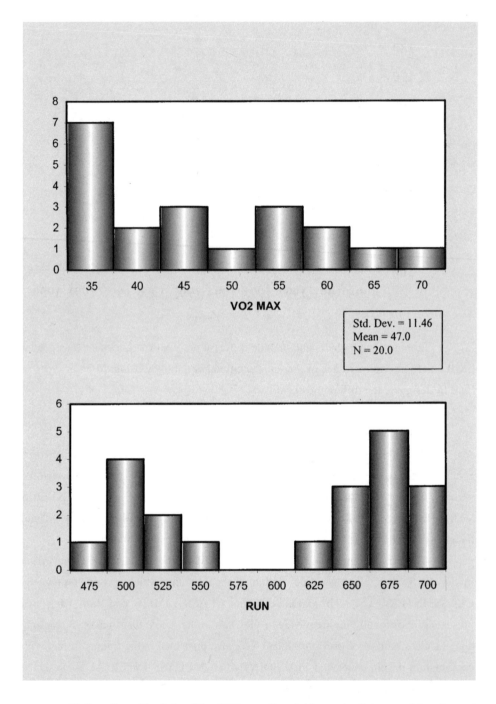

Std. Dev. = 11.46
Mean = 47.0
N = 20.0

Notice, the midpoints of the "VO$_2$max" variable are in distance of 5 units, and therefore the histogram represents the following distribution.

Lower Limit	Mid-Point	Upper Limit	Frequency	%	Cumulative %
32.5	35	37.5	7	35	35
37.5	40	42.5	2	10	45
42.5	45	47.5	3	15	60
47.5	50	52.5	1	5	65
52.5	55	57.5	3	15	80
57.5	60	62.5	2	10	90
62.5	65	67.5	1	5	95
67.5	70	72.5	1	5	100
			n = 20	*100%*	

The histogram can be presented by using the PERCENTAGES of the CLASS INTERVALS instead of the FREQUENCIES. As one may notice, in the "RUN" histogram, two class intervals have missing values. It is an indication that within these ranges (575 ± 12.5 and 600 ± 12.5), there were no times recorded. The histogram indicates that there are two groups of runners, one is a fast one (left side of the histogram) and the other is the slow one (right side of the histogram). It is the decision of the investigator how many class intervals he/she wishes to present in a graphical form.

A FREQUENCY POLYGON is a continuous line formed by plotting the midpoints of each class interval against the class frequency. An example of a frequency polygon looks as follows:

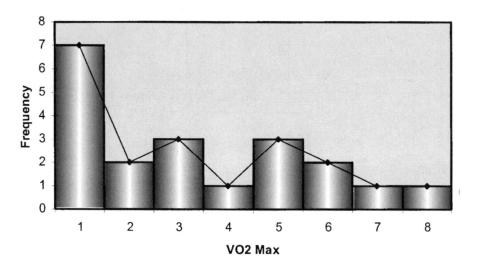

or

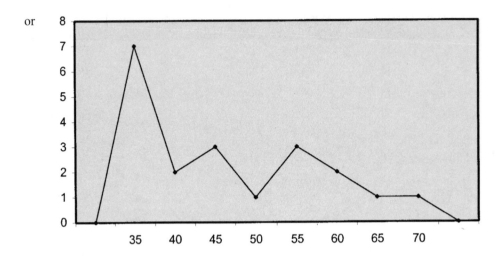

Notice some area of the histogram is excluded, however IDENTICAL area is included. Thus, relatively, identical area remains under the histogram and the polygon. This is true only when the distances of the starting and ending points of the polygon from the first and last bars are equal to the distances between the midpoints of these bars and their lower and upper class intervals, respectively.

Frequency Polygons can be described in curve shapes such as these:

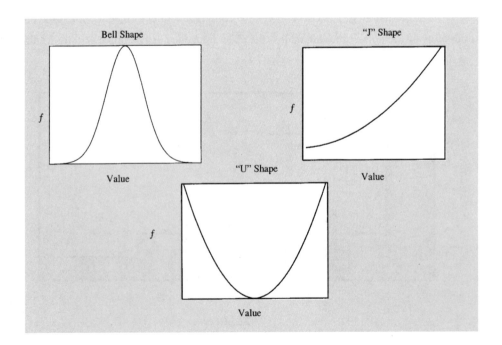

If we are interested to know the accumulated cases until a given scaled value, instead of using the frequency as on Y-axis indicator, we use the CUMULATIVE FREQUENCY (CF) as an indicator. An increase in value results usually in accumulated frequency, such as presented below:

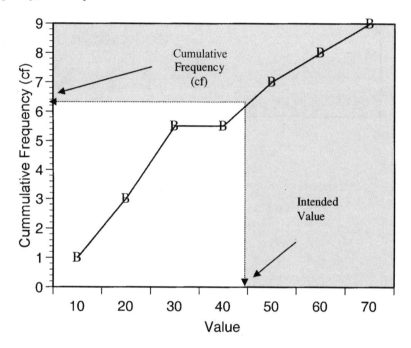

The "OGIVE" shape of the CUMULATIVE FREQUENCY vs. the VARIABLE VALUE indicates that until the class with midpoint 30 there was a steady increase in the number of observations. However from 30 to 40 there were no observations, and from 40 and on, additional values were added. The ogive shape allows us also to estimate how many values/observations were in the distribution until any certain value. The dotted arrowed lines demonstrate this process.

3.7   X-Y Plots-Association

The X-Y plots are used for two main reasons: (a) to see the ASSOCIATION between two or more variables, and (b) to detect any OUTLIER or EXCEPTIONAL values, which were mistakenly, or purposefully coded/entered into the data matrix. Here are two simple examples of plotting the "RUN" vs. the "VO$_2$max" values from the previous data matrix. The first figure shows the data points for the whole sample and the second one for each group/gender separately.

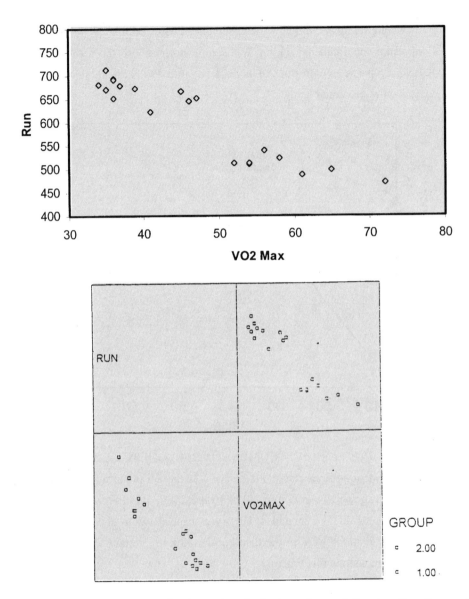

As one may immediately notice, in both males and females (together and separately), the higher the maximal oxygen consumption the faster (lower values) the long run. This is an indication of a positive linear association between the two variables (note that "run" is a "reversal" variable, i.e., the lower the values the "better"/faster is the runner). Later these data plots will be accompanied with numerical estimators of association such as CORRELATION and LINEAR or NON-LINEAR FUNCTIONS, but the visual presentation of these various statistics is of vital importance.

(4) Measures of Central and Dispersion Tendency

Nominal scales are summarized (aggregated) by frequencies, proportions, and percentages. Such summaries provide meaning to names, categories, and other elements. However data that represent interval or ratio scales can be represented by a more sophisticated estimation. On one hand we are interested in an estimator that best represent the CENTRALITY of the data, and on the other hand, we are interested in estimations of DISPERSION. Once we know the central and dispersion characteristics of the data, we can make judgements that relate to:

CENTRALITY: HOW GOOD, BAD, HIGH, LOW, ANXIOUS ... ARE THE SAMPLED PERSONS?

DISPERSION: HOW DISTRIBUTED ARE THESE PERSONS IN RELATION TO THE VARIABLE THEY WERE MEASURED? ARE THEY HOMOGENEOUS OR HETROGENEOUS, do they look alike or vary?

4.1 Measures of Central Tendency

The best-known and used measures of central tendency are the ARITHMETIC MEAN, MODE, and MEDIAN. The "strongest" and most representative is the mean.

The Arithmetic Mean

The arithmetic mean is the most common and the most powerful estimator of the data central tendency. A population mean is notated by the symbol μ, and of a sample of subjects from the population as m or $\bar{x}$. The arithmetic mean is the sum of all the observations in a distribution divided by the number of observations.

If the observations are

$x_1, x_2, x_3, x_4 ..... x_n$

and their order (1, 2, 3 ... n) is signified as i then

$sum = x_1 + x_2 + x_3 + ... x_n$ or Σx_i

and the arithmetic mean is

$$\bar{x} = sum/n = \sum_{i=1}^{n} x_i/n \qquad (6)$$

The sum of the observation distances from the mean is zero. This is an indication of its CENTRALITY.

In mathematical term

$$\sum_{i=1}^{n} (x_i - \bar{x}) = 0$$

This can be proved as follows:

$$\sum_{i=1}^{n} (x_i - \bar{x}) = \sum_{i=1}^{n} x_i - \sum_{i=1}^{n} \bar{x}$$

Since $\bar{x}$ is a constant, we may express it as

$$\sum_{i=1}^{n} \bar{x} = n\bar{x} = n \cdot \sum_{i=1}^{n} x_i/n = \sum_{i=1}^{n} x_i$$

Integrating this term in the previous equation

$$\sum_{i=1}^{n} (x_i - \bar{x}) = \sum_{i=1}^{n} x_i - \sum_{i=1}^{n} \bar{x} = \sum_{i=1}^{n} x_i - \sum_{i=1}^{n} x_i = 0$$

We can demonstrate it by example: we measured push-ups in 8 young boys. The number of push-ups were as follows: 20, 25, 30, 15, 42, 28, 24, 16. Their mean is
$$\bar{x} = (16 + 24 + 28 + 42 + 15 + 30 + 25 + 20)/8 = 200/8 = 25.$$

The eight distances from their means are:

20 – 25 =	-5
25 – 25 =	0
30 – 25 =	5
15 – 25 =	-10
42 – 25 =	17
28 – 25 =	3
24 – 25 =	-1
16 – 25 =	-9
$x_i - \bar{x}$	$\sum (x_i - \bar{x}) = 0$

$$(-5 + 0 + 5 - 10 + 17 + 3 - 1 - 9) = 0$$

When we sample all the population (N) the mean will be

$$\mu = \sum x_i/N \qquad (7)$$

Once the data is presented in class intervals, the mid-point (m_i) of each class is used as representative of the central value. The mid-point value is multiplied by the number of observations that signifies the class (f_i). This is like summing up all the values within the class. Summing up $f_i m_i$ across all class intervals and dividing by the total number of observations (n), will result in the arithmetic mean.

$$\bar{x} = \Sigma f_i m_i / n \qquad\qquad (8)$$

where $m_i = (l_{min} + l_{max})/2$, l_{min} and l_{max} are the lower and higher limits of each class interval, for example,

Class Interval	Central Value (m$_i$)	Frequency (f$_i$)	f$_i$m$_i$
36-40	38	5	190
41-45	43	8	344
46-50	48	9	432
51-55	53	12	636
56-60	58	8	464
61-65	63	6	378
66-70	68	4	272
		n = Σf_i = 52	$\Sigma f_i m_i$ = 2716

$$\bar{x} = \sum_{i=1}^{k} f_i m_i / n = 2716/52 = 52.23$$

Class intervals may be replaced by values, and the number of observations associated with them:

Observation (x$_i$)	Frequency (f$_i$)	X$_i$f$_i$
25	5	125
35	4	140
41	3	123
52	5	260
60	7	420
73	8	584
	n = Σf_i = 32	$\Sigma x_i f_i$ = 1652

$$\bar{x} = \sum_{i=1}^{k} x_i f_i / n = 1652/32 = 5.625$$

Weighted, Harmonic, and Geometric Mean

The WEIGHTED MEAN enables us to calculate a representative mean from all the given means. This signifies different samples which represent a given population of observations. For example, assume that we measured the physical fitness of 3 samples of young adults located in big cities, towns, and villages as follows:

Sample	Size	Mean
Cities	20,000	52
Towns	2,500	56
Villages	2,000	50

Since each mean represents a different number of observations, the overall weighted mean should be taken it into account. The number of observations/cases in each sample is n_i, the mean of each sample is $\bar{x}_1$, k is the number of samples, and N is the total number of observations ($n_1 + n_2 + n_3 = N$). Thus the weighted mean (M_w) is

$$M_w = \sum_{i=1}^{k} n_i x_i / N \qquad (9)$$

and in the above example
$$M_w = (20{,}000 \bullet 52 + 2{,}500 \bullet 56 + 2{,}000 \bullet 50)/(20{,}000 + 2{,}500 + 2{,}000)$$
$$= 1{,}222{,}000/24{,}500$$
$$= 52.25$$

The weighted fitness mean of the 24,500 cases in the distribution is 52.25. Frequently, the weighted mean can be calculated by assigning a given weight to a given category of cases so that all the weight sum-up to 100%. In such cases the weighted mean (M_w) will be

$$M_w = \sum w_i x_i / \sum w_i \qquad (10)$$

Two additional means which are useful, but not as frequently used, are the HARMONIC MEAN (M_h) and the GEOMETRIC MEAN (M_g). These can be calculated through the following equations:

$$M_h = n / \sum_{i=1}^{n} 1/x_i \qquad (11)$$

and

$$M_g = \sqrt[n]{(x_1)(x_2) \dots (x_n)} \qquad (12)$$

Median

For an odd number of cases, the median is the value in the distribution that is located exactly in the middle of the RANK-ORDERED distribution (from low to high or vice-versa). For an even number of cases, the median is the average of the two middle observations for the RANK-ORDERED distribution.

There are TWO main VALUES associated with the median. One is its LOCATION and the other is its CORRESPONDING VALUE. The median (M_d) in simple ranked order data is calculated as follows

	Location		Value
	1		1
	2		2
	3		5
(l) location →	4	→	6 ← value (M_d)
	5		8
	6		12
	7		22

The LOCATION (l) is calculated by the equation

$$l = (n + 1)^2 \qquad (13)$$

and in the example,

l = (7 + 1)/2 = 8/2 = 4.

Now we know that the 4th observation in the distribution represents the median's value (M_d). In this example

$$M_d = 6$$

or $\quad$ $l = 4 \; ; M_d = 6$

and in odd number of observations the procedure is similar:

Location	Value
1	1
2	3
3	5
4	6
(l) location → 4.5 →	7 ← value (M_d)
5	8
6	12
7	22
8	24

the location (l) of the median (M_d) is

$$l = (8 + 1)/2 = 9/2 = 4.5$$

between the 4th and 5th observations. The two values which correspond to these locations are 6 and 8 and their average is (6 + 8)/2 = 7. Theoretically, each number between the two central values can be regarded as a median, but their average value is the most commonly used one.

The LOCATION and VALUE of the MEDIAN are not altered when observational values change. If for example, the 8th observation would be 2400 instead of 24, the median's location (4.5) and value (7) will remain the same. The MEAN, in contrast, will change accordingly. Thus the MEAN is more SENSITIVE to the VALUE's MAGNITUDES than is the MEDIAN.

Mode

The mode is the most common (frequent) observation in the distribution of data. For example, in a distribution such as

5, 7, 12, 22, 34, 65

each value appears only ONCE. Therefore, there is no mode in such a distribution. In the following distribution

> 5, 7, 7, 12, 22, 34, 65

the observation "7" appears twice, more than any other observation, and therefore is regarded as the mode. In the next distribution

> 5, 6, 6, 12, 22, 22, 34, 65

there are two modes, 6 and 22. Both appear twice. Once the number of observations is large, the data are presented in a table such as below:

Class Interval	Frequency (f_i)
1-5	5
6-10	6
11-15	18
16-20	22
21-25	31
26-30	16
31-35	12
36-40	8
41-45	4

The most frequent class interval is 21-25 as it contains 31 observations, more than any other class interval. The mid-point of this class interval is $(21 + 25)/2 = 23$, and 23 is considered to be the mode (M_0) of this distribution. In case of equality in the number of observations at two or more class intervals, there will be more than one mode.

Mean, Median and Mode in One Distribution

Previously we have mentioned the median is not affected by extremely high and low values. The MEDIAN is a central value that relates to the LOCATION of the values and/or observations in the data distribution once they are RANKED-ORDERED. In contrast, any VALUE CHANGES will be immediately reflected in the ARITHMETIC MEAN.

Though the median is a popular central measure in ordered scales, there is some discussion whether the mean is a suitable central measure in rank-ordered scales. The fact that the mean is a more stable central measure than the median in various samples makes it more appropriate and it is used not only in interval and ratio scales, but also in rank-ordered scales. It is a well-known fact in inferential statistics that means of different samples are closer to each other than their respective medians. Thus, the mean is a better central tendency estimator, since it is more GENERALIZABLE to the population. However, in cases where the DISTRIBUTION of OBSERVATIONS is NOT SYMETRIC (i.e., SKEWED), the MEDIAN may be a preferable central tendency estimator than the MEAN. The location of the MEAN (μ), MEDIAN (M_d) and MODE (M_o) with respect to the OBSERVATION DISTRIBUTION is presented in a figure 2.2.

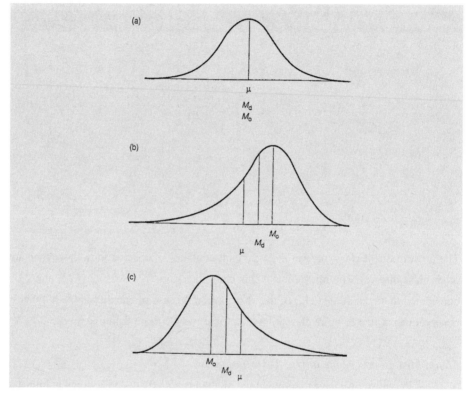

Figure 2.2   The location of the Mean, μ, Median, M_d, and Mode, M_o, in Normal (a) and Skewed Distributions (b and c).

The mean is affected by extreme values, and therefore will tend to shift towards these values, in contrast to the median. The mode remains always with the most frequent value in the distribution, and therefore will not change its location, no matter how skewed the distribution. However, in cases where there is more than one mode, like in the BI-MODAL distribution, the median and mean will share locations at the bottom center while two modes will indicate the tops of the two hills (Figure 2.3).

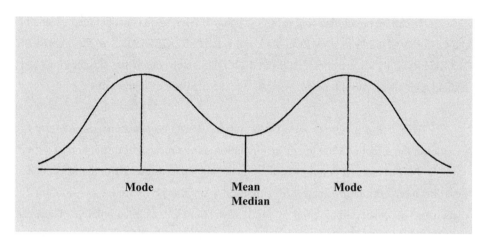

Figure 2.3   A Bimodal Distribution.

4.2   Measures of Dispersion

Measures of dispersion complement the measures of central tendencies. The means of two samples may be very similar to each other, but the samples they have been drawn from are very different. For example, see Figure 2.4.

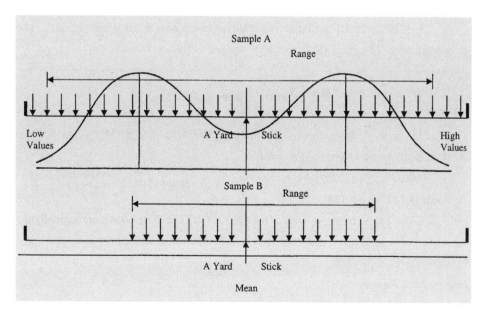

Figure 2.4   Two Samples (A and B) with Identical Mean but Different Range of Observations.

It can be concluded that samples A and B have similar or identical means but the OBSERVATIONS in SAMPLE A are more HETEROGENEOUS while SAMPLES' B OBSERVATIONS are more HOMOGENEOUS. How much the observations vary around their own central tendency measure is the measure of dispersion.

Dispersion measures are also important when the researcher is interested in examining the effect of a treatment/manipulation on the mean and dispersion of a given variable. Furthermore, it is not possible to make any conclusions about the effect of any IV (i.e., intervention or change of conditions) on the DV without considering the dispersion of observations prior to and after the IV was manipulated. Thus, the MEASURES OF DISPERSION are DESCRIPTIVE STATISTICS, which indicate how general the observations in the sample are.

Range

The RANGE is the DIFFERENCE between the LARGEST and SMALLEST VALUES in the SAMPLED DISTRIBUTION. In the following distribution:
41, 39, 17, 32, 29, 24
the RANGE is 41-17 = 24.

In class intervals the range is the difference between the mid-point of the two extreme classes. The range (RA) can be expressed as follows:

$$RA = X_{max} - X_{min} \qquad (14)$$

Its main disadvantage is its SENSITIVITY to EXTREME values. If the previous distribution of observation was
141, 39, 12, 32, 29, 24
the range is 141—17 = 124!

Thus, one extreme value that may be an OUTLIER may alter dramatically the range. To avoid such cases, the INTERQUARTILE RANGE is used.

Interquartile Range

The INTERQUARTILE RANGE (IQR) is the DIFFERENCE between the upper limits of the FIRST QUARTILE and the THIRD QUARTILE. It is the range that describes the MIDDLE 50% of the rank-ordered cases (see Figure 2.5).

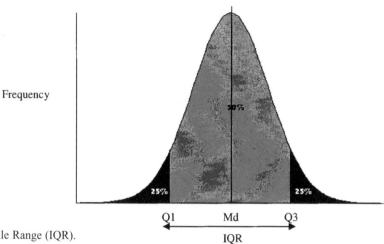

Figure 2.5

The Interquartile Range (IQR).

There are 25% of the observations under the first Quartile (Q1) and similarly there are 25% of the observations above third quartile (Q3). Thus, to calculate the IQR we need first to find the LOCATIONS of Q_1 and Q_3 (similarly to the M_d), their VALUES, and then the distance. Q_1 is located at the 25/100 =? of the range, and Q_3 at the 75/100 =? of the range. For example, in the following distribution (rank-ordered):

Value: 5, 7, 12, 14, 16, 17, 18, 20, 24, 25, 27, 30
Sequence number: 1 2 3 4 5 6 7 8 9 10 11 12

There are 12 observations, the locations of Q_1 and Q_3 are:

$Q_1 = 12 \bullet 1/4 = 3$

$Q_3 = 12 \bullet 3/4 = 9$

The values that correspond to these locations are

$Q_1 = 3 \rightarrow 12$

$Q_3 = 9 \rightarrow 24$

Therefore,

$$IQR = Q_3 - Q_1 = 24 - 12 = 12 \qquad (15)$$

When n is not divided into integers, the average between the two numbers which correspond to Q_1 and Q_3 should be average and thus IQR be calculated.

Mean Deviation

The MEAN DEVIATION (MD) is specified by the ABSOLUTE DISTANCES of the observations from their means divided by the number of observations. In fact, this MD is just like the MEAN to the OBSERVATIONS' VALUES, but applied to the DISTANCES.

$$MD = \left[\sum_{i=1}^{n} |x_i - \bar{x}| \right] / n \qquad (16)$$

For example, the observation

24, 19, 18, 15, 12, 7

share the following mean

$\bar{x} = (7 + 12 + 15 + 8 + 19 + 24) / 6 = 15.83$

and the MD is

$MD = \left[|7 - 15.83| + |12 - 15.83| + |15 - 15.83| + |8 - 15.83| + |19 - 15.83| + |24 - 15.83| \right] / 6$
$= (8.83 + 3.83 + 0.83 + 2.17 + 3.17 + 8.17) / 6 = 4.50$

One can conclude that the mean deviation of the observations from their mean is 4.50. Though the MD seems to be a good dispersion measure, it has several limitations: (a) absolute values are limited in their exposure to mathematical manipulation, (b) absolute values are limited in describing normal distributions, and (c) absolute values are limited when applied to inferential statistical procedures.

Standard Deviation

Similar to the MD, the STANDARD DEVIATION (SD or S) attempts to capture the DISTANCE of each OBSERVATION in the distribution from the MEAN. Every distance is first squared before all the distances are summed. The summation of the squared distances are then averaged by dividing by the number of observations (i.e., which is equal to the number of distances from their mean). To get a final standard deviation, the root square of the mean squared deviation is performed. In mathematical terms, this procedure is presented as follows:

$$S = \sqrt{\sum_{i=1}^{n} (x_i - \bar{x})_2 / (n - 1)} \qquad (17)$$

for a sample, and

$$\theta = \sqrt{\sum_{i=1}^{n} (x_i - \mu) / n} \qquad (18)$$

for the population and S^2 or θ^2 are termed VARIANCE.

The two equations define the standard deviation of the sample (S) and population (θ) as the average of the distances of the observations x_i from their own means, or μ. For example, the observations

7, 12, 15, 18, 19, 24 share the following mean:

$\bar{x} = (7 + 12 + 15 + 8 + 19 + 24) / 6 = 15.83$

the differences of the 6 observations from their mean and their squared values are

$(7 - 15.83)^2 + (12 - 15.83)^2 + (15 - 15.83)^2 + (18 - 15.83)^2 + (19 - 15.83)^2 + (24 - 15.83)^2$

$= (-8.83)^2) + (-3.83)^2 + (-0.83)^2 + (2.17)^2 + (3.17)^2 + (8.17)^2$

$= 77.969 + 14.669 + 0.689 + 4.709 + 10.049 + 66.749$

$= 174.834,$

and the standard deviation is

$$S = \sqrt{174.834/(6 - 1)} = \sqrt{34.967} = 5.913$$

For easier calculations of the standard deviation, equation 19 is more convenient

$$S = \sqrt{\frac{\sum x_i - \frac{(\sum x_i)^2}{n}}{n - 1}} \qquad (19)$$

with the similar previous six observations the standard deviation is

$7^2 + 12^2 + 15^2 + 18^2 + 19^2 + 24^2$

$= 49 + 144 + 225 + 324 + 361 + 579$

$= 1682$

$\Sigma x_i = (7 + 12 + 15 + 18 + 19 + 24) = 95$

$(\Sigma x_i)^2 = 95^2 = 9025$, and

$$S = \sqrt{\frac{1682 - \dfrac{9025}{6}}{5-1}} = \sqrt{\frac{1682 - 1504.17}{5}} = \sqrt{\frac{174.83}{5}}$$

$$= \sqrt{34.967} = 5.913$$

Once the distribution is presented in class intervals, the mid-points (m_I) of each class are used as the observation that represents all the observations in its class. Thus, the distance of the mid-point from the mean is

$m_i - \bar{x}$ and its squared value is

$(m_i - \bar{x})^2$

However, each class consists of several observations, f_i, and therefore the standard deviation is

$$S = \sqrt{\sum_{i=1}^{k} f_i(m_i - \bar{x})_2/(u-1)} \qquad (20)$$

where f_i is the number of observations in each class interval and k is the number of class intervals.

Coefficient of Variation

There are cases where the researcher is interested in the standard deviation/mean ratio. This ratio is termed COEFFICIENT OF VARIATION (CV) and is expressed as

$$\mathbf{CV} = S/\bar{x} \text{ or } (S/\bar{x})100 \text{ (in percentage).} \qquad (21)$$

For example, two samples were examined with respect to the number of push-ups in two conditions. The mean number of push-ups and standard deviations in the two modes were 12 and 14 and 4 and 6 respectively. The CVs of the two modes were 4/12 = 0.33 (33%) and 6/14 = 0.43 (43%).

Asymmetry

In cases where the distribution of observations deviates from normality, the distance between the mean and the median increases. The increase in this distance causes the distribution to be SKEWED. The most commonly used measure of ASYMMETRY is termed SKEWNESS and is calculated as follows:

Skewness = $3(\bar{x} - m_d)/S$ (22)

In a distribution like this:

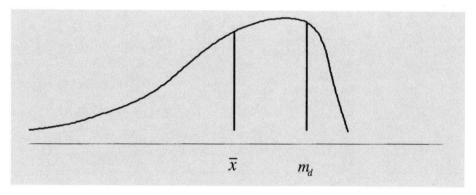

and therefore the difference is negative. However, once the observations distribute as follows:

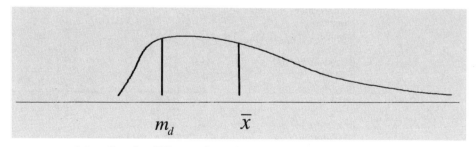

and therefore the difference is positive. A perfect normal distribution results in identical and m_d values, and therefore the skewness is zero.

The computerized statistical programs help us to avoid errors while computing the various equations. A typical output (SPSS, version 11.0) of the CENTRAL and DISPERSION MEASURES are as follows (we use the "RUN" and "VO$_2$max" as two DV and "sport" and "group" (gender as two grouping/categorical variables):

Descriptive Statistics

	SPORT			Statistic	Std. Error
VO$_2$MAX	1.00	Mean		45.7500	6.5112
		95% Confidence	Lower Bound	25.0284	
		Interval for Mean	Upper Bound	66.4716	
		5% Trimmed Mean		45.7222	
		Median		45.5000	
		Variance		169.583	
		Std. Deviation		13.0224	
		Minimum		34.00	
		Maximum		58.00	
		Range		24.00	
		Interquartile Range		23.2500	
		Skewness		.015	1.014
		Kurtosis		-5.853	2.619
VO$_2$MAX	2.00	Mean		53.8333	6.2685
		95% Confidence	Lower Bound	37.7196	
		Interval for Mean	Upper Bound	69.9471	
		5% Trimmed Mean		53.8704	
		Median		57.5000	
		Variance		235.767	
		Std. Deviation		15.3547	
		Minimum		35.00	
		Maximum		72.00	
		Range		37.00	
		Interquartile Range		31.0000	
		Skewness		-.381	.845
		Kurtosis		-1.791	1.741
	3.00	Mean		40.5000	4.5000
		95% Confidence	Lower Bound	-16.6779	
		Interval for Mean	Upper Bound	97.6779	
		5% Trimmed Mean			
		Median		40.5000	
		Variance		40.500	
		Std. Deviation		6.3640	
		Minimum		36.00	
		Maximum		45.00	
		Range		9.00	
		Interquartile Range		.	
		Skewness		.	.
		Kurtosis		.	.
	4.00	Mean		46.6000	2.9428
		95% Confidence	Lower Bound	38.4295	
		Interval for Mean	Upper Bound	54.7705	
		5% Trimmed Mean		46.6111	
		Median		47.0000	
		Variance		43.300	
		Std. Deviation		6.5803	
		Minimum		39.00	
		Maximum		54.00	
		Range		15.00	
		Interquartile Range		13.0000	
		Skewness		-.076	.913
		Kurtosis		-2.554	2.000

				Statistic	Std. Error
	5.00	Mean		39.6667	3.1798
		95% Confidence	Lower Bound	25.9851	
		Interval for Mean		53.3482	
		5% trimmed Mean			
		Median		37.0000	
		Variance		30.333	
		Std. Deviation		5.5076	
		Minimum		35.00	
		Maximum		46.00	
		Range		10.00	
		Interquartile Range			
		Skewness		1.668	1.225
		Kurtosis			
	GROUP			Statistic	Std. Error
VO$_2$MAX	1.00	Mean		51.0000	3.8326
		95% Confidence	Lower Bound	42.3300	
		Interval for Mean	Upper Bound	59.6700	
		5% Trimmed Mean		50.6667	
		Median		50.5000	
		Variance		146.889	
		Std. Deviation		12.1198	
		Minimum		36.00	
		Maximum		72.00	
		Range		36.00	
		Interquartile Range		20.0000	
		Skewness		.349	.687
		Kurtosis		-.811	1.334
	2.00	Mean		42.9000	3.0639
		95% Confidence	Lower Bound	35.9689	
		Interval for Mean	Upper Bound	49.8311	
		5% Trimmed Mean		42.3889	
		Median		38.0000	
		Variance		93.878	
		Std. Deviation		9.6891	
		Minimum		34.00	
		Maximum		61.00	
		Range		27.00	
		Interquartile Range		17.5000	
		Skewness		.885	.687
		Kurtosis		-.693	1.334

Stem and Leaf Plot

Stem and leaf plots graphically and numerically present the shape of the data distribution. The first DIGIT of each individual value of the VO_2max data (the "tens") is a STEM and the second digit (the "unit") is a LEAF. The stem values are arranged vertically from the smallest to the largest, next to a vertical line. Working through the scores, each leaf value is then centered next to its stem, so we obtain an arrangement of data, which is very similar to a histogram. For the VO_2max data, the histogram and stem and leaf are presented as follows:

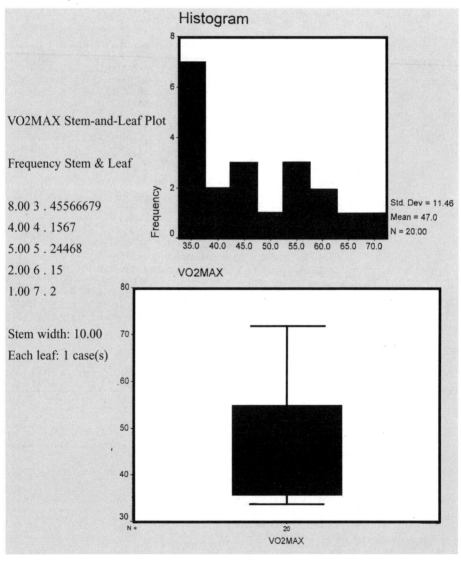

VO2MAX Stem-and-Leaf Plot

Frequency Stem & Leaf

8.00 3 . 45566679

4.00 4 . 1567

5.00 5 . 24468

2.00 6 . 15

1.00 7 . 2

Stem width: 10.00

Each leaf: 1 case(s)

The similarity between the histogram and stem and leaf plots is obvious. We see that the distribution is greatly skewed toward the left as most (f = 8) of the values are within the 30-40-interval class (34, 35, 35, 36 ... 39 in the stem and leaf plot) and only one value above 70 (72 in the stem and leaf plot). Similarly, the "RUN" results are as follows:

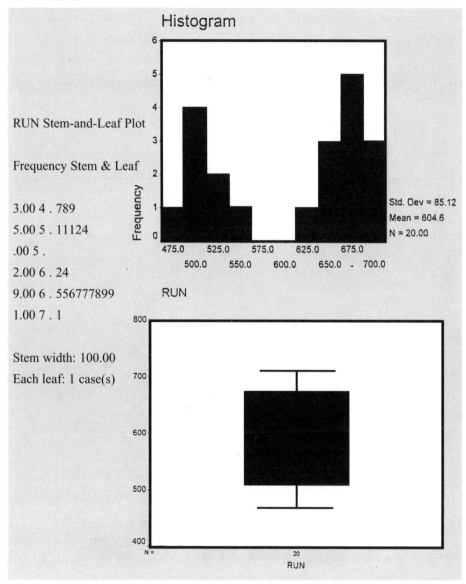

RUN Stem-and-Leaf Plot

Frequency Stem & Leaf

3.00 4 . 789

5.00 5 . 11124

.00 5 .

2.00 6 . 24

9.00 6 . 556777899

1.00 7 . 1

Stem width: 100.00

Each leaf: 1 case(s)

These plots can be established for each sport-type or gender separately, and then be contrasted each against the other.

Box and Whisker Plot

Knowledge of the median and the interquartile range provides an additional way of displaying data in a graphical fashion. The Box and Whisker plot displays the central location of the data, the spread (dispersion) and the EXTREMITIES, which are termed TAILS. The Box and Whisker plots are drawn on a number line with the middle 50% of data (between the quartiles) represented by a BOX. Whiskers are then drawn from the quartiles to the OUTLIERS—the highest and the lowest values. This plot enables the researcher to examine the distribution within its central limits (upper and lower quartiles) and its extremities, which are above and beneath these limits (Figure 2.6).

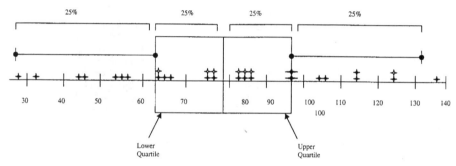

Figure 2.6   Box and Whisker Plot for Hypothetical Data.

For the VO$_2$max and RUN data, the Box and Whisker for 5 sport-types and the VO$_2$max for the two gender groups are displayed as follows:

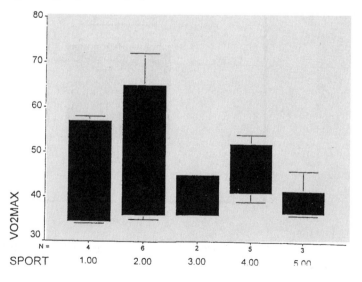

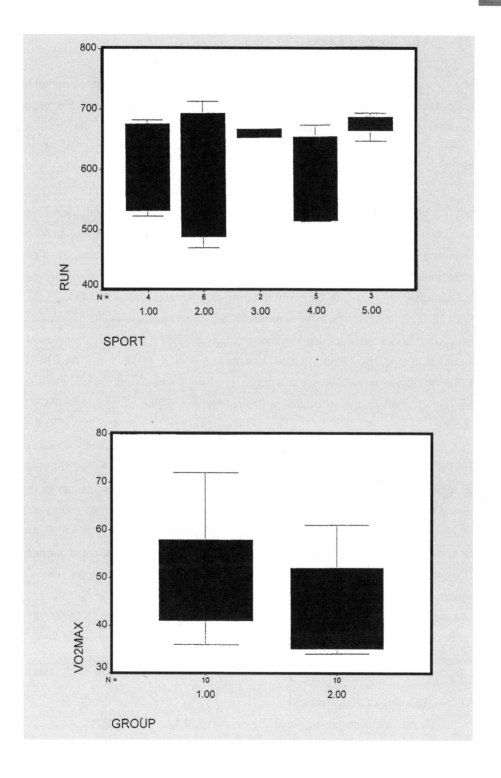

(5)   The Normal Curve

Each of the data sets collected by the researcher is distributed in some kind of shape. The FORM/SHAPE of these various DISTRIBUTIONS has a significant role in the sort of ANALYSES that are appropriate and can be applied to the data set. Inappropriate analyses of the data, which stem from the lack of meeting the MAIN ASSUMPTIONS OF DATA DISTRIBUTION, may jeopardize the examination of hypotheses, and consequently the theory, which reflects its foundation.

The NORMAL DISTRIBUTION of observations is a distribution that enables the researcher to apply LINEAR STATISTICS. When sufficient numbers of observations are made, the normal distribution represents the nature of many variables in the populations, mainly in the social and behavioral sciences, but also in the physical and natural sciences. When the distribution of observations is NOT NORMAL, then NON-LINEAR statistics are more appropriate to infer relationships and commonalities among the various variables that have been measured. There are, however, procedures, which enable us to TRANSFORM a data set, which violates the NORMAL ASSUMPTIONS into a data set that meets its assumptions. At this stage, we shall describe in detail the main features and characteristics of the CLASSIC NORMAL CURVE.

The NORMAL CURVE is a UNIDIMENSIONAL CURVE, which is PERFECTLY SYMMETRICAL, is ASSYMPHOTIC, and represents the function between the VALUE of a variable and its FREQUENCY. The perfect symmetry of the normal curve enables us to estimate various AREAS, which lie within any two values, whether real or theoretical. Once the REAL UNITS of the variable are TRANSFORMED into STANDARDIZED UNITS, areas can be calculated and numbers of observations are derived. Also NORMS can be developed so that people who are measured on the variable can be compared to their "assigned group" distribution. This procedure can be applied in a simple manner through the MEAN and the STANDARD DEVIATION of the NORMAL DATA DISTRIBUTION. But before we describe this procedure, a short introduction about measurement and its meaning is presented.

5.1   Meaning of Measurement

Each variable that is measured shares UNITS of MEASUREMENT, which give MEANING to the MEASURE. A distance is measured by units of kilometers, meters, centimeters, etc; speed and velocity by units or hours, minutes, seconds, etc; heat and temperature by degrees centigrade (Celsius), Fahrenheit, Kelvin, and so on. Every MEASURE has a MEANING once we know its MAGNITUDE and have gathered sufficient INFORMATION about the NATURE of the VARIABLE. Thus, we know that a long jump of 8.83 m, and a 100 m run of 9.95 seconds are exceptionally high and a temperature of 40°C means very hot weather, but not sufficient enough to boil water and prepare coffee.

When several variables are measured, we are interested in knowing "how much" of one variable is more, less, or equal to "how much" in another variable. For example, which distance in long jump is equal to the speed time in 100 m run? Once many observations are collected, and they share normal distribution, we may estimate the percentages that are associated with different scores of each of the variables separately. By doing so, we STANDARDIZE the two distributions so that a COMPARISON between the two or more variables can be made. Furthermore, a PROFILE of STANDARDIZED SCORES can be drawn, despite the different units of measurement that each variable shares. The idea is to STANDARDIZE the LOCATIONS of VALUES using the NORMAL CURVE as a REFERENCE POINT. The locations have NO UNITS but instead STANDARDIZED LOCATIONS. The standardized locations reflect the RELATIVE LOCATIONS of each score from its MEAN in STANDARD DEVIATION UNITS. By using STANDARDIZED SCALES for different variables (termed, Z, T, H, Stanines, etc) we can answer the question of "how much" of a variable is equal or is more or less than "how much" of another variable.

5.2   Normal Curve and its Standard Units

The mean and the standard deviation (S) are used for STANDARDIZATION of the AREAS under the NORMAL CURVE. A standard score has the notation Z and is determined through the equation

$$Z_i = (x_i - \bar{x})/S \qquad\qquad (23)$$

which is the difference (distance) between any score x_i from its mean, divided by the standard deviation (S) of the distribution of observations. For example, if the mean push-ups for boys in grade 9 is 12 and the standard deviation 3, then a boy who performed 9 push-ups has a Z score of

$Z_9 = (9—12)/3 = -3/3 = -1.00$

which is ONE STANDARD DEVIATION UNDER THE MEAN. Another student who performed 16 push-ups is located accordingly

$Z_{16} = (16—12)/3 = 4/3 = 1.33$

which means 1.33 STANDARD DEVIATIONS ABOVE THE MEAN. The NORMAL DISTRIBUTION enables us to use the NORMAL AREA DISTRIBUTION TABLE to estimate the LOCATION of each SCORE in PROPORTION or PERCENT relative to the MEAN and STANDARD DEVIATION of the distribution. This is done by using the table of AREAS UNDER THE STANDARD NORMAL CURVE. It is important to remember that NO MATTER the SHAPE of the NORMAL CURVE, the RELATIVE AREAS UNDER THE CURVE REMAINS IDENTICAL (see Figure 2.7).

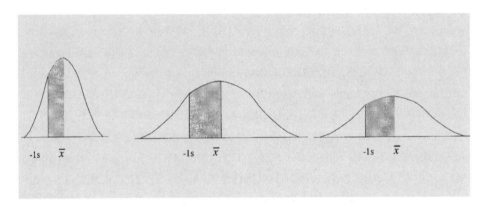

Figure 2.7   Normal curves of Different Shapes. The Areas under Identical Standardized Units Remain always Identical. The Area between the Mean () and one Standard Deviation below the Mean (-1S) is Identical in all the 3 Curves. This Remains True for any Distance from the Mean of each Respective Curve.

Let's return for a moment to the two students who performed the push-ups exercise. Knowing their STANDARDIZED LOCATIONS (-1.00 and +1.33) from the MEAN, we can estimate how "good" they are in push-ups RELATIVE to the characteristics of the sample of students for whom the normal distribution was established. The table of AREAS UNDER THE NORMAL CURVE can be found in Appendix 1. We use the two standardised scores (Z_i) and the area table (Appendix 1) to compare the two scores. In figure 2.8, the two push-ups scores are located within the normal distribution frame.

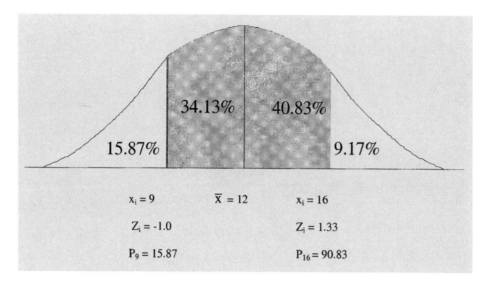

Figure 2.8   The Area between Two Scores (9 and 10) under the Normal Curve.

Accordingly, 1 standard deviation (which corresponds to $x_i = 9$) is equal to 34.13% of the total area (100%), while 1.33 standard deviation (which correspond to x_i = 16) is equal to 48.83% of the area. Thus the student who performed 9 push-ups performed MORE PUSH-UPS THAN 15.87% of the students (50—34.13 = 15.89) while his/her friend with 16 push-ups performed better than 90.83% of his/her counterparts (50 + 40.83 = 90.83). Only 9.17% of the students performed more push-ups than him/her. We can say that the student who performed 9 push-ups is located in the 15.87 percentile (or centile) and the one that performed 16 push-ups is located in the 90.83 centile ($P_{15.87}$ and $P_{90.23}$, respectively).

The AREAS under the normal curve represent the RELATIVE FREQUENCY of the NUMBER OF CASES in the DISTRIBUTION. These values have PROBABILISTIC MEANING. For example, if we know that the mean intelligence of the population is IQ = 100 and S = 15, then what is the probability that if we randomly sample a person, his/her IQ will be greater then 110. To answer this question, we first calculate the Z score that corresponds to IQ = 110.

$Z_{110} = (110—100)/15 = 10/15 = 0.67$

and graphically it is presented as follows:

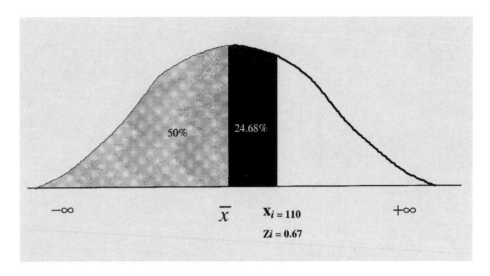

The AREA UNDER THE NORMAL CURVE which corresponds to Z = 0.67 equals 24.68%. 50% of the area is located between the mean to $+\infty$ or $-\infty$. Thus, a score of IQ = 110 means that 74.68% of the people in the population are expected to score lower than 110 and 25.14% (100 - 74.68) are expected to score above 110. We can conclude that the PROBABILITY to randomly choose a person with IQ > 110 is 25.14% and IQ <110 - 74.86%. It should be noted that PROBABILITY corresponds only to AREAS and NOT TO SINGLE POINTS or VALUES. This is because there are infinite points and therefore the probability of a point tends to zero. Thus, the probability corresponds to areas and not to single points in the normal curve.

The MEAN of the STANDARDIZED DISTRIBUTION is ZERO and its standard deviation is 1 (= 1). The areas between ±1S, ±2S, and ±3S are presented in Figure 2.9.

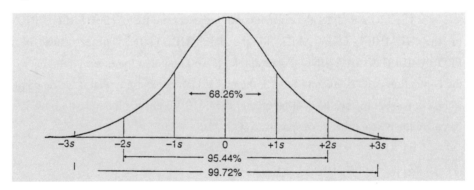

Figure 2.9   Areas between ±1S, ±2S, and ±3S under the Normal Curve.

It can be seen that 68.26% of the area/cases/observations lie within ±1S, 95.44% within ±2S, and 99.72% within ±3S. Thus, only 0.28% of the area/cases lie above (0.14%) or below (0.14%) the −3 and +3 standard deviations. In this line, it is possible to calculate the areas above and beneath each value in the normal distribution, or between two values in the normal distribution, and convert the Z-values into percentages and probabilities (see Figure 2.10 for general example and Table 2.5 for specific Z values).

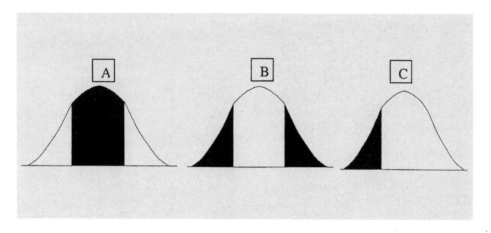

Figure 2.10   Areas under the Normal Curve between two Values (A), beyond two Values (B), and beyond one Value (C)

Table 2.5

Areas under the Normal Curve (between Points, beyond Points, and beyond one Point).

z (standard deviation units)	Area under curve between points	Area under curve beyond both points	Area under curve beyond one point
±0.1	0.080	0.920	0.460
±0.2	0.159	0.841	0.4205
±0.3	0.236	0.764	0.382
±0.4	0.311	0.689	0.3445
±0.5	0.383	0.617	0.3085
±0.6	0.451	0.549	0.2745
±0.7	0.516	0.484	0.242
±0.8	0.576	0.424	0.212
±0.9	0.632	0.368	0.184
±1	0.683	0.317	0.1585
±1.1	0.729	0.271	0.1355
±1.2	0.770	0.230	0.115
±1.3	0.806	0.194	0.097
±1.4	0.838	0.162	0.081
±1.5	0.866	0.134	0.067
±1.6	0.890	0.110	0.055
±1.645	0.900	0.100	0.050
±1.7	0.911	0.089	0.0445
±1.8	0.928	0.072	0.036
±1.9	0.943	0.057	0.029
±1.96	0.950	0.050	0.025
±2	0.954	0.046	0.023
±2.1	0.964	0.036-	0.018
±2.2	0.972	0.028	0.014
±2.3	0.979	0.021	0.0105
±2.4	0.984	0.016	0.008
±2.5	0.988	0.012	0.006
±2.6	0.991	0.009	0.0045
±2.7	0.993	0.007	0.0035
±2.8	0.995	0.005	0.0025
±2.9	0.996	0.004	0.002
±3	0.997	0.003	0.0015
±3.1	0.998	0.002	0.0001
±3.2	0.9986	0.0014	0.0007
±3.3	0.9990	0.0010	0.0005
±3.4	0.9993	0.0007	0.0003
±3.5	0.9995	0.0005	0.00025
±3.6	0.9997	0.0003	0.00015
±3.7	0.9998	0.0002	0.0001
±3.8	0.99986	0.00014	0.00007
±3.9	0.99990	0.00010	0.00005
±4	>0.99990	<0.00010	<0.00005

5.3 T and H Values

T and H values are similar to Z values but avoid the negative (minus) sign, which signifies that the value is being located under the mean. The T method consists of dividing the normal curve into 10 standard deviations on a scale, which ranges from 0-100. The MEAN is 50 and the STANDARD DEVIATION is 10 (100/10 = 10). In Z-scores the MEAN is 0. Each standard deviation of Z equals 10 points in T units. Thus to transform a Z value into a T value, the constant 50 should be added to the multiplication of Z by 10. The equation is

$$T = 50 + 10Z \qquad (24)$$

If a Z score of a person equals 1.3, his T score is
$T = 50 + 10 \cdot 1.3 = 50 + 13 = 63$
and if the Z score is −1.93 then
$T = 50 + 10(-1.93) = 50 - 19.3 = 30.7$.

As can be seen, T scores remain positive and range between 0-100, which is a comfortable range with which to work. However, one can notice that 99.73% of the values of a normal distribution lie within the +3.0 - (-3.0) range of Z values. Therefore, 99.23% of the values in the normal curve lie within the 20-80 T-values range because Z = 3.0 is T = 50 + 10 (3) = 80, and Z = -3 implies that T = 50 + 10(-3) = 20.

The H standardized values are very similar to the T values. However the normal curve is divided into 7 sections instead of 10 in the T method. The mean of H is 50 with 3.5 standard deviations above the mean and 3.5 below the mean. The H value range is 0-100 and therefore each standard deviation equals 100/7 = 14.28 points (instead of 10 points in the T method). For reasons of simplicity 14.28 is rounded to 14.3. The Z to H transformation is

$$H = 50 + 14.3Z \qquad (25)$$

Thus for example, if Z = 1.3 then
$H = 50 + 14.3 \cdot 1.3 = 50 + 18.59 = 68.59$
And if Z = -1.93 then
$H = 50 + 14.3(-1.93) = 50 - 27.60 = 22.40$.

Since about 100% of the values fall within the ±3.5 standard deviation range, the value range is 0-100, while in T they range between 20-80 and in Z between –3.0–3.0.

5.4   Standardized Values, Tables, and Norms

Once we know the mean and standard deviation of the data distribution, it is relatively simple to transform the values into one of the standardized values methods Z, T, and H. The Z, T, and H standardized values are shown in Table 2.6.

Table 2.6

Standardized Values: Z, T, and H Methods

Z −	Z +	T −	T +	H −	H +
-3.000	3.000	20.000	80.000	7.100	92.900
-2.900	2.900	21.000	79.000	8.530	91.470
-2.800	2.800	22.000	78.000	9.960	90.040
-2.700	2.700	23.000	77.000	11.390	88.610
-2.600	2.600	24.000	76.000	12.820	87.180
-2.500	2.500	25.000	75.000	14.250	85.750
-2.400	2.400	26.000	74.000	15.680	84.320
-2.300	2.300	27.000	73.000	17.110	82.890
-2.200	2.200	28.000	72.000	18.540	81.460
-2.100	2.100	29.000	71.000	19.970	80.030
-2.000	2.000	30.000	70.000	21.400	78.600
-1.900	1.900	31.000	69.000	22.830	77.170
-1.800	1.800	32.000	68.000	24.260	75.740
-1.700	1.700	33.000	67.000	25.690	74.310
-1.600	1.600	34.000	66.000	27.120	72.880
-1.500	1.500	35.000	65.000	28.550	71.450
-1.400	1.400	36.000	64.000	29.980	70.020
-1.300	1.300	37.000	63.000	31.410	68.590
-1.200	1.200	38.000	62.000	32.840	67.160
-1.100	1.100	39.000	61.000	34.270	65.730
-1.000	1.000	40.000	60.000	35.700	64.300
-0.900	0.900	41.000	59.000	37.130	62.870
-0.800	0.800	42.000	58.000	38.560	61.440
-0.700	0.700	43.000	57.000	39.990	60.010
-0.600	0.600	44.000	56.000	41.420	58.580
-0.500	0.500	45.000	55.000	42.850	57.150
-0.400	0.400	46.000	54.000	44.280	55.720
-0,300	0.300	47.000	53.000	45.710	54.290
-0.200	0.200	48.000	52.000	47.140	52.860
-0.100	0.100	49.000	51.000	48.570	51.430
0.000	0.000	50.000	50.000	50.000	50.000

When a NORM TABLE is established, VALUES of DIFFERENT VARIABLES can be COMPARED to each other. We will now demonstrate how such a table can be created. Above and below the mean there are 50 points in both T and H methods. If the standard deviation (S) is known, 5S = 50 points. Thus, if we divide 50 points by 50 (50/50 = 1), a precision of 1 will result, and 5S/25 is 50/25 = 2 points precision, 50/10 = 5 points precision, and 50/5 = 10 points precision. Similarly with H values: 3.5S = 50 points, and therefore 3.5S/50 = 1 point precision, 3.5S/25 = 2 points precision and so on. These precision values are shown in Table 2.7.

Table 2.7

Transformation Equations for Raw Data into Standardized T and H Values

Precision	T values	H values
1	$\bar{x} \pm 5S/50$	$\bar{x} \pm 3.5S/50$
2	$\bar{x} \pm 5S/25$	$\bar{x} \pm 3.5S/25$
5	$\bar{x} \pm 5S/10$	$\bar{x} \pm 3.5S/10$
10	$\bar{x} \pm 5S/5$	$\bar{x} \pm 3.5S/5$

For example, assume we measured long jump (LJ) and 60 m run (R) scores in students. The mean LJ was 4.00 m and S = 0.15 m and the mean for 60 m run was 9.2 sec., and S = 0.6 sec. If we are interested in applying the T method with 1 point precision, we shall use the 5S/50 transformation. First, we ask 'how many meters in LJ and how many seconds of 60 m RUN equal ONE POINT of T values?"

The solution is as follows:
5S/50 = (5 · 0.15)/50 = 0.75/50 = 0.015 m for LJ
5S/50 = (5 · 0.60)/50 = 3/50 = 0.06 sec for R.
In H values ONE POINT is equal
3.5S/50 = (3.5 · 0.15)/50 = 0.0105 for LJ
3.5S/50 = (3.5 · 0.60)/50 = 0.042 for R.

The NORM TABLE can now be constructed in a manner described in Table 2.8.

Table 2.8

Norm Construction Using T and H Standardized Values

Z	T	60 m (sec)	Long Jump (m)	H	60 m (sec)	Long Jump (m)
3.0	80	7.40	4.450	100	7.100	4.525
.	.	.	.	.	.	.
.	.	.	.	.	.	.
.	.	.	.	.	.	.
.	.	.	.	.	.	.
0.5	55	8.90	4.075	55	8.990	4.0525
0.4	54	8.96	4.060	54	9.032	4.0420
0.3	53	9.02	4.045	53	9.074	4.0315
0.2	52	9.08	4.030	52	9.116	4.0210
0.1	51	9.14	4.015	51	9.158	4.0105
0.0	**50**	**9.20**	**4.000**	**50**	**9.200**	**4.0000**
-0.1	49	9.26	3.985	49	9.242	3.9895
-0.2	48	9.32	3.970	48	9.284	3.9790
-0.3	47	9.38	3.955	47	9.326	3.9685
-0.4	46	9.44	3.940	46	9.368	3.9580
-0.5	45	9.50	3.925	45	9.410	3.9475
.	.	.	.	.	.	.
.	.	.	.	.	.	.
.	.	.	.	.	.	.
-3.0	20	11.00	3.550	0	11.300	3.475

First, the Z-score column is established from –3.0 to +3.0 and similarly the T column from 0-80 and H from 0-100. The means 0, 50 and 50 are placed respectively with the means of the LJ (4.00 m) and R (9.20 sec.). Now, add to the T values column in LJ 0.015 m for each one T point (upwards) and subtract 0.015 m (downwards). Continue doing so until T = 20 points which is equivalent to 4.0 - (3.0 · 0.015) = 3.550 m, and T = 80 where 4.0 + (30 · 0.015) = 4.450 m. Perform the same operations with the RUN (R) variable, being careful and REVERSE the ascending and descending values (Running fast means lower values and vice versa).

T and H values can be transformed back to Z-scores and be compared by using the NORMAL CURVE areas and probability values. They can be simply transformed into percentages.

5.5 Stanines

Stanines are standardized values, which consist of dividing the normal distribution into nine parts between 2.25S to –2.25S. Thus each part equals 0.5S. The 5th stanine includes the mean of all the observations. From the mean (0), 0.25S are added and subtracted to constitute the upper and lower limits of the 5th stanine. From here on 0.5S are added to the upper limit of the 5th stanine and subtracted from the lower limit of this stanine until the upper and lower limits of the 9th and 1st stanine are determined. In Figure 2.11 the stanine construction is presented.

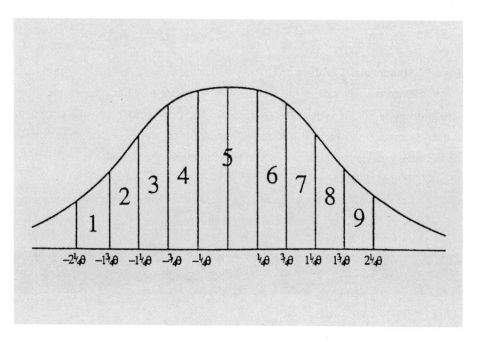

Figure 2.11   The Stainine Standardized Method.

The number and percentage of observations in each stanine decreases as we move to the left and right tails of the distribution. The percent and number of cases can be derived from the normal distribution table. The percent of observation for each of the nine stanines is presented in Table 2.9.

Table 2.9

Stanine Distribution and % of Observations in each Stanine.

Stanine	Lower limit	Upper limit	% Observations
1	$\bar{x} - 2.25S$	$\bar{x} - 1.75S$	4
2	$\bar{x} - 1.75S$	$\bar{x} - 1.25S$	7
3	$\bar{x} - 1.25S$	$\bar{x} - 0.75S$	12
4	$\bar{x} - 0.75S$	$\bar{x} - 0.25S$	17
5	$\bar{x} - 0.25S$	$\bar{x} + 0.25S$	20
6	$\bar{x} + 0.25S$	$\bar{x} + 0.75S$	17
7	$\bar{x} + 0.75S$	$\bar{x} + 1.25S$	12
8	$\bar{x} + 1.25S$	$\bar{x} + 1.75S$	7
9	$\bar{x} + 1.75S$	$\bar{x} + 2.25S$	4

5.6 Standardized Profiles

Once the raw data of the various variables were transformed into one of the standardized scores, it is possible to compare the performance of each person on different variables and PROFILE it. It is also possible to compare different individuals on the same variable or a number of variables simultaneously. Now all the VARIABLES SHARE EQUAL UNITS.

Let's assume that we measured 10 grade class students in high jump, long jump, and sit-ups, and the mean ($\bar{x}$) and standard deviation (S) were:

	High jump (m)	Long jump (m)	Sit-ups (number)
$\bar{x}$	1.22	4.12	38
S	0.51	0.45	14

Two students in the class achieved the following results:

Student	High jump	Long jump	Sit-ups
A	1.52 m	4.80 m	25
B	1.14 m	3.64 m	46

The Z-value of each of the scores is $Z_i = (x_i - \bar{x})/S$ and we can now calculate the Z-scores for each of the students as follows:

Student	High jump	Long jump	Sit-ups
A	(1.52 - 1.22)/0.51 = 0.59	(4.80 - 4.12)/0.45 = 1.51	(25 - 38)/14 = -0.93
B	(1.14 - 1.22)/0.51 = -0.16	(3.64 - 4.12)/0.45 = -1.07	(46 - 38)/14 = 0.54

These values mean that student A high jumped 0.59 standard deviation above the mean of his/her classmates, 1.51S above the mean in long jump, but 0.93S below the mean in sit-ups. In contrast, student B was 0.16S and 1.07S below his/her classmate's mean in high and long jumps, respectively, but 0.54S above the mean in sit-ups. The differences between the two and their profiles can be displayed in a graph:

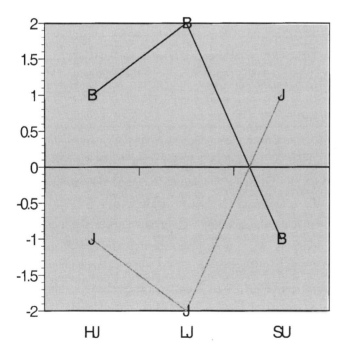

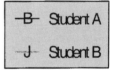

The same graph could be established if T or H scores were preferable to Z scores.

All the standardized values and their distributions are presented in Figure 2.12.

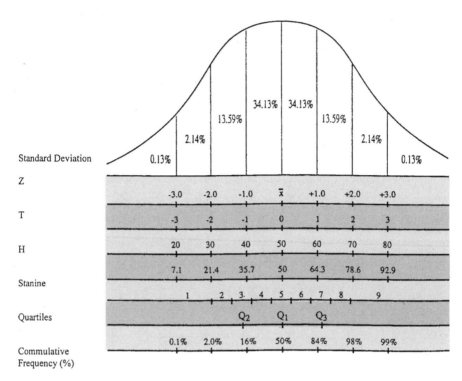

Figure 2.12 Standardized Values and their Distributions in the Normal Curve

Summary

A large data set usually does not make too much sense when all cases data are observed. The techniques which were introduced aimed at the REDUCTION and the process of MAKING SENSE of the large amount of INFORMATION inherent in the data. Specifically, the central and dispersion measures are used for this purpose. These measures REDUCE the amount of information and make it easier to make conclusions and decisions. When these measures are introduced visually, they make much more sense. When required, the use of PROFILES is recommended for making comparison WITHIN GROUPS (i.e., different individuals within the same group) and BETWEEN GROUPS. What the eyes SEE cannot be replaced by any other statistics.

Reference

Argyrous, G. (1996). *Statistics for Social Research.* Melbourne: Mcmillan.

In this chapter the essence of the concept termed ASSOCIATION is introduced. Theories help us to understand the world. They consist of abstract constructs that are related to each other. The RELATIONS among the constructs constitute the concept and the model, which the research aims to EXPLORE or CONFIRM.

The chapter begins with the illustration of how the term association/relation is perceived and implemented. Later, we introduce how different methods were developed to satisfy and meet these basic requirements in different levels of measurement, namely nominal, ordinal, and ratio/interval.

The implications of estimating relations among two or more variables are greater in scope than merely the estimation itself. The methods which are termed "correlational" allow us to PREDICT (i.e., account for) events which rely on other events, to SELECT groups of observations which share similarities in a given trait, to GROUP/CLUSTER observations which share some common traits, and distinguish them from other groups/clusters on these traits. They also allow us to EXPLORE new structures/factors/dimensions/clusters, which are unknown, but are not clear to us at a particular point, and to CONFIRM a concept which we already know.

The general concept of this chapter is illustrated graphically below, followed by the specific contents which operationalize it.

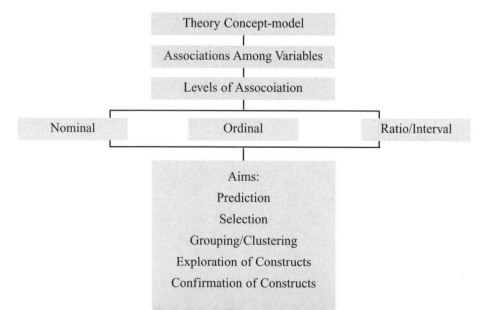

Contents

(1) The Essence of Association Among Variables

The association between two or more variables is the essence of a theory. The researcher attempts to QUANTIFY (i.e., determine the STRENGTH of) the association. "Association exists if the distribution of one variable is related to the distribution of another variable. Measures of association indicate, in quantitative terms, the extent to which a change in the value of one variable is related to a change in the value of another variable" (Argyrous, 1996). For example, associations exist if people who VARY IN MAXIMAL OXYGEN CONSUMPTION VARY SIMILARLY or REVERSELY in LONG RUN, and if so, HOW STRONG is this SIMILARITY? To estimate the STRENGTH and DIRECTION of the ASSOCIATION, statistical procedures are applied. However, before introducing the mathematical procedures, we introduce the logic of the term ASSOCIATION, and the different conceptual frameworks associated with it.

Assume that A and B are two variables.

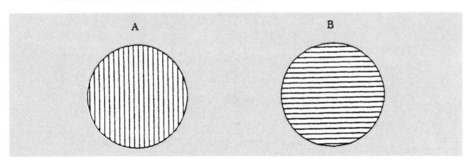

We can conclude from observing the distance between A and B that they are not related. They do not overlap and each remains a separate entity and does not share anything with the other. In the next example, A and B are closer to each other. Some of their areas overlap (A′B′), but still much of the area remains unique, B - A′B′ and A - A′B′.

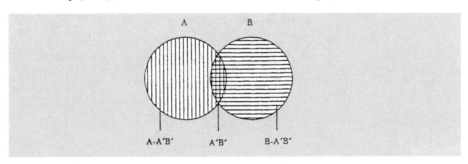

Notice that the COMMON AREA A'B' is relatively small compared to the areas which do not overlap. In the third example, the overlap area A'B' increased substantially

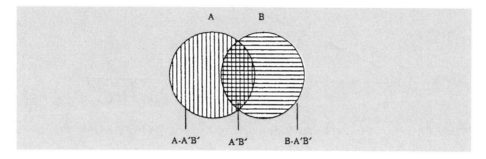

and in the fourth example A'B' is greater than the unique area of entities A and B separately.

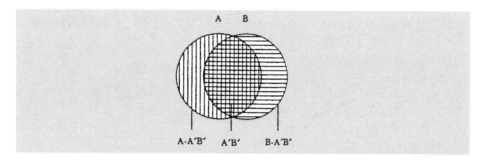

We may say that the more entities A and B have in COMMON, the stronger the ASSOCIATION between them, and the less they have in common, the weaker the association between them. Thus ASSOCIATION can be perceived as the RATIO between the COMMON of A and B and the UNIQUENESS of A and B, or

$$r_{AB} = f [A'B' | (A - A'B'), (B - A'B')]$$

where r_{AB} is the association between entities A and B, A'B' is the overlap (i.e., commonality) between the two, and A-A'B' and B-A'B' are the uniqueness of A and B respectively. In statistics, the overlap is termed COVARIANCE and the uniqueness is termed VARIANCE.

The association or relationship between variables X and Y can be demonstrated by an X-Y plot. Five observations of X and Y are presented in Figure 3.1

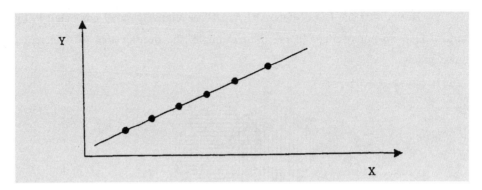

Figure 3.1   A Perfect Positive Linear Relation Between Variables X and Y.

In figure 3.1 a POSITIVE LINEAR RELATION exists between variables X and Y. Every increase in variable X results in an increase in variable Y and vice-versa. We also may say in this example that the relations between X and Y are PERFECT. Similarly a PERFECT NEGATIVE LINEAR RELATION between X and Y is presented in Figure 3.2

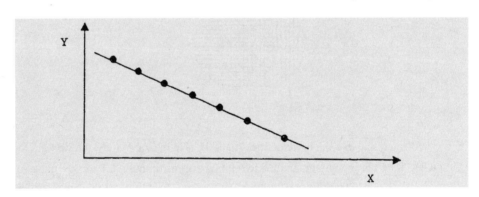

Figure 3.2   A Perfect Negative Relation Between Variables X and Y.

In this example every increase in variable X results in a decrease in variable Y and vice-versa. When we connect the X-Y observations in Figures 3.1 and 3.2, we get a LINEAR LINE. When all the X-Y observations are located on a linear line, the relationship between variables X and Y is PERFECT (i.e., very very strong). In most of the experiments, the relationships among the various variables are NOT PERFECT, i.e., the X-Y observations are not located perfectly on the linear line. In Figure 3.3, the linear line is of a positive trend, as the X-Y observations are located around it. The TREND of the RELATION seems to be positive but not perfect.

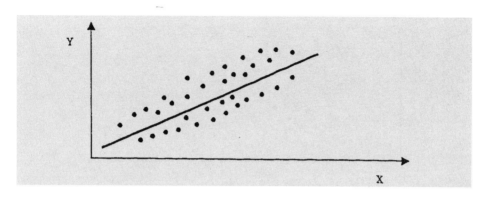

Figure 3.3   A Positive Relationship Between X and Y.

Similarly a non-perfect but NEGATIVE relationship between X and Y is presented in Figure 3.4

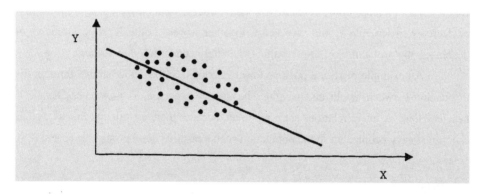

Figure 3.4   A Negative Relationship Between X and Y.

The X-Y plots in the figures above show that the observations X_iY_i within the X-Y space create a condensed elliptic shape toward the linear line. The closer this elliptic shape is toward the line, the stronger the relations are between X and Y.

Once all the observations are located on the linear line, the X-Y relations are perfect (positive or negative). As the elliptic shape which represents the X_iY_i values "opens" and turn into a circle, the X-Y relations weaken and in the case presented in Figure 3.5 we can see that NO RELATION exist between variables X and Y.

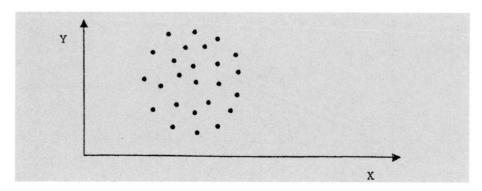

Figure 3.5   Lack of Linear Relationship Between Variables X and Y.

If we wish to describe the relationship between variables X and Y in Figure 3.5, we may conclude that infinite number of lines could be drawn to represent the $X_i Y_i$ observations spread. The "no relations" between variables X and Y can be phrased as follows: each increase in the value of variable X does not necessarily follow an increase or decrease in variable Y, and vice-versa. In other words, as the X value increases or decreases, the probability of any Y value occurring is equal to other values.

An example of strong positive linear relations can be demonstrated through the association between height and weight. The taller the person, in most cases he/she is heavier. However, these relations are not perfect, because there are tall and thin as well as short and heavy people, but in the population such a positive trend exists (see Figure 3.6).

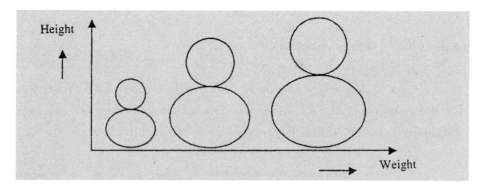

Figure 3.6   Positive Relations Between Height and Weight.

In contrast, a strong negative relation exists between age and hair quantity in males (see Figure 3.7).

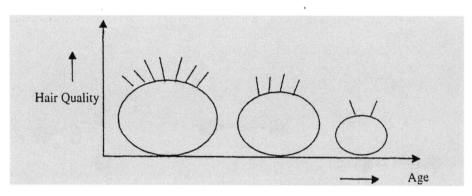

Figure 3.7   Negative Relations Between Age and Hair Quantity.

To summarize, we can conclude that RELATIONS between VARIABLES have a DIRECTION and a MAGNITUDE. The DIRECTION indicates whether the relations are POSITIVE, NEGATIVE, or tend toward NO-RELATION. The MAGNITUDE indicates whether the relations are STRONG, MODERATE, or WEAK. The closer the X_iY_i observations are to a linear line that gradually increases or decreases, the stronger the relations become, and the weaker the relations become as the X_iY_i observations are more spread.

Associations among variables can be of several types. MUTUAL RELATIONS (SYMETRICAL) mean that the VARIABLES SHARE VARIANCES. They affect each other.

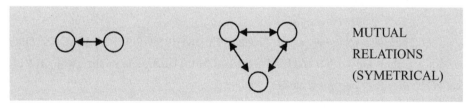

MUTUAL
RELATIONS
(SYMETRICAL)

Relations can be UNIDIRECTIONAL (ASSYMETRIC) where the VARIANCE of a variable or a set of variables ACCOUNT for the VARIANCE of another variable or a set of variables (i.e., can predict the other variable).

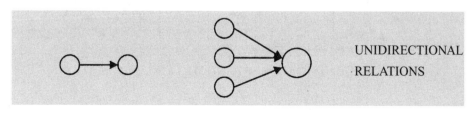

UNIDIRECTIONAL
RELATIONS

There are relations in which MODERATORS affect the relations among other variables.

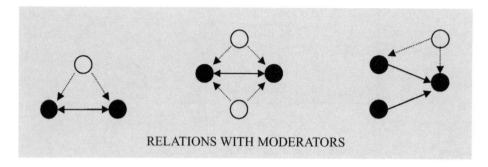

RELATIONS WITH MODERATORS

A relation can also occur through a MEDIATOR, i.e., one variable has a unidirectional relation with another variable via a mediator variable.

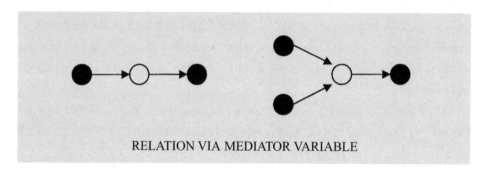

RELATION VIA MEDIATOR VARIABLE

There are relations, which produce CLUSTERS/GROUPS/FACTORS. Once several variables are ASSOCIATED WITH EACH OTHER more so than with OTHER variables, they may become a cluster.

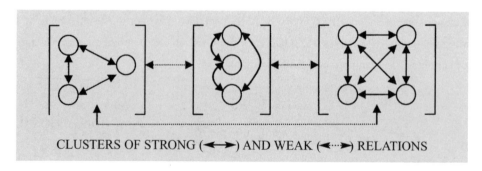

CLUSTERS OF STRONG (◄━►) AND WEAK (◄┄►) RELATIONS

(2) Choosing the Association Method

There are many measures of association, depending on the LEVEL of MEASUREMENT (nominal, ordinal, interval/ratio) of the variables in the model. There are methods for each level; however, the most appropriate one is determined by the LOWEST LEVEL of the two or more variables which are to be associated. Thus if an association between sport-type (nominal) and aggressiveness (interval) is desired, the measure of association will be determined by the nominal association method.

(3) Magnitude of an Association Between Variables

The simplest method of an association can be demonstrated by the following example. Assume that we ask 100 athletes from two countries whether they prefer "home" games or "away" games, and their responses are as follows:

Country	Game location	
	A	B
A (n = 50)	100%	0%
B (n = 50)	0%	100%

We can say that there is a PERFECT association between the location of the country and the preferences of game location. However, if the responses were distributed as follows:

Country	Game location	
	A	B
A (n = 50)	50%	50%
B (n = 50)	50%	50%

we cannot know anything more than the athletes from both countries A and B prefer equally "home" and "away" games. Thus, the country cannot determine the preferred game location. We say in this case that the two variables are not associated each with the other. However, if the responses were as follows:

Country	Game location	
	A	B
A (n = 50)	80%	20%
B (n = 50)	20%	80%

We see now that the association is not perfect but is STRONG. Athletes of country A prefer "away" games by majority of 80%, while the athletes of country B prefer "home" games by majority of 80%. The athletes of the two countries tend *strongly* to have *different* preferences about "home" and "away" games.

Measures of association range from –1 to +1 or 0 to 1. When both VARIABLES are measured on an interval, ordinal, or ratio scale, the MAGNITUDE of the ASSOCIATION ranges between (-1) - 0 - (+1). When at least one variable is measured by a nominal scale the range is 0 - 1. The SEMANTIC DESCRIPTORS and the DIRECTION of the ASSOCIATION are seen in Figure 3.8.

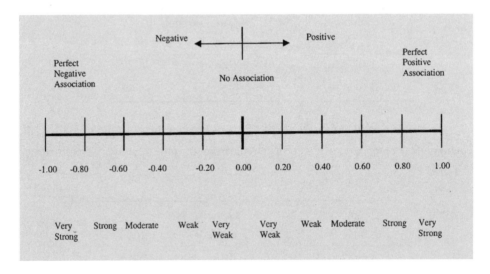

Figure 3.8   Direction and Semantic Descriptors of Association Between Variables Measured on Ordinal, Interval, or Ratio Scales. When at Least One Variable is Measured by a Nominal Scale the Range is from 0-1.

The association becomes weaker toward the center line (zero), and stronger toward the two extremes until becoming perfect. The MAGNITUDE of the association is the MAIN INTEREST. Its significance depends on the number of observations which were used to estimate the ASSOCIATION COEFFICIENT. A very large sample of observations usually results in significance of every association regardless of its magnitude. A strong association may result in a non-significant correlation when the number of observations is small. In such a case it is worth examining the association in a larger sample of the population.

(4) Associations Between Variables with Nominal-Level Values

Nominal level scales do not allow us to calculate mean, standard deviation, and other statistics that are available in ordinal, interval, or ratio level scales. However there are statistics and parameters which can be estimated to represent the association between the two nominal variables. The first step is to establish a TABLE, which COMBINES THE TWO VARIABLES' DISTRIBUTIONS. This procedure is termed CROSS TABULATION (i.e., CROSSTAB) or a BIVARIATE TABLE. For example, a hypothetical study was carried out to measure the association between the level of exercise participation (professional, amateur, and recreational) and attitudes toward the use of banned drugs in sport (for, against, no opinion). Their responses are presented in Table 3.1.

Table 3.1

Hypothetical Attitudes Toward the use of Banned Drugs in Sport by Different Level Participants in Sport (Numbers Represent Frequencies)

Sport-type	Use of Drugs in Sport			Total
	For	Against	No opinion	
Recreational	50	70	20	140
Amateurs	80	40	50	170
Professionals	100	10	20	130
Total	230	120	90	440

The COUNTS (i.e., frequencies) within the cells can be interpreted in various ways. Considering the TOTAL COUNTS of the ROWS as a CRITERION, we can conclude that 35.71% [(50/140) x 100] of the recreational, 47.06% of amateur, and 76.92%

of professional athletes support the use of banned drugs in sport, respectively. Negative attitudes by recreational, amateur, and professional athletes in percent are: 50%, 23.53%, and 7.69% respectively. Neutral opinion is shared by 14.29%, 29.41%, and 15.38%, respectively. We are interested in examining whether these DIFFERENCES are SUBSTANTIAL and MEANINGFUL, as well as whether they are SIGNIFICANT. If indeed the DIFFERENCES are MEANINGFUL, we can conclude that there is an ASSOCIATION between the level of participation in sport and the attitudes toward the use of banned drugs to enhance performance. It can be therefore exerted that

DIFFERENCE = ASSOCIATION/RELATION

once the results indicate it.

The RELATIVE COUNTS in Table13.4.1 can also be presented in relation to the COLUMN TOTALS. Of the 230 athletes who expressed positive attitudes toward the use of drugs, 21.74% [(50/230)100] were recreational athletes, 34.78% [(80/230)100] were amateurs, and 43.48% [(100/230)100] were professionals. Similarly, attitudes against the use of drugs were distributed: 58.73%, 30%, and 8.33% respectively, and neutral attitude were distributed: 22.22%, 55.55%, and 15.38% respectively.

It can be seen that the TOTALS of both the ROWS and the COLUMNS are important, and we shall refer to them shortly. In CROSS TABULATION the NUMBER of CELLS is determined by the NUMBER of CATEGORIES/LEVELS of each of the TWO VARIABLES. In the above example there were three levels of exercise participation and three levels of attitudes toward the use of banned drugs. Thus the number of cells is 3 x 3 = 9. We can conclude that the number of cells in a cross tabulation is:

NUMBER OF CELLS = No. of V1 levels x No. of V2 levels
and the TOTALS are termed MARGINALS.

The use of the computer eases the calculations. We have used the SPSS-PC version 8.0 to calculate the percent of athletes who show positive, negative, and neutral attitudes toward the use of banned drugs in each of the sport types separately (i.e., row percent). These are presented in Table 3.2.

Table 3.2

Distribution of Attitudes Toward Banned Drugs by Participation Level (ROW%)

		drug attitude			Total
		for	against	neutral	
sport	recreational	35.7%	50.0%	14.3%	100.0%
level	amature	47.1%	23.5%	29.4%	100.0%
	professional	76.9%	7.7%	15.4%	100.0%
Total		52.3%	27.3%	20.5%	100.0%

Similarly the distribution in percent of athletes of different sports with respect to the attitudes (i.e., column percent) is shown in Table 3.3.

Table 3.3

Distribution of Participants of Different Sport Levels by Drug Attitude Levels (COLUMN%)

		drug attitude			Total
		for	against	neutral	
sport	recreational	21.7%	58.3%	22.2%	31.8%
level	amature	34.8%	33.3%	55.6%	38.6%
professional		43.5%	8.3%	22.2%	29.5%
Total		100.0%	100.0%	100.0%	100.0%

These two tables can be combined into one table (see Table 3.4).

Table 3.4

Introduction of Cell Proportions by Drug Attitude and Participation Level (Row and Column %)

			drug attitude			Total
			for	against	neutral	
sport	recreational	% within sport level	35.7%	50.0%	14.3%	100.0%
	Level	% within drug attitude	21.7%	58.3%	22.2%	31.8%
	amateur	% within sport level	47.1%	23.5%	29.4%	100.0%
		% within drug attitude	34.8%	33.3%	55.6%	38.6%
	professional	% within sport level	76.9%	7.7%	15.4%	100.0%
		%within drug attitude	43.5%	8.3%	22.2%	29.5%
Total		% within sport level	52.3%	27.3%	20.5%	100.0%
		%within drug attitude	100.0%	100.09%	100.0%	100.0%

A graphical presentation is an easier way to capture the information before applying inferential statistics to the data. From the three figures below we can immediately recognize that in our sample there are more amateur athletes than recreational and professional athletes. We also can see that the majority of the athletes in the sample exhibit positive attitudes toward the use of banned drugs, and when considering the attitudes within each sport-type, the positive attitudes toward the use of drugs is attributed to the attitudes of the professional athletes. Amateur and recreational athletes do not share the same attitudes. It seems that these DIFFERENCES point out toward the conclusion that there is an ASSOCIATION between the two variables, sport-level and drug attitudes. To examine this view, a statistical test, which is appropriate to two nominal-level variables, is required.

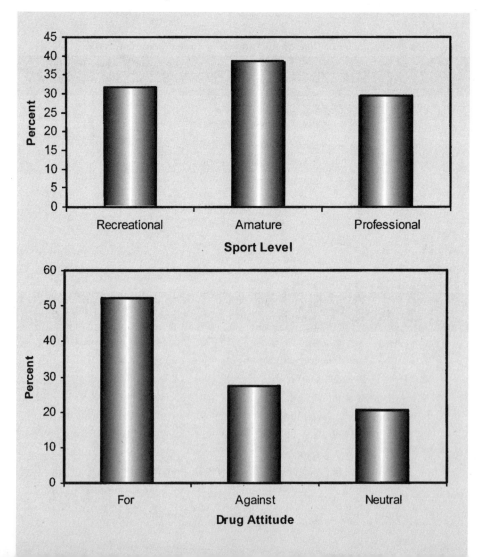

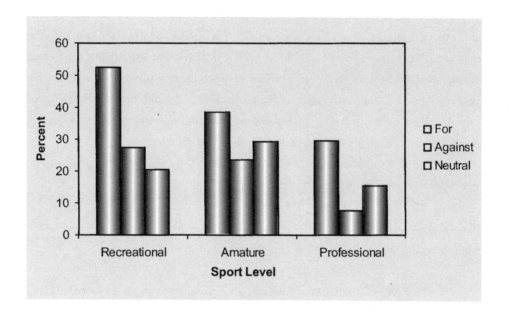

4.1 Chi-Square (χ^2) Test for Independence

When two variables are said to be STATISTICALLY INDEPENDENT it means that the COUNTS (i.e., frequencies) of ONE VARIABLE'S levels are NOT RELATED to the COUNTS of the other variable's levels. In our example, a test of independence between two variables examines whether the attitudes that athletes hold toward banned drug use are dependent (related) or independent of their enjoyment in different sport-types. In this example, it can be argued that the test of independence examines whether the TYPE of SPORT athletes are engaged in determines their attitude toward the use of forbidden drugs in sport (one-way dependence).

The hypotheses, which we desire to examine, are:

H_0: Attitudes toward forbidden drug use is independent of the athlete's sport-type.

H_1: Attitudes toward forbidden drug use is dependent on the athlete's sport-type.

To examine which of the two HYPOTHESES we verify and which we REJECT, a CHI SQUARE (χ^2) TEST is carried out.

The principle of the χ^2 test is that under the FULL HYPOTHESIS of INDE-PENDENCE the RELATIVE COUNTS (i.e., frequencies) within each of the CELLS should be EQUAL. Thus there are EXPECTED COUNTS within each cell and there are

OBSERVED COUNTS within each cell. Once the DIFFERENCE between the observed and expected increase, the CHANCES of DEPENDENCE between the two variables increase (thus verifying the H_1). The MORE SIMILAR the expected and observed counts, the CHANCE of INDEPENDENCE between the two variables decreases (thus verifying the H_0). The distribution is the probability χ^2 distribution of the chi square statistic of an infinite number of random samples of the same size drawn from a population in which the variables are independent of each other.

The χ^2 equation is

$$x^2 = \sum \frac{(f_o - f_e)^2}{f_e} \tag{1}$$

where f_o is the observed cell count, f_e is the expected cell count.

The EXPECTED CELL COUNTS are calculated from the MARGINALS of the ROWS and COLUMNS. The DIFFERENCE, f_o - f_e, is squared and therefore χ^2 is always positive. The greater the χ^2, the greater the difference between the observed and expected counts. Indeed if two variables are completely independent in the population, then f_o - f_e = 0 and χ^2 = 0.

However, the greater the difference

$(f_o - f_e) > 0$ then $\chi^2 > 0$

the greater the probability of dependence/relations between the two variables.

The χ^2 is determined by the counts and not by the percentages associated with the counts. Furthermore, it is assumed that the SAMPLES were RANDOMLY SELECTED and are INDEPENDENT each of the other. The χ^2 curve varies with different degrees of freedom (df) and is probabilistic in nature. Several examples, each with different df, are presented in Figure 3.9.

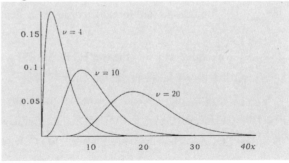

Figure 3.9

Distributions with Different df(V).

χ^2 distributions vary from 0 to ∞ and have right skewness which modifies with increases in df(V). The χ^2 distribution can be perceived as a distribution of the sum of independent squared standardized values, which are normally distributed. A χ^2 distribution is additive, i.e., two independent χ^2 distributions with V_1 and V_2 degrees of freedom will be distributed with $V_1 + V_2$ degrees of freedom.

Now we shall use the example presented in Table 3.1 to illustrate the concept of the χ^2 test. As mentioned earlier, under the NULL HYPOTHESIS all the CELL COUNTS should be EQUAL. Thus the EXPECTED COUNTS should be EQUAL RELATIVE to the ROW AND COLUMN MARGINALS (TOTALS). Each CELL consists of an INTERACTION between a COLUMN and a ROW. See the following example using a 2 x 2 table in Table 3.5.

Table 3.5

Counts (Frequencies) in a 2 x 2 Table

a	b	a + b
c	d	c + d
a + c	b + d	N = a + b + c + d

where a, b, c, d are counts. The EXPECTED COUNTS (f_e) for each cell so that RELATIVELY ALL CELL COUNTS are EQUAL is:

a: $(a + b)(a + c)/N$
b: $(a + b)(b + d)/N$
c: $(c + d)(a + c)/N$
d: $(c + d)(b + d)/N$

In other words, f_e is determined by multiplying the MARGINAL of the COLUMNS by the MARGINAL of the ROW and dividing this sum by the TOTAL NUMBER of OBSERVATIONS (N). The sum of the EXPECTED and OBSERVED COUNTS should be EQUAL. With respect to Tables 3.1 and 3.5, the EXPECTED COUNTS are calculated and presented in Table 3.6.

Table 3.6

Calculating the Expected Counts (Frequencies) under the Null Hypothesis

Participants	Use of Drugs in Sport			
	For	Against	No opinion	Total
Recreational	(140·230)/440	(140·120)/440	(140·90)/440	140
Amateurs	(170·230)/440	(170·120)/440	(170·90)/440	170
Professional	(130·230)/440	(130·120)/440	(130·90)/440	130
Total	230	20	90	440

The computer does it faster. In Table 3.7 the observed (f_o) at expected (f_e) counts in each cell are presented.

Table 3.7

Observed and Expected Counts for the Sport-type and Attitudes Toward Drugs in Sport Variables

		Drug Attitude			
		For	Against	Neutral	Total
Sport	**Recreational** Count	50	70	20	140
Level	Expected Count	73.2	38.2	28.6	140.0
	Amature Count	80	40	50	170
	Expected Count	88.9	46.4	34.8	170.0
	Professional Count	100	10	20	130
	Expected Count	68.0	35.5	26.6	130.0
Total		230	120	90	440
		230.0	120.0	90.0	440.0

Notice that the marginals of f_o and f_e are equal for both the columns and the rows. Once f_e and f_o are known, we should follow the χ^2 equation and estimate the MAGNITUDE of the χ^2. This is presented in Table 3.8.

Table 3.8

χ^2 *Estimation.*

Cell	f_o	f_e	$f_o - f_e$	$(f_o - f_e)^2$	$(f_o - f_e)^2/f_e$
11	50	73.18	-23.18	537.31	7.34
12	70	78.18	31.82	1012.51	20.52
13	20	28.64	-8.64	74.65	2.61
21	80	88.86	-8.86	78.50	0.88
22	40	46.36	-6.36	40.45	0.87
23	50	34.77	15.23	231.95	6.67
31	100	67.95	32.05	1027.20	15.12
32	10	35.45	-25.45	647.70	18.27
33	20	26.59	-6.59	43.43	1.63
Total	440	440			79.91

Thus

$$\chi^2 = \sum \frac{(f_o - f_e)^2}{f_e} = 79.91$$

This equation can be shortened as follows

$$\chi^2 = \sum \frac{(f_o - f_e)^2}{f_e} = \sum \frac{f_o - 2f_o f_e + f_e^2}{f_e}$$

$$= \sum \frac{f_o^2}{f_e} - 2\sum f_o + \sum f_e$$

since $\sum f_o$ and $\sum f_e$ are both equal to N

$$\chi^2 = \sum \frac{f_o^2}{f_e} - N \qquad (2)$$

and this is much easier to calculate (see Table 3.9).

Table 3.9

χ^2 Estimation

Cell	f_0	f_e^2	f_0^2/f_e
11	50	2500	34.16
12	70	4900	128.34
13	20	400	13.97
21	80	6400	72.02
22	40	1600	34.51
23	50	2500	71.90
31	100	10000	147.17
32	10	100	2.02
33	20	400	15.04
			519.93

and $\chi^2 = 519.93 - 440 = 79.93$.

The very minor difference between the two χ^2 values is due to the "rounding" of numbers. The χ^2 calculated by the computer is as follows:

	Value	df	Asymp. Sig. (2-sided)
Pearson Chi-Square	79.909[a]	4	.000
Likelihood Ratio	80.664	4	.000
Linear-by-Linear Association	16.709	1	.000
N of Valid Cases	440		

Let's use r to designate rows and c to designate columns, then the number of cells will be r x c. To generalize:

$i = 1, 2, 3 \dots$ r for rows, and

$j = 1, 2, 3 \dots$ c for columns

and n_{ij} = number of observed counts in each cell ij

e_{ij} = number of expected count in each cell ij under the assumption of independence.

Thus, total number of counts in a row is

$$n_{i\bullet} = \sum_{j=1}^{c} n_{ij} \quad \text{for } i = 1, 2, 3 \dots r$$

and for column

$$n_{\bullet j} = \sum_{j=1}^{r} n_{ij} \quad \text{for } j = 1, 2, 3 \dots r$$

The χ^2 is then

$$X^2 = \sum_{i=1}^{r} \sum_{j=1}^{c} \frac{(n_{ij} - e_{ij})^2}{e_{ij}} \tag{3}$$

but

$$e_{ij} = N \bullet \frac{n_i}{N} \bullet \frac{n_{\bullet j}}{N} = \frac{N_i - N_{\bullet j}}{N}$$

and the χ^2 equation will be

$$X^2 = N \left[\sum_{i=1}^{r} \sum_{j=1}^{c} \frac{n_{ij}^2}{n_{i\bullet} \bullet n_{\bullet j}} - 1 \right] \tag{4}$$

and this allows us to estimate χ^2 without the need to calculate the expected cell values. Most of the statistical computer programs allow us to observe the RAW, STANDARD-IZED, and ADJUSTED RESIDUALS. Once the χ^2 is significant, we know that there are discrepancies between observed and expected counts. The RAW RESIDUAL, d, is

$$d = f_o - f_e.$$

For each cell the differences between the counts are calculated and one should observe the SIGNS of the RESIDUAL (positive, negative, or zero) so that one can make a LOGICAL INTERPRETATION of the FINDINGS. The next question related to the MAGNITUDE of the RESIDUAL: How large does it need to be in order to be considered important? To elaborate on this question, the residuals should be transformed because raw residuals are affected by the total counts and cannot be compared across tables. The two types of transformations are termed STANDARDIZED and ADJUSTED RESIDUALS.

A standardized residual S is defined as

$$S = (f_o - f_e)/ \sqrt{f_e} \hspace{4cm} (5)$$

for the C_{11} (recreational athletes supporting use of banned drugs) cell in table 15.1, where $f_o = 50$ and $f_e = 73.2$

$$S_{11} = (50 - 73.2)/ \sqrt{73.2} = -23.2/8.55 = -2.71.$$

These standardized values are termed COMPONENTS of PEARSON CHI SQUARE because the sum of the squared standardized residuals equals χ^2. The ADJUSTED RESIDUALS are more complex and are not introduced here. The SPSS 11.0 output for the counts in Table 3.1 is presented here:

Sport Level * Drug Attitude Crosstabulation

		Drug Attitude			
		For	Against	Neutral	Total
Sport	**Recreational** Count	50	70	20	140
Level	Residual	-23.2	31.8	-8.6	
	Std. Residual	-2.7	5.1	-1.6	
	Adjusted Residual	-4.8	7.3	-2.2	
	Amature Count	80	40	50	70
	Residual	-8.9	-6.4	15.2	
	Std. Residual	-.9	-.9	2.6	
	Adjusted Residual	-1.7	-1.4	3.7	
	Professional Count	100	10	20	130
	Residual	32.0	-25.5	-6.6	
	Std. Residual	3.9	-4.3	-1.3	
	Adjusted Residual	6.7	-6.0	-1.7	
Total Count		230	120	90	440

Notice that the bigger the raw residuals, the bigger the standardized and adjusted residuals. The - and + signs indicate the DIRECTION of the data. Thus the value −23.2 (50 - 73.2) indicates that recreational athletes are *less than expected* in endorsing the use of banned drugs in sport compared to the participants who were sampled.

4.2   Likelihood-Ratio Chi-Square

The LIKELIHOOD RATIO (LR) is another statistic for GOODNESS OF FIT and is termed LIKELIHOOD-RATIO CHI SQUARE, symbolized as G^2 or L^2. The G^2 values distribute approximately as the natural log, termed ln is used to represent the likelihood ratio. The LR(G^2) equation is:

$$G^2 = 2\sum obslog\frac{obs}{exp} \qquad\qquad (6)$$

but since log(a/b) = log a—log b

$$G^2 = 2\sum obs\ (\log\ obs\ -\ \log\ exp) \qquad\qquad (7)$$

summed across all cells. The G^2 statistics for our data are presented earlier along with the χ^2. Its interpretation is also similar to that of the χ^2.

Degrees of Freedom and Significance Level

The term SIGNIFICANCE is a key term in statistics but mainly in interpreting the data at hand. When findings are significant, then we believe that we can GENERALIZE them beyond the sample from which they have been obtained. This issue has been under great dispute during the last 20-40 years. We dedicate a special section to this dispute later in this book.

We already know that the larger the difference between the expected and observed counts in the crosstabs, the higher the probability that there is a meaningful relationship between the two variables. The larger these discrepancies, the greater the χ^2 or G^2 value. The significance of the χ^2 and G^2 statistics to infer SIGNIFICANCE depends on their MAGNITUDE and the DEGREES OF FREEDOM. The magnitude signifies the EFFECT or RELATIONSHIP and the DEGREES OF FREEDOM relate to the minimum number of observations needed to know all about the data. In a 2 x 2 table, if we know the marginal of each row and column, it is sufficient to know the count (frequency) of one cell of the four so that f_e can be calculated for all the cells. In a 2 x 2 table the degrees of freedom is 1. Thus, the degrees of freedom are:

$$df = (r - 1)(c - 1) \qquad (8)$$

Where r is the number of rows and c is the number of columns.

For 2 x 2: $df = (2—1)(2—1) = 1 \cdot 1 = 1$
For 3 x 3: $df = (3—1)(3—1) = 2 \cdot 2 = 4$
For 2 x 3: $df = (2—1)(3—1) = 1 \cdot 2 = 2$

Once the χ^2 or G^2 magnitudes are known, we use the df and the χ^2 distribution to decide about their SIGNIFICANCE LEVEL. The principle is to locate the CRITICAL χ^2 VALUE and to decide on the SIGNIFICANCE LEVEL at which we desire to examine our HYPOTHESIS. Usually there is a "sacred" agreement to use 95% confidence and 5% error, which is symbolized as $p \le .05$ or $\alpha \le .05$. This indicates that if H_1 is verified, in 5 out of 100 other studies the results may be different (i.e., a $5/100 = 1/20$ probability of falsification). More conservative researchers prefer $p < .01$, $p < .001$, and even $p < .0001$. The lower the PROBABILITY FOR ERROR, the sounder and more generalizable are the findings (so the researchers believe). In our example the df are:

$$df = (3—1)(3—1) = 2 \times 2 = 4$$

the critical values
for $p < .05$ is $\chi^2 = 9.48$
for $p < .01$ is $\chi^2 = 13.28$
for $p < .001$ is $\chi^2 = 18.46$.

The CALCULATED PEARSON χ^2 was 79.909, substantially greater than each of the $\chi^2{}_c$ and therefore we accept H_1 and reject H_0, i.e., we conclude that very strong and significant ($p < .001$) relations exist between sport-type and attitudes toward the use of banned drugs in sport. However, we have three groups of athletes. We may wish to know which type is different from the other. Additional χ^2 statistics can be performed for each pair separately as follows:

Sport Type		For	Against	No opinion
Recreational	F_o	50	70	20
	F_e	58.71	49.68	31.68
Amateur	F_o	80	40	50
	F_e	71.29	60.32	38.39
	$\chi^2 = 25.29$	df = 2	p < .001	
Recreational	F_o	50	70	20
	F_e	77.78	41.48	20.74
Professional	F_o	100	10	20
	F_e	72.22	38.52	19.26
	$\chi^2 = 61.38$	df = 2	p < .001	
Amateur	F_o	80	40	50
	F_e	102.00	28.33	39.67
Professional	F_o	100	10	20
	F_e	78.00	21.67	30.33
	$\chi^2 = 22.25$	df = 2	p < .001	

These results indicate that the null hypothesis is rejected in all the three paired comparisons. However the greatest differences can be seen by the χ^2 magnitudes. In our hypothetical example the second comparison, recreational vs. professional athletes, the $\chi^2 = 61.38$. Look at the observed and expected counts and interpret the findings.

In a 2 x 2 table, χ^2 statistic can be calculated from the cell counts and their row and column marginals as follows:

a	b	a + b
b	d	c + d
a + c	b + d	N = a + b + c + d

and

$$\chi^2 = \frac{N(ad - bc)^2}{(a+b)(c+d)(a+c)(b+d)} \qquad (9)$$

However, this type of calculation may result in extremely large numbers and logarithmic transformation is recommended to simplify it. The equation indicates that $\chi^2 = 0$ when the diagonal counts multiplications are equal, and a·b = b·c. The more similar the two, the higher the probability NOT to reject H_0.

The χ^2 statistic requires a large number of counts because only large numbers can satisfy the χ^2 distribution. The assumption of course is that the curve, which represents the χ^2 values is continuous. Once the number of counts is small, a correction is performed; half a unit is added and subtracted to each direction from the f_0. The correction equation is

$$x^2 = \frac{N(ad - bc - N/2)^2}{(a+b)(c+d)(a+c)(d+b)} \qquad (10)$$

for example,

7(a)	15(b)	22 (a + b)
(10.06)	(11.94)	
9(c)	4(d)	13 (c + d)
(5.94)	(7.06)	
16 (a + c)	19 (b + d)	35 (N)

$$x^2 \frac{n(ad - bc)^2}{(a+b)(c+d)(a+c)(d+b)} = \frac{35(7 \cdot 4 - 15 \cdot 9)^2}{22 \cdot 13 \cdot 16 \cdot 59} = \frac{400{,}715}{86{,}944} = 4.61$$

The expected counts, f_e for cells a, b, c, d were 10.06, 11.94, 5.94, and 7.06, respectively. The correction consists of subtracting 0.5 points from the observed count f_0 toward the direction of the expected count, f_e as follows:

9.5(a)	14.5(b)	22 (a + b)
(10.06)	(11.94)	
8.5(c)	4.5(d)	13 (c + d)
(5.94)	(7.06)	
16 (a + c)	19 (b + d)	

and

$$x^2 = \frac{d(\,|ad-bc|-N/2\,)^2}{(a+b)(c+d)(a+c)(d+b)} = \frac{35(\,7.5\cdot 4.5 - 14.5\cdot 8.5 - \frac{35}{2}\,)^2}{22\cdot 13\cdot 16\cdot 19}$$

$$= \frac{181{,}440}{86{,}944} = 2.09$$

with df = (c - 1)(r - 1) = (2 - 1)(2 - 1) = 1, a significance level of $p \le .05$, and the critical χ^2 value, $\chi^2_c = 3.84$. If the correction was not applied to the χ^2 equation, we would reject H_0 because $\chi^2_0 > \chi^2_c$ (4.61 > 3.84). However, after applying the correction $\chi^2_0 < \chi^2_c$ (2.09 < 3.84) and H_0 is not rejected, the relationship between the two variables cannot be pronounced and generalized. The correction equation is recommended in cases where the counts of at least one cell is smaller than 10. Once the sample of counts is very large almost every difference becomes significant. We recommend logically determining how large the residuals are to infer real differences/relations between the two variables.

4.3   Fisher Exact Test

Statisticians argue that data, which consists of a 2 x 2 table of counts, should be always treated by the Fisher Exact Test rather than the χ^2 procedure. Though it is some-what complicated, we shall introduce it here in detail. The Fisher test is an exact test because it does not consist of estimated probabilities. Assume that the 2 x 2 table is

a	b	a + b
c	d	c + d
a + c	b + d	N

and assuming that the null hypothesis, H_0, is true, i.e., as proportional differences among the counts exist, then the probability for that to occur in the population is

$$P_k = \frac{(a+b)!(c+d)!(a+c)!(b+d)!}{N!\,a!\,b!\,c!\,d!} \qquad (11)$$

This equation is derived from the hypergeometric distribution based on a constant unchangeable distribution. The assumption is that the data represent repeated samples taken from the population of N possible observations. Accordingly we relate to the samples as if they are the population itself within the cells. If a + c observations are in the first column and a + b in the first row, etc, then what is the probability that of a + b counts in the first row there will be a count in the first column and b in the second column? If we randomly sampled a + b counts and located them in the first column and the rest joined the second column, then we assume that the cells are "filled-up" randomly, and we ask how probable it is that the counts we have will stay that way.

From the hypergeometric distribution, the probability to exert precisely a and b counts in the first and second column is

$$p(a_1b_1) = \frac{\binom{a+c}{a}\binom{b+d}{b}}{\binom{N}{a+b}}$$

To further develop this equation

$$P_{(a,b)} = \frac{\dfrac{(a+c)!(b+d)!}{a!(a+c-a)!b!(b-d-b)!}}{\dfrac{N!}{(a+b)!(N-a-b)!}} = \frac{\dfrac{(a+c)!(b+d)!}{a!c!b!d!}}{\dfrac{N!}{(a+b)!(c+d)!}}$$

$$= \frac{(a+c)!(b+d)!(a+b)!(c+d)!}{N!\,a!\,b!\,c!\,d!}$$

This indicates that if a+b sample of counts were chosen and located in the first column, identical results would be obtained.

The probability equation in a 2 x 2 table consists of nine factors and the calculations are complex. Since we are interested in knowing all the possibilities to get different count combinations, and not only the one that was first obtained, we should add to the first probability additional probabilities toward the same direction. Let's assume that the observed counts, f_0, in a 2 x 2 table were as follows:

4	12	16
8	5	13
12	17	29

If we assume that the marginals of the rows and columns are constant, there are additional 4 combinations which are less probable than this one:

3	13	16	**(1)**
9	4	13	
12	17	29	

2	14	16	**(2)**
10	3	13	
12	17	29	

1	15	16	**(3)**
11	2	13	
12	17	29	

0	16	16	**(4)**
12	1	13	
12	17	29	

In the above example, we subtracted one count each time from cells a and c and added one count in cells b and d, until one of the cells has reached "0". Assuming that cell a contains always the lowest number of counts, we shall use the symbol P_0 to note the probability for "0" counts in cell a under the null hypothesis, P_1 is the probability on one count, P_2 of two counts, and so on. In this example, the sum of all the probabilities is

$$P_0 + P_1 + P_2 + P_3 + P_4$$

in order to calculate the probability of at least four counts in cell a. Because we apply a one-tailed test, the probability level should be multiplied by two if direction was not hypothesized.

Instead of estimating P_I by the original equation, it is preferable to calculate P_0 directly and the rest of the Ps as a simple function of P_0. Instead of using the symbols a, b, c, and d to represent the marginals of the row and the columns, we shall use the letter k to describe the smallest cell a. If k counts are present in cell a, the counts in the cells are a_k, b_k, c_k, and d_k. Since the marginals are constant, k remains the same if we subtract one count from a_k and d_k and add one count to b_k and c_k just like the numbers in the previous example. The P_0 equation can be simplified since $a_o = 0$, therefore $a_o! = 1$ by definition, $(a_o + c_o) = c_o!$, $(a_o + b_o)! = b_o!$, the number of factors decreases and

$$P_0 = \frac{(c_o + d_o)!(b_o + d_o)!}{N!d_o!}$$

The nominator decreased from four factors into two factors, which consist of all the counts in cells $(b_0 + d_0)$ and $(c_0 + d_0)$. The denominator consists not only of N! and d_0. d_0 can be calculated from the last table presented previously. In our example

$$d_0 = 1, N = 29, (b_0 + d_0) = 17, (c_0 + d_0) = 13$$

and P_0 can be easily calculated using the above equation.

To calculate P_1, P_2, P_3, and P_4 a general equation for P_{k+1} based on P_k should be developed. The cells were symbolized as a_k, b_k, c_k, and d_k, respectively. Because the rows and columns marginally remain constant,

$$P_k = \frac{(a+b)!(c+d)!(a+c)!(b+d)!}{N!a_k!b_k!c_k!d_k}$$

and

$$P_{k+1} = \frac{(a+b)!(c+d)!(a+c)!(b+d)!}{N!(a_k+1)!(b_k+1)!(c_k-1)!(d_k+1)}$$

The denominator in P_{k+1} is different than that of P_k since one count was added to cells a and d, and one count was subtracted from cells b and c. Dividing the terms P_{k+1} by P_k, the following will emerge:

$$\frac{P_{k+1}}{P_k} = \frac{a_k!b_k!c_k!d_k!}{(a_k+1)!(b_k-1)!(c_k-1)!(d_k+1)!}$$

but $a_k!/(a_k+1)! = 1(a_k+1)$ and subsequently, $d_k!/(d_k+1)!$, $b_k!/(b_k-1)!$, and $c_k!/(c_k-1)!$ so

$$\frac{P_{k+1}}{P_k} = \frac{b_k c_k}{(a_k+1)(d_k+1)}$$

or

$$P_{k+1} = P_k \frac{b_k c_k}{(a_k+1)(d_k+1)}$$

Now it is easier to calculate the factors as we can use this equation to estimate P_1 and P_0 and later P_2 and so on. We return to the example and calculate P_0, P_1, P_2, P_3, and P_4.

$$P_0 = \frac{13!\,17!}{29!\,1!} = 0.3 \cdot 10^{-6}$$

and therefore

$$P_1 = P_0 \frac{b_0 c_0}{(a_0+1)(d_0+1)} = (0.3 \cdot 10^{-6}) \frac{16 \cdot 12}{1 \cdot 2} = 28.8 \cdot 10^{-6}$$

To estimate P_2 we should use a_1, b_1, c_1, and d_1 and not the values used in estimating P_1.

$$P_2 = P_1 \frac{b_1 c_1}{(a_1+1)(d_1+1)} = (28.8 \cdot 10^{-6}) \frac{15 \cdot 11}{2 \cdot 3} = 792 \cdot 10^{-6}$$

$$P_3 = P_2 \frac{b_2 c_2}{(a_2+1)(d_2+1)} = (792 \cdot 10^{-6}) \frac{14 \cdot 10}{3 \cdot 4} = 9,240 \cdot 10^{-6}$$

$$P_4 = P_3 \frac{b_3 c_3}{(a_3+1)(d_3+1)} = (9,240 \cdot 10^{-6}) \frac{13 \cdot 9}{4 \cdot 5} = 54,054 \cdot 10^{-6}$$

All the terms in the nominator decrease by 1 when calculating P_{k+1} from P_k while the terms in the denominator decrease by 1. When summing up all the probabilities we get

$$P_0 + P_1 + P_2 + P_3 + P_4 = (0.3 + 28.8 + 7.92 + 9,240 + 54,054) \cdot 10^{-6}$$
$$= 64,115 \cdot 10^{-6} = 0.0641$$

Thus, the probability that four or less counts occur in cell a under the null hypothesis is 0.0641 and a decision should be made whether to accept or reject this hypothesis. The Fisher Exact Test is more conservative than the χ^2 test; usually their values are lower than that of the χ^2 and it is harder therefore to reject the H_0. The χ^2 with the correction for continuity is therefore easier to apply and when more than five counts per cell exist, the final probabilities are very similar to that of the Fisher Exact Test.

χ^2 test allows us to verify and reject the H_0 and H_1 hypotheses. If H_0 was rejected we are still unable to determine the MAGNITUDE of the ASSOCIATION between the two variables. The significance level is not a sufficient statistic for this purpose because the more observations made, the higher the probability is for significance, but the MAGNITUDE is still undetermined. If for example we sampled 60 counts as follows:

20	10	30
10	20	30
30	30	60

χ^2 will be 6.73. If the counts were doubled (N = 120)

40	20	60
20	40	60
60	60	120

χ^2 will become 13.37. If the two Σ counts in the two tables are converted into percentages, they will look identical, but the χ^2 in the second one is doubled. As a rule, if the number of counts increase by k, also χ^2 will increase by k times the χ^2

$$\chi^2 = \sum \frac{(kf_o - kf_e)^2}{kf_e} = \sum \frac{k(f_o - f_e)^2}{kf_e} = k \sum \frac{(f_o - f_e)^2}{f_e}$$

and the χ^2 statistics will be a multiplication of the previous χ^2 by k.

The χ^2 and Fisher Exact Tests are good measures for examining associations between variables when at least one of them is measured at the nominal level. The χ^2 is a statistic that indicates the extent to which the data depart from the null hypothesis assumption, i.e., proportional equality among all the cells. The greater this departure, the greater the χ^2, the stronger the relations between the variables, and the more confidence the researcher gains as to its generalizability in accepting the alternative hypothesis, i.e., that different levels of one variable result in different counts in the levels of the second variable. However, the χ^2 as previously mentioned, is influenced by the number of observations/counts and ranges from 0 to ∞. The following measures were developed to limit the association strength into more reasonable limits which are similar in concept to the correlation measure used for interval and ratio level variables.

4.4 Q^2 Value

As previously shown, the χ^2 statistic is proportional to the number of counts, N. Q^2 is the χ^2 divided by the number of counts.

$$Q^2 = \chi^2/N \qquad (12)$$

and it ranges between 0 (complete lack of association) and 1 (perfect association) in 2 x k tables. For example,

35	0	35
0	35	35
35	35	70

$\chi^2 = 70$, $N = 70$ and then

$Q^2 = 70/70 = 1.0$ which indicates a perfect association.

4.5 T^2 Value

In r x c type of tables, Q^2 may result in values which are greater than 1.0. In such cases the use of a statistic which takes χ^2/N into account but with 1.0 as its upper limit is recommended. The T value (Tschuprow's T) is defined as

$$\chi^2 = \sum \frac{(kf_o - kf_e)^2}{kf_e} = \sum \frac{k(f_o - f_e)^2}{kf_e} = k \sum \frac{(f_o - f_e)^2}{f_e} \qquad (13)$$

The T^2 value can be 1.0 only when the number of rows is equal to the number of columns. In other words, for example 2 x 3 or 5 x 2, the upper limit of T^2 is always smaller than 1.00. Dividing the T^2 value by the maximum T^2 is recommended, but the following statistics are preferable.

4.6 Cramer's V

Cramer's V consists of dividing the χ^2 value by the number of counts (N) multiplied by the number of levels that is the smaller among the two variables.

$$V^2 = \frac{x^2}{N \cdot min(r-1, c-1)} = \frac{Q^2}{min(r-1, c-1)} \qquad (14)$$

The simplest and more convenient equation is

$$V = \sqrt{\frac{x^2}{N(k-1)}} \tag{15}$$

where k is the number of row or columns which is smaller.

In the previous example the χ^2 value for the sport-type and attitudes toward banned drugs was 79.909 (p < .001), N = 440, and the total consisted of 3 x 3 (c x r). Thus

$$V = \sqrt{\frac{79.909}{440(3-1)}} = \sqrt{\frac{79.909}{880}} = 0.30$$

which indicates a weak-moderate association between the two variables.

4.7   Phi (ϕ) Value

The Phi measure of association is defined as

$$\phi = \sqrt{\frac{x^2}{N}} \tag{16}$$

ϕ may be greater than 1.00 for tables greater than 2 x 2. As can be observed, ϕ is a special case of Cramer's V.

4.8   Pearson's Contingency Coefficient (C)

The Pearson's Contingency Coefficient is defined as:

$$C = \sqrt{\frac{x^2}{x^2 + N}} \tag{17}$$

Its lowest limit is "0" when the two variables are completely unrelated. The upper limit of C depends on the number of rows and columns. In a 2 x 2 table the upper limit of C is $\sqrt{N/N} + N$ because χ^2 may get the maximum value of N. Then $\sqrt{N/2N} = \sqrt{1/2} = 0.707$ which is the maximal contingency value. With increase of N, the maximal C value increases, but will always remain smaller than 1.00. Since the C value is restricted in its upper limit, in a 2 x 2 Table, the C value is always divided by 0.707.

Using the SPSS 11.0 version, the Phi, Cramer's V, and Pearson's Contingency Coefficient (C) for the sport-type and attitude toward banned drugs use were:

Symmetric Measures

		Value	Approx. Sig.
Nominal by Nominal	Phi	.426	.000
	Cramer's V	.301	.000
	Contingency Coefficient	.392	.000
N of Valid Cases		440	

4.9   Yule's Q

So far, all the association statistics introduced relied on the χ^2. χ^2 is a somewhat problematic statistic because it weights cells with low counts relatively more than cells with many counts. The Yule's Q is applied only to 2 x 2 tables and is defined as

$$Q = \frac{ad - bc}{ad + bc} \qquad (18)$$

where a, b, c, and d are the counts in each of the cells. When the nominator is squared and multiplied by N, the Q gets the value of χ^2. Q is 0 when the variables are independent of each other, i.e., when the diagonal multiplications are equal. Q's values range between −1.0 to 1.0 when one of the cells equal "0". Examples:

15	0	35
(a)	(b)	
0	35	35
(c)	(d)	
35	35	70

$$Q = \frac{(35 \bullet 35) - (0 \bullet 0)}{(35 \bullet 35) + (0 \bullet 0)} = 1.00$$

in this case, the counts of b and c were "0". Let's assume that on b = 0 and c = 10, then

$$Q = \frac{(35 \cdot 35) - (0 \cdot 10)}{(35 \cdot 35) + (0 \cdot 10)} = \frac{1225}{1225} = 1.00$$

When the rows and columns marginals do not indicate an association as the previous one, the association magnitude decreases:

35	20	55
15	45	60
50	50	115

$$Q = \frac{(35 \cdot 45) - (20 \cdot 15)}{(35 \cdot 45) + (20 \cdot 15)} = \frac{1275}{1875} = 0.68$$

and a reversed association:

20	35	55
45	15	60
65	50	115

$$Q = \frac{(20 \cdot 15) - (35 \cdot 45)}{(20 \cdot 15) + (35 \cdot 45)} = \frac{-1275}{1875} = -0.68$$

The association between the two variables decreases compared to the perfect association where at least one cell has "0" counts. The + and – signs are interpreted in relation to their respective levels (categories).

4.10 Goodman and Kruskal's Tau (*t*)

Goodman and Kruskal's Tau (τ) shares a probabilistic nature. The association ranges between 0 and 1. A and B are two variables, A is independent and B is the dependent variable. Assume we interview 1000 athletes and their distribution was as follows:

	A1	A2	Total
B1	100	200	300
B2	200	100	300
B3	200	200	400
Total	500	500	1000

Because 300 counts were included in category B1 at variable B, in fact 700 of 1000 do not belong to this category (B1) and should expect to have 300 (700/1000) = 210 errors for the long run. With this logic in mind, 300 counts were observed in category B2 and therefore 700 of the 1000 counts do not belong to this category. Again we may expect 210 errors in classifying people to this category. In other words, only 300-210 = 90 counts are really valid counts. Respectively, the number of errors expected in category B3 is 400(600/1000) = 240. Thus overall we expect to make

$$210 + 210 + 240 = 660$$

errors in locating 1000 counts. Much above the 50% chance of flipping a coin!

Next we ask additional questions to get more information about the sampled data. For example, if variable A is known, and the distribution of counts into A1 and A2 is given, can we use this information to reduce the number of errors that we might make when we classify counts into the various B categories? If A and B are completely independent of each other, then knowing A will not help us to know about B, and the number of errors we make in A will be similar to the number that we make in B. In contrast, if A and B are perfectly associated, it will enable us to perfectly classify B by knowing A. The Goodman and Kruskal's Tau enables us to reduce the relative error when A is given.

Given a count in category A1, we ought to classify 100 of 500 counts in column A1 and B1, and the other 200 counts in B1 were assigned to A2. Because 400 of 500 counts in A1 do not belong to B1, we expect to make 100(400/500) = 80 errors in this classification. Respectively, of 200 counts in A1 located in B2, we may make 200(300/500) = 120 errors and 120 errors in B3.

Now we shall relate to the 200 counts in A2, which are assigned to B1. Of 500 counts in A2, 200 belong to B1 and the other 300 to B2 and B3. Similarly to the previous calculations, we expect

200(300/500) = 120 errors of classification in B1, 100(400/500) = 80 in B2, and 120 in B3. All the possible errors we may do when A is known are:

$$80 + 120 + 120 + 120 + 80 + 120 = 640.$$

The τ_B is known to be a measure of PROPORTIONAL REDUCTION OF ERRORS (PRE).

$$\tau_B = \frac{[\text{errors without information on A}] - [\text{errors with information about A}]}{\text{errors without information on A}} \qquad (19)$$

In the hypothetical example,

$$\tau_B = \frac{660 - 640}{660} = \frac{20}{660} = 0.03$$

In this case 30 errors were reduced from 600 possible errors. The error reduction rate was only 3%. The τ_B values, like 0.50 or 0.75 indicate a 50% and 75% error reduction. When A classification is desired from B classification, the statistic is termed τ_a. The values of τ_a and τ_B are not identical. In a 2 x 2 table, $\tau_a = \tau_B = Q^2$.

4.11   Lambda (λ)

The Lambda, λ, value is similar to that of τ in its symmetry in the relation between A and B. If B is the dependent (to be predicted) variable, the number of errors will be minimal when all the counts will be located in the largest categories of B. In the previous example, the 1000 counts should be located in category B3 instead of only 400 counts. If indeed this was the case, we would conduct 600 errors, the number of counts in categories B1 and B2. This error is smaller than that in the τ_B equation (660). Assume we know the category of A to which a count belongs. If we can categorize the 500 counts in A1 to B2, that contains many counts of A1, we shall conduct 500-300 = 200 errors. If all the 500 counts of A2 were classified to B1, we could have made 500-300 = 200 errors. Thus, when the A categories are known and we can classify the counts, we assume that we could conduct 200 + 200 = 400 errors. λ_B as a statistic of PROPORTIONAL REDUCTION OF ERRORS (PRE) is

$$\lambda = \frac{E_1 - E_2}{E_1} \tag{20}$$

where E_1 is the number of errors without information on the independent variable and E_2 is the number of errors with the information on the independent variable. In our example

$$\lambda = \frac{600 - 400}{600} = \frac{200}{600} = 0.333$$

If $E_2 = 0$, then $\lambda_B = E_1/E_1 = 1.0$, and this is an indication of perfect association between A and B. λ is easier to calculate than τ because the reduction in errors is unlimited and therefore its value is also larger. λ can be "0" when the marginal of one row of B attracts the majority of counts. We used the data from the sport-type by attitudes toward banned drugs in sport to calculate the Lambda and Tau values presented earlier. Here are the results:

Directional Measures

			Value	Asymp. Std. Error[a]
Nominal by Nominal	Lambda	Symmetric	.146	.046
		drug attitude Dependent	.095	.050
		sport level Dependent	.185	.057
	Goodman and Kruskal tau	drug attitude Dependent	.b00	.021
		sport level Dependent	.087	.019
	Uncertainty Coefficient	Symmetric	.087	.018
		drug attitude Dependent	.090	.019
		sport level Dependent	.084	.018

Directional Measures

			Aoorox. T[b]	Approx. Sig.
Nominal by Nominal	Lambda	Symmetric	3.015	.003
		drug attitude Dependent	1.833	.067
		sport level Dependent	2.965	.003
	Goodman and Kruskal tau	drug attitude Dependent		.000[c]
		sport level Dependent		.000[c]
	Uncertainty Coefficient	Symmetric	4.728	.000[d]
		drug attitude Dependent	4.728	.000[d]
		sport level Dependent	4.728	.000[d]

a. Not assuming the null hypothesis.

b. Using the asymptotic standard error assuming the null hypothesis.

c. Based on chi-square approximation.

d. Likelihood ratio chi-square probality.

4.12   Odd Ratio

An additional measure of association developed by Goodman *et al.* is termed Odd Ratio (α). In 2 x 2 table as this

a	b
c	d

the ratios a/c, b/d, a/b, c/d allow us to compare the different ratios of counts in the different variables. For example,

School	Sport Participation		Total
	Yes	No	
Elementary	25	30	55
High	15	40	55
Total	40	70	110

The data suggests that among the elementary students, the ratio of being an athlete relative to not being an athlete is 25/30 = 0.83 and among high school students it is 15/40 = 0.375. If these two ratios were identical then we could conclude that there is no association between the school grade and participation in sport. Thus, α can be defined as

$$\alpha = (a/b)/(c/d) = ad/bc \qquad (21)$$

and in the above example

$\alpha = 0.83/0.375 = 2.21$.

The ratio will stay constant if we multiply the counts by any number k. The ratio does not accept negative values, however when a cell contains "0" count the ratio can not be defined. In some cases a logarithmic transformation is performed on the proportions as follows:

P1	P2
1 - P1	1 - P2
1.0	1.0

The ratio in the first column is P1/(1 - P1) and thus

$$\text{Log}[P1/(1 - P1)] = \log P1 - \log(1 - P1)$$

If ln (natural log on e basis) is used instead the values are termed LOGITS.

4.13 Hypothesis Testing for Two Proportions

An additional method for examining a pattern of dependence between two nominal variables (i.e., 2 x 2 bivariate table) is the Z-test for proportions, which is considered as a special curve of the χ^2 test.

Assume that a researcher is interested in knowing the link between sport-type (team vs. individual) and attitudes (positive vs. negative) toward the use of banned drugs in sport. If team and individual athletes equally endorse or reject the use of banned drugs in sport, then proportionally they are equal, i.e., independent.

However, if one of the groups is proportionally more or less than the other on that issue, we may say that one type of athletes endorse or reject the use of such drugs more than the other, i.e., dependence between the two variables. Thus, if we say the proportion of team sport athletes who endorse the use of drugs is P_i and similarly the proportion of individual athletes who endorse the use of drugs is P_j, then under the null hypothesis

$$H_0: P_i = P_j$$

only if the samples fully represent the population of team and group athletes.

Assume a hypothetical example as follows:

Sport-type	Attitude toward the use of banned drugs in sport		
	Endorse	Against	Total
Individual	100	100	200
Team	20	180	200

The proportion of individual and team athletes who endorse the use of drugs is:

P_i (individual) = 100/200 = 0.50

P_j (team) = 20/200 = 0.10

The question is whether this difference is a TRUE difference (i.e., significant) or a difference which is random, i.e., non-significant.

To further examine these differences we should estimate the weighted average of the two sample proportion. This is

$$P_u = \frac{N_i P_i + N_j P_j}{N_1 + N_2} \quad (22)$$

In the hypothetical example P_u is

$$P_u = \frac{200(0.50) + 200(0.10)}{200 + 200} = \frac{100 + 20}{400} = \frac{120}{400} = 0.30$$

The standard error (SE) of the sampling distribution of all possible sample differences is

$$\theta_{P_i - P_j} = \sqrt{P_u(1 - P_u)} \cdot \sqrt{\frac{N_i + N_j}{N_i N_j}} \quad (23)$$

and in our example $\quad \theta_{P_i - P_j} = \sqrt{0.30(1 - 0.30)} \cdot \sqrt{\frac{200 + 200}{200 \cdot 200}}$

$$= 0.458 \cdot 0.1 = 0.0458$$

$$= 0.458 \cdot 0.1 = 0.0458$$

The difference between the proportions of the two samples in endorsing the use of banned drugs in sport in standard deviation units is:

$$Z_{sample} = (P_i - P_j)/\theta_{Pi-Pj} \quad (24)$$

which is

$$Z_{sample} = (0.50 - 0.10)/0.0458 = 8.734$$

This value, like the χ^2 observed value is compared to the Z values which correspond to the distribution of Z with 95% or 99% (or $p \leq .05$ or $p < .01$, respectively) to conduct a type I error. The Z-value in the table is termed $Z_{critical}$, and again if

$$Z_{observed} \leq Z_{critical}$$

then we conclude that proportionally the attitudes of individual and team athletes toward banned drugs are similar. However if

$$Z_{observed} > Z_{critical}$$

we then say that the two samples differ from each other. In our example, $Z_{obs} > Z_c$ and therefore we can conclude that individual athletes endorse the use of banned drugs in sport more than do team athletes.

4.14   Log Linear Analysis

Log linear analysis is used to explain or account for a dependent variable (DV) or a criterion variable that is genuinely categorical. It applies only when the predictors/ explanatory variables are also categorical (i.e., placed on a nominal scale). We recommend Bakeman and Robinson's (1994) book *'Understanding log-linear analysis with ILOG: An interactive approach'* to further elaborate on this topic. Here we shall use their illustration of two dimensional frequency tables. So far the test of association of nominal scales assumed only two variables. The log-linear analysis allows us to examine the effect (or association) of a number of variables (IV) on one dependent variable (DV) simultaneously.

The previous statistical procedures relied on a GENERIC INDEPENDENCE MODEL for testing INDEPENDENCE of ROW and COLUMN FACTORS (sampling allows row and column margins to vary) or HOMOGENEITY of PROPORTION (either row or column margins are fixed). However there are other models which can be arranged in a HIERARCHICAL SERIES (each successive model incorporates all terms included in earlier models), and the difference between the models in the series can be tested.

A HIERARCHICAL LOG-LINEAR MODEL includes all lower order terms by higher order ones. A HIERARCHICAL SERIES of LOG-LINEAR MODEL refers to a series of nested models in which successively more complex models incorporate all terms included in less sampled ones (Bakeman and Robinson, 1994). The FIT of each model (i.e., how much the data fit the model under the null hypothesis assumption—the expected values) is examined by using the Pearson χ^2 or the likelihood-ratio χ^2 (G^2). By using the differences between G^2 or the successive models (partial χ^2), it is possible to test the significance of the additional terms (i.e., more complex model).

To illustrate the various terms of the log-linear analysis we shall use the data from the previous hypothetical example where individual and team sport athletes were asked about their attitudes toward the use of banned drugs to enhance performance. We sampled 400 athletes. If we did not have any information about the sample distribution, we would assume that half of them were individual and half were team athletes, and that half of each of them endorsed the use of banned drugs. This model is termed EQUIPROBABLE MODEL or the NULL MODEL because it ignores any potential effect of one of the variables. This is symbolized as [0]. The observed values (their *ln* are in parenthesis) were:

	Attitudes		Total
	Endorse	Against	
Individual athletes	100	100	200
	(4.60)	(4.60)	
Team athletes	20	180	200
	(2.99)	(5.99)	
Total	120	280	400

Under the [0] model the distribution (nature log of count in parenthesis) will be:

	Attitudes		Total
	Endorse	Against	
Individual athletes	100	100	200
	(4.60)	(4.60)	
Team athletes	100	100	200
	(4.60)	(4.60)	
Total	200	200	400

The likelihood-ratio χ^2 for the [0] model is

$$G^2 = 2\sum obs(\log obs - \log exp) \qquad (25)$$

or in our case

$$G^2 = 2\sum obs(\ln obs - \ln exp)$$
$$G = 2[100(4.60 - 4.60) - 100(4.00 - 4.00) + 20(2.99 - 4.60) + 180(5.19 - 4.60)]$$
$$= 2(-32.2 + 106.2)$$
$$= 148.00$$

with df $= 4-1 = 3$ [4 cells counts; not as in the case of 2 x 2 χ^2, where df $= (c - 1)(r - 1)$]. The critical value for χ^2 with df $= 3$ and p$\leq$ .05 is 7.82; thus $G^2(3) = 148$ is very significant and indicates that the null model [0] <u>does not fit</u> the data well.

The second model assumes that we have knowledge of ONE FACTOR (fixed by the researcher). For example, we know that 200 individual and 200 team athletes were sampled, but we do not know how many of them endorsed the use of banned drugs. Thus we distribute the individual and team athletes evenly between the two columns, which represent those endorsing and opposing drug use in sport. Since it is a model that represents sport-type only, we shall term this model [S]. The distribution of counts and the natural logs (ln) are presented as follows:

	Attitudes		Total
	Endorse	Against	
Individual athletes	100	100	200
	(4.60)	(4.60)	
Team athletes	100	100	200
	(4.60)	(4.60)	
Total	200	200	400

Because the number (counts) of individual and team athletes are identical (200 each), the [S] and the [0] models result in identical G^2. However the df in the S model are 2 instead of 3 in the [0] model. This is because we begin with 4 cells and therefore df $= 4$. We constrain all cells to sum to the total observed as well. The first constraint is the grand total, N and the second constraint is the first row thus df $= 4-2 = 2$. The critical value for χ^2 (2) $= 5.99$ with p $\leq$ .05, therefore the [S] model is significant and again indicates a bad fit between the model and the data (counts). The change in G^2 between the [0] and [S] which is zero with df $= 1(3 - 2 = 1)$ is not significant and therefore does not change the fit.

The third model assumes knowledge of both factors/dimensions, the distribution of athletes by sport-type and attitudes toward banned drugs. We know that there are 200 individual and 200 team athletes and we know that 120 endorsed and 280 rejected the use of banned drugs. Taking the marginal totals into account, we would expect that the 200 marginal counts in row 1 and the 200 marginal counts in row 2 to be distributed into the cells like the column marginal totals: 120/280 or 12/28 or 6/14 or 3/7. This model takes into account the marginal tables for both sport-type and attitude categories, so we term it the sport-type PLUS attitude model, and it is symbolized as [S][A] model. The expected frequencies according to the [S][A] model and their ln values (in parenthesis) are as follows:

	Attitudes		Total
	Endorse	Against	
Individual athletes	3/10 x 200 = 60	7/10 x 200 = 140	200
	(4.09)	(4.94)	
Team athletes	3/10 x 200 = 60	7/10 x 200 = 140	200
	(4.09)	(4.94)	
Total	120	280	

Considering the observed counts and their ln values and the expected counts by the [S][A] model counts, the G^2 is

$G^2 = 2[100(4.60 - 4.09) + 100(4.60 - 4.94) + 20(2.99 - 4.09) + 180(5.19 - 4.94)] = 2(51 - 34 - 22 + 45)$

$= 2 \cdot 40 = 80$ with df = 1 (4 cells, constrain the total, first row and first column margin total, thus 4-3 = 1).

The critical value of χ^2 (1) = 4.43 per P ≤ .05. Thus the [S][A] model does not fit the data well. The change in G^2 between the [S] and [S][G] models is 148—80 = 68.0 with 1 df (2—1) is very significant which means that knowing the distribution of athletes' attitudes toward banned drugs, we know more than if this information was not known. However, we shall still keep in mind that the [S][A] model does not fit the observed data well. Thus the [S][A] model of independence or homogeneity fails to fit the data.

The fourth and last model assumes knowledge of the frequencies within the cells. Such a model is termed a SATURATED MODEL and the counts generated by it fit the observed counts perfectly. Thus it is termed here the [S][A][SA] model or [SA] model. Counts that satisfy the [SA] model, cross-classification of the two variables necessarily satisfy the [S] (rows) and the [A] (columns) marginal constraints as well. Once [SA] is specified, there is no reason to include the [S] and [A] to it. The [SA] is a hierarchical model. The G^2 of the [SA] model is zero with 0 df. The expected and observed counts are identical. The 4 df are completely exhausted by the [SA] constraint and therefore df = 4 - 4 = 0. The [SA] model is as follows:

	Attitudes		Total
	Endorse	Against	
Individual athletes	100	100	200
	(4.60)	(4.60)	
Team athletes	20	180	200
	(2.99)	(5.19)	
Total	120	280	400

In reality, the obvious starting point is with the saturated [SA] model, which by definition fits perfectly the later model (i.e., expected = observed counts), and then use backward procedures to eliminate terms. The goal is to find the SIMPLEST MODEL that FITS THE DATA whose G^2 remains NON-SIGNIFICANT. The G^2 indicates how well the model expected counts fit the observed counts. The importance of the term, effect, or constraint deleted at that step is indicated by the partial . To summarize the previous results we can use the G^2 in a hierarchical order shown in Table 3.10.

Table 3.10

A Hierarchical Series of Models for the Sport-type Drug Attitude Hypothetical Data

Step	Model	G^2	df	Term deleted	ΔG^2	Δdf
1	[SA]	0	0	—	—	—
2	[S][A]	80^*	1	SA	80^*	1
3	[S]	148^*	2	A	68^*	1
4	[0]	148^*	3	S	0.0	1

Note: S and A represent sport-type and attitudes toward banned drugs; ΔG^2 and Δdf represent change in G^2 and degrees of freedom; * $p < .05$.

In our example, none of the models fit the data except the saturated model. Neither sport-type nor knowing the attitudes distribution are sufficient enough to account for the observed data, though knowing the attitudes of athletes helped improve the prediction to some degree. It is concluded that indeed sport-type and attitudes toward banned drugs are dependent and their association is strong. Individual athletes endorse it much more than team athletes.

(5)   Measures of Association for Ordinal Data

Ordinal data contain more information than nominal data. We know how the values of a variable are ORDERED/RANKED with respect to their MAGNITUDE. When at least one of the variables is described in ranked/ordered nature, then measures of association for ordinal data should be applied if we wish to know how the variables are associated.

5.1   Gamma

GAMMA is a symmetric measure of association, not considering that one of the variables is dependent and the other independent. However causality may be inferred by merely logical inferences.

The GAMMA coefficient is based on a simple logic, which we shall try to demonstrate, by an example. Assume that we wish to know the association between age categories (young, and young adults) and their perceived exertion under a standardized condition of running on a treadmill (easy, moderate, hard, very hard) when exactly reaching 80% of their maximal oxygen uptake. The results are demonstrated as follows:

Age Category	Perceived Exertion at 80%			VO$_2$max	Total
	Easy	Moderate	Hard	Very Hard	
Young	5	10	10	15	40
	(12.5%)	(25%)	(25%)	(37.5%)	(100%)
Young Adults	12	22	5	1	40
	(30%)	(55%)	(12.5%)	(2.5%)	(100%)

The distribution of young and young adults into the categories of ordered perceived exertion shows that these groups differ in their perceived exertion once they are in their 80% of VO$_2$max. More young people tend to perceive it harder than young adults. However, to examine the magnitude of the relations between age and perceived exertion, the GAMMA coefficient is calculated next. First we have to determine HOW MANY CONCORDANT PAIRS and DISCORDANT PAIRS are in our data. CONCORDANT PAIRS are two cases that are RANKED the SAME on the TWO VARIABLES. DISCORDANT PAIRS are two cases that are RANKED DIFFERENTLY on the two variables. Thus, POSITIVE ASSOCIATION between the variables will result when many concordant and few discordant pairs will occur. A NEGATIVE ASSOCIATION will result when many discordant and few concordant pairs exist. NO ASSOCIATION will result once the number of concordant and discordant pairs are equal. Thus GAMMA is defined as

$$G = \frac{N_c - N_d}{N_c + N_d} \qquad (26)$$

where N_c is the number of concordant pairs, and N_d is the number of discordant pairs.

In the data on age category and rate of perceived exertion, we shall count first HOW MANY CONCORDANT PAIRS are in the distribution:

	Young	Young Adults	
Easy	5	12	
Moderate	10	22	
Hard	10	5	$1(10 + 10 + 5) = 1 \cdot 25 = 25$
Very Hard	15	1	
Easy	5	12	
Moderate	10	22	
Hard	10	5	$5(5 + 10) = 5 \cdot 15 = 75$
Very Hard	15	1	
Easy	5	12	
Moderate	10	22	
Hard	10	5	$22(5) = 110$
Very Hard	15	1	

$N_c = 25 + 75 + 110 = 210.$

Second, we count how many DISCORDANT cases are in the distribution.

	Young	Young Adults	
Easy	5	12	
Moderate	10	22	
Hard	10	5	$15(12 + 22 + 5) = 15 \cdot 39 = 585$
Very Hard	15	1	
Easy	5	12	
Moderate	10	22	
Hard	10	5	$10(12 + 22) = 10 \cdot 34 = 340$
Very Hard	1 5	1	
Easy	5	12	
Moderate	10	22	
Hard	10	5	$10(12) = 120$
Very Hard	1 5	1	

$$N_d = 585 + 340 + 120 = 1045$$

and Gamma equals

$$G = \frac{N_c - N_d}{N_c + N_d} = \frac{210 - 1045}{210 + 1045} = \frac{-835}{1255} = -0.67$$

which is a moderate to strong relation between age and perceived exertion at 80% VO_2max. It indicates that with age increase, people lower their perceived exertion when practicing at 80% of their maximal aerobic capacity. Why? This is a different question. The Gamma ranges between –1 to 1. A "1" means that every higher rank on one variable is equivalent to higher rank in the other variable. A "-1" indicates the reversed trend, i.e., a high value in one variable is always lower in rank in the other variable. A "0" means that a rank in one variable cannot predict a rank in the other variable. Using SPSS 11.0 the output for the same data is as follows:

Age Category * Rate of Perceived Exertion Crosstabulation

	Rate of Perceived Exertion				
	1.00	2.00	3.00	4.00	Total
Age	5	10	10	15	40
Category	12	22	5	1	40
Total	17	32	15	16	40

Symmetric Measures

		Value	Asymp Std. Error	Approx. T^b.	Approx. Sig.
Ordinal by Ordinal	Gamma	-.665	.113	-5.058	.000
N of Valid Cases		80			

a. Not assuming the null hypothesis.

b. Using the asymptotic standard error assuming the null hypothesis.

5.2   Spearman Rank-Order Correlation Coefficient

Spearman's rank order correlation, known also as SPEARMAN'S RHO is the most frequently used measure of association between two variables which share ordinal data. The ordinal data consists of many categories, which are RANKED, in MAGNI-TUDE. If one of the two variables shares an interval/ratio level, then its values should be first transformed into an order level.

To illustrate the RHO method of association we shall use hypothetical data for long and high jumps. The 10 participants were ranked on long jump and measured on high jump. Thus to enable an estimation of RHO, we are required to transfer its value into ordered fashion.

Student	Long jump (rank) x_i	High jump (m)	High jump (rank) y_i	Difference $d = x_i - y_i$	d^2 $(x_i - y_i)^2$
1	7	1.20	8.5	-1.5	2.25
2	10	1.10	10	0	0.00
3	4	1.48	4	0	0.00
4	1	1,55	1	0	0.00
5	2	1.50	2.5	-0.5	0.25
6	9	1.20	8.5	0.5	0.25
7	6	1.30	5	1	1.00
8	5	1.25	7	-2.00	4.00
9	3	1.50	2.5	0.5	0.35
10	8	1.28	6	2.0	4.0
					$\Sigma d^2 = 12.00$

First we have converted the interval scale of high jump values to ordered values. Student no. 4 with the highest jumped was ranked no. 1. Students 5 and 9 jumped 1.50 m and shared the 2nd and 3rd place. Therefore the ranks were averaged, $(2 + 3)/2 = 2.5$ and so on. The first and 6th students jumped 1.20 m and shared the 8th and 9th ranks, and therefore were assigned the rank $(8 + 9)/2 = 8.5$. Then the ranks at y_i (high jump) were subtracted from the ranks of x_i (long jump) to estimate their differences $(d = x_i - y_i)$. If the ranks of the students in the two variables were identical, then all the differences were "0", and their summation was also "0". This is an indication of perfect positive association. If the differences were very large, then the association will be very negative. This concept is introduced in the Spearman RHO correlation coefficient:

$$r_s = 1 - \frac{6\sum D^2}{N(N^2 - 1)} \qquad (27)$$

In our hypothetical example the correlation is

$$r_s = \frac{6 \cdot 12}{10(10^2 - 1)} = \frac{1 - 72}{990} = 1 - 0.073 = 0.93$$

which indicates a very strong association between high and long jumps. The values of RHO range from "-1.00" (perfect negative association) through "0" (no association) to "+1.00" (perfect positive association). Using SPSS 11.0 for estimating RHO and the high/ long jumps plot we get the following output:

Correlations

			long jump	high jump
Spearman's rho	long jump	Correlation Coefficient	1.000	.927**
		Sig. (2-tailed)	.	.000
		N	10	10
	high jump	Correlation Coefficient	.927**	1.000
		Sig. (2-tailed)	.000	.
		N	10	10

** *Correlation is significant at the .01 level (2-tailed).*

5.3 Somer's D

Like Gamma, Somer's D takes into account the concordant and discordant pairs, but uses the tied cases on the dependent variable.

$$d = \frac{N_c - N_d}{N_s + N_d + T_y} \qquad (28)$$

where T_y is the number of tied cases on the DV.

5.4 Kendall's tau-b

Kendall's tau-b is a symmetric association of two ordinal-level variables. It uses the tied cases on the DV and IV:

$$tau-b = \frac{N_s - N_d}{\sqrt{(N_s + N_d + T_y)(N_s + N_d + T_x)}} \qquad (29)$$

where T_y is the number of tied cases on the DV, T_x is the number of tied cases on the IV.

Kendall's tau-b ranges between "-1" to "1" only when the number of rows in the bivariate table equals the number of columns. Using SPSS 11.0 for the long-high jump variables we get:

Correlations

			long jump	high jump
Spearman's rho	long jump	Correlation Coefficient	1.000	.841**
		Sig. (2-tailed)	.	.001
		N	10	10
	high jump	Correlation Coefficient	.841**	1.000
		Sig. (2-tailed)	.001	.
		N	10	10

** Correlation is significant at the .01 level (2-tailed).

(6)   Measures of Association for Interval/Ratio Data

At the beginning of this chapter when we introduced the "essence of ASSOCIATION among VARIABLES", we classified the concept of COVARIANCE, i.e., how much variance is SHARED or ACCOUNTED FOR by two variables, and how much variance is UNSHARED, i.e., unique to each variable.

The more two variables COVARY, the STRONGER the ASSOCIATION is between them; the less they vary, the weaker their association. Once the two variables are measured on an interval-level scale, the PEARSON PRODUCT-MOMENT CORRELATION is the most representative estimate of the association between them. We shall introduce it next.

6.1   Pearson Product-Moment Correlation

If x and y are two variables and n is the number of observations, then we have n times $x_i y_i$ points. These points can be plotted on x-y axis. The ASSOCIATION between variables x and y becomes stronger when the observations (values) of both "behave" in a similar (whether positive or negative) manner.

For example, if observations low in x are low also in y, moderate in x - moderate in y, high in x - high in y, we can say that there is a STRONG and POSITIVE RELATION between them (see Figure 3.10).

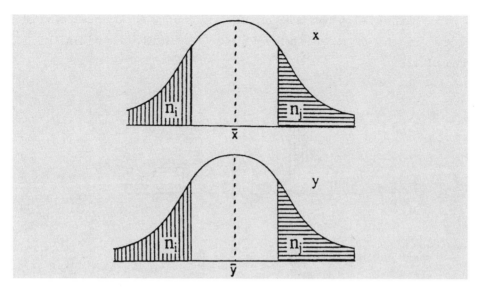

Figure 3.10 Positive Relations Between Variables x and y. Low, Moderate, and High Values of x. Correspond to Low, Moderate, and High Values of y, Respectively.

This is analogous to the plot in figure 3.11

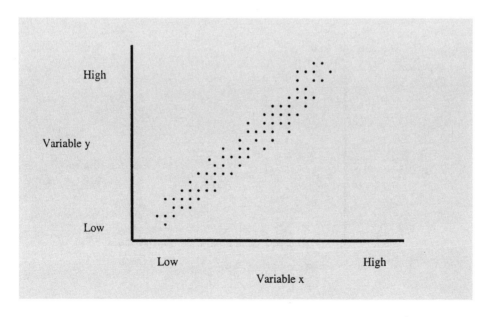

Figure 3.11 A Representation of Figure 13.6.1 as a x-y Plot: Positive Relations Between x and y.

Similarly, when high values of variable x correspond to low values of variable y, and vice-versa, the relations between x and y are STRONG but NEGATIVE (see Figure 3.12).

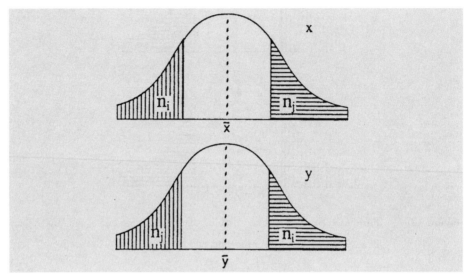

Figure 3.12   Negative Relations Between Variables x and y. Low and High Values of Variable x Correspond to High and Low Values of Variable y, Respectively.

This is analogous to the plot in Figure 3.13

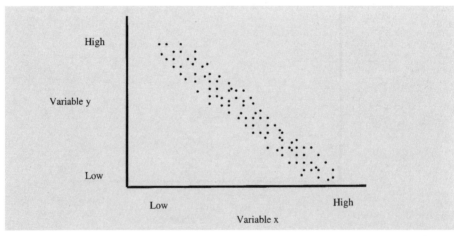

Figure 3.13   A Representation of Figure 13.6.3 as a x-y Plot—Negative Relations Between x and y.

The relationship between variables x and y are termed CORRELATION. To represent the concept of a correlation in mathematical terms, we first calculate the mean of the two variables, x and y, and then the distance of each observation x_i from its mean $\bar{x}$ $(x_i - \bar{x})$ and similarly y_i from $\bar{y}$ $(y_i - \bar{y})$. Assume that x is long jump and y is high jump and we have examined 10 students. Here are their results and PEARSON PRODUCT MOMENT CORRELATION estimation (Table 3.11)

Table 3.11

Estimation of Pearson Product Moment Correlation

Student	Long jump (x_i) m	High jump (y_i) m	$x_i - \bar{x}$	$y_i - \bar{y}$	COVARIANCE $(x_i - \bar{x})(y_i - \bar{y})$	$(x_i - \bar{x})^2$	$(y_i - \bar{y})^2$
1	4.20	1.20	-0.44	-0.136	0.0639	0.221	0.018
2	3.30	1.10	-1.37	-0.236	0.3233	1.877	0.056
3	5.10	1.48	0.43	0.144	0.0619	0.185	0.021
4	6.20	1.55	1.53	0.214	0.3274	2.341	0.046
5	5.60	1.50	0.93	0.164	0.1525	0.865	0.027
6	3.40	1.20	-1.27	-0.136	0.1727	1.613	0.018
7	4.70	1.30	0.03	-0.036	-0.0011	0.001	0.001
8	4.80	1.25	0.13	-0.086	-0.0112	0.017	0.007
9	5.50	1.50	0.83	0.164	0.1361	0.689	0.027
10	3.90	1.28	-0.77	-0.056	0.0431	0.593	0.003
	$\bar{x} = \Sigma x_i/n$ $= 46.7/10$ $= 4.67$	$\bar{y} = \Sigma y_i/n$ $= 13.76/10$ $= 1.336$			$\Sigma(x_i - \bar{x})(y_i - \bar{y})$ $= 1.2686$	$\Sigma(x_i - \bar{x})^2$ $= 8.402$	$\Sigma(y_i - \bar{y})^2$ $= 0.2177$

From the $x_i - \bar{x}$ and $y_i - \bar{y}$ columns it can be seen that in 8 of the 10 observations, higher values in x are associated with higher values of y and vice-versa. Thus we expect to have positive relationships between variables x and y. Also because the COVARIANCE between x and y is strong (they "behave" in a similar fashion), we expect to have strong relationships between variables x and y. The COVARIANCE corresponds to the sum (Σ) of MULTIPLICATIONS between the distances of x_i and y_i

from their respective means, $(x_i - \bar{x})(y_i - \bar{y})$. If the SUM is POSITIVE it means that we multiplied $(+)\cdot(+)$ or $(-)\cdot(-)$ and therefore the COVARIANCE is positive -x and y "behave" similarly. However when the sum of the covariance is negative, it means that we multiplied $(-)\cdot(+)$ or $(+)\cdot(-)$, i.e., values under the mean of x correspond to values above the mean of y and vice-versa. In this case the sum of covariances will be negative and indicates negative relations between variables x and y. It can be seen that it is the COVARIANCE, which dictates the DIRECTION of the RELATION between the two variables. The VARIANCES $\Sigma(x_i - \bar{x})^2$ and $\Sigma(y_i - \bar{y})^2$ can only be positive.

The covariance between x and y was 1.2686. To complete the calculations we estimate the standard deviations of the two variables, S_x and S_y as follows:

$$S_x = \sqrt{\frac{\sum_{i=1}^{n}(x_i - \bar{x})^2}{n-1}} = \sqrt{\frac{8.402}{9}} = 0.966$$

$$S_y = \sqrt{\frac{\sum_{i=1}^{n}(y_i - \bar{y})^2}{n-1}} = \sqrt{\frac{0.2177}{9}} = 0.155$$

The Pearson Product Moment Correlation is

$$r_{xy} = \frac{\sum_{i=1}^{n}(x_i - \bar{x})(y_i - \bar{y})}{N \cdot S_x \cdot S_y} \qquad (30)$$

and in our case

$$r = \frac{1.2626}{10 \cdot 0.966 \cdot 0.155} = 0.923$$

which indicates a very strong and positive relation between variables x and y.

Using SPSS 11.0 we get the following output:

Correlations

			long jump	high jump
Spearman's rho	long jump	Correlation Coefficient	1.000	.923**
		Sig. (2-tailed)	.	.000
		N	10	10
	high jump	Correlation Coefficient	.923**	1.000
		Sig. (2-tailed)	.000	.
		N	10	10

** Correlation is significant at the .01 level (2-tailed).

We demonstrate now another hypothetical data set on 15 participants (maximal oxygen uptake-VO$_2$max, long-run-RUN, and motivation-motive) and use SPSS 11.0 to estimate Pearson Correlation between VO$_2$max and long RUN. The data are as follows:

	Vo$_2$max	Run	Motivation
1	56.00	576.00	56.00
2	35.00	720.00	37.00
3	71.00	510.00	60.00
4	37.00	700.00	50.00
5	24.00	810.00	42.00
6	67.00	540.00	55.00
7	37.00	710.00	40.00
8	65.00	536.00	51.00
9	62.00	581.00	55.00
10	53.00	561.00	43.00
11	57.00	548.00	57.00
12	42.00	687.00	39.00
13	48.00	667.00	43.00
14	39.00	688.00	45.00
15	34.00	705.00	37.00

Plotting VO$_2$max against long RUN results in the following figure:

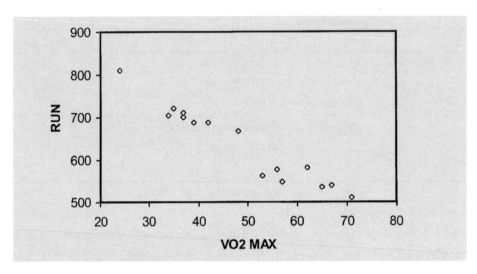

We notice immediately that higher values of VO_2max are associated with lower values of long run and therefore a negative association/correlation between them will result. This is in fact true, the Pearson Correlation among the two variables is –0.969, a very strong negative correlation:

Descriptive Statistics

	Mean	Std. Deviation	N
maximal oxygen uptake	48.4667 1.000	14.2471	15
aerobic performance	635.9333	89.8479	15

Correlations

		max. oxygen uptake	aerobic performance
maximal oxygen uptake	Pearson Correlation	1.000	-.969**
	Sig. (2-tailed)	.	.000
	N	15	15
aerobic performance	Pearson Correlation	-.969**	1.000
	Sig. (2-tailed)	.000	.
	N	15	15

*** Correlation is significant at the .01 level (2-tailed).*

This means that people with higher oxygen uptake have lower times in long run, that is, they run faster. Thus, we should keep in mind that once one of the variables is REVERSED, we may get a NEGATIVE CORRELATION, but we should INTERPRET it as POSITIVE CORRELATION. In the above case, the higher the VO_2max, the faster the long run, just as expected.

The SPSS statistical package, like other similar statistical programs provides the SIGNIFICANCE LEVEL of the associations. The $r = -0.969$ was found to be very very significant ($p<.000$) which means that it can be generalized to the population from which our sample was derived. In case we desire to examine the hypotheses

$H_0: r = 0$

$H_1: r \neq 0$

then we apply a t-statistic as follows

$$t_{sample} = r\sqrt{\frac{N-2}{1-r^2}} \qquad (31)$$

In our example

$$t_{sample} = -0.969\sqrt{\frac{15-2}{1-0.969^2}} = \sqrt{\frac{13}{0.06}} = \sqrt{216.67} = 14.72$$

For $p < 0.01$, $df = 14$, the critical value of t is 4.14. Therefore $t_{obs} > t_c$, and the correlation obtained between VO_2max and long run is very significant. H_1 was verified, H_0 was rejected.

The STRONGER the CORRELATION is, the CLOSER the x_iy_i observations are to a LINEAR LINE. The CORRELATION indicates the MAGNITUDE and DIRECTION between the variables but it cannot tell us by HOW MUCH ONE VARIABLE CHANGES when the OTHER VARIABLE CHANGES. For this we need to DEFINE a LINEAR LINE. This linear line is termed a REGRESSION LINE. We describe it later in this chapter.

6.2   Partial Correlation

Correlation coefficients may indicate that there are MUTUAL RELATIONS between two or more variables. We cannot infer CAUSALITY, i.e., that changes in one variable (IV) are causing changes in the other variable (DV). Logically we may say that the relations seem to be UNIDIRECTIONAL. In our previous example, maximal oxygen consumption (VO_2max) determines the speed of long run and not vice-versa. However, there may be other variables, which potentially and practically may affect this relation. For example, one may claim that highly motivated people train more, and therefore, run faster than those less motivated. The researcher in this case may be interested in the "net relationships" between VO_2max and long run, PARTIALLING OUT the influence of motivation on both VO_2max and running performance. In statistical terms we ask the question: "What is the relationship between maximal oxygen uptake and long run when motivation is kept constant?"

The partial correlation is a measure of linear relations between two variables that continues to exist once all the other relations are held constant. Assume that n participants were chosen from a population N and variables, x_1, x_2, and x_3 are measured. There are three possible correlations among the three variables: r_{12}, r_{13}, and r_{23}.

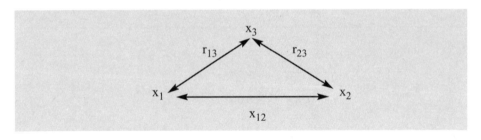

The number of correlations of k variables is $[k(k - 1)]/2$. Now we may assume that the value x_{3i}, i.e., $(x_i - \bar{x})$ for the values x_{3i} will remain constant for each case i. What then will be the correlation between x_1 and x_2? x_3 should be held constant in estimating the r_{12}. It is symbolized $r_{12.3}$ and is calculated

$$r_{12.3} = \frac{r_{12} - r_{13} \cdot r_{23}}{\sqrt{(1 - r_{13}^2)(1 - r_{23}^2)}} \qquad (32)$$

The partial correlation is the correlation between the error terms in predicting x_1 by x_3 and x_2 from x_3. Since none of the mentioned errors are dependent on x_3, the correlation between the errors represents the partial correlation between variables x_1 and x_2 while the effect of x_3 is controlled.

In our example the correlations and matrix among the three variables are:

Correlations

		aerobic performance	maximal oxygen uptake	motivation
Pearson Correlation	aerobic performance	1.000	-.969	-.777
	maximal oxygen uptake	-.969	1.000	.806
	motivation	-.777	.806	1.000
Sig. (1-tailed)	aerobic performance		.000	.000
	maximal oxygen uptake	.000		.000
	motivation	.000	.000	
N	aerobic performance	15	15	15
	maximal oxygen uptake	15	15	15
	motivation	15	15	15

One variable, aerobic performance (long run) is scored in a reversed format, i.e., the higher the score the worse and vice-versa. Therefore the correlations between aerobic performance and the other two variables are negative, and positive between motivation and maximal oxygen uptake. All of the correlations are very significant and therefore can be generalized to the population from which the observations were derived. To partial out the correlations with motivation (x_3) from the correlation between VO$_2$max and run (x_1 and x_2), we follow the equation and find

$$r_{12.3} = \frac{-0.969 - (0.806 \cdot -0.777)}{\sqrt{(1 - 0.806^2)(1 - (-0.777)^2)}} = \frac{-0.969 + 0.6262}{\sqrt{0.35 \cdot 0.3963}}$$

$$= \frac{-0.3428}{0.3724} = -0.92$$

and using SPSS 11.0 we get similar partial correlation.

Partial Correlation Coefficients

Controlling for MOTIV

	VO$_2$MAX	RUN
VO$_2$MAX	1.0000	-.9197
	(0)	(12)
	P= .	P= .000
RUN	-.9197	1.0000
	(12)	(0)
	P= .000	P= .

(Coefficient / (D.F.) / 2-tailed Significance)
" . " is printed if a coefficient cannot be computed

Similarly we can partial out any variable from the correlations of the other two variables by applying the following equations:

$$r_{13.2} = \frac{r_{13} - r_{12} \cdot r_{23}}{\sqrt{(1 - r_{12}^2)(1 - r_{23}^2)}} \tag{33}$$

$$r_{23.1} = \frac{r_{23} - r_{12} \cdot r_{13}}{\sqrt{(1 - r_{12}^2)(1 - r_{13}^2)}} \tag{34}$$

The SPSS 11.0 output is as follows:

Controlling for.. RUN

	VO₂MAX	MOTIV
VO₂MAX	1.0000	.3395
	(0)	(12)
	P= .	P= .235
MOTIV	.3395	1.0000
	(12)	(0)
	P= .235	P= .

(Coefficient / (D.F.) / 2-tailed Significance)
" . " is printed if a coefficient cannot be computed

Controlling for.. VO₂MAX

	MOTIV	RUN
MOTIV	1.0000	.0253
	(0)	(12)
	P= .	P= .932
RUN	.0253	1.0000
	(12)	(0)
	P= .932	P= .

(Coefficient / (D.F.) / 2-tailed Significance)
" . " is printed if a coefficient cannot be computed

The results of this procedure show that partialling out motivation from the running-VO_2max relations somewhat reduces the strength of these relations from –0.97 to –0.92, but this relation remains very strong and significant (p < .000). However when running performance (aerobic performance) is controlled, the relationship between VO_2max and motivation is reduced from 0.806 to 0.339. Similarly, when VO_2max is controlled, the relationship between motivation and running performance reduces from –0.777 to 0.025. It means that VO_2max is the main determinant of long running performance, and motivation is of less importance, though still necessary. It should be kept in mind that we use hypothetical data, which do not necessarily represent the reality. Also, the partialling out of possible variables in models should be based on THEORETICAL and LOGICAL GROUNDS before applying any statistical procedure to the data.

Partial correlations can be applied to more than controlling one variable. For example, if we measured four variables, x_1, x_2, x_3, and x_4 and desire to estimate the net correlation between x_1 and x_2, controlling for x_3 and x_4, the equation will be:

$$r_{12.34} = \frac{r_{12.3} - r_{14.3} \cdot r_{24.3}}{\sqrt{(1 - r_{14.3}^2)(1 - r_{24.3}^2)}} \qquad (35)$$

This is a SECOND LEVEL PARTIAL CORRELATION. First we control for x_3 (FIRST LEVEL PARTIAL CORRELATION), and then use the result for the second level partial correlation. In this way we can control for as many variables as we desire. The control of various variables, as previously mentioned, is determined by theoretical concepts. Models can have forms such as:

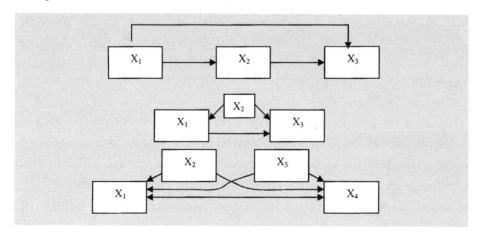

In addition to many other forms. Today these more complicated models are dealt with by simultaneous regression, better known as STRUCTURAL EQUATION MODELLING. This procedure is introduced in more detail later in this chapter.

6.3 Linear Regression

Linear regression is FITTING a LINE which BEST REPRESENTS the scatter plot of the $x_i y_i$ values. In BEST FIT we mean a line from which the DISTANCES of ALL the $x_i y_i$ values are MINIMAL.

A linear line has two characteristics (i.e., parameters), a SLOPE and an INTERSECTION POINT. In Figure 3.14, two hypothetically different lines represent the $x_i y_i$ values.

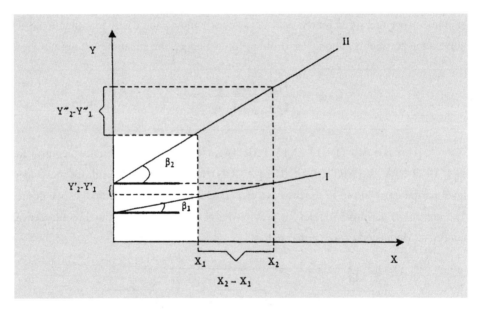

Figure 3.14   y Values as Dependent on x Values Represented by Two Linear Lines.

The two lines are different in both parameters. Line II is steeper than line I and its intersection with the y-axis is also higher. When we move from point x_1 to point x_2 on the x-axis, and try to see by what distance this move will result on y, if line I represent the $x_i y_i$ observation, then the respective change in y will be very small, $y'_2 - y'_1$. However if line II represents the $x_i y_i$ observations, then the same move on the x-axis will result in a larger change in y, $y''_2 - y''_1$. A very strong correlation can be obtained if the x_iy_i observations were close to either one of the linear lines, I or II. Although if x predicts y, then any change in x will result in different change in y. To complement the correlation coefficient we need to estimate the PARAMETERS of the REGRESSION LINE, i.e., the SLOPE (β_1 or β_2 in Figure 3.14) and the INTERSECTION of the line with the y-axis (also termed CONSTANT).

The simplest LINEAR MODEL, which represents REGRESSION LINE, is presented in Figure 3.15

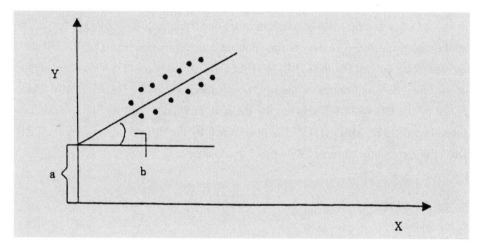

Figure 3.15   A Simple Regression Model. $Yi = a_0 + bx_i + e_i$

a_0 is a constant that adds up to each value of y_i of observation i, b represents the slope of the line, and e_i represents the error we make when predicting y from x. If the xy correlation is not perfect (i.e., 1.0 or −1.0) then we do not predict perfectly y from x. We perform some error, e. This error becomes greater and greater when the correlation between the variables becomes weaker and weaker. Under a perfect correlation, the error term, e is 0, and therefore

$$y_i = a_0 + bx_i$$

or, if $e_i = 0$, then all the x_iy_i observations are located on a linear line. The x_iy_i observations can also represent a NON-LINEAR relation. We shall elaborate on that later in this chapter.

If y values are predicted from x values, we can transform the x and y values into standardized values Zx and Zy by

$$Zy = (y_i - \bar{y})/S_y$$
$$Zx = (x_i - \bar{x})/S_x$$

The linear predictive model is

$$Zy' = A + BZx$$

where A and B are CONSTANTS and $Zx \neq Zy'$.

Only when the $x_i y_i$ observations share one linear line, $Zx = Zy'$. In Figure 3.16, all the standardized $x_i y_i$ values are spread around the regression line. The PREDICTED Zy' values are located ON the LINE, NOT the OBSERVED ones. The linear line in most of the cases does not represent the $x_i y_i$ observations perfectly. The ERROR is determined by the DISTANCES between the PREDICTED and OBSERVED $x_i y_i$ observations. The ERROR MAGNITUDE is determined by the difference between the PREDICTED Zy' and the observed Zy when Zx is known.

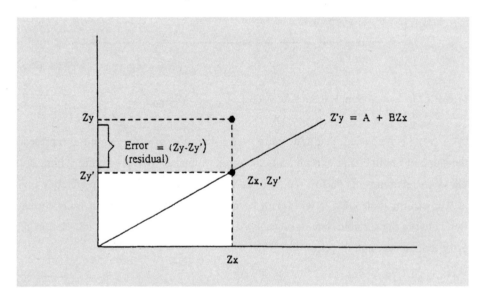

Figure 3.16   Determining the Standardized Error by the Distance Between the Standardized Predicted and Observed Values of Variable y from the Standardized Values of x.

As previously mentioned, the best line, which FITS the data, is the line from which the ZxZy values are MINIMAL.

The LEAST SQUARE (LS) METHOD is used to estimate the two CONSTANTS A and B of the linear line. These constants determine the line from which the DISTANCES of ZxZy are MINIMAL. Therefore, for each case i, a predicted value $Z'y_i$ is determined. $Z'y_i$ will not be identical to Zy_i and the ERROR TERM will be

$$E_I = Z'y_i - Zy_i$$

We then have to choose constants A and B so that

$$\sum_{i=1}^{n} (Z'y_i - Zy_i)/n$$

will be minimal. When the LS method is applied to standardized values, the constant A (i.e., intercept) is always 0, so that the linear function has the form $Z'y_i = BZx_i$.

Developing the mean squared error and integrating it to the function $Z'y = A + BZx$ will result in

$$\frac{\sum_{i=1}^{n}(Z'y_i - Zy_i)^2}{n} = \frac{\sum_{i=1}^{n}[(BZx_i - Zy_i) + A]^2}{n}$$

by squaring each i and summing up we get

$$\frac{\sum_{i=1}^{n}[BZx_i - Zy_i) + A]^2}{n} = \frac{\sum_{i=1}^{n}(BZx_i - Zy_i)^2}{n} + 2A\frac{\sum_{i=1}^{n}(BZx_i - Zy_i)}{n} + \frac{\sum_{i=1}^{n}A^2}{n}$$

$$= \frac{\sum_{i=1}^{n}(BZx_i - Zy_i)^2}{n} + A$$

because A and B are constants and the means and are always 0. Assuming B is constant, for which value of A can the expression be minimal? The first term is describing the squared differences and should therefore be positive and A should also be a positive number. Therefore, the minimal value is when A = 0, and according to the LS method, the value of A in standardized values should be 0.

According to the LS method, the constant B for predicting Z values should be

$$B = \frac{\sum_{i=1}^{n} Zx_i \cdot Zy_i}{n} = r_{xy} \qquad (36)$$

We know already that in standardized form A = 0 so

$$\frac{\sum_{i=1}^{n}(Z'y_i - Zy_i)^2}{n} = \frac{\sum_{i=1}^{n}(BZx_i - Zy_i)^2}{n}$$

Squaring the whole term

$$\frac{\sum_{i=1}^{n}(Z'y_i - Zy_i)^2}{n} = \frac{B^2\sum_{i=1}^{n}Zx_i^{\,2}}{n} + \frac{2B\sum_{i=1}^{n}Zx_i \cdot Zy_i}{n} + \frac{\sum_{i=1}^{n}Zy_i^{\,2}}{n}$$

$$= B^2 - 2Br_{xy} + 1$$

However, the variance of standardized values $(S_Z{}^2)$ is always 1. We assume that B is different from r by the value c (whether positive or negative). Replacing r + c instead of B we get

$$\frac{\sum_{i=1}^{n}(Z'y_i - Zy_i)^2}{n}$$

$$= (r + c)^2) - 2(r + c)r + 1$$
$$= r^2 + 2rc + c^2 - ar^2 - 2rc + 1$$
$$= (1 - r^2) + c^2$$

When B = r_{xy}, so that c = 0, the squared error should be minimal:

$$\frac{\sum_{i=1}^{n}(Z'y_i - Zy_i)^2}{n} = (1 - r_{xy}{}^2)$$

and for each value c ≠ 0 the value should be 1 - r^2_{xy} plus a positive value c. Therefore B = r_{xy} is the minimal predicted error in standardized linear regression. The term $Z'y_i = r_{xy} \cdot Zx_i$ is known as a REGRESSION EQUATION or as a PREDICTIVE EQUATION where Zy is predicted by Zx. The constant B is termed STANDARD REGRESSION COEFFICIENT or WEIGHT. Thus when RAW DATA is transformed into STANDARDIZED DATA

$$B = r_{xy}$$

In raw data, the regression coefficient is somewhat different. The squared mean error, termed as the SAMPLE VARIANCE OF ESTIMATE is

$$S^2_{Zy\,Zx} = \frac{\sum_{i=1}^{n}(Z'y_i - Zy_i)^2}{n} = 1 - r_{xy}{}^2$$

The greater the $(Z'y_i - Zy_i)^2$ the less predictive is the regression line. In some cases this term is written as

$$S_{Z'yZx} = \sqrt{1 - r^2_{xy}} \qquad (37)$$

and termed SAMPLE STANDARD ERROR. It can be seen that there is a strong relationship between the correlation among the variable x and y and the error term. Under perfect correlation ($r_{xy} = 1.0$ or -1.0), the error term becomes 0, and the weaker the relationship ($r_{xy} \to 0$), the greater the error term becomes.

The Correlation (r)-Regression Coefficient (b) Relationship

We shall skip the algebraic development of the r and b relationship and say that when the correlation coefficient r_{xy} was calculated, the regression coefficient, b, which represents the slope of the linear line, can be calculated by

$$b_{y \cdot x} = r_{xy}(S_y/S_x) \qquad (38)$$

Using the VO_2max-Run data, we get the following statistics from the SPSS 11.0.0:

Descriptive Statistics

	Mean	Std. Deviation	N
aerobic performance	635.9333	89.8479	15
maximal oxygen uptake	48.4667	14.2471	15

Correlations

		aerobic performance	maximal oxygen uptake
Pearson Correlation	aerobic performance	1.000	-.969
	maximal oxygen uptake	-.969	1.000
Sig. (1-tailed)	aerobic performance	.	.000
	maximal oxygen uptake	.000	.
N	aerobic performance	15	15
	maximal oxygen uptake	15	15

To estimate b from this data where

$r_{xy} = -0.969$

$S_x = 14.2471$

$S_y = 89.8479$

we calculate

$b_{y \cdot x} = r_{xy}(S_y/S_x) = -0.969(89.8479/14.2471)$

$b_{y \cdot x} = -6.0858$

and

$$a = \bar{y} - b\,\bar{x} \qquad (39)$$

and in our data

$a = 635.9373 - (-6.08) \cdot 48.4667 = 635.9333 + 294.67754$

$= 930.6108$

and the standardized regression coefficient is r_{xy} which is -0.969. Using SPSS 11.0, we received the following output (minor changes are due to rounding numbers).

Coefficients[a]

Model		Unstandardized Coefficients		Standardied Coefficients		
		B	Std. Error	Beta	t	Sig.
1	(Constant)	932.091	21.791		42.775	.000
	maximal oxygen uptake	-6.111	.432	-.969	-14.129	.000

Coefficients[a]

Model		95 % Confidence Interval for B	
		Lower Bound	Upper Bound
1	(Constant)	885.015	979.167
	maximal oxygen uptake	-7.045	-5.176

[a] *Dependent Variable: aerobic performance*

The regression line of predicting long run (y) by aerobic capacity (maximal oxygen uptake, x) is $Y = 932.091 - 6.11\,x$

The computer also supplies 95% confidence intervals for the parameters in the population. Thus we expect that the regression lines of many possible samples in the population will vary in both the slope and constant (intercept) parameters. In 95 of 100 samples, the intercept will fall between 885.015 - 979.167 and the slope between –7.045 - (-5.176).

The negative regression coefficient (b = -6.11) indicates that the regression line has a negative trend. With increase in x (VO$_2$max) the run is faster (i.e., decreases). This can be seen in the SPSS 11.0 graphs:

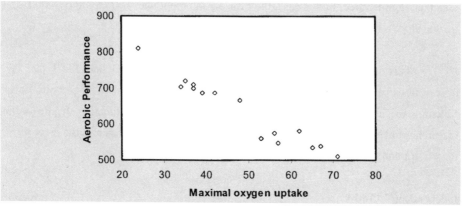

Independent:	VO$_2$MAX						
Dependent	Mth	Rsq	d.f.	F	Sigf	b0	b1
RUN	LIN	.939	13	199.62	.000	932.091	-6.1105

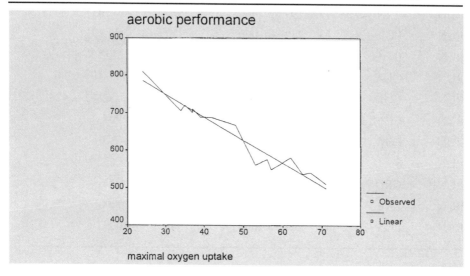

In SPSS 11.0, the constant a is symbolized by b_0 and the regression coefficient b_1. We notice that the observed values are very close to the predicted linear regression line. The predicted-observed differences, which determine the error term, are examined by a simple F-test (introduced in the next part of this book).

We can see that F = 199.62 and p < .000 which means that the regression line represents very strongly the observed values. Both parameters (constants) B and A have error terms. SPSS calculates them and via simple t-test (introduced in the next part), examines their significance. In this case, the t for the intercept was 42.775 and p < .000, and for the slope –14.129, and p < .000.

This indicates that the regression line can be trusted and FITS the $x_i y_i$ observations very well. SPSS 11.0 allows us to examine additional linear and non-linear functions to fit the data. It produces a significant test to each function. It allows the researcher to choose the best function that fits the data. The criteria are: the error term, the r^2(rsq), and the magnitude of F. Here is the output:

Independent: VO_2MAX

Dependent	Mth	Rsq	d.f.	F	Sigf	Upper bound	b0	b1	b2	b3
RUN	LIN	.939	13	199.62	.000		932.091	-6.1105		
RUN	LOG	.947	13	232.88	.000		1711.14	-280.19		
RUN	INV	.904	13	122.64	.000		378.408	11402.3		
RUN	QUA	.950	12	114.63	.000		1051.49	-11.431	.0546	
RUN	CUB	.951	11	70.64	.000		989.835	-7.0624	-.0428	.0007
RUN	COM	.942	13	209.60	.000		1004.50	.9904		
RUN	POW	.934	13	183.66	.000		3377.80	-.4376		
RUN	S	.874	13	90.20	.000		6.0476	17.6320		
RUN	GRO	.942	13	209.60	.000		6.9122	-.0096		
RUN	EXP	.942	13	209.60	.000		1004.50	-.0096		
RUN	LGS	.942	13	209.60	.000		.0010	1.0097		

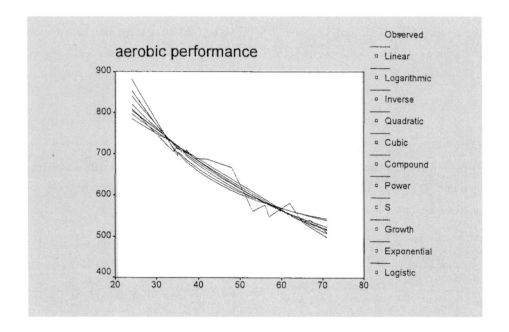

aerobic performance

Observed
□ Linear
□ Logarithmic
□ Inverse
□ Quadratic
□ Cubic
□ Compound
□ Power
□ S
□ Growth
□ Exponential
□ Logistic

6.4   Concerns in Regression Analysis

There are several concerns associated with regression analysis. We shall briefly relate to each of them so that the learner may further elaborate on them.

Index of Fit

The GOODNESS OF FIT represents the degree to which the regression line MATCHES the $x_i y_i$ observations. The CORRELATION COEFFICIENT between the OBSERVED DV, y, and the PREDICTED $\hat{y}$ estimated by the regression line is the estimate of fit. In most of the cases the square of the correlation, R^2, is used since it indicates the DV PERCENTAGE of VARIANCE accounted for by the IV when multiplied by 100. The R^2 may be written as

$$R^2 = 1 - \frac{\sum (y_i - \hat{y}_i)^2}{\sum (y_i - \overline{y})^2} \qquad (40)$$

where y_i is the observed DV, $\hat{y}$ is the predicted DV, and y is the mean of the observed DV which is the proportion of total variability in y that is explained by x. If R^2 is close to 1 or 100% it means that the variance y is very much accounted for by the x variance. To examine the R^2 significance, i.e., the null hypothesis $H_0(p=0)$ or $H_1(p\neq0)$ where p is the population correlation, a t-statistic is used:

$$t = \frac{|R|\sqrt{n-2}}{\sqrt{1-R^2}} \quad \text{with df = 2} \quad \text{with df = 2} \tag{41}$$

The fit can be evaluated by plotting the DV(y) against the IV(x) with the regression line. The higher the R^2, the closer the $x_i y_i$ to the line, the better the fit between the data and the line. Figure 3.17 shows several hypothetical examples.

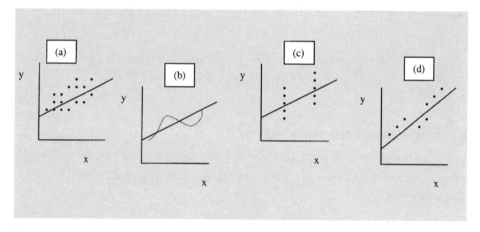

Figure 3.17   Hypothetical x-y Plots Around A Linear Regression Line.

As can be seen, the $x_i y_i$ observations in (d) fit best the regression line. Plots (b) and (c) need a non-linear function in order to fit, and in (a) a linear function may fit best, but not convincingly.

Analysis of Residuals

Detection of outliers and various deficiencies in the data are best done by the examination of the residuals. A residual is defined as

$$e_i = y_i - \hat{y}_i \tag{42}$$

and the standardized residual is

$$e_{iS} = e_i/S \qquad (43)$$

where S is the standard deviation of the residuals

$$S^2 = \frac{\sum (y_i - a - b_i x_{1i})^2}{n-2} \qquad (44)$$

The e_{iS} are distributed normally with mean 0. Though not independently distributed, this violation may be ignored if a sufficient number of observations exist. Standardized residuals are best represented by plots such as:

1) e_{iS} against the fitted value, $\hat{y}$

2) e_{iS} against the independent/dependent variables

3) the time order in which the observation occur. (Chatterjee and Price, 1977).

An example from the VO_2max-long run (aerobic performance) data is introduced to illustrate the concept (SPSS11.0).

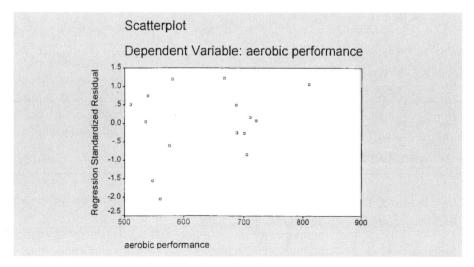

The residuals seem to be normally distributed within ±2 SD with mean 0. Except for two residuals (located about −1.5 and −2.0 beneath the mean) the residuals seem to be spread equally along the aerobic performance axis. In this case, corrections are not needed before proceeding with further analysis.

To illustrate how exceptional values can completely change the regression coefficients, we added an exceptional value to the data and asked SPSS11.0 to produce for us a scatter plot of the residuals. This above plot was altered to become the following plot:

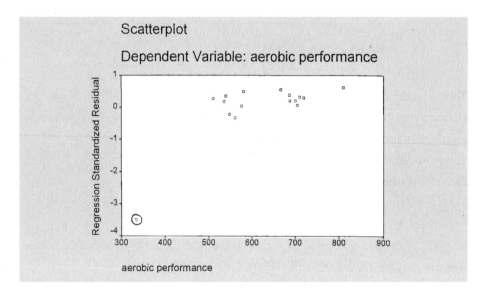

The standardized residuals are spread around their 0 mean, except one residual value which is located –3.5 SD beneath it. This one single value has caused the following changes to the original regression:

	Previous	Current
a (intercept/constant)	$932.09 \pm 21.79 \rightarrow$	894.02 ± 81.17
b (regression coefficient)	$-6.11 \pm 0.43 \rightarrow$	-5.74 ± 1.62

Thus with "casewise diagnostics" the 16th standardized residual of –3.495 should be removed prior to any further analysis.

Transformation of Variables' Values

The most commonly violated assumptions are those which relate to the linearity of the data and constancy of the error variance. Here are several models, which are all linear:

$$y = a + bx + e$$
$$y = a + b_1x + b_2x^2 + e$$
$$y = a + b_1 \log x + e$$
$$y = a + b\sqrt{x} + e$$

This is because b, the statistic of the model enters linearly. However a model like

$$y = a + e^{b_1x} + \mu$$

is non linear because the statistic b does not enter the model linearly. Thus sometimes we need to transform the variable so that linear regression can be applied to the data. Here are the most common examples taken from Chatterjee and Price (1977):

Table 3.12

Linearizable Functions with Corresponding Transformation (from Chatterjee and Price, 1977, Regression Analysis by Example, N.Y.: Wiley)

Function	Transformation	Linear form	Graph shown in Figure
$y = \alpha x^\beta$	$y' = \log y, \quad x' = \log x$	$y' = \log \alpha + \beta x'$	2.5a, b
$y = \alpha e^{\beta x}$	$y' = \ln y$	$y' = \ln \alpha + \beta x$	2.5c, d
$y = \alpha + \beta \log x$	$x' = \log x$	$y = \alpha + \beta x'$	2.5e, f
$y = \dfrac{x}{\alpha x - \beta}$	$y' = \dfrac{1}{y}, \quad x' = \dfrac{1}{x}$	$y' = \alpha - \beta x'$	2.5g, h
$y = \dfrac{e^{\alpha + \beta x}}{1 + e^{\alpha + \beta x}}$ [a]	$y' = \ln\left(\dfrac{y}{1-y}\right)$	$y' = \alpha + \beta x$	2.5i

[a] *In Chapter 5 we describe an application using this transformation.*

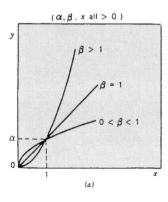

(α, β, x all > 0)

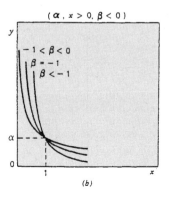

($\alpha, x > 0, \beta < 0$)

(a)   (b)

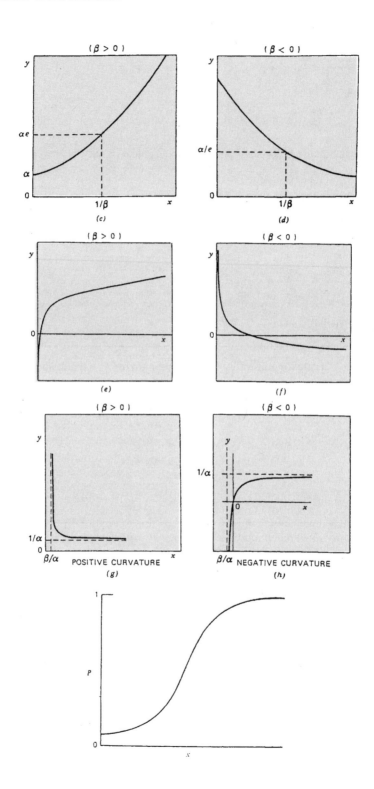

$(\beta > 0)$

$(\beta < 0)$

(c)

(d)

$(\beta > 0)$

$(\beta < 0)$

(e)

(f)

$(\beta > 0)$

$(\beta < 0)$

POSITIVE CURVATURE

NEGATIVE CURVATURE

(g)

(h)

Detection and Removal of Heteroscedastic Errors

Heteroscedasticity occurs when the residual plot (standardized residuals, e_i vs. the independent measure x_i) shows that error variance tends to increase with x as presented in Figure 3.18.

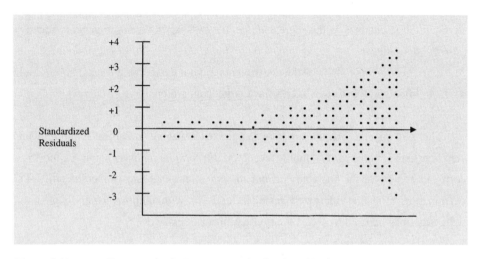

Figure 3.18   Heteroscedastic Errors—Standardized Residual Vary with Increase of x.

This phenomenon means that with increase of the IV (x), the ERROR VARIANCE INCREASES or DECREASES. When the residuals behave in such a fashion, some transformations should take place (y/x and 1/x as DV and IV, respectively) and the fitted model should take the form of

$$\frac{y}{x} = a' + \frac{b'}{x}$$

and then the fitted model in terms of original variables is

$$y = b' + a'x$$

Qualitative/Dummy Variables

Qualitative variables can be used as explanatory variables in regression analysis. Factors such as gender, marital status, country of residency, etc. can be represented by indicator or dummy variables. These dummy variables do not reflect a qualitative ordering of categories, but are used for identifying categories. We shall not elaborate on this topic in this book, but refer the reader to several sources, which describe this procedure in detail.

Detection and Correction of Multicollinearity

Multicollinearity is the presence of strong linear relationships among all or some of the independent variables. It results in unstable estimates of the regression coefficients. Indications of multicollinearity are:

1)   Large changes in regression coefficients when a variable is added or deleted,

2)   Large changes in the regression coefficients when an observation is added or deleted,

3)   The algebraic signs of the coefficients are not in line with the equations, and

4)   Main variables' coefficients have large standard error.

The size of the correlation between the explanatory variables (IVs) indicates clearly whether collinearity among these variables exists. However, low to moderate correlations among the variables do not always indicate absence of collinearity. The examination of the standardized residuals and R^2 with additional variables in the regression may be used to detect the multicollinearity existence.

Besides deleting variables on a theoretical basis, or alternatively, using variables within clusters (hierarchical regression; introduced later in this chapter), it is also possible to impose constraints on the model. One constraint is to equalize the regression coefficients, $\beta_1 = \beta_2$; $\beta_1 = \beta_4 = \beta_6$, etc. However the complexity of this issue is described in more detail in books which concentrate solely on regression analysis.

6.5   Multiple Regression Model

So far we introduced a simple linear model with one DV and one IV (explanatory, predictor). But usually more than one IV is used to predict one DV. A simple linear regression looks like this

$$\boxed{x} \rightarrow \boxed{y}$$

A multiple regression model looks like this

$$\boxed{x_n} \cdots \boxed{x_4} + \boxed{x_3} + \boxed{x_2} + \boxed{x_1} \rightarrow \boxed{y}$$

One should keep in mind that the IVs may correlate among themselves, so that if x_1 is the first predictor of y, and x_2 is the second one, the correlation between x_1 and x_2 should be partialled out from the association of each of them separately with y. When

x_3 is entered to the regression, its associations with x_1 and x_2 should be partialled out from the association with y. Thus the overall contribution of $x_1, x_2, x_3 \ldots x_n$ in predicting y cannot exceed 100%. Ideally the predictors $x_1, x_2, x_3 \ldots x_n$ should have low to moderate correlations among themselves (to avoid collinearity) and strong correlations with the DV, y. When this happens, the additional variance of y accounted for by the variances of the IVs is high and significant. Once the additional predictor variables do not add to the accounted variance of y, there is no sense in considering them in the regression equation. A data set, which may be used for a multiple regression, looks as follows:

ID	y	x_1	x_2	x_3	...	x_p
1	y_1	x_{11}	x_{21}	x_{31}		x_{p1}
2	y_2	x_{12}	x_{22}	x_{32}		x_{p2}
3	y_3	x_{13}	x_{23}	x_{33}		x_{p3}
4	y_4	x_{14}	x_{24}	x_{34}		x_{p4}
$\vdots$	$\vdots$	$\vdots$	$\vdots$	$\vdots$		$\vdots$
N	y_n	x_{1n}	x_{2n}	x_{3n}		x_{pn}

The relationship between y and $x_1, x_2, x_3 \ldots x_p$ is represented as a linear model as follows:

$$y_i = a + b_1 x_{1i} + b_2 x_{2i} + \ldots b_p x_{pi} + \varepsilon_i$$

where $b_1, b_2 \ldots b_p$, and a are constants of the linear regression coefficient and ε_i is a random disturbance (error). It is assumed that for the IVs $x_1, x_2 \ldots x_p$, a linear equation provides an acceptable approximation of the true relationship between the DV, y, and the IVs, x_s. It is assumed that ε_i are random quantities which are independently and normally distributed with means of 0 and constant variance θ^2. The regression coefficient β_i determines the increment in y corresponding to a unit increase in x_i when all other variables are held constant. Similar to the simple regression, the b's are estimated by minimizing the residual sum of squares (MLS). We shall skip the algebraic calculation of the statistics a, $b_1, b_2 \ldots b_p$, and instead use our previous data on VO_2max, run (aerobic performance), and motivation (motiv), to illustrate how two IVs (VO_2max and motivation) predict (account for) the DV (long run-aerobic performance).

	VO$_2$max	Run	Motivation
1	56.00	576.00	56.00
2	35.00	720.00	37.00
3	71.00	510.00	60.00
4	37.00	700.00	50.00
5	24.00	810.00	42.00
6	67.00	540.00	55.00
7	37.00	710.00	40.00
8	65.00	536.00	51.00
9	62.00	581.00	55.00
10	53.00	561.00	43.00
11	57.00	548.00	57.00
12	42.00	687.00	39.00
13	48.00	667.00	43.00
14	39.00	688.00	45.00
15	34.00	705.00	37.00

First we start with a correlational matrix among all the variables:

Correlations

		aerobic performance	maximal oxygen uptake	motivation
Pearson Correlation	aerobic performance	1.000	-.969	-.777
	maximal oxygen uptake	-.969	1.000	.806
	motivation	-.777	.806	1.000
Sig. (1-tailed)	aerobic performance	.	.000	.000
	maximal oxygen uptake	.000	.	.000
	motivation	.000	.000	.
N	aerobic performance	15	15	15
	maximal oxygen uptake	15	15	15
	motivation	15	15	15

We notice that maximal oxygen uptake (VO$_2$max) is associated almost perfectly with the DV, aerobic performance (run). Also motivation is correlated strongly with the DV. The two IVs are strongly correlated (0.806) which indicates that collinearity between the DVs does exist. In this example we shall not make any corrections or adjustments which are required in such situations. We will proceed in the analysis. The descriptive statistics of the three variables are shown next. It is advisable to also examine the skewness and kurtosis, as well as multivariate distribution, in order to eliminate, or alternatively transform, some of the variables to run the regression analysis without any major violations.

Descriptive Statistics

	Mean	Std. Deviation	N
aerobic performance	635.9333	89.8479	15
maximal oxygen uptake	48.4667	14.2471	15
motivation	47.3333	7.9072	15

The first predictor (IV) in the equation is maximal oxygen uptake. The SPSS 11.0 produces the following analysis:

Variables Entered/Removed[b]

Model	Variables entered	Variables removed	Method
1	maximal oxygen uptake[a]	.	Enter

[a] All requested variables entered.
[b] Dependent variable: aerobic performance.

Model Summary[b]

Model	R	R Square	Adjusted R Square	Std. Error of the estimate
1	.969a	.939	.934	23.0555

[a] Predictors: (Constant), maximal oxygen upptake.
[b] Dependent variable: aerobic performance.

ANOVA[b]

Model		Sum of Squares	df	Mean Square	F	Sig.
1	Regeression	106106.725	1	106106.725	199.616	.000[a]
	Residual	6910.208	13	531.554		
	Total	113016.933	14			

[a] Predictors: (Constant), maximal oxygen upptake.

[b] Dependent variable: aerobic performance.

Coefficients[a]

Model		Unstandardized Coefficients		Standardied Coefficients s		
		B	Std. Error	Beta	t	Sig.
1	(Constant)	932.091	21.791		42.775	.000
	maximal oxygen uptake	-6.111	.432	-.969	-14.129	.000

[a] Dependent variable: aerobic performance.

Residuals Statistics[a]

	Minimum	Maximum	Mean	Std. Deviation	N
Predicted Value	498.2424	785.4379	635.9333	87.0577	15
Std. Predicted Value	-1.582	1.717	.000	1.000	15
Standard Error of Predicted Value	5.9563	12.1413	8.2316	1.8266	15
Adjusted Predicted Value	494.4200	776.0126	635.1207	87.0038	15
Residual	-47.2322	28.2151	5.684E-14	22.2168	15
Std. Residual	-2.049	1.224	.000	.964	15
Stud. Residual	-2.129	1.292	.016	1.026	15
Deleted Residual	-51.0011	33.9874	.8126	25.2720	15
Stud. Deleted Residual	-2.534	1.329	-.013	1.109	15
Mahal. Distance	.001	2.949	.933	.867	15
Cook's Distance	.000	.301	.070	.086	15
Centered Leverage Value	.000	.211	.067	.062	15

[a] Dependent variable: aerobic performance.

We see that the correlation between the predictor (VO_2max) and the predicted (aerobic performance-run) is 0.969, R^2 is 0.939 and R^2 adjusted for the number of participants is 0.934. This indicates that 93.4% of the aerobic performance variance is accounted for by maximal oxygen uptake. The analysis of variance (ANOVA, discussed in Part IV, Chapter 16) indicates that the regression is very significant ($p < .000$). Then the unstandardized and standardized regression coefficients are introduced (note that the standardized intercept, a, is zero). Both a and b are very significant. Next the standardized residual statistics are introduced. According to the regression line, the lowest and highest predicted values of aerobic run are given along with the mean and standard deviation. The standardized predictive values follow (mean = 0, SD = 1) along with the two residuals, which vary between –47.23 and 28.21 and in standardized form between –2.049 and 1.224, which is an indication of satisfactory conditions.

The second predictor, motivation, is entered second. Here are the various statistics supplied by SPSS 11.0.

Coefficients[a]

Model		B	Std. Error	Beta	t	Sig.
		Unstandardized Coefficients		Standardied Coefficients s		
1	(Constant)	9929.017	41.807		22.221	.000
	maximal oxygen uptake	-6.164	.760	-.977	-8.114	.000
	motivation	.120	1.369	.011	.088	.932

a Dependent variable: aerobic performance.

Residuals Statistics[a]

	Minimum	Maximum	Mean	Std. Deviation	N
Predicted Value	498.5528	786.1096	635.9333	87.0596	15
Residual	-46.4703	28.7092	7.958E-14	22.2097	15
Std. Predicted Value	-1.578	1.725	.000	1.000	15
Std. Residual	-1.937	1.197	.000	.926	15

a Dependent variable: aerobic performance.

CHARTS

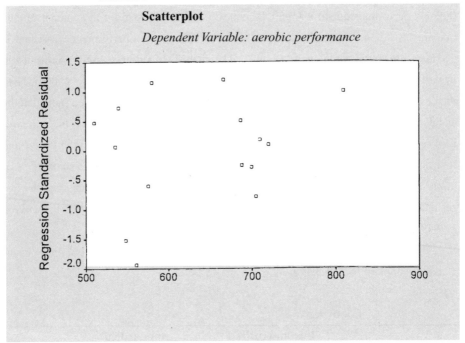

Scatterplot

Dependent Variable: aerobic performance

We can see that the coefficients a and b have not changed dramatically with the inclusion of motivation into the regression equation. However, because motivation is highly correlated with both VO_2max and aerobic performance, its regression coefficient was not significantly different from 0 and thus can be deleted from the equation. The standardized residuals were within the acceptable zone of -1.937 - 1.197.

Since motivation has not added significantly to the prediction of aerobic performance, we cannot rely on the R^2 change to indicate whether this change is significant. These statistics are of vital importance because it allows the researcher to decide whether he/she desires to include another variable in the model for relatively low contribution or not.

Just for curiosity, the residual statistics and 95% confidence interval for the regression coefficients when the two predictors are included in the equation are given and presented:

Residuals Statistics[a]

	Minimum	Maximum	Mean	Std. Deviation	N
Predicted Value	498.5528	786.1096	635.9333	87.0596	15
Std. Predicted Value	-1.578	1.725	.000	1.000	15
Standard Error of Predicted Value	7.9546	14.7814	10.5789	1.8466	15
Adjusted Predicted Value	494.3789	771.4880	635.7500	86.2462	15
Residual	-46.4703	28.7092	7.958E-14	22.2097	15
Std. Residual	-1.937	1.197	.000	.926	15
Stud. Residual	-2.173	1.277	.003	1.039	15
Deleted Residual	-58.4975	38.5120	.1833	28.1088	15
Stud. Deleted Residual	-2.672	1.316	-.036	1.143	15
Mahal. Distance	.606	4.382	1.867	1.013	15
Cook's Distance	.000	.408	.091	.129	15
Centered Leverage Value	.043	.313	.133	.072	15

[a] *Dependent variable: aerobic performance.*

Coefficients[a]

	95 % Confidence Interval for B	
Model	Lower Bound	Upper Bound
1 (Constant)	837.927	1020.107
maximal oxygen uptake	-7.819	-4.509
motivation	-2.863	3.102

[a] *Dependent Variable: aerobic performance*

The scatterplot of the observed and predicted regression values of aerobic performance looks as follows:

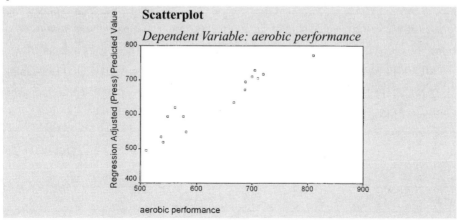

Scatterplot
Dependent Variable: aerobic performance

which is an indication of a very nice fit of the predicted to the observed aerobic performance observations.

Selection of Variables in a Regression Equation

There is no way to determine which method of selection of variables into the regression equation is the best. We may state that it is the strength of the THEORY which determines this. However, the PURPOSE for which an equation is constructed determines the criteria for selecting and evaluating the contributions of different variables. With respect to choosing the most appropriate set of variables into the regression equation, there may be several sets which represent several alternative solutions, and these solutions can be compared to each other later. "In fact, the process of variable selection should be viewed as an intense analysis of the correlational structure of the independent variables and how they individually and jointly affect the dependent variable under study" (Chatterjee and Price, 1977).

Regression equations are used for (a) description and model building, (b) estimation and prediction, and (c) control (the equation is viewed as a response function, with y as the "response variable" to changes in the x_i variables).

Criteria for Evaluating Equations

The most common way to evaluate the adequacy of fitted regression equations is through the RESIDUAL MEAN SQUARE (RMS). With k terms, the RMS is defined as:

$$(RMS)_k = \frac{(SSE)_k}{n-k} \tag{45}$$

where $(SSE)_k$ is the residual sum of squares for a k-term equation. Among various equations, the one with the smallest (RMS) is usually preferred. $(RMS)_k$ is associated with the MULTIPLE CORRELATION COEFFICIENT, R_k and the ADJUSTED (for sample size) MULTIPLE CORRELATION, R_{ak} as strong criteria of FIT. The relationship between $(RMS)_k$ and these measures is as follows:

$$R_k^2 = 1 - (n-k)\frac{(RMS)_k}{SST} \tag{46}$$

and

$$R_{ak}^2 = 1 - (n-1)\frac{(RMS)_k}{SST} \tag{47}$$

where

$$SST = \Sigma (y_i - \bar{y})^2$$

which is the total sum of squares.

Another measure of fit is through the examination of the MEAN SQUARE ERROR of the PREDICTED VALUE rather than the variance. This value is termed J_k and we shall avoid its presentation here.

Selection of Variables: Stepwise Procedures

In cases where many IVs exist, the stepwise procedure consists of adding or deleting IVs in the equation one at a time. With q variables, at most q + 1 equations are possible. There are two main classifications in stepwise procedure: (a) forward selection (FS) and (b) backward elimination (BE). We shall shortly discuss each of these next.

Forward Selection Procedure. This procedure begins with an equation that contains no IVs, but a constant term. The first IV in the equation is then chosen based on its highest simple correlation with the DV, y. If the regression coefficient of this IV is significantly different from 0, it is retained in the equation. The second IV is then chosen based on the highest correlation with the DV, y, after y has been adjusted for the association of the first IV, that is, the variable with the highest correlation coefficient with the residual from the previous step. The significance of the second variable is tested, and if it significantly differs from 0, a third IV is selected using identical criterion. The procedure is terminated once any of the remaining variables significantly contribute to the explained variance of the DV.

Backward Elimination Procedure. This procedure begins with the inclusion of all the variables in the equation and then dropping one variable at a time. The elimination consists of their contribution to the reduction of error sum of squares. The first variable eliminated is the one with the smallest contribution to the error sum of squares reduction (equivalent to having the smallest t ratio of its regression coefficient). The equation with the remaining q - 1 variables is then fitted and the t ratios for the new regression coefficients are examined. The procedure is terminated when all the t-ratios are significant, or all but one IV has been deleted.

6.6 Hierarchical (Cluster) Linear Regression

In cases where the sample of participants is relatively small, the number of variables is relatively large, and many of the variables share a latent trait, hierarchical linear regression may be one of the best solutions to examine how much variance of the DV can be accounted for by the "clusters" of the IVs.

We shall demonstrate this concept by example, without introducing the algebraic equations related to it. The principles of the hierarchical regression are similar to that of simple linear multivariate regression. In our example, 47 people who varied in age were tested for maximal oxygen consumption. A week later they were asked to run on a treadmill as long as they could while controlling their load on 90% VO_2max. They were given a "perceived exertion scale" every 30 seconds. Once they indicated "hard", the time lapse between this point and ceasing the run was termed "time in the zone of exertion tolerance". They were given several questionnaires which were clustered under three traits/states: goal orientation, coping strategies, and determination. Based on a sound theory, the order of entrance of clusters into the regression equation was predetermined. The results are presented in Table 3.13.

Table 3.13

Hierarchical Regression Coefficients using "Time in the Zone of Exertion Tolerance" as a DV and Goal Orientation, Coping Strategies, and Determination as IV Clusters

Dependent variable = *Time in the 'zone of exertion tolerance'*

Step	Variables	β	Multiple R	R^2	$\triangle R^2$
1	**Goal Orientation**		0.55	0.29	—
	Ego	0.21			
	Will to Win	-0.11			
	Competitive	-.03			
	Win	-0.35*			
	COI Outcome	-0.58*			
	Task	0.03			
	COI Performance	0.32*			
	Goal	0.13			
	Composite	-0.58*			

2	**Coping Strategies**		0.66		0.44	0.14
	Self Control	0.20				
	Perceived Physical Ability	0.02				
	Perceived Self Presentation	-0.14				
	Confidence	-0.07				
3	**Determination**		0.69		0.48	0.04
	Amount of Effort	-0.06				
	Commitment to Task	0.11				
	Perception of Tolerance	0.42*				

*$p < .05$

Goal orientation accounted for 29% of the variance of the DV, coping strategies added an additional 14% of accounted variance, and determination an additional 4% to be added to 48% accounted variance. The R^2 change is examined for significance, similar to the procedures described before. Among the regression coefficients of all the individual variables, only five were found to be significant.

If we decided to alter the entrance order of the clusters, then we could decide whether to delete the "determination" cluster from the regression equation or retain it, however this is a theoretical issue which should be determined by the researcher.

We then performed an additional and similar analysis, but the age of the participants was entered first and then the order remained similar to that of the previous equation. The results are presented in Table 3.14.

Table 3.14

Hierarchical Regression Coefficients using "Time in the Zone of Exertion Tolerance" as a DV and Age, Goal Orientation, Coping Strategies, and Determination as IV Clusters

Dependent variable = *Time in the 'zone of exertion tolerance'*

Step	Variables	β	Multiple R	R^2	$\triangle R^2$
1	*Age*	0.42*	0.42*	0.18	
2	*Goal Orientation*		0.63*	.40	0.22
	Ego	0.17			
	Will to Win	-0.05			
	Competitive	0.01			
	Win	-0.33*			
	COI Outcome	-1.39*			
	Task	0.02			
	COI Performance	1.27*			
	Goal	0.03			
	Composite	-2.20*			
3	*Coping Strategies*		0.67*	0.45	0.05
	Self Control	0.27			
	Perceived Physical Ability	0.06			
	Perceived Self Presentation	-0.13			
	Confidence	-.71*			
4	*Determination*		0.73*	0.53	0.08
	Amount of Effort	0.05			
	Commitment to Task	-0.03			
	Perception of Tolerance	0.34*			

*$p < .05$

It is clear that "age" was a strong determinant of exertion tolerance. It accounted for 18% of the DV variance. However, goal orientation added 22% accounted variance, which is very substantial. The coping strategies and determination clusters added 5% and 8% respectively to account for 53% of the exertion tolerance variance.

It should also be noticed that the inclusion of age as the first factor seriously altered some of the regression coefficients of the individual variables. This may be an indication of collinearity between age and these variables that has to be further remedied.

6.7   Multi-level (Hierarchical; Nested) Linear Models

Multi-level analysis refers to analysis of observations, which are NESTED within different levels. For example, we may observe performance of athletes in different countries, different clubs, and different coaches. All of these variables can be considered as units in the analysis where coaches are nested within clubs and clubs are nested within countries. This kind of analysis is termed MULTI-LEVEL or HIERARCHICAL.

Multi-level analysis is also reflected in longitudinal studies where multiple observations on persons are recorded. The observations are taken under various conditions and therefore the personal growth curves result in different trajectories. Also quantitative integration of findings of many studies can be viewed as multi-level if studies are nested within different research methods, use of instrumentation, treatments, etc. The number of levels is dependent on how many levels are nested with a broader level of categorization.

Bryk and Raudenbush (1992) describe in detail the properties, concepts, and the algebraic development of various types of multi-level linear models. Here we shall introduce the logic of these models as described by them. Let's assume that we measure attitudes toward banned drugs in sport as a function of the skill-level of athletes in one location. In this case

$$y_i = a + b_1 x_i + \varepsilon_i$$

or graphically as:

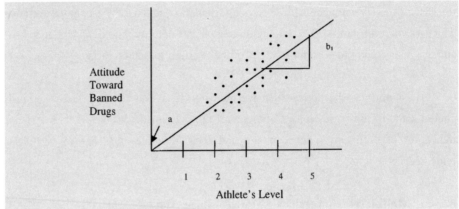

Figure 3.19   A Regression Line with Constants a and b_1 which Determine the Relations Between Athletic Level and Attitude Toward Banned Drugs in Sport.

where a is the expected attitudes of an athlete whose athletic level is 0. The slope b_1, is the expected change in attitude associated with one unit increase in athletic level. The error, ε_i, is associated with the unique effect of person i, ε_i' s are assumed to be normally distributed with mean 0 and variance θ^2, $\varepsilon_i \sim N(0, \theta^2)$. It is suggested to "center" the IV (athlete's level) by subtracting the mean of athletic level from each score: $x_i - \bar{x}_o$ where $\bar{x}_o$ is the mean athletic level in the club. When this is applied, the intercept a is the mean attitude toward banned drugs and the slope, b_1, remains unchanged. (Figure 3.20)

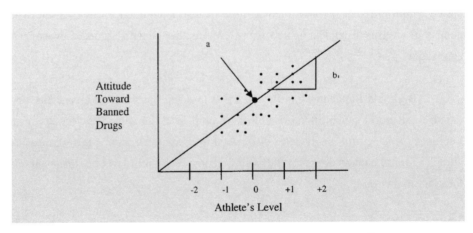

Figure 3.20   Figure 3.19 with Centering of Athletic Level (a) by $x_i - \bar{x}_o$.

Assume that the same attitude scale was administered to athletes in two different countries. For each country a "centered" regression line is computed and the scatterplot is presented in Figure 3.21.

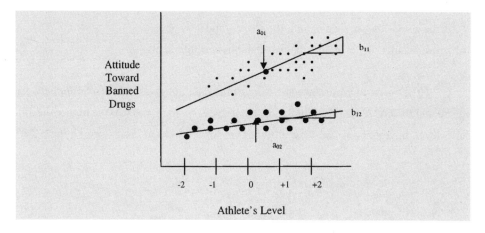

Figure 3.21   Regression Lines for Athletes of Two Countries after Centering (x_i –) each
Score in the Two Samples, Separately.

We can see that the mean attitude is higher in country 1 than in country 2 ($a_{01} > a_{02}$). Also athletes' level is more predictive of attitudes toward banned drugs in country 1 ($b_{11} > b_{12}$). The "effect" is indicated by the centered means of the two slopes ($a_{01} > a_{02}$) and the "equity" by the slopes ($b_{11} > b_{12}$).

Assume that attitudes toward banned drugs were sampled randomly in j countries in the world. The relationship between athletes' attitude and athletes' level within each j country is

$$y_{ij} = a_{0j} + b_{1j} (x_{ij} - \bar{x}_{oj}) + E_{ij} \qquad (46)$$

where ε_{ij} is normally distributed with homogeneous variance across countries, $\varepsilon_{ij} \sim N(0, \theta^2)$. Each country now has a unique intercept and slope (j) (i.e., each country has a unique a_{0j}-mean and b_{1j}-slope). It is assumed that a_0 and b_1 have a bivariate normal distribution across the population of countries.

$E(a_{0j}) = \gamma_0$, $var(a_{0j}) = \tau_{00}$

$E(b_{1j}) = \gamma_1$, $var(b_{1j}) = \tau_{11}$

$Cov(a_{0j}, b_{1j}) = \tau_{01}$

where

γ_0 is the average country mean for population of countries,

γ_{00} is the population variance among the country means,

γ_1 is the average athlete's level-attitude slope for the countries,

γ_{11} is the countries variance among the slopes, and

γ_{01} is the population covariance between slopes and intercepts.

The variance/covariance structure of the data indicates the correlation between the IV and the DV. A positive population covariance, τ_{01} indicates that the higher the athlete's level, the more positive their attitudes are toward banned drugs (see Figure 3.22).

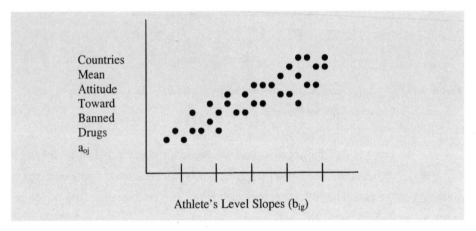

Figure 3.22   The Covariance (τ_{01}) Between Athlete's Level Slopes (b_{1j}) and Countries' Mean Attitudes (a_{0j}).

The correlation (p) between b_{1j} and a_{0j} is

$$P(a_{0j}, b_{1j}) = \tau_{01}/(\tau_{00} \cdot \tau_{11})^{1/2} \qquad (47)$$

Now when the countries vary in the mean and slopes which describe their athletes' attitudes toward banned drugs in sport, a model which predicts a_{0j} and b_{1j} from the data is required. In the example that was introduced, level 1 units are the athletes and the level 2 units are their countries. The PARAMETERS a and b in the LEVEL 1 MODEL are LEVEL 1 COEFFICIENTS and γ_s are the LEVEL-2 COEFFICIENTS. Bryk and Raudenbush (1992) further develop the various regression models associated with multilevel data structure, and show how intercepts and slopes of outcomes in each level are treated in the subsequent linear regression model. We refer the advanced students in statistics and matrix algebra to their book.

6.8   Canonical Analysis

The association between a set of dependent and a set of independent variables, or between two sets of variables, is termed a CANONICAL CORRELATION. The two sets, p and q, should be equal or greater than 2, p could be predictors and q criteria, or alternatively, the two sets could be mutually associated without a definite direction. As previously indicated, the direction is determined by the theory and logic. The idea is to form two linear combinations for x_p and x_q variables by differentially weighting them to obtain maximal possible associations between the two sets of variables. The linear combination, referred to as CANONICAL VARIATES, is the CANONICAL CORRELATION R_c. R^2_c represents the shared variance between the two canonical variates. However, as Pedhazur (1997) notes "R^2 is *not* an estimate of the variance shared between x_p and y_q, *but of linear combinations of these variables*" (p. 926).

Like in multiple regressions, canonical analysis seeks to determine a set of weights that will maximize the correlation coefficient. However, unlike in regression analysis where only the DVs are weighted, in canonical analysis both the Xs and Ys are differentially weighted. The principle consists of obtaining the pair x-y which yields the largest R_c in the given data set. The second R_c is then the linear combination of x's and y's which is the least correlated with the first pair and at the same time yields the second largest R_c in the data and so on. The largest number of pairs that can enter into the canonical analysis is equal to the number of the variables in the smallest set when $p \neq q$.

For example, assume we have laboratory tests and physical performance measures as follows:

Laboratory (x_p)	Field (y_q)
VO$_2$max	(a) 12 minute run
Anaerobic capacity:	
(1) average power	(b) 40 m sprint
(2) maximal power	(c) push-ups- 1 min
Anaerobic threshold	(d) pull-up (bar)

We measure N subjects in the four laboratory tests and the four field tests. The matrix of data consists of N subjects by p + q (or $x_p + y_q$) variables as follows:

Subject	x_p (laboratory)				y_q (field)			
1	x_{11}	x_{12}	x_{13}	x_{14}	y_{11}	y_{12}	y_{13}	y_{14}
2	x_{21}	x_{22}	x_{23}	x_{24}	y_{21}	y_{22}	y_{23}	y_{24}
3	x_{31}	x_{32}	x_{33}	x_{34}	y_{31}	y_{32}	y_{33}	y_{34}
4	x_{41}	x_{42}	x_{43}	x_{44}	y_{41}	y_{42}	y_{43}	y_{44}
$\vdots$	$\vdots$	$\vdots$	$\vdots$	$\vdots$	$\vdots$	$\vdots$	$\vdots$	$\vdots$
N	x_{N1}	x_{N2}	x_{N3}	x_{N4}	y_{N1}	y_{N2}	y_{N3}	y_{N4}

N = number of cases, p = number of x variables, q = number of y variables.

Usually the data is transformed into deviations or standard scores. Correlations are computed among the variables to constitute a correlation matrix R. This matrix is also partitioned. In Table 3.15, the broken line signifies the partitioning.

Table 3.15

Partitioned Correlation Matrix for Canonical Analysis

	x			y		
	1	2	... p	1	2	... p
1 2 $\vdots$ p	Rxx			Rxy		
1 2 $\vdots$ q	Ryx			Ryy		

The four partitions of the matrix are succinctly stated as

$$R = \begin{bmatrix} R_{xx} & R_{xy} \\ R_{yx} & R_{yy} \end{bmatrix}$$

where R is the supermatrix of all possible correlations, R_{xx} are the correlations among the x_p variables, R_{yy} are the correlations among the y_q variables, R_{xy} are the correlations between the x_p and the y_q variables, and R_{yx} is the transpose of R_{xy}. These matrices are used in the solution of the canonical analysis problem. As previously mentioned, the number of canonical correlations is equal to the number of variables in the smaller set of variables. The canonical correlations are equal to the square roots of the eigenvalues, or characteristic roots of the determinatal equation that we shall not present in this book. We refer the readers to Pedhazur (1997, pp. 924-959) for detailed analyses and calculations which require understanding in matrix algebra.

In illustrating q = 2, p = 2 correlational matrix, Pedhazur arrived at two eigenvalues:

$$\lambda_1 = 0.27740$$
$$\lambda_2 = 0.00490$$

Taking the positive square roots of the λ's

$$R_{c1} = \sqrt{\lambda_1} = \sqrt{.27740} = .52669$$
$$R_{c2} = \sqrt{\lambda_2} = \sqrt{.00490} = .07000$$

R_c^2 indicates the proportion of variance shared by a pair of canonical variates to which it corresponds. The first pair shared about 28% and the second pair about 0.7%. This can be examined for significance; however, $R_c^2 < .10$ (10% shared variance) is considered to be not meaningful.

CANONICAL WEIGHTS are then calculated for each R_c that is retained. The canonical weights are used to exert MEANINGFULNESS or STATISTICAL SIGNIFI-CANCE of the R_c. The λ values are used for this purpose. With respect to the above λ values, Pedhazur (1997, pp. 930-933) calculated two weights for the two DV, y_1 and y_2 which are 0.49304 and 0.59086. These are standardized coefficients (2 scores) which are associated with the first canonical correlation R_{c1}. This weight is symbolized as β_1. The canonical weights of the x's were 0.74889 for x_1 and 0.35141 for x_2. These standardized canonical weights are interpreted similarly to the interpretation given to linear regression weights. From the results demonstrated here one may conclude that the weights of y_1 and y_2 (0.49 and 0.59) are both important, but the weight of x_1 is much more important than the weight of x_2 (0.74 > 0.35). As canonical weights have several shortcomings, several statisticians recommend using STRUCTURE COEFFICIENT instead.

STRUCTURE COEFFICIENTS (i.e., LOADINGS) are the CORRELATION between ORIGINAL variables and CANONICAL VARIATES. In other words, structure coefficient is the correlation between a given variable and the canonical variate scores on a given function. In calculating these correlations, Pedhazur (1997, p. 933) found that the correlation between x_1 and the first canonical variate is 0.96, and that between x_2 and the first canonical variate is 0.80. Similarly x_1 and x_2 correlate with the second canonical variate -0.28 and 0.60 respectively. The results for the y's were 0.90 and 0.93 between y_1 and y_2 and the first variate, and 0.42 and -0.35 with the second variate. These findings are shown in the form:

$$S_x \qquad\qquad S_y$$
$$\begin{bmatrix} .95974 & -.28194 \\ .80074 & .59586 \end{bmatrix} \begin{bmatrix} .90664 & .42170 \\ .93600 & -.35236 \end{bmatrix}$$

As a rule of thumb, a structure coefficient ≥ 0.30 is treated as meaningful. Since the second canonical correlation was not meaningful, its structural coefficient (-0.28) was not meaningful. With larger numbers of variables, the structure coefficients on given canonical variates are interpreted similarly to loadings in factor analysis. They provide means of identifying the dimensions on which they load. If, for example, we had only two variables of the laboratory test (x_p) with meaningful weights on the first canonical variate, say VO_2max and anaerobic threshold, we could conclude that the first canonical variate reflects "aerobic capacity". Similar interpretation is given to the y's, in our previous example—field tests (y_q).

The structure coefficients can easily be transferred into "accounted variance" proportion. In Pedhazur's example the first canonical variate accounts for about 92% of the variance of x_1 (0.95974^2 x 100) and for about 64% (0.80074^2 x 100) of the variance of x_2. Similarly the first canonical variate accounts for about 82% and 88% of the variance of y_1 and y_2, respectively.

The sum of squared structure coefficients of a set of variables (i.e., x's or y's) on a given canonical variate indicates the amount of variance of the set that is accounted for by the canonical variate. Dividing the amount of variance extracted by the number of variables in the set (i.e., p for the x's and q for the y's) yields a proportion of its total variance that is extracted by the canonical variate. In pp. 934-936 Pedhazur demonstrates the calculations of PV_{xj} and PV_{yj}—the proportion of the total variance of the x's extracted by canonical variate j and similarly for y's by q variables. He found that:

$PV_{x1} = 0.78114 \rightarrow$ 78% of the total variance extracted by the 1st canonical variate

$PV_{x2} = 0.21727 \rightarrow$ 22% of the total variance extracted by the 2nd canonical variate

$PV_{y1} = 0.84965 \rightarrow$ 85% of the total variance of y's is extracted by the 1st canonical variate

$PV_{y2} = 0.15099 \rightarrow$ 15% of the total variance of y's is extracted by the 2nd canonical variate.

Note that the sum of variance extracted by the canonical variates is always 1.00 (100%). When the sets consist of unequal number of variables, this sum will be smaller than 1.00. The PV's are playing an important role in the examination of REDUNDANCY, but it should be kept in mind that those canonical weights and structures should be cross-validated before any generalization can be made.

The REDUNDANCY (Rd) is defined as:

$$Rd_{xj} = PV_{xj} \, R^2_{cj} \qquad (48)$$

In the Pedhazur example $PV_{x1} = 0.78114$ and $PV_{x2} = 0.21727$, $R^2_{c1} = 0.27740$ and $R^2_{c2} = 0.00490$, and therefore

$Rd_{x1} = (0.78114)(0.27740) = 0.21669$

which indicates that about 22% of the total variance of the x's is accounted for by the first canonical variate (linear combination) of the y's, and

$Rd_{x2} = (0.21727)(0.00490) = 0.00106$

which means that only 0.1% of the total variance of the x's is accounted for by the second canonical variate (linear combination) of the y's.

The total redundancy of x, given all linear combinations of y's is

$$\overline{Rd_x} = \sum Rd_{xj} \qquad (49)$$

and in the Pedhazur example

$$\overline{Rd}_x = 0.21669 + 0.00106 = 0.21775$$

and this is equal to the average of squared multiple correlations of each of the x's with all the y's (see Pedhazur, 1997, p. 937). Similarly,

$$Rd_{yj} = PV_{yj}R^2_{cj} \qquad (50)$$

and in the Pedhazur example

$$Rd_{y1} = (0.84905)(0.27746) = 0.23553$$

which means that about 24% of total variance of y's is predictable from the first linear combination (canonical variate) of the x's, and

$$Rd_{y2} = (0.15099)(0.00490) = 0.0074$$

In other words, 0.07% of the total variance of y's is predictable with the second canonical variate of the x's.

$$\overline{Rd}_y = \Sigma\, Rd_{yj} \qquad (51)$$

and $\qquad \overline{Rd}_y = 0.23553 + 0.00074 = 0.23627$

that is, about 24% of the y's variance is accounted for by the two canonical variates. As can be seen $\overline{Rd}_{yj} \neq \overline{Rd}_{xy}$.

Pedhazur also introduces the Bartlett's (1947) test of Wilk's Λ (lambda) to examine the significance of Rc^2 using x^2 distribution with df = (p-1)(q-1) (see pp. 939-940). He then introduces a CANONICAL ANALYSIS with a CATEGORICAL INDEPENDENT VARIABLE (pp. 947-951) which we recommend reading.

6.9   Factors, Clusters, Groups - Associations

An additional application of the association among variables is the REDUCTION of the number of variables based on the relations among them. A correlation between two variables does not automatically indicate that they belong to the same domain, content, or concept. Once a concept has been developed, clusters of variables have been established, and variables operationalized, the correlational-based analysis is designed to EXPLORE or CONFIRM the relationships and their directions. Basically there are two processes: EXPLORATORY and CONFIRMATORY.

The EXPLORATORY process of clustering/factoring variables is applied when the researcher establishes a new concept and operational definitions (i.e., instrumentation). At a second stage, the relations among the variables are estimated in an exploratory nature. The researcher is not imposing his/her concept on the relationship among the variables. Thus the variables, $V_1, V_2 \ldots V_{10}$ can have the following structure (see Figure 3.23).

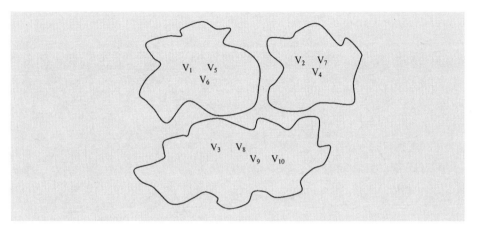

Figure 3.23   Possible Structure of 10 Variables.

In the hypothetical example, the relationships among the variables within the shapes are stronger than the relationships between them and the variables in the other shapes. However, if the researcher was not confident that indeed these relationships definitely do exist, he/she then explores them, and is required to CROSS-VALIDATE it in more samples. The relationships among the 10 variables could be different (see Figure 3.24).

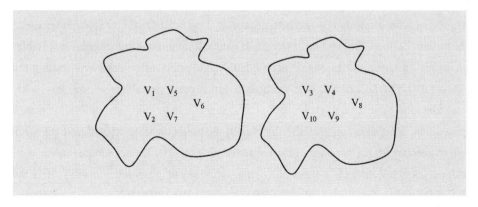

Figure 3.24   Possible Structure of the 10 Variables.

The CONFIRMATORY process consists of a WELL ESTABLISHED CONCEPT/THEORY, which postulates precisely the relations among the variables. For example, five tests of aerobic (A) capacity should be more strongly correlated among themselves than with five tests of anaerobic (An) capacity. The aerobic tests do not have to share very strong associations, but stronger than with the anaerobic tests and vice-versa (see Figure 3.25).

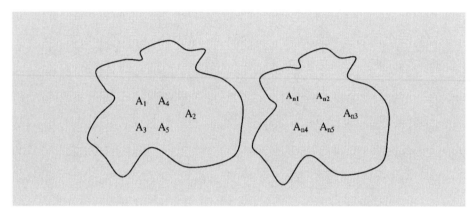

Figure 3.25   Two Clusters/Factors of Aerobic (A) and Anaerobic (An) Tests.

Our presentation will start with EXPLORATORY FACTOR ANALYSIS, a procedure that helps the researcher to explore the relationships among many variables and clarify the dimensions/clusters/factors, which underlie them.

6.10   *Exploratory Factor Analysis (EFA)*

Factor analysis (FA) results usually in DATA REDUCTION. When clusters/factors are defined, the scores of individuals can be transformed from scores on variables to scores on clusters/dimensions/factors. Unlike the previous correlational techniques, FA is an INTERDEPENDENCE method in which many variables are simultaneously considered to be related to each other. Unlike regression or canonical analysis, the purpose of FA is not to account for the variance of the predictor variable or variate (cluster), but to account for the variance of the entire variable set. The factor (variate) can be considered as a DV, that is, a function of the entire set of observed variables. It is the IDENTIFICATION OF A STRUCTURE (i.e., INTERDEPENDENCE). In exploratory FA (EFA), no constraints are imposed on the data set (i.e., measured variables).

Thus, the aim of EFA is to condense the number of variables into several variates (factors) without losing too much information. According to Hair *et al.* (1995), EFA has three objectives:

(1) Identification of relationships among either variables or respondents. R-FA identifies the dimensions that are latent (not observed). Q-FA identifies groups of respondents which share similar clusters of responses.

(2) Identification of the most representative variables for subsequent analyses.

(3) Establishment of new variable set for use in subsequent analyses.

To pursue FA, one should take care of several issues:

(1) The measurement of the variables should be metric (interval/ratio, but also ordered, like attitude scales). If the response format is dichotomous, other methods of analysis should be applied.

(2) A sufficient number of variables should a priori share a content or dimension, even though the procedure is exploratory and not confirmatory. At least five variables per dimension/factor are typically recommended.

(3) The rule of thumb is to sample at least five times more observations than variables. Some propose even 20 times more observations. When k variables are measured, $k(k-1)/2$ correlations result. Twenty variables will result in 20 $(20-1)/2 = 190$ correlations. Thus considering $p < .05$, 9-10 correlations will be significant by chance, and we would never know which of these were true. A high observation by variable ratio is desirable.

Any departure from normality, homoscendastivity, and linearity may diminish the observed correlations, and subsequently the resulting factors. Some collinearity among the variables is required, because variables that share variance are expected to share the same factor/dimension.

We shall illustrate now, by example, the procedures and results of EFA. We use data gathered on 10 variables, VAR1, VAR2, ..., VAR10 which represent motives for children's participation in sport after school hours. The sample was comprised of 607 children from an urban environment, ranging in age between 14 and 16 years. The 10 items had a Likert-type format ranging from "1"—not at all to "5"—very much. We used the SPSS 11.0 version to factor analyze the data. The descriptive statistics (means and standard deviations) and the correlations among the 10 variables [10(10-1)/2 = 45 correlations] are presented below:

Factor Analysis

Descriptive Statistics

	Mean	Std. Deviation	Analysis N
VAR00001	3.6030	.9676	607
VAR00002	3.2273	1.1291	607
VAR00003	3.1269	1.1149	607
VAR00004	3.2735	1.0629	607
VAR00005	3.0840	1.1708	607
VAR00006	3.0692	1.0939	607
VAR00007	2.6903	1.0653	607
VAR00008	2.9176	1.0146	607
VAR00009	3.4152	1.0207	607
VAR00010	3.3081	1.0368	607

Correlation Matrix

		VAR00001	VAR00002	VAR00003	VAR00004	VAR00005	VAR00006
Correlation	VAR00001	1.000	.722	.334	.430	.290	.378
	VAR00002	.722	1.000	.412	.482	.357	.443
	VAR00003	.334	.412	1.000	.603	.682	.335
	VAR00004	.430	.482	.603	1.000	.581	.360
	VAR00005	.290	.357	.682	.581	1.000	.302
	VAR00006	.378	.443	.335	.360	.302	1.000
	VAR00007	.322	.421	.533	.487	.592	.493
	VAR00008	.348	.428	.488	.486	.539	.442
	VAR00009	.398	.383	.258	.327	.270	.394
	VAR00010	.458	.512	.333	.445	.365	.341

	VAR00007	VAR00008	VAR00009	VAR00010
Correlation VAR00001	.322	.348	.398	.458
VAR00002	.421	.428	.383	.512
VAR00003	.533	.488	.258	.333
VAR00004	.487	.486	.327	.445
VAR00005	.592	.539	.270	.365
VAR00006	.493	.442	.394	.341
VAR00007	1.000	.746	.281	.357
VAR00008	.746	1.000	.371	.410
VAR00009	.281	.371	1.000	.484
VAR00010	.357	.410	.484	1.000

KMO and Bartlett's Test

Kaiser-Meyer-Olkin Measure of Sampling Adequacy.		.868
Bartlett's Test of Sphericity	Approx. Chi-Square	2931.723
	df	45
	Sig.	.000

From the examination of means, standard deviations, and normality (skewness and kurtosis—not in this output), it was evident that there were no deviations from normality, and therefore the correlational analysis could proceed. The magnitude of the correlations indicates that the majority of them are above 0.30. It is possible to further examine these correlations by asking for PARTIAL CORRELATIONS or ANTI-IMAGE correlations (the negative value of the partial correlation) to ensure that after partialling out the other variables, variance remains meaningful (i.e., controlling for the accounted variance of other variables). Small partial correlations are indicative of "true" factors existence. The Bartlett test or sphericity (i.e., test of presence of correlations among the variables) shows that the 45 correlations share a high degree of association among them. Also the Measure of Sampling Adequacy (MSA; Kaiser-Meyer-Olkin) indicates that the sample is highly adequate (0.90-1.00—very high; .80-.89—high; .70-.79—middle; .60-.69—mediocre; .50-.59—low; <.50—unacceptable).

Once the correlations were computed, a decision about the method and number of extracted factors should be made. Two basic methods are of use for meeting this aim: COMMON FA and PRINCIPLE COMPONENT ANALYSIS (PCA). The total variance in FA consists of (1) common, (2) specific (unique), and (3) error. COMMON VARIANCE is the variance shared by each variable and all the other variables in the analysis. SPECIFIC/UNIQUE VARIANCE is the one which characterizes ONLY the VARIABLE. ERROR VARIANCE is due to MEASUREMENT ERROR (i.e., UNRE-LIABILITY) or RANDOM COMPONENT in the MEASUREMENT. Thus, in Principle Component Analysis (PCA) we derive factors that contain much common variance and small unique variance. COMMUNALITIES are ESTIMATES of SHARED/COMMON VARIANCE and are used to extract the factors/dimensions, which underlie the variables' associations/correlations. In our example the communalities were moderate to high, indicating high common variance.

Communalities

	Initial	Extraction
VAR00001	1.000	.686
VAR00002	1.000	.700
VAR00003	1.000	.674
VAR00004	1.000	.589
VAR00005	1.000	.730
VAR00006	1.000	.420
VAR00007	1.000	.700
VAR00008	1.000	.641
VAR00009	1.000	.495
VAR00010	1.000	.555

Extraction Method: Principal Component Analysis

Now we must decide about the CRITERIA for the number of factors to be extracted. Theoretically, the extraction of the largest and most representative number of factors is recommended, and then after examination of the data, to reduce the number of variables within each factor. The most often used Criterion for this purpose is termed

LATENT ROOT or EIGENVALUE (λ). Only $\lambda > 1.00$ is considered substantial. Usually factors with $\lambda < 1.0$ are disregarded because their additional common variance is negligible. Another criterion is the A PRIORI CRITERION, which is applied when the researcher planned in advance the items and clusters, and is now interested in verifying them. However, in such cases we recommend the application of the CONFIRMATORY FA techniques. The eigenvalue indicates the PERCENT of EXPLAINED OR ACCOUNTED for VARIANCE. Usually when $\lambda < 1.0$, the additional variance accounted for is very small. The SCREE TEST is frequently used to identify the optimal number of factors that should be extracted before the amount of unique variance dominates the common variance (particularly the factors in which $\lambda < 1.0$). In the Scree Test the latent roots are plotted against the number of factors in their order of extraction. The shape of the curve is used to determine the number of extracted factors. Below is the Scree Test for our data:

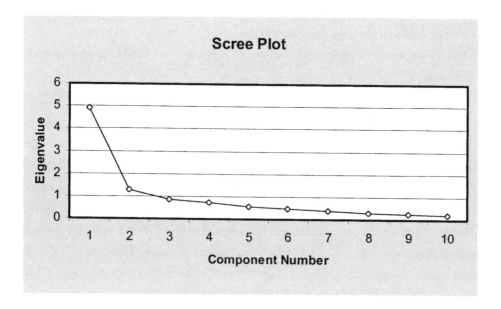

The first and second factors share $\lambda > 1.0$, however from the 3rd factor on the line becomes horizontal. The point where the line straightens out is used as a "cutting point" of the number of factors to be extracted. In the above example it is clear that two factors are sufficient to account for the portion of total variance. The computer program follows this criterion as well.

Initial Eigenvalues			Extraction Sums of Squared Loadings			Rotation
Component	% of	Cumulative		% of	Cumulative	Sums of
Total	Variance %		Total	Variance %		Total
1 4.915	49.149	49.149	4.915	49.149	49.149	4.235
2 1.275	12.750	61.899	1.275	12.750	61.899	3.896
3 .842	8.417	70.316				
4 .726	7.260	77.576				
5 .567	5.675	83.251				
6 .476	4.760	88.011				
7 .400	4.001	92.012				
8 .306	3.056	95.068				
9 .262	2.615	97.684				
10 .232	2.316	100.000				

Extraction Method: Principal Component Analysis

[a] *When components are correlated, sums of squared loadings cannot be added to obtain a total variance.*

The first component with $\lambda = 4.91$ accounted for 49.15% of the total variance while the second component with $\lambda = 1.275$ accounted for an additional 12.75% of the variance, totalling together 61.9% of the accounted variance. The other components together accounted for 38.1% of the variance. Had we decided to choose three factors, 70.32% (61.899 + 8.417) of the total variance was accounted for. With four factors 77.58% (70.316 + 7.260) variance was accounted for. It is the researcher who should make this decision. The computer extracts the number of variables based on $\lambda > 1.0$. In our example the number of factors is two. It should be noted that the FIRST FACTORS DISCRIMINATE less than the LATEST FACTORS among the participants who responded to the stimuli. This is an additional component that should be taken into consideration when deciding upon the number of extracted factors. As Hair *et al.* (1995) state "the factor analyst should always strive to have the most representative and parsimonious set of factors possible" (p. 379).

To further determine the variables which LOAD (i.e., are associated) on the higher-level dimension, several methods exist. An UNROTATED SOLUTION consists of estimation of LOADINGS of each VARIABLE, which represent the best linear combination of variables among the other possible linear combinations. Thus, the 1st factor is viewed as representing the best linear relation among the variables; the second factor is viewed as the second best linear choice that is ORTHOGONAL to the FIRST FACTOR, and so on with the third, fourth, etc. It should be noted that EACH SUBSEQUENT FACTOR being orthogonal to the previous one means that its accounted variance relates to the REMAINING VARIANCE left by the previous factors (i.e., it accounts for the RESIDUAL VARIANCE). The FACTOR LOADINGS represent the CORRELATION between the VARIABLES and the FACTORS. The higher the LOADING on the FACTOR, the more representative the variable is on that factor. However, to better account for the total variance and to reduce the residual variance, it is desired to ROTATE the FACTORS so that a more OPTIMAL solution can be found. The un-rotated solutions for our data with two proposed factors are as follows:

Component Matrix[a]

	Component	
	1	2
VAR00001	.661	.499
VAR00002	.736	.398
VAR00003	.723	-.389
VAR00004	.752	-.153
VAR00005	.724	-.455
VAR00006	.631	.147
VAR00007	.761	-.348
VAR00008	.762	-.244
VAR00009	.572	.409
VAR00010	.663	.340

Extraction Method: Principal Component Analysis

[a] *2 components extracted.*

It can be seen that ALL 10 variables load higher on the first factor than on the second one. Now we shall examine whether a ROTATION of the FACTORS will alter or sustain this factor structure.

ROTATION of factors means that the REFERENCE AXES of the factors are turned about the origin until some position is reached. The rotation redistributes the variance from the factors extracted earlier to achieve a more sensitive and representative clustering solution. When the axes are rotated in 90°, the rotation is termed ORTHOGONAL. When not constrained to 90°, the rotation is termed OBLIQUE (see Figure 3.26).

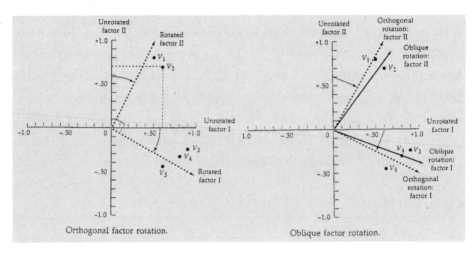

Figure 3.26   Orthogonal (Upper Panel) and Oblique Factor Rotation (from Hair *et al.* 1995, p. 381).

As can be seen, the oblique rotation is much more flexible than the orthogonal rotation because the axes can move (iterate) until the best solution is found. In this regard, an orthogonal solution is a special case of oblique rotation. The oblique rotation assumes that the factors/dimensions are correlated among themselves. Only rarely two or more dimensions do not share any variance. There are several orthogonal solutions (QUARTIMAX, VARIMAX, and EQUIMAX) and several oblique rotations (OBLIMIN, PROMAX, ORTHOBLIQUE, OQUART, DOBLIMIN, and ORTHOBLIQUE). They all result in a very similar FACTOR STRUCTURE (see Hair *et al.* 1995, pp. 384-385 for a short and clear explanation).

A loading above 0.30 or under –0.30 is considered to be associated with the dimension on which it loads; 0.40 or 0.50 are more conservative estimates. Loadings, more than correlations, are subjected to error and therefore should be treated more carefully than correlations. One can use a POWER level with a given probability (say $p < .05$), and number of responses to decide upon acceptance of the factor loadings. Significance is determined with sample size as follows:

Load	Sample Size Required for Significance
.30	350
.35	250
.40	200
.45	150
.50	120
.55	100
.60	85
.65	70
.70	60
.75	50

Hair *et al.* (1995) summarizes the criteria for choosing variables' loading as representing a factor/dimension as follows:

(1) the larger the sample size, the smaller the loading to be considered significant.

(2) the larger the number of variables, the smaller the loading to be considered significant.

(3) the larger the number of factors, the larger the size of the loadings on the later factors to be considered significant for interpretation as they contain more unique and error variance.

SPSS 11.0 was used to rotate the two factors of our data. OBLIMIN (OBLIQUE) ROTATION was applied. Two matrices, similar to canonical analysis, were obtained, one PATTERN MATRIX and the second STRUCTURE MATRIX. The Pattern matrix is more DISCRIMINATIVE among the two, though the final solutions are similar.

Since the two factors correlate 0.537, many items load significantly on the two factors. It is recommended to leave the higher of the two in its location and to keep in mind that it accounts also for the variance of the other factors.

Though not a desirable situation, it occurs many times. In our example the first factor consists of the following variables: 3, 4, 5, 7, 8, and the second factor consists of variables: 1, 2, 6, 9, 10.

Pattern Matrix

	Component	
	1	2
VAR00001	-8.784E-02	.872
VAR00002	6.057E-02	.803
VAR00003	.844	-4.557E-02
VAR00004	.625	.222
VAR00005	.911	-.115
VAR00006	.247	.481
VAR00007	.827	1.835E-02
VAR00008	.724	.129
VAR00009	5.326E-02	.731
VAR00010	7.320E-02	.703

Extraction Method: Principal Component Analysis.

Rotation Method: Oblimin with Kaiser Normalization.

[a] *Rotation converged in 6 iterations.*

Structure Matrix

	Component	
	1	2
VAR00001	.380	.825
VAR00002	.491	.835
VAR00003	.820	.407
VAR00004	.744	.558
VAR00005	.849	.374
VAR00006	.505	.614
VAR00007	.837	.462
VAR00008	.793	.518
VAR00009	.339	.702
VAR 00010	.451	.742

Extraction Method: Principal Component Analysis.

Rotation Method: Oblimin with Kaiser Normalization.

Component Correlation Matrix

Component	1	2
1	1.000	.537
2	.537	1.000

Extraction Method: Principal Component Analysis.
Rotation Method: Oblimin with Kaiser Normalization.

To make MEANING of the factors/dimensions which underlie the 10 variables, one should return to the items/variables contents. The 10 items represent motives of children to participate in sport after school hours. Here are the items' contents, which correspond to each factor:

Factor 1: AFFECTIVITY		Factor 2: FITNESS/ATTRACTIVENESS	
3	fun	1	strong
4	happiness	2	fit
5	enjoyment	6	look good
7	enthusiasm	9	healthy
8	tension reduction	10	attractive

It is clear that the five items in the first factor relate to emotions and enjoyment (i.e., affectivity) while the other five items relate to fitness, health, and attractiveness. Thus, the CONTENT and ESSENCE of the items enable us to LABEL or find the COM-MON CONCEPT that underlies the items, tests, components, etc. It should be noted that though the first factor accounted for most of the variance, this does not mean that it is perceived as the most important. To exert this, one should establish two scales, one for affectivity and another for fitness/attractiveness, standardize their scores (Z-transformation or sum of items/number of items), calculate means, standard deviations, and conduct the appropriate test for the significance of mean difference.

Hair *et al.* (1995) recommends that several procedures should be taken into account when interpreting the factor analysis results:

(1)   Observe the PATTERN MATRIX, which represents loading of the unique contribution of each variable to the factor. Then observe the STRUCTURE

MATRIX, which contains correlation between the variables and the factors (contains both unique variance and correlations among the factors). Most analysts report the pattern matrix.

2)   Underline the highest loading of each variable among all the factors (go from right to left for each variable throughout all the columns).

(3)   Variables with low communalities (say half of the variance of each variable should be accounted for) and non-significant loadings be considered for deletion.

(4)   Name the factors based on the content they SHARE (items with higher loading deserve more attention in this matter). Signs of loadings are interpreted as correlations are interpreted. A negative or positive sign of the loading relates ONLY to the FACTORS to which it is assigned.

Factor scores, which derive from the factor loadings, can be rotated again to verify whether HIGHER-ORDER DIMENSIONS exist. This is particularly true when the resulting factors correlate moderately to strongly. This concept is presented in Figure 3.27:

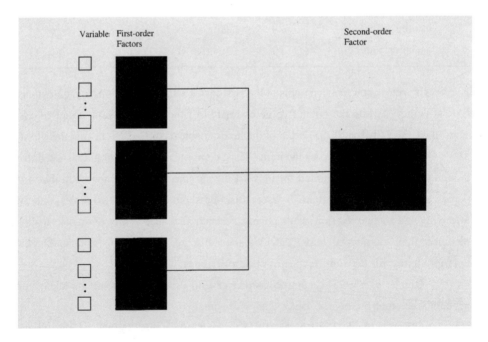

Figure 3.27   First-order and Second-order Factor Structure.

Generalizability can be obtained by cross-validation of the factors. Different samples from different locations, countries, regions, etc. can be measured on the same variables and an EFA be performed on their responses. Once a theory was established, a confirmatory FA (CFA) can be used to evaluate the replicability of the results. A multi-group CFA can also be carried out for this purpose. To ensure stability of the factor pattern/structure, a sufficient number of observation/variable ratios is required. Needless to say that screening the data prior to the analysis for outlier detection and normality assumptions confirmation are of the utmost importance.

Factor Analysis allows us to establish FACTOR SCORES for each individual in the sample. Factor scores or summated scales/surrogate variables are used for further analyses which are aimed by the research objectives and questions. If the further analyses are performed on the same sample, then factor scores are preferable.

However, factor scores are different for different samples, because both the loadings and the correlations among the factors vary. Therefore, summated scores are preferable in such cases.

6.11   Cluster Analysis

Cluster analysis enables us to search for "natural" structures among observations based on multivariate profiles. Individuals or items within the clusters share more variance among them than with individuals or items in other clusters with respect to predetermined selection criteria.

The distances (plotted geometrically) between individuals and clusters indicate how strongly they are associated. The CLUSTER VARIATE consists of several variables, which represent the traits/states under examination, and is determined by the researcher. Thus cluster analysis COMPARES OBJECTS on the VARIATE, but does not estimate the variate itself. The researcher concept and operational definitions are of utmost importance.

Cluster analysis groups OBJECTS while factor analysis groups VARIABLES. Cluster analysis can be demonstrated by plotting two variables on which a sample of subjects should be measured. The plot is presented in Figure 3.28.

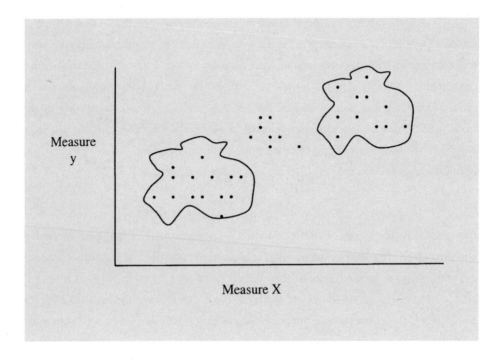

Figure 3.28   Plotting Observations on Measures x and y.

We can see that the observations can be classified into two independent clusters. The measures which are not classified to either of the clusters are termed ENTROPY GROUP.

Cluster analysis can be EXPLORATORY or CONFIRMATORY, depending on the state and soundness of the theory. The variables, which are selected for the establishment of clusters, should be derived from this theory. Variables that are not distinctive across the clusters should be eliminated, so that the other variables under consideration may better classify the objects/measures which constitute the sample of observations.

The first stage in performing cluster analysis is DETECTION of OUTLIERS. Outliers distort the TRUE STRUCTURE and therefore the resulting clusters do not reliably represent the population. Outliers can be identified by plotting PROFILES of the observation on all the variables, as presented in Figure 3.29.

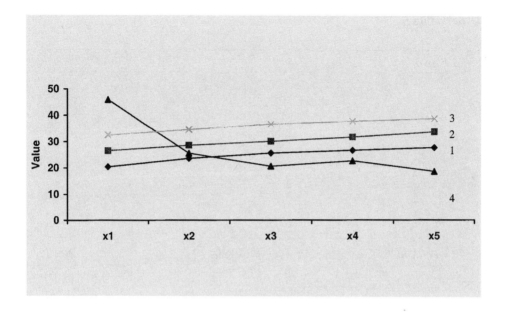

Figure 3.29   Profiles of Observations.

The profile of observation four is substantially different from the others, and therefore, should be deleted. When the number of variables and/or observations is very large, residual analysis, or multivariate normality procedures can be applied to detect outliers.

Like in factor analysis, INTEROBJECT SIMILARITY is a measure which is carried out to indicate how similar the observations are in the data set. When the similarity characteristics are defined, all pairs of objects are compared to each other. In this process, similar observations are grouped together.

Three methods dominate the cluster establishment: CORRELATIONAL MEASURES, DISTANCE MEASURES, and ASSOCIATION MEASURES. The former two consist of matrix data and the last one of non-metric data.

To achieve a PATTERN CORRESPONDENCE across characteristics, the data (rows and columns) are inverted, i.e., columns represent the observations and rows the variables, such as in the following chart:

Observation

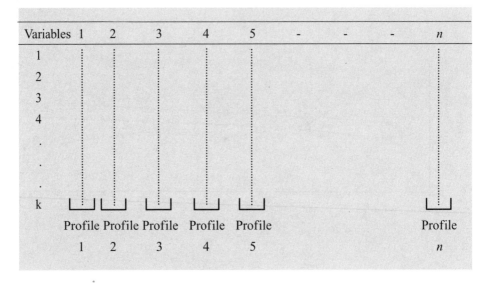

Variables	1	2	3	4	5	-	-	-	n
1									
2									
3									
4									
.									
.									
.									
k									

Profile 1　Profile 2　Profile 3　Profile 4　Profile 5　　　　Profile n

Thus, the numbers of profiles are equal to the number of observations, but the correlations indicate HOW MUCH the PROFILES are ASSOCIATED with each other (like a Q-type factor analysis). The CORRELATION represents a PATTERN ACROSS THE VARIABLES.

High correlations indicate that the observations share similar profiles/patterns and vice-versa. In cluster analysis, correlations are rarely used because the magnitudes are of the utmost importance. Instead DISTANCE MEASURES, which represent PROXIMITY of observations across all VARIABLES in the CLUSTER VARIATE, are used more frequently.

Small distances among the measures are indicators of greater similarity. Correlational clusters indicate similar patterns. Distance clusters indicate similarity in values across the set of variables, but not necessarily similar patterns.

The EUCLIDEAN DISTANCE is the most commonly used measure to illustrate the similarity between two observations:

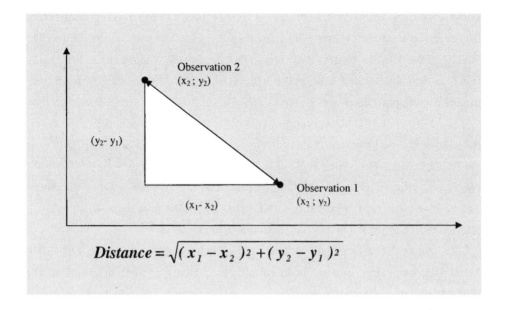

$$Distance = \sqrt{(x_1 - x_2)^2 + (y_2 - y_1)^2}$$

Also used are the SQUARED or ABSOLUTE EUCLIDEAN DISTANCES (the sum of squared distances without taking the squared root). The sum of ABSOLUTE DIFFERENCES, termed the CITY-BLOCK APPROACH, is used to approximate the distances among the variables, but has several serious limitations. Standardization of the variables avoids major disputes among the different distance estimation approaches. The MAHALANOBIS DISTANCE is such a method. It also sums the pooled within-group variance-covariance, which adjusts for the intercorrelations among the variables. The Mahalanobis distance is similar to R^2 in regression analysis.

When the units of different variables vary substantially so will their standard deviations. The larger standard deviation in this case will dominate the Euclidean distance. Therefore, the data for all the variables should be normalized by transforming all observations into standardized scores (x). This procedure is termed NORMALIZED DISTANCE FUNCTION. The distances will then be presented in Z-scores. In attitudinal-type data, WITHIN-CASE or ROW-CENTERING STANDARDIZATION is needed to remove response effect (each response is standardized with respect to the person's mean and SD).

After choosing the variables and number of clusters desired, it is necessary to decide on the PROCEDURE which should be used to CLASSIFY observations into

GROUPS/CLUSTERS (i.e., CLUSTER ALGORITHM). The algorithm maximizes the differences among the clusters with respect to the variation within each cluster. The RATIO of the between cluster (BC) variation to the average within-cluster (WC) variation is comparable to the F-ratio in the analysis of variance procedure. The most common clustering procedures are HIERARCHICAL and NONHIERARCHICAL.

HIERARCHICAL procedures of clustering have a tree-like structure. There are two commonly used methods in this category: AGGLOMERATIVE and DIVISIVE. In the AGGLOMERATIVE METHOD each observation is viewed as a cluster. Then the two closest clusters are combined into a cluster, and a third observation is combined. Then each earlier stage of clustering is NESTED within the next stage. This process is referred to as a DENDOGRAM (i.e., tree-like figure).

An opposite procedure to that of the agglomerative one is the DIVISIVE METHOD. One large cluster made of all observations is first determined. The observations that are the most dissimilar are separated into other clusters until individual clusters are established.

Agglomerative procedures use different LINKAGES to establish clusters. The SINGLE-LINKAGE PROCEDURE consists of the shortest distance between two observations and places them as the first cluster. The next shortest distance is then computed so that a third observation is added and a new cluster of two is established. This process continues until all observations structure one cluster. The COMPLETE LINKAGE is the opposite of SINGLE LINKAGE because it begins with the largest distance that observations are linked. The two methods can be viewed as reflecting the "similarity of most similar pair or least similar pair of objects" (Hair *et al.*, 1995). The AVERAGE LINKAGE method is similar to the previous two, but the cluster criterion consists of the average distance of observations within each cluster to the other clusters' mean distances. Therefore, this method is not as biased toward extreme values as are the other two methods. In WARD'S METHOD the distance between two clusters consists of the sum of squares between two clusters summed over all variables. In the CENTROID METHOD the distance between clusters is the distance between the mean values of each cluster (i.e., centroid). With additional observations, centroids alter.

NONHIERARCHICAL METHODS do not form a tree-like structure. The assignment of observations into clusters is done once the clusters are identified and specified. The principle is to find a CLUSTER SEED, assign observations around it, find another seed with observations around it, and continue the process until the last observation is assigned. Then reclassification takes place to better fit the observations into their seeds. This procedure is also termed K-MEANS CLUSTERING.

K-MEANS CLUSTERING consists of three common methods. SEQUEN-TIAL THRESHOLD METHOD begins with one seed and includes observations around it. Another seed with observations is then established until the last observation is assigned to a cluster. PARALLEL THRESHOLD METHOD simultaneously selects seeds and assigns observations to their nearest seed. Thresholds are adjusted with the ongoing process. Far distance observations may not be classified. OPTIMIZATION METHOD permits alterations in the observations cluster assignment. The main problem associated with non-hierarchical methods is the determination of the seeds. Both the order of observation and random order cause problems with regard to all seeds' determination. It is advisable by Hair *et al.* (1995) to use both methods in order to take advantage of each of them separately (see pp. 441-442). The number of clusters can be determined by theoretical assumptions or practical reasons determined by the researcher. Sometimes it is preferable to set an upper and lower limit of clusters (say 2-5), perform each of them separately, and see which provides the most elegant and useful solution. It is recommended to randomly divide the sample of observations (particularly when it is a large sample) into two or three sub-samples and run the same cluster procedure for all the samples separately. This process will ensure that the clusters are stable or not (i.e., cross-validation of clusters).

We use SPSS 11.0 to cluster 10 variables on a sample of 57 observations (note that we classify here the variables, not the observations, though in principle the procedure is identical). We ran "QUICK CLUSTER" (hierarchical) and have chosen the Ward's method to minimize the within cluster differences. The observations were randomly selected (10%) from 570 observations. First a PROXIMITY MATRIX is computed on the standardized scores. We can observe the distances among all the 10 variables. For example VAR4 and VAR5 are relatively far in distance from VAR6 (74.714 and 85.583, respectively) and so are VAR3 and VAR9 (71.119). In contrast, VAR1 and VAR2 are close to each other (28.002) and so are VAR2 and VAR 10 (28.879).

Proximities

Case Processing Summary[a]

	Cases					
Valid		Missing		Total		
N	Percent	N	Percent	N	Percent	
57	96.6%	2	3.4%	59	100%	

[a] *Squared Euclidean Distance Used*

Cluster

Proximity Matrix

	Matrix File Input						
Case	VAR00001	VAR00002	VAR00003	VAR00004	VAR00005	VAR00006	VAR00007
VAR00001		28.002	56.708	45.022	67.084	46.035	50.996
VAR00002	28.002		46.367	49.513	66.846	40.084	40.762
VAR00003	56.708	46.367		49.761	38.405	74.786	51.026
VAR00004	45.022	49.513	49.761		56.790	74.714	62.854
VAR00005	67.084	66.846	38.405	56.790		85.583	45.422
VAR00006	46.035	40.084	74.786	74.714	85.583		56.266
VAR00007	50.996	40.762	51.026	62.854	45.422	56.266	
VAR00008	46.207	39.894	60.420	62.317	59.902	54.497	24.993
VAR00009	48.704	48.853	71.119	82.834	82.213	43.021	64.117
VAR00010	44.238	28.879	58.198	46.450	50.046	57.946	47.069

Proximity Matrix

	Matrix File Input		
Case	VAR00008	VAR00009	VAR00010
VAR00001	46.207	48.704	44.238
VAR00002	39.894	48.853	28.879
VAR00003	60.420	71.119	58.198
VAR00004	62.317	82.834	46.450
VAR00005	59.902	82.213	50.046
VAR00006	54.497	43.021	57.946
VAR00007	24.993	64.117	47.069
VAR00008		52.186	40.520
VAR00009	52.186		60.190
VAR00010	40.520	60.190	

Next the cluster analysis is performed with each case included along with the clustering coefficient (the within-cluster sum of squares). In the other method, the squared Euclidean distances replace the within-cluster sum of squares. The smaller the coefficient, the more homogeneous the established cluster.

Agglomeratin Schedule

	Cluster Combined			Stage Cluster First Appears		
Stage	Cluster 1	Cluster 2	Coefficients	Cluster 1	Cluster 2	Next Stage
1	7	8	24.993	0	0	5
2	1	2	28.002	0	0	3
3	1	10	33.707	2	0	5
4	3	5	38.405	0	0	8
5	1	7	39.156	3	1	7
6	6	9	43.021	0	0	9
7	1	4	43.848	5	0	8
8	1	3	48.739	7	4	9
9	1	6	53.508	8	6	0

Two very different clusters are indicated by large coefficient differences. Similarly to the Scree test in factor analysis, large increases in the coefficients are indicative of a new cluster.

As we can see, large changes are obtained when moving from one to two clusters (53.508 - 48.739 = 4.769) followed by moving from two to three clusters (48.739 - 43.848 = 4.891). The VERTICAL ICICLE DIAGRAM also may help in this decision (see Hair *et al.*, 1995, pp. 449-451).

The dendrogram and the agglomeration schedule are used to detect outliers. In the dendrogram, a long branch that does not join until very late is an outlier.

****** H I E R A R C H I C A L   C L U S T E R   A N A L Y S I S

Dendrogram using Average Linkage (Within Group)

Rescaled Distance Cluster Combine

```
C A S E                 0      5      10     15     20     25
Label          Num      + ------- + ------- + ------- + ------- + ------- +
VAR00007        7       +                    +
VAR00008        8       +                    +            +
VAR00001        1             +      +       I            I
VAR00002        2             +      +       +            +      +
VAR00010       10                    +                    I      +      +
VAR00004        4                                         +      I      I
VAR00003        3                           +                    +      I
VAR00005        5                           +                           I
VAR00006        6                                  +                    +
VAR00009        9                                  +
```

The dendrogram reflects when clusters are established, i.e., at what stages the variables (usually observations) are joined to establish a cluster.

In the non-hierarchical cluster analysis, an initial two clusters were established with two centers (seeds). The final clusters are then established and the observations within each cluster are used to examine whether the distances are significant using Analysis of Variance (ANOVA). As we can see, 23 and 34 observations were in the first and second clusters respectively (n = 57). The distances between the two clusters were significant (p < .001) in all the variables. For further interpretation of the clusters, see Hair *et al.* (1995, pp. 453-456).

Initial Cluster Centers

	Cluster	
	1	2
VAR0001	1.00	5.00
VAR0002	1.00	5.00
VAR0003	1.00	5.00
VAR0004	2.00	5.00
VAR0005	2.00	5.00
VAR0006	1.00	5.00
VAR0007	1.00	5.00
VAR0008	1.00	5.00
VAR0009	1.00	4.00
VAR00010	2.00	5.00

Iteration History

	Changes in Cluster Centers	
Iteration	1	2
1	3.630	3.981
2	.000	.000

Final Cluster Centers

	Cluster	
	1	2
VAR0001	2.61	4.12
VAR0002	2.13	3.94
VAR0003	2.57	4.03
VAR0004	2.70	3.85
VAR0005	2.39	3.62
VAR0006	2.43	3.35
VAR0007	1.91	3.21
VAR0008	2.13	3.47
VAR0009	2.39	3.65
VAR00010	2.35	3.82

References

Argyrous,G. (1996). *Statistics for Social Research*. Melbourne: Mcmillan.

Bakeman, R., and Robinson, B.F. (1994). *Understanding Log-Linear Analysis with Ilog: An Interactive Approach*. Hillsdale, NY: Lawrence Erlbaum Associates.

Bartlett, M.S. (1947). Multivariate Analysis. *Journal of the Royal Statistical Society, Series B, 9,* 176-197.

Bryke, A.S. and Randenbush, S.W. (1992). *Hierarchical Linear Models*. Newbury Park, CA: Sage.

Chatterjee, S., and Price, B. (1997). *Regression Analysis by Example*. New York: Wiley.

Hair, J.F., Anderson, R.E., Tatham, R.L., and Black, W.C. (1995). *Multivariate Data Analysis with Readings (4th Edition)*. London: Prentice-Hall.

Pedhazur, E.J. (1997). *Multiple Regression in Behavioural Sciences (3rd Edition)*. New York: Holt, Rinehart, and Winston.

Recommended Literature:

All the books listed above (except Bartlett, 1947) are recommended to advance the knowledge on the various topics discussed in this chapter.

6.12   Structural Equation Modeling in Sport and Exercise Sciences

Ronit Hanegby, School of Education, Tel-Aviv University, Israel

David Kaplan, School of Education, University of Delaware, USA

In sport and exercise sciences researchers often test theories, which postulate relationships between theoretical constructs. For example, one may be interested in testing the relationship between "motivation" and "performance", "self-efficacy" and "perceived ability", or "motivation" and "self-satisfaction". These theoretical constructs are not directly observed. Rather, we try to obtain multiple empirical measures and derive LATENT VARIABLES that we assume to coincide with the theoretical construct of interest. We are typically not interested in any one of these empirical measures, per se, but rather the construct itself.

Moreover, any one of these measures is, itself, unreliable to some extent and its use in regression analysis would lead to biased estimates of relationships. Through the use of factor analysis we can obtain a direct estimate of the constructs. The goal is to employ the constructs directly into our regression relationships so as to obtain unbiased estimates of relationships. The methodology that combines factor analysis and regression analysis is referred to as STRUCTURAL EQUATION MODELING (SEM) and is the subject of this chapter.

From Path-analysis to SEM

Let us assume we would like to test a theory about sport motivation and self-satisfaction. The purpose of this analysis would be to better understand how students' perceptions of motivation affect their self-satisfaction derived from participating in-competitive sports in school. Using eight Likert-type scale items with a four category format (1= not apply to me at all....4= apply to me very much), students were asked why they chose to participate in the competitive sport-school clubs. These eight items reflected intrinsic and extrinsic motives to engage in sport. In addition the students were asked to indicate how satisfied they are from various aspects of the sport club activities. This was measured with six items which share a Likert-type scale (1= not satisfied at all....4= very satisfied). Based on the theory, the following path model was specified, assuming relations between intrinsic and extrinsic motivation and self-satisfaction.

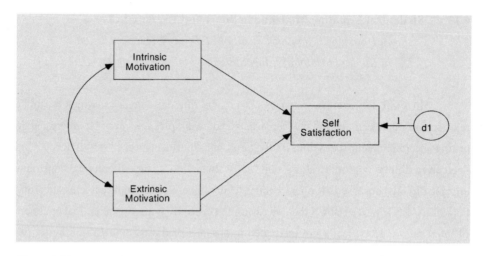

Figure 3.30.   Path Diagram of a Structural Model.

The example given above refers to the simple case of a regression relationship between the variables, portraying these relationships as a PATH ANALYSIS. In constructing the path diagram, we represent the relationships between variables with arrows. A straight arrow indicates a direct casual relationship while the double-headed arrow between variables indicates a correlation between the variables. Figure 1 shows a simple model, in which both intrinsic and extrinsic motivations are predictors for self-satisfaction, with a curved arrow between them. This double-headed arrow represents the correlation between intrinsic and extrinsic motivation.

Typically we are interested in more complex relationships among variables that are derived from deeper theoretical knowledge. Indeed, it may be the case that some of the variables of interest are simultaneously related as, for example, "self-satisfaction" and "self-efficacy" or "perceived ability" and "physical self-concept". That is, higher levels of perceived ability may lead to higher physical self-concept which, in turn, may lead to higher levels of performance.

The variables measured in our example above (Figure 3.30) consist of the summation or the average score that each subject obtained on each variable. In doing so, we represent each of the variables in Figure 1 as manifest variables. Instead of using average or summation scores of scales, we can incorporate those variables as "latent variables". In this case, the manifest variables are referred to as "indicators" of the latent variables. In order to explain this process, we need to consider the issue of factor analysis.

Exploratory Factor Analysis (EFA) Vs. Confirmatory Factor Analysis (CFA)

Factor analysis is a multivariate statistical procedure that is designed to extract common underlying factors - referred to synonymously as "constructs", "factors", or "latent variables", based on the pattern of correlations among the observed variables. Unlike the similar procedure of principal component analysis, factor analysis explicitly accounts for measurement error in the observed variables. Thus, the latent variables can be considered "measurement error-free" variables.

In the diagram, the observed variables are represented as cubes while latent variables are represented in ellipses. In our example (Figure 3.31), variables x1- x4 are the indicators of the latent variable "intrinsic motivation", x5—x8 are the indicators of the latent variable "extrinsic motivation". Items S1—S6 are observed variables of self-satisfaction. The decision to use these particular items to measure the latent variable may have been based on a preliminary EXPLORATORY FACTOR ANALYSIS followed up by a CONFIRMATORY FACTOR ANALYSIS.

Figure 3.31 represents the same model shown in Figure 3.30. An inspection of Figure 3.31 shows that the model contains two parts: the structural part, which is represented by the path diagram of the relationships between the latent variables, and the measurement part, that is represented by the relationships between the observed variables and the latent variables. Structural equation modelling, which has its roots in econometric simultaneous equation modelling, can incorporate these simultaneous relations in addition to addressing the problems of measurement error.

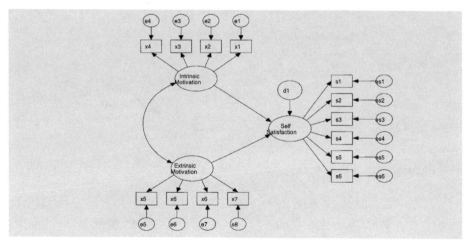

Figure 3.31.   Path Diagram of Structural Model Among Latent Variables.

General Model

Structural equation models are composed of two parts (Jöreskog, 1973; Kessling, 1972; Wiley, 1973).

The measurement part relates observed measures to latent variables via confirmatory factor analysis (CFA), and the structural part relates ENDOGENOUS (dependent) latent variables to each other and to EXOGENOUS (independent) latent variables via path analysis. Two general types of models can be considered. The first type is referred to as RECURSIVE, where all relationships are uni-directional. The second type, often found in economic modeling, is referred to as NON-RECURSIVE, where endogenous latent variables can be simultaneously related to each other.

Let us take our example of motivation and self-satisfaction and add another latent variable to the model of self-efficacy. Now we have two endogenous variables that can be implemented into the model. In the first form, Figure 3.32a presents a recursive model, which specifies that self-efficacy mediates the relationship between motivation and self-satisfaction. Although self-efficacy in this model is both endogenous and exogenous, the model is recursive since all relationships are unidirectional. In the second form, Figure 3.32b, self-efficacy is both endogenous and exogenous, but the relations are non-recursive.

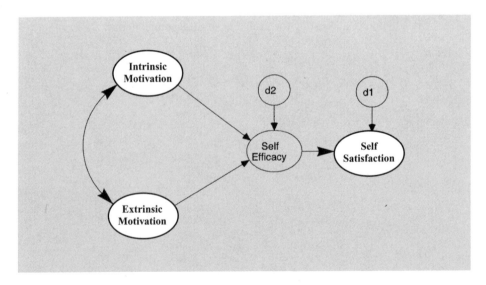

Figure 3.32a. A recursive model.

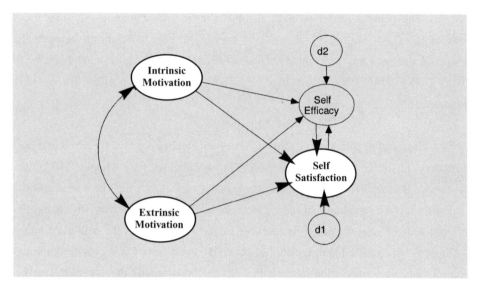

Figure 3.32b. A non-recursive model.

The general model can be written as follows:

$$\eta = B\eta + \Gamma\xi + \zeta, \qquad (52)$$

where η is a vector of endogenous latent variables, ξ is a vector of exogenous latent variables, **B** is a matrix of regression coefficients relating the latent endogenous variables to each other, Γ is a matrix of regression coefficients relating endogenous variables to exogenous variables, and ζ is a vector of disturbance terms.

The latent variables are linked to observable variables via measurement equations for the endogenous variables and exogenous variables. That is,

$$y = \Lambda_y\eta + \varepsilon, \qquad (53)$$

and

$$x = \Lambda_x\xi + \delta, \qquad (54)$$

where $_y$ and $_x$ are matrices of factor loadings, respectively, and ξ and δ are vectors of measurement errors, respectively.

The general model is quite flexible allowing for numerous sub-models as special cases. An important sub-model concerns only the relationship between the observed measures and the latent variables. In the context of SEM, this model is referred to as CONFIRMATORY FACTOR ANALYSIS and can be specified using either Equation (52) or Equation (53).

It is useful, perhaps, to distinguish between exploratory factor analysis and confirmatory factor analysis. In exploratory factor analysis (see Mulaik, 1972), the researcher is interested in determining the number of factors which best represent the measured variables loadings. In some special cases, an investigator may wish to explicitly test a hypothesis regarding the number of factors[1], however, the pattern of factor loadings is not specified beforehand. Moreover, the initial set of factors is arbitrary and subject to a choice of rotation schemes that can serve to simplify the structure. The two common rotations are the orthogonal rotation and the oblique rotations[2].

In contrast to exploratory factor analysis, confirmatory factor analysis requires that the investigator species exactly which measures load on which factors based on a theoretical model. The remaining loadings are typically set to zero. Moreover, confirmatory factor analysis also allows for factors to be correlated and hence there is no rotational choice that needs to be made. Thus, confirmatory factor analysis provides a statistical representation of Thurstone's idea of simple structure (Thurstone, 1947). Here, the null hypothesis is that there are a pre-specified number of factors *and* that the relationship between the observed measurements and the factors take on a particular pattern as specified by the theory. For a discussion of confirmatory factor analysis, see Bollen (1989).

Confirmatory factor analysis has been used in the sports sciences literature. One example of CFA is the study by Bartholomew, Edwards, Brewer, Van Raalte, and Linder (1998) on the sport pain inventory. These researchers failed to confirm the five proposed subscales of the sport pain inventory: Coping, Cognitive, Avoidance,

---

[1] Statistical methods of estimation in exploratory factor analysis, such as maximum likelihood, allow for testing the null hypothesis that there are k number of factors underlying the data. The alternative hypothesis is that there may be more, less, or no common factions underlying the data.

Catastrophizing, and Body Awareness. Through their work, it has been shown that there are some theoretical issues that must be modified before the inventory can be used as an assessment tool.

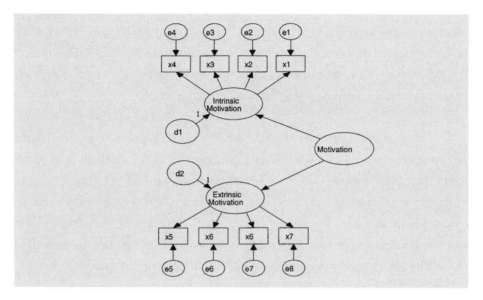

Figure 3.33. Second order factor analysis of motivation.

An interesting extension of factor analysis (both EFA and CFA) is that it is possible to specify and assess the existence of a higher order factor. A higher order factor is one that supposedly accounts for the covariation among lower order factors. We can refer to motivation as multidimensional concept, which consists of intrinsic and extrinsic motivation, and represent it in second-order factor analysis (Figure 3.33).

An example of higher order factors using CFA is that of Marsh and Redmayne (1994). They examined the multidimensional construct of physical self-concept (physical appearance, physical ability, strength, balance, flexibility, and endurance) and its relation to multiple components of physical fitness (endurance, flexibility, balance, strength, and speed (shuttle run)).

---

[2] The most common form of orthogonal rotation is called *varimax* (Kaiser, 1958). Among the class of oblique rotations, the two most common are *direct oblimin* and *promax*.

Another important sub-model of SEM allows latent endogenous variables to be regressed on observed exogenous variables. This model is referred to as the MULTIPLE INDICATORS-MULTIPLE CAUSES (MIMIC) model (Jöreskog & Goldberger, 1975). A special case of this model allows the exogenous variables to take on nominal values reflecting group membership. In this case the regression coefficients reflect group differences in the latent variable. This is similar to analysis-of-variance (ANOVA) except that the outcome is a latent variable. Indeed, this model can be extended to incorporate exogenous variables reflecting designed experimental situations.

An example is the study of gender differences in self-satisfaction in sport. Here, self-satisfaction constitutes a latent variable measured by multiple indicators, as shown before. The gender variable is an observed nominal scale (e.g. male = 1, female = 0). The model can be extended to include ethnicity (e.g. Black = 1, White = 0) and the interaction of gender and ethnicity. The regression coefficients relating self-satisfaction in sports to these exogenous variables would give the main effect of gender, the main effect of ethnicity and the gender by ethnicity interaction. To illustrate this concept, Figure 3.34 presents a MIMIC model of gender, ethnicity and self-satisfaction in sport.

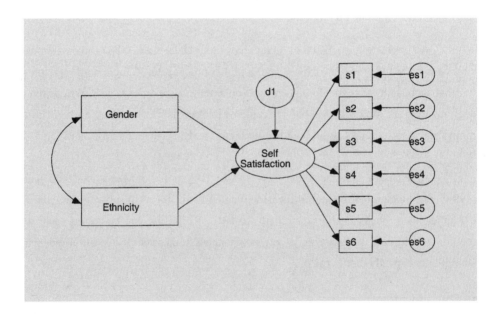

Figure 3.34   MIMIC Model for gender, ethnicity and self-satisfaction.

Multigroup Structural Equation Modeling

Let us consider further the analysis of group differences. We will use the previous example of motivation and self-satisfaction. Our interest is two fold: first, whether the measurement model holds for both females and males, and second, whether the structural relationship between motivation and self-satisfaction is the same for both genders. To use the example above, the sequence of testing is as follows: First, we test the relationships among the variables that measure intrinsic and extrinsic motivation and self-satisfaction as given by the sample covariance matrices, and examine their equality across gender groups[3].

Generally, we would want to reject this hypothesis because if the sample covariances are equal, then the data can be pooled and multiple group modeling is unnecessary. Assuming that the sample covariance matrices are unequal, the next step is to test whether the factor loadings that relate the observed variables to the latent variables are equal across gender groups. Assuming that the factor loadings are invariant, the next step is to test the equality of factor loadings and measurement error variances across groups. Finally, given the invariance of measurement structure, we add a test of equality of structural relationships across groups to the model.

A methodology for studying the equivalency of measurement and structural relationships across groups, such as males and females, was given by Jöreskog (1971). Jöreskog's approach allows for testing increasingly restrictive hypotheses, beginning with testing the invariance of the measurement structure (factor loadings followed by measurement of error variances) across groups, and concluding with invariance of measurement and structural relationships across groups.

Finally, it is possible to study mean differences on the factors themselves. For example, it may be of interest to study not only whether the factor structure for motivational orientation is the same for males and females, but whether males exhibit higher levels of motivational orientation. This is referred to as mean structure modeling and was developed by Sörbom (1974). The procedure for testing mean structures is much the same as that described above for testing group differences in measurement and structural relationships. However, in terms of data, we require not only the covariances of the observed data but also the means of the variables. Typical practice would require that the

---

[3] The stategy we are describing treats the three constructs as a three-factor CFA. It is possible to parameterize structural models as CFA models.

factor mean differences be assessed only after equality of measurement and structural relationships have been found to hold.

Outline of Steps in Structural Equation Modeling

Bollen and Long (1993) characterize five steps in the application of structural equation modeling: (1) model specification, (2) identification, (3) estimation, (4) model evaluation, and (5) model modification. We will consider each in turn.

Model Specification

Model specification concerns the initial formulation of the equations of the model based on a theory. The theory should, ideally, suggest the general pattern of relationships among the variables. We can distinguish between three types of relationships among variables. The first type we refer to as "free" relationships, in which variables are assumed to be related to each other. Since a free parameter is a parameter that is unknown and needs to be estimated, we allow the software program to estimate the magnitude and direction of that relationship. The model shown in Figure 3.35 assumes free relationships between gender, ethnicity and motivation (intrinsic and extrinsic), self-efficacy and self-satisfaction. The second type is referred to as a "fixed" relationship. A fixed parameter is fixed to a specified value, typically either zero or one. Usually, this means the absence of a relationship as suggested by theory.

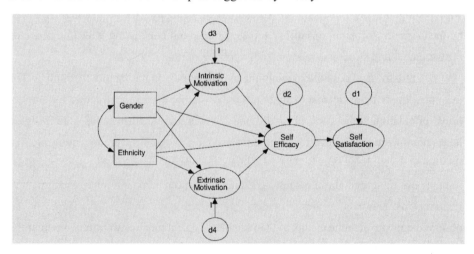

Figure 3.35   A structural equation model for gender, ethnicity, motivation, self-efficacy and self-satisfaction in sport.

For example in the model shown in Figure 3.35, no relationships exist between gender, ethnicity, and self-satisfaction. Fixed relationships could also mean that the relationship is fixed to some preassigned non-zero constant. Finally, the third relationship is referred to as a "constrained" relationship wherein two or more sets of relationships are set equal to each other. Typical examples of constrained parameters occur when testing models across groups. For example Li and Harmer (1996a) tested whether a model for sports motivational scales is invariant across gender.

Generally, as noted before, a path diagram aids the specification of a structural model. The standard approach to drawing a path diagram uses squares to represent observed variables, circles to represent latent variables, and arrows to represent directions of relationships (see Markland & Hardy, 1997 for an example). There are some minor variations to the drawing of a path diagram, however it should be emphasized that path diagrams are visual representations of the statistical equations that make up the model and should not be confused with the theory itself.

Identification

Identification refers to whether it is possible to assign unique values for the parameters of the model. It relates to the relationships between the parameters that ought to be estimated and the information in the variances/covariance structure of the data used to estimate the parameters of the model. Sometimes this is referred to as "pieces of information" since this is the input we use to solve the unknown parameters in the equations. To be concrete, if there are p observed variables in model, then there will be $s = \frac{p(p+1)}{2}$ elements in the covariance matrix. For example, consider that we have three observed variables (see Figure 13.6.21), so that there are $3(4)/2 = 6$ "pieces of information" (three sample variances and their three covariances).

The number of parameters that are to be estimated, say t, are the number of variances and covariances of the exogenous variables (observed or latent), the variances and covariances of disturbance terms (measurement errors and structural disturbances), and all free regression coefficients. In our example, the number of parameters to be estimated is two regression coefficients, three variances of the independent variables (two exogenous variables and one disturbance term variance of the endogenous variable), and one covariance among the exogenous variables.

For the model to be identified there must be $t \leq s$ parameters to be estimated. If $t = s$ then the model is just identified (0 degrees of freedom). If t $< s$ then the model is over-identified. Finally, if $t > s$ then the model is not identified. Duncan (1975) has referred to this rule as the COUNTING RULE.

There is a direct relationship between the identification status of a model and the degrees-of-freedom used to test the model. The degrees of freedom are equal to the number of observed variances and covariances minus the number of free parameters - i.e., parameters that will be estimated. A model that is just identified has zero degrees of freedom (model shown in Figure 3.30). In this case, the parameters can be estimated (see below), but the model cannot be tested. A model that is over-identified has positive degrees-of-freedom (model shown in Figure 3.31). Here, the parameters can be estimated and the model as a whole can be tested. A model that is not identified has negative degrees-of-freedom and cannot be estimated or tested.

It should be noted that establishing identification by the counting rule is only a necessary condition for identification. In other words, this condition could be met and the model still not be identified. Generally speaking, the counting rule works well for recursive structural equation models. For non-recursive structural equation models, however, somewhat more stringent rules need to be met. In particular, a necessary condition for identification of non-recursive structural equation models is that the number of excluded variables (endogenous or exogenous) in any equation must be at least one less than the number of equations in the model. Figure 3.36a represents a non-recursive model that is not identified since the rule discussed above had not been addressed, and all exogenous variables serve as predictors of both endogenous variables (self-efficacy and self-satisfaction). An identified non-recursive model is present in Figure 3.36b where gender serves as a unique predictor of self-satisfaction and ethnicity serves as a unique predictor of self-efficacy.

This is referred to as the *order condition* of identification. A necessary and sufficient condition for identification is the so-called RANK CONDITION of identification. A full description of the rank condition is beyond the scope of this chapter (see Bollen, 1989, for a more complete description). Suffice to say, however, that the rank condition requires that each equation be distinct from every other equation in the system and that no equation can be derived as a linear combination of another equation in the model (Duncan, 1975, p. 83).

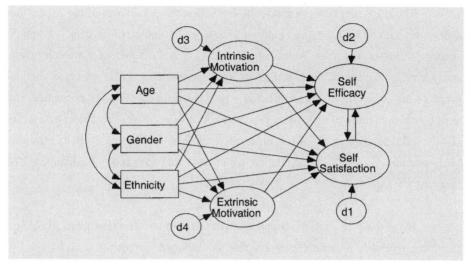

Figure 3.36a   A non-recursive model—not identified.

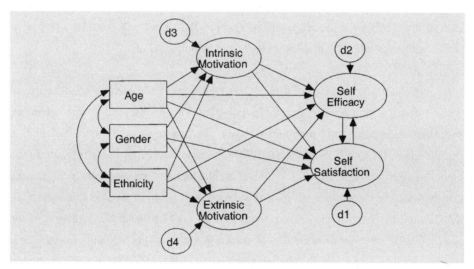

Figure 3.36b   A non-recursive identified model.

Estimation

Assuming that the model is identified (either just identified or over identified), the next step in SEM is the estimation of the free parameters of the model, i.e. the parameters that we intend to estimate and that were not fixed. Estimation of the parameters' values of the model enables us to examine the extent to which the data predicted from the model matches the observed data.

There are numerous methods for estimating the parameters of the model that differ from each other in their assumptions about the distribution of the data. A common assumption underlying many statistical procedures is that the measures are continuous and normally distributed. For structural equation modeling, it is assumed that all variables are jointly normally distributed - referred to as multivariate normality. The most common method of estimating this assumption is *maximum likelihood estimation (MLE)*. A full description of MLE is beyond the scope of this chapter. Suffice to say, that MLE provides estimates of population parameters that maximize the likelihood of obtaining the sample data.

If the data are continuous and multivariate normal, then maximum likelihood estimation will yield parameter estimates that are unbiased, efficient, and asymptotically normal - allowing for parameters to be tested for statistical significance. Other estimators besides MLE are available for structural equation modelling, but a full discussion of each of them is beyond the scope of this chapter. Below, we will consider some alternative estimators when we discuss issues of the assumptions of SEM.

Sometimes, the kinds of data encountered in sport and exercise sciences are not derived from a multivariate normal population. This is especially true when we encounter categorical and non-normal data. For example, the Sport Orientation Questionnaire (SOQ; Gill and Deeter, 1988) is comprised of 25 items measured on a 5-point Likert scale. Even if the univariate histograms showed relatively normal distributions, the categorical nature of this data is a violation of the continuous normality assumption - even if the univariate histograms are "bell-shaped". Violation of the assumption of multivariate normality is known to yield serious problems for structural equation models. For example, Muthén and Kaplan (1985, 1992) among others showed that non-normal data yields incorrect standard errors of parameter estimates and inflated tests of model fit (to be described below). Here, parameter estimates themselves appear to be unaffected by non-normality.

Over the past fifteen years, exceptional developments have been made in the estimation of structural equation models in the presence of non-normal data. For example, Browne (1982, 1984) developed an estimation procedure based on weighed least squares that takes into account the skewness and kurtosis of the observed variables.

His procedure is referred to as asymptotically distribution free (ADF) estimation. Studies of the ADF estimator (e.g. Browne, 1982; Muthén and Kaplan, 1985, 1992) showed that if the observed variables are continuous and non-normal, the ADF estimator yields unbiased estimates and standard errors, as well as correct measures of model fit. However, a major disadvantage of the ADF estimator is that in practice it requires very large sample sizes (often in excess of 5000 units) and/or models with limited number of variables.

As noted above, some data encountered in sport sciences are categorical in nature. The categorical nature of the variables is, by itself, a violation of the assumption of normality. One approach to estimating structural equation models with non-normal data was offered by Muthén (1984). Muthén's approach can be outlined as follows. First, it is assumed that underlying each categorical variable is a continuous latent response variable that is assumed to be normally distributed. For example, consider measuring student sport participation as either 'yes' or 'no'. It is assumed that underlying this dichotomous variable is a propensity to participate, which is observed as a participant's propensity to participate exceeds some threshold. Otherwise, the student omits attending sport activities. In this case there is one threshold. However, for 5-point Likert scales, for example, four such thresholds exist. In general, if a scale has C categories, then there will be $C - 1$ thresholds.

Next, assume we have another dichotomous variable, like parental involvement in sports with a 'yes' or 'no' response format. Muthén's approach requires the calculation of a correlation coefficient between these two variables. The association between these two variables is referred to in the classic psychometric literature as the 'phi' coefficient. However, this coefficient does not account for the underlying normality assumption. In fact, the phi correlation will typically underestimate the true correlation between the underlying latent response variables. Thus, the correlation in this case is between the underlying latent response variables. The correct correlation coefficient for dichotomous scored variables is referred to as the TETRACHORIC correlation.

When measured by Likert scales, the correlation between the variables is referred to as the POLYCHORIC correlation and is used as a replacement for the product-moment correlation when both variables are measured by ordinal scales with three or more categories. Again, the polychoric correlation assumes that underlying the categories is a continuous and normally distributed response variable. Finally, another type of correlation within this class is the BISERIAL correlation, which relates a dichotomous response variable with a polychotomous variable (i.e., a metrically measured variable is associated with another binary measured variable). Muthén's (1984) approach allows one to estimate structural models based on correlation matrices whose elements are any combination of the above correlations, including standard Pearson correlations. This approach has been referred as Categorical Variable Methodology (CVM). Again, its major advantage lies in accurate estimation of parameters, standard errors, and tests of model fit. Its major disadvantages are two-fold. First, there is the additional assumption that the response variables are normally distributed. If this assumption does not hold, then Muthén's procedure may give inaccurate results[4]. Second, Muthén's procedure suffers from the same limitations as ADF, namely, very large sample sizes and/or very restricted models are required for the method to work.

Despite the limitations of the estimation methods we have described, considerable thought should be given to the choice of method. Every attempt should be made to use estimation methods that are appropriate for the underlying distributional assumptions. If one is required to use a method that is inappropriate for the data, then the limitations of the method vis-a-vis should be spelled out, and inferences should be made with great caution.

For example, we have chosen a maximum likelihood estimation method for the model presented in Figure 3.36b. The estimates we were interested in were the loadings of each of the indicators on each of the latent variables, and the coefficients between the exogenous and the endogenous variables. A parameter is considered to be a good estimator if it is in the expected direction and is significantly different from zero (p < .05). The parameters that are being estimated can be in two forms: unstandardized and standardized. Most of the programs also provide squared multiple (R^2) correlations for the endogenous variables.

---

[4] Muthén and Hofacker (1988) show how to test for the assumption of underlying bivariate normality for the polychoric case and underlying tri-variate normality in the tetrachoric case.

Model Evaluation

Once the model parameters are estimated, the next step is to evaluate whether the model is consistent with the data. The main approach is to reproduce the sample data (e.g. covariance matrix or correlation matrix) based on the model and compare it to the actual sample data. The difference between the data implied by the model and actual data yields a residual matrix. Estimation algorithms such as maximum likelihood are designed to yield estimates that minimize the residuals as much as possible. If the residuals are "small", we tentatively conclude that the model fits the data. However, inspecting the residuals is not the most reliable method of assessing the fit of the model to the data. Instead, we tend to prefer statistical tests of model fit.

The most popular statistical approach for assessing model fit is through the use of the likelihood ratio chi-square statistic. The likelihood ratio chi-square tests the null hypothesis that specifies a model of interest that fits the data. The alternative hypothesis is that the covariance (or correlation) matrix may not support any model.

Often confusion arises in the interpretation of statistical significance in the SEM setting. When the discrepancy between the sample covariance matrix and the implied covariance matrix is minimal (e.g. not significant) then the model may be a good representation of the process that generated the data in the population. The more the implied and sample covariances differ from each other, the larger the χ^2 statistics, and the stronger the evidence that the model does not fit the data in the population.

A major problem with the likelihood ratio chi-square test, and one that has dominated the literature on SEM, is sample size sensitivity. The problem arises from the fact that the equation for the likelihood ratio chi-square statistic is the product of the sample size and the discrepancy between the covariance matrix implied by the model and the sample covariance matrix. Thus, unless the model fits perfectly (i.e. the discrepancy is zero), sample size will magnify even trivial discrepancies because the sample size is multiplying a non-zero discrepancy value.

Although this issue is one of statistical power (see Kaplan, 1995), the response in the literature has been to develop alternative methods of model fit that are purportedly less sensitive to sample size.

There are numerous ways to classify fit indices. Perhaps the simplest is to consider four families of indices: goodness-of-fit measures, comparative fit indices, indices based on approximate fit, and model selection indices. To begin, two goodness-of-fit measures that do not depend on sample size are the goodness-of-fit index (GFI), and the adjusted goodness-of-fit index (AGFI), proposed by Jöreskog and Sörbom (1989). The GFI measures how much better the hypothesized model fits the data relative to no model assumed for the covariance matrix at all. The AGFI adjusts the GFI by a penalty function for estimating each parameter involving the degrees-of-freedom of the model. Ideally, one would prefer values of the GFI and AGFI to be close to each other. Both measures theoretically range from zero to one, where one represents excellent fit of the model to the data. In practice, both measures could be negative indicating that one's model fits worse than no model at all.

The second class of fit indices involves comparative fit. Comparative fit indices use the notion of a baseline model to test against the model of interest. The baseline model is typically a model that specifies complete independence among all variables. The chi-square test for this model will be, obviously, quite large. The chi-square for the model of substantive interest is compared to the chi-square of the independence model and the fit index is scaled in such a way as to lie between zero and one. A comparative fit index value of zero means that one's model is worse than a model of complete independence, whereas a value of one means that the model fits the data (in this sense) perfectly.

The development of comparative fit indices has dominated the methodological literature for many years. Several indices of this type include (1) non-normed fit index (NNFI, TLI), (2) the incremental fit index (IFI), (3) the parsimonious goodness-of-fit index (PGFI), and the comparative fit index (CFI) to name just a few. The major advantage of these indices is their ease of use. However, the major disadvantage to the use of these indices is that the model of substantive interest is being compared to a model that states that the variables are completely uncorrelated - a very unrealistic and scientifically useless comparison (see Sobel and Bohrnstedt, 1985). One could argue, however, that in a purely exploratory mode of research, such indices may be valuable.

The third class of alternative fit indices is based on the notion of approximate fit. Specifically, it may be unreasonable to assume that a model will fit perfectly even in the population. However, this is precisely what the likelihood ratio chi-square statistic is testing. Rather, it may be more reasonable to assume that a model fits only approximately well in the population. Thus, it would be useful to have a way of gauging the degree of model misfit in the population.

Based on work of Browne and Cudeck (1993) and Steiger (1990) a fit index referred to as the *root mean square error of approximation* (RMSEA) was developed. The RMSEA is bounded below by zero indicating no misfit in the population. In addition, the RMSEA has an associated probability value that allows one to test the inexact directional null hypothesis that the RMSEA is less than 0.05[5]. The alternative hypothesis is that the RMSEA is greater than 0.05. Quoting Browne and Cudeck (1993) "Practical experience has made us feel that a value of the RMSEA of about .05 or less would indicate a close fit of the model in relation to the degrees of freedom. This figure is based on subjective judgment. It cannot be regarded as infallible or correct, but it is more reasonable than the requirement of exact fit with the RMSEA = 0.0. We are also of the opinion that a value of about 0.08 or less for the RMSEA would indicate a reasonable error of approximation and would not want to employ a model with a RMSEA greater than 0.1." (p. 114).

The fourth class of fit indices is based on information measures of cross-validation. These include the Akaike Information Criterion (AIC) and the Expected Cross-Validation Index (ECVI) to name only two. These indices do not represent stand-alone measures of model fit. That is, their numbers have no reference in isolation. Rather, these numbers are used to compare models and choose among them. The basis for this choice is that the model with the lowest information value among a set of competing values will be the model that will cross-validate best in a new sample of the same size and sampled in the same way. An example of the use of cross-validation indices in the sport sciences literature is that of Markland and Hardy (1997).

In the interest of space, we did not cover all the indices available. In addition, there are numerous ways of classifying indices of fit. The interested reader may wish to consult Tanaka (1993) or Hu and Bentler (1995) for further discussions of this topic.

---

[5] The value of 0.05 does not refer to the standard alpha level of Type I error probability. It is simply a baseline value.

Finally, the use of these indices is not without their critics (see Kaplan, 1990a 1990b and articles therein for a debate on this topic). Nevertheless, alternative fit indices are widely used in applied SEM research. A review of the sport and exercise sciences literature wherein SEM has been applied also reveals that alternative fit indices are widely used (e.g. Li and Harmer, 1996). It is important to recognize, however, that alternative indices give very different and sometime conflicting information about the fit of the model.

Reporting many different types of indices becomes confusing insofar as it is unclear how the model is being evaluated. Therefore, when one is considering the use of these indices it is important to carefully consider which fit indices will give the information the researcher actually needs in order to answer the question he/she is interested in.

Model Modification

Rarely do we find that models fit data even when the assumptions underlying the estimation procedure are not violated. We often wish to bring our models closer in line with the data. In addition, we wish to develop models that are as parsimonious as possible. Therefore we often engage in a process of model modification.

To begin, recall that models contain fixed and free parameters. Fixed parameters are typically fixed to zero representing the absence of a relationship. Assuming that all of the assumptions underlying the estimation procedure are met, then if the model is a true representation of the data, these fixed parameters will be zero in the population. However, if the model is not true, then one or more of these fixed parameters may not be zero. In this case, the restrictions that we have imposed on our model are inconsistent with the data and may need to be relaxed.

A methodology for gauging whether a restriction should be relaxed utilizes a statistic referred to as the *Lagrange multiplier* or the *modification index* (Sörbom, 1989). The modification index gives the expected decrease in the model chi-square if the parameter associated with the modification index is freed. The relaxation of this restriction results in a loss of one degree of freedom. Moreover, if the fixed effect is truly nonzero in the population, the modification index is a one degree-of-freedom non-central chi-square that can be used to obtain an estimate of the power of the test to detect the effect. Two examples of the use of the modification index in the sport and exercise sciences literature are Li and Harmer (1996a). In their study they suggest testing a simplex model for sport motivation scale. Figure 3.37a shows the model for males and females. It was assumed from the model that the simplex structure underlying the sport motivation scale could be structured as paths occurring only between adjacent levels.

After testing the model for the two groups, the authors found, based on the program's modification indices that, for the male sample, a path should be free between external regulation and intrinsic motivation (Figure 3.37b). As for the female sample, a path from amotivation to intrinsic motivation should be free based on the model indices (Figure 3.37c). Freeing those paths resulted in significant coefficients and improved model fit indices.

The modification index does not indicate the size or sign of the parameter that is being considered for freeing. Therefore a researcher may end up freeing many parameters that are of minimal statistical or theoretical importance and thus capitalize on chance features of that particular data set. To assist in choosing modifications to be made, Saris, Satorra and Sörbom (1987) developed the expected change statistic. This statistic gives the expected size and sign of the parameter when the parameter is freed.

With the modification index and expected change statistic in hand, one can consider four possible variations to model modification. These have been described by Saris, Satorra and Sörbom (1987) and Kaplan (1990). First, one can encounter a large modification index associated with a large expected change. If it makes theoretical sense to free this parameter, then to do so would result in a large improvement in model fit coupled with the addition of a substantively large and important parameter estimate in the model.

Second, one can encounter a large modification index associated with a small-expected change. Here one may not want to free this parameter because it would only improve fit at the expense of adding a trivial parameter that might not replicate in a future sample (see Kaplan, 1991).

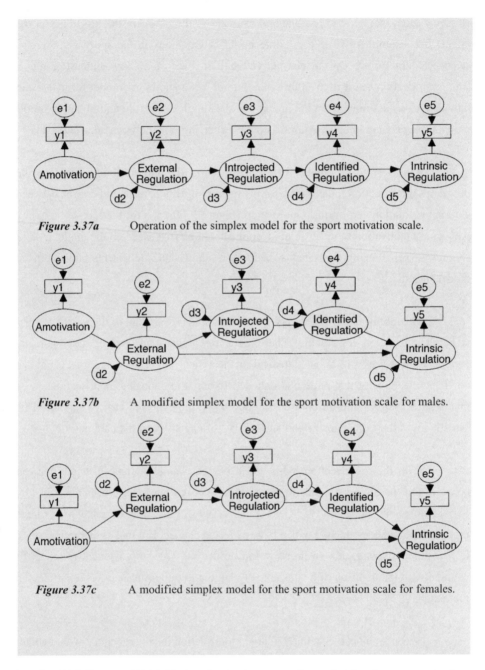

Figure 3.37a   Operation of the simplex model for the sport motivation scale.

Figure 3.37b   A modified simplex model for the sport motivation scale for males.

Figure 3.37c   A modified simplex model for the sport motivation scale for females.

based on Li & Harmer (1996a). Testing the simplex assumption underlying the sport motivation scale: A structural equation modeling analysis. *Research Quarterly for Exercise and Sport, 67,* 396-405.

Third, one can encounter a small modification index associated with a large expected change. In this case the problem may be that the test has too little power to detect this large effect - perhaps due to a small sample size. A more detailed power analysis as described by Satorra and Saris (1985) may be warranted. Finally, one may encounter a small modification associated with a small expected change. Here, it probably does make sense to free this parameter in so far as it does not contribute to improvement in model fit or add new substantive information to the model.

Clearly, the approach described above adds paths to the model and renders the model less parsimonious. However, parsimony is a desirable quality in a statistical model and thus we do not wish to retain parameters that do not contribute in a meaningful way to our understanding of the phenomenon of interest. One way to make a model more parsimonious is to remove paths that are statistically or substantively non-significant. Assuming that it is theoretically justified to remove a path, one can use statistical criteria to gauge the impact on the model as a whole when a path is removed.

Associated with each free parameter is an estimate of its standard error. The ratio of the estimate to its standard error yields a statistic that has a z-distribution, which can be then compared to the table of the standard normal distribution to determine statistical significance. It is known that the square of this z-statistic is a one degree-of-freedom chi-square, which can be compared to a chi-square table to judge for statistical significance.

This statistic is referred to as the WALD test and gives an estimate of the increase in the overall model chi-square when the particular free parameter in question is fixed. A strategy similar to that used in the context of freeing parameters can also be used for fixed parameters as well.

The strategies of model modification described above represent only one way of improving the fit of a model or making a model more parsimonious. When one decides to engage in model modification, the modifications may be pertinent to the particular data set and not generalizable to other data sets obtained from new samples. This is the issue of cross-validation and it represents an important problem in SEM. There are essentially two ways to engage in cross-validation. The first requires that one estimates a model on a particular sample and modifies the model as needed. Then, one obtains a new sample (of the same size and same sampling procedures), and applies the model, with paths fixed at their values from the first analysis, to the data of the second sample. One compares the chi-squares from the model applied to the first and second samples to judge the adequacy of cross-validation.

The difficulty with the approach just described is that it requires the investigator to either obtain two samples or split a large sample randomly in half. As such, obtaining large samples may represent a practical difficulty in typical research settings. Thus, it would be helpful to have a way of gauging the effects of model modification on cross-validation adequacy in a single sample.

A second approach based on cross-validation in single samples utilizes the AIC and ECVI cross-validation described above. Ideally, each modification should result in a decrease in the AIC or ECVI suggesting that the addition of this path would cross-validate in a future sample of the same size and sampled in the same way.

An Example

The example presented here was based on data from the study "The school sport club" (Feigin, Hangeby & Bareli, 1998). The study focused on students' attitudes toward participation in school sport clubs, their perceptions of the function of these clubs to school, and their satisfaction with participation in school sport clubs. For this example, we chose to present a model that examines the relationships between five latent variables: three exogenous variables that deal with the reasons for choosing to participate in school sport club, a mediating variable that measures the perception of sports to the student and school (function), and an endogenous variable of student satisfaction from school sport club. Each of these variables is presented as a latent variable based on the indicators below.

Using Likert-type scale items with a 4 category format (1= does not apply to me at all....4= applies to me very much), students were asked why they chose to partic-ipate in the competitive school sport clubs. The indicators were as follow:

Choice based on security and comfort reasons:

V1—It is much nicer to play with friends in school than in sport association clubs.

V2—The conditions at school are much better than in sport association clubs.

V3—My parents feel that it is safer to engage in sport in the school club.

V4—It is much easier to get to sport activities in the school club compared to other clubs.

Choice based on physical educator's encouragement

V5—The PE teacher encouraged me to join the school sport club.

V6—The PE teacher encouraged me to participate in this sport field.

Choice based on external reasons

V7—I had no information about other opportunities to be involved in sport.

V8—My parents advised me to choose the school sport club.

V9—Some of my friends chose this sport.

V10—This is what was offered in the school sport club.

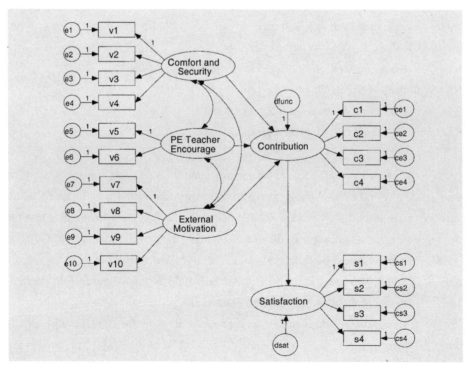

Figure 3.38   The Base Model.

As shown in Figure 3.38, all indicators are represented by squares and the latent variables are represented by ellipses. Each of the indicators is measured with an error, sometimes referred to as 'uniqueness' (represented in circles).

In addition, the students were asked to indicate how they perceived the contribution of sport to them and to the school and to indicate how satisfied they were with various aspects of the sport club activities. The mediating variable, contribution, was measured with the following indicators, requiring students to rate the extent to which they agree with each statement (1 = strongly disagree ... 4 = strongly agree).

The SCHOOL SPORT CLUB in your school caused:

C1—Higher identification of students with school,

C2—Involvement of non-PE teachers in sport events,

C3—Interest of Non PE teachers in sport, and

C4—Encouragement of students to participate in sport activities.

The exogenous variable, satisfaction, was measured with 4 indicators, requiring students to rate the extent to which they are satisfied with the school sport club (1 = not satisfied at all ... 4 = Very satisfied):

S1—With the practice program offered in the school sport club.

S2—With the level of coaching in the school sport club.

S3—With improving my own sport achievements.

S4—With the school team achievements.

We incorporated the five latent variables into a base model (Figure 3.38), which consists of the theory. All exogenous variables were correlated and for each latent variable one indicator is given a fixed value of one that assigns the measurement unit for the latent variable. The number of distinct elements in the covariance matrix is 171. The number of parameters to be estimated is 43. Therefore, the number of degrees-of-freedom is 128 and the model is over-identified according to this counting rule (Bollen, 1989). Estimates of the parameters were obtained using ML estimation.

The results of this model are presented in diagram 3.39 (using AMOS program). First, it is necessary to evaluate the general fit of the model because serious evidence of lack of fit would call into question the interpretation of specific effects. The results show that this model did not fit the data according to the minimum value of discrepancy (χ^2=253.65, df=128, p=.00). However according to the other fit indices, this model was shown to fit the data well (GFI=.93; AGFI=.91; CFI=.93; RMSEA=.05).

On the basis of evidence of approximate fit, we will proceed to interpret the effects in the model. The base model indicated a significant effect of comfort and security choice (β = .58) and of PE encouragement (β = .15) on contribution. External choice did not have a significant effect on contribution. A significant effect was found for the effect of contribution on satisfaction (β= .37). As for the measurement part of the model, all indicators were significantly loaded on the latent variables. The correlations among the exogenous latent variables were all highly significant.

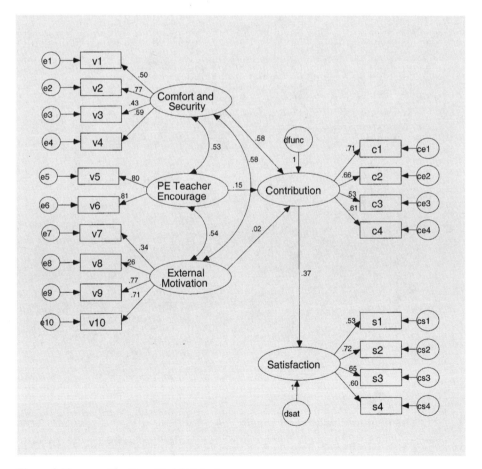

Figure 3.39   The Base Model Output.

As we explained earlier in this chapter one should consider two kinds of modification: the first is to remove non-significant paths based on their associated *t*-values, and
the second is to add paths based on modification indices suggested by theory in combination with information provided by the program. In our example we modified the model
by removing the non-significant path between external motivation and contribution. We
then re-estimated the model once again without this path. No modification indices were
suggested to improve the model. Since the external choice variable did not relate to any of
the variables in the model, we eliminated it from the model and estimated the model once
again without this variable. The modified and final model is presented in Figure 3.40.

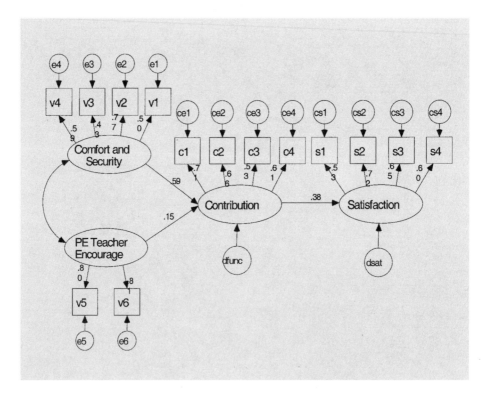

Figure 3.40   The Final Modified Model.

The final-modified model (Figure 3.40) had a significant discrepancy value
(χ^2=162.99, *df*=73, *p*=.00) but some of the other fit indices improved (GFI=.95;
AGFI=.92; GFI=.93; RMSEA=.05). The explained variance was 46% for contribution
and 14% for satisfaction.

To conclude, the satisfaction of students derived from participation in school sport clubs is mediated by how the students perceived the contribution of school sport clubs. Students that tend to choose the school sport club based on comfort and security reasons tend also to have high positive attitudes toward the function of the school sport club. The relations between the variables of choice (comfort and security, PE teacher engorgement, external motivation) and the satisfaction from school sport clubs is mediated through the contribution attitudes and had no significant direct effect on satisfaction.

In this example we laid down the basic procedures of estimation. In the second part of this chapter we will address advanced topics.

Additional Topics in Structural Equation Modeling

In this section we consider some additional issues in structural equation modeling. We will begin with a discussion of missing data problems and how they are addressed in the SEM context. This will be followed by a discussion of modeling data that arise from hierarchical structures, such as athletes nested within clubs. Finally, we will consider the problem of change over time and how this is modelled within an SEM context.

Missing Data

Missing data is a ubiquitous problem in all branches of the social and behavioral sciences. Generally, structural equation modeling assumes that each unit of analysis has complete data. However, for numerous reasons, units may have missing values on one or more of the variables under investigation. Standard approaches to handling missing data, such as listwise deletion or pairwise deletion, have numerous disadvantages. More modern approaches, as we will see, are theoretically sound, but often are unable to be implemented in practice.

To begin, we will consider a standard terminology for missing data problems. Consider first the case of missing values in one variable, say number of hours that a student participates in athletic activities. The effect of missing values in the univariate case is to reduce the sample from size n to size m. Statistical summaries of the data, such as the sample mean and variance are based on m units who responded to the question. If the m observed units are a random sample from the n total sample, then the missing data are said to be *missing-at-random* (MAR) and the missing data mechanism is *ignorable*. However, if students with few hours of athletic participation tend not to report their hours of participation, then the probability of observing a value for the number of hours of participation depends on their level of participation and hence the missing data are not MAR and the mechanism generating the missing data is *non-ignorable*.

Consider next the case of two variables with missing data occurring for only one variable. This is referred to as a monotone missing data pattern. To place this problem in a substantive context consider examining the number of hours of participation and motivation to participate in athletics for a sample of students, with missing values again occurring for number of hours of participation. Following Rubin's (1976) terminology, three cases are possible. First, if missing values for hours of participation are independent of both motivation and hours of participation - i.e. that the number of hours of participation are unrelated to the pattern of omitted responses on both variables - then the missing data are MAR and the observed data are *observed-at-random* (OAR), and thus the missing data are *missing-completely-at-random* (MCAR). Second, if missing values on hours of participation are dependent on values of motivation, we say that the missing values on participation are MAR. Although the observed values on participation are not a random sample from the original sample, they are a random sample within sub-groups defined on motivation (Little, 1987). Finally, if the probability of responding to participation depends on participation, then the data are neither MAR or OAR. Here again, the missing data mechanism is non-ignorable.

There are essentially three approaches to handling missing data in the SEM context. The first is to use *listwise deletion*. Listwise deletion involves deleting any observation that has any missing value on the variables used in the analysis. The advantage of this approach is its obvious simplicity. The disadvantages to this approach are twofold. First, this approach may result in a dramatic loss of sample size depending on the amount missing data. Second, it assumes that the missing data are MCAR, which is a very restrictive assumption.

The second approach to handling missing data is to use *pairwise deletion*. Here, observations are deleted if there are any missing values on any pair of variables under consideration. The advantage to pairwise deletion is also its simplicity. However, there are two disadvantages to pairwise deletion: first, as with listwise deletion, pairwise deletion assumes that the missing data are MCAR. Second, pairwise deletion results in variances and covariances calculated on different sample sizes. This is a major problem for SEM for the following reason: sample covariance matrices are sample statistics and hence have sampling distributions. The sampling distribution of a sample covariance matrix is called the Wishart distribution. There is a direct correspondence between the Wishart distribution and the multivariate normal distribution, such that maximum likelihood estimation can be derived from both. Hence, a violation of the Wishart distribution assumption will have the same effect on maximum likelihood estimation as will a violation of the multivariate normality assumption. The current view is that pairwise deletion should be avoided if possible, and only be used if the amount of missing data is quite small and MCAR. Here, however, listwise deletion may be preferable.

The third approach to handling missing data in the SEM context is to formally model the process that gives rise to missing data. In SEM, an approach to formally modeling the missing data mechanism was offered simultaneously by Muthén, Kaplan, and Hollis (1987) and Allison (1987). Their approach considered missing data as a problem of selection. That is, they considered how observations were selected to be observed and modelled the selection process as a function of the variables or factors in the model. Their approach can work well for designed missing data problems such as found in the administration of national assessments of achievement (see Kaplan, 1995 for an example using the National Assessment of Educational Progress). In the context of sports sciences this approach could be useful when measuring physical fitness wherein not all athletes are measured on all fitness sub-tests but where we wish to estimate a fitness factor. This approach might also work well for longitudinal studies on different cohorts. Again, in the sport and exercise sciences field, this approach might be useful for modeling perseverance in sports activities taking into account drop out over time.

The disadvantage of the model-based approach to handling missing data is that, in general, it does not work well for typically encountered patterns of missing data. New approaches, such as the full information maximum likelihood approach of Arbuckle (1996) appear promising but little is known about the procedure at this time. Thus, the problem of missing data within the SEM context remains an open area of scholarship. Therefore, when encountering missing data in applications of SEM, the preferred ad hoc approach is listwise deletion.

Sampling Problems

Up to now our discussion of SEM has assumed that observations were obtained under simple random sampling and that the observations were independent of one another. In research on any organization such as athletic teams, observations are usually drawn from multi-stage random sampling. For example, in the area of sports one may wish to draw a random sample of athletic teams, followed by a random sample of athletes within the teams. The outcome of interest might be a measure of "sense of coherence".

When observations are drawn from this type of sampling it is not appropriate to ignore hierarchical structure of the data - assuming that the team level has no effect. The reason is two-fold. First, if data are disaggregated to the level of the athlete, then any analysis involving the "sense of coherence" (e.g. regression analysis) would result in a violation of the standard assumption of independent observations. This is because the athletes share observable and unobservable characteristics of the team in common such that athletes within a team are more similar amongst themselves then they are amongst athletes in other teams.

Second, if the data are aggregated to the team level there can be a substantial loss of variability due to individual differences among athletes. This loss of variability results in inflated correlations among other variables aggregated in the same manner. Thus, neither approach for handling hierarchical data is optimal. Instead, we wish to have a method that accounts for the multilevel structure of the data and allows each level to contribute to the prediction of the outcome of interest.

In Chapter IV of this book there is a discussion of multilevel modeling - a class of methodologies that are specifically suited for this kind of data (see e.g. Bryk & Raudenbush, 1992). However, multilevel modeling suffers from two limitations. First, it is not suited for the incorporation of latent variables. Thus, problems of measurement error might affect inferences. Second, standard multilevel models cannot model the complexity of relationships within and between levels of an organization. Recently, advances have been made extending multilevel methods to the SEM context. However, this is a very advanced topic that is beyond the scope of this chapter. Interested readers should refer to theoretical and didactic papers by Muthén, (1991, 1994), Muthén and Satorra (1989), and Kaplan and Elliott (1997a, 1997b).

Growth Modeling

So far, our discussion of structural equation modeling has focussed on cross-sectional data. Of major importance to sport and exercise sciences is change over time and specifically the predictors of change over time. For example, it might be of interest to model the change in measures of motivation in sports over the junior high school years (e.g. 7th grade through 9th grade). A methodology for estimating change over time and relating change to hypothesized predictors of change is referred to as growth curve modeling (see Muthén, 1991; Willett & Sayer, 1994).

Growth curve modeling is a special case of general multilevel modeling where time is viewed as nested within individuals. This allows each individual to bring his/her own unique growth trajectory into the analysis. The first step in growth curve modeling is to estimate the initial status and growth rate over the time period. Using the motivation in sports example, the initial starting point might be 7th grade, though it is perfectly appropriate to choose another grade level. The initial status parameter is the mean motivation score for the sample of participants at time t (e.g. 7th grade). The growth rate gives the rate of change in motivation over the time period. Finally, one can obtain the correlation between the initial status and growth rate. This correlation would provide information as to whether variation in starting level relates to rate of change over time. For example, if one is highly motivated at time t we would not expect much change in motivation over time.

Next, it might be of interest to add predictors into the growth curve model. Two kinds of predictors can be distinguished. The first predictors are referred to as *time-invariant predictors* of initial status and growth rate. As the name implies, these predictors are not assumed to vary over time. A good example of a time-invariant predictor is gender. To take the example of motivation in sports, we may find that males start out with higher levels of motivation compared to females, but that females have a higher rate of change in motivation as compared to males over time. Other time-invariant predictors can be added as well.

The second type of predictors is referred to as *time-varying predictors*. Time-varying predictors are assumed to predict the "ups and downs" of the growth curve. An example of a time-varying predictor might be parental encouragement for sports over time. We might expect that as parental encouragement wanes over time, the reported motivation for sports by the child might also decrease.

Finally, it is possible to incorporate more than one outcome which changes over time. For example, we may add reported satisfaction with sports activities as an outcome. In this example, we can estimate two initial status parameters, two slopes and the correlations among these four parameters. In this case, the correlation between the initial status parameters would reveal whether motivation at time t is related to satisfaction at time t. The correlation between the slopes would indicate whether the rate of change in motivation is related to the rate of change in satisfaction. Other correlations are similarly interpreted.

Growth curve modeling is a very flexible and increasingly popular methodology. It has recently been extended to cover changes in dichotomous outcomes as representing changes in the probability of an event over time (Muthén, 1996). The potential use of growth curve modeling for forecasting has been explored by Kaplan and George (1998). It can be incorporated in multilevel programs such as HLM (Bryk, Raudenbush, & Congdon, 1994), and SEM programs such as LISREL (Jöreskog & Sörbom, 1993). The advantage of the SEM approach is that it tends to be more flexible in handling complex growth curves and can incorporate latent variable outcomes over time.

Concluding Remarks

The purpose of this chapter was to provide an overview of the method of structural equation modeling. We considered the general specification of the model, issues of estimation and identification, model testing, and model evaluation. In addition, we considered some advanced topics, including missing data, sampling problems, and growth curve modeling.

Structural equation modeling is, arguably, the most popular advanced methodology in the social and behavioral sciences. The popularity of the methodology is attested to by a journal specifically devoted to structural modeling as well as a very active electronic listserv called SEMNET[6]. Moreover, there are several statistical software programs on the market that can be used to conduct structural equation modeling. These include LISREL (Jöreskog & Sörbom, 1991), EQS (Bentler, 1995), AMOS (Arbuckle, 1996), and Mx (Neale, 1997), to name a few. A very good review of these and other software programs can be found in Hox (1995). Since this review a new program referred to as Mplus (Muthén & Muthén, 1999) has been developed which can handle complex multilevel structural models and growth models in a simple way.

A key feature of most of these software programs is their user-friendly graphical interface. The ease of use of these software programs, however, comes at a price. Specifically, it is possible that the ease of these software programs can come at the expense of understanding the statistical theory and inherent limitations of structural equation modeling. For example, current software programs make model modification a matter of simply drawing the desired path on the computer screen. Therefore, the temptation to fit the model to the data may be great. A novice user may not understand the problems associated with capitalization on chance in fitting models to data. Therefore, easy to use software programs are no substitute for substantive theoretical considerations and a solid understanding of the statistical underpinnings of the method.

Although important advances have been made in the theory of structural equation modeling, the future of the methodology lies in its ability to reveal insights into the relationships among constructs that could not otherwise be obtained via simpler procedures. The knowledge gained from the application of structural equation modeling has been, and promises to be, an important contribution to the body of theoretical literature in sports science.

---

[6] To subscribe to SEMNET send an email message to LISTERV@BAMA.UA.EDU and in the body of the email write SUBSCRIBE SEMNET *first name last name*.

References

Allison, P. D. (1987). Estimation of linear models with incomplete data. In C. C. Clogg (Ed.), *Sociological Methodology 1987* (pp. 68-119). San Francisco: Jossey-Bass.

Arbuckle, J. L. (1996). Full information estimation in the presence if incomplete data. In G. A. Marcoulides & R.

E. Schumacker (Eds.) *Advanced Structural Equation Modeling: Issues and Techniques* (pp. 243-277).

Mahwah: Lawrence Erlbaum and Associates.

Bartholomew, J. B., Edwards, S. M., Brewer, B. W., Avn Raalte, J. L., & Lindrer, D. E. (1998). The sport inventory for pain: A confirmatory factor analysis. *Research Quarterly for Exercise and Sport, 69*, 24-29.

Bentler, P. M. (1995). *EQS Structural Equation Program Manual*. Encino, Ca.: Multivariate Software Inc.

Bollen, K. A. (1989). *Structural Equations with Latent Variables*. New York: Wiley.

Bollen, K. A., & Long, J. S. (Eds.). (1993*). Testing Structural Equation Models*. Newbury Park, Ca: Sage Publication.

Browne, M. W. (1982). Covariance structures. In Hawkins, D. M. (ed.). *Topics in Applied Multivariate Analysis* (pp.72-141). Cambridge: Cambridge University Press.

Browne, M. W. (1984). Asymptotically distribution-free methods for the analysis of covariance structures.

British Journal of Mathematical and Statistical Psychology, 37, 62-83.

Browne, M. W., & Cudeck, R. (1993). Alternative ways of assessing model fit. In K. A. Bollen & Long, J. S.

(Eds*.) Testing Structural Equation Modeling* (pp. 136-162). Newbury Park, CA: Sage Publications.

Bryk, A. S., & Raudenbush, S. W. (1992). *Hierarchical Linear Models: Applications and Data Analysis Methods*. Newbury Park, CA: Sage Publications.

Bryk, A. S., Raudenbush, S. W., & Congdon, R. T. (1994). *HLM 2/3*. Chicago: Scientific Software International.

Duncan, O. D. (1975). *Introduction to Structural Equation Models*. New York: Academic Press.

Fejgin, N., Hanegby, R., & Bareli, M. (1998). *The School Sport Club in Israel* . Netanya: Zinman College of PE and Sport Sciences & Israeli Sport Authority. (In Hebrew).

Gill, D. L. & Deeter, T. E. (1988). Development of the sport orientation questionnaire. Research *Quarterly for*
Exercise and Sport, 59, 191-202.

Hox, J. J. (1995). AMOS, EQS, and LISREL for Windows: A comparative review. *Structural Equation Modeling, 2,* 79-91.

Hu, L., & Bentler, M. P. (1995). Evaluating model fit. In R.H. Hoyle (Ed.). *Structural Equation Modeling: Concepts, Issues and Applications* (pp. 76-99). Thousand Oaks, CA: Sage.

Jöreskog, K. G. (1971). Simultaneous factor analysis in several populations. *Psychometrika, 36,* 409-426.

Jöreskog, K. G. (1973). A general method for estimating a linear structural equation - system. In A. S. Goldberger & O. D. Duncan (Eds.), *Structural Equation Models in the Social Sciences* (pp. 85-112). New York: Academic.

Jöreskog, K. G & Goldberger, A. S. (1975). Estimation of a model with multiple indicators and multiple causes of a single latent variable. *Journal of the American Statistical Association, 10,* 631-639.

Jöreskog, K. G., & Sörbom, D. (1989). *LISREL 7 User's Reference Guide.* Chicago: Scientific Software.

Jöreskog K. G. & SÖrbom, D. (1993*). LISREL 8: Structural Equation Modeling with SIMPLIS command language.* Hillsdale, NJ: Erlbaum.

Kaplan, D. (1990a). Evaluation and modification of covariance structure models: A review and recommendation. *Multivariate Behavioral Research, 25,* 137-155.

Kaplan, D. (1990b). Rejoinder on evaluating and modifying costructure models. *Multivariate Behavioral Research, 25,* 197204

Kaplan, D. (1991). On the modification and predictive validity of covariance structure models. *Quality and Quantity, 25,* 307-314.

Kaplan, D. (1995). Statistical power in structural equation modeling. In R. H. Hoyle (ed.), *Structural Equation Modeling: Concepts, Issues, and Applications* (pp. 100-117). Newbury Park, CA: Sage Publications, Inc.

Kaplan, D. & Elliott. P. R. (1997a). A model-based approach to validating education indicators using multilevel structural equation modeling. *Journal of Educational and Behavioral Statistics, 22,* 323 348.

Kaplan, D., & Elliott, P. R. (1997b). A didactic example of multilevel structural equation modeling applicable to the study of organizations. *Structural Equation Modeling: A Multidisciplinary Journal, 4,* 1-24.

Kaplan, D., & George, R. (1998). Evaluating latent variable growth models through ex post simulation. *Journal of Educational and Behavioral Statistics, 23,* 216-235.

Kessling, J. W. (1972). *Maximum Likelihood Approaches to Causal Analysis. Unpublished Doctoral Dissertation,* University of Chicago.

Li, F., & Harmer, P. (1996a). Testing the simplex assumption underlying the sport motivation scale: A structural equation modeling analysis. *Research Quarterly for Exercise and Sport, 67,* 396-405.

Li, F., & Harmer, P. (1996b). Confirmatory factor analysis of the group environment questionnaire with and intercollegiate sample. *Journal of Sport and Exercise Psychology, 18,* 49-63.

Little, R. J. A., & Rubin, D. B. (1987). *Statistical Analysis with Missing Data.* New York: John Wiley & Sons.

Markland, D. & Hardy, L. (1997). On the factorial and construct validity of the intrinsic motivation inventory:
Conceptual and Operational Concerns. *Research Quarterly for Exercise and Sport, 68,* 20-32.

Marsh, H. W. & Remayne, R. S. (1994). A multidimensional physical self-concept and its relations to multiple components of physical activity. *Journal of Sport and Exercise Psychology, 16,* 43-55.

Mulaik, S. (1972). *The Foundations of Factor Analysis.* New York: McGraw-Hill.

Muthén, B. (1996). Growth modeling with binary responses. In A. von Eye and C. C. Clogg (eds.), *Categorical Cariables in Developmental Research.* New York: Academic Press.

Muthén, B. (1994). Multilevel covariance structure analysis. *Sociological Methods and Research, 22,* 376-398.

Muthén, B. (1991). Multilevel factor analysis of class and student achievement components. Journal of *Educational Measurement, 28,* 338-354

Muthén, B. (1984). A general structural equation model with dichotomous, ordinal, categorical, and continuous latent variable indicators. *Psychometrika, 49,* 115-132.

Muthén B. & Hofacker (1988). Testing the assumptions underlying tetrachoric correlations. *Psychometrika, 53*, 563-578.

Muthén B. & Muthén L. (1999). *Mplus User's Guide.* Los Angeles: Muthén & Muthén.

Muthén B. & Kaplan D. (1985). A comparison of some methodologies for the factor analysis of non-normal Likert variables. *British Journal of Mathematical and Statistical Psychology, 38,* 171-189.

Muthén B. & Kaplan D. (1992). A comparison of some methodologies for the factor analysis of non-normal Likert variables: A note on the size of the model. *British Journal of Mathematical and Statistical Psychology, 45,* 19-30.

Muthén B. & Satorra A. (1989). Multilevel aspects of varying parameters in structural models. In R. D. Bock (ed.), *Multilevel Analysis of Educational Data* (pp. 87-99). San Diego, CA: Academic Press.

Muthén, B., Kaplan, D., & Hollis (1987). On structural equation modeling with data that are not missing completely at random. *Psychometrika, 51*, 431-462.

Neale, M. C. (1997). *Mx: Statistical Modeling.* Richmond, Va.: Department of Psychiatry.

Rubin, D. E. (1976). Inference and missing data. *Biometrika, 63,* 581-592.

Saris, W. E., Satorra, A., & Sörbom, D. (1987). The detention and correction of specification errors in structural equation models. In C. C. Clogg (Ed.), *Sociological Methodology 1987* (pp. 105-129). San Francisco: Jossey-Bass.

Satorra, A., & Saris, W. E. (1985). Power in the likelihood ratio test in covariance structure analysis. *Psychometrika, 50*, 83-90.

Sobel, M., & Bohrnstedt, G. W. (1985). Use of null models in evaluating the fit of covariance structural models. In N.. Tuma (Ed.), *Sociological Methodology 1985* (pp. 152-178). San Francisco: Jossey-Bass.

Sonstroem, R. J., Harlow, L. L., & Josephs, L. (1994). Exercise and self-esteem: Validity of model expansion and exercise Associations. *Journal of Sport and Exercise Psychology, 16*, 29-42.

Sörbom, D. (1974). A general method for studying differences in factor means and factor structure between groups. *British Journal of Mathematical and Statistical Psychology, 27,* 229-239.

Sörbom, D. (1989). Model modification. *Psychometrika, 54*, 371-384.

Steiger, J. H. (1990). Structural model evaluation and modification: An interval estima tion approach. *Multivariate Behavioral Research, 25*, 173-180.

Tanaka, J. S. (1993). Multifaceted conception of fit in structural equation models. In K. A. Bollen & J. S. Long (Eds.), *Testing Structural Equation Models* (pp. 10-39). Newbury Park, Ca: Sage Publication.

Thurstone, L. L. (1947). *Modern Factor Analysis*. Chicago: University of Chicago Press.

Wiley, D. E. (1973). The identification problem for structural equation models with unmeasured variables. In A. S. Goldberger & O. D. Duncan (Eds.), *Structural Equation Models in the Social Sciences* (pp. 69-83). New York: Academic.

Willett, J. B, & Sayer, A. G., (1994). Using covariance structure analysis to detect correlates and predictors of individual change over time. *Psychological Bulletin, 116*, 363-381.

Summary

Chapter 3 introduced one of the most important groups of methods, which are used in science in general, and sport and exercise sciences in particular. The use of the methods for estimation of simple correlations among variables, and their more advanced implications, such as predictions, selections, clustering/grouping, exploration and confirmation of concepts, are believed to be clear by now. It is not just the mathematical procedures which are important to comprehend, but also the match between the scientific questions and the methods, which are aimed at giving answers to these questions. Each of the methods which were introduced has weaknesses and limitation. When applying these methods, one should be aware of one's strengths and limitations. It is through this awareness, that its vast applications can be better understood.

CHAPTER IV: EXPERIMENTAL AND QUASI-EXPERIMENTAL METHODS

This chapter describes experimental designs and the statistical principles associated with them. It is aimed at understanding what is meant by the term TRUE DIFFERENCES or RELIABLE DIFFERENCES between two or more groups or within the same group of people or objects on different occasions. In other words, we shall discuss the CONDITIONS under which we can TRUST that DIFFERENCES are RELIABLE with a GIVEN PROBABILITY. This enables the researcher to reduce an ERROR in JUDGEMENT and be more CONFIDENT that under similar conditions, similar differences will be repeated. This chapter also explores the reasons WHY differences between or within groups occur. Some differences between groups occur because people belong to different cultures, live under different conditions, eat different food, share different life habits and so on. But differences may also occur because various planned and natural manipulations, interventions, and events happen which cause people to change on one or more variables. The researcher is the one who decides which VARIABLES are OBSERVED and what should be taken into account, so that ALTERNATIVE EXPLANATIONS to the study's results will be minimal.

The conductance of errors that people make is illustrated here by a story from the court house.

A suspect person is brought to the court house. She is accused of burglary. After the testimonies have been heard and evidence shown, the judge makes a decision whether to find the suspect guilty or innocent of the charges against her. If many witnesses could identify the accused person and the accused person could not show a strong alibi, the judge has a case to find the accused guilty or innocent of the crime. However, if very few witnesses appeared, did not see the person, only heard her voice, and she has a strong alibi, it is probable that the judge will find the person innocent. Under what conditions will the judge find it hard to decide whether the person is guilty or innocent?

The answer is simple, when evidence brought to the judge is doubtful and unreliable. Under such conditions the judge will probably free the person, but the person could still be the thief! Such cases are very well known in the legal system: doubt in evidence leads to an "innocence" decision, even if it may be wrong! Assume that the judge in the above case was seeking more evidence that will enable him/her to make justice to both sides and such evidence could be found. Then the decision of the judge REDUCES the PROBABILITY of making an ERROR in his/her decision. His/her decision is made with more CONFIDENCE that justice was made. REDUCTION in ERROR allows a more COMPETENT and RELIABLE DECISION to be achieved. This example should be kept in mind, because SCIENTIFIC INQUIRY is about asking questions, and designing a study which is aimed at answering these questions. Based on the EVIDENCE, the scientist makes the DECISION about the PROBABILITY that one of the HYPOTHESES is ACCEPTED and the alternative one is REJECTED. Experimental designs are aimed at this target. A SOUND EXPERIMENTAL DESIGN is one which REDUCES the ERROR and INCREASES the PROBABILITY of the scientist making RELIABLE DECISIONS.

In the first part of this chapter we shall introduce the BASIC TERMS and ASSUMPTIONS, which are required to be present when simple or complex studies are planned. The different research designs will then be introduced with examples in the domain of exercise and sport. The construction of this chapter is illustrated in a graph, and the contents of this chapter are introduced next.

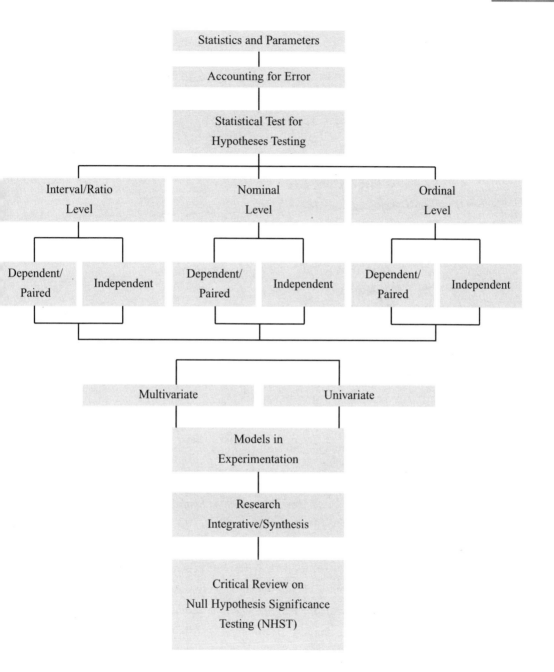

Contents

(1)   Sampling Distributions, Statistics, and Parameters

Earlier we have described how a sample, which represents the population, is derived. Various methods were introduced to enable the researcher or surveyor to reliably ensure the REPRESENTATIVENESS of the sample of the population. The DATA COLLECTION and SUMMATION/REDUCTION of observations made on the sample is aimed at deriving conclusions about the population, otherwise GENERALIZATION of the FINDINGS could not be made. A study, which uses ALL the population, is termed CENSUS and the descriptive measures are termed PARAMETERS. Thus a PARAMETER is a NUMERICAL VALUE that DESCRIBES SOMETHING in the POPULATION. Parameters of the population are usually unknown unless ALL the population is sampled. Parameters are denoted by Greek symbols (μ for mean, θ for standard deviation, etc.).

The descriptive measures in the sample are termed STATISTICS and they are denoted by Roman symbols ($\bar{x}$ or m for mean, S or SD for standard deviation, etc.). The statistics are OBSERVED and KNOWN MEASURES, and they usually change from one sample of the population to another one. The MEAN of the POPULATION in any variable is CONSTANT, and does not change at a certain point in time. The mean of the various samples do CHANGE. We therefore may ask when verifying the hypothesis in a study, HOW WELL DO THE STATISTICS of our SAMPLE represent the POPULATION from which it was derived? We attempt to verify the PARAMETERS by using the STATISTICS to MAKE DECISIONS. The question is, which STATISTICAL TEST should we use to arrive at these DECISIONS? It should be noted and reminded that the scientific enquiry derives from a SOUND THEORY. A sound theory is the foundation of HYPOTHESES DERIVATION (introduced in detail in Part II, Chapter 6). The methods we describe in this chapter are aimed at verification of these hypotheses.

To ensure that the SAMPLE statistics represent the population, INFERENTIAL STATISTICS are applied. Inferential statistics are "the numerical techniques used for making conclusions about a population, based on the information obtained from a random sample drawn from that population" (Argyrous, 1996, p. 104). Statistical inference depends on:

- RAW DATA—the numbers, which represent the measure of the variables in each case of the sample.
- DESCRIPTIVE DATA—summary values such as the mean, median, mode, range, and standard deviation that represent the sample on a variable.
- INFERENTIAL STATISTICS—statistical test's values which enable us to make a generalization about the population.

If theoretically we derive an infinite number of samples from the population and they share an equal number of observations, their means will be NORMALLY DISTRIBUTED around the POPULATION MEAN. This distribution of means is termed SAMPLING DISTRIBUTION. This distribution is a THEORETICAL one because in reality we do not use an infinite number of samples for examining our research hypotheses. We prefer to use various and limited numbers of samples from the population and examine how close their statistics are. If we choose a random sample of n observations from a population with mean μ, and variance (squared standard deviation) θ^2, we assume that the sample is drawn from a NORMAL MEAN DISTRIBUTION with MEAN μ, and a STANDARD ERROR $\theta_{\bar{x}}$ which is the STANDARD DEVIATION of the MEANS of the HYPOTHETICAL SAMPLES had they been used. The standard error of the mean is

$$\theta_{\bar{x}} = \theta/\sqrt{n} \qquad (1)$$

As can be seen, the larger the sample n, the smaller is the standard error . It reminds us of the "court story" previously mentioned: the more evidence brought to the judge, the smaller are the chances for him/her to make a wrong decision. Figure 4.1 demonstrates the decrease in standard error as a function of the number of observations, n. The mean remains in an almost identical location.

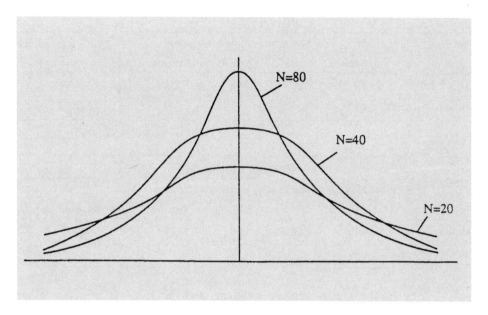

Figure 4.1 Distribution of Means (Standard Error of the Mean) as a Function of Sample Size n.

An example of means and standard errors is illustrated below. We sampled 637 observations and calculated their mean, standard deviation, and standard error of the mean. Then we repeated the same procedures for approximately 10% and 30% of these numbers respectively using SPSS 11.0. The standard errors (SE), $(SD/\sqrt{n})$ for each sample were:

N	SD	SE=$(SD/\sqrt{n})$	Mean
637	0.97	0.038	3.61
69	1.03	0.124	3.65
190	0.98	0.070	3.66

Descriptive Statistics

	N	Minimum	Maximum	Mean		Std.
	Statistic	Statistic	Statistic	Statistic	Std. Error	Statistic
VAR00001	637	1.00	5.00	3.6091	3.847E-02	.9710
Valid N (listwise)	637					

Descriptive Statistics

	N	Minimum	Maximum	Mean	Std.	
	Statistic	Statistic	Statistic	Statistic	Std. Error	Statistic
VAR00001	69	1.00	5.00	3.6522	.1236	1.0265
Valid N (listwise)	69					

Descriptive Statistics

	N	Minimum	Maximum		Mean	Std.
	Statistic	Statistic	Statistic	Statistic	Std. Error	Statistic
VAR00001	190	1.00	5.00	3.6579	7.095E-02	.9780
Valid N (listwise)	190					

The means remain almost identical, but the standard error increased substantially with the reduction in the number of observations. Fewer observations indicate less evidence that the statistics represent reliably the population parameters. Thus, for a smaller sample we should have larger CONFIDENCE INTERVALS around the STATISTICS calculated on the sample to ensure that the POPULATION PARAMETERS fall within this range. The more observations we sample the smaller is this confidence interval.

In sum, we refer to three distributions when we use inferential statistics. One distribution is that of the population with mean μ and standard deviation θ. This normal distribution is denoted as $NOR(\mu, \theta^2)$. The second distribution is that of the sample drawn from the population. Once this sample of observations is large, its values are normally distributed. This is the only REAL distribution we have. The third distribution is that of the STATISTICS (the means of the samples). The distribution of means is assumed to be normal with smaller standard deviation than that of the population. The contrast between the sampling and population distributions is shown in Figure 4.2.

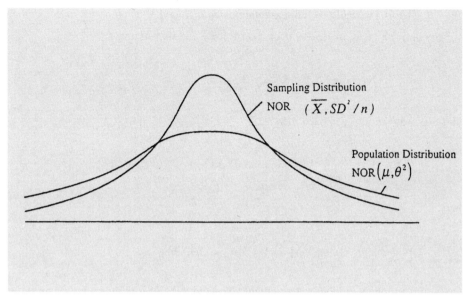

Figure 4.2   Population and Sampling Distributions.

The sampling distribution is used in SIGNIFICANCE TESTS for HYPOTHESES EXAMINATION using PROBABILITY RULES. The means and standard deviations of each of the three distributions are as follows:

population $\rightarrow \mu$ (mean), θ (standard deviation)

sample $\rightarrow \overline{X}$ (mean), S (standard deviation)

sample distribution $\rightarrow \mu$ (mean), $\theta/\sqrt{n}$ (standard error).

The theory postulates that with increased number of observations, the sample mean more precisely approximates the population mean, as the number of observations get closer to the number of subjects in the population (i.e., the big numbers law). Also, when n is large, the means will vary less among themselves. The greater the SAMPLE'S HOMOGENEITY (θ^2 smaller), the smaller the standard error ($\theta/\sqrt{n}$) and the more similar are the hypothetical means. This principle can be shown by a simple linear combination. The mean is a linear function of observation X_i because

$$\overline{X} = \frac{1}{n}(X_1 + X_2 + X_3 + ... X_n)$$

If Y is a variable with linear relations with X_i and X_i is randomly selected, then we can derive a mathematical expected term for y and its variance

$$Y = C_1 X_1 + C_2 X_2 + ... C_n X_n$$

and if x_i was randomly chosen then

$$E(Y) = C_1 E(X_1) + C_2 E(X_2) + ... C_n E(X_n)$$

and

$$VarY = \theta Y^2 = C_1^2 \theta X_1^2 + C_2^2 \theta X_2^2 + C_n^2 \theta X_n^2$$

When the sample is randomly derived, the expected Y, E(Y) is μ. If we decide that $C_i = 1/n$, then Y becomes the sample's means and

$$E(\overline{X}) = E(Y) = \frac{1}{n} (\mu + \mu + ... + \mu) - \frac{1}{n} (n\mu) = \mu$$

and since

$$C_1^2 = C_2^2 ... = C_n^2 = \frac{1}{n^2}$$

$$\theta_Y^2 = \theta_{\overline{x}}^2 = \frac{1}{n^2} \theta X_1^2 + \frac{1}{n^2} \theta X_2^2 + ... + \frac{1}{n^2} \theta X_n^2$$

$$= \frac{1}{n^2} (\theta^2 + \theta^2 + ... \theta^2) = (n\theta^2) = \theta^2/n$$

and therefore

$$E(X) = \mu$$
$$\theta_{\overline{x}}^2 = \theta^2/n \rightarrow \theta_{\overline{x}} = \theta/\sqrt{n}$$

which is the STANDARD ERROR of the MEAN when each observation has EQUAL CHANCE to be selected from the population. When the sample is smaller than 30 (n < 30) it is recommended to use equation 2.

$$SE_{\overline{x}} = S/\sqrt{n-1} \qquad\qquad (2)$$

One of the basic theorems in sampling distribution theory is the CENTRAL LIMIT THEOREM which states that the SAMPLING DISTRIBUTION of the MEANS will APPROXIMATE NORMALITY REGARDLESS of its FORM in the POPULATION DISTRIBUTION, provided that the sample size is sufficiently large and population variance is finite. The more the normal curve is distorted, the larger the sample of observations needed for the theorem to hold.

(2) Characteristics of a Good Estimator

How good is a statistic as an estimate of a parameter? The first CRITERION is BIAS. A good statistic is one that its SAMPLING DISTRIBUTION will be equal to the PARAMETER of which it estimates. This is more a matter of the method used for SAMPLING. "What one implies is that in the long run the mean of such statistics computed from a large number of samples of equal size will be equal to the parameter. If the statistic $\hat{\theta}$ is an estimator of the parameter θ, and if

$$E(\hat{\theta}) = \theta + C,$$

then the bias of the estimator is of magnitude C" (Winer, 1971, p. 7). Thus the mean $\overline{X}$ of a random sample is unbiased because the sampling distribution of $\overline{X}$ has an expected value of μ. When more RANDOM SAMPLES are derived from the population and their means are unequal, the AVERAGE of these MEANS has a greater PRECISION as an ESTIMATE of the POPULATION MEAN than each of the sample's means separately.

A good estimate is PRECISE, i.e., its STANDARD ERROR is very small. When the sample size increases, the standard error decreases, being $S/\sqrt{n}$, and the precision increases.

The EFFICIENCY of an unbiased estimator is calculated through the relation between the squared standard error of a sample and the BEST unbiased estimator.

An estimator is expected to be CONSISTENT. The CONSISTENCY of an estimator is reached "if the probability that it differs from the parameter by any amount approaches zero as the sample size increases" (Winer, 1971, p. 8). Also CONSISTENT estimators are ASYMPTOTICALLY UNBIASED ESTIMATORS.

A parameter is described by a NUMBER that is also termed POINT ESTIMATE. A RANGE OF NUMBERS which describes a parameter is termed INTERVAL ESTIMATE of the PARAMETERS. The difference between the smallest and largest numbers is the WIDTH of the INTERVAL.

The SAMPLING DISTRIBUTION of a statistic provides information about the RELATIVE FREQUENCY (PROBABILITY) of a STATISTIC in a GIVEN INTERVAL. This allows us to predict the relative frequency with which statistics of a GIVEN MAGNITUDE will occur if it truly represents the population.

Two important questions that are frequently addressed are: (1) given a sample, what is the LIKELIHOOD that it was drawn from a specified set of parameters, and (2) given a sample, what is the CONFIDENCE that the population from which it was drawn has specified parameters within a given range? R.A. Fisher introduced the MAXIMUM-LIKELIHOOD ESTIMATORS in which MAXIMUM PRECISION (MINIMUM STANDARD ERROR) is achieved. Another principle is that of LEAST SQUARE in which its estimators have minimum variance. There are also BAYES ESTIMATORS, which consist of some function of the sample observations that minimizes the expected values of a RISK.

An INTERVAL ESTIMATE is referred to as a CONFIDENCE INTERVAL for a PARAMETER. It consists of lower and upper bounds within which there is a specific likelihood/confidence that the parameter will be located. We shall refer to confidence interval next.

(3)   Confidence Interval of a Sample's Mean

When a random sample is drawn from a population and a mean is calculated, it is desirable to know within which limits the mean of the population is located. Since we do not observe all the population on the variable/s of interest, the CONFIDENCE

INTERVAL around the mean statistic allows us to know the RANGE within which μ of the population is located. The SMALLER this RANGE, the more EFFICIENT, PRECISE, and UNBIASED is the estimator $\overline{X}$.

The confidence interval is calculated by using the standard error of the mean $SE_{\overline{X}}$ derived from the standard deviation S, and the number of observations n, where

$$SE_{\overline{X}} = S/\sqrt{n}$$

assuming that the mean's distribution is normal with standard deviation $S/\sqrt{n}$ which is $SE_{\overline{X}}$. To set the confidence interval, the NORMAL CURVE AREAS are used. We already know that about 68% of the area lies between ±1S from the mean; between ±2S about 95%, and between ±3S about 99.7%. Thus the confidence intervals of the sample mean $\overline{X}$ are:

$$\overline{X} \pm 1S/\sqrt{n} = \overline{X} \pm 1SE_{\overline{X}} \quad \text{for 68.26\% confidence,}$$
$$\overline{X} \pm 2S/\sqrt{n} = \overline{X} \pm 2SE_{\overline{X}} \quad \text{for 95.46\% confidence, and}$$
$$\overline{X} \pm 3S/\sqrt{n} = \overline{X} \pm 3SE_{\overline{X}} \quad \text{for 99.73\% confidence.}$$

If 36 students were observed for sit-up performance, their mean $\overline{X} = 36$ and standard deviation S = 10, the standard error is

$$SE_{\overline{X}} = 10\sqrt{36} = 10/6 = 1.67$$

The confidence intervals will be accordingly

$30 \pm 1.67 = 28.33 - 31.67$ for 68.26% confidence,

$30 \pm 2 \cdot 1.67 = 30 \pm 3.34 = 26.66 - 33.34$ for 95.46% confidence, and

$30 \pm 3 \cdot 1.67 = 30 \pm 5.01 = 24.99 - 35.01$ for 99.97% confidence.

It can be clearly seen that the confidence interval becomes larger with increase in confidence. A 68.26% confidence is with 3.34(31.67 – 28.33) sit-ups, and 10.02(35.01 – 24.99) for 99.97% confidence. Thus the probability that the population mean sit-ups μ is between the values 24.99 – 35.01 is much higher than between the values 28.33 – 31.67.

Researchers usually prefer the 95% and 99% confidence intervals. 95% refers to the values ±1.96 in the normal curve area, and 99% refers to ±2.58. In Figure 4.3 these two intervals are presented.

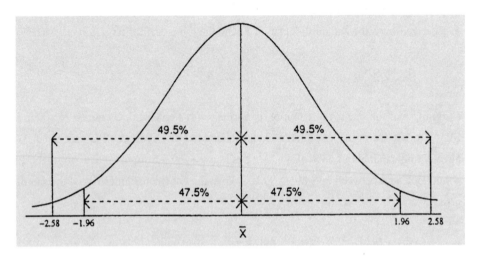

Figure 4.3 Area under the Normal Curve which Pertain to 95% and 99% of the Normal Curve.

Thus, the population mean, μ will be located within

$\overline{X} \pm 1.96SE_{\overline{X}}$ with 95% confidence, and

$\overline{X} \pm 2.58SE_{\overline{X}}$ with 99% confidence,

$95\% \rightarrow 30 \pm 1.96 \cdot 1.67 = 30 \pm 3.2732 = 26.7268 - 35.2732$

$99\% \rightarrow 30 \pm 2.58 \cdot 1.67 = 30 \pm 4.3086 = 25.6914 - 34.3086$

It can be seen from the term $S/\sqrt{n}$ that the confidence interval depends on how homogeneous or heterogeneous the sample is on the measured variable (S), and on the number of observations sampled. The higher the S (heterogeneity), the larger the $SE_{\overline{X}}$ and subsequently the confidence interval. The more observations are conducted, the smaller is $SE_{\overline{X}}$ and subsequently the interval.

When n < 30, it is recommended to subtract 1 from n, so that

$SE_{\overline{X}} = S/\sqrt{n-1}$

and then calculate the confidence interval. In some statistical books, confidence interval is denoted as ci and the value extracted from the normal distribution is denoted Z (represents any two values from the normal curve that pertains to the area under these values). Then, the equation for ci is

$$ci = \overline{X} \pm Z(S/\sqrt{n}) \qquad (3)$$

or for $n < 30$

$$ci = \overline{X} \pm Z(S/\sqrt{n-1}) \qquad (4)$$

The confidence interval ci can change accordingly to the researcher's wishes. If one wishes 80% confidence, then 40% should be above and below the mean, respectively. The Z value that corresponds to 40% is 1.28 and therefore

$$ci = \overline{X} \pm 1.28 \cdot S/\sqrt{n} \quad or \quad ci = \overline{X} \pm 1.28 \cdot S/\sqrt{n-1}$$

When we estimate the confidence interval with 99% confidence we take 1% chance of error that the population mean μ is above or below the upper or lower limits respectively (0.5% above and 0.5% below the interval limit). Similarly with 95% confidence we take 5% chance of an error (2.5% and 2.5% above and below the interval limit). The error-rate is denoted α (alpha) or p. In the above cases $\alpha = 0.01$ (1%) and $\alpha = 0.05$ (5%) respectively. In complex designs, the error term associated with different statistics has to be estimated first, before confidence intervals for the statistics are calculated.

Confidence intervals can be computed for means of several groups. Here is an example of 95% and 99% confidence intervals for five different age groups. In the second age group the number of observations was much larger than the others, and therefore the ci boundaries of $\overline{X}$ are much smaller. The 5th age category consisted only of 17 observations and therefore the ci boundaries of its mean $\overline{X}$ are very large. Note the SPSS 11.0 changes in the Y-axis values associated with 95% and 99% ci boundaries.

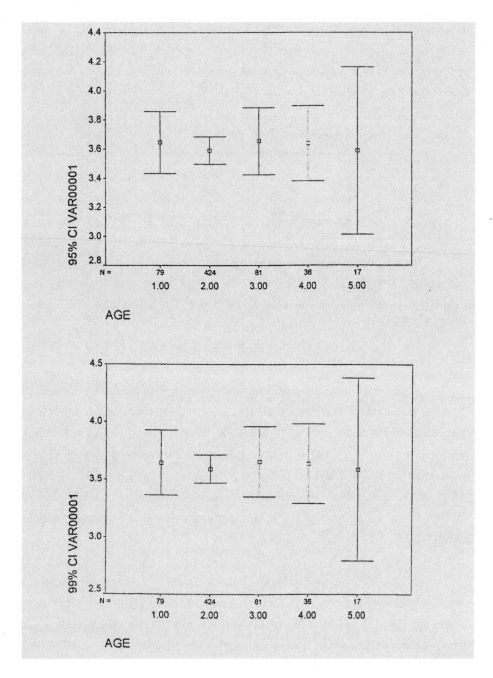

We further asked for $\overline{X} \pm 2SE_{\overline{X}}$, and in contrast $\overline{X} \pm 2S$ (the last DOES NOT relate to ci but rather to the SAMPLE DISTRIBUTION).

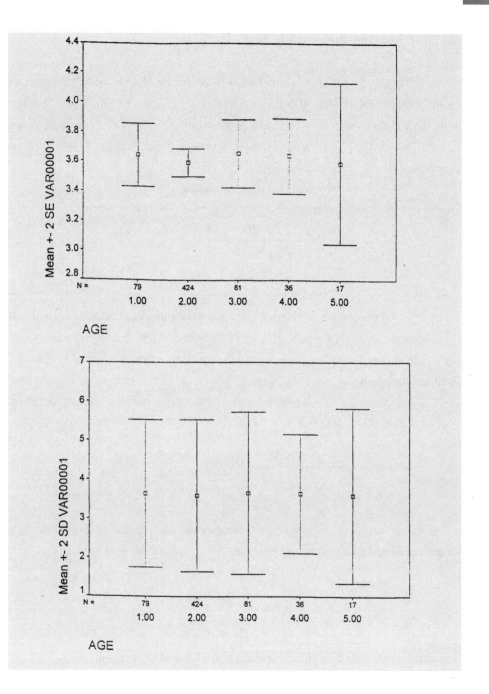

(4)   Choosing the Sample Size

Usually sample sizes are not easy to determine. The procedure depends on HOW MANY FACTORS (DVs) we have, what is the EFFECT we consider SUBSTANTIAL enough to be regarded as SIGNIFICANT, the LEVEL of confidence, i.e., PROBABILITY, ERROR-RATE we are ready to take, and the POWER of our conclusions that we shall introduce in the next section.

A very simple procedure is using the equation

$$N = \frac{Z^2 \cdot \theta^2}{\left(\dfrac{width}{2}\right)^2} \tag{5}$$

where θ^2 is the population variance, Z is the normal standardized value associated with the confidence interval (normally 95% or 99% where Z = 1.96 or 2.58 respectively) and the "width" is a pre-specified range around the mean. For example, the maximal oxygen uptake of the population precision range we wish is say, 2 mm/kg/min, we are interested in 95% confidence (i.e., Z = 1.96) and we know that the population standard deviation, θ, is 10.5. Thus the sample size is

$$N = \frac{1.96 \cdot 10.5^2}{\left(\dfrac{2}{2}\right)^2} = \frac{216.09}{1} = 216.09$$

which means that about 216 people are needed in this study. However, less conservative range, say 5 mm/kg/min and more precision (99% → Z = 2.58) will result in

$$N = \frac{2.58 \cdot 10.5^2}{\left(\dfrac{5}{2}\right)^2} = \frac{284.445}{6.25} = 45.51$$

a smaller sample size of 45-46 observations is needed now for higher precision but larger range of values around the mean. It is a decision the researcher has to make.

(5)   Uses of the Term Probability

The use of the term PROBABILITY is two-fold: (1) A PRIORI probability –
prior to sampling we are ready to take a RISK in making an error, say 5% in rejecting
the null hypothesis, H_0. It is common to use 0.05 (5/100 = 1/20), 0.01 (1/100) or even
0.001 (1/1000) as probability for an error in rejecting H_0. These p or α levels are
arbitrary and stay with us during the 20th century. Any researcher can choose a different
level of a priori probability for an error to occur, (2) POSTERIORI PROBABILITY –
after the sampling was conducted we determine the probability of rejecting H_0.

For example, assume that we are ready to take a 5% risk in making an error
rejecting H_0 (p $\leq$.05). Then we chose the sample out of the population; calculate
statistics and its standard error, say $Z_{\bar{X}}$ = 2.0. Accordingly the risk to reject H_0 and
conducting unidirectional error is 0.023, smaller than 0.05 that we determined
apriorically. There are cases in which we set an apriori probability, p, but get a lower p
after testing the data. This indicates that we may get a stronger effect than we have
expected. All the statistical programs provide the p (or α) value along with the statistical
tests of the hypotheses. We should be cautious in interpreting them.

(6)   Inferential Errors and Power

Verification of hypotheses can be seen as decision-making between correct and
wrong statements. Assume that 16-17 year old students in the country perform on the average
57 sit-ups and their standard deviation is 16. A special treatment was suggested to increase
these parameters to 61 ± 16. A researcher has applied this intervention on 100 students and
found that his/her student performed on the average 60 sit-ups. Can he/she argue that the
special treatment works? There are two PRECISE HYPOTHESES in this case:

H_0: μ = 57

H_1: μ = 61.

The sampling distribution was normal (i.e., population), and the standard error
of the 100 participants was $16/\sqrt{100} = 16/10 = 1.6$. Choosing p < .05 for a false rejection
of one-tailed H_0, he/she needs Z ≥ 1.65. The statistic Z is

$$Z = (\bar{X} - \mu_{\bar{X}})/S_{\bar{X}} = (60 - 57)/1.6 = 3/1.6 = 1.88$$

and since $1.65 < 1.88$, H_0 is rejected and it can be concluded the treatment is of value. The RISK FOR AN EFFOR in this example is termed TYPE-I ERROR. This error is defined as REJECTING H_0 WHEN H_0 IS CORRECT (termed also as α, alpha).

We may also ask what are the chances that the decision we make is NOT an error, indeed H_0 is NOT correct, and is our decision justified? To answer this question we ought to know the precise value of μ under H_1. In the above example we know μ under H_1, and we also know that the sit-up distribution was normal with mean $61 (\mu_{\overline{X}} = \mu$ under $H_1)$ and standard error

$$\theta_{\overline{X}} = 16/\sqrt{100} = 16/10 = 1.6.$$

Now we should look for the CRITICAL-Z (Z_c) that corresponds to the H_0 probability. In fact we transform Z_c under H_0 to a raw score that corresponds to the critical statistic – the mean. To estimate the critical mean, $\overline{X}_c$ we add to μ (under H_0) the multiplication Z_c (under H_1) by $\theta_{\overline{X}}$:

$$\overline{X}_c = (Z_{c(H_1)} \cdot \theta_{\overline{X}}) + \mu_{(H_0)}$$

and using the above example

$$\overline{X}_c = (1.65 \cdot 1.6) + 57 = 59.64$$

Then we estimate the standard score that corresponds to $\overline{X}_c$ under H_1:

$$Z_{c(H_1)} = (59.64 - 61)/1.6 = -1.36/1.6 = -0.85$$

The normal curve's values indicate that $Z = -0.85$ divides the area under the curve into two parts. The one on the right with 80.23% of the possible samples' means under H_1 and 19.77% of the possible samples' means under H_1 to the left. The 5% risk for an error divided the area under the normal curve into two parts under H_1: the right to with 80.23% of the area, and left to with 19.77% of the area. This is illustrated in Figure 4.4.

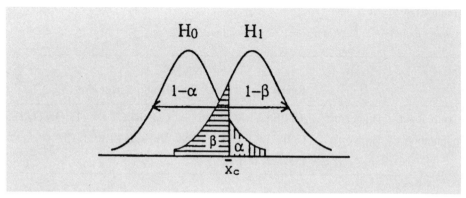

Figure 4.4 The Probability for Correct Decisions and Inferential Risk Errors in Hypotheses Verification.

The area to the right of $\overline{X}_c$ describes the PROBABILITY we are after, i.e., the probability that H_0 is WRONG and we correctly rejected it (H_1 is the correct one). This PROBABILITY is denoted as $1 - \beta$ and is termed POWER OF A TEST.

Let's assume that the sample's mean was not 60 sit-ups per minute but instead $\overline{X} = 58$. Previously we showed that $\overline{X}_c = 59.64$ and therefore it is clear that with $\overline{X} = 58$, H_0 was ACCEPTED and H_1 REJECTED because $58 < 59.64$. Thus, if $\overline{X} = 58$, TYPE-I ERROR (α, alpha) was not a problem since H_0 was not rejected. Instead we could ask the complementary question of $1 - \alpha$ which is the PROBABILITY of ACCEPTING H_0 as a CORRECT DECISION. This probability is 95% because we decided to take 5% risk of error ($p \leq .05$).

We shall now turn and examine the probability that our last decision is WRONG. Not rejecting H_0 will mean in fact acceptance of H_1. What is the probability that we may conduct an error, because H_0 is after all NOT the correct decision (H_1 is the correct one)? This probability is determined by the area located at the left of $\overline{X}_c$ under H_1 (in our example $-.85$). This area (19.77% under H_1) determines the error risk we take not to reject H_0 (i.e., reject H_1) because the truth about the population is that H_0 is not true (i.e., H_1 is correct). We term this error TYPE-II error, or β (beta). Decision-making, which corresponds to HYPOTHESES TESTING, is summarized in Table 4.1.

Table 4.1

Correct and Error in Decisions which Correspond to Hypotheses.

		Decision	
		Reject H_0	Do not reject H_0
Truth about	H_0 correct	TYPE I ERROR (α)	CORRECT DECISION ($1-\alpha$)
population	H_0 wrong	CORRECT DECISION POWER ($1-\beta$)	TYPE II ERROR (β)

If the truth is that H_0 is correct, but was rejected in favor of H_1, we committed a TYPE-I error. If the truth is that H_1 is the correct hypothesis, but H_0 was not rejected in favor of H_1, we made a TYPE-II error. $1 - \alpha$ is the probability of making a correct decision not to reject H_0 when it is true. $1 - \beta$ is the probability termed POWER, which indicates the probability of a correct decision to reject H_0 when it is wrong in favor of H_1. In our example we gave a one-tailed hypothesis. We shall expand our discussion on two-tailed hypotheses later in this chapter, though in principle it shares similar logic and procedures.

It should be noted that probabilities as the ones we have demonstrated can be estimated only when H_0 and H_1 have PRECISE VALUES. In the behavioral and social sciences, H_0 is known but usually H_1 is missing. Therefore we lack the knowledge about β and the POWER of the STATISTICAL TESTS. We can estimate these probabilities indirectly.

In reality it is impossible to prevent an error of inference. On one hand we keep being conservative with the probability to conduct type-I error ($p < .05$ or $.01$), and on the other hand we strive for more power ($1 - \beta$) in our statistical test. This is because the probability of $1 - \beta$ determines the probability to reject justifiably H_0, or simply stated, that an effect that exists really emerged.

In the previous example we have shown how POWER is estimated. We summarize now this procedure (for means) and remind the readers that for power to be estimated, a PRECISE ALTERNATIVE HYPOTHESIS (i.e., real value) is required:

(a) Estimate $\theta_{\bar{X}}$

(b) Estimate the critical value of $\bar{X}$

$$\bar{X}_c = (Z_{c(H_0)} \cdot \theta_{\bar{X}}) + \mu_{(H_0)}$$

(c)   Calculate the standard score Z which corresponds to $\overline{X}_c$ under H_1

(d)   Estimate the POWER $(1 - \beta)$ through the normal curve areas table.

There are several factors, which affect the statistical test power:

(a) *The "DISTANCE" of H_1.* The Power of the statistical test varies with the "distance" between different hypotheses. In our example, assume that μ under H_1 is 62 instead of 61. Thus, $\theta_{\overline{x}} = 1.6$, $\overline{X}_c = 59.64$, ($\overline{X}_c$ stays constant because all the components which determine it do not alter: $\mu_{(H_0)}$, $\theta_{\overline{x}}$, $Z_{c(H_0)}$). The critical Z, Z_c, under H_1 is therefore

$$Z_{c(H_1)} = \frac{59.64 - 62}{1.6} = -1.475$$

Accordingly $1 - \beta$ will be 93% and $\beta = 7\%$. As a consequence of a distance increase between the H_0 and H_1 distributions, β decreases and the power $(1 - \beta)$ increases. This concept is presented in Figure 4.5.

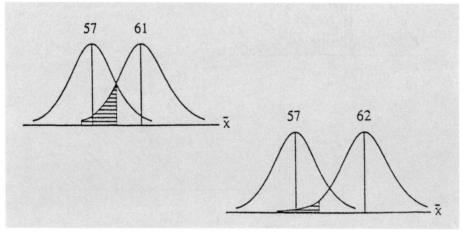

Figure 4.5 The Effect of the H_0 and H_1 Distributions' Distance on the Power of the Statistical Test.

It can be argued that the greater the distance is between the means of H_1 and H_0 distribution, the greater the test power, and the lower the probability to conduct type-II error. The smaller this distance, the smaller the test's power, and the higher are the chances to conduct a type-II error (calculate the power with $\mu_{(H_1)} = 60$ and see!).

(b) *The magnitude of* α. Assume that instead of $\alpha = .05$ we decide to become more conservative about type-I error and use a $\alpha = .01$. Under H_0, $Z_{(H_0)}$ will be now $Z_{(H_0)} = 2.33$ (see normal curve table). Since $\theta_{\bar{x}} = 1.6$,

$$\bar{X}_c = (2.33 \cdot 1.6) + 60.728$$

and the $\bar{X}_c$ under H_1 will be

$$Z_{c(H_1)} = \frac{60.728 - 61}{1.6} = -.17$$

The power $(1 - \beta)$ is 56.75% and $\beta = 43.25\%$. Figure 4.6 illustrates this concept.

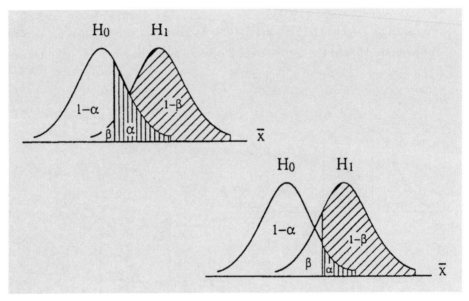

Figure 4.6   The Effect of α Magnitude on Two Statistical Tests' Power.

Decrease in α results in β increase and consequently $1 - \beta$ decreases (i.e., decrease in power). In an experiment where the EXPERIMENTAL EFFECT exists, we desire to reject H_0 if indeed it is not true. We can do so by decreasing the α level. But we decrease the statistical power of the test. Thus, it is recommended to increase the power by decreasing the standard error of the statistic through increase of the sample size.

(c) *Sample size*. Assume that a researcher has used a random sample of 36 observations (instead of 100). As a result:

$\theta_{\bar{X}} = 16/\sqrt{36} = 2.60$ and

$\bar{X}_c = (1.65 \cdot 2.66) + 57 = 61.389$, so that

$$Z_{c(H_1)} = \frac{61.389 - 61}{2.66} = 0.146$$

The power is therefore 44.3% and $\beta = 55.7\%$. This concept is illustrated in Figure 4.7.

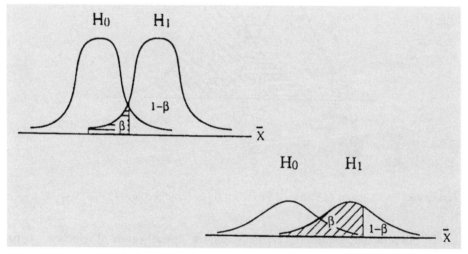

Figure 4.7   The Effect of Sample Size on the Statistical Test's Power.

As a result of sample decrease, the sampling distribution variance increases and consequently power decreases as a result of greater overlap between the H_0 and H_1 distributions (in the lower panel of figure 4.7, the overlap area is so large, that β occupies most of the area under H_1).

When given a population with standard deviation θ, the standard error of the mean depends on the sample size, $\theta_{\bar{X}} = \theta/\sqrt{n}$, as there is a reversed relationship between n and $\theta_{\bar{X}}$. Thus, increase in sample size, n, increases the power of the statistical test, considering the other components remain unchanged. When $\theta_{\bar{X}}$ increases, the statistical power decreases once $1 - \beta > \alpha$.

(d) *Directionality of the hypothesis and location of the alternative hypothesis.* In our example the alternative hypothesis was stated as unidirectional (one-tailed). When the alternative hypothesis is two-tailed, the power of the test decreases. This is because α is divided by 2, becomes smaller, and we already know the decrease in α automatically results in power decrease. The addition area of $1 - \beta$ in the other distribution tail (opposite to that of H_1) is illustrated in Figure 4.8.

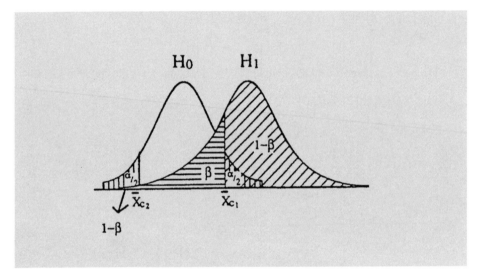

Figure 4.8   Power of Statistical Test when H_1 is Two-directional $(1 - \beta > \alpha)$.

In principle, the test has two-tails, and two critical values of rejection – upper limit $(\overline{X}_{c1})$ and lower limit $(\overline{X}_{c2})$ compared to one-tailed $\overline{X}_c$. $\overline{X}_{c1}$ becomes more extreme and $1 - \beta$ results in value decrease. Since β is "trapped" between $\overline{X}_{c1}$ and $\overline{X}_{c2}$ it should be taken into account in estimating $1 - \beta$ the area to the left of $\overline{X}_{c2}$ under H_1. The area is usually small, and therefore frequently ignored. However, this area does exist! A two-tailed or one-tailed hypotheses decision should be based on theoretical grounds. When the DIRECTION is CERTAIN and JUSTIFIABLE, then we examine the data using unidirectional concept. If not, a two-directional concept should be applied.

Let's examine the situation where the hypothesis is stated in a unidirectional fashion, and the true alternative is in the same direction, Figure 4.9 (A). The opposite direction is illustrated in Figure 4.9 (B).

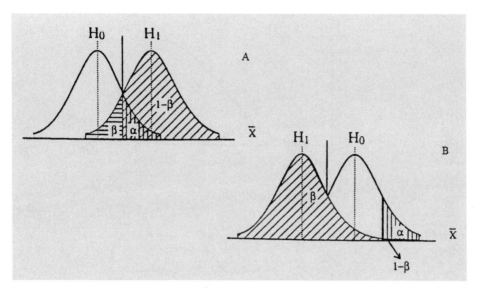

Figure 4.9 Power of a Test Under Uni-directional $H_1(\beta > \alpha)$ (A) and Bi-directional $(1 - \beta < \alpha)$ (B).

When the true alternative is located at the opposite end of the "rejection area", $1 - \beta$ becomes very small. In this case $(1 - \beta < \alpha)$, increase of sample size, n, will not result in subsequent power increase, and in fact the opposite is true. This point raises the question of choice between unidirectional or bi-directional hypotheses. The THEORY should GUIDE the DECISION, so that the "rejection areas" are defined accordingly. This DECISION should be made PRIOR to DATA COLLECTION. Unidirectional hypothesis may result in "benefit" in power when the results are in line with H_1, but a "cost" when the results are in contrast to H_1. Some argue that it is "safer" to state bi-directional H_1 and "ignore" the costs associated with the mismatch between the unidirectional and opposite results.

To describe the PROBABILITY of discovering an EFFECT we use POWER FUNCTIONS. The power function links the MAGNITUDE of the EFFECTS to the POWER of the STATISTICAL TEST. Different functions exist for various statistical tests. A test may have several functions depending on the COMPONENTS, which have an effect on the statistical power, as discussed above. This concept is illustrated in Figures 14.10, 14.11, and 4.12. Figure 4.10 describes the relation between the statistical power and the true value of $\mu_{(H_1)}$ under constant α. Figure 4.11 illustrates power curves under varying α, and Figure 4.12 presents power functions as a function of sample size.

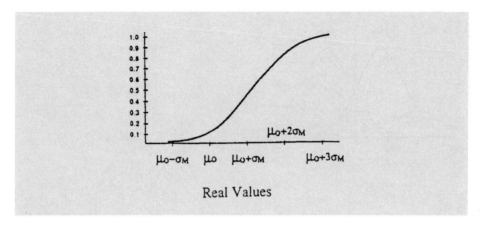

Figure 4.10 Power Function for Unidirectional H_1 with Constant α.

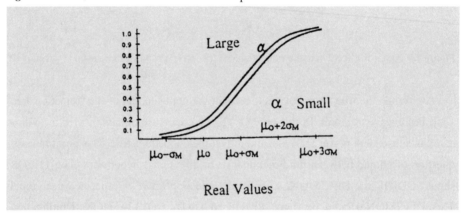

Figure 4.11 Power Function for Two Tests with Identical Sample Size and Different α.

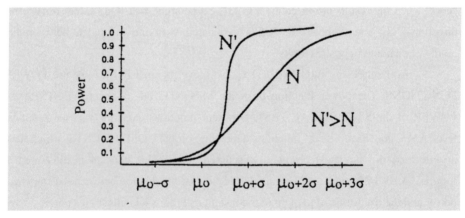

Figure 4.12 Power Function for Two Tests with Identical α and Different Sample Sizes, $N' > N$.

(7)   Choosing the Statistical Test

In order to choose a statistical test to examine the underlying hypotheses (H_0 and H_1), the following factors ought to be considered:

(a)   Level of measurement (nominal, ordinal, interval/ratio),

(b)   Sample size,

(c)   Number of samples from which inferences are being made,

(d)   Information we have about the population, and

(e)   Whether the samples are dependent (same subjects under different conditions or same conditions in different occasions), or independent. (Argyrous, 1996, p. 142).

We shall introduce next all the most common tests for the examination of hypotheses in which we have ONE DEPENDENT VARIABLE (DV). Later in this chapter we shall introduce more complicated tests where more than one DV exists.

Before we introduce the various statistical tests, one should CHOOSE the SIGNIFICANCE LEVEL (alpha, α, or p-probability) for verifying, accepting, or rejecting H_0 or H_1. The ALTERNATIVE HYPOTHESIS, H_1, should be stated as BIDIRECTIONAL or UNIDIRECTIONAL so that the OBSERVED statistic will be compared to the appropriate ONE or TWO-TAILED STATISTICS. Also the SAMPLE SIZE should be determined to ensure that the NORMALITY ASSUMPTIONS are met. Remember, the probability we choose (α) and the sample size DETERMINE the CRITICAL VALUE against which the CALCULATED STATISTIC can be compared. Similarly, this determines if H_0 will be verified or rejected for H_1. (See critical values for two-tailed hypothesis when $\alpha \leq 0.05$ in Figure 4.13)

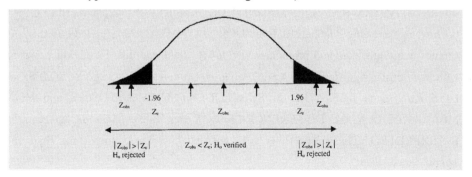

Figure 4.13   Critical Regions for Two-tailed Test, $\alpha = 0.05$.

The most common values for the Z_c are:

α	Two-tailed $|Z|$	One-tailed $|Z|$
$0.01\rightarrow$	2.58	2.33
$0.05\rightarrow$	1.96	1.645
$0.10\rightarrow$	1.645	1.28

Z observed is

$$Z_{obs} = \frac{\overline{X} - \mu}{\theta_{\overline{x}}}$$

and

$$\theta_{\overline{x}} = \theta/\sqrt{n}$$

if $Z_{obs} > Z_c$ then H_1 is verified, but if $Z_{obs} < Z_c$, H_0 is verified and H_1 rejected. This is how decision-making in accepting and rejecting scientific hypotheses works. SIGNIFICANCE means that the DIFFERENCE BETWEEN TWO OR MORE MEANS is a TRUE one, not a random one that in other similar samples drawn from the population, the reverse will be found. However, as we shall later see, almost every difference, given a large sample size, will become SIGNIFICANT. When we collect data which represent NATIONS, a significance test is useless. Every difference between populations (PARAMETERS) is a TRUE DIFFERENCE, or SIGNIFICANT one. Say that in nation I, the average hours people exercise is 2.7 h/week and in another nation 2.8 h/week. This is a TRUE DIFFERENCE. The question that follows is the most important question: WHAT IS THE MAGNITUDE of the DIFFERENCE between TWO OR MORE MEANS? WHAT is the MAGNITUDE of an EXPERIMENTAL EFFECT? A 0.1 h/week exercising may be TRUE but DOES NOT MEAN ANYTHING. In the 20th century many mistakes and prejudices were established and distributed which started with the term "significance". Again, what matters is HOW MANY TIMES the DIFFERENCE is REPEATED in SUBSEQUENT TRIALS/STUDIES and HOW MEANINGFUL is the DIFFERENCE/EFFECT that makes SENSE and can be INTERPRETED. These questions and answers are more important than the "significance" itself.

(8)   Tests of Significance for Interval/Ratio Level Measurement

8.1   A Z-Test for a Simple Mean (Population, Standard Deviation is Known)

A physical education instructor reads in a magazine that the average maximal oxygen uptake in young adults aged 15-17 is 42.6 ml/min/kg and $\theta = 8.6$. He/she developed a PE curriculum, which enhances aerobic capacity while exercising twice a week for 1 hour each session. To examine whether his/her program works, 100 students were randomly selected from the 15 to 17-age range in school. All 100 students underwent a direct VO_2max test in the laboratory. The 100 values of VO_2max were averaged to 45.9 ml/min/kg. The teacher was eager to know whether he/she can rely on this difference and conclude that the PE program TRULY results in higher values of aerobic capacity in the trained students. The statistics and parameters are as follows:

$$\text{For sample} \quad \begin{bmatrix} N = 100 & \mu = 42.6 \\ \overline{X} = 45.9 & \theta = 8.6 \end{bmatrix} \text{For population}$$

The hypotheses are precise ones:
$$H_0: \mu = 42.6$$

which postulates that in the population of students in the school VO_2max is equal to the VO_2max in the general population of young adults aged 15 to 17. In contrast
$$H_1: \mu > 42.6$$
which postulates that the students at the particular school developed higher VO_2max than their counterparts in the population with mean of 42.6.

As we can notice, H_1 is unidirectional (one-tailed). We set the level of significance (α or p) at 0.05 (5% chance of making an error in rejecting H_0). With these data, a critical Z value can be determined by observing the tables with the areas under the normal curve.

$$Z_{c, N = 100, \alpha = .05} = 1.65$$

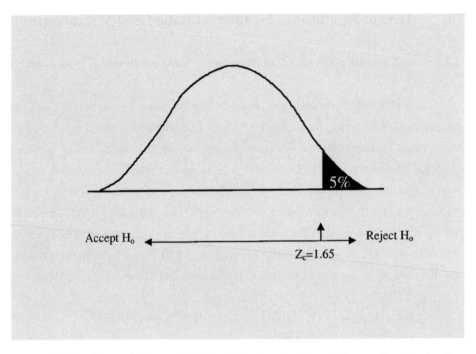

If the observed, Z_{obs}, will fall within the rejection of H_0 area then the teacher can be certain in 95% confidence that his/her program works according to expectations. To estimate Z_{obs}, the standard error of the sample's mean is:

$$\theta_{\bar{x}} = \theta/\sqrt{n} = 8.6/\sqrt{100} = 8.6/10 = 0.86$$

and Z_{obs}

$$Z_{obs} = \frac{\bar{X} - \mu}{\theta_{\bar{x}}} = \frac{45.9 - 42.6}{0.86} = 3.837$$

Thus

$$Z_{obs} > Z_c \ (3.837 > 1.650)$$

and therefore H_0 is rejected and H_1 verified, meaning that the PE program designed by the teacher works accordingly to their expectations. At least in 95% of similar random samples, a higher VO_2max in the school's sample then the population is expected to occur if the program will be similarly implemented.

At this stage the teacher may ask whether this effect is true also with $\alpha = 0.01$ (only 1% chance for conducting type-I error). For one-tailed test

$$Z_{c, \alpha = 0.01} = 2.33$$

and the $Z_{obs} = 3.837$. The answer is YES; this difference is also true for $\alpha < .01$.

8.2   A t-Test for a Single Mean

In most of the cases, the mean and the standard deviation of the population of the variable of interest are unknown. Thus the Z_c cannot be derived from the "areas under the normal curve". For this reason STUDENT t-distribution and t-test are used. T-distribution looks like Z-distribution but is flatter.

However, with a large sample of observations, the two curves are much alike. A t-test is used under the assumption that when the sample of observations is small, the sampling distribution of sampling means will have t-distribution only where the population is normally distributed. If this assumption is not met, non-parametric tests are recommended instead of a parametric test such as the t-test.

In the t-table DEGREES OF FREEDOM (df) are used instead of the number of observations (N). We have elaborated previously on df when we presented the TESTS OF ASSOCIATIONS. If we have 10 values which with a given mean, nine of the values can vary, but once they are determined the tenth must be a definite score to produce the same average. Thus, 1 df was lost and we remained with 9 df, because we imposed certain results on the data, and therefore $df = N - 1$.

The t-test assumes that the S (standard deviation) of the sample is equal to the population θ, which is unknown, and therefore we lose 1 df. Instead of using N, we use df which in fact is N minus the number of restrictions we impose on the data. The df affects the critical t-value, t_c. The larger the sample, the smaller the t_c and the higher the probability that the differences between means will be significant. A t-distribution with its df, and one and two-tailed test (α) is presented in Table 4.2.

Table 4.2

t-Distribution (df, and One and Two-tailed Tests (α)).

Degrees of freedom (df)	Level of significance for one-tail test (α)				
	0.10	0.05	0.025	0.01	0.005
	Level of significance for two-tail test (α)				
	0.20	0.10	0.05	0.02	0.01
1	3.078	6.314	12.706	31.821	63.657
2	1.886	2.920	4.303	6.965	9.925
3	1.638	2.353	3.182	4.541	5.841
4	1.533	2.132	2.776	3.747	4.604
5	1.476	2.015	2.571	3.365	4.032
6	1.440	1.943	2.447	3.143	3.707
7	1.415	1.895	2.365	2.998	3.499
8	1.397	1.860	2.306	2.896	3.355
9	1.383	1.833	2.262	2.821	3.250
10	1.372	1.812	2.228	2.764	3.169
11	1.363	1.796	2.201	2.718	3.106
12	1.356	1.782	2.179	2.681	3.055
13	1.350	1.771	2.160	2.650	3.012
14	1.345	1.761	2.145	2.624	2.977
15	1.341	1.753	2.131	2.602	2.947
16	1.34	1.746	2.120	2.583	2.921
17	1.333	1.740	2.110	2.567	2.898
18	1.330	1.734	2.101	2.552	2.878
19	1.328	1.729	2.093	2.539	2.861
20	1.325	1.725	2.086	2.528	2.845
21	1.323	1.721	2.080	2.518	2.831
22	1.321	1.717	2.074	2.508	2.819
23	1.319	1.714	2.069	2.500	2.807
24	1.318	1.711	2.064	2.492	2.797
25	1.316	1.708	2.060	2.485	2.787
26	1.315	1.706	2.056	2.479	2.779
27	1.314	1.703	2.052	2.473	2.771
28	1.313	1.701	2.048	2.467	2.763
29	1.311	1.699	2.045	2.462	2.756
30	1.310	1.697	2.042	2.457	2.750
40	1.303	1.684	2.021	2.423	2.704
60	1.296	1.671	2.000	2.390	2.660
120	1.289	1.658	1.980	2.358	2.617
∞	1.282	1.645	1.960	2.326	2.576

Assume that the teacher who developed the aerobic program desired to compare the mean of his/her students to the mean population, but the standard deviation of the population was unknown. Here the assumption is that the standard deviation of the sample, S, assume 10.7, represents the population standard deviation, θ. The t_{obs} is then estimated similarly to the previous Z_{obs}.

$$\theta_{\overline{x}} = S/\sqrt{N-1}$$

and

$$t_{obs} = \frac{\overline{X} - \mu}{\theta_{\overline{x}}}$$

In our example

For sample | $N = 100$ | $\mu = 42.6$ | for population
$X = 45.9$
$S = 10.7$

The critical t value, t_c is first examined with df $= 100 - 1 = 99$ and say $\alpha \le .01$ one-tailed (see table 16.2)

$t_{c, \alpha = .01, df = 99} = 2.39$ (look at df $= 60$ as the differences for df: 60-120 are very minor).

If t_{obs} results in a greater value than 2.39, the teacher will reject H_0 and conclude that the program results in higher VO_2max values than that of the population in 99% of the cases.

$$\theta_{\overline{x}} = S/\sqrt{N-1} = 10.7/\sqrt{100-1} = 10.7/9.9498 = 1.075$$

and

$$t_{obs} = \frac{\overline{X} - \mu}{\theta_{\overline{x}}} = \frac{45.9 - 42.6}{1.075} = 3.069$$

Again $t_{obs} > t_c$ (3.069 > 2.39) under $\alpha \le .01$ and the teacher may conclude that the program is very beneficial in developing aerobic capacity in young adult students.

Note that t_{obs} can be negative when the sample's mean is smaller than the population mean. Here t_{obs} values should be always converted to ABSOLUTE values, $|t_{obs}|$.

We illustrate the t-test for single mean by using the SPSS 11.0 software and the data set on VO_2max and run test times (in seconds), which we used to describe ASSOCIATIONS. The data set and its means and standard deviations are presented below:

VO_2max	Run
56.00	576.00
35.00	720.00
71.00	510.00
37.00	700.00
24.00	810.00
67.00	540.00
37.00	710.00
65.00	536.00
62.00	581.00
53.00	561.00
57.00	548.00
42.00	687.00
48.00	667.00
39.00	688.00
34.00	705.00

Descriptives
Descriptive Statistics

	N	Minimum	Maximum	Mean	Std. Deviation
maximal oxygen uptake	15	24.00	71.00	48.4667	14.2471
aerobic performance	15	510.00	810.00	635.9333	89.8479
Valid N (listwise)	15				

In this example the researcher is interested to know whether the VO_2max and aerobic performance (run) of the sample is different from the population from which the sample of 15 observations was drawn. The researcher knows the population mean in both variable but not θ.

$$\mu_{VO_2max} = ml/min/kg$$

$$\mu_{run} = 665 \text{ seconds.}$$

The results are shown in the output below:

T-Test

One-Sample Statistics

	N	Mean	Std. Deviation	Std. Error Mean
maximal oxygen uptake	15	48.4667	14.2471	3.6786

One-Sample Test

	Test Value = 42.6					
					95% Confidence Interval of the Difference	
	t	df	Sig. (2-tailed)	Mean Difference	Lower	Upper
maximal oxygen uptake	1.595	14	.133	5.8667	-2.0231	13.7565

T-Test

One-Sample Statistics

	N	Mean	Std. Deviation	Std. Error Mean
aerobic performance	15	635.9333	89.8479	23.1986

One-Sample Test

	Test Value = 665					
					95% Confidence Interval of the Difference	
	t	df	Sig. (2-tailed)	Mean Difference	Lower	Upper
aerobic performance	-1.253	14	.231	-29.0667	-78.8228	20.6894

The output shows the sample means, S, and $\theta_{\bar{x}}$, and then the t_{obs} with N-1(15 − 1 = 14)df. The mean difference for two-tailed test was not significant at $\alpha = .05$ for both variables. The 95% confidence interval of the difference contains ZERO in both variables, which means that there is a high probability that the sample's mean and population mean are equal, and therefore, the difference between them may be zero. In this example

$$\bar{X} = \mu$$

so that H_0 was verified and H_1 rejected. The researcher may conclude that the VO_2max and run scores of the sample he/she used represent the population it was drawn from. However, one should be cautious with such conclusions. Similar results with df = 200 could reverse the researcher's conclusions! The decision turns again to the logic of what constitutes a MEANINGFUL DIFFERENCE!

9   **A Z-Test for the Equality of Two Independent Means**

A researcher designed a study to answer the question whether individual athletes are higher in practice determination than team athletes. He asked 70 individual and 60 team athletes to respond to a "determination" scale. The variances of the individual and team athletes' population are known:

$$\theta_i^2 = 420$$
$$\theta_t^2 = 420$$

The means of the two samples were as follows:

$$\overline{X}_i = 120$$
$$\overline{X}_t = 100$$

The hypotheses were:

H_0: $\mu_i - \mu_t = 0$ or $\mu_i = \mu_t$
H_1: $\mu_I - \mu_t > 0$ or $\mu_i > \mu_t$

We assume that the differences, d,($\mu_i - \mu_t$), between any two randomly selected samples of individual and team athletes will be normally distributed. Relying on the populations' variances, we can estimate the variance of d, which is $\theta_{\overline{d}}$ as follows:

$$\theta_{\overline{d}} = \theta^2_{(\overline{X}_i - \overline{X}_t)} = \theta^2_{X_i} + \theta^2_{X_t} = \frac{\theta_i^2}{N_i} + \frac{\theta_t^2}{N_t}$$

$$= \frac{420}{60} + \frac{630}{70} = 7 + 9 = 16$$

and

$$\theta_{\overline{d}} = \sqrt{16} = 4$$

We choose now the significance α to reject H_0 using the areas under the normal distribution curve (95% to the left of Z_c since the researcher postulated one-tailed alternative hypothesis). Thus

$Z_c < 1.65$ is the acceptance of the zone

$Z_c \geq 1.65$ is the rejection of the zone.

The Z statistic is

$$Z_{obs} = \frac{\overline{X}_i - X_t}{\theta_{\overline{d}}} = \frac{120 - 100}{4} = \frac{20}{4} = 5$$

Since $Z_{obs} > Z_c$ (5 > 1.65) we reject H_0 and accept H_1 i.e., individual athletes are indeed more determined than team athletes in their practice session.

10   A t-Test for the Equality of Two Independent Means

So far we assumed that the population's variance and/or mean is known. However, in the majority of the cases this does not happen. This variance is usually estimated by the sample's statistics.

One of the most important criterions for evaluating a statistic is its unbiased estimation of the population's parameter. A statistic is an unbiased population's estimate when its sampling distribution (E) is equal to the parameter. The sample's mean and proportion are unbiased estimators as $E(\overline{X}) = \mu$ and $E(\overline{P}) = p$. In contrast, the sample's variance, S^2, is not an unbiased estimator of the population's variance, θ^2, because it can be shown that:

$$E(S^2) = \theta^2 - \theta_{\overline{x}}^2 \qquad\qquad (6)$$

In simple words, the expected sample's variance, $E(S^2)$, is equal to the difference between the population's variance, θ^2, and the sample's mean variance. Since the sample size cannot be infinite, the sampling distribution can never average 0. Thus the sample's variance, S^2, is a biased variance estimator of the population. From equation (6) we can exert that:

$$E(S^2) = \theta^2 - \frac{\theta^2}{n} = \frac{n\theta^2 - \theta^2}{n} = \frac{\theta^2(n-1)}{n} \tag{7}$$

and we can correct this bias by

$$\hat{S}^2 = \frac{n}{n-1} \cdot S^2 \tag{8}$$

$\hat{S}^2$ is an unbiased estimator because

$$E(\hat{S}^2) = \frac{n}{n-1} E(\hat{S}^2) = \frac{n}{n-1} \cdot \frac{n-1}{n}\theta^2 = \theta^2$$

so if we calculate $\hat{S}^2$ directly from the sample, we should multiply the sample's variance by the term n/(n-1), so we get

$$\hat{S}^2 = \frac{\sum_{i=1}^{n}(X_i - \overline{X})^2}{n} \cdot \frac{n}{n-1} = \frac{\sum_{i=1}^{n}(X_i - \overline{X})^2}{n-1}$$

Thus, the unbiased standard deviation of the sample is

$$S = \sqrt{\frac{\sum_{i=1}^{n}(X_i - X)^2}{n-1}}$$

i.e., instead of dividing the "summed squared deviation from the mean" by n, we divide them by n – 1. Once the sample size, n, is very large, n – 1 does not make any change in the estimation of the sample's variance. But when n < 30, it does! Unlike Z, we do not know the population's variance, and therefore the t-statistic is

$$t = \frac{\overline{X} - \mu_x}{\hat{S}_{\overline{X}}} \tag{9}$$

where $\hat{S}^2$ is an estimator of θ^2, and $\hat{S}_{\overline{X}} = \hat{S}/\sqrt{n}$ is the estimator or $\theta_{\overline{X}} = \theta/\sqrt{n}$. The theoretical distribution of the t values is called "t distribution".

t-distribution assumes that the dependent variable (DV) is normally distributed, and are mutually independent. t, not like Z, is not normally distributed. If X is normally distributed, also then t and Z are similar. But unlike in Z, the denominator of t, is not a constant and it VARIES from one sample to the other, and therefore t is not necessarily normally distributed.

A t-distribution is symmetric and has a bell shape, which depends on the degrees of freedom. It looks like a normal distribution curve when the mean and median of t are 0. A t-distribution is more flat than the Z-distribution: lower in the center and higher in the tails (see Figure 4.14).

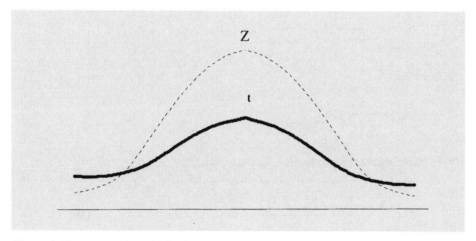

Figure 4.14   t and Z Distributions.

As previously mentioned, Z is one distribution. In contrast t, is a "family distribution" for different degrees of freedom (df). The fewer are the df, the flatter, the t-distribution becomes. Thus the probability of an extreme t-value occurring is higher than in the Z distribution. With an increase in sample size, n, and θ^2 become closer and t-distribution approximates the normal curve distribution. The t-statistic is compared to t_c that is derived from the t-table (see Table 4.2), and the hypotheses are examined similarly to the procedures described earlier.

Assume a researcher is interested in comparing the efficiency of two training methods. Efficiency is determined by the time required to reach a certain criterion. The researcher randomly divided the participants into two groups and applied to each of them a different training method. The results were as follows:

	Method A	Method B
n:	42	42
$\overline{X}$:	55 (hours)	50 (hours)
S:	20.1246	18.00
S^2:	405	324

The population variance is unknown and therefore we estimate the VARIANCE and the STANDARD ERROR of the DIFFERENCE. We already know that

$$\hat{S}^2 = S^2 \cdot \frac{n}{n-1} ; S_{\overline{X}}^2 = \frac{S^2}{n-1}$$

and therefore

$$\hat{S}_{\overline{X}_A}^2 = \frac{S_A^2}{n_A - 1} ; \hat{S}_{\overline{X}_B}^2 = \frac{S_B^2}{n_B - 1}$$

if the sample's sizes are greater than 30 the t-statistic is

$$t = \frac{(\overline{X}_A - \overline{X}_B) - (\mu_A - \mu_B)}{\hat{S}_{(\overline{X}_A - \overline{X}_B)}} \qquad (10)$$

When the sample sizes are small (n < 30), we assume that the VARIANCES of the POPULATIONS from which the samples have been drawn are EQUAL

$$\theta_A^2 = \theta_B^2 = \theta^2$$

The standard error of the mean difference is

$$\theta_{(\overline{X}_A - \overline{X}_B)}^2 = \frac{\theta_A^2}{N_A} + \frac{\theta_B^2}{N_A} = \theta^2 \left(\frac{1}{N_A} + \frac{1}{N_B} \right)$$

$$\theta_{(\overline{X}_A - \overline{X}_B)} = \theta \sqrt{\frac{1}{N_A} + \frac{1}{N_B}} \qquad (11)$$

Based on the two samples' statistics,

$$\hat{S} = \sqrt{\frac{n_a S_a^2 + n_b S_b^2}{n_a + n_b - 2}}$$

and the standard error of the difference is

$$\hat{S}_{(\overline{X}_A - \overline{X}_B)} = \sqrt{\frac{n_A S_A^2 + n_B S_B^2}{n_a + n_b - 2}} \cdot \sqrt{\frac{n_A + n_B}{n_A \cdot n_B}} \qquad (12)$$

with df = $n_1 + n_2 - 2$, and

$$t = \frac{(\overline{X}_A - \overline{X}_B) - \mu_{(\overline{X}_A - \overline{X}_B)}}{\hat{S}_{(\overline{X}_A - \overline{X}_B)}} \qquad (13)$$

To answer the question about the efficiency of the two training methods, we follow these equations and first state the hypotheses:

$$H_0 : \mu_A - \mu_B \leq 0 \text{ or } \mu_A = \mu_B$$
$$H_1 : \mu_A - \mu_B > 0 \text{ or } \mu_A > \mu_B$$

Applying equation (12) to estimate the standard error of the difference we get

$$\hat{S}_{(\overline{X}_A - \overline{X}_B)} = \sqrt{\frac{42 \cdot 405 + 42 \cdot 324}{42 + 42 - 2}} \cdot \sqrt{\frac{42 + 42}{42 \cdot 42}}$$

$$= \sqrt{\frac{17010 + 136 \cdot 8}{82}} \cdot \sqrt{\frac{84}{1764}} = 19.3233 \cdot 0.2182$$

$$= 4.2167$$

with df = 42 + 42 − 2 = 82 and $\alpha \leq .05$
(one-tailed) $t_c < 1.65$ for accepting H_0
               $t_c \geq 1.65$ for rejecting H_0

The t-statistic is

$$t = \frac{(\overline{X}_A - \overline{X}_B) - 0}{\hat{S}_{(\overline{X}_A - \overline{X}_B)}} = \frac{55 - 50}{4.2167} = 1.18$$

and since $t_{obs} < t_c$ (1.18 < 1.65) we do NOT reject H_0 and therefore the researcher cannot claim that method A is more efficient than method B in reaching the performance criterion he/she stated.

Using statistical software saves us the calculations and the time required for manual calculations. We applied the t-test for independent means to data that was previously shown. It consists of two groups of participants, 10 in each, who underwent VO_2max and running performance tests. Then we used SPSS 11.0 to perform two independent t-tests, one comparing the two groups in VO_2max, and the other in running performance. The data and the analyses are presented next.

	Name	VO_2max	Run	Group
1	1.00	56.00	540.00	1
2	2.00	35.00	670.00	2
3	3.00	58.00	523.00	1
4	4.00	34.00	682.00	2
5	5.00	72.00	470.00	1
6	6.00	54.00	510.00	2
7	7.00	65.00	497.00	1
8	8.00	35.00	712.00	2
9	9.00	36.00	693.00	1
10	10.00	61.00	488.00	2
11	11.00	45.00	667.00	1
12	12.00	36.00	652.00	2
13	13.00	47.00	653.00	1
14	14.00	52.00	512.00	2
15	15.00	41.00	623.00	1
16	16.00	39.00	672.00	2
17	17.00	54.00	513.00	1
18	18.00	37.00	679.00	2
19	19.00	36.00	691.00	1
20	20.00	46.00	645.00	2

T-Test

Group Statistics

	GROUP	N	Mean	Std. Deviation	Std. Error Mean
VO2MAX	1.00	10	51.0000	12.1198	3.8326
	2.00	10	42.9000	9.6891	3.0639
RUN	1.00	10	587.0000	86.7141	27.4214
	2.00	10	622.2000	84.1834	26.6211

Independent Samples Test

		Levene's Test for Equality of Variances	
		F	Sig.
VO2MAX	Equal variances assumed	.553	.467
	Equal variances not assumed		
RUN	Equal variances assumed	.236	.633
	Equal variances not assumed		

Independent Samples Test

		t-test for Equality of Means			
		t	df	Sig. (2-tailed)	Mean Difference
VO2MAX	Equal variances assumed	1.651	18	.116	8.1000
	Equal variances not assumed	1.651	17.168	.117	8.1000
RUN	Equal variances assumed	-.921	18	.369	-35.2000
	Equal variances not assumed	-.921	17.984	.369	-35.2000

In the upper table we can see the means, S, and $SE_{\bar{x}}$ of the two samples in VO_2max and running performance. In the second table Levene's test for variance equality (not introduced here) shows that the two samples' variances on VO_2max and run are not significantly different each from the other, i.e., do not violate an important assumption of the t-test statistics. Thus in the lower table we see that differences between the two groups in VO_2max and run are NOT significant (p's > .05), and therefore we cannot claim that the means of the two populations in the two variables are significantly different each from the other (i.e., H_0 was not rejected). From the additional statistics presented below, we can see that when 95% confidence intervals (CIs) are computed for the $SE_{\bar{D}}$, a zero is included within this interval, meaning that the difference between the two means can be zero. Therefore, these means cannot be regarded as different each from the other.

| | | t-test for Equality of Means | 95% Confidence Interval of the Difference | |
		Std. Error Difference	Lower	Upper
VO2MAX	Equal variances assumed	4.9068	-2.2088	18.4088
	Equal variances not assumed	4.9068	-2.2447	18.4447
RUN	Equal variances assumed	38.2180	-115.4931	45.0931
	Equal variances not assumed	38.2180	-115.4981	45.0981

11 A t-test for the Equality of Two Dependent (Paired) Means

When the same sample is measured twice with or without an intervention between the two tests, and there are hypotheses about any changes/differences between the two means, then the SECOND observation is DEPENDENT (i.e., correlated) on the FIRST observation. In cases where two different samples are observed on a given variable, and the two are PERFECTLY MATCHED on ALL the INTERVENING and OTHER VARIABLES, BUT the DV, then a paired t-test can be also performed.

Assume a researcher is interested in the examination of the effect of physical activity (PA) on mood state. He/she sampled four participants before and after the participants underwent one month of planned PA. The data were as follows:

Participants	Mood state	
	Before	After
1	119	113
2	116	116
3	125	115
4	92	98

Since the observations are PAIRED, the MEAN DIFFERENCE is an UNBIASED ESTIMATE of the PAIRED POPULATION, because

$$E(\overline{X}_1 - \overline{X}_2) = \mu_1 - \mu_2$$

But the standard error of the difference is NOT $\theta_1^2/n_1 + \theta_2^2/n_2$ because the two, θ_1^2 and θ_2^2 covary (i.e., correlate) by $2cov_{(x_1, x_2)}$. However the difference between each PAIR can be viewed as attributed to ONE SAMPLE. Thus a difference, d_i, can be computed for each pair of observations so that

$$d_i = X_{1i} - X_{2i}$$

and

$$\overline{d} = \frac{\sum\limits_{i=1}^{n} d_i}{n} - \frac{\sum\limits_{i=1}^{n} X_{1i} - \sum\limits_{i=1}^{n} X_{2i}}{n} = \overline{X}_1 - \overline{X}_2 \qquad (14)$$

and

$$\hat{S}_{\overline{d}} = \sqrt{\frac{\hat{S}_d^2}{n}} = \frac{\hat{S}_d}{\sqrt{n}} \qquad (15)$$

where n is the number of paired observations.

In the above example, the one-tailed hypotheses are:

$$H_0 : \mu_1 - \mu_2 \geq 0 \text{ or } \mu_1 \geq \mu_2$$
$$H_1 : \mu_1 - \mu_2 < 0 \text{ or } \mu_1 < \mu_2$$

(assuming of course that the lower the score the more comfortable is the mood state). To verify these hypotheses, estimation of $\overline{d}$ $\hat{S}_{\overline{d}}$ and are computed:

Participant	Mood state		Difference (d_i)	d_i^2
	Before	After		
1	119	113	6	36
2	116	116	0	0
3	125	115	10	100
4	92	98	-6	36
			$\Sigma d_i = 10$	$\Sigma d_i^2 = 172$

$$\bar{d} = \frac{\sum_{i=1}^{n} d_i}{n} = \frac{10}{4} = 2.5$$

$$\hat{S}_d^2 = \frac{n}{n-1}\left(\frac{\sum_{i=1}^{n} d_i^2}{n} - \bar{d}^2\right) = \frac{4}{3}\left(\frac{172}{4} - 2.5^2\right) = 49$$

$$\hat{S}_{\bar{d}} = \sqrt{\frac{\hat{S}_d^2}{n}} = \sqrt{\frac{49}{4}} = 3.5$$

with one-tailed and df = 4 – 1 = 3, $\alpha \le .05$

$t_{obs} < 2.353$, H_0 is accepted

$t_{obs} \ge 2.353$, H_0 is rejected.

The dependent (paired)-t is

$$t_{dep} = \frac{\bar{d} - \mu_{\bar{d}}}{\hat{S}_{\bar{d}}} \qquad (16)$$

and in the present case

$$t = \frac{2.5 - 0}{3.5} = 0.714$$

and since $t_{obs} < t_c$, H_0 is not rejected, and we cannot conclude that PA affects mood state in this population, relying on four paired observations.

We now demonstrate the same procedure on 30 observations that were tested twice on an anxiety test with two-tailed alternative hypothesis. The data are as follows:

Anxiety1	Anxiety2
56.00	59.00
43.00	41.00
65.00	56.00
73.00	45.00
23.00	34.00
45.00	23.00
34.00	45.00
23.00	65.00
45.00	45.00
65.00	34.00
45.00	56.00
34.00	71.00
54.00	23.00
34.00	43.00
56.00	54.00
43.00	65.00
23.00	34.00
23.00	23.00
45.00	45.00
34.00	34.00
23.00	65.00
45.00	54.00
65.00	34.00
64.00	23.00
34.00	45.00
23.00	34.00
45.00	25.00
34.00	46.00
23.00	34.00
43.00	65.00

and the SPSS 11.0 output is

T-Test

Paired Samples Statistics

		Mean	N	Std. Deviation	Std. Error Mean
Pair 1	ANXIETY1	42.0667	30	15.0125	2.7409
	ANXIETY2	44.0000	30	14.4437	2.6370

Paired Samples Correlations

		N	Correlation	Sig.
Pair 1	ANXIETY1 & ANXIETY2	30	-.052	.786

Paired Samples Test

		Paired Differences					
		Mean	Std. Deviation	Std. Error Mean	95% Confidence Interval of the Difference Lower	Upper	t
Pair 1	ANXIETY1 - ANXIETY2	-1.9333	21.3637	3.9005	-9.9107	6.0440	-.496

Paired Samples Test

		df	Sig. (2-tailed)
Pair 1	ANXIETY1 - ANXIETY2	29	.624

The mean, S, and $SE_{\bar{x}}$ are presented first followed by the correlation between the two sets of observations (r = -0.05 which indicate complete independence). Then, the paired difference mean (-1.93) with its S, $S_{\bar{d}}$ and its 95% CI are presented along with the t-statistic (-.496). In the lower panel the df and two-tailed significance level (p) are shown. The results indicate that the mean paired difference (-1.93) is not significant and therefore the null hypothesis, H_0, cannot be rejected. The anxiety levels of the participants did not differ in the two measurement sessions.

(12) Hypotheses Testing with More than Two Independent Samples: One-Way Analysis of Variance (ANOVA)

In comparing two groups, the questions were whether they were drawn from ONE POPULATION, from TWO POPULATIONS with EQUAL MEANS, or from DIFFERENT POPULATIONS. When more than two groups exist, the number of possible comparisons is $k(k-1)/2$, where k is the number of groups. Thus for 3, 5, and 10 groups the number of paired comparisons are:

$$3 \rightarrow 3(3-1)/2 = 3$$
$$5 \rightarrow 5(5-1)/2 = 10$$
$$10 \rightarrow 10(10-1)/2 = 45.$$

From a PRACTICAL VIEW, the number of comparisons increases substantially, $\binom{k}{2}$, with additional groups, and therefore it is inconvenient to estimate many Z, t, and θ values. From a STATISTICAL VIEW the multi-comparisons procedure causes a more serious problem. When the "rejection zone" is determined (say $\alpha \leq .05$), we declare a 5% risk in rejecting H_0. Among 100 paired mean comparisons, it is expected that no more than five will result in $t_{obs} > t_c$ that was determined under H_0, conditional on independent sampling procedures. Thus when more and more comparisons are added, more rejections of H_0, which are false, will occur and we shall not be able to determine which is true and which is random. In other words, type-I error will be uncontrolled. From a SCIENTIFIC VIEW, groups can be CLUSTERED, and thus be compared in CLUSTERS to each other. Multi paired t-tests are a limited method to handle such questions efficiently.

In k-INDEPENDENT SAMPLES the null hypothesis assumes equality among the k-samples' means,

$$H_0: \mu_1 = \mu_2 = \mu_3 = ... = \mu_k$$

The alternative hypothesis can be stated in different ways, depending on the THEORETICAL FOUNDATION, which led to the HYPOTHESES POSTULATION. For example, in the case of four independent samples (k = 4)

$$H_1: \mu_1 > (\mu_2 = \mu_3 = \mu_4)$$
$$H_1: (\mu_1 = \mu_2) < (\mu_3 = \mu_4)$$
$$H_1: (\mu_1 = \mu_2 = \mu_3) > \mu_4$$

and of course other possibilities also exist.

To examine and verify these hypotheses an ANALYSIS OF VARIANCE F-test (ANOVA) is used. The F-test examines the null hypothesis that the samples are drawn from populations with equal means for a variable measured at the interval/ratio level. It overcomes the type-I error that was previously described.

Before we proceed to the mathematical presentation of ANOVA, we introduce the concept that guides it. The k number of means which represent DIFFERENT POPULATIONS have a VARIANCE around them. These variances around the k means are their UNIQUE VARIANCE. This variance is termed WITHIN SUBJECTS VARIANCE (see Figure 4.15).

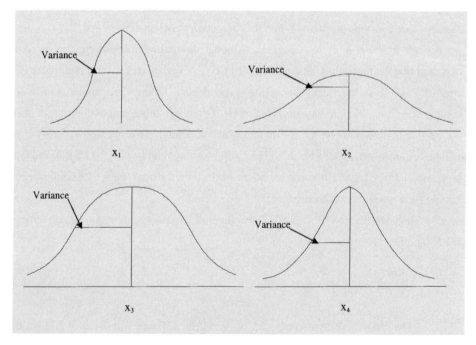

Figure 4.15   A Demonstration of Unique-Within Variance in Four Samples Drawn Independently from Four Populations.

Each of the mean, $\overline{X}_i$, has also a STANDARD ERROR, which allows us to determine confidence intervals, CI, around it. If $\overline{X}_1, \overline{X}_2, \overline{X}_3$, and $\overline{X}_4$ are very far in distance from each other, and the confidence intervals do not OVERLAP, they are probably representing POPULATIONS with DIFFERENT MEANS. However, when the means are very close to each other, and their $SE_{\overline{x}}$ overlap, it indicates that the MEANS of the POPULATION from which they were drawn DO NOT DIFFER from each other. The DISTANCES of the MEANS from a GRAND MEAN, $\overline{X}_{\bullet\bullet}$, which represents ALL the POPULATIONS, are termed a BETWEEN SUBJECTS VARIANCE (see Figure 4.16).

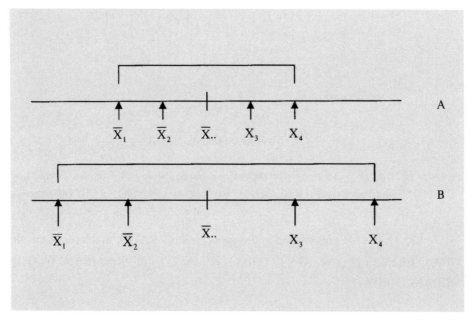

Figure 4.16 Small (A) and Large (B) Variances among Four Means of Independent Samples Drawn from Four Populations.

Now, it can be concluded that the GREATER the BETWEEN SUBJECTS VARIANCE, and the SMALLER the WITHIN SUBJECTS VARIANCE will result in TRUE DIFFERENCES among the populations' means. The SMALLER the BETWEEN VARIANCE and the LARGER the WITHIN SUBJECTS VARIANCE will result in NO TRUE DIFFERENCES among the populations' means. This concept is presented in Figure 4.17.

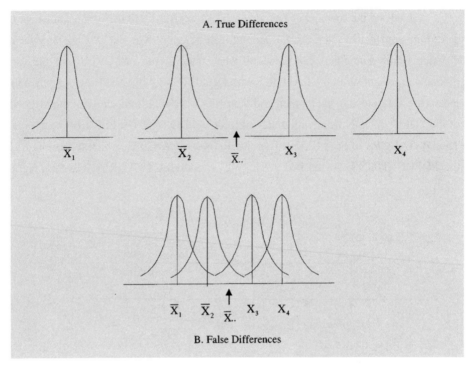

Figure 4.17 True (A) and False (B) Differences among Means of Samples Drawn from Four Populations as a Function of "Between" and "Within" Subjects Differences.

The F-test is a presentation of this concept. It is a RATIO, which represents the MEAN BETWEEN VARIANCE (MBV) RELATIVE to the MEAN WITHIN VARIANCE (MWV).

$$F = MBV/MWV$$

and it can be realized that F increases linearly with MBV increase and decreases linearly with MWV increase, just as described in Figures 4.16 and 4.17.

F-tests consist of comparisons between two different sources of variances. One important assumption of F-test is that the variances of the samples, θ^2, are equal,

$$\theta_1^{\,2} = \theta_2^{\,2} = \theta_3^{\,2} = \dots \theta_k^{\,2}$$

Assume the following data:

Subject	Sample A	Sample B	Sample C
1	8	5	2
2	5	4	4
3	4	7	3
4	7	7	2
5	6	7	4

To estimate the within and between subjects variances, we shall begin with the former one. There are three samples, which represent three populations. If subjects are denoted as i and samples as j, then expected within subject variance $\hat{S}_w^2$ will be:

$$\hat{S}_w^2 = \frac{\sum_{j=1}^{j} \hat{S}_j^2}{j} \tag{16}$$

or

$$\hat{S}_w^2 = \frac{\sum_{i=1}^{n} (X_{ij} - \overline{X}_j)^2}{n_j - 1} \tag{17}$$

so within each of the three samples:

The means of the three samples are as follows:
$\overline{X}_1 = (8 + 5 + 4 + 7 + 6)/5 = 6$
$\overline{X}_2 = (5 + 4 + 7 + 7 + 7)/5 = 6$
$\overline{X}_3 = (2 + 4 + 3 + 2 + 4)/5 = 3$

and the within Ss (WS) variances are:

$$\hat{S}_1^2 = \frac{(8-6)^2 + (5-6)^2 + \ldots + (6-5)^2}{5-1} = \frac{10}{4} = 2.5$$

$$\hat{S}_2^2 = \frac{(5-6)^2 + (4-6)^2 + \ldots + (7-5)^2}{5-1} = \frac{8}{4} = 2$$

$$\hat{S}_3^2 = \frac{(2-3)^2 + (4-3)^2 + \ldots + (4-3)^2}{5-1} = \frac{4}{4} = 1$$

and

$$\hat{S}^2_w = \frac{2.5 + 2 + 1}{3} = \frac{5.5}{3} = 1.83$$

with $j(n-1)$ degrees of freedom.

To estimate the between subjects (BS) variance we calculate first the GRAND MEAN ($\overline{X}_{..}$) and then estimate the differences between each sample's mean and the grand mean.

$$\overline{X}_{..} = \sum_1^j \overline{X}_j/j$$

if the groups are of equal size. If not, a weighted mean should be calculated:

$$\overline{X}_{..} = \sum_1^j W\overline{X}_j/N$$

In the above example

$$\overline{X}_{..} = (3 + 6 + 6)/3 = 5$$

and $\hat{S}^2_{\overline{X}}$ is

$$\hat{S}^2_{\overline{X}} = \frac{\sum_{j=1}^j (\overline{X}_j - \overline{X}_{..})}{j - 1} \tag{18}$$

which in our example is

$$\hat{S}^2_{\overline{X}} = \frac{(6-5)^2 + (6-5)^2 + (3-5)^2}{3-1} = \frac{6}{2} = 3.$$

The population variance can be estimated from the sample variance since we know that

$$\theta_x^2 = \frac{\theta^2}{n}$$

so that $\hat{S}^2_B$ is

$$\hat{S}^2_B = n \cdot \hat{S}^2_{\bar{x}} \text{ with } j - 1 \text{ df}$$

in our example $\hat{S}_B = 5 \cdot 3 = 15$.

PARTITIONING the WITHIN and BETWEEN SOURCES OF VARIANCE INDEPENDENTLY from each other enables us to verify H_0. If H_0 is TRUE, the within $\hat{S}^2_W$ and $\hat{S}^2_B$ ratio will be small (small mean differences and large within subjects variance), meaning that both are influenced by random individual factors. However, if H_0 is FALSE, large MEAN DIFFERENCES ($\hat{S}^2_B > \hat{S}^2_W$)exist and there is a REASON for that. The F-test, which expresses this ratio, is

$$F = \frac{\hat{S}^2_B}{\hat{S}^2_W} \tag{19}$$

with df = j-1, j(n-1).

The larger the F, the higher the probability to reject H_0 (equality among the means) and vice-versa.

In many books the within variance is termed Sum of Squares Within (SSW)

$$SSW = \Sigma(X_i - \bar{X}_S)^2$$

and the between variance is termed Sum of Squares Between (SSB)

$$SSB = \Sigma N_S(\bar{X}_S - \bar{X}_{..})^2$$

so that the total variance (Total Sum of Squares) is

$$TSS = SSB + SSW$$

which in fact is

$$TSS = \sum_i (X_i - \bar{X})^2 \tag{20}$$

where $\overline{X}_S$ is the mean of each sample.

N_S is the number of observations in each sample.

$$TSS = \sum_i X_i^2 - N\overline{X}_{..}^2 \qquad (21)$$

is an alternative equation to equation (20) and easier to compute.

Accordingly

$$F = \frac{SSB / (k-1)}{SSW / (N-k)} = \frac{MSB}{MSW} \qquad (22)$$

which is another presentation of equation (19).

It should be kept in mind that:

$$df_{total} = df_{between} + df_{within}$$

or

$$N - 1 = (J - 1) + (N - J)$$

and

$$MST = \frac{SST}{df_t} = \frac{\sum\limits_{j=1}^{j}\sum\limits_{i=1}^{n_j}(X_{ij} - \overline{X}_{..})^2}{N-1} \qquad (23)$$

$$MSW = \frac{SSW}{df_w} = \frac{\sum\limits_{j=1}^{j}\sum\limits_{i=1}^{n_j}(X_{ij} - \overline{X}_{j})^2}{N-J} \qquad (24)$$

$$MSB = \frac{SSB}{df_b} = \frac{\sum\limits_{j=1}^{j}n_j(\overline{X}_{j} - \overline{X}_{..})^2}{J-1} \qquad (25)$$

If the three groups represent three different treatments, then a large mean difference among the three means may be attributed to the MAGNITUDE and DIFFERENT EFFECTS they had on the participants which took part in each of them. The DIFFERENCES among the participants WITHIN EACH TREATMENT represent an ERROR VARIANCE. These differences are attributed to random factors which differentiate the participants among themselves. They can be personality differences, intelligence, attitudes, motor, physical, fitness, and many other differences. An F-test is also the ratio between the EFFECT and the ERROR

$$F = EFFECT/ERROR$$

where   EFFECT = TREATMENT + ERROR (MSB)
            ERROR = INDIVIDUAL DIFFERENCES (MSW).

The F-ratio (F_{obs}) is contrasted to the F_c, which is derived from the Table, which represents the F distribution. There are several F-distributions, each representing different α level. The F tables consist of df for between Ss (samples), k-1, or j-1 in the upper column and df for the within Ss (N – k or N – j) in the left column. The F_c table for $\alpha = 0.05$ is presented below (Table 4.3). In our example

$$F_{obs} = \frac{MSB}{MSW} = \frac{15}{1.83} = 8.182$$

with j-1, N-j (3-1 = 2, 15-3 = 12)df.

In Table 4.3, F_c with 2, 12 df equals 3.68 for $\alpha \leq .05$, and since $F_{obs} > F_c$ we reject H_0 and accept H_1, i.e., there are differences among the three means. The legitimate subsequent question is: AMONG WHICH PAIRS of MEANS are there TRUE DIFFERENCES? 1-2?, 1-3?, 2-3? For that reason POST-HOC Multiple Comparison Tests were developed. We shall introduce them next.

Table 4.3

F-distribution ($\alpha = 0.05$).

Degrees of freedom for estimates of variance within samples (N − k)	Degrees of freedom for estimates of variance between samples (k−1)									
	1	2	3	4	5	6	7	8	9	∞
1	161.4	199.5	215.07	224.6	230.2	234.0	236.8	238.9	240.5	254.3
2	18.51	19.00	19.16	19.25	19.30	19.33	19.35	19.37	19.38	19.50
3	10.13	9.55	9.28	9.12	9.01	8.94	8.89	8.84	8.81	8.53
4	7.71	6.94	6.59	6.39	6.26	6.16	6.09	6.04	6.00	5.63
5	6.61	5.79	5.41	5.19	5.05	4.95	4.88	4.82	4.77	4.36
6	5.99	5.14	4.76	4.53	4.39	4.28	4.21	4.15	4.10	3.67
7	5.59	4.74	4.35	4.12	3.97	3.87	3.79	3.73	3.68	3.23
8	5.32	4.46	4.07	3.84	3.69	3.58	3.50	3.44	3.39	2.93
9	5.12	4.26	3.86	3.63	3.48	3.37	3.29	3.23	3.18	2.71
10	4.96	4.10	3.71	3.48	3.33	3.22	3.14	3.07	3.02	2.54
11	4.84	3.98	3.59	3.36	3.20	3.09	3.01	2.95	2.90	2.40
12	4.75	3.88	3.49	3.26	3.11	3.00	2.91	2.85	2.80	2.30
13	4.67	3.80	3.41	3.18	3.02	2.92	2.83	2.77	2.71	2.21
14	4.60	3.74	3.34	3.11	2.96	2.85	2.76	2.70	2.65	2.13
15	4.54	3.68	3.29	3.06	2.90	2.79	2.71	2.64	2.59	2.07
16	4.49	3.63	3.24	3.01	2.85	2.74	2.66	2.59	2.54	2.01
17	4.45	3.59	3.20	2.96	2.81	2.70	2.61	2.55	2.49	1.96
18	4.41	3.55	3.16	2.93	2.77	2.66	2.58	2.51	2.46	1.92
19	4.38	3.52	3.13	2.90	2.74	2.63	2.54	2.48	2.42	1.88
20	4.35	3.49	3.10	2.87	2.71	2.60	2.51	2.45	2.39	1.84
21	4.32	3.47	3.07	2.84	2.68	2.57	2.49	2.42	2.37	1.81
22	4.30	3.44	3.05	2.82	2.66	2.55	2.46	2.40	2.34	1.78
23	4.28	3.42	3.03	2.80	2.64	2.53	2.44	2.38	2.32	1.76
24	4.26	3.40	3.01	2.78	2.62	2.51	2.42	2.36	2.30	1.73
25	4.24	3.38	2.99	2.76	2.60	2.49	2.40	2.34	2.28	1.71
26	4.22	3.37	2.98	2.74	2.59	2.47	2.39	2.32	2.27	1.69
27	4.21	3.35	2.96	2.73	2.57	2.46	2.37	2.30	2.25	1.67
28	4.20	3.34	2.95	2.71	2.56	2.44	2.36	2.29	2.24	1.65
29	4.18	3.33	2.93	2.70	2.54	2.43	2.35	2.28	2.22	1.64
30	4.17	3.32	2.92	2.69	2.53	2.42	2.33	2.27	2.21	1.62
40	4.08	3.23	2.84	2.61	2.45	2.34	2.25	2.18	2.12	1.51
60	4.00	3.15	2.76	2.52	2.37	2.25	2.17	2.10	2.04	1.39
120	3.92	3.07	2.68	2.45	2.29	2.17	2.09	2.02	1.96`	1.25
∞	3.84	2.99	2.60	2.37	2.21	2.09	2.01	1.94	1.88	1.00

Using SPSS 11.0 for the same data we get:

Oneway

Descriptives

	N	Mean	Std. Deviation	Std. Error	95% Confidence Interval for Mean		Minimum	Maximum
					Lower Bound	Upper Bound		
1.00	5	6.0000	1.5811	.7071	4.0368	7.9632	4.00	8.00
2.00	5	6.0000	1.4142	.6325	4.2440	7.7560	4.00	7.00
3.00	5	3.0000	1.0000	.4472	1.7583	4.2417	2.00	4.00
Total	15	5.0000	1.9272	.4976	3.9327	6.0673	2.00	8.00

DV

Test of Homogeneity of Variances

Levene Statistic	df1	df2	Sig.
.727	2	12	.503

DV

Anova

	Sum of Squares	df	Mean Square	F	Sig.
Between Groups	30.000	2	15.000	8.182	.006
Within Groups	22.000	12	1.833		
Total	52.000	14			

The results are identical to those we have computed by hand. In addition, Levene's test of homogeneity shows that the assumption that the three population variances are equal was not violated. There were no significant differences among the three populations' variances. The SPSS output also supplies a clue about the possible pair of means, which are different, from each other by showing these means graphically.

Means Plots

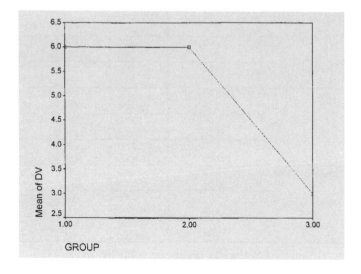

It looks as if groups one and two have an identical mean while group three has a substantially lower mean than the other two groups. Are these differences statistically significant? The post-hoc tests compare each pair of means separately and supply answers about whether the differences between the means are TRULY (SIGNIFICANTLY) different from zero. There are several POST-HOC TESTS that we shall briefly introduce next. The SPSS 11.0 output that is displayed shows Tukey HSD, Scheffe, LSD, and Bonferroni procedures that are more frequently reported in the literature. They ALL indicate that the means of GROUPS one and two are higher than the mean of GROUP three, and the means of groups one and two can be clustered together against the mean of group three.

Post Hoc Tests

Multiple Comparisons

Dependent Variable: DV

	(I) GROUP	(J) GROUP	Mean Difference (I-J)	Std. Error	Sig.	95% Confidence Interval Lower Bound	95% Confidence Interval Upper Bound
Tukey HSD	1.00	2.00	.0000	.856	1.000	-2.2846	2.2846
		3.00	3.0000*	.856	.011	.7154	5.2846
	2.00	1.00	.0000	.856	1.000	-2.2846	2.2846
		3.00	3.0000*	.856	.011	.7154	5.2846
	3.00	1.00	-3.0000*	.856	.011	-5.2846	-.7154
		2.00	-3.0000*	.856	.011	-5.2846	-.7154
Scheffe	1.00	2.00	.0000	.856	1.000	-2.3871	2.3871
		3.00	3.0000*	.856	.015	.6129	5.3871
	2.00	1.00	.0000	.856	1.000	-2.3871	2.3871
		3.00	3.0000*	.856	.015	.6129	5.3871
	3.00	1.00	-3.0000*	.856	.015	-5.3871	-.6129
		2.00	-3.0000*	.856	.015	-5.3871	-.6129
LSD	1.00	2.00	.0000	.856	1.000	-1.8658	1.8658
		3.00	3.0000*	.856	.004	1.1342	4.8658
	2.00	1.00	.0000	.856	1.000	-1.8658	1.8658
		3.00	3.0000*	.856	.004	1.1342	4.8658
	3.00	1.00	-3.0000*	.856	.004	-4.8658	-1.1342
		2.00	-3.0000*	.856	.004	-4.8658	-1.1342
Bonferroni	1.00	2.00	.0000	.856	1.000	-2.3802	2.3802
		3.00	3.0000*	.856	.013	.6198	5.3802
	2.00	1.00	.0000	.856	1.000	-2.3802	2.3802
		3.00	3.0000*	.856	.013	.6198	5.3802
	3.00	1.00	-3.0000*	.856	.013	-5.3802	-.6198
		2.00	-3.0000*	.856	.013	-5.3802	-.6198

*. The mean difference is significant at the .05 level.

Homogeneous Subsets

DV

	GROUP	N	Subset for alpha = .05	
			1	2
Tukey HSD[a]	3.00	5	3.0000	
	1.00	5		6.0000
	2.00	5		6.0000
	Sig.		1.000	1.000
Scheffe[a]	3.00	5	3.0000	
	1.00	5		6.0000
	2.00	5		6.0000
	Sig.		1.000	1.000

Means for groups in homogeneous subsets are displayed.

a. Uses Harmonic Mean Sample Size = 5.000.

12.1 *Post-Hoc Multiple Comparison Tests*

Multiple Comparison Tests (MCT) are used to make a decision about TRUE DIFFERENCES among PAIRS of MEANS AFTER an F-test resulted in SIGNIFICANCE, i.e., REJECTION of H_0.

A COMPARISON or CONTRAST between two means is designed by the symbol $\hat{\psi}_i$.

$\hat{\psi}_i = \overline{X}_j - \overline{X}_{j'}$ is a contrast between two means for treatment j and j'.

For K=3 treatments

$$\hat{\psi}_1 = \overline{X}_1 - \overline{X}_2$$
$$\hat{\psi}_2 = \overline{X}_1 - \overline{X}_3$$
$$\hat{\psi}_3 = \overline{X}_2 - \overline{X}_3$$

Comparison/contrast can be also performed between a different combination of means such as

$$\hat{\psi}_1 = \frac{\overline{X}_1 + \overline{X}_2}{2} - \overline{X}_3$$

or/and

$$\hat{\psi}_1 = \frac{\overline{X}_1 + \overline{X}_3}{2} - \overline{X}_2$$

or/and

$$\hat{\psi}_1 = \frac{\overline{X}_2 + \overline{X}_3}{2} - \overline{X}_1$$

The first 3 contrasts can be written as follows:

$$\hat{\psi}_1 = C_j(\overline{X}_1) + C_{j'}(\overline{X}_2) = 1(\overline{X}_1) - 1(\overline{X}_2)$$
$$\hat{\psi}_2 = C_j(\overline{X}_1) + C_{j'}(\overline{X}_3) = 1(\overline{X}_1) - 1(\overline{X}_3)$$
$$\hat{\psi}_3 = C_j(\overline{X}_2) + C_{j'}(\overline{X}_3) = 1(\overline{X}_2) - 1(\overline{X}_3)$$

where the COEFFICIENTS C_j and $C_{j'}$ are 1 or -1 respectively. These coefficients can be 1/3, 1/2, 1/4 or any other combination that we wish to contrast means.

A PRIORI or PLANNED COMPARISONS relate to SPECIFIC HYPOTHESES PRIOR to conducting the experiment. The t-statistics for carrying out multiple comparisons among means when the number of observations, n, in each treatment is equal is

$$t = \frac{C_j(\overline{X}_j) + C_{j'}(\overline{X}_{j'})}{\sqrt{\frac{2MS_{error}}{n}}} \qquad (26)$$

and if the n's are not equal

$$t = \frac{C_j(\overline{X}_j) + C_{j'}(\overline{X}_{j'})}{\sqrt{MS_{error}\left[\frac{(C_j)^2}{n_j} + \frac{(C_{j'})^2}{n_{j'}}\right]}} \qquad (27)$$

where MS_{error} is the unbiased estimate of the population error variance (i.e., the WG variance) where

$$MS_{WG} = \left[\sum_1^k \sum_1^n X_{ij}^2 - \sum_1^k \frac{(\sum_1^n X_{ij})^2}{n}\right] / (N - k) \qquad (28)$$

For the DIFFERENCE between each pair of means, a CONFIDENCE INTERVAL (CI) is drawn using

$$CI = t_{\alpha/2,V} \sqrt{MS_{error} \left[\frac{(C_j)^2}{n_j} + \frac{(C_{j'})^2}{n_{j'}} \right]} \qquad (29)$$

where V designates the df associated with the ERROR VARIANCE, and $t_{\alpha/2}$ is a two-tailed t value for the α chosen (usually for $\alpha = 0.05$ or $\alpha = 0.01$). The probability of obtaining at least one significant comparison by chance is

$$1 - (1 - \alpha)^C \cong C\alpha \qquad (30)$$

DUNN's MCT consists of the following equation

$$d = t'D_{\alpha/2;C,V} = \sqrt{MS_{error} \left[\frac{(C_j)^2}{n_j} + \frac{(C_{j'})^2}{n_{j'}} + \ldots + \frac{(C_{j''})^2}{n_{j''}} \right]} \qquad (31)$$

where $t'D_{\alpha/2}$ is a coefficient obtained from a table (not included in this book), C is the number of comparisons for k means and V is the df for experimental errors.

POSTERIORI COMPARISONS are performed when the hypotheses could not identify precisely the direction of means, and the F-test indicated that there are significant differences.

The LEAST SIGNIFICANT DIFFERENCES (LSD) was the first one developed by Fisher (1949) and consists of equation (32):

$$LSD = t_{\alpha/2,V} \sqrt{\frac{2MS_{error}}{n}} \qquad (32)$$

where $t_{\alpha/2,V}$ is the upper percentage point from student's t distribution for V df (denominator of the F ratio). A DIFFERENCE higher than the LSD is DECLARED SIGNIFICANT.

Another posteriori comparison test is termed Tukey's HONESTLY SIGNIFICANT DIFFERENCE (HSD):

$$HSD = q_{\alpha,V} \sqrt{\frac{MS_{error}}{n}} \tag{33}$$

where q is obtained from the distribution of the studentized range statistics.

$$q = \frac{C_j(\overline{X}_j) + C_{j'}(\overline{X}_{j'})}{\sqrt{\dfrac{MS_{error}}{n}}} \tag{34}$$

with Confidence Interval, CI

$$(\overline{X}_j - \overline{X}_{j'}) \pm q_{\alpha,V} \sqrt{\frac{MS_{error}}{n}} \tag{35}$$

SCHEFFE procedure is described as

$$S = \sqrt{(k-1)F_{\alpha;V_1 V_2}} \cdot \sqrt{MS_{error} \left[\sum_{j=1}^{k} \frac{(C_j)^2}{n_j} \right]} \tag{36}$$

where is derived from the F distribution with V_1 and V_2 df, k is the number of treatment levels or number of groups, C_j is a coefficient of the contrast, and n_j is the number of observations in the jth treatment/group level. A difference value above S is declared significant.

NEWMAN-KEULS Test consists of

$$W_r = q_{r,\alpha:r,V} \sqrt{\frac{MS_{error}}{n}} \tag{37}$$

where q_r is obtained from the distribution of the studentized range statistic and r designates the number of steps separating ordered means.

There are additional procedures, which vary in CONSERVATISM from each other. For an excellent review see Kirk (1968, pp. 69-98).

12.2 *Expressing Differences Between Means in Standardized Units-Effect Sizes*

We already know that with large sample sizes almost every difference among pairs of means results in significance. The question remains whether SIGNIFICANCE infers also MEANINGFULNESS and in our opinion this is not the case. The meaning of a difference depends primarily on its MAGNITUDE. Next we shall show how a difference between means can be expressed as a STANDARDIZED VALUE. This standardized difference also allows us to compare MAGNITUDES of different scales and measures, since standardized units do not have typical units like length (meter, cm, mm, km, etc.), temperature (C°, F°, etc.), volumes (m^3, cm^3, etc.), and others, but they signify HOW FAR is the DIFFERENCE from the center of the normal curve (0). This standardized unit is termed an EFFECT-SIZE (ES) and can be transformed into PERCENTAGE VALUE by using the AREAS UNDER the NORMAL CURVE. Therefore, effect-sizes are used in META ANALYSIS, an integrative method which consists of transformation of means' differences and using them for SECONDARY ANALYSIS. We shall refer to it later in this chapter.

An EFFECT SIZE (ES) is expressed as:

$$\text{ES} = \frac{\overline{X}_1 - \overline{X}_2}{S_c} \quad \text{or} \quad \frac{\overline{X}_1 - \overline{X}_2}{S_p} \tag{38}$$

where $\overline{X}_1$ and $\overline{X}_2$ are the means of the two groups, S_c is the standard deviation of the control group (in experimental designs), and S_p is the pooled standard deviation of the two groups. In most cases S_p is more recommended than the standard deviation of the control group. S_c signifies a standard deviation that was unchanged due to experimental manipulation, and therefore should be used instead of S_p.

Using the means and S_c of the previous example (one-way ANOVA), the statistics of the three groups were:

Group	Mean	SD
Group 1	6.00	1.5811
Group 2	6.00	1.4142
Group 3	3.00	1.000
Total	5.00	1.9272

The effect sizes using equation (38) are:

$$ES_{1-2} = \frac{6.00 - 6.00}{1.9272} = \frac{0}{1.9272} = 0$$

$$ES_{1-3} = \frac{6.00 - 3.00}{1.9272} = \frac{3}{1.9272} = 1.556$$

$$ES_{2-3} = \frac{6.00 - 3.00}{1.9272} = \frac{3}{1.9272} = 1.556$$

The means of group 1 and group 2 are equal and therefore there were no differences between them. However, the differences between these two means and the mean of group 3 were 1.556 of a standard deviation. We used S_p as a denominator because we refer to the means as representing groups and not as treatment group vs. a control group. A 1.556 of a standard deviation can be expressed in percentage as follows:

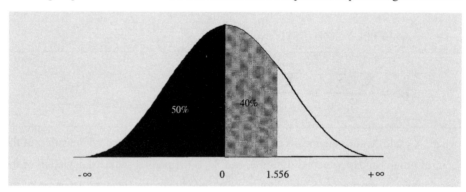

About 44% of the total area is located between the mean (0) and 1.556 standard deviations. Including the 50% of the mean from the mean to -∞, an advantage of 94% is noted. This means that the AVERAGE PARTICIPANT in GROUPS 1 and 2 is ABOVE 94% of the PARTICIPANTS in GROUP 3. An effect size that has a negative sign is interpreted as follows: assume the effect size was –0.53.

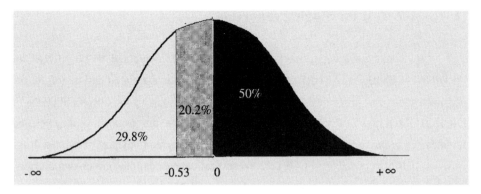

This means that the second group is lower than the first group. The average student in group two is above 29.8% of the students in the first group. One should keep in mind that the average participant in the first group is above 50% of his/her own peers.

In pre-post designs, where two groups, say a control and an experimental, have two means at the outset and at the end, the effect-size is:

$$ES = \frac{(\overline{X}_2 - \overline{Y}_2) - (\overline{X}_1 - \overline{Y}_1)}{S_{p_1}} \quad \text{or} \quad \frac{(\overline{X}_2 - \overline{Y}_2) - (\overline{X}_1 - \overline{Y}_1)}{S_{y_1}} \quad (39)$$

where X is the experimental group, Y is the control group, S_{P_1} is the pooled standard deviation at the outset of the study of the two groups, S_{y_1} and is the standard deviation of the control group at the outset of the study. Graphically the ES looks as follows:

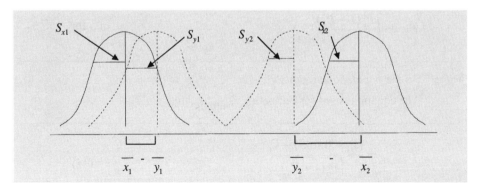

In fact, the difference $\overline{X}_1 - \overline{Y}_1$ at the outset of the study is PARTIALLED OUT from the difference at the end of the study. The control or pooled standard deviation at the outset of the study is used as the denominator. Like before, the ES can be expressed in percentage.

(13) A Z-Test for Single Proportion

In some cases where the variable of interest is expressed by NOMINAL or ORDINAL LEVEL MEASUREMENT, a mean cannot be estimated and therefore, the previous statistical procedures cannot be applied. In such cases, PROPORTION or DICHOTOMOUS-TYPE variables describe, for example, the proportion of males and females in a group, or the rate of people who oppose or agree to the use of banned drugs in sport. It is also possible to COLLAPSE several categories into one or two clusters, establish a dichotomous-type variable, and then COUNT how many people endorse or reject each "cluster". In such a manner a BINOMIAL DISTRIBUTION represents natural dichotomous variables (i.e., gender) or clustered variables (the proportion of students running 100 m faster and slower than 17.5 seconds).

When PROPORTIONS are calculated on a SAMPLE, inferences about the POPULATION PROPORTION are needed (i.e., proportion of many samples which share equal size). An infinite number of samples with equal size will establish a distribution, which approximates normality with a MEDIAN PROPORTION equal to the population value. Though binomial is a discrete variable, and normal curve is continuous, large sample size approximate normality with STANDARD ERROR of SAMPLING DISTRIBUTION, θ_p,

$$\theta_p = \sqrt{\frac{P_u(1-P_u)}{N}} \qquad (40)$$

where P_u is the population proportion.

The equations used for estimating Z_{sample} are:

$$Z_{sample} = \frac{(P_s - 0.005) - P_u}{\sqrt{\dfrac{P_u(1-P_u)}{N}}} \qquad (41)$$

where $P_s > P_u$
and

$$Z_{sample} = \frac{(P_s + 0.005) - P_u}{\sqrt{\dfrac{P_u(1 - P_u)}{N}}} \qquad (42)$$

where $P_s < P_u$

P_s is the sample proportion

P_u is the population proportion.

The 0.005 is termed a CONTINUITY CORRECTION, but with less than 30 observations, an EXACT BINOMIAL PROBABILITY should be calculated instead of the Z-approximation.

For example, assume we sampled 100 athletes on the use of banned drugs in sport – agree or disagree. Of 100 responses, 20 athletes "agree". Thus

N = 100 and

$$P_s = \frac{20}{100} = \frac{1}{5} = 0.20$$

The figures of a large population showed that the proportion is higher than that,

$P_u = 0.32$.

The question is whether our sample is different in its attitude to banned drugs to that of the population. The hypotheses will be stated as follows:

H_0: $P_u = 0.32$; Our sample shares similar attitudes toward the use of banned drugs as the population sample, and

H_1: $P_u < 0.32$; Our sample is more negative toward the use of banned drugs in sport. To examine these hypotheses we know that

$P_s < P_u$

and therefore we use equation (42) to estimate Z_{sample},

$$Z_{sample} = \frac{(0.20 + 0.005) - 0.32}{\sqrt{\dfrac{0.32(1 - 0.32)}{100}}} = \frac{-0.115}{0.0466} = 2.4678$$

Assume we are comfortable with $\alpha = 0.05$, one-tailed, the area under the curve which corresponds to 95% (to the left of the Z_c value) is 1.64:

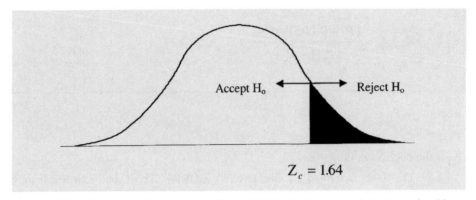

$$Z_c = 1.64$$

Since $Z_{sample} > Z_c$, we reject H_0 and claim that our sample is less tolerable to drugs than the population.

Confidence intervals can be computed for proportion similarly to confidence intervals of means. With proportion it is done using equation (43),

$$\textbf{ci} = \textbf{P}_s \pm \textbf{Z} \sqrt{\frac{\textbf{P}_s(1 - \textbf{P}_s)}{\textbf{N}}} \qquad\qquad \textbf{(43)}$$

Assume that in our example the sample represents the population, and therefore

$$ci = 0.20 \pm Z \sqrt{\frac{0.20(1 - 0.20)}{100}}$$

For 95% confidence interval, we already know from looking at the areas under the normal curve that $Z = 1.96$, and therefore

$$ci = 0.20 \pm 1.96 \sqrt{\frac{0.20(1 - 0.20)}{100}} = 0.20 \pm 1.96 \cdot 0.04$$

$$ci = 0.20 \pm 0.0784$$

and the proportion of the population that agrees with the use of banned drugs in sport is:

$L_u = 0.20 + 0.0784 = 0.2784$ (upper limit)

$L_L = 0.20 - 0.0784 = 0.1216$ (lower limit)

which means that between 12.16% to 27.84% of the athletes approve the use of banned drugs in sport.

(14)   Ordinal Tests for Two or More Independent Samples

Ordinal data are used mainly to describe attitudes that people hold. Categorical types of responses such as "1" (not at all), "2" (moderately), and "3" (very much) are typical responses to a variety of statements which describe opinions, attitudes, moods, and personalities of people who respond to these questions/ideas/statements. In many instances the summation or mean of these responses indicate "how much" a person is on the measured trait or state, as if the ordered response categories had a meaningful unit of measurement. We discussed this issue in chapter 11, and concluded that measurements, which share an ORIGIN, EQUAL UNIT, LINEARITY, and are SAMPLE-FREE can be considered as interval/ratio and subjected to statistical inferences which assume interval/ratio level of measurement. In many cases, where NORMAL RESPONSE DISTRIBUTION on the measured ordinal scales are satisfied, researchers tend to apply inferential statistics under the assumption that the ordinal scale has properties similar to interval/ratio scale. The following statistical tests which we present next, do not take this assumption into consideration.

14.1   *Runs Test (Wald Wolfowitz)*

In the Runs test we assume that two independent samples were drawn from a population and then measured on an ordinal-level scale. It is hypothesized that the two populations are identical and therefore can be compared to each other on the variable of interest. The distribution of responses has no apriori requirements. The QUESTION we are aimed at answering is whether the two samples are similar or different on the measured variable.

The procedure of the Runs test consists of ORDERING the response of both samples on a continuum, which signifies some quantity on which the scores of both samples can be located. If A and B represent scores of two samples, a hypothetical order can be as follows:

A A A A A B A B B B B B B.

In this example, most of the A scores are located on the left side of the continuum and the B scores on the right. This probably indicates that the two samples differ each from the other, and therefore, H_0 will be rejected and H_1 be accepted.

The method of counting the sequence consists of counting the A's until a B appears, and then counting the B's until an A appears. A small number of "runs" is an indication that H_0 is representing the data, while a large number of "runs" indicate a probable rejection of H_0.

H_0 assumes that the two samples are drawn from populations which equally share the continuum. When more than 20 subjects are measured, the sampling distribution of r (runs) is assumed to be normal with

$$\text{mean } \mu_r = \frac{2N_1N_2}{N_1+N_2}+1 \tag{44}$$

and

$$\text{standard deviation } \theta_r = \sqrt{\frac{2N_1N_2(2N_1N_2-N_1-N_2)}{(N_1+N_2)^2(N_1+N_2-1)}} \tag{45}$$

The mean $(\overline{X})$ and standard deviation (s) are estimated from the counts (frequencies) of the two samples. The Runs test does not take into consideration any DIRECTION, and the alternative hypothesis is usually unidirectional.

In larger samples, when H_1 has a definite direction, the probability of conducting an error is doubled since H_1 is tested against half of the distribution. Since A and B are independent of each other, the probability of significant difference with 0.05 level without a definite direction is:

P(A&B) = P(A)P(B) = (0.5)(0.05) = 0.025.

This principle is applied when the sample distribution is symmetric and not unidirectional. If we had three samples with a defined direction, $\overline{X}_1 \geq \overline{X}_2 \geq \overline{X}_3$, the probability for significant differences in this direction is 1/6 assuming $\mu_1 = \mu_2 = \mu_3$.

For example, runners from two populations were united and ordered as following:

$\underline{1\ 2\ 3}\ \overline{4\ 5}\ \underline{6\ 7\ 8}\ \overline{9\ 10}\ \underline{11\ 12\ 13}\ \overline{14\ 15}\ \underline{16}\ \overline{17}\ \underline{18}\ \overline{19}$

The locations of sample A are underlined and sample B overlined. Since the sample is small ($n < 20$), instead of using the normal distribution values, we use Table 4.4 to infer significance level. The mean and standard deviation of the "runs" under H_0 (no sample difference) is:

$$\mu_r = \frac{2(10)(9)}{10+9} + 1 = 10.47$$

$$\theta_r = \sqrt{\frac{2(10)(9)[2(10)(9)-10-9]}{(19^2)(18)}} = 2.11$$

The actual number of counts (number of underlined and overlined runs) is 10. Then

$$Z = \frac{r - \mu_r}{\theta_r} = \frac{10 - 10.47}{2.11} = -0.22.$$

The number of runs is less than expected (10.47) and therefore Z is negative. The critical value of Z for $p < .05$ is 1.96. Since the calculated Z is much smaller than the critical Z, we accept H_0 and conclude that the two populations are equal in running. Using SPSS 11.0 we get:

Wald-Wolfowitz Test

Frequencies

	GROUP	N
RUN	1.00	10
	2.00	9
	Total	19

Test Statistics[b,c]

		Number of Runs	Z	Exact Sig. (1-tailed)
RUN	Exact Number of Runs	10[a]	.000	.510

a. No inter-group ties encountered

b. Wald-Wolfowitz Test

c. Grouping Variable: GROUP

Table 4.4

Critical Values for Runs Test. In the Runs Test for Two Samples, each Value that is smaller or equal to the Tabled Critical Value is Significant at the 0.05 Level when the Direction is Unknown. For Undirectional Hypothesis, the Probability is 0.025.

N_1 \ N_2	2	3	4	5	6	7	8	9	10	11	12	13	14	15	16	17	18	19	20
4			2																
5		2	2	3															
6		2	3	3	3														
7		2	3	3	4	4													
8	2	2	3	3	4	4	5												
9	2	2	3	4	4	5	5	6											
10	2	3	3	4	5	5	6	6	6										
11	2	3	3	4	5	5	6	6	7	7									
12	2	3	4	4	5	6	6	7	7	8	8								
13	2	3	4	4	5	6	6	7	8	8	9	9							
14	2	3	4	5	5	6	7	7	8	8	9	9	10						
15	2	3	4	5	6	6	7	8	8	9	9	10	10	11					
16	2	3	4	5	6	6	7	8	8	9	10	10	11	11	11				
17	2	3	4	5	6	7	7	8	9	9	10	10	11	11	12	12			
18	2	3	4	5	6	7	8	8	9	10	10	11	11	12	12	13	13		
19	2	3	4	5	6	7	8	8	9	10	10	11	12	12	13	13	14	14	
20	2	3	4	5	6	7	8	9	9	10	11	11	12	12	13	13	14	14	15

14.2 Mann-Whitney (U)/Wilcoxon (W)

Like in the "Runs" test, in the Mann-Whitney test the scores of the two variables are unified into one sequence, but the focus is on ONE SAMPLE. Then each value in this sample is used as a criterion from which the number of ranks higher than that value are present in the other sample. The numbers are summed up and constitute the statistic U. The distribution of "U" values is exact when the number of scores is low. If there are many values the normal curve values are used. If U is very low or very large, we reject the hypothesis that the values were derived from the same population.

We shall use the example of the Runs test to illustrate the Mann-Whitney test.

Runner's Group	Rank
A	1, 2, 3, 7, 8, 11, 12, 13, 16, 18
B	4, 5, 6, 9, 10, 14, 15, 17, 19

The U distribution tables are introduced at the end of this section. The tables represent various n_1 and n_2 combinations in the upper row and U values in the left column. The probability values constitute the table. For example, if $n_1 = 4$, and $n_2 = 5$, n_2 is the larger sample, if U = 2 then the probability U ≤ 2 for to occur is 0.032 if the direction is predicted. In all the tables the critical U values are given. For example, for $p \le .001$ under known hypothesized direction, $n_1 = 10$ and $n_2 = 13$, to reach significance U must be greater than 17. When the samples are big, the U values approximate the normal distribution values with

$$\text{mean } \mu_U = \frac{N_1 N_2}{2} \qquad (46)$$

and

$$\text{standard deviation } \theta_U = \sqrt{\frac{N_1 N_2 (N_1 + N_2 + 1)}{12}} \qquad (47)$$

where N_1 is the size of the first sample

        N_2 is the size of the second sample.

In the sample above, the second sample contains 9 cases, and we shall count the number of cases in the first sample which are located above each value of the first sample. Above rank 4 are 7 cases in sample A. Similarly, in sample A there are 7 cases above rank 5, and 7 cases are above 6, 5 cases above 9 – and so on.

    U = 7 + 7 + 7 + 5 + 5 + 2 + 2 + 1 + 0 = 36.

If the criterion was sample A, then the number of cases above each of the B sample values was

    U = 9 + 9 + 9 + 6 + 6 + 4 + 4 + 4 + 2 + 1 = 54.

Each of these U values can be used for significance testing. But the tables are arranged in such a manner that the smallest U value of the two is considered. There is no need to count both U's. If one is known, the second U statistic is

$$U' = N_1 \cdot N_2 - U' \quad \text{or} \quad U' = N_1 \cdot N_2 - U \qquad (48)$$

In our example, U = 36 then

U = (10·9) − 36 = 90 − 36 = 54.

Once N_1 and N_2 are very large, the RANKS (R) of each sample should be summed up to constitute R_1 and R_2 as follows:

SAMPLE A ($N_1 = 10$)	SAMPLE B ($N_2 = 9$)
1	4
2	5
3	6
7	9
8	19
11	14
12	15
13	17
16	19
18	
$R_1 = 99$	$R_2 = 91$

and apply the following equations

$$U = N_1 \cdot N_2 + \frac{N_1(N_2 + 1)}{2} - R_2 \qquad (49)$$

$$U' = N_1 \cdot N_2 + \frac{N_1(N_1 + 1)}{2} - R_1 \qquad (50)$$

To check

$$R_1 + R_2 = \frac{N(N + 1)}{2}$$

$$91 + 99 = \frac{19(20)}{2} = 190$$

when N is the number of cases in both samples,

$$U = 10(9) + \frac{9(10)}{2} - 99 = 90 + 45 - 99 = 36$$

and

$$U' = 10(9) + \frac{10(11)}{2} - 91 = 90 + 55 - 91 = 54$$

Identical statistics to the previous were obtained. If we unify the equation for U and U', the similarity to the parametric t-test is obvious:

$$Z = \frac{R_1 - R_2 - (N_1 - N_2)(N + 1)/2}{\sqrt{N_1 N_2 (N + 1)/3}} \tag{51}$$

The nominator contains the difference $R_1 - R_2$ together with a term that signifies the acceptance of H_0. The correction factor is needed because we calculated a difference between sums and not means. If N_1 and N_2 are equal, the correction term in the nominator becomes 0. Therefore, the Mann-Whitney test is also termed RANK SUM TEST.

In the U distribution table we notice that with 10 and 9 cases, U should be ≤ 20 (for $p \leq .05$, and undefined direction) to reject H_0. Since in our example U = 36, we failed to reject H_0 and conclude that the runners in the two samples are not different from each other in rankings. If H_1 was unidirectional, U should be ≤ 24 when $p \leq .05$. If the number of cases is large, we use the equation, which approximates the normal curve:

$$Z = \frac{U - N_1 \cdot N_2 / 2}{\sqrt{N_1 N_2 (N_1 + N_2 - 1)/12}} \tag{52}$$

and with our data

$$Z = \frac{36 - (10 \cdot 9)/2}{\sqrt{10(9)(20)/12}} = \frac{36 - 45}{\sqrt{150}} = \frac{-9}{12.247} = -0.73$$

If U was substituted by U' (54) then

$$Z = \frac{54 - 45}{\sqrt{150}} = \frac{9}{12.247} = +0.73$$

with the previous equation

$$Z = \frac{91 - 99 - (10 - 9)(20)/2}{\sqrt{10(9)(20)/3}} = \frac{-8 - 10}{\sqrt{600}} = \frac{-18}{24.49} = -0.73$$

Comparing this value to the normal distribution values with $p \leq .05$ we shall reject H_1 and accept H_0. When the ranks in the two samples are equal, the average rank is given to each one. For example, if two scores share the 8th and 9th locations then each will be considered as $(8 + 9)/2 = 8.5$. If three cases share locations 12, 13, 14, then each is assigned $(12 + 13 + 14)/3 = 13$. Since the correction factor is the standard error of U which is in the denominator, the Z equation is

$$Z = \frac{U - N_1 N_2 / 2}{\sqrt{[N_1 N_2 / N(N-1)][N^3 - N]/12 - \sum T_i}} \qquad (53)$$

where $N_1 + N_2 = N$

$T_i = (t^3 - t_i)/12$ where t is the number of identical locations for a given rank.

If for example we had two identical cases for two locations, and three identical cases for three locations, then

$$\sum T_i = T_1 + T_2 = \frac{t_1^3 - t_1}{12} + \frac{t_3^3 - t_2}{12} \qquad (54)$$

$$= \frac{2^2 - 2}{12} + \frac{3^2 - 3}{12} = \frac{6}{12} + \frac{24}{12} = 2.5 \ \text{ and}$$

$$Z = \frac{36 - 45}{\sqrt{\frac{10(9)}{19 \cdot 8}\left(\frac{19^3 - 19}{12}\right) - 2.5}} = \frac{-9}{\sqrt{\frac{90}{342}(557.5)}} = \frac{-9}{12.112} = -0.74$$

This correction has not changed the fact that H_1 was rejected and H_0 accepted. Once the number of identical locations is large, the Smirnov-Kolmogorov test is preferable. The Wilcoxon Rank Sum Test is very similar to the Mann-Whitney test and most statistical packages allow the use of both tests simultaneously. Using SPSS 11.0 the results of the data are as follows:

Two-Sample Kolmogorov-Smirnov Test

Mann-Whitney Test

Ranks

	GROUP	N	Mean Rank	Sum of Ranks
RUN	1.00	10	9.10	91.00
	2.00	9	11.00	99.00
	Total	19		

Test Statistics[b]

	RUN
Mann-Whitney U	36.000
Wilcoxon W	91.000
Z	-.735
Asymp. Sig. (2-tailed)	.462
Exact Sig. [2*(1-tailed Sig.)]	.497[a]

a. Not corrected for ties.

b. Grouping Variable: GROUP

Next we introduced probability tables for critical U values observed in the Mann-Whitney test when the hypotheses are unidirectional. In the case of bidirectional hypotheses, the probability values shall be multiplied by 2. The tables for the examination of Mann-Whitney U statistics located in Appendix C1.

14.3   *Kolmogorov-Smirnov (KS) Test*

Kolmozorov-Smirnov (KS) assumes no identical scores in the two samples. It shares the same fundamental assumptions of the Mann-Whitney/Wilcoxon (MW) tests. In cases where the values are ordered and then grouped, the KS test is preferable over the other tests. In the KS test, if H_0 is verified then the two samples, which were randomly chosen from the same population, share a similar CUMULATIVE FREQUENCY (CF). The KS test consists of the largest DIFFERENCE between the CFs of the two samples. If the greatest difference is larger than expected at random, it means that the gap between the CFs does not indicate equality between the samples. The H_1 can be unidirectional or bi-directional.

Assume that we have drawn two groups of athletes. One has high expectations for future success and the other low expectations. The two samples are also limited with respect to their skill level: very low, low, moderate, high, and very high. We relate to the first criterion by assuming that the two samples were derived from a larger population of athletes. We expect that athletes with high expectations for success will be also those with higher skill level. Can we conclude that such an association be significant at $p \leq .01$?

Since the basic assumptions of the KS test are identical to those of the MW-U test and the Runs test, the D (difference) distribution (the largest difference between the two samples) when $n \leq 40$ and $n_1 = n_2$ can be tested by using the MW test. If the number of cases is large and $n_1 \neq n_2$, or $n_1 = n_2$, the D value should be at least

$$1.36\sqrt{\frac{n_1 + n_2}{n_1 \cdot n_2}} \quad \text{for p} < .05$$

in order to reject H_0. Similarly

$$\text{for} \quad 1.22\sqrt{\frac{n_1 + n_2}{n \cdot n_2}} \quad \text{for } p \leq .10$$

$$\text{for} \quad 1.63\sqrt{\frac{n_1 + n_2}{n_1 \cdot n_2}} \quad \text{for } p \leq .01$$

$$\text{for} \quad 1.95\sqrt{\frac{n_1 + n_2}{n_1 \cdot n_2}} \quad \text{for } p \leq .001$$

If the H_1 is bidirectional, the coefficient (1.22, 1.63, 1.95, etc.) can be replaced by the estimated χ^2. The χ^2 is

$$\chi^2 = 4D^2 \frac{n_1 \cdot n_2}{n_1 + n_2} \quad \text{with df} = 2 \tag{55}$$

We demonstrate the KS test by example:

Physical/Motor Skill	Expectations for Future Success	
	Very Low	Very High
Very Low	52	25
Low	42	34
Moderate	30	20
High	31	52
Very High	28	63
Total	183	194

We hypothesize that very high expectations will be associated with higher skills (H_1 – unidirectional) and decide on $p \leq .01$. The hypothesis will be tested using χ^2. First we add the frequencies to establish the cumulative frequencies (cf) in each sample separately. In the second stage we represent each cumulative frequency by P, the proportion of cf and the total number of observations in each sample.

Physical/Motor Skill	cf_1 $(f_{1i} + f_{2i} + \dots f_{ki})$	P_1 (f_i/N_1)	cf_2 $(f_{1j} + f_{2j} + \dots + f_{kj})$	P_2 (f_j/N_2)	D $(P_1 - P_2)$
Under Low	52	.284	25	.129	.155
Under Moderate	94	.514	59	.304	.219
Under High	124	.678	79	.407	.271 ←
Under Very High	155	.847	131	.675	.172
Total	183	1.000	194	1.000	

$$x^2 = 4D^2 \frac{N_1 \cdot N_2}{N_1 + N_2} = 4(.271)^2 \frac{183(194)}{183 + 194} = 27.663.$$

The greatest difference between the proportions is 0.271 and is designated by an arrow →. χ^2 is then calculated using this value. The χ^2 is a function of this difference. The larger the difference, the greater χ^2 is. The critical χ^2 in the table for $p \leq .01$ and df = 2 is 9.21. This means that H_0 is rejected and equality between the two groups does not exist $(\chi_0^2 > \chi_c^2)$. χ^2 can be also used in small samples. In the above case, if H_1 is bidirectional the D value should be at least

$$1.63\sqrt{\frac{183+194}{183\cdot194}} = 1.63\cdot0.103 = 0.168.$$

To reject H_0, the largest difference, 0.271 (in absolute terms) should be larger than 0.168. Indeed 0.271 > 0.168, and therefore H_1 is accepted and H_0 rejected. The P_1 and P_2 values indicate that high expectations are related to higher physical/motor skill level and vice-versa.

14.4 Kruskal-Wallis H and Median Tests for More Than Two Samples

The Kruskal-Wallis H-test (KW-H) allows us to compare more than two samples on any given, ordinal variable. In reality we can use any of the previous tests on two samples each time. However KW-H examines all the possibilities at once. Like the Mann-Whitney (U) and Wilcoxon (W) tests, it compares the rank sums for each sample in the comparison. It has assumptions of χ^2 and H_0 assumes equality of distributions on the ordinal measure.

In the SPSS example we examined three groups of 59 subjects on an attitude scale which ranges from 0-10. The KW χ^2 with df = 2 was 2.8411 and non-significant. Therefore, the three possible pairs (1 vs. 2, 1 vs. 3, and 2 vs. 3) were not compared each to the other. The second test was the MEDIAN test. The test consists of locating the median of the three groups (Md = 5 in the output) and counting the number of observations above (GT – greater than) and equal or below the median (LE – lower equal). A χ^2 test is applied to this 2 x 3 table of counts. With df = 2, [(3-1)(2-1) = 2·1 = 2], the χ^2 = 4.2394 and is non-significant. This indicates that H_0 was not rejected and the three groups are equal in attitude.

Kruskal-Wallis 1-way Anova

Attitude by Group

Mean Rank	Cases	
28.66	19	GROUP=1
35.00	20	GROUP=2
36.27	20	GROUP=3
	—	
	59	Total
Chi Square	D.F	Significance
2.8411	2	.2416

Median Test

Attitude by group

Attitude	Group				
	1	2	3		
GT Median	6	11	5		
LE Median	13	9	15		
Cases	Median	Chi Square	D.F	Significance	
59	5.00	4.2394	2	.1201	

(15) Ordinal/Nominal Tests for Paired/Dependent Samples

15.1 *The McNemar Test for Binomial Distributions*

The McNemar test is applied to pre-post design where the variables share binomial nature. It can be applied also to pairs of subjects who are believed to be similar with respect to all variables except the manipulation/intervention given to some of them and prevented from others.

Assume we ask athletes a month before the Olympic games whether they agree or disagree with letting professional athletes participate in the games and then we ask them the same question again immediately after the closing ceremony. The design we have is as follows:

After

Yes (a) ← no change

Yes

No (b) ← change

Before

Yes (c) ← no change

No

No (d) ← change

If the Olympic games have not changed their opinion, then cells "a" (yes;yes) and "d" (no;no) will NOT CHANGE. If the Olympic experience has changed their opinion, then cells "b" (yes; no) and "c" (no;yes) will show a dramatic change. The McNemar test relates to cells "b" and "c" to examine any possible change. The observed-expected difference is similar to the χ^2 concept and therefore

$$x_M^2 = \frac{(N_b - N_c - 1)^2}{N_b + N_c} \tag{56}$$

where N_b is the observed number of counts in cell b

N_c is the observed number of counts in cell c.

Assume the following data was collected:

After

		Yes	No
	Yes	50	32
		(a)	(b)
Before			
	No	15	60
		(c)	(d)

The number of athletes who have NOT CHANGED their opinion was:

a + d = 50 + 60 = 110.

The number of athletes who CHANGED their opinion was:

$b + c = 32 + 15 = 47$

Are the 47 athletes who change their opinion a number that is sufficient to reject the H_0?
We apply the McNemar statistics and get

$$x_2^2 = \frac{(N_b - N_c - 1)^2}{N_b + N_c} = \frac{(32 - 15 - 1)^2}{32 + 15} = \frac{256}{47} = 5.45$$

The critical χ^2 with df = 1 at $p \le .01$ is 6.635. Thus we can not reject H_0 and accept H_1, i.e., the Olympic games have not changed the athletes opinion to a degree that can be generalized to ALL athletes. The results using SPSS 11.0 are as follows:

NPar Tests

Descriptive Statistics

	N	Mean	Std. Deviation	Minimum	Maximum
BEFORE	157	1.4777	.5011	1.00	2.00
AFTER	157	1.5860	.4941	1.00	2.00

McNemar Test

Crosstabs

Before & After

BEFORE	AFTER 1	2
1	50	32
2	15	60

Test Statistics[b]

	BEFORE & AFTER
N	157
Chi-Square[a]	5.447
Asymp. Sig.	.020

a. Continuity Corrected

b. McNemar Test

Keep in mind that if we were less conservative on our judgement to reject H_0, and decided on $p \le .05$, then χ^2 (1) = 3.84 and we could conclude that the Olympic games did CHANGE the athletes' opinions about professionalism in sport. The SPSS output shows us that (1) = 5.447 is significant at the $p < .02$ level. Here again, it is the researcher who must make the decision whether to accept or reject H_0.

15.2 Wilcoxon Signed-Ranks Test

The Wilcoxon Signed-Ranks test counts the negative ranks (before – "yes" and after – "no") – 32, positive rank (before – "no" and after – "yes") – 15, and ties (no-no, yes-yes; 50 + 60) – 110, and estimates a Z statistic taking into account the total number of count (N = 157). The SPSS 11.0 output is as follows:

Sign Test

Frequencies

		N
AFTER - BEFORE	Negative Differences[a]	15
	Positive Differences[b]	32
	Ties[c]	110
	Total	157

a. AFTER < BEFORE
b. AFTER > BEFORE
c. BEFORE = AFTER

Test Statistics[a]

	AFTER - BEFORE
Z	-2.334
Asymp. Sig. (2-tailed)	.020

a. Sign Test

Note that the significance level of the McNemar and Sign tests are identical.

15.3 Wilcoxon Signed-Ranks Test for Ordinal Data

In the McNemar and Sign tests the analyses were performed on nominal data: yes-no, agree-disagree, accept-reject, etc. In cases where ordinal data are collected, the Wilcoxon Signed-ranks test is the appropriate one under PAIRED conditions (i.e., some participants measured in two occasions, or two samples who are paired on all other variables but one).

Assume that instead of asking the athletes to respond "yes" or "no", we have given them an attitudinal-type of question with response format that ranges between "1" (completely disagree) through "2", "3", "4", and "5" (completely agree), before and after the Olympic games. To simplify the hard calculation we shall choose only 10 athletes.

Athlete	Olympics		Difference
	Before	After	
1	5	4	-1
2	2	2	0
3	1	3	2
4	3	1	-2
5	4	2	-2
6	5	5	0
7	4	4	0
8	2	5	3
9	4	1	-3
10	3	3	0

Four athletes (2, 6, 7, 10) did not change their attitudes toward professionalism in the Olympics. Next we order the "difference" values from the smallest to the largest as follows:

Athlete	1	3	4	5	8	9
Difference	-1	2	-2 -	2	3	-3
Rank	1	3	3	3	5.5	5.5

As there are six athletes where change was recorded, there are six ranks. Athlete 1 had the smallest change, athletes 3, 4, and 5 showed a change of $|2|$ and share location 2, 3, 4 thus averaging 3. Athletes 8 and 9 share the 5th and 6th location and averaged 5.5. If the positive and negative changes are equally distributed through the ranks, the ranks will be equal and can be calculated as follows:

$$\mu_T = \frac{N(N+1)}{4} \qquad (57)$$

$$\mu_T = \frac{6(6+1)}{4} = \frac{6 \cdot 7}{4} = 10.5$$

This is the value we use for examining the null hypothesis:

H_0: $\mu_T = 10.5$

This is the rank sum we expect from samples drawn from a population of athletes asked about including professional athletes in the Olympic games. We summarize the negative and positive changes separately as follows:

Sum of Positive Ranks: $\Sigma R+ = 3 + 5.5 = 8.5$

Sum of Negative Ranks: $\Sigma R- = 1 + 3 + 3 + 5.5 = 12.5$.

Now we may ask what is the probability that H_0 is true under $\Sigma R+ = 8.5$ and $\Sigma R- = 12.5$? The sample statistic Wilcoxon's T is the smallest rank sum, which in this case is for the negatives. A Z-test is conducted on the difference between μ_T and the sample value T:

$$Z = \frac{T - \mu_T}{\theta_T}$$

where $\theta_T = \sqrt{\dfrac{N(N+1)(2N+1)}{24}}$

For our hypothetical data, we get

$$\theta_T = \sqrt{\frac{6(6+1)(2 \cdot 6 + 1)}{24}} = \sqrt{\frac{42 \cdot 13}{24}} = \sqrt{22.75}$$

$$= 4.769$$

and

$$Z = \frac{8.5 - 10.5}{4.769} = \frac{-2.0}{4.769} = -0.42$$

Comparing the Z observed with Z critical with df = 5 we conclude that we cannot reject H_0, and the Olympic games have not changed the attitude of the athletes about professionalism in the Olympics. Using SPSS 11.0 with the data described we get:

NPar Tests

Wilcoxon Signed Ranks Test

Ranks

		N	Mean Rank	Sum of Ranks
AFTER - BEFORE	Negative Ranks	4[a]	3.13	12.50
	Positive Ranks	2[b]	4.25	8.50
	Ties	4[c]		
	Total	10		

a. AFTER < BEFORE

b. AFTER > BEFORE

c. BEFORE = AFTER

Test Statistics[b]

	AFTER - BEFORE
Z	-.425[a]
Asymp. Sig. (2-tailed)	.671

a. Based on positive ranks.

b. Wilcoxon Signed Ranks Test

Table 4.5

Critical Values for the Wilcoxon Signed-Ranks Test.

N	Significance Level (Unidirectional)		
	.025	.01	.005
	Significance Level (Bidirectional)		
	.05	.02	.01
6	0	–	–
7	2	0	–
8	4	2	0
9	6	3	2
10	8	5	3
11	11	7	5
12	14	10	7
13	17	13	10
14	21	16	13
15	25	20	16
16	30	24	20
17	35	28	23
18	40	33	28
19	46	38	32
20	52	43	38
21	59	49	43
22	66	56	49
23	73	62	55
24	81	69	61
25	89	77	68

(16) Hypotheses Testing with k Independent Factors (DV = Interval/Ratio Level Measurement)

Previously we introduced the one-way ANOVA as a statistical procedure of testing hypotheses, which relate to ONE DV (measured on an interval/ratio level) and ONE IV that is termed also a GROUPING VARIABLE. For example, to test the hypothesis that athletes who are engaged in aerobic-type of activity will tolerate exertion for a longer period of time than anaerobic athletes and non-athletes, the IV is the activity type. The DV is the time all the participants in the study can squeeze a handle bar of a dynamometer 70% of the maximal squeeze capacity or running 90% of their personal maximal oxygen uptake as long as they can. This experiment is graphically presented as follows:

Activity-Type	Exertion Tolerance
Aerobic	$\bar{X}_1, S_1$
Anaerobic	$\bar{X}_2, S_2$
None	$\bar{X}_3, S_3$
$\underbrace{\qquad}$	$\underbrace{\qquad}$
ONE IV	ONE DV
(grouping)	(interval/ratio level)

This simple design can be expressed as:

$$X_{ij} = \mu + \beta_j + \varepsilon_{ij} \qquad\qquad (58)$$

where X_{ij} is the exertion tolerance (DV) of person i within one of the three j groups (aerobic, anaerobic, no activity), μ is the grand mean, β_j is the group effect, and ε_{ij} is the within Ss error. The matrix that represents such an experiment looks as follows:

$$\begin{bmatrix} X_{i1j} \\ X_{i2j} \\ \vdots \\ X_{ipj} \end{bmatrix} = \begin{bmatrix} \mu_1 \\ \mu_2 \\ \vdots \\ \mu_p \end{bmatrix} + \begin{bmatrix} \beta_{1j} \\ \beta_{2j} \\ \vdots \\ \beta_{pj} \end{bmatrix} + \begin{bmatrix} \varepsilon_{i1j} \\ \varepsilon_{i2j} \\ \vdots \\ \varepsilon_{ipj} \end{bmatrix}$$

$$X_{ij} = \mu + \beta_{ij} + \varepsilon_{ij}$$

$$\underbrace{DV}\ =\ \underbrace{\text{Grand}}\ \underbrace{\text{Group}}\ \underbrace{\text{Error}}$$
$$\qquad\qquad \text{Mean} \quad \text{Effect}$$

This is termed a SINGLE FACTOR model where β can be a GROUP or any TREATMENT/INTERVENTION. The H_0 in this model is:

$$H_0 = \mu_1 = \mu_2 = \dots \mu_k.$$

However, assume we have TWO FACTORS or MORE that can affect exertion tolerance such as gender and activity type. Now we say that exertion tolerance (DV) is a function of (a) activity-type, (b) gender, and (c) their combination/interaction. A research design, which corresponds, to the questions raised here is as follows:

Activity-Type (j)	Gender (k)	DV = Exertion Tolerance
Aerobic	⌈ Female (1)	X_{11}, S_{11}
(1)	⌊ Male (2)	X_{12}, S_{12}
Anaerobic	⌈ Female (1)	X_{21}, S_{21}
(2)	⌊ Male (2)	X_{22}, S_{22}
None	⌈ Female (1)	X_{31}, S_{31}
(3)	⌊ Male (2)	X_{32}, S_{32}
TWO FACTORS		ONE DV (interval/ratio level)

Here we have a model that can be expressed as:

$$X_{ijk} = \mu + \beta_j + \gamma_k + \beta_j\gamma_k + \varepsilon_{ijk} \qquad (59)$$

DV	Grand Mean	Activity-type Effect	Gender Effect	Activity by Gender Effect	Error

Each of these SOURCES OF VARIANCE (EFFECTS) can be illustrated as follows:

ACTIVITY-TYPE EFFECT:

Activity-Type Effect	Mean	Mean-Grand Mean	Diff
(1) Aerobic ———— (males + females)	$\bar{X}_1$ ⟶	$\bar{X}_1 - \bar{X}_{..}$	⌉ 3 means
(2) Anaerobic ———— (males + females)	$\bar{X}_2$ ⟶	$\bar{X}_2 - \bar{X}_{..}$	are contrasted
(3) None ———— (males + females)	$\bar{X}_3$ ⟶	$\bar{X}_3 - \bar{X}_{..}$	to each other ⌋

or

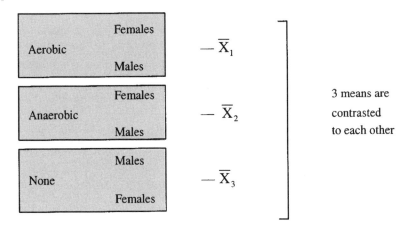

Thus the effect of ACTIVITY-TYPE consists of the difference among the three means ACROSS GENDER. The gender effect is illustrated as follows:

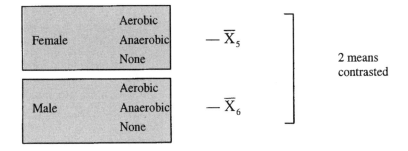

or

The interaction between activity-type and gender consists of more means than each of the factors separately, because it relies on the levels of both factors rather than each of them separately.

Activity-Type	Gender	Mean	Mean-Grand Mean Diff	
Aerobic	Female	$\overline{X}_7$	$\overline{X}_7 - \overline{X}_{\bullet\bullet}$	
	Male	$\overline{X}_8$	$\overline{X}_8 - \overline{X}_{\bullet\bullet}$	6 means
Anaerobic	Female	$\overline{X}_9$	$\overline{X}_9 - \overline{X}_{\bullet\bullet}$	are contrasted
	Male	$\overline{X}_{10}$	$\overline{X}_{10} - \overline{X}_{\bullet\bullet}$	each to the other
None	Female	$\overline{X}_{11}$	$\overline{X}_{11} - \overline{X}_{\bullet\bullet}$	
	Male	$\overline{X}_{12}$	$\overline{X}_{12} - \overline{X}_{\bullet\bullet}$	

The effects of each of the two factors are termed MAIN EFFECTS, and their combined effect is termed INTERACTION. Here are illustrations of possible main and interactional effects:

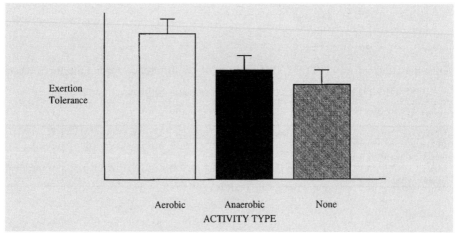

Figure 4.18   A Hypothetical Main Effect of Activity-type on Exertion Tolerance.

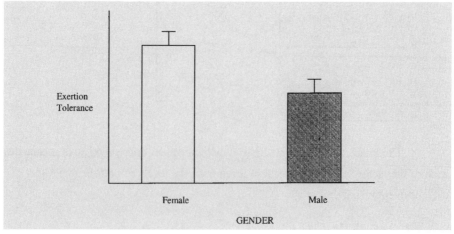

Figure 4.19   A Hypothetical Main Effect of Gender on Exertion Tolerance.

In both figures, 4.18 and 4.19, if the F-test assigned to activity-type and gender, separately, were significant ($\alpha \leq .05$) so it seems that aerobic athletes (males and females) tolerate exertion for a longer period of time than anaerobic athletes (males and females) and non-exercisers (males and females). However, this argument has to be verified by applying POST-HOC TESTS to the three pairs of means. The second main effect is that of gender. Females (aerobic, anaerobic, and non-exercisers) can tolerate exertion for a longer time than males (aerobic, anaerobic, and non-exercisers). In this case a post-hoc test is not required because there are only two levels of gender and a significant F statistic indicates significant differences among only males and females. A possible 2-way interaction may look as follows:

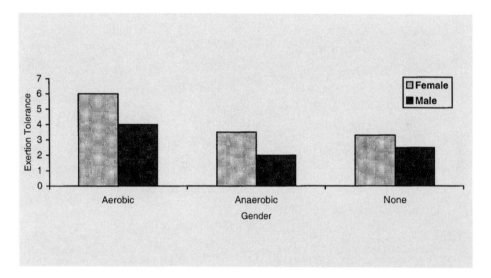

Figure 4.20 A Hypothetical Activity Type by Gender Interactional Effect on Exertion Tolerance.

Figure 4.20 consists of six means (3 x 2), which pertain to all the possible combinations. In this particular example it can be noticed that the greatest mean differences in exertion tolerance is evidenced between male and female aerobic athletes. Aerobic female athletes can tolerate exertion the highest of ALL the six subgroups comprised of activity-type and gender, while male aerobic athletes are slightly higher than their male anaerobic counterparts. Thus an interaction may result from ONE MEAN that is different from the OTHERS or TWO, THREE or MORE that are different from the others. Again, POST-HOC TESTS are required to verify these differences.

Several considerations should be kept in mind in k-factorial designs:

(A)   More than one alternative hypothesis can be stated and examined. For example:

H_0: $\mu_f > \mu_m$ (Females tolerate exertion more than males)

H_1: $\mu_a > \mu_a > \mu_n$ (Aerobic athletes tolerate exertion longer than anaerobic athletes, who in turn tolerate exertion longer than non-exercisers)

H_1: $\mu_{fa} > \mu_{ma}$ (Female aerobic athletes tolerate exertion longer than male aerobic athletes), depending on the THEORY, which was the FOUNDATION of the postulated HYPOTHESES and RESEARCH PLAN.

(B)   The degrees of freedom (df) associated with each effect are different. Assume we had 60 participants in each activity-type, and within each, 30 were males and 30 were females. Thus, the design consists of:

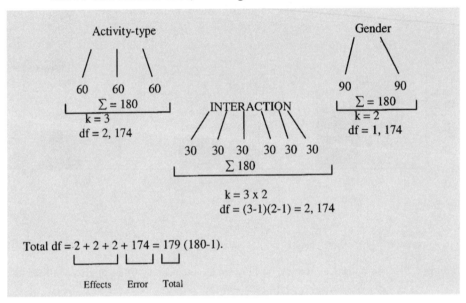

The df associated with the ERROR TERM comes from the WITHIN Ss VARIANCE, i.e., the 180 participants in the study. Thus, the SUM of SQUARES (SS) which represent the differences among the three activity types are divided by 2 (3 – 1) to estimate its MEAN SS (MSS). The gender differences are divided by 1 (2-1) to estimate the MSS associated with gender. Similarly the differences among the six means of the interaction are divided by 5 (6-1) to estimate the MSS associated with the gender by activity type interaction. Each of these MSS is divided by the ERROR SUM OF SQUARES to yield an F-test for each of the three effects.

$$F = \frac{MSS_{effect}}{MSS_{error}} \text{ with (k-1), error df.}$$

(C)   A TREAD ANALYSIS can be performed where the IV has a LOGICAL
       QUALITATIVE or QUANTITATIVE INCREMENT. For example, if an
       intervention consists of more hours of training, then the researcher may assume
       that also motor performance will subsequently increase. The question is how
       this will increase: Linearly? In a quadratic shape? Cubic shape? Here are three
       examples:

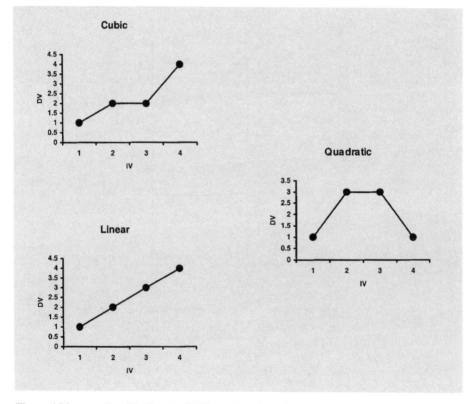

Figure 4.21   Possible Trends of DV as a Function of IV.

(D)   The more IVs (i.e., factors) are included in the research design, the more
       interactions will result, and more OBSERVATIONS will be needed. For
       example, in a 3-factorial design, we shall have the following effects:

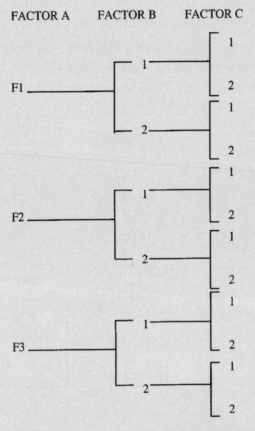

FACTOR A   FACTOR B   FACTOR C

MAIN EFFECTS: FACTOR A (FA)
                       FACTOR B (FB)
                       FACTOR C (FC)

TWO-WAY INTERACTIONS: FA by FB
                        FA by FC
                        FB by FC

THREE-WAY INTERACTIONS: FA by FB by FC

In the example above, FA has 3 levels and FA and FB have 2 levels each. Therefore the smallest cell in this design consists of the 3-way interactions 3 x 2 x 2 = 12 cells. As a rule of thumb, at least 30 observations are required to satisfy the normality assumption of the smallest cell. Therefore we need at least 30 observations within each of the 12 cells, i.e., at least 12 x 30 = 360 observations. This does not exclude the requirement to examine the data for normality by using the appropriate univariate and multivariate methods. If the 3 factors had 3 levels each, the number of the smallest cells was 3 x 3 x 3 = 27, and the minimal number of observations needed was 27 x 30 = 810.

An example of SPSS 11.0 output for two-factorial design is given next. (The number of observations is too small and inappropriate. This example is used merely for demonstrating the concept introduced above.) The data consist of 12 participants divided into two groups (i.e., factors): anxiety (low – 1, high – 2) and tension (1 – low, 2 – high). All were tested on a motor performance task, termed here "trial 1".

	Subject	Anxiety	Tension	Trial 1
1	1	1	1	18
2	2	1	1	19
3	3	1	1	14
4	4	1	2	16
5	5	1	2	12
6	6	1	2	18
7	7	2	1	16
8	8	2	1	18
9	9	2	1	16
10	10	2	2	19
11	11	2	2	16
12	12	2	2	16

First, two ONE-WAY ANOVAS were conducted for "trial 1" to illustrate the effect of anxiety and tension on performance without taking into account their interaction.

Oneway

Descriptives

Trial 1

	N	Mean	Std. Deviation	Std. Error	95% Confidence Interval for Mean		Minimum	Maximum
					Lower Bound	Upper Bound		
1	6	16.17	2.71	1.11	13.32	19.02	12	19
2	6	16.83	1.33	.54	15.44	18.23	16	19
Total	12	16.50	2.07	.60	15.19	17.81	12	19

Test of Homogeneity of Variances

Trial 1

Levene Statistic	df1	df2	Sig.
3.312	1	10	.099

Anova

Trial 1

	Sum of Squares	df	Mean Square	F	Sig.
Between Groups	1.333	1	1.333	.292	.601
Within Groups	45.667	10	4.567		
Total	47.000	11			

Means Plots

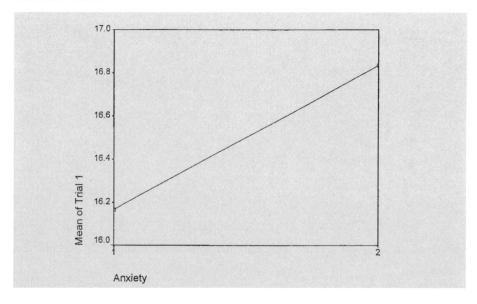

Oneway

Descriptives

Trial 1

	N	Mean	Std. Deviation	Std. Error	95% Confidence Interval for Mean		Minimum	Maximum
					Lower Bound	Upper Bound		
1	6	16.83	1.83	.75	14.91	18.76	14	19
2	6	16.17	2.40	.98	13.65	18.69	12	19
Total	12	16.50	2.07	.60	15.19	17.81	12	19

Test of Homogeneity of Variances

Trial 1

Levene Statistic	df1	df2	Sig.
.005	1	10	.944

Anova

Trial 1

	Sum of Squares	df	Mean Square	F	Sig.
Between Groups	1.333	1	1.333	.292	.601
Within Groups	45.667	10	4.567		
Total	47.000	11			

Means Plots

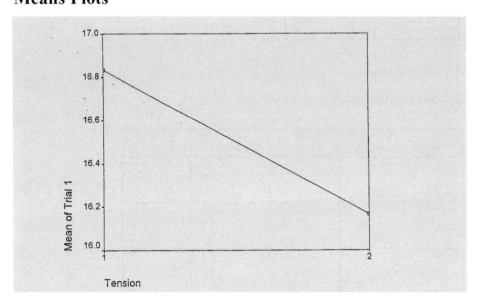

The means, standard deviations, ranges, and 95% CIs for the two groups which vary in anxiety and tension are introduced first. The Levene's Homogeneity of Variance tests show that the variances of the groups do not differ each from the other. Finally, the F-test indicates no significant differences between either the two anxiety level groups, or the two tension groups (α's > .05), thus H_0 was not rejected. The mean plots for the groups (given in the figure) were <u>not</u> large enough in relation to the standard errors to result in significant differences.

Next a TWO-WAY FACTORIAL ANOVA is presented. The design and descriptive data are introduced first followed by Levene's test of equality of error variances. The test ensured that the assumption of variance homogeneity was not violated. The ANOVA TABLE (test of between Ss effect) indicates that the MAIN EFFECT (anxiety and tension, respectively) and the TWO-WAY INTERACTIONAL EFFECT (anxiety by tension) were non-significant, thus not rejecting H_0. Eta squared values indicate the proportion of trial 1 variance explained by the two factors and their interactions. These values were very minor.

Between-Subjects Factors

		N
Anxiety	1	6
	2	6
Tension	1	6
	2	6

Descriptive Statistics

Dependent Variable: Trial 1

Anxiety	Tension	Mean	Std. Deviation	N
1	1	17.00	2.65	3
	2	15.33	3.06	3
	Total	16.17	2.71	6
2	1	16.67	1.15	3
	2	17.00	1.73	3
	Total	16.83	1.33	6
Total	1	16.83	1.83	6
	2	16.17	2.40	6
	Total	16.50	2.07	12

Levene's Test of Equality of Error Variances[a]

Dependent Variable: Trial 1

F	df1	df2	Sig.
1.319	3	8	.334

Tests the null hypothesis that the error variance of the dependent variable is equal across groups. a. Design: Intercept + ANXIETY + TENSION + ANXIETY * TENSION

Test of Between-Subjects Effects

Dependent Variable: Trial 1

Source	Type III Sum of Squares	df	Mean Square	F	Sig.	Eta Squared
Corrected Model	5.667[c]	3	1.889	.366	.780	.121
Intercept	3267.000	1	3267.000	632.323	.000	.988
ANXIETY	1.333	1	1.333	.258	.625	.031
TENSION	1.333	1	1.333	.258	.625	.031
ANXIETY * TENSION	3.000	1	3.000	.581	.468	.068
Error	41.333	8	5.167			
Total	3314.000	12				
Corrected Total	47.000	11				

Estimated Marginal Means

1. Grand Mean

Dependent Variable: Trial 1

Mean	Std. Error	95% Confidence Interval	
		Lower Bound	Upper Bound
16.500	.656	14.987	18.013

2. Anxiety

Dependent Variable: Trial 1

Anxiety	Mean	Std. Error	95% Confidence Interval	
			Lower Bound	Upper Bound
1	16.167	.928	14.027	18.307
2	16.833	.928	14.693	18.973

3. Tension

Dependent Variable: Trial 1

Tension	Mean	Std. Error	95% Confidence Interval	
			Lower Bound	Upper Bound
1	16.833	.928	14.693	18.973
2	16.167	.928	14.027	18.307

4. Anxiety * Tension

Dependent Variable: Trial 1

Anxiety	Tension	Mean	Std. Error	95% Confidence Interval	
				Lower Bound	Upper Bound
1	1	17.000	1.312	13.974	20.026
	2	15.333	1.312	12.307	18.360
2	1	16.667	1.312	13.640	19.693
	2	17.000	1.312	13.974	20.026

(17)   Multivariate Analysis of Variance (MANOVA)

In the UNIVARIATE analysis of variance, the effect of a factor (or treatment) or several factors (or treatments) on a SINGLE VARIABLE, X, was examined. In the MULTIVARIATE ANOVA, SEVERAL VARIABLES are examined SIMULTANEOUSLY, X_1, X_2 ... X_p. For example, physical exercise may affect simultaneously heart-rate, blood pressure, and respiratory functioning. Each OBSERVATION is considered to be a VECTOR rather than a SCALAR.

When each of the X_1, X_2 ... X_p variables is analyzed separately, the correlations among these variables are ignored. In the univariate ANOVA the hypothesis (H_0) is

H_0: $\mu_1 = \mu_2 = ... = \mu_k$

and the corresponding multivariate hypothesis is

$$
\begin{bmatrix} \mu_{11} \\ \mu_{21} \\ \vdots \\ \mu_{p1} \end{bmatrix}
=
\begin{bmatrix} \mu_{12} \\ \mu_{22} \\ \vdots \\ \mu_{p2} \end{bmatrix}
= \ldots =
\begin{bmatrix} \mu_{1k} \\ \mu_{2k} \\ \vdots \\ \mu_{pk} \end{bmatrix}
$$

$$
\mu_1 \quad = \quad \mu_2 \quad = \ldots = \quad \mu_k
$$

for two or more DVs the model has the following structure:

	Factor/Treatment 1 X_1 X_2		Factor/Treatment 2 ... X_1 X_2			Factor/Treatment k X_1 X_2	
	X_{111}	X_{121}	X_{112}	X_{122}	...	X_{11k}	X_{12k}
	X_{211}	X_{221}	X_{212}	X_{222}	...	X_{21k}	X_{22k}
	$\vdots$	$\vdots$	$\vdots$	$\vdots$		$\vdots$	$\vdots$
	$\underline{X_{n11}}$	$\underline{X_{n21}}$	$\underline{X_{n12}}$	$\underline{X_{n22}}$	...	$\underline{X_{n1k}}$	$\underline{X_{n2k}}$
Total	T_{11}	T_{21}	T_{12}	T_{22}		T_{1k}	T_{2k}
	$G_1 = \Sigma T_{1j}$		$G_2 = \Sigma T_{2j}$		...	$G_k = \Sigma T_{kj}$	

The computation necessitates knowledge in matrix algebra and can be read in Winer (1971, pp. 232-240). In general terms MULTIVARIATE ANOVA has the following form:

$$
\underbrace{Y_1 + Y_2 + \ldots + Y_n}_{\text{Interval/Ratio level}} = \underbrace{X_1 + X_2 + \ldots + X_n}_{\text{Categorical/Grouping level}}
$$

while UNIVARIATE ANOVA has the term of

$$
\underbrace{Y_1}_{\text{Interval/Ratio}} = \underbrace{X_1 + X_2 + \ldots + X_n}_{\text{Categorical/Grouping}}
$$

MANOVA is a statistical procedure which examines differences and variations between groups or experimental conditions of SEVERAL DEPENDENT VARIABLES in a COMBINED manner that decreases the probability of conducting a type-I error had the analysis been performed separately for each of the DVs (i.e., univariate ANOVAs).

HOTELLING's T^2 is a useful statistic, which is aimed at the verification of the greatest group difference formed by the DVs, and at the same time controls for type-I error inflation. This is done by a single overall test of group differences across all DVs at a given probability (α) level. Hotelling's T^2 values are contrasted to a known distribution of "no treatment effect" on any set of the DVs. It is an F distribution with p and $N_1 + N_2 - 2 - 1$ df after adjustment (p is the number of DVs). The critical value of T^2, T_c^2 is

$$T_c^2 = \frac{p(N_1 + N_2 - 2)}{N_1 + N_2 - p - 1} \cdot F_c \qquad (60)$$

and T_{obs} is contrasted to T_c to verify H_0 to all the tests previously mentioned. If $T_{obs}^2 > T_c^2$ then H_0 is rejected and there is a difference between the two groups on the VECTORS of the DVs.

When more than two groups are compared on VECTORS of DVs, a DISCRIMINANT FUNCTION specifies the weights which maximize the DIFFERENCES among the GROUPS, which also maximize the F-value, and allow us to compute the GREATEST CHARACTERISTIC ROOT STATISTIC (GCR)

$$GCR = \frac{(k-1)F_{max}}{N-k} \qquad (61)$$

again to examine the H_0 of mean vector's equality to GCR distribution. When $GCR_{obs} > GCR_c$, H_0 is rejected and the groups differ on the mean vectors they were measured.

It should be noted that when the DVs are correlated (i.e., multicollinearity), MANOVA is a more powerful statistical test than many univariate tests. MANOVA detects COMBINED DIFFERENCES, which cannot be detected via univariate tests. The univariates are formed into CLUSTERS/DIMENSIONS, which may DISTINGUISH among the GROUPS/TREATMENT more strongly than univariate does. However, the VARIABLES should SHARE a SOUND CONCEPTUAL/ THEORETICAL BASE. The ORDER of the DV may also share a logical sequence and a STEPDOWN ANALYSIS can examine the statistical differences among the groups on the VECTORS in a SEQUENTIAL FORM, similar to multiple linear regressions.

For example, a UNIVARIATE QUESTION like: "Are trained and untrained subjects different in respiratory rate and respiratory depth?"

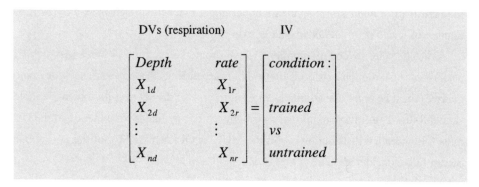

A MULTIVARIATE QUESTION may be: "Are training conditions and gender affecting aerobic capacity?"

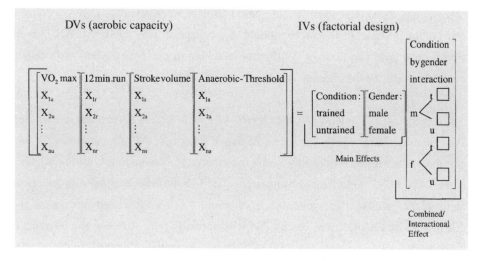

The sample size for a MANOVA should be greater than for an ANOVA as there are more variables to be considered. In the second panel of the above example, a main effect of GENDER refers to the differences between males and females on the four DVs which comprise of aerobic capacity. A CONDITION main effect refers to the difference in the four DVs between trained and untrained subjects. The GENDER by CONDITION INTERACTIONAL EFFECT refers to the four cells in the right side of the panel. It may result from different combinations. For example, trained females may be characterized by different patterns of the four DVs than the other three groups. Or for example, males untrained are similar to female trained subjects in the four DVs, but males trained and females untrained differ on the four DVs. POST-HOC tests or PLANNED tests are required if (a) a main effect or interactional effect reached significance, and (b) if the number of levels with the DV is greater than two.

There are several assumptions which should be examined when a MANOVA is performed: (a) the observations must be independent, (b) the variance-covariance matrices must be equal for all treatment groups, and (c) the set of p-dependent variables should follow a multivariate normal distribution (i.e., any linear combination of the DVs must follow such a distribution). Also the MULTICOLLINEARITY of the DVs should be carefully considered.

INDEPENDENCE. When subjects are given similar questions within a short time interval or under conditions which bring them to respond similarly, this causes the observations to be dependent. If for some reason a set in the data shows correlated observations, these observations should be collapsed into ONE MEAN. Lower significance level (say 0.01 or 0.001) may also help in preventing type-I error due to dependence among the observations.

EQUALITY of VARIANCE-COVARIANCE MATRICES. All groups (levels of the IVs) should share equal variance-covariance matrices. All the covariances and correlations are tested for equality across the groups. The common test for this equality is the BOX TEST. Significant results necessitate transformation of the data in one or more of the variables. To avoid such a violation, it is recommended to examine the distribution of each DV, and ensure that it is normally (i.e., Kurtosis and Skewness) distributed. Lack of equality may also result from substantial differences in the number of observations in each of the groups.

NORMALITY. All the variables ought to be MULTIVARIATE NORMAL. Lack of violation in univariate normality does not guarantee multivariate normality, but only rarely does this occur.

LINEARITY and MULTICOLLINEARITY. An examination of the data is needed to assess any non-linear relations among the DVs. The DVs should not share too high multicollinearity, which creates redundancy and decreases the statistical efficiency.

OUTLIERS. Analysis of residuals is needed to examine the lack of HETEROSCEDASTICITY. Outliers should be detected to avoid type-I errors.

The most popular criteria for MULTIVARIATE SIGNIFICANCE are: PILLAI's TRACE, WILKS' LAMBDA, HOTELLING's TRACE, and ROY's LARGEST ROOT. The ROY's GCR measures the differences on only the first canonical root (or discriminant function) among the DVs. It is an efficient test when the DVs are related. Wilks' Lambda refers to more discriminant function (p or k-1 where p is the number of DVs and k the number of groups; whichever is the smaller). Thus all combinations of the DVs are examined. Wilks' Lambda values are transformed into F-values for significance testing. Pillai's Trace and Hotelling's Trace are similar to Wilks' Lambda and are transformed to F values for significance (hypotheses) testing.

POWER. To avoid type-II (beta) error discussed earlier, three criteria are used: significance level (α), the effect-size (ES; standardized difference between means), and sample-size (number of observations). As α increases, β decreases, and vice-versa. It is important therefore to keep a "reasonable" α (e.g. .05) and a power of about .80. The larger the ES, the higher the power is, though ES is hard to control. However, increasing the number of observations reduces the sampling error and increases the power of the statistical test. When the sample size is very large, almost any difference becomes significant. At this point the power and the ES are more important in making SENSE and giving MEANING to the OBSERVED DIFFERENCES.

For good practice it is recommended to hypothesize A PRIORI about the ES and then to determine the SAMPLE SIZE to identify such an ES. The ES can be hypothesized by relying on the LITERATURE (previous RESEARCH) and on THEORETICAL/CONCEPTUAL grounds. A convenient Table, which combines power, ES magnitudes, and number of groups, is presented in Hair *et al.* (1995).

Table 4. 6

Sample Size Requirement per Group for Achieving Statistical Power of .80 in MANOVA (From Hair et al., 1995, p. 279).

Effect Size	Number of Groups											
	3				4				5			
	No. of DVs				No. of DVs				No. of DVs			
	2	4	6	8	2	4	6	8	2	4	6	8
Very large	13	16	19	21	14	18	21	23	16	21	24	27
Large	26	33	38	42	29	37	44	48	34	44	52	58
Medium	44	56	66	72	50	64	74	84	60	76	90	100
Small	98	125	145	160	115	145	165	185	135	170	200	230

We have used SPSS 11.0 on a data set, which contained questions about attitudes toward banned drugs in sport. Each question was rated on a 1-5 Likert-type scale. We shall demonstrate the MANOVA on the first five first questions (VAR1-VAR5) as DVs and Gender (male/female) and Educational Level (EDUC: 1, 2, 3, and 5; category 4 had five respondents and therefore was excluded from the analysis) as IVs.

Only the relevant information of the output is given next. The between Ss factors and the number of observations in each is presented first.

Between Subjects Factors

		N
GENDER	1.00	219
	2.00	401
EDUC	1.00	416
	2.00	114
	3.00	53
	5.00	37

Then descriptive statistics (means, Ss, and N) are provided for each of the five DVs by Gender and Educational level (we avoid their presentation here). To examine the equality of covariance matrices, Box's test is provided.

Box's Test of Equality of Covariance Matrices'

Box's M	118.296
F	1.054
df1	105
df2	32900
Sig.	.333

Tests the null hypothesis that the observed covariance matrices of the dependent variables are equal across groups. a. Design: Intercept+GENDER+EDUC+GENDER * EDUC

As can be seen, the lack of significance (α = .33) indicates that the variance/covariance matrices in all the groups do not vary. The Multivariate Tests are given next.

Multivariate Tests[d]

Effect		Value	Hypothesis F	df	Error df	Sic.
Intercept	Pi tai's Trace	.888	960.259°	5.000	608.000	.000
	Wilks' Lambda	.112	960.259^{1}	5.000	608.000	.000
	Hotelling's Trace	7.897	960.259^{1}	5.000	608.000	.000
	Roy's Largest Root	7.897	960.259^{1}	5.000	608.000	000
GENDER	Pillai's Trace	.011	1.327°	5.000	608.000	.251
	Wilks' Lambda	.989	1.327^{1}	5.000	608.000	.251
	Hotelling's Trace	.011	1.327^{1}	5.000	608.000	.251
	Roy's Largest Root	.011	1.327^{1}	5.000	608.000	.251
EDUC	Piilai's Trace	.036	1.490	15.000	1830.000	.100
	Wilks' Lambda	.964	1.492	15.000	1678.822	.100
	Hotellfing's Trace	.037	1.493	15.000	1820.000	.099
	Ray's Largest Root	.025	3.033°	5.000	610.000	.010,
GENDER ' EDUC	Pillai's Trace	.023	.955	15.000	1830.000	.502
	Wilks' Lambda	.977	.953	15.000	1678.822	.503
	Hotelling's Trace	.024	.952	15.000	1820.000	.505
	Roy's Largest Root	.013	1_622°	5.000	610.000	.152

Multivariate Tests[d]

Effect		Eta Scuared	Noncent. Parameter	Observed Power'
Intercept	Pillafs Trace	.888	4801.296	1.000
	Wilks' Lambda	.888	4801.296	1.000
	Hotelling's Trace	.888	4801.296	1.000
	Ray's Largest Root	.888	4801.296	1.000
GENDER	Piilai s Trace	.011	6.633	.472
	Wilks' Lambda	.011	6.633	.472
	Hotelling's Trace	.011	6.633	.472
	Roy's Largest Root	.011	6.633	.472
EDUC	Pillai's Trace	.012	22.351	.877
	Wilks' Lambda	.012	20.580	.840
	Hoteliing's Trace	.012	22.393	.877
	Ray's Largest Root	.024	15.167	.867
GENDER ' EDUC	Piilai s Trace	.008	14.320	.647
	Wilks' Lambda	.008	13.153	.599
	Hotelling's Trace	.008	14.277	.645
	Roy's Largest Root	.013	8.112	.567

a. Computed using alpha =.05

b. Exact statistic

c. The static is an upper bound on F that yields a lower bound on the significance level.

d. Design: Intercept + GENDER + EDUC + GENDER * EDUC

The results show that males and females do not vary on the five additional questions. Also the gender by education level resulted in non-significant multivariate statistics. However, education level (main effect) was very close to significance by three criterions and significant ($\alpha < .01$) by Roy's Largest Root test. The effect of educational level had also a strong power (.84 - .88).

Before proceeding to the Tests of Between Subjects Effects to locate source of variation (in this example, "educational level") the Levene's Test of Equality of Error (Sampling) Variance is provided.

Levene's Test of Equality of Error Variances[a]

	F	df1	df2	Sig.
VAR00001	.398	7	612	.903
VAR00002	.445	7	612	.874
VAR00003	.717	7	612	.658
VAR00004	1.915	7	612	.065
VAR00005	.803	7	612	.585

Tests the null hypothesis that the error variance of the dependent variable is equal across groups,

a. Design: Intercept+GENDER+EDUC+GENDER * EDUC

With 7,612 df, no major violation in sampling error was noted. VAR4 was somewhat different than the other four variables. The tests of BS effects are presented next.

Tests of Between-Subjects Effects

Source	Dependent Variable	Type III Sum of Squares	df	Mean Square	F	Sig.
Corrected Model	VAR00001	11.644[11]	7	1.663	1.784	.088
	VAR00002	5.749°	7	.821	.635	.727
	VAR00003	15.530'	7	2.219	1.785	.088
	VAR00004	11.195[d]	7	1.599	1.433	.189
	VAR00005	13.036[e]	7	1.862	1.375	.213
Intercept	VAR00001	3593.658	1	3593.658	3854.791	.000
	VAR00002	2825.615	1	2825.615	2184.714	.000
	VAR00003	2497.389	1	2497.389	2008.744	.000
	VAR00004	2803.287	1	2803.287	2512.530	.000
	VAR00005	2442.381	1	2442.381	1803.208	.000
GENDER	VAR00001	3.691	1	3.691	3.959	.047
	VAR00002	.756	1	.756	.584	.445
	VAR00003	.101	1	.101	.081	.776
	VAR00004	.149	1	.149	.133	.715
	VAR00005	.158	1	.158	.117	.732
EDUC	VAR00001	3.358	3	1.119	1.201	.309
	VAR00002	.485	3	.162	.125	.945
	VAR00003	12.471	3	4.157	3.344	.019
	VAR00004	4.766	3	1.589	1.424	.235
	VAR00005	8.429	3	2.810	2.074	.102
GENDER * EDUC	VAR00001	1.557	3	.519	.557	.644
	VAR00002	1.267	3	.422	.326	.806
	VAR00003	1.279	3	.426	.343	.794
	VAR00004	2.921	3	.974	.873	.455
	VAR00005	2.219	3	.740	.546	.651
Error	VAR00001	570.542	612	.932		
	VAR00002	791.534	612	1.293		
	VAR00003	760.874	612	1.243		
	VAR00004	682.822	612	1.116		
	VAR00005	828.932	612	1.354		
Total	VAR00001	8639.000	620			
	VAR00002	7236.000	620			
	VAR00003	6803.000	620			
	VAR00004	7321.000	620			
	VAR00005	6726.000	620			
Corrected Total	VAR00001	582.185	619			
	VAR00002	797.284	619			
	VAR00003	776.405	619			
	VAR00004	694.018	619			
	VAR00005	841.968	619			

Tests of Between-Subjects Effects

Source	Dependent Variable	Eta Squared	Noncent. Parameter	Observed Power'
Corrected Model	VAR00001	.020	12.490	.725
	VAR00002	.007	4.445	.277
	VAR00003	.020	12.492	.725
	VAR00004	.016	10.034	.610
	VAR00005	.015	9.624	.588
Intercept	VAR00001	.863	3854.791	1.000
	VAR00002	.781	2184.714	1.000
	VAR00003	.766	2008.744	1.000
	VAR00004	.804	2512.530	1.000
	VAR00005	.747	1803.208	1.000
GENDER	VAR00001	.006	3.959	.511
	VAR00002	.001	.584	.119
	VAR00003	.000	.081	.059
	VAR00004	.000	.133	.065
	VAR00005	.000	.117	.063
EDUC	VAR00001	.006	3.602	.323
	VAR00002	.001	.375	.073
	VAR00003	.016	10.031	.760
	VAR00004	.007	4.272	.379
	VAR00005	.010	6.223	.532
GENDER' EDUC	VAR00001	.003	1.670	.165
	VAR00002	.002	.979	.114
	VAR00003	.002	1.029	.117
	VAR00004	.004	2.618	.241
	VAR00005	.003	1.638	.163
Error	VAR00001			
	VAR00002			
	VAR00003			
	VAR00004			
	VAR00005			
Total	VAR00001			
	VAR00002			
	VAR00003			
	VAR00004			
	VAR00005			
Corrected Total	VAR00001			
	VAR00002			
	VAR00003			
	VAR00004			
	VAR00005			

a. Computed using alpha =.05
b. R Squared =.020 (Adjusted R Squared =.009)
c. R Squared = .007 (Adjusted R Squared = -.004)
d. R Squared =.016 (Adjusted R Squared = .005)
e. R Squared = .015 (Adjusted R Squared = .004)

The "intercept" significant results indicate that the means of all the DVs (VAR1-VAR5) are significantly different from zero. In line with the multivariate analysis, most of the effects were non-significant. Males and females differed on VAR1 ($\alpha<.05$) but since the Multivariate MANOVA failed to show it, we do not accept the BS test as a significant effect. However, the only significant means' differences were obtained for VAR3 ($\alpha<.02$) with respect to education. The descriptive statistics and post-hoc test are provided next to locate the source of differences among the educational level means in VAR3.

1. Grand Mean

Dependent Variable	Mean	Std. Error	95% Confidence Interval Lower Bound	Upper Bound
VAR00001	3.605	.058	3.491	3.719
VAR00002	3.196	.068	3.062	3.331
VAR00003	3.005	.067	2.873	3.137
VAR00004	3.184	.064	3.059	3.308
VAR00005	2.972	.070	2.834	3.109

2. GENDER

Dependent Variable	GENDER	Mean	Std. Error	95% Confidence Interval Lower Bound	Upper Bound
VAR00001	1.00	3.489	.084	3.323	3.655
	2.00	3.720	.080	3.564	3.877
VAR00002	1.00	3.144	.099	2.949	3.339
	2.00	3.249	.094	3.064	3.433
VAR00003	1.00	2.986	.098	2.794	3.178
	2.00	3.024	.092	2.843	3.205
VAR00004	1.00	3.207	.092	3.025	3.388
	2.00	3.161	.087	2.989	3.332
VAR00005	1.00	2.996	.102	2.796	3.196
	2.00	2.948	.096	2.759	3.136

3. EDUC

Dependent EDUC Variable		Mean	Std. Error	95% Confidence Interval	
				Lower Bound	Upper Bound
VAR0001	1.00	3.587	.053	3.484	3.691
	2.00	3.508	.091	3.330	3.686
	3.00	3.491	.133	3.230	3.753
	5.00	3.832	.159	3.520	4.144
VAR0002	1.00	3.179	.062	3.057	3.301
	2.00	3.231	.107	3.021	3.440
	3.00	3.135	.157	2.827	3.443
	5.00	3.241	.187	2.874	3.609
VAR0003	1.00	3.212	.061	3.093	3.331
	2.00	2.853	.105	2.647	3.058
	3.00	3.006	.154	2.704	3.309
	5.00	2.949	.183	2.589	3.309
VAR0004	1.00	3.307	.058	3.194	3.420
	2.00	3.081	.099	2.886	3.275
	3.00	3.184	.146	2.898	3.470
	5.00	3.164	.174	2.823	3.505
VAR0005	1.00	3.145	.063	3.020	3.269
	2.00	2.872	.109	2.658	3.087
	3.00	2.869	.161	2.553	3.184
	5.00	3.001	.191	2.626	3.377

4. GENDER' EDUC

Dependent Variable	GENDER	EDUC	Mean .	Std. Error	95% Confidence Interval Lower Bound	Upper Bound
VAR00001	1.00	1.00	3.496	.089	3.320	3.671
		2.00	3.350	.125	3.105	3.595
		3.00	3.500	.197	3.113	3.887
		5.00	3.611	.228	3.164	4.058
	2.00	1.00	3.679	.056	3.569	3.789
		2.00	3.667	.131	3.409	3.925
		3.00	3.483	.179	3.131	3.835
		5.00	4.053	.222	3.618	4.488
VAR00002	1.00	1.00	3.060	.105	2.853	3.266
		2.00	3.183	.147	2.895	3.472
		3.00	3.167	.232	2.711	3.623
		5.00	3.167	.268	2.640	3.693
	2.00	1.00	3.298	.066	3.168	3.427
		2.00	3.278	.155	2.974	3.582
		3.00	3.103	.211	2.689	3.518
		5.00	3.316	.261	2.803	3.828
VAR00003	1.00	1.00	3.197	.103	2.994	3.399
		2.00	2.817	.144	2.534	3.099
		3.00	2.875	.228	2.428	3.322
		5.00	3.056	.263	2.539	3.572
	2.00	1.00	3.227	.064	3.101	3.354
		2.00	2.889	.152	2.591	3.187
		3.00	3.138	.207	2.731	3.545
		5.00	2.842	.256	2.340	3.344
VAR00004	1.00	1.00	3.222	.098	3.030	3.414
		2.00	3.050	.136	2.782	3.318
		3.00	3.333	.216	2.910	3.757
		5.00	3.222	.249	2.733	3.711
	2.00	1.00	3.391	.061	3.271	3.511
		2.00	3.111	.144	2.829	3.393
		3.00	3.034	.196	2.649	3.420
		5.00	3.105	.242	2.629	3.581
VAR 00005	1.00	1.00	3.085	.108	2.874	3.297
		2.00	2.967	.150	2.672	3.262
		3.00	2.875	.238	2.408	3.342
		5.00	3.056	.274	2.517	3.594
	2.00	1.00	3.204	.067	3.072	3.336
		2.00	2.778	.158	2.467	3.089
		3.00	2.862	.216	2.438	3.286
		5.00	2.947	.267	2.423	3.472

We shall not introduce ALL the post-hoc tests. Instead the post-hoc tests, which correspond to VAR3 with respect to educational level, will be introduced.

Multiple Comparisons

Dependent Variable		(I) FDUC	(J) EDUC	Mean Difference (I-J)	Std. Error	Sia.
VAR00003	Tukey HSD	1.00	2.00	.3679*	.118	.010
			3.00	.1999	.163	.608
			5.00	.2728	.191	.483
		2.00	1.00	-.3679*	.118	.010
			3.00	-.1680	.185	.802
			5.00	-9.5069E-02	.211	.970
		3.00	1.00	-.1999	.163	.608
			2.00	.1680	.185	.802
			5.00	7.292E-02	.239	.990
		5.00	1.00	-.2728	.191	.483
			2.00	9.507E-02	.211	.970
			3.00	-7.2922E-02	.239	.990
	Scheffe	1.00	2.00	.3679*	.118	.022
			3.00	.1999	.163	.680
			5.00	.2728	.191	.566
		2.00	1.00	-.3679*	.118	.022
			3.00	-.1680	.185	.844
			5.00	-9.5069E-02	.211	.977
		3.00	1.00	-.1999	.163	.680
			2.00	.1680	.185	.844
			5.00	7.292E-02	.239	.993
		5.00	1.00	-.2728	.191	.566
			2.00	9.507E-02	.211	.977
			3.00	-7.2922E-02	.239	.993

Based on observed means.

Both Tukey's HSD and Scheffe's tests indicate that there are significant ($\alpha < .01$) differences between educational level 1 and level 2 in VAR3. Observing the means of VAR3 shows that level 1 has a mean of 3.21 ± 0.06 ($SE_{\bar{x}}$) and level 2 has a mean of 2.85 ± 0.10, a difference of 0.3679. This difference can be shown graphically using bar-charts.

Finally, homogeneous subset for the four educational levels was computed for VAR1 through VAR5 separately. The results showed ONE SUBSET for all five DVs. This means that the four educational levels can be seen as one subset in relating to the five questions on the use of banned drugs in sport. An example of Tukey HSD and Scheffe test for VAR1 is introduced.

VAR00001

			Subset
	EDUC	N	1
Tukey HSD	3.00	53	3.4906
	2.00	114	3.5000
	1.00	416	3.6274
	5.00	37	3.8378
	Sig		.144
Scheffe	3.00	53	3.4906
	2.00	114	3.5000
	1.00	416	3.6274
	5.00	37	3.8378
	Sig		.210

Means for groups in homogeneous subsets are displayed. Based on Type III Sum of Squares. The error term is Mean Square (Error) = .932.

a. Uses Harmonic Mean Sample Size = 70.088

b. The group sizes are unequal. The harmonic mean of the group sizes is used. Type I error levels are not guaranteed.

c. Alpha = .05

To summarize briefly, once the assumptions are satisfied, the multivariate analysis can be performed. Significant effects should be then re-examined for each of the main and interactional effects separately followed by post-hoc tests, if necessary (for k > 2). Graphical presentations of the main and/or interactional effects are a MUST.

(18)   Analysis of Covariance: Accounting for "Intervening Variables"

In both UNIVARIATE (ANOVA) and MULTIVARIATE (MANOVA) analyses, variables that are considered to INTERVENE the effect of the IDs on the IVs can be CONTROLLED, or ACCOUNTED FOR. In statistical terms such variables are called COVARIATES. When an ANOVA or MANOVA includes covariates, they are termed ANCOVA or MANCOVA. When the covariates are measured on an interval/ratio level and they are taken care in the experimental design, their inclusion is aimed at removing EXTRANEOUS INFLUENCES from the DV, i.e., increasing the WITHIN GROUP VARIANCE (MS_W; Error variance). Similarly to regression analysis, ANCOVA or MANCOVA are carried out after "adjustment" to the covariates' influence were made.

An example can be the effect of PHYSICAL CAPACITIES on FIELD TEST/S (PERFORMANCE). It is possible that people with higher physical capacities have also higher motivation, perceived competencies, and task-specific self-efficacy which enhance their performance and increase the mean differences in field performance between them and the people with lower physical capacities. To account for the influence of the intervening variables, their effect should be partialled out from the REAL EFFECT of physical capacities on physical performance; otherwise we may accept an INFLATED EFFECT which is NOT a true effect. This concept for univariate and multivariate analyses is presented in Figure 4.22.

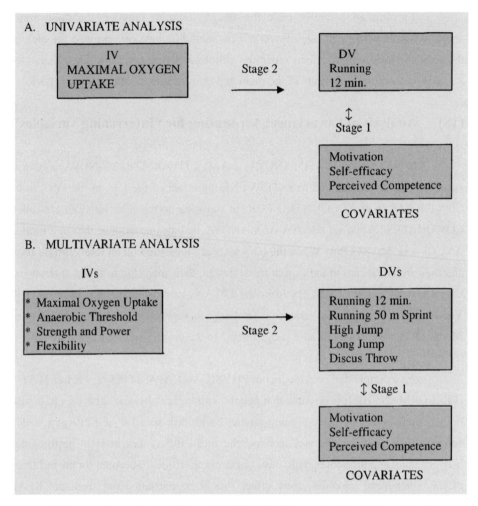

Figure 4.22   Removing the Effect of COVARIATES from the Main Effect of the IV on the DV in a Univariate and Multivariate Design.

The covariates should be variables that are theoretically STRONGLY CORRELATED with the DVs but not with the IVs. In such a case some of the variance can be explained by the covariates and the error term of the DV decreases (MS_W decreases).

The number of covariates is in debate. Some argue that it is the CONCEPT/THEORY that determines the number of variables that COVARY with the DVs. Others argue for statistical considerations such as:

$$0.10n - (k - 1) \qquad\qquad (62)$$

where n is the number of observations and k is the number of groups. For example, for three groups and 150 observations, the number of covariates should not exceed

$(0.10 \cdot 150) - (3 - 1) = 15 - 2 = 12$.

It is assumed that the covariates have SIMILAR EFFECTS on all the groups in the study and they correlate with the DVs.

An example of ANCOVA is as follows: 15 participants were assigned randomly to either control or experimental (physical training) groups. After completing the treatment (physical for experimental Ss and attention to controls), the subjects were asked to perform a long run. The following data was collected: run is the DV, treatment is the IV, and motivation for running was measured by a highly reliable questionnaire and is used here as a covariate, which may affect the running performance. The data look like that:

VO_2max	Run	Motive	Treatment
56.00	576.00	56.00	1.00
35.00	720.00	37.00	2.00
71.00	510.00	60.00	1.00
37.00	700.00	50.00	2.00
24.00	810.00	42.00	2.00
67.00	540.00	55.00	1.00
37.00	710.00	40.00	2.00
65.00	536.00	51.00	1.00
62.00	581.00	55.00	1.00
53.00	561.00	43.00	1.00
57.00	548.00	57.00	1.00
42.00	687.00	39.00	2.00
48.00	667.00	43.00	2.00
39.00	688.00	45.00	2.00
34.00	705.00	37.00	2.00

First we analyzed the data without including "motivation" as a covariate. The results are as follows:

Tests of Between-Subjects Effects

Dependent Variable: aerobic performance

Source	Type III Sum of Squares	df	Mean Square	F	Sig.	Eta Squared
Corrected Model	96278.630[b]	1	96278.630	74.776	.000	.852
Intercept	5937965.03	1	5937965.03	4611.790	.000	.997
TREATMEN	96278.630	1	96278.630	74.776	.000	.852
Error	16738.304	13	1287.562			
Total	6179185.00	15				
Corrected Total	113016.933	14				

Tests of Between-Subjects Effects

Dependent Variable: aerobic performance

Source	Noncent. Parameter	Observed Power[a]
Corrected Model	74.776	1.000
Intercept	4611.790	1.000
TREATMEN	74.776	1.000
Error		
Total		
Corrected Total		

a. Computed using alpha = .05
b. R Squared = .852 (Adjusted R Squared = .841)

Estimated Marginal Means

Treatment

Dependent Variable: aerobic performance

TREATMEN	Mean	Std. Error	95% Confidence Interval	
			Lower Bound	Upper Bound
1.00	550.286	13.562	520.986	579.585
2.00	710.875	12.686	683.468	738.282

It can be seen that the treatment effect was very strong $F(1,13) = 74.776$, $\alpha \leq$ .000, power $= 1.00$, meaning that the difference between the means of the treatment and control groups (550.286 vs. 710.875 seconds) were very significant. In standardized units this difference is equal to:

$$ES = \frac{550.2857 - 710.8750}{89.8479} = -1.78773$$

standard deviations using the pooled S of the long run, or

$$ES = \frac{550.2857 - 710.8750}{43.2284} = -3.7149$$

standard deviation, using the control group S of the long run. The negative sign is due to the nature of the DV – the faster one runs the smaller is the numerical value and vice-versa. Thus the treatment group participants showed a substantial and significant advantage over the control participants. But, it may be attributed to their MOTIVATION. We treated the same data by using motivation as a covariate (ANCOVA instead of ANOVA). The results were as follows:

Tests of Between-Subjects Effects

Dependent Variable: aerobic performance

Source	Type III Sum of Squares	df	Mean Square	F	Sig.	Eta Squared
Corrected Model	96768.970[b]	2	48384.485	35.735	.000	.856
Intercept	65548.075	1	65548.075	48.411	.000	.801
MOTIV	490.340	1	490.340	.362	.559	.029
TREATMEN	28547.151	1	28547.151	21.084	.001	.637
Error	16247.964	12	1353.997			
Total	6179185.00	15				
Corrected Total	113016.933	14				

Tests of Between-Subjects Effects

Dependent Variable: aerobic performance

Source	Noncent. Parameter	Observed Power[a]
Corrected Model	71.469	1.000
Intercept	48.411	1.000
MOTIV	.362	.086
TREATMEN	21.084	.987
Error		
Total		
Corrected Total		

a. Computed using alpha = .05

b. R Squared = .856 (Adjusted R Squared = .832)

Estimated Marginal Means

Treatment

Dependent Variable: aerobic performance

			95% Confidence Interval	
TREATMEN	Mean	Std. Error	Lower Bound	Upper Bound
1.00	558.403[a]	19.374	516.190	600.616
2.00	703.772[a]	17.566	665.501	742.044

a. Evaluated at covariates appeared in the model: motivation = 47.3333.

Now with the inclusion of motivation into the linear model, the effect of treatment was reduced to $F(1,12) = 21.084$, $\alpha<.001$, power = 0.987. Still very significant, the treatment is worthwhile in improving long run performance. The means though were adjusted as well, and they are not identical to the means we got without taking into account the motivation of the participants for running. The standardized difference between the adjusted means, taking the control group S as a denominator is:

$$ES = \frac{558.403 - 203.772}{46.4752} = \frac{145.369}{46.4752} = -1.78773$$

standard deviations, somewhat smaller than without motivation (-3.7149).

The application of covariates in MANOVA are almost identical to this in ANOVA.

(19)   Analysis of Repeated Measures (Trials) Designs

REPEATED MEASURES/TRIALS are used when the RESEARCH PLAN exposes the SAME SUBJECTS to several treatments or to several measurement occasions in different times without any manipulation. Thus the simplest repeated measure design is when ONE or MORE MEASURES are taken for the same subjects. The same subjects can also undergo several treatments in a COUNTER-BALANCED ORDER or SAME ORDER (if there is a strong theory that suggests such an order). These are illustrated in Figure 4.22.

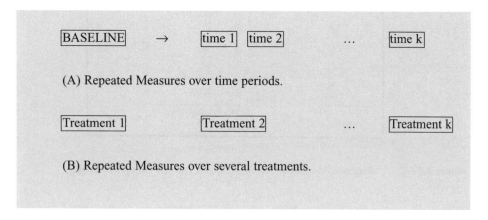

Figure 4.22   Repeated Measures over Time (A) and Treatments (B).

In Figure 4.23 one may notice that the MAIN ASSUMPTION of INDEPENDENCE is strongly VIOLATED. The repeated measures are usually STRONGLY CORRELATED. The DV scores in time 2 are correlated with the scores of time 1, and similarly scores of treatment 2 are correlated with scores of treatment 1. This is the MAIN CONCERN of REPEATED MEASURES ANOVA or MANOVA.

Repeated Measures can have BETWEEN SUBJECTS COMPONENTS. For example, gender, activity-type, anthropometric and demographic data (height, weight, nationality, etc) can be used, if required, as GROUPING VARIABLES (between subjects). This is illustrated in Figure 4.24.

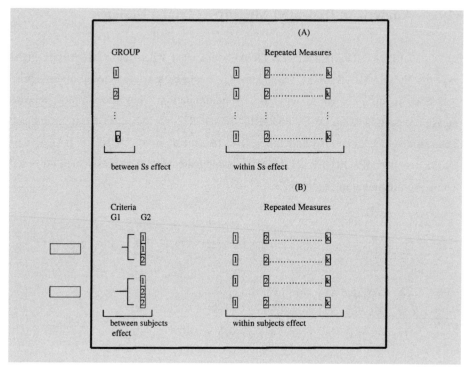

Figure 4.24   Repeated Measures with One (A) and Two (B) Grouping Variables.

Repeated measures can have also several WITHIN SUBJECTS level. For example, assume that some participants (males and females) were exposed to three different music styles and one silence condition within each of two experimental conditions (competition vs. single run). The order of the repeated measures was counter-balanced so that the participants were exposed to the eight conditions in a different order. The design is illustrated in Figure 4.25.

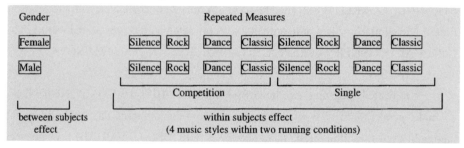

Figure 4.25   Repeated Measures with One Grouping Variable (Gender) and Two within Ss Factors (Music Styles Nested within Running Conditions).

The more GROUPING VARIABLES and WITHIN Ss FACTORS, the more main effects will result for each of them separately, and the more 2-way, 3-way, and k-way interactions will be obtained (i.e., the more sources of variance – EFFECTS may account for the study's results).

To account for the DEPENDENCE of the observations in the REPEATED TRIALS/TREATMENTS, the TREATMENT EFFECT for each subject, i, is measured RELATIVE to the AVERAGE RESPONSE made by subject i on ALL TREATMENTS/TRIALS. Thus, each subject is a control for himself or herself where the MAIN CRITERION is his/her INDIVIDUAL DEVIATION from his/her AVERAGE MEASURE obtained on ALL TRIALS/TREATMENTS. In this way variability assigned to average individual responsiveness is eliminated from the experimental error.

We follow Winer's (1971) notation to describe the RM Model:

Person	Treatment/Trial						Total	Mean
	1	2	...	j	...	k		
1	X_{11}	X_{12}		X_{1j}		X_{1k}	P_1	$\bar{P}_1$
2	X_{21}	X_{22}		X_{2j}		X_{2k}	P_2	$\bar{P}_2$
⋮	⋮	⋮		⋮		⋮	⋮	⋮
i	X_{i1}	X_{i2}		X_{ij}		X_{ik}	P_i	$\bar{P}_i$
⋮	⋮	⋮		⋮		⋮	⋮	⋮
n	X_{n1}	X_{n2}		X_{nj}		X_{nk}	P_n	$\bar{P}_n$
Total	T_1	T_2		T_j		T_k	G	
Mean	$\bar{T}_1$	$\bar{T}_2$		$\bar{T}_j$		$\bar{T}_k$		$\bar{G}$

X_{11} represent the measurement of person 1 under treatment/trial 1, X_{12} the measurement of the same person (1) under treatment/trial 2, X_{ij} the measurement of person 1 under treatment j. The first subscript to an X is the person's identification and the second one indicates the treatment/trial under which the observation was made. P_1 denotes the sum of k observations on person 1, P_2 the same for person 2, and P_i the sum of k observations on person i.

Thus

$$P_i = \Sigma X_{ij}$$

with a mean of

$$\overline{P}_i = \frac{P_i}{k}$$

T_1 is the sum of all n observations under treatment 1. T_2 is the same for treatment 2, and T_j the sum of observations under treatment j. Thus

$$T_j = \sum_i X_{ij},$$

with a mean of

$$\overline{T}_j = \frac{T_j}{n}$$

The sum of kn observations in the experiment, designated G is

$$G = \Sigma P_i = \Sigma T_j = \Sigma X_{ij}$$

which is the sum over ALL the OBSERVATIONS in the experiment. The GRAND MEAN is designated and is

$$\overline{G} = \frac{G}{kn} = \frac{\Sigma \overline{P}_i}{n} = \frac{\Sigma \overline{T}_j}{k}$$

Thus, the TOTAL VARIATION is divided to (a) differences between the MEANS of the SUBJECTS, and (b) the POOLED VARIATION WITHIN the PERSONS. The total variation is

$$SS_{.total} = \sum\sum(X_{ij} - \overline{G})^2 \tag{63}$$

This source of variation has kn-1 df and that part of the total variation due to differences among the means of the persons is

$$SS_{b.people} = k\sum(\overline{P}_i - \overline{G})^2 \tag{64}$$

The between-people variation is the squared deviations of the means for the persons about the grand mean. This source of variance is attributed to the differences between all POSSIBLE PAIRS (i.e., the larger the difference, the larger this effect). Since n persons share n means, this variation source shares n-1 df.

The variations within each person i is:

$$SS_{\text{w.person i}} = \sum_{j} (X_{ij} - \overline{P}_i)^2$$

This source of variance (effect) has k-1 df, and the pooled within-person variation, $SS_{\text{w.people}}$ is

$$SS_{w.people} = \sum_{i} SS_{w.personi} = \sum\sum (X_{ij} - \overline{P}_i)^2 \qquad (65)$$

The pooled within person variations has n(k-1) df.

The between and within subjects sources of variance are statistically independent, so that they are additive and

$$SS_{\text{total}} = SS_{\text{b.people}} + SS_{\text{w.people}}$$

with

kn-1 = n-1 + n(k-1) degrees of freedom.

Winer (1971, pp. 261-267) further partitions the total variation and the df associated with each source of variation. We recommend the learner to read his conceptual and mathematical description and the computational example provided. His presentation can be conceptually viewed in Figure 4.26.

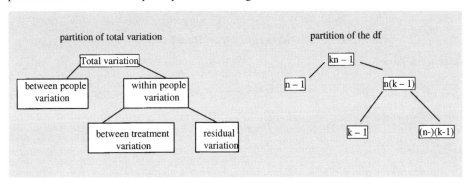

Figure 4.26   Schematic Representation of Repeated Measures Design (adapted from Winer, 1971, table 4.2-1 p. 266).

The sum of squares are divided by their respective df to yield a mean square that establishes the F statistic for hypothesis examination

$$F_{obs} = \frac{MS_{treatment/trial}}{MS_{residual}}$$

which is compared to the F value derived from F-distribution with 1 and n-1 df to test H_0.

We shall use a previous example with 12 persons who perform a motor task under 4 different conditions (trial1-trial4; within people source of variance), and were divided into high and low with respect to two factors (between Ss source of variance: anxiety and tension). The data, which are presented, next were analyzed by using SPSS 11.0.

	Subject	Anxiety	Tension	Trial 1	Trial 2	Trial 3	Trial 4
1	1	1.00	1.00	18.00	14.00	12.00	6.00
2	2	1.00	1.00	19.00	12.00	8.00	4.00
3	3	1.00	1.00	14.00	10.00	6.00	2.00
4	4	1.00	2.00	16.00	12.00	10.00	4.00
5	5	1.00	2.00	12.00	8.00	6.00	2.00
6	6	1.00	2.00	18.00	10.00	5.00	1.00
7	7	2.00	1.00	16.00	10.00	8.00	4.00
8	8	2.00	1.00	18.00	8.00	4.00	1.00
9	9	2.00	1.00	16.00	12.00	6.00	2.00
10	10	2.00	2.00	19.00	16.00	10.00	8.00
11	11	2.00	2.00	16.00	14.00	10.00	9.00
12	12	2.00	2.00	16.00	12.00	8.00	8.00

As a special case of MANOVA, the general linear model was as follows:

General Linear Model

Between-Subjects Factors

		N
Anxiety	1	6
	2	6
Tension	1	6
	2	6

The multivariate tests were then applied. First we introduce the BETWEEN PERSONS (SUBJECT) EFFECTS and then the WITHIN SUBJECTS EFFECTS and their interactions. The multivariate analysis which pertains to the two grouping variables (anxiety and tension) resulted in the following effects:

Multivariate Tests[c]

Effect		Value	F	Hypothesis df	Error df	Sig.
Intercept	Pillai's Trace	.990	118.223[b]	4.000	5.000	.000
	Wilks' Lambda	.010	118.223[b]	4.000	5.000	.000
	Hotelling's Trace	94.578	118.223[b]	4.000	5.000	.000
	Roy's Largest Root	94.578	118.223[b]	4.000	5.000	.000
ANXIETY	Pillai's Trace	.961	30.586[b]	4.000	5.000	.001
	Wilks' Lambda	.039	30.586[b]	4.000	5.000	.001
	Hotelling's Trace	24.469	30.586[b]	4.000	5.000	.001
	Roy's Largest Root	24.469	30.586[b]	4.000	5.000	.001
TENSION	Pillai's Trace	.926	15.663[b]	4.000	5.000	.005
	Wilks' Lambda	.074	15.663[b]	4.000	5.000	.005
	Hotelling's Trace	12.530	15.663[b]	4.000	5.000	.005
	Roy's Largest Root	12.530	15.663[b]	4.000	5.000	.005
ANXIETY * TENSION	Pillai's Trace	.964	33.938[b]	4.000	5.000	.001
	Wilks' Lambda	.036	33.938[b]	4.000	5.000	.001
	Hotelling's Trace	27.150	33.938[b]	4.000	5.000	.001
	Roy's Largest Root	27.150	33.938[b]	4.000	5.000	.001

We intentionally avoided the Eta Squared (similar to effect size) and Power statistics of the effects to simplify the presentation. It can be clearly seen that ACROSS all four trials (physical performances) anxiety and tension were significant determinants of performance. Furthermore, their interaction was also very significant. Averaging the performance of low and high anxiety and tension subjects, separately across the four performance trials yields an illustration of the two main between subjects effects:

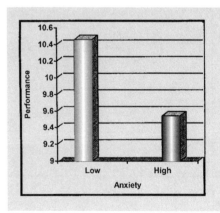 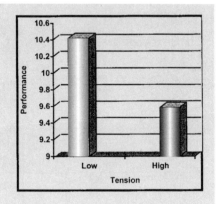

The high anxious and tense participants exhibited lower performances than their low anxious and tense counterparts across the four trials. The significant anxiety by tension interactional effect is shown next:

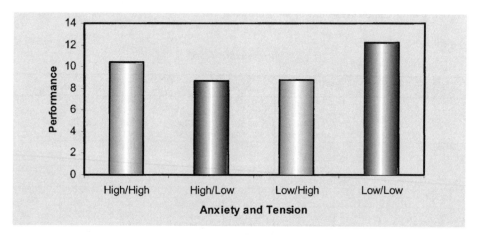

Test Between-Subjects Effects

Source	Dependent Variable	Type III Sum of Squares	df	Mean Square	F	Sig.
Corrected Model	Trial 1	5.667[b]	3	1.889	.366	.780
	Trial 2	33.000[c]	3	11.000	2.750	.112
	Trial 3	20.917[d]	3	6.972	1.287	.343
	Trial 4	72.250[e]	3	24.083	10.704	.004
Intercept	Trial 1	3267.000	1	3267.000	632.323	.000
	Trial 2	1587.000	1	1587.000	396.750	.000
	Trial 3	720.750	1	720.750	133.062	.000
	Trial 4	216.750	1	216.750	96.333	.000
ANXIETY	Trial 1	1.333	1	1.333	.258	.625
	Trial 2	3.000	1	3.000	.750	.412
	Trial 3	8.333E-02	1	8.333E-02	.015	.904
	Trial 4	14.083	1	14.083	6.259	.037
TENSION	Trial 1	1.333	1	1.333	.258	.625
	Trial 2	3.000	1	3.000	.750	.412
	Trial 3	2.083	1	2.083	.385	.552
	Trial 4	14.083	1	14.083	6.259	.037
ANXIETY * TENSION	Trial 1	3.000	1	3.000	.581	.468
	Trial 2	27.000	1	27.000	6.750	.032
	Trial 3	18.750	1	18.750	3.462	.100
	Trial 4	44.083	1	44.083	19.593	.002
Error	Trial 1	41.333	8	5.167		
	Trial 2	32.000	8	4.000		
	Trial 3	43.333	8	5.417		
	Trial 4	18.000	8	2.250		
Total	Trial 1	3314.000	12			
	Trial 2	1652.000	12			
	Trial 3	785.000	12			
	Trial 4	307.000	12			
Corrected Total	Trial 1	47.000	11			
	Trial 2	65.000	11			
	Trial 3	64.250	11			
	Trial 4	90.250	11			

The interactional effect is quite clear: across the four trials, subjects with both low anxiety and tension performed the best, seconded by subjects with high levels of both anxiety and tension. The combination of high anxiety-low tension and vice-versa was detrimental to physical performance. To substantiate these findings, POST-HOC tests are required. We shall now proceed to the Tests of Between-Subjects effects for EACH VARIABLE SEPARATELY. This is conditional on the significant results obtained in the multivariate analysis introduced above. The results are shown in the table on the left page.

This analysis indicates that the differences between high and low anxious and tense participants were due mainly because of their performance on trial 4, but not on the first three trials. These are seen in the following two Tables:

2. Anxiety

Dependent Variable	Anxiety	Mean	Std. Error	95% Confidence Interval	
				Lower Bound	Upper Bound
Trial 1	1	16.167	.928	14.027	18.307
	2	16.833	.928	14.693	18.973
Trial 2	1	11.000	.816	9.117	12.883
	2	12.000	.816	10.117	13.883
Trial 3	1	7.833	.950	5.642	10.024
	2	7.667	.950	5.476	9.858
Trial 4	1	3.167	.612	1.755	4.579
	2	5.333	.612	3.921	6.745

3. Tension

Dependent Variable	Tension	Mean	Std. Error	95% Confidence Interval	
				Lower Bound	Upper Bound
Trial 1	1	16.833	.928	14.693	18.973
	2	16.167	.928	14.027	18.307
Trial 2	1	11.000	.816	9.117	12.883
	2	12.000	.816	10.117	13.883
Trial 3	1	7.333	.950	5.142	9.524
	2	8.167	.950	5.976	10.358
Trial 4	1	3.167	.612	1.755	4.579
	2	5.333	.612	3.921	6.745

The differences can be expressed also in standardized units (ES), but the mean differences in trial 4 are clearly seen. The interaction occurred mainly in trials two and four. The table of means shows it clearly:

4. Anxiety * Tension

Dependent Variable	Anxiety	Tension	Mean	Std. Error	95% Confidence Interval Lower Bound	Upper Bound
Trial 1	1	1	17.000	1.312	13.974	20.026
		2	15.333	1.312	12.307	18.360
	2	1	16.667	1.312	13.640	19.693
		2	17.000	1.312	13.974	20.026
Trial 2	1	1	12.000	1.155	9.337	14.663
		2	10.000	1.155	7.337	12.663
	2	1	10.000	1.155	7.337	12.663
		2	14.000	1.155	11.337	16.663
Trial 3	1	1	8.667	1.344	5.568	11.765
		2	7.000	1.344	3.901	10.099
	2	1	6.000	1.344	2.901	9.099
		2	9.333	1.344	6.235	12.432
Trial 4	1	1	4.000	.866	2.003	5.997
		2	2.333	.866	.336	4.330
	2	1	2.333	.866	.336	4.330
		2	8.333	.866	6.336	10.330

In trial 2 and trial 4, participants with low anxiety and low tension performed particularly well compared to the other anxiety by tension combinations.

Now we turn to the Within Subjects source of variation (i.e., 4 trials and their interactions with the between subjects factors). The multivariate tests excluding Eta Squared and Power are as follows:

Multivariate Tests[c]

Effect		Value	F	Hypothesis df	Error df	Sig.
TRIAL	Pillai's Trace	.985	127.686[b]	3.000	6.000	.000
	Wilks' Lambda	.015	127.686[b]	3.000	6.000	.000
	Hotelling's Trace	63.843	127.686[b]	3.000	6.000	.000
	Roy's Largest Root	63.843	127.686[b]	3.000	6.000	.000
TRIAL * ANXIETY	Pillai's Trace	.756	6.183[b]	3.000	6.000	.029
	Wilks' Lambda	.244	6.183[b]	3.000	6.000	.029
	Hotelling's Trace	3.091	6.183[b]	3.000	6.000	.029
	Roy's Largest Root	3.091	6.183[b]	3.000	6.000	.029
TRIAL * TENSION	Pillai's Trace	.639	3.546[b]	3.000	6.000	.088
	Wilks' Lambda	.361	3.546[b]	3.000	6.000	.088
	Hotelling's Trace	1.773	3.546[b]	3.000	6.000	.088
	Roy's Largest Root	1.773	3.546[b]	3.000	6.000	.088
TRIAL * ANXIETY * TENSION	Pillai's Trace	.672	4.099[b]	3.000	6.000	.067
	Wilks' Lambda	.328	4.099[b]	3.000	6.000	.067
	Hotelling's Trace	2.050	4.099[b]	3.000	6.000	.067
	Roy's Largest Root	2.050	4.099[b]	3.000	6.000	.067

Of the four sources of variance (i.e., effects), only two resulted in an acceptable significance in rejecting H_0 ($\alpha < .05$). These were TRIAL and TRIAL by ANXIETY interaction. Though trial by tension and trial by anxiety by tension were not significant, they tended toward significance. We recommend observing them by graphical presentation, and seeing if in subsequent studies a similar pattern results. Here we demonstrate only the significant effect. The trial effect can be seen in the following table:

1. Grand Mean

Dependent Variable	Mean	Std. Error	95% Confidence Interval Lower Bound	Upper Bound
Trial 1	16.500	.656	14.987	18.013
Trial 2	11.500	.577	10.169	12.831
Trial 3	7.750	.672	6.201	9.299
Trial 4	4.250	.433	3.251	5.249

Even without POST-HOC tests it can be seen that performance decreases sharply from trial 1 to trial 4. A subsequent contrast analysis showed that a LINEAR function is more appropriate than the QUADRATIC and CUBIC function in describing this decrease, $F(1,8) = 247.845$, $\alpha < .000$. The trial by anxiety-level effect on performance is illustrated as follows:

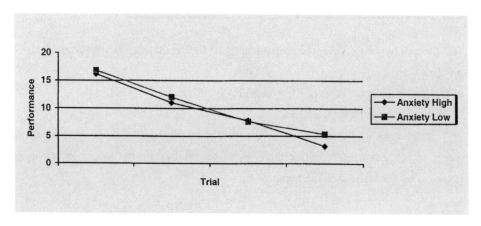

In trials 1 and 2 low anxious subjects performed slightly better than high anxious subjects. In trial 3 they were equal, but in trial 4 high anxious subjects were much below their low anxious subjects.

The Mauchly's Test of Sphericity shows that the variance-covariance matrices were not equal, but this is due to the low number of observations used in this example.

Mauchly's Test of Sphericity[b]

Measure: MEASURE 1

Within Subjects Effect	Mauchly's W	Approx. Chi-Square	df	Sig.
TRIAL	.187	11.254	5	.049

Test the null hypothesis that the error covariance matrix of the orthonormalized transformed dependent variables is proportional to an identity matrix.

Levene's test of equality of error variance among the four trials showed no violation of this main assumption.

Levene's Test of Equality of Error Variances[a]

	F	df1	df2	Sig.
Trial 1	1.319	3	8	.334
Trial 2	.000	3	8	1.000
Trial 3	1.020	3	8	.433
Trial 4	.762	3	8	.546

Test the null hypothesis that the error variance of the dependent variable is equal across groups.

a. Design: Intercept + ANXIETY + TENSION + ANXIETY * TENSION

Within Subjects Design: TRIAL

The results should always be interpreted in relation to the hypotheses and the theory which was used to derive them. Repeated studies are needed in order for the results to be generalized to the population.

(20) *Common Models in Experimentation*

Previous sections in this chapter introduced LINEAR MODEL with FIXED VARIABLES, MULTIVARIATE ANOVA, REPEATED MEASURES as a special case of MANOVA, and ANCOVA-MANCOVA procedures. These statistical methods are the most commonly used in the sport and exercise science domain. In all these models, the determination of the FACTORS is the crucial issue besides the MEASUREMENT and

OBSERVATION issues. Most of the research/analysis methods fall into a "family" of methods, which is termed SINGLE-FACTOR experimentation or FACTORIAL EXPERIMENTATION. Here we briefly overview the different experimental designs to enable the learner to categorize his/her research plans appropriately.

20.1   *Completely Randomized Design (CRD)*

The CRD is the simplest and most convenient design. When more than two groups are needed, subjects are randomly assigned to each of the $k > 2$ groups and later the groups are compared on ONE DV. For many years ONE EXPERIMENTAL group was compared to ONE CONTROL group, assuming that randomization of sampling ensured initial equality, and therefore an effect of the treatment could be inferred. We recommend using MORE than one control group in which the subjects give attention and vary only in the treatment nature. These measures ensure that the external validity of the EFFECT results.

The DV scores are designated as X_{ij} where i is the order/rank of the subject in the control or treatment groups j. A typical 3-groups/treatments design is shown in Table 4.7.

Table 4.7

A Completely Randomized Design with 3 Groups/Treatments.

	Treatment/Group		
	b_1	b_2	b_3
	X_{11}	X_{12}	X_{13}
	X_{21}	X_{22}	X_{23}
	X_{31}	X_{32}	X_{33}
	$\vdots$	$\vdots$	$\vdots$
	X_{n1}	X_{n2}	X_{n3}
Mean:	$X_{\bullet 1}$	$X_{\bullet 2}$	$X_{\bullet 3}$ $\overline{X}_{\bullet\bullet}$ - Grand Mean

The CRD model can be expressed as a linear model

$$X_{ij} = \mu + \beta_j + \varepsilon_{ij} \qquad\qquad (66)$$

where X_{ij} is the DV, μ is the population mean, β_j is the treatment/group effect, and ε_{ij} is the error term which comes from the subjects' internal and external sources. Parameters μ, β_j and ε_{ij} are unknown but they are estimated in the sample as $\hat{\mu}$, $\hat{\beta}_j$ and $\hat{\varepsilon}_{ij}$. The maximum likelihood method assures that these are unbiased estimators of the population

$$\hat{\mu} = \overline{X}_{\bullet\bullet} \longrightarrow \mu$$
$$\hat{\beta}_j = (\overline{X}_{\bullet j} - \overline{X}_{\bullet\bullet}) \longrightarrow \beta_j$$
$$\hat{\varepsilon}_{ij} = (X_{ij} - X_{\bullet j}) \longrightarrow \varepsilon_{ij}$$

In this model the estimated error term is

$$\hat{\varepsilon}_{ij} = X_{ij} - \hat{\beta}_j - \hat{\mu}$$

20.2 Randomized Block Design (RBD)

The RBD consists of dividing the subjects to BLOCKS. Blocks are established for subjects who are more similar to each other. The reasons can differ: geographical location, sport-type, culture, etc. Thus WITHIN each BLOCK the assignment of subjects is randomized.

In Table 4.8 the differences among the columns' means signify the differences between the treatments and the differences among the rows' means signify the blocks' differences.

Table 4.8

Randomized Block Design (Three Treatments and n Blocks).

Block	Treatment b_1	b_2	b_3	Block Mean
P_1	X_{11}	X_{12}	X_{13}	$\overline{X}_{1\bullet}$
P_2	X_{21}	X_{22}	X_{23}	$\overline{X}_{2\bullet}$
$\vdots$	$\vdots$	$\vdots$	$\vdots$	$\vdots$
P_n	X_{n1}	X_{n2}	X_{n3}	$\overline{X}_{n\bullet}$
Treatment Mean	$\overline{X}_{\bullet 1}$	$\overline{X}_{\bullet 2}$	$\overline{X}_{\bullet n}$	Grand Mean = $\overline{X}_{\bullet\bullet}$

The linear model of RBD is

$$X_{ij} = \mu + \beta_j + \pi_i + \varepsilon_{ij} \qquad (67)$$

and the unbiased parameter estimators using the statistics are:

$$\hat{\mu} = \overline{X}_{\bullet\bullet} \longrightarrow \mu$$
$$\hat{\beta}_j = (\overline{X}_{\bullet j} - \overline{X}_{\bullet\bullet}) \longrightarrow \beta_j$$
$$\hat{\pi}_i = (\overline{X}_{i\bullet} - \overline{X}_{\bullet\bullet}) \longrightarrow \pi_i$$
$$\hat{\varepsilon}_{ij} = (X_{ij} - \overline{X}_{\bullet j} - \overline{X}_{i\bullet} + \overline{X}_{\bullet\bullet}) \longrightarrow \varepsilon_{ij}$$

π_{ij} represents the block effect. The other terms are similar to the previous CRD model. The error term in RBD is

$$\hat{\varepsilon}_{ij} = X_{ij} - \hat{\beta}_j - \hat{\pi} - \hat{\mu}$$

while in the CRD it was

$$\hat{\varepsilon}_{ij} = X_{ij} - \hat{\beta}_j - \hat{\mu}$$

which are similar except of the block effect, π_i.

20.3   *Latin Square Design (LSD)*

In the LSD at least two NUISANCE sources (variables) are controlled by blocks. The assumption is that within the blocks subjects are more homogeneous. The nuisance variables' levels are presented in both the rows and columns of the model. The treatment levels are designated within each of the cells. The treatment levels, C_k are assigned randomly to each of the 9 cells in the example but the treatment level should appear in a row and a column only once (see Table 4.9).

Table 4.9

Latin Square Model (LSM) with Two Blocks (with Three Levels each) and One Treatment (with Three Levels).

	Block 1	Block 2		Mean Block 1
	b_1	b_2	b_3	
a_1	c_1	c_2	c_3	$\overline{X}_{1\bullet\bullet}$
	X_{111}	X_{122}	X_{133}	
a_2	c_2	c_3	c_1	$\overline{X}_{2\bullet\bullet}$
	X_{212}	X_{223}	X_{231}	
a_3	c_3	c_1	c_2	$\overline{X}_{3\bullet\bullet}$
	X_{313}	X_{321}	X_{332}	
Mean Block 2	$\overline{X}_{\bullet1\bullet}$	$\overline{X}_{\bullet2\bullet}$	$\overline{X}_{\bullet3\bullet}$	
General Mean	$\overline{X}_{\bullet\bullet}$			

Mean Treatment 1: $c_1 = (X_{111} + X_{321} + X_{231})/3 = \overline{X}_{\bullet\bullet1}$
Treatment 2: $c_2 = (X_{212} + X_{122} + X_{332})/3 = \overline{X}_{\bullet\bullet2}$
Treatment 3: $c_3 = (X_{313} + X_{223} + X_{133})/3 = \overline{X}_{\bullet\bullet3}$

To establish a LSM, the number of rows, columns, and treatments should be equal. In table 4.9, the number of observations would be always a multiplication of 9. The linear LSD is:

$$X_{ijk} = \mu + \alpha_i + \beta_j + \gamma_k + \pi_i + \varepsilon_{ijk} \tag{68}$$

where X_{ijk} is the DV, μ is the population mean, α_i, β_j, and γ_k are the effects of the two blocks and treatment, respectively and ε_{ijk} is the error term. If the blocks result in a significant and meaningful effect, this model is more powerful than the CRD and RBD models because

$$\hat{\varepsilon}_{ij} = X_{ijk} - \hat{\alpha}_i - \hat{\beta}_j - \hat{\gamma}_k - \hat{\mu}$$

20.4   *Incomplete Block Design (IBD)*

In some circumstances some, blocks and/or treatment levels cannot contain observations. When this happens, an IBD is appropriate to use. The IBD is illustrated in Table 4.10.

Table 4.10

Incomplete Block Design with Three Block and Three Treatment Levels

Block	Treatment Level			Mean Block
	b_1	b_2	b_3	
P_1	X_{11}		X_{13}	$\overline{X}_{1\bullet}$
P_2		X_{22}	X_{23}	$\overline{X}_{2\bullet}$
P_3	X_{31}	X_{32}		$\overline{X}_{3\bullet}$
Mean Treatment	$\overline{X}_{\bullet 1}$	$\overline{X}_{\bullet 2}$	$\overline{X}_{\bullet 3}$	Grand Mean $\overline{X}_{\bullet\bullet}$

The linear model, which represents IBD, is

$$X_{ij} = \mu + \beta_j + \pi_i + \varepsilon_{ij} \tag{69}$$

This design is also termed "a balanced incomplete block design" because it requires equal number of observations within each treatment by block cell.

20.5   *Factorial Designs*

Factorial designs enable the researcher to investigate the combined effect of two or more FACTORS on ONE DV. This is achieved by combining the levels of the factor simultaneously (see Figure 4.27).

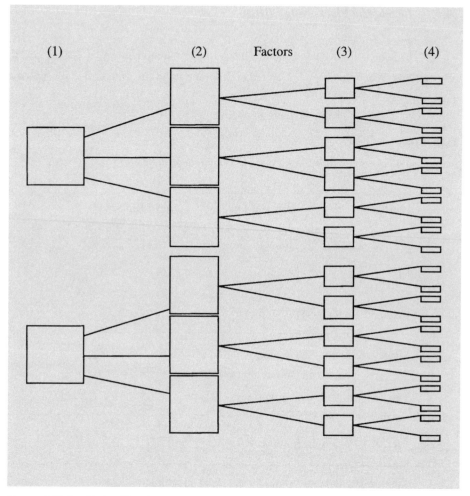

Figure 4.27 Combining Simultaneously Four Factors with Two Levels (Factors 1, 3, and 4) and Three Levels (Factor 2).

The most commonly used factorial models are: Completely Randomized Factorial Design (CRFD) and Randomized Block Factorial Design (RBFD), which were introduced before.

Assume the researcher is interested in investigating treatments in comparison to a control condition in two temperatures, say 10°C and 28°C. In Table 4.11 this design is illustrated.

Table 4.11

A Completely Randomized Factorial Design (CRFD).

Temperature	Treatments/Control			Mean Temperature
	b_1	b_2	b_3	
(1) 10°C	X_{111}	X_{121}	X_{131}	$\overline{X}_{1\bullet\bullet}$
	X_{112}	X_{122}	X_{132}	
	$\vdots$	$\vdots$	$\vdots$	
	X_{11n}	X_{12n}	X_{13n}	
(2) 28°C	X_{211}	X_{221}	X_{231}	
	X_{212}	X_{222}	X_{232}	$\overline{X}_{2\bullet\bullet}$
	$\vdots$	$\vdots$	$\vdots$	
	X_{21n}	X_{22n}	X_{23n}	
Mean Treatment	$\overline{X}_{\bullet1\bullet}$	$\overline{X}_{\bullet2\bullet}$	$\overline{X}_{\bullet3\bullet}$	Grand Mean $\overline{X}_{\bullet\bullet}$

The first two subscripts besides each observation designates the two factors, temperature and treatment, and the third are the number of the observations within its cell. In CRFD we assume that ALL OBSERVATIONS were RANDOMLY divided into the six cells. In RBFD (Table 4.12) the two factors are randomly divided within each block. In RBFD the three subscripts denote temperature level, treatment level, and the block. The mathematical representations of the two models are as follows:

For CRFD:

$$X_{ijm} = \mu + \alpha_i + \beta_j + \alpha\beta_{ij} + \varepsilon_{m(ij)} \qquad (70)$$

and for RBFD:

$$X_{ijm} = \mu + \alpha_i + \beta_j + \pi_m + \alpha\beta_{ij} + \varepsilon_{ijm} \qquad (71)$$

Table 4.12

Randomized Block Factorial Design (RBFD) with 2 x 3 Levels in Two Factors and Three Blocks.

Block	Temperature:	a_1	a_1	a_1	a_2	a_2	a_2	Block
	Treatment:	b_1	b_2	b_3	b_1	b_2	b_3	Means
P_1		X_{111}	X_{121}	X_{131}	X_{211}	X_{221}	X_{231}	$\overline{X}_{\bullet\bullet 1}$
P_2		X_{112}	X_{122}	X_{132}	X_{212}	X_{222}	X_{232}	$\overline{X}_{\bullet\bullet 2}$
P_3		X_{113}	X_{123}	X_{133}	X_{213}	X_{223}	X_{233}	$\overline{X}_{\bullet\bullet 3}$
Row Mean:		$\overline{X}_{11\bullet}$	$\overline{X}_{12\bullet}$	$\overline{X}_{13\bullet}$	$\overline{X}_{21\bullet}$	$\overline{X}_{22\bullet}$	$\overline{X}_{23\bullet}$	
Grand Mean:	$\overline{X}_{\bullet\bullet}$							

Temperature a_1 Mean: $\overline{X}_{1\bullet\bullet} = (X_{111} + X_{112} + X_{113} + X_{121} + \ldots + X_{133})/9$

Temperature a_2 Mean: $\overline{X}_{2\bullet\bullet} = (X_{211} + X_{212} + X_{213} + X_{221} + \ldots + X_{233})/9$

Treatment b_1 Mean: $\overline{X}_{\bullet 1\bullet} = (X_{111} + X_{112} + X_{113} + X_{211} + X_{212} + X_{213})/6$

Treatment b_2 Mean: $\overline{X}_{\bullet 2\bullet} = (X_{121} + X_{122} + X_{123} + X_{221} + X_{222} + X_{223})/6$

Treatment b_3 Mean: $\overline{X}_{\bullet 3\bullet} = (X_{131} + X_{132} + X_{133} + X_{231} + X_{232} + X_{233})/6$

The temperature in the linear models is designated as α_i, the treatment as β_j, their interaction as $\alpha\beta_{ij}$, the block as π_m and the error term as $\varepsilon_{m(ij)}$. The models enable us to examine the main effects of the two factors separately (temperature and treatment), their interaction, and the effect of the block. Blocks do not interact with factors. The error in CRFD is:

$$\hat{\varepsilon}_{m(ij)} = X_{ijm} - \hat{\alpha}_i - \hat{\beta}_j - \hat{\alpha\beta}_{ij} - \mu$$

If τ_{ij} integrates the factors/treatments effect, then

$$\hat{\varepsilon}_{m(ij)} = X_{ijm} - \hat{\tau}_{ij} - \hat{\mu}$$

which is identical to the CRD where

$$\hat{\varepsilon}_{ij} = X_{ij} - \hat{\beta}_j - \hat{\mu}.$$

In the RBFD the error term is

$$\hat{\varepsilon}_{ijm} = X_{ijm} - \hat{\alpha}_i - \hat{\beta}_j - \hat{\pi}_m - \hat{\alpha\beta}_{ij} - \hat{\mu}.$$

Again, if τ_{ij} integrates the effects of factors/treatments,

$$\hat{\varepsilon}_{ijm} = X_{ijm} - \hat{\tau}_{ijm} - \hat{\pi}_m - \mu$$

similarly to the RBD where

$$\hat{\varepsilon}_{ij} = X_{ij} - \hat{\beta}_j - \hat{\pi}_i - \mu \, .$$

POST-HOC tests and Linear Trend Analysis (LTA) can be performed to examine hypotheses which postulate a TREND of the DV as a function of the IV (see Figure 4.28).

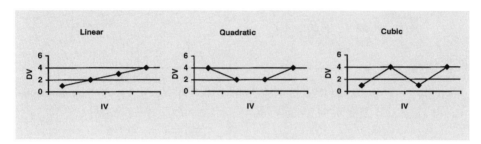

Figure 4.28   Linear Trends, which Postulate the Dependence of the DV on the IV.

20.6   *Nested Factors (Hierarchical Designs)*

Assume that the researcher is interested in examining the effectiveness of two training methods. One will be given to athletes in training centers 1, 2, and 3, and the other in centers 4, 5, and 6. Thus centers are NESTED within the training methods. Effects which are restricted to a SINGLE LEVEL of a FACTOR are considered NESTED within that factor (see Figure 4.29).

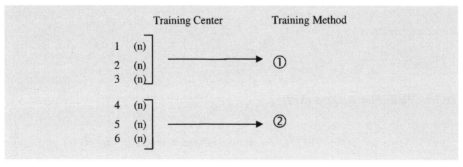

Figure 4.29   Nesting Training Centers within 2 Training Methods.

The training centers in this example are nested under one of two training centers. Therefore, the training center by training method interaction cannot be estimated. Only if each training center had randomly assigned athletes to the two different training methods, an interaction between the two could be possible. This is a two-factor experiment; when one factor is nested under the other, an interaction cannot be estimated.

If factor B is nested under factor A, the Nested Factorial Model (NFM) is

$$\overline{AB}_{ij} = \mu + \alpha_i + \beta_{j(i)} + \overline{\varepsilon}_{ij} \tag{72}$$

where $\beta_{j(i)}$ is the effect of level b_j nested under level a_i. No $\alpha\beta_{ij(i)}$ interaction is noted. The df associated with NFM models are:

(1)   training method $2 - 1 = 1 \rightarrow p - 1$

(2)   training method within Center $1 \rightarrow 3 - 1 = 2 \rightarrow q - 1$

(3)   training method within Center $2 \rightarrow 3 - 1 = 2 \rightarrow q - 1$

(4)   within training centers $\rightarrow 6(n-1) \rightarrow pq(n-1)$.

With 3-factor hierarchical design the df are:

A $\rightarrow$ p-1

B within A $\rightarrow$ p(q-1)

C within (A and B) $\rightarrow$ pq(r-1)

Experimental error $\rightarrow$ pqr(n-1)

Total: npqr - 1.

20.7   Split-Plot Designs (SPD)

Split-plot design (SPD) is a design in which levels of one factor apply to a whole plot, and levels of a second factor apply only to subplots of the whole plot. A graphical presentation of SPD can be seen in Figure 4.30.

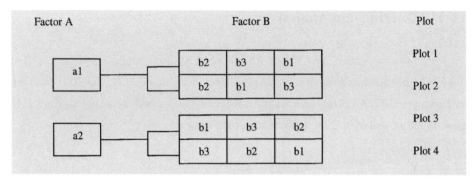

Figure 4.30 A Split-Plot Design (SPD) with Two Factors and Four Plots.

Differences between the A levels cannot be independently estimated between groups of plots. The linear expression of SPD is:

$$X_{ijk} = \mu + \alpha_i + \pi_{k(i)} + \beta_j + \alpha\beta_{ij} + \pi^1_{k(ij)} + \varepsilon_{ijk} \qquad (73)$$

where $\pi_{k(i)}$ designates the effect of plot k within level a_i (plot nested within the levels of factor A), $\pi_{k(ij)}$ designates residual subplot effect. The df associated with such a design are: $\rightarrow p(q-1)(n-1)$

$$\text{Between plots} \} \rightarrow \frac{np-1}{p-1}$$

<u>A</u>

plots within a_1
⋮ $\rightarrow p(n-1)$
plots within a_p

$$\text{Within plots} \} \rightarrow \frac{np(q-1)}{q-1}$$

<u>B</u>

$AB \rightarrow (p-1)(q-1)$

$$\left.\begin{array}{l}\text{B x plots within } a_1 \\ \text{B x plots within } a_p\end{array}\right\} \rightarrow p(q-1)(n-1)$$

For more computational details and extended examples of these models and variations, we direct the reader to Winer (1971) and Kirk (1968).

(21) Discriminant Analysis

The purpose of DISCRIMINANT ANALYSIS is to establish a FUNCTION of VARIABLES measured on an interval/ratio level, which can DISTINGUISH between one or more CATEGORIES of a variable, measured on an ordinal or nominal level. In general terms, a discriminant analysis looks as follows:

$$\boxed{Y_i} \quad = \quad \boxed{X_1 + X_2 + ... + X_n}$$

DV   **IVs**

(categorical/ordinal)   (interval/ratio)

The IVs, X_1, X_2 ... X_n are used to identify the group of Y where an observation belongs. In linear regression, the IVs (categorical or interval/ratio) account for the DV, Y_i, variance that is measured on an interval/ratio level and has VARIANCE. In discriminant analysis, the correct/incorrect CLASSIFICATION rate of observations made by a function of the IVs is the "ACCOUNTED VARIANCE" of the DV. In sport sciences a possible discriminant function can be illustrated as follows:

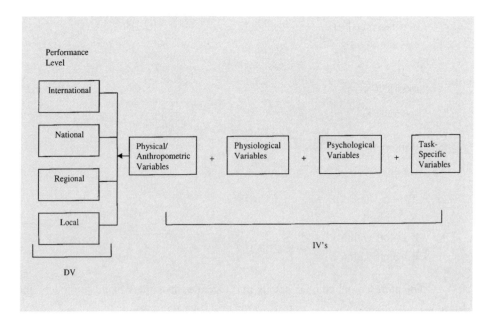

In this function, physical/anthropological variables can be height, weight, body mass, strength, length of limbs, physiological variables can be aerobic and anaerobic capacities, psychological skills may be mental toughness, determination, self-efficacy, perceived ability, goal-orientation, and task-specific skills may be movement efficiency, dribbling, faking, etc. There may be many other variables, depending on what should be classified. In the present example the performers are classified into four levels of achievements. Therefore, the procedure is termed "MULTIPLE DISCRIMINANT ANALYSIS (MDA)".

The linear combination of two or more IVs is termed a VARIATE. The best discrimination power is obtained when WEIGHTS are assigned to the IVs so that the Between Ss variance is maximized and the Within Ss variance (i.e., error) is minimized. The final function, which satisfies this condition, is termed a "DISCRIMINANT FUNCTION". Thus a discriminant function has the form of:

$$Z = W_1 X_1 + W_2 X_2 + \dots + W_n X_n \qquad (74)$$

where Z is the discriminant value, W_i is the discriminant weight for variable i, and X_i is the IV i.

The Null NYPOTHESIS tested by a discriminant analysis is that MEANS of a SET of IVs of two or more groups are equal. After the DISCRIMINANT WEIGHTS are determined, the EXPECTED VALUES/SCORES of each observation are estimated and classified. By averaging the discriminant scores for all the individuals within each group, a group mean, termed CENTROID, is determined. The centroid of the groups indicates how far apart the standardized distances among them are. These distances are then subjected to significance tests (as the centroids have a distribution of individual discriminant scores around them). Figure 4.31 illustrates different levels of discrimination between two groups. The shaded areas are probabilities associated with misclassification of observation (i.e. elite athletes to regional athletes and vice-versa). It should be noted that there are usually more than one discriminant function and each observation is classified by all the functions. The number of functions is k − 1, where k is the number of groups for classification.

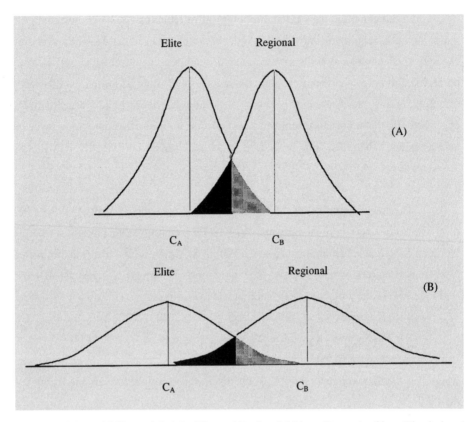

Figure 4.31 Centroid (C_A and C_B) for Elite and Regional Athletes Determined by a Discriminant Function. The Discrimination Power of Function B is Stronger than that of Function A.

A powerful discriminate function is one which MAXIMIZES the DIFFERENCES among groups by assigning weights to variables to establish the most appropriate VARIATES for that purpose.

The desired number of observations for a discriminant analysis is 20 or more observations for each predictor variable. Also, each category of the DV must have at least 20 observations. It should be kept in mind that the proportion of observations in each category should not favour dramatically one category over the other, otherwise a classification without the help of a discriminant function will be equally or more accurate. For example, if the classification into categories is 90% to one category and 10% to the other category, then by chance one can classify the observations to the 90% category very precisely. It is recommended to use a large sample of observations in the following manner: to divide it randomly into two sub samples. Then, use one subsample as an ANALYSIS SAMPLE to establish the discriminant function, and one as a HOLDOUT SAMPLE to test the discriminant function. This procedure is termed CROSS-VALIDATION.

Several assumptions should be met prior to conducting a discriminant analysis. The first is MULTIVARIATE NORMALITY of the IVs and EQUAL DISPERSION and COVARIANCE STRUCTURES (MATRICES) for the groups defined by the DV. When this assumption is not met, a LOGISTIC REGRESSION is preferable to use for the data. The second assumption is that of MULTICOLLINEARITY among the IVs. High associations among the IVs reduce the power of the discriminant function. This is particularly felt when a stepwise procedure rather than a simultaneous procedure is employed (similarly to stepwise linear regression). The third assumption is that all the relationships among the IVs are linear (similarly to all the multivariate techniques). OUTLIERS should be detected before any analysis takes place. Their presence may distort completely the discriminant coefficients and the power of the function.

The significance of the discriminant function is determined by tests which were introduced in the MANOVA section: Wilks' lambda, Hotelling's trace, Pilliai's criteria, and Roy's largest root (only the first function). In a STEPWISE METHOD, the MAHALANOBIS D^2 and Rao's V tests are most appropriate. Similarly to cluster analysis, the Mahalanobis D^2 consists of the generalized squared Euclidean distance adjusted for unequal variance. Like stepwise regression, to maximize Mahalanobis distance (D^2) is the aim of adding variables to the discriminant function.

Significant tests of the discriminant function are insufficient to exert sound conclusions. With a large sample, a small centroid distance can be significant. Thus the ACCURACY and POWER of the function should be estimated via FIT STATISTICS (similar to R^2 in regression analysis and x^2 in structural equation modelling). In discriminant analysis the PERCENTAGE OF CORRECT CLASSIFICATION (i.e., HIT RATIO) is the R^2 or FIT of the discriminant function.

To establish a CLASSIFICATION MATRIX a CUTTING SCORE is required, so that each observation is given a SCORE determined by the function and this score is classified into one of the CATEGORIES of the DV. The researcher seeks to determine the OPTIMUM CUTTING SCORE, CRITICAL Z VALUE. Under equal sample size, the Critical Z is located at the center of the GROUP CENTROID, thus

$$Z_C = \frac{Z_A + Z_B}{2} \qquad (75)$$

where Z_A and Z_B are the centroids of group A and B respectively, assuming equal sample sizes. For this reason it is vital to determine whether the groups/categories of the DV are expected to have 50/50 ratio or any other ratio, say 35/65, 40/60, etc., otherwise a 50/50 is assumed for two groups, 33/33/33 in three groups, 25/25/25/25 in four groups, etc. (equal chances of occurrance). If the probabilities are unknown, then the sample actual grouping determines this probability. Say that we have 80% team athletes and 20% individual athletes in our sample, and we do not have the population distribution statistics, the ratio we should choose is 80/20. When the groups are not equal in size, the Z_C should be determined by a weighted optimal cutting score:

$$Z_{CW} = \frac{N_A Z_A + N_B Z_B}{N_A + N_B} \qquad (76)$$

where Z_{CW} is the critical weighted cutting value for unequal groups' size, N_A and N_B are the number of observations in groups A and B, and Z_A and Z_B are the centroids of both groups, assuming normal distribution around the centroids. This concept is illustrated in Figure 4.32.

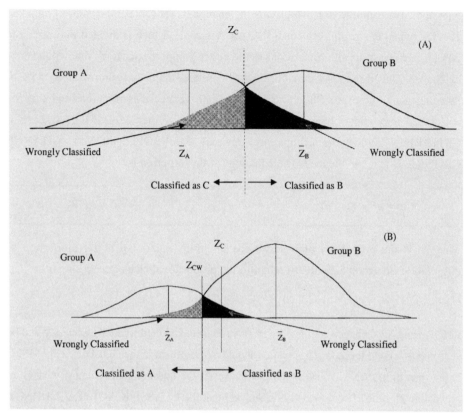

Figure 4.32 Optimal Cutting Point Z_C (Unweighted and Weighted; Z_C, Z_{CW}) for Equal (A) and Unequal (B) Samples' Sizes. Wrong Classifications (B→A and A→B) are Indicated in Shadowed Areas.

The classification (HIT RATIO) can be examined by a t-test for significance. It can be perceived as a TEST of CLASSIFICATION ACCURACY. For two equal groups the equation is:

$$t = \frac{p - 0.5}{\sqrt{\dfrac{0.5(1.0 - 0.5)}{N}}} \qquad (77)$$

where p is the proportion of correct classification and N is the sample size.

The PREDICTIVE ACCURACY is a "subjective" question. One can claim that 90% is an excellent hit ratio while the other may claim that 70% is "good enough". This determination should take into account the CHANCE CLASSIFICATION (i.e., guessing). For example, for two groups the chance (C) is (50/50). For more groups, k, C = 1/k (when the groups are equal in size). A sample, which is divided into 80% and 20%, if one classifies all observations to the larger group, the accuracy rate will be 80% by chance. Thus if the discriminant function classifies the observation with say 85% or 88% accuracy, these are 5% and 8% better than chance classification, and may be considered important. Chance by the largest group is termed MAXIMUM CHANCE CRITERION. When the groups are unequal the PROPORTIONAL CHANCE CRITERION is recommended. The equation for this criterion is:

$$C_p = p^2 + (1-p)^2 \qquad\qquad (78)$$

where p is the proportion of observations in group 1 and 1-p is the proportion of observations in group 2. With .90/.10 ratio the proportional chance criterion is:

$C_p = .90^2 + (1 - .90^2) = 0.81 + .01 = .82$

which means 82% chance compared with 90% chance, and therefore 90% accuracy will be accepted as a good hit ratio. These ratios should be examined in the HOLDOUT SAMPLE rather than in the ANALYSIS SAMPLE. However, the question still remains: what is an acceptable hit ratio? Hair *et al.* (1995) suggest that the CLASSIFICATION ACCURACY will be at least ONE-FOURTH GREATER than that achieved by CHANCE. Thus:

  for 50% → 62.5% (50 + 0.25· 50)
  for 30% → 37.5% (30 + 0.25 · 30)
  for 85% → 100% (85 + 0.25 · 85 = 106.25).

The statistic used for examination of the classification matrix compared to the chance model is PRESS's Q STATISTIC. The correct classifications are contrasted against the number of observations and groups and compared to x_c^2 with df = 1 and α<.05 (or smaller).

$$Q_p = \frac{\{N - (n\cdot k)\}^2}{N(k-1)} \qquad\qquad (79)$$

where N is the number of observations, n is the number of correct classifications, and k is the number of groups (categories). Assume that we have data that look like this:

N = 150, n = 120, k = 3 and $\alpha < .01$

$$Q_p = \frac{[150 - (120 \cdot 3)]^2}{150(3-1)} = \frac{44100}{300} = 147.$$

The critical for $\alpha < .01$ is 6.63 and therefore the predictions of the discriminant functions are much higher than chance.

To further elaborate on the discriminant function, one should examine the STANDARDIZED DISCRIMINANT WEIGHTS (COEFFICIENTS). The larger the coefficient of a variable, the higher is its predictive/classification power. The sign (negative or positive) is an indicator of the DIRECTION of its relationship with the DV (similarly to linear regression analysis). Attention should be given to the DISCRIMINANT LOADING (STRUCTURE CORRELATIONS), which are used as indicators of the relations between each of the IVs and the DV. When using stepwise approach in the discriminant analysis, the PARTIAL F VALUES associated with each step are of much value for deciding which variable contributes to the classification of the DV.

Just like factor analysis, discriminant functions can be ROTATED to find a better account for the classification of the DV. The original structure and reliability of the functions are preserved, but they may become "stronger". When more than one discriminant function results, a summary measure is useful in accounting for the contribution of variables across all the significant functions. This measure is termed POTENCY INDEX.

We shall use a simple example where two IVs, maximal oxygen uptake (VO_2max) and long run performance are used to classify participants into two groups (i.e., GROUP). We use SIMULTANEOUS PROCEDURES to the data presented here (the number of observations is too small and we use the data for illustration of the concept).

Name	VO$_2$max	Run	Group
1.00	56.00	540.00	1
2.00	35.00	670.00	2
3.00	58.00	523.00	1
4.00	34.00	682.00	2
5.00	72.00	470.00	1
6.00	54.00	510.00	2
7.00	65.00	497.00	1
8.00	35.00	712.00	2
9.00	36.00	693.00	1
10.00	61.00	488.00	2
11.00	45.00	667.00	1
12.00	36.00	652.00	2
13.00	47.00	653.00	1
14.00	52.00	512.00	2
15.00	41.00	623.00	1
16.00	39.00	672.00	2
17.00	54.00	513.00	1
18.00	37.00	679.00	2
19.00	36.00	691.00	1
20.00	46.00	645.00	2

The SPSS 11.0 program was used to analyze the data. The group descriptive statistics are presented first. It can be seen that group 1 has higher VO$_2$max values and faster run times, but the ANOVAs showed that these differences were non-significant.

Group Statistics

GROUP		Mean	Std. Deviation	Valid N (listwise) Unweighted	Valid N (listwise) Weighted
1.00	VO2MAX	51.0000	12.1198	10	10.000
	RUN	587.0000	86.7141	10	10.000
2.00	VO2MAX	42.9000	9.6891	10	10.000
	RUN	622.2000	84.1834	10	10.000
Total	VO2MAX	46.9500	11.4592	20	20.000
	RUN	604.6000	85.1163	20	20.000

Tests of Equality of Group Means

	Wilks' Lambda	F	df1	df2	Sig.
VO2MAX	.869	2.725	1	18	.116
RUN	.955	.848	1	18	.369

Then the Eigenvalues and canonical correlations are computed for the discriminant function and Wilks' Lambda (or other significance test) is applied. The function with its standardized coefficient (no constant as it is 0) and its loadings (structure matrix) are presented next. It can be seen that the canonical correlation of 0.50 was not significant ($\alpha<.086$) though tended toward significance (with more observations significance would result). The standardized coefficients (2.68 and 2.14) are quite impressive and the loadings (0.673 and -0.375) large. These indicate that VO$_2$max is a stronger variable than running time in classifying the observation into two groups (the minus sign of the running loading indicates a negative relation between this variable and the DV, however, keep in mind that the faster one runs, the lower is his/her value. Thus, conceptually these relations are positive).

Eigenvalues

Function	Eigenvalue	% of Variance	Cumulative %	Canonical Correlation
1	.335[a]	100.0	100.0	.501

a. First 1 canonical discriminant functions were used in the analysis

Wilks' Lambda

Test of Function(s)	Wilks' Lambda	Chi-square	df	Sig.
1	.749	4.908	2	.086

Standardized Canonical Discriminant Function Coefficients

	Function 1
VO2MAX	2.681
RUN	2.141

Structure Matrix

	Function 1
VO2MAX	.673
RUN	-.375

Pooled within-groups correlations between discriminating variables and standardized canonical discriminant functions Variables ordererd by absolute size of correlation within function.

The unstandardized coefficients of the discriminant function are also presented (this time with a constant/intercept coefficient) and the group centroids given. The distance between the two groups was large (0.549 + 0.549 = 1.098). We considered that the prior probability of being classified into one of the two groups was 0.50 (10 to each of the two groups). Then the classification function is determined and the observations classified.

Canonical Discriminant Function Coefficient

	Function 1
VO2MAX	.244
RUN	.025
(Constant)	-26.616

Unstandardized coefficients

Functions at Group Centroids

GROUP	Function 1
1.00	.549
2.00	-.549

Unstandardized canonical discriminant functions evaluated at group means

Classification Statistics

Prior Prohabilities for Groups

GROUP	Prior	Cases Used in Analysis Unweighted	Cases Used in Analysis Weighted
1.00	.500	10	10.000
2.00	.500	10	10.000
Total	1.000	20	20.000

Classification Function Coefficients

	GROUP	
	1.00	2.00
VO2MAX	8.459	8.191
RUN	1.099	1.072
(Constant)	-539.097	-509.881

Fisher's linear discriminant functions

Classification Results[a]

			Predicted Group Membership		
		GROUP	1.00	2.00	Total
Original	Count	1.00	6	4	10
		2.00	2	8	10
	%	1.00	60.0	40.0	100.0
		2.00	20.0	80.0	100.0

a. 70 % of original grouped cases correctly classified

The discriminant function was accurate in 70% of its classifications (6 out of 10 in the first group (60%) and 8 out of 10 (80%) in the second group). If Q_p was applied, then

$$Q_p = \frac{[20 - (14 \cdot 2)]^2}{20(2-1)} = \frac{(20-28)^2}{20} = \frac{-8^2}{20} = \frac{64}{20} = 3.2$$

which is smaller than x_c^2 for $\alpha < .01$ (6.63). Thus, this classification is not better than chance, and the discriminant function cannot be used for classification. It should be noted that with larger sample size, these results would certainly be significant. Therefore REPEATABILITY and VALIDATION are required to make a GENERALIZATION.

(22)   Integrating Research Findings: Meta Analysis

When a theory is verified through a research plan and appropriately performed, the results of the study confirm, reject, or modify the hypotheses, which were derived from the theory. We stated in several occasions throughout this book that in order to GENERALIZE the findings of research projects, the same or SIMILAR findings ought to be demonstrated in more than one study. This is the requirement of REPLICATION. The procedure, which consists of using results of several studies, aimed at similar questions, and verifying whether they share similar results is termed SECONDARY ANALYSIS or alternatively, RESEARCH SYNTHESIS and RESEARCH INTEGRATION. After Glass (1976, 1981) it was termed META ANALYSIS. Thus, research integration is conducted on UNITS, which represent a STUDY. For example, the means and variation of experimental and control groups in a study are used as ONE OBSERVATION in the meta analysis. The number of observations/units for analysis is usually the number of studies, which were aimed toward similar questions.

The main problem associated with integration of research findings is the VARIABILITY that exists among many FEATURES of the studies that are used for the analysis. This variability is the MAIN SOURCE of VARIANCE ERROR that has to be accounted for. The studies do NOT follow similar METHODOLOGICAL PLANS, do not always use similar types of SAMPLES and SAMPLING PROCEDURES, and use different MEASUREMENT TOOLS (and therefore reliability and validity of measurement – internal sources of error variance are included). There are many other variations among the studies that can be considered within the major sources of error-variance mentioned above. For example, lack of equality in sample size, gender, age, skills, background, education, training, measurement techniques, tasks performed, scoring performance, data analysis, treatment and control conditions, are all only a few examples where error variance may become a major obstacle in making conclusions about ANSWERS to QUESTIONS which are theoretically founded.

In general, research integration can be seen as arriving to conclusions about questions, which have theoretical base ACROSS ALL possible SOURCES of VARIANCE ERROR. This concept is seen in Figure 4.33.

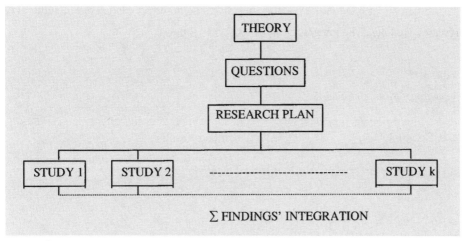

Figure 4.33 The Concept of Research Integration-Meta Analysis.

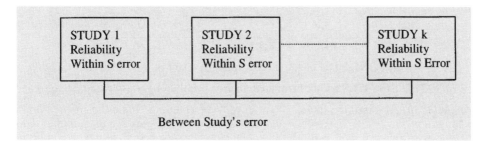

Figure 4.34 Within Studies and Between Studies Sources of Error.

However, the plethora or abundance of studies aimed at each question is very substantial and therefore needs integration in order to be accountable. Glass (1976) was the first who introduced methods to estimate the mean effect of treatments on outcome variables across a large sample size of STUDIES. He termed it META ANALYSIS. Raw data of studies are used for PRIMARY ANALYSIS. These are used as UNITS in the META-ANALYSIS.

In meta-analysis the TREATMENT EFFECT is termed EFFECT SIZE (ES) and designates the STANDARDIZED DIFFERENCE/EFFECT that exists between EXPERIMENTAL and CONTROL GROUPS. However, specific factors (intervening, moderators) that may affect the ES are taken into account similarly to other experimental designs. Subsets of data are excluded from the large sample of studies with respect to their conceptual homogeneity and ESs are estimated for them separately. Such subsets can be: gender, age, publication source and year, measurement types, etc.

In the past, counting positive, negative, and no-effect carried out integration of research findings. The integrating table looked as follows:

Table 4.13

Summary of Research Findings.

Study	Treatment Results		
	Positive	Negative	No Change
1	✓	⋮	⋮
2	✓	✓	⋮
3	⋮	✓	✓
⋮	⋮	⋮	✓
k	⋮	⋮	⋮
Total	Σ✓	Σ✓	Σ✓

The MAGNITUDE of the effects was not taken into account and therefore a WEIGHTED EFFECT was not estimated, or had been wrongly estimated. Hedges and Olkin (1980) criticized the statistical power of "vote counting" (type II error).

Rosenthal (1984) offered the Stouffer method, which consists of transforming the PROBABILITY VALUES of the significance test, p_i into Z VALUES, summing them up across all the studies and dividing by the square root of their number, k. The Z values are normally distributed and can be transformed back into probability, p, values. Thus:

$$p_i \rightarrow Z_i$$
$$Z_0 = \sum Z_i / \sqrt{k} \qquad (80)$$

and
$$Z_0 \rightarrow p_0$$

where the symbol 0 is designating "overall". The pooled sample size of combined studies is much stronger than for each single study separately. Rosenthal (1984) offers also a method of testing the HOMOGENEITY of the Z values by estimating their variance:

$$x^2 = \sum (Z_i - \overline{Z})^2 \tag{81}$$

with df = k-1

where Z_i is the individual study's Z_i converted from the p_i and $\overline{Z}$ is the mean of all Z_i values. When the χ^2 is significant it means that the VARIABILITY of the EFFECT SIZES, Z, is large and probably there are more homogeneous subsets of Z values within the studies surveyed. The MAGNITUDE of the ES (Z) can be converted into an ASSOCIATION ESTIMATE (correlation, r) by

$$r = Z_0 / \sqrt{N} \tag{82}$$

where N is the total sample size comprised of all the samples in the surveyed studies. As we know many non-significant results have smaller chance to be published. To estimate how many studies with no effect are needed in order to invalidate a significant overall p, the following equation is used:

$$N_{f, \alpha < .05} = \left(\sum Z_i / 1.645 \right)^2 - k \tag{83}$$

The p values, however, are not as strong indicators of the ES as the MEANS and STANDARD DEVIATIONS are in the experimental and control groups. Statistics such as t-test values can be transformed to Z and ES, d, values so that the standardized difference MAGNITUDE between the groups can be illustrated (Cohen, 1977). The most common estimator of ES is the standardized mean difference (Glass, 1976) symbolized as g

$$g = \frac{\overline{X}_e - \overline{X}_c}{S_c} \text{ or } \frac{\overline{X}_e - \overline{X}_c}{S_p} \tag{84}$$

where $\overline{X}e$ and $\overline{X}_c$ are the means of the experimental and control group respectively and S_c and S_p are the control group and pooled (both groups) standard deviations respectively. When the control participants do not receive any treatment, they represent better a non-treated population, and therefore it is recommended to use S_c as the denominator. When the control participants receive attention or some "other" treatment, we recommend using the S_p. When S_p is preferred, it is computed as:

$$S_p^2 = [(n_c - 1)(S_e)^2 + (n_c - 1)(S_c)^2]/(n_e + n_c - 2) \quad (85)$$

The ES estimator, g, is biased for small sample size. Hedges and Olkin (1985) suggested a correction estimator which is unbiased. The correction factor, c, is:

$$c = 1 - \frac{3}{4m - 9} \quad (86)$$

where $m = N_e + N_c - 2$ when S_p is used. Thus the UNBIASED ES, is

$$d = c \cdot g \quad (87)$$

The RANDOM EFFECT MODEL (Hedges & Olkin, 1985) suggests that the observed ESs represents the TRUE VARIANCE of the POPULATION ESs. As previously illustrated, the observed variability in sample estimates of ESs is partly due to the variability in the underlying population parameters and partly due to sampling error. Thus the variance of the ESs is divided into two components where

population variance = observed variance – sampling error

and the percent of observed variance made up by sampling error is

$$\% \text{ of observed variance} = \frac{\text{sampling error}}{\text{observed variance}} \times 100$$

and this illustrates the HOMOGENEITY/HETEROGENEITY of the ESs. If 100% of the observed variance is accounted for as a sampling error, the data is very homogeneous (ESs do not vary among themselves). If say 30% are explained by sampling error, then the residual variation of 70% is due to systematic factors that should be detected.

It should be noted that in REPEATED MEASURES DESIGNS the ES could be computed as follows:

$$ES = \frac{(\overline{Y}_e - \overline{Y}_c) - (\overline{X}_e - \overline{X}_c)}{S_{px}}$$

where Y is the post-test (second trial), X is the pre-test (first trial), S_{px} is the pooled standard deviation of the pre-test, and e and c symbolize the experimental and control groups, respectively. Sometimes, S_{cx} is used instead of S_{px} when it is justified on conceptual grounds.

Also correlation can be transformed into Z scores and then analyzed using the same meta-analysis procedures. The ESs can be displayed graphically as a STEM and LEAF display. The average Z_i (transformed from r values) are computed to yield an overall association measure between the variables. Both mean ESs, r and p transformed ESs should be WEIGHTED with respect to the SAMPLE SIZE they were computed from. Samples with many observations more accurately represent the population ES than ESs which consist of small sample sizes. Thus d and r should be d_W and r_W.

Sampling errors are smaller with large sample sizes and sampling error increases the variance across studies. The correlation between sampling error variance and population variance is additive and therefore observed variance of correlations is regarded as the sum of the two variance components. The Schmidt-Hunter method approximates the error variance S_e^2 as:

$$S_e^2 = [(1 - \overline{r}^2) \cdot k] / N \qquad (88)$$

where is the squared weighted mean of the ES, k is the number of studies, and N is the total sample size (Hunter et al., 1982). From this the population variance S_{rex}^2 is:

$$S_{res}^2 = S_r^2 - S_e^2 \qquad (89)$$

It is desirable that the observed variance, S_r^2 will be accounted for by the sampling error, S_e^2, and that the residual variance S_{rex}^2 will be zero. Then the variance accounted for by sampling error will be 100%, which is an indication of complete homogeneity. At least 75% of the observed variance should be accounted for by sampling error in order to obtain homogeneity and not seek for further factors, which may account for the unexplained variance (Hunter et al., 1982). CLUSTER ANALYSIS follows a test of homogeneity if the χ^2 test is significant. The CLUSTERS are comprised of ESs, which share common features. There may be factors, which relate to sampling, treatments, procedures and method of investigation, measurement tools, or other moderators. Outlier ESs are increasing the unexplained errors and should be treated similarly to regression analysis.

(23) Critical Review on Null Hypothesis Testing (NHT) and the Bayesian Alternative

At this stage the learner is believed to be competent in the use of many techniques, which he or she can choose from to approach the specific questions that ought to be studied. However, we may always ask ourselves whether we used the appropriate research methodology to tackle these questions. Does our statistical approach have a sound theoretical basis? The more we question, the more we become sceptical but creative in seeking far better and advanced procedures. We introduce here part of Tenenbaum and Fogarty's (1997) article on the debate of Null Hypothesis Testing (NHT), which we think is very important mainly to researchers who develop their skills at the beginning of the third millennium.

Because most research in our field still relies on conventional tests of significance – after all, that is the approach still advocated in most textbooks – it is important that we review the arguments for and against significance testing and consider whether we need to change the way we do things. Our own summation of the debate is that it comes down to a question of reliability: the faith one has in one's experimental outcomes. We suggest a number of ways in which researchers in sport and exercise sciences can improve the confidence they have in the results of single studies.

According to Cohen (1994) who quotes Morrison and Henkel (1970) and earlier researchers, the NHST "has not only failed to support the advancement of psychology as a science but also has seriously impeded it" (p. 997). It is mainly the 0.05 significance level on which H_0 is rejected that concerns Cohen. The importance of the base rate was advocated by the Bayesian theorem; however the base rate is often neglected before testing any hypothesis. This error often results in the adoption of a low and arbitrary probability such as 0.05. Loftus (1996) further argues that "… reliance on NHST has channelled our field into a series of methodological cul-de-sacs, and it has been my observation over the years … that conclusions made entirely or even primarily based on NHST are at best severely limited, and at worst highly misleading" (p. 162).

To make sense out of NHST one should specify what is meant by a "difference" between two or more means of the population. The probability that the means will be identical is zero and therefore "meaningful" differences should be proposed. Thus, instead of asking whether there are differences between two or more means, the question should be "how big are the differences? Are they big enough to the investigator to care about and, if so, what pattern do they form?" (Loftus, 1996, p. 163). When simply testing for mean differences, "rejecting a typical null hypothesis is like rejecting the proposition that the moon is made of green cheese… [You may think,] yes, okay, but so what" (Loftus, 1996, p. 163). The null hypothesis according to Schmidt (1992) is always false and therefore the rate of Type I error is zero resulting only in Type II error. Thus, our science is going nowhere due to false results, which rely on significance levels rather than magnitudes of effects. "Amounts" are more important than "directions" when verifying a theory. It is for this reason that regression coefficients are more stable than correlation coefficients and therefore recommended.

Loftus (1996) argues, "… investigators, journals, journal editors, reviewers, and scientific consumers often forget … and behave as if the .05 cut-off were somehow real rather than arbitrary. Accordingly, the world of perceived psychological reality tends to become divided into "real effects" ($p<=.05$) and "non-effects" ($p>.05$) … no wonder there is an epidemic of "conflicting" results in psychological research" (p. 164). It is for this reason that meta-analytical studies end up with zero effect-size. When appropriate measures are applied and magnitudes estimated, base-rates could be determined and used for testing hypotheses. The 0.05 level of significance would no longer be the ultimate criterion for accepting or rejecting theories.

What then should we do in order to advance the domain of sport and exercise science? We summarise the recommendations made by Cohen (1994) and Loftus (1996) in the following Table 4.14.

Table 4.14

Recommendation to Improve the Statistical Procedures in the Social and Behavioral Sciences.

Cohen (1994)	Loftus (1996)
(1) Use graphical presentation.	(1) Plot data rather than present in Tables plus F and p values.
(2) Use effect-sizes to show magnitudes and confidence-intervals (CI) to replace p values in NHST. The smaller the CIs the greater the power.	(2) Provide Confidence Intervals (CI) to assess the statistical power of the results. It visually shows how the pattern of means reflects the population means-pattern (see Loftus & Masson, 1994 for review).
(3) Decide upon a "good enough" range to test hypotheses. Determine differences in units such as effect-size; logits; etc. (see Seplin & Lapsley, 1993 for review).	(3) Compute effect-sizes for single studies and overall ES plus variation and CI for a set of studies. Control for independent variables such as gender, culture, instrumentation, ego, type of task/treatment, duration of interventions, etc.
(4) Challenge the results with alternative explanations (perceptual control over independent variables).	(4) Set a quantitative hypothesis about the underlying pattern of means (i.e., assign weights) and correlate with observed means (i.e., "planned comparison").
(5) Add likelihood ratios and Bayesian methods (Goodman, 1993; Greenwald, 1975).	(5) When interaction emerges, instead of focusing on differences between the dependent variable at a fixed level of the independent variables (vertical differences), look at differences between the independent variable (horizontal differences) at a fixed level of the dependent variable.
(6) Rely on replication.	

These are all good suggestions and are echoed by others in the literature. Hammond (1996), for example, advocates the use of confidence intervals and effect sizes. He also recommends the use of replication to improve reliability. Gonzalez (1994) lists four principles to guide psychological research:

- The theoretical model should play a central role in guiding the analysis;
- The theoretical model should suggest parameters to estimate;
- The researcher should create a design that permits proper estimation of the parameters;
- Intervals should be placed around parameter estimates.

Gonzalez goes on to advocate the use of a Bayesian approach wherein one has to estimate one's *prior belief* in a hypothesis and then compute a *posterior belief* on the basis of data gathered in the study. The essence of the Bayesian approach is the moderation of one's beliefs in the light of empirical data. Gregson (1997) argues that the problem is more serious than simply replacing a "significance" test by a confidence interval and also agrees with Gonzalez that a Bayesian approach is the preferred option.

Grayson, Pattison, and Robins (1997) made an interesting contribution to the debate when they summarised the alternatives as follows:

- continue as at present with objective tests of null hypotheses that severely limit what we can say about the results of a study;
- move towards a Bayesian approach that is intuitively appealing but where the requirement for prior knowledge poses some difficulties;
- adopt some intermediate position, such as a "commonsense approximation to Bayesian confidence intervals in the absence of prior knowledge …".

Grayson and his colleagues stopped short of recommending any particular approach, preferring instead to urge researchers to be more flexible in their thinking about the role of statistical inference in research: "We also believe that the context of a problem may well affect the interpretive position that one might wish to adopt. In one situation, meta-analysis of existing, focused, pertinent research may be very useful; in another scientifically new, exploratory context, the null hypothesis could well be a very important speculation at which to address evidence; in another well-studied situation, a more quantitative Bayesian approach to inference about parameter values may be especially valuable" (p. 70).

The important point made by Grayson et al. (1997) is that there is unlikely to ever be any resolution of the debate over preferred statistical approaches and that scientists should not adopt a passive role, waiting to see which side emerges the victor. Rather, scientists should recognize that they are in the best position to judge how data should be interpreted.

It would be pointless if we were to advise researchers in our fields to abandon the NHST when it is still so widely accepted (and expected) by journal editors and reviewers. Nor would we wish to do so. The NHST is so well-entrenched that it is likely to take many years before it ceases to be the dominant paradigm. Certainly it will retain this status whilst the textbooks continue to favor the NHST position. Instead, we would urge researchers to take the not-quite-so-adventurous steps of reporting effect sizes and confidence intervals rather than relying solely on a test of the null hypothesis. This will give researchers wider scope for the interpretation of research findings. We would also argue that the real crux of the NHST debate hinges on the question of reliability: it is a debate not so much about alpha levels and confidence intervals as it is about the confidence we are prepared to place in our own experimental findings. Basically, with the NHST approach, one can make two kinds of errors: a Type I error where one has rejected the null hypothesis when it was inappropriate to do so; or a Type II error where one failed to reject the null hypothesis when it should have been rejected. These errors will only be detected with replications that fail to support the original decisions; hence Hammond's (1996) emphasis on replication. To improve the reliability of research outcomes, we agree with Hammond (1996) that replication is important, but we would disagree that it is the only way of improving reliability. Another way of improving reliability is by improving the measures one uses in a study and also by increasing the number of measures.

Summary

This chapter summarized the main concepts, methods, and procedures, which are used in experimentation of quantitative nature. Some methods (for interval/ratio level measures) are more appropriate for such disciplines as exercise physiology, biochemistry, sport medicine, biomechanics, and others (ordinary and nominal levels of measurement) are more appropriate in research fields such as psychology and sociology of sport and exercise, though the use of all these techniques can be seen in all the above disciplines. It is important to note that whatever experimental method is chosen, the experimenter should be aware of the main requirements and assumptions underlying the method, and find the appropriate explanations for the obtained findings. The key to a successful research plan is to be aware of the limitations of the various methods, and accordingly suggest new alternatives and explanations to advance the study, which was aimed at specific concerns. Finally, the integration of findings from various research projects is required to shed more light on the questions that are researched. As the learner may see, new and innovative methods, just like human beings, strive for further explorations and development. The more the researcher will adopt and use the innovations (with intended consciousness), the more science will be advanced.

References

Argyrous, G. (1996*). Statistics for Social Research*. Melbourne: Mcmillan

Cohen, J. (1997). *Statistical Power Analysis for the Behavioral Sciences*. New York: Academic Press.

Cohen, J. (1994). The earth is round (p<.05*). American Psychologist, 49*, 997-1003.

Glass, G.V. (1976), Primary, secondary and meta-analysis of research, *Educational Researcher, 10*, 3-8.

Gonzalez, R. (1994). The statistical ritual in psychological research. *Psychological Science, 5*, 321-325.

Goodman, S.N. (1993). P values, hypothesis tests, and likelihood implications for epidemiology: implications of neglected historical debate. *American Journal of Epidemiology, 137*, 485-496.

Grayson, D., Pattison, P., and Robins, G. (1997). Evidence, inference, and the "rejection" of the significance test. *American Journal of Psychology, 49,* 64-70.

Greenwald, A.G. (1975). Consequences of prejudice against the null hypothesis. *Psychological Bulletin, 82*, 1-20.

Gregson, R.A.M. (1997). Signs of obsolescence in psychological statistics: significance verses contemporary

theory. *Australian Journal of Psychology, 49*, 59-63.

Hair, J.F., Anderson, R.E., Tatham, R.L., and Black, W.C. (1995*). Multivariate Data Analysis with Readings (4th Edition)*. New Jersey: Prentice Hall.

Hammond, G. (1996). The objections to null hypothesis testing as a means of analysing psychological data. *Australian Journal of Psycholgy, 49,* 104-106.

Hays, W. (1981). *Statistics (3rd Edition)*. New York: Holt, Reinhart and Winston.

Hedges, L.V., and Olkin, I. (1985). *Statistical Methods for Meta-Analysis*. New York: Academic Press.

Hunter, J.E., Schmidt, F.L., and Jackson, G.B. (1982*). Meta-Analysis. Cumulating Research Findings Across*

Studies. Beverly Hills, CA: Sage.

Kirk, R.E. (1968). *Experimental Design: Procedures for the Behavioural Sciences*, Belmont, CA: Brooks/Cole.

Loftus, G.F. (1996). Psychology will be a much better science when we change the way we analyze data. *Current Directions in Psychological Sciences, 54*, 161-170.

Loftus, G.R., and Masson, M.E.J. (1994). Using confidence intervals in within-subject designs. *Psychonomic Bulletin and Review, 1*, 476-490.

Morrison, D.E., and Henkel, R.E. (Eds.). (1970*). The Significance Test Controversy.* Chicago: Aldine.

Rosenthal, R. (1984). *Meta-Analytic Procedures for Social Research.* Beverly Hills, CA: Sage.

Schmidt, F.L. (1992). What do data really mean? Research findings, meta-analysis, and cumulative knowledge in psychology. *American Psychologist, 47*, 1173-1181.

Seplin, A.A., and Lapsley, D.K. (1993). Rational appraisal of psychological research and the good-enough principle. In G. Keren & C Lewis (Eds.). *A Handbook for Data Analysis in the Behavioral Sciences* (pp. 199-228). Hillsdale, NJ: Erlbaum.

Tenebaum, G., and Golding, E. (1989). A meta-Analysis of the effect of enhanced instructions: cues, participation, reinforcement and feedbacks and correctives (CPR+FB/C) on motor skill learning. *Journal of Research and Development in Education, 22*, 53-63.

Tenebaum, G., and Forgarty, G. (in press). Moving with times: Keeping up with trends and statistical analysis in research design. In R. Lidor and M. Bar-Eli (Eds.). *Linking Theories and Practice.* Morgantow, WV: Fitness Information Tecnologies.

Tenenbaum, G., and Fogarty, G. (1997). Applications of the Rasch Analysis to sport and exercise psychology measurement. In J. Duda (Ed.), *Advancements in Sport and Exercise Psychology Measurement.* Morgentown, M.V.: Fitness Information Technologies.

Winer, B.J. (1971). *Statistical Principles in Experimental Design (2nd Edition).* New York: McGraw-Hill.

Whitley, B.E. (1996). *Principles of Research in Behavioural Science.* Mountain View, CA: Mayfield.

Recommended Literature

Anderson, N.H. (2001). *Empirical Direction in Design and analysis.* Mahwah, NJ: Lawrence Erlbaum.

Argyrous, G. (1996). *Statistics for Social Research*, Melbourne: Mcmillan.

Glass, G.V., and Hopkins, K.D. (1996). *Statistical Methods in Education and Psychology (3rd Edition)*. Boston, MA: Allyn and Bacon.

Hair, J.F., Anderson, R.E., Tatham, R.L., and Black, W.C. (1995). *Multivariate Data Analysis with Readings* (4th edition). New Jersey: Prentice Hall.

Kirk, R.E. (1968). *Experimental Design: Procedures for the Behavioural Sciences*, Belmont, CA: Brooks/Cole.

Maxwell, S.E., and Delaney, H.D. (2004). Designing Experiments and Analyzing Data: A model Comparison Perspective (2nd Edition). Mahwah, NJ: Lawrence Erlbaum.

Winer, B.J. (1971). *Statistical Principles in Experimental Design* (2nd Edition). New York: McGraw-Hill.

(24)   Single Subject Research: Roots, Rational and Methodology
Eitan Eldar

"Science is, of course, more than a set of attitudes. It is a search for
order, for uniformities, for lawful relations among the events in nature.
It begins, as we all begin, by observing single episodes, but it quickly
passes on to the general rule, to scientific law. If we could not find
some uniformity in the world, our conduct would remain haphazard
and ineffective" (Skinner, 1969, p. 13).

Single subject research (SSR) is also referred to as single case, intensive, within-
subject, repeated measures, and time series experimental designs. The roots of SSR
methodology go back to the early work of B. F. Skinner. His initial behavioral research
(1930-1937) led him to distinguish between respondent behavior and operant behavior.
In a series of experiments, he made repeated observations and manipulations of a well-
defined behavior of a single subject (rats and pigeons), in a controlled context. The
concluding chapter of his first book "The Behavior of Organism" (Skinner, 1938),
discusses the differences between group and SSR, calling for a further refinement of
SSR, as the basic methodology for studying human behavior. "Tactics of Scientific
Research – Evaluating Experimental Data in Psychology" (Sidman, 1960), is a highly-
cited book, providing comprehensive and rich guidelines of how to do and how to judge
research in experimental psychology. In his work, Sidman offers a direct and systematic
replication for achieving reliability and generality of research findings.

The development of Applied Behavior Analysis (ABA) is associated with the
seminal article "Current Dimensions of Applied Behavior Analysis" (Baer, Wolf, &
Risley, 1968), published in the first issue of The Journal of Applied Behavior Analysis
(JABA). This article sets the ground rules for SSR in applied settings. Another
significant contribution is "Strategies and Tactics of Behavioral Research" (Johnston &
Pennypacker, 1980, 1993). This book, which derives from the classic work of Sidman,
presents a complete and coherent rationale and description of behavioral research
methods. The 1993 edition is much more communicative than the first one, allowing
students and researchers to relate the SSR methodology in a clear and sound theoretical

foundation. Numerous experimental, technical, theoretical and philosophical SSR articles can be found in The Journal of Applied Behavior Analysis (JABA), The Journal of Behavioral Education, The Behavior Analyst, The Journal of Experimental Analysis of Behavior (JEAB), and others.

The methodology presented in this chapter has been implemented in various educational (mostly special education) settings. It is suggested here as an exceedingly appropriate paradigm for studying behavior in sport contexts. The hypothetical examples provided in this chapter are intended to assist in generalizing the methodology into the sport and exercise sciences.

This chapter describes the basic features of SSR as the foundation for its experimental reasoning. It compares SSR to group research, and evaluates its potential contribution to the study of behavior in sport contexts. The major judgment tool in SSR – VISUAL ANALYSIS of graphic data is described and explained, followed by a detailed description of the BASELINE LOGIC, guiding the construction of all single subject designs. Once the logic has been formulated, five major designs (WITHDRAWAL, MULTIPLE BASELINE, CHANGING CRITERION, MULTITREATMENT, and ALTERNATING TREATMENT) and their variations are described. Each design is discussed in terms of its implementation, the demonstration of experimental control, and advantages and limitations. The chapter concludes with a discussion of SSR potential and adaptability in sport contexts.

24.1   *Basic Features of Single Subject Research*

The SSR methodology corresponds to the clinical / empirical orientation of applied behaviour analysis. It is focusing on socially important behaviors, and is committed to their improvement. The basic features characterizing SSR are closely related to the following comprehensive "working" definition of behavior.

> The behavior of an organism is that portion of an organism's interaction with its environment that is characterized by detectable displacement in space through time of some part of the organism and that results in a measurable change in at least one aspect of the environment. (Johnston & Pennypacker, 1993, p. 23).

Some basic features, derived from the essence of applied behavior analysis, led to the development of the SSR methodology. These are:

1. **Behavior is emitted by individuals**. Groups are comprised of individuals. Each individual has a specific interaction with the environment. Therefore, it is the individual's behavior that is studied, and not an average behavior of a group to which this individual belongs.

2. **Behavior takes time, and therefore requires repeated measurement**. Every behavioral event has a measurable duration. The frequency of the behavior within a specific duration is also amenable to measurement. Because behavior changes over time, it is essential to measure it systematically and reliably. Measuring behavior over time is vital to SSR, because experimental control is presented with the same participant, and not by a comparison to other (control) individuals. Therefore, data are collected prior to implementation of the independent variable, and throughout the study. Maintaining a reliable data collection should guarantee stability of data, and control of variables, extraneous to the context of study.

3. **Behavior is determined by the environment**. The "deterministic law" applies to all behaviors. It is subjected to logic and to order, like any other scientific phenomenon. Therefore, behavior analysts look for "functional relations" between the behavior and environmental events. This empirical orientation contributed to the development of SSR, focusing on causality rather than description or correlation.

4. **Behavior is systematic.** It is possible to identify stability in data of repeated behaviors, which is fundamental to all SSR. Variability in data is caused by interaction with the environment and can be explained. If variability is detected, an experimental manipulation is conducted, to control for it.

5. **Behavior is flexible - calling for a creative investigation.** The basic core of SSR is quite simple. The designs are built as a combination of "building blocks", tailored to answer a specific research question. The "baseline logic" serves all designs, while creative judgment is required to adjust it to the specific research context.

6. **Individuals respond to similar stimuli in a similar way.** Therefore, the reliability and the external validity (generality) of research findings in SSR is established if replication of previous procedures, produce similar outcomes (Johnston & Pennypacker, 1993; Sidman, 1960).

24.2 *Single Subject Design versus Group Design*

The essence and the implementation of SSR and "group research" (GR) differ substantially. SSR apply when the main concern is with individuals rather than with groups. GR provides information representing many individuals. Such data is not accurate for any specific individual in that group. "A prediction of what the average individual will do is often with little or no value in dealing with a particular individual. The actuarial tables of life insurance companies are of no value to a physician in predicting the death or survival of a particular patient" (Skinner, 1953, p. 19). Similarly, data showing a substantial motivation improvement of 20 players in a soccer team may not indicate that the most valuable player for that team (e.g., the scorer) has also been improved, following the implementation of a specific motivation program. In fact it may be that this player's motivation has actually regressed due to this specific intervention.

In GR participants are randomly assigned to groups. The analysis of the data is based on the assumption that measures of central tendency for each group represent the larger group (i.e., population) from which it was drawn. Analyzing groups' averages may "mask" important information regarding specific participants. Such an analysis, based on combined scores, does not allow drawing conclusions about an individual member of the group. This problem may be crucial for the coach, who's tactical plans are concentrated in a specific player. Therefore, empirical strategy and tactic in sport should be based on individual data.

Both group and SSR are methods of investigating the effect of the manipulation of the independent variable on the dependent variables. However, there are some conspicuous differences between the two. These are:

1. The source for EXPERIMENTAL CONTROL in SSR lies in comparing research conditions of the same participant. GR compares the differences among groups of participants.

2. Internal validity in SSR is determined by the contribution of the intervention to the target behavior of the participant. The significance of change depends on the unique characteristics of each individual (social validity). In GR the criteria for experimental validity are much more rigid. The level of significance is based on fixed statistical measures, determined ahead of time.

3. Data analysis in SSR is based on visual analysis of graphic data. In GR, it is based on statistical inference.

4. The ongoing measurement of behavior in SSR, followed by a continuous graphic presentation, enables the researchers to detect fluctuations that are sensitive to specific timing or context. A post-test measure in GR can not detect such process characteristics.

5. The graphic process analysis in SSR may also yield serendipitous findings or phenomena. Although unrelated to the research question, such information may contribute significantly to the area of study.

6. External validity in SSR is determined by replicating the intervention in similar context and with similar participants. In SR, the sampling methods and the population they represent confirm the external validity.

The above comparison has emphasized the advantages of SSR in the study of behavior and sport context. However, the criteria for selecting the research methodology should not necessarily be philosophical or paradigm dependent. They should serve the research question in the most appropriate way. If we are interested in a certain population (e.g., the whole team), then GR should be used to study the effect of the intervention (e.g., the effect of motivation training on "team spirit").

24.3   *Visual Analysis of Graphic Data*

The visual analysis of graphic data is the major "judgement tool" of behavior analysts. It is possible to detect a behavior change of an individual or a small group without the employment of statistical tools. Most independent variables studied in ABA lead to a clear and abrupt change in the dependent variables. Such a change is amenable to visual inspection (Baer, 1977).

The following advantages of graphic display of behavioral data are described in various publications (Baer, 1977; Cooper, Heron, & Heward, 1987; Michael, 1974; Parsonson & Baer, 1978; Sidman, 1960; Skinner, 1956). Visual analysis is a conservative approach, requiring a notable and stable behavior change, in order to be accepted as an important one. However, the analysis is relatively simple and may be administered with most computer programs available at homes, clubs, universities, and schools. The presentation is compact - displaying a detailed summary of all conditions in the research, time spent in each one, the design employed, the independent and dependent variables, the relationships between them, and follow-up details. The familiar presentation mode allows participants to understand and follow the process. It may also serve as an intervention, due to the reactive effect of posted graphs (e.g., provide the athletes with a weekly graph of their performance). The direct, immediate and continuos contact with the graphic data enables an ongoing formative evaluation of the process (e.g., if data show a decrease in motivation when the assistant coach is leading the practice, a personal adaptation may be implemented).

GRAPHIC PRESENTAIONS are visual illustrations of verbal statements and numeric data. They show at a glance the whole process, allowing a holistic evaluation of the intervention. In SSR a series of measures collected at each phase represent the dependent variables. The more data points collected at each phase, the more representative (i.e., valid) these data are of the target behavior. The following graphic tendencies serve as important judgment tools for the visual analysis of graphic data:

1. **LEVEL**. The value of the data path on the vertical axis. The mean level line (has an equal amount of data points above and under) represent the magnitude of the data in each phase of the research.
2. **TREND.** The direction of the data path across time. Trend may increase, decrease, or show a zero slope (horizontal). Trend value depends upon the nature of the target behavior. (e.g., an increase in the athlete's anxiety may be positive or negative).
3. **STABILITY / VARIABLITY.** The range in data points in the same phase. The closer data points are distributed around the mean data path, the greater the stability. An opposite situation means a high variability.

The analysis of graphic data is done within and between conditions, while only one variable is changed at each condition. Each condition should include a minimum of three separate and preferably, consecutive data points. The more variable the data are, the longer the condition should last. A within-condition analysis is concerned with the stability of data. The between-condition analysis compares the level and trend of data. A convincing demonstration of experimental control should show large and abrupt change in level (e.g., from low to high), and a remarkable change in trend direction (e.g., from decreasing or horizontal, to increasing). An overlap in data paths of two adjacent conditions, and high variability, weaken the experimental control and call for a further analysis.

Baseline Logic for Internal Validity

The first phase in implementing Single Subject Methodology is collecting "BASELINE DATA". These data provide information about the target behavior under "natural conditions", with no planned intervention related to the ongoing research or clinical treatment. It is the repeated measurement of behavior in units of frequency, duration, latency, or magnitude. A baseline is not necessarily a situation of no treatment or learning – it is the absence of the independent variable that defines it as such. Baseline data are the result of objective observations. They are not based on subjective judgments of the clinician or the researcher.

BASELINE DATA serve two functions – descriptive and predictive.

1. **Description of the target behavior**. Graphic and anecdotal descriptions of behavior provide objective knowledge about the participant's performance, the antecedents for the target behavior and the consequences of maintaining it. Such information is essential for programming the intervention.

2. **Prediction of future performance**. Stable baseline data enable the researcher to predict future probabilities of the target behavior, if the intervention had not been applied. Such PREDICTION enables the clinician to plan an appropriate success criterion for the subject and provides the researcher with a measure against which to compare the intervention data.

Baseline Logic – Defined

Single subject research methodology is based on BASELINE LOGIC (Sidman, 1960). It requires the repeated measurement of behavior, under at least two conditions: baseline (A) and intervention (B). A measurable change in the behavior following the intervention, when compared to baseline data, may lead to the conclusion that it is the intervention that caused the change.

BASELINE LOGIC is not a research design in itself – it is a set of guidelines for planning and decision-making in order to achieve functional relationships (also referred to as causality / experimental control) between the independent variable and the dependent variable. Measuring behavior under two conditions (A & B) does not demonstrate functional relationships (the behavior caused the change). Various strategies have been developed to verify such an assumption, all based on extension and adaptation of the A-B paradigm.

Baseline Logic – Components

BASELINE LOGIC provides basic methodological principles demonstrating that the change in behavior is related to the independent variables and not to confounding / extraneous variables. Such variables are events or situations that are not controlled by the researcher, but may have an effect on the target behavior. It consists of four components that should be present in every design demonstrating causality: PREDICTION, INTERVENTION, VERIFICATION, and REPLICATION. Another component – FOLLOW UP, is included in most designs, in order to ensure generalization and maintenance of the behavior change. This chapter presents baseline logic as it appears in the withdrawal design. A similar logic applies to all other designs. Baseline logic components are presented in Figure 4.35.

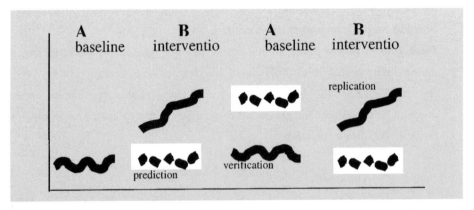

Figure 4.35 The Four Components of Baseline Logic – Baseline, Intervention, Verification and Replication, as they Appear in a Hypothetical ABAB Design. (The solid lines are actual baselines and interventions. The doted lines are predictions, if intervention had not been applied / removed).

PREDICTION is the assumption that baseline data will maintain level, trend and stability, if intervention is not applied. This is an extrapolation of a situation in which baseline condition would have remained unchanged. Intervention data are measured and compared against this extrapolation (Johnston & Pennypacker, 1993; Kazdin, 1982).

Effective Baseline Data

The following baseline characteristics are recommended for ensuring effective PREDICTION:

1. **Baseline length**. Baseline should include enough data points representing all aspects of the target behavior and not missing special events. On the other hand, it should not be too extended because it may withhold an effective intervention. Three data points are the minimal requirement for PREDICTION (Hersen & Barlow, 1976), but more information is usually required. If the target behavior is severe or risky, an immediate intervention should be implemented. A design with no initial baseline (e.g., B-A-B) should be employed in such a case.

2. **Baseline stability**. Baseline phase should be maintained until clear data STABILITY has been demonstrated (Baer, Wolf, & Risley, 1968). If data are variable the behavior should be further defined, and data collection reliability should be examined. Research in applied context leads to greater data VARIABILITY because some variables are difficult to control. Such variability should be treated as a natural part of individual functioning (Sidman, 1960). A baseline is considered stable if it does not include data points exceeding 50% of the average value of all points (Barlow & Hersen, 1984; Repp, 1983; Sidman, 1960). This is an arbitrary criterion that should be judged according to the research context.

3. **Baseline trend**. Data TREND is comprised of three or more data points, and can show increases, decreases, or zero trends. It is recommended to terminate a baseline with a deteriorating trend, or one that shows no change. Such data should support the need for intervention.

Intervention

The second phase in all single subject research designs includes measuring the behavior under intervention. The level and trend of data provide information about the effectiveness of the treatment. It is assumed that without INTERVENTION, baseline data would have remained unchanged (PREDICTION). It is also assumed that the intervention will have a positive effect on the target behavior.

Following a stable baseline, only one independent variable is administered. Intervention should be the least restrictive one for the participant, yet still effective. There are three possible outcomes for intervention:

1. **No change**. There are three methodological options for the researcher: a) continue with intervention, assuming a delay in the behavior change; b) modify the intervention; c) change the intervention.
2. **Improvement**. There are three options: a) maintain the successful intervention. This option (A-B) does not demonstrate causality, but it satisfies clinical judgment; b) apply intervention to other behaviors of the same subject (MULTIPLE BASELINE DESIGN); and c) withdraw the effective intervention or administer a placebo (WITHDRAWAL DESIGN). This is a powerful experimental tactic that is rarely implemented in educational settings because of the need to withdraw intervention.
3. **Deterioration.** In this case, intervention should be terminated, and an alternative one should be considered.

Verification

VERIFICATION provides assurance of the preceding PREDICTION, suggesting that without intervention, behavior would have remained unchanged. Verification contradicts the assumption that other variables, extraneous to the research design, are responsible for the change. One way of achieving verification is by withdrawing the intervention. If data reverse towards the previous baseline, it may be concluded that without intervention, no change would have occurred. Verification is based on the prediction that intervention effect would have been remained the same, if intervention had not been removed.

It should be noted that intervention withdrawal does not necessarily lead to a complete reversal to baseline. Some aspects of the behavior could already be acquired, causing a slow reversal.

Verification is strengthened if extraneous variables are controlled, and the reliability of data collection is improved. Verifying the prediction allows for claiming causality, but replicating the intervention effect increases the internal validity of the independent variable.

Replication within the Research

REPLICATION is a reintroduction of the independent variable. It reduces the probability that other extraneous variables caused the change in the dependent variables. The more an intervention be replicated, the more its believability will be strengthened (Baer, Wolf, & Risley, 1968). This principle is commensurate with single subject research methodology that is flexible and allows for adaptations.

It is recommended to extend the last intervention to ensure that data are stable and that the behavior has been acquired. Follow-up data, gathered after intervention is terminated, should provide information about the long-term effect of the independent variable.

Replication for Reliability and External Validity

Replication across studies is the repetition of a given experiment by the same experimenter, while keeping the independent variable and the participants constant (Sidman, 1960). This version of replications is called "DIRECT" because it repeats all aspects of the research. A series of successful direct replications, producing the same effect, strengthen the reliability of the results.

In SYSTEMATIC REPLICATION some aspects of the study are slightly and systematically varied (Cooper, Heron, & Heward, 1987). A successful systematic replication with different participants, with a slight change in the intervention or setting, should increase the reliability and the generality (external validity) of the results.

Direct replication is impossible in sport settings, because they are dynamic in nature. However, the systematic replication of an intervention may be an integral part of a training program. An example is having a sport psychologist "working" with an athlete on improving self-control. Once positive results are achieved, and experimental control (internal validity) is demonstrated, another study is initiated with a second athlete, then a third one, etc. The replication of effect with all participants, strengthen the generality of the results.

24.4   A-B Designs

A, B, and A-B designs do not demonstrate experimental control, but may contribute significantly to the professional's work. They present reliable data, enabling coaches and athletes to support their decisions with objective judgment.

"**A**" and "**B**" designs are also referred to as "case study" due to their descriptive nature. They describe the behavior prior to intervention (A), and during or after intervention has been employed (B). Unlike other case studies, based on narrative descriptions of a certain context or event, these designs present quantitative data. The graphic presentation of the data draws the level and trend of the target behavior, in a specific time frame and in a well-defined context.

A-B, also termed "simple time series design," is fundamental to all single subject designs. It presents behavior data in baseline phase and in the following intervention (first two phases in Figure 4.24). A-B is most suitable for evaluating educational and training goals that do not require experimental control. A-B is preferable to "A" because it measures the independent variable after presenting the behavior in its natural condition - with no intervention. It can also indicate that changes are not due to time (maturation), if an abrupt change, different than the stable baseline data path, is demonstrated with the presentation of intervention. This design is simple and therefore recommended highly for the practitioner who strives for success. It may demonstrate effective treatment, but cannot control for extraneous variables.

24.5   Withdrawal Designs

WITHDRAWAL (reversal) designs entail the programmed repeated introduction and withdrawal of the independent variable. Data comparison before, during, and after intervention enables the verification and replication of experimental control (as demonstrated in figure 1). The basic withdrawal design – ABAB, will be described here at length, followed by a short description of some withdrawal variations.

ABAB – Implementation

The following procedures are required for the implementation of ABAB:

1. A clear definition of the target behavior, and a description of other behaviors that could "react" to the planned intervention.
2. Collections of continuous baseline data, until clear and stable level and trend have been achieved.
3. Presentation of intervention following a deteriorating or "no change" baseline.
4. Continue intervention until the criterion for the target behavior has been achieved, or until a clear therapeutic trend has been demonstrated. Intervention phase length should be similar to baseline length, if possible.
5. Withdraw intervention when one of the two conditions (in #4) is met. Baseline 2 is similar to baseline 1, because there is no intervention, and data are collected in the same context.
6. Re-introduce the intervention (replication) after data in baseline 2 show no improvement or a deteriorating stable trend.
7. Continue intervention until therapeutic data are stable. It is recommended to collect follow-up data to ensure maintenance of the positive behavior change.

Experimental Control

WITHDRAWAL DESIGNS attain experimental control when data path shows improvement whenever intervention is introduced, and shows deterioration and return to baseline upon its removal. Every withdrawal and replication, followed by deterioration or improvement, strengthens the internal validity of the independent variable. This is a powerful strategy demonstrating causality with the same subject and with the same target behavior. BASELINE LOGIC components of withdrawal designs are described in the previous section (baseline logic).

An abrupt change detected immediately with the presentation of the intervention increases its internal validity. However, an abrupt change is not essential for claiming causality. In some cases, a gradual change is observed, because behavior has been acquired partially, or due to a carry-over effect of the intervention. In such cases, the stability of data plays a more significant role in determining experimental control.

Advantages

The major advantage of ABAB is the powerful experimental control it demonstrates. This is a simple design that is easy to explain and discuss. It is clear to the eye of the scientist, the practitioner, and the consumer.

The final phase of ABAB involves presentation of the independent variable. Ending a study with an effective treatment is warranted, enabling the maintenance of improvement. It also provides the researcher with extension possibilities for further study and refinement of the independent variable, or for comparison with other treatments.

Limitations

The limitations of ABAB are related to clinical and ethical, rather than experimental considerations. There is no sense in withdrawing an effective intervention prior to the acquisition of the target behavior. Such a conflict between clinical and experimental judgments should be considered when planning a withdrawal design.

Another limitation is related to acquired / irreversible behaviors (e.g., learning the correct kick in soccer). They do not lend themselves to withdrawal, and no reversal in data should be expected. An exception would be evidence with motivation problems interfering with the improvement of acquired behaviors. In such cases, the data trend should deteriorate upon withdrawal of the motivation program.

Variations of Withdrawal Designs

WITHDRAWAL DESIGNS are flexible to meet the needs of the participants and the context of the study. All variations adhere to the BASELINE LOGIC, presenting and withdrawing intervention.

ABA is the minimal withdrawal design demonstrating experimental control (the first three phases in Figure 16.35). This is an extension of an AB design, withdrawing intervention after stable data have been achieved. ABA is not frequently used in educational settings because it is terminated with a contratherapeutic change. It does not show a continuation of improvement as demonstrated in ABAB.

BAB design presents intervention at the first phase (no initial baseline), followed by withdrawal, and reintroduction of intervention. This design is applied when the target behavior is dangerous or unethical (e.g., a player may injure teammates during the practice), or when collecting baseline data is technically inappropriate (e.g., the training program has already started). It lacks the preliminary information about the target behavior in its "natural" context. However, it provides an immediate intervention, and is terminated with a continuation of treatment, enabling maintenance of the behavior change.

A **"probe" phase** in which an intervention is removed for a short period (e.g., one or two data points) may be applied when there is an abrupt deterioration in the target behavior. An immediate change in trend and level following reintroduction of intervention provides VERIFICATION of its effect. Probe data are taken when an extended withdrawal of intervention is either unethical or inappropriate (e.g., may jeopardize an already acquired skill).

Despite its limitations, the WITHDRAWAL DESIGN may be very effective in sport settings. There are many cases in which the withdrawal is an inevitable part of the process. For example, (a) The head coach is not present in some practices due to other duties (e.g., scouting); (b) in some games, certain players do not participate; (c) the athlete may try a certain diet or pre-competition arrangement. Such procedures, whether pre-planned or involuntary, may be included in a withdrawal design, enabling the evaluation of their contribution to the team / athlete.

24.6 *Multiple Baseline Designs*

The most frequently used design in educational settings is the multiple baseline (MB). This is a series of AB designs, in which BASELINE DATA are collected simultaneously, and intervention is introduced sequentially to each one of the target behaviors, participants or settings.

The MB design was formulated by Sidman (1960) and first introduced by Baer, Wolf and Risley (1968) as an alternative to reversal / withdrawal designs. It enables the measurement of a few dependent variables at the same time, when one is under experimental condition and the others are controlled. Figure 4.36 describes a hypothetical MB design across three different behaviors. It shows the BASELINE LOGIC components as they apply to this design.

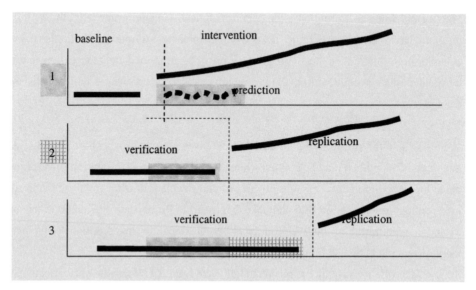

Figure 4.36 A Hypothetical Multiple Baseline Design. (The shaded area in tiers 2 & 3 serve as verification for the prediction for tier 1. The grid/shaded lines in tier 3 verify the prediction for tier 2).

Basic Forms

The basic arrangement of control and experimental conditions may be applied in three different forms:

1. **Multiple baselines across behaviors**. The effect of the independent variable is studied against different behaviors of the same participant or group. For example, the effect of a concentration training (independent variable) on the accuracy of passes, foul shots and assists in basketball (dependent variables).

2. **Multiple baselines across participants**. The effect of the independent variable is studied against different participants or groups, performing the same target behavior, in similar conditions. For example, the effect of a motivation program (independent variable) on the frequency of successful tackles (dependent variable) of three different soccer players, at the last 10 minutes of league games.

3. **Multiple baselines across settings**. The effect of the independent variable is studied in different settings in which the same behavior of the same participant/s is performed. For example, employing a self-control intervention for a "problematic" athlete in practices, competitions, and team gatherings.

Implementation

Each one of the three MB forms include two basic measures:

1. A simultaneous and continuous measure of baseline for all dependent variables.
2. A sequential presentation of intervention to all dependent variables.

The first step includes the collection of baseline data for all dependent variables, and setting criteria for a successful intervention. Once the baselines have been established, an intervention is applied to one variable, but not to the others, remaining under baseline condition. Then, rather than withdrawing intervention (as in withdrawal designs), it is applied to the next baseline, and so on. The following guidelines should be kept when implementing MB.

- The dependent variables should be FUNCTIONALLY INDEPENDENT. This means that there is no interaction among variables, and introducing the treatment to the first variable will not cause changes in the other unexposed variables. For example, changing the athlete's verbal inappropriate behavior may eliminate confrontations with referees. Therefore these are functionally dependent variables that are not amenable to the same MB design.
- The dependent variables should be FUNCTIONALLY SIMILAR so that they will respond to the same intervention. For example, cooperating with teammates and with the coach is functionally similar in that they may both be responsive to "social training". On the other hand, foul shooting and cooperation are not similar enough to respond to the same intervention (whether it is social or concentration training).
- The scale of measurement should be the same with all variables (e.g., percent of accuracy), to enable data analysis.
- Intervention should be introduced to stable baselines.
- Intervention should be introduced to the next variable, when the previous one has reached the target criterion, or when data trend is improving for three consecutive data points.
- Intervention condition is continued where applied, and baseline data are taken for all variables that were not exposed yet to treatment.
- It is recommended to vary the length of the unexposed baselines to control for extraneous variables such as "cyclic effect".
- Treatment is eventually applied to all variables.

Experimental Control

Experimental control is demonstrated when "where intervention is applied, change occurs; where it is not, change does not occur" (Horner & Baer, 1978, p. 189). It is the intention of the experimenter to show that each dependent variable is changing, in succession, only when the independent variable is introduced. Other unexposed baselines remain unchanged or vary just slightly (Baer et al., 1968).

Prediction. When baseline data are stable for the first variable, predictions are made that the level and trend will remain the same if all contextual variables will remain constant. A similar prediction is made with all other stable baselines.

Intervention. At this stage, intervention is implemented for baseline one, while all other baselines remain constant. If it is followed by a therapeutic change, it may be assumed that intervention is associated with the change in the dependent variable (as in AB design).

Verification. Continued baseline data of the other variables showing no change in stability, level, and trend, serve as verification for the prediction made for the previous baseline exposed to intervention. These baselines are still exposed to the same conditions under which the changed baseline had been measured. The fact that they have not changed, controls for time dependent extraneous variables such as specific / seasonal period of time, history and maturation. At the same time, only the dependent variables exposed to the intervention were changed.

Replication. The successive introduction of the intervention to unexposed baselines serves as replication of effect, if they are followed by a therapeutic change. No absolute rule can be given about the number of replications needed. Each additional one strengthens the internal validity and further controls for the "threat" of other extraneous variables. As with all other single subject designs, the decision about the number of replications is flexible and is left to the clinician and the researcher's judgment (Baer et. al., 1968). It has been demonstrated that a two-tier MB is sufficient enough to demonstrate causality (Cooper, Heron, & Heward, 1987). However, three or for tiers are frequently used in most MB designs.

Figure 4.36 shows the four components of baseline logic mentioned above, as they apply to the MB design.

Advantages

The MB design is empirically and practically oriented. It has the advantage of not withdrawing an effective treatment, thus supporting the maintenance of the behavior change. The prolonged data collection for several behaviors, participants, or settings, enables an empirical evaluation of the athlete or the program goals. Furthermore, the MB is consisted of a series of AB designs, providing ongoing information about the dependent variables before and after intervention.

The MB design enables the evaluation of generalization of behavior change. For example, the measurement of the same target behavior (e.g., concentration) in three different settings (individual practice, scrimmage, and competition) shows the degree of generalization attained.

Limitations

The MB design presents a weaker internal validity than in the withdrawal design. The reason lies in the VERIFICATION procedure. Verification in the MB design is achieved through other variables (participants, behaviors, or settings), remaining unchanged while the data for the variable under intervention show change. In withdrawal designs, verification is achieved within the same participant – if behavior data deteriorate when intervention is removed.

The MB design requires a delay in the delivery of intervention for the second and subsequent independent variables. Such a delay may not be appropriate if an immediate intervention is essential.

Other limitations are technical, relating to time required for implementing the MB design, and the interference that the prolonged baselines may cause to the participants and their surroundings.

24.7   *Variations to MB Designs*

Delayed MB. This variation has been constructed to overcome the limitation of prolonged baselines (Heward, 1978; Risley & Hart, 1968; Watson & Workman, 1981). While the first baseline data are being collected, other baselines are not yet measured. It is important to add the next baseline prior to implementation of intervention to the first baseline. This baseline overlap (a minimum of three data points) enables the

VERIFICATION element. If there is no such overlap, no causality may be claimed. Other baselines are added in the same delayed fashion.

The delay in measurement eliminates the need for extended baseline that may result in reactive effect (i.e., the observation procedure changes the target variables). This design may save resources in cases where they are limited. The delayed MB is flexible, enabling the addition of new variables, not available or relevant while the initial one was studied. If the first intervention is successful, other baselines, not presented initially, may be added, to strengthen the internal validity. Thus, a delayed MB has both advantages (i.e., flexibility and sensitivity to clinical procedures), and drawbacks (internal validity).

The limitations of this variation lay in the incomplete baselines. It may not be sufficient to collect only a few data points in each subsequent baseline, before the presentation of the intervention. Without an initial and concurrent measure of all variables, it may be difficult to provide an acceptable control for confounding variables such as history. The addition of delayed measurements of new variables to an already functioning MB should maintain a powerful internal validity, yet enable the required flexibility.

Multiple Probe Design. In this variation (Cuvo, 1979; Horner & Baer, 1978), data are not collected continuously on variables that have not yet been exposed to the independent variable. Probe measurements, interspersed throughout the unexposed baselines, are presumed to represent the level and trend of these variables. While intervention is presented to the first variable, probe data are intermittently collected for subsequent variables. It is advised to probe all variables when the first intervention reaches the desired criterion. Such a simultaneous measure increases internal validity. At least three consecutive data points are collected in the second tier, prior to the introduction of the second intervention. During the second intervention phase, intervention probes are conducted for the first variable, and baseline probes are taken for the third variable.

Both the probe and the delayed designs are suitable for coaches who wish to measure their athletes' progress, but lack the time and resources required for extended measurements. They may also reduce the intrusive effect of data collection during practices. Due to their functional similarities, both designs suffer similar limitations (see above).

Changing Criterion Design. The CHANGING CRITERION DESIGN (CCD) is ideal for sports contexts. It enables the athlete and the coach to evaluate gradual and systematic changes in performance, and therefore, to motivate progress. The CCD (Hartmann & Hall, 1976; Sidman, 1960) involves a successive change of the planned criterion for success (i.e., reinforcement contingencies), in graduated steps, from baseline to the desired terminal goal. Each phase of the design provides a baseline for the following one. Improvement in performance is presumed to occur concurrently with changes in the planned and stated task contingencies. Figure 4.37 describes the basic format of the CCD.

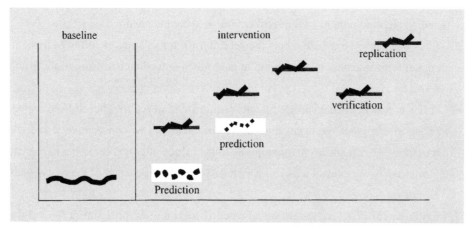

Figure 4.37 A Hypothetical Changing Criterion Design. (The dotted lines are predictions of data if intervention had not been applied).

Implementation

Implementing the CCD is comparable to operating a training program. Due to the applicable nature of this design, the following steps should be carefully executed, to maintain acceptable empirical outcomes:

1. A specific target behavior should be selected and behaviorally defined.
2. Baseline data should be taken to set a clear initial criterion for intervention, and to determine a desired criterion for terminating the intervention. Baseline data are taken here in the same manner used in all other single subject designs. Criterion changes must be large enough so they are visible, but not too large to frustrate the athlete and slow down the training program.

3. An intervention program is designed to meet the final criterion. Each intervention phase is defined clearly in terms of criterion, and the time in which it should be attained. These phases are the steps in the ladder the athlete should climb to reach the top rung. The criterion for each step is based on professional estimation of the athlete's ability, and knowledge of the target behavior. It is recommended that each successive performance step be based on the same difference as the previous one. For example, if baseline data show that only 10% of the athlete's moves are accurate, the criterion for the first phase may be 15% accuracy, for the second – 20%, and so on.

4. After a stable baseline has been achieved, the first phase of intervention is presented, and so on. A minimum of four replications is recommended.

5. Each performance, which meets the set criterion for success, is followed by some sort of reinforcement to the athlete (e.g., a positive feedback in front of the whole team).

6. A few consecutive and successful data points are required to proceed from a given phase to a higher one. The minimal requirement is two consecutive successful measures, or two successful data points out of three attempts (e.g., the basketball player has two games in a row in which he/she had a frequency of 4 assists per 10 minutes).

7. Criterion for progress should be adjusted if reaching the criterion is too easy or too difficult.

8. The procedure is terminated when the target criterion has been achieved and maintained.

Experimental Control

The CCD is based on the match between the pre-established success criterion for each phase, and the actual value of the dependent variable at this phase. Experimental control is achieved when the level and the trend of the target behavior, vary concurrently with the manipulated change in the criterion and the contingent feedback it yields.

The change in the new phase should be immediate and should follow a stable level and trend in the preceding phase. The reason is that each phase serves as a baseline for the following one.

A short reversion to the previous criterion level may strengthen the experimental control. This can be done, by setting a lower requirement for reinforcement, after a higher one has already been achieved. A regression in performance in this case will verify that change in the performance was due to the intervention and not to other variables or to natural improvement. Varying the length of each phase should also control for extraneous variables and serve as VERIFICATION.

Advantages

The CCD is a positive practical procedure in that it supports a gradual improvement of performance to achieve experimental control. The CCD is tailored for complex behaviors and for extended acquisition periods. The sub-phases of this design are parallel to the phases in shaping (Cooper, Heron, & Heward, 1987; Skinner, 1953), which arrange successive approximations to the behavior, by repeatedly reinforcing minor improvements towards the terminal performance. It also supports behavior change programs, based on gradual change (e.g., force development).

The CCD is ideal for evaluating motivational programs designed to improve the performance of an individual athlete or a team. It can be used with accelerating (e.g., increasing running distance) and decelerating programs (e.g., weight loss) due to its stepwise graphic display.

Limitations

The CCD does not demonstrate a powerful experimental control. This is an extended procedure that may not be appropriate when an abrupt and immediate change is essential (e.g., when preparing for an upcoming competition). The CCD is appropriate only for evaluating already acquired behaviors.

24.8   *Comparative Designs*

Single subject research designs are mostly associated with studying a single participant and a single independent variable. This section describes another group of designs, comparing the effect of two or more independent variables, across one or more participants or behaviors. These designs are termed "COMPARATIVE", because they assess the relative effectiveness of a few interventions.

Multitreatment Design

The MULTITREATMENT DESIGN (MTD) is an extension of the withdrawal design, using the same baseline logic. Unlike the withdrawal design - presenting and withdrawing the same intervention, the MTD (Kratochwill, 1978) presents and removes different independent variables. The MTD may serve coaches who are considering different training methods, and are looking for empirical validation of the preferred one. Figure 4.38 presents an illustration of the MTD using hypothetical data.

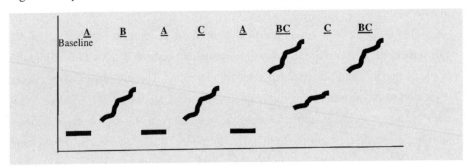

Figure 4.38 A Hypothetical Multitreatment Design Comparing Three Different Independent Variables (B, C, BC). Implementation.

As in withdrawal design, the MTD requires baseline measures of the target behavior to assess the athlete's present level of performance. Once a stable baseline is achieved, the independent variables are sequentially presented with a return to baseline following each presentation. It is important to determine in advance the order in which intervention will be introduced. If several participants take part in the study, the presentation order should be counterbalanced, to control for order effect.

The presentation of the first intervention is actually an ABA design. Then, the next intervention (C) is presented and reversed, with a notation A-B-A-C-A. Additional interventions may be introduced in the same manner. It is important to terminate the study with the most effective intervention (e.g., A-B-A-C-A-D-A-D).

It is also possible to evaluate a package of a few interventions and to compare their effect to other interventions. For example, two training methods (B & C) that show a moderate effect, may be combined (BC). This package is then compared to baseline condition (A-B-A-C-A-BC-A-BC), or to the separate treatments (A-B-A-C-A-BC-B-BC-C-BC). This variation stresses the flexibility of SSR, enabling modification of the design to meet the superior outcomes.

Experimental Control

Experimental control is demonstrated when the intervention is followed by a change in the dependent variable (see description for withdrawal design). Since there are a few compared interventions, they may be compared to each other (e.g., A-B-C-B-C) and not to a mediating baseline (e.g., A-B-A-C-A-C). In this case, one intervention (the less effective) serves as an active baseline for the other (the more effective). This presentation enables a direct comparison of the two interventions. It should be noted though, that only adjacent conditions might be compared. Non-consecutive conditions are subject to sequence effect and other interference, caused by the other conditions and by time elapsed between them.

External validity is achieved by replicating the intervention effect in different settings, with different behaviors and with different participants.

Advantages and Limitations

The MTD compares a few interventions in simple and clear fashion. It resembles the didactic logic of designing training programs, while attempting to reach the most effective procedure. Historical and maturation threats are substantial for this design because it introduces different interventions in a time lagged sequence. Another threat to internal validity is a carryover from one condition to another, and sequence effect, masking the pure contribution of each intervention.

24.9   Alternating Treatment Design

The ALTERNATING TREATMENT DESIGN (ATD) presents different interventions in alternation, and compares their effect on the dependent variable. The ATD (Barlow & Hayes, 1979) has also been referred to as multiple schedule design, alternating condition design, multi element baseline design, and simultaneous treatment design.

The most widely used definitions of ATD involve rapidly alternating two or more treatments or conditions, with the same person – within or between observational sessions (Barlow & Hersen, 1984). Most studies reported in the literature as a simultaneous treatment design have employed the same above definition of ATD. Figure 14.24.5 describes the prototype of the ATD.

Only one study (Browning, 1967) implemented a pure simultaneous presentation of treatments. It involves the concurrent presence of two or more treatments available at the same time for the participant's choice. The participant selects the most appropriate intervention at each given session. Therefore, this variation is actually measuring treatment preference rather than its effectiveness.

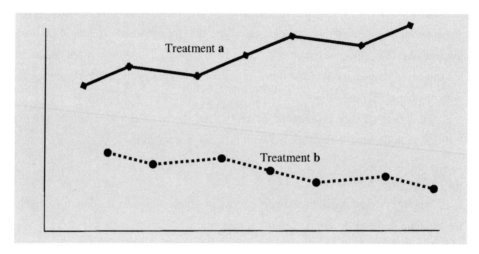

Figure 4.39 A Hypothetical Alternating Treatment Design, (comparing two different independent variables (A, B), with no baseline).

Implementation

Baseline data provide the researcher with clear and accurate "pictures" of the participant's ability. Target interventions are selected and scheduled for presentation prior to initiation of the study. The essence of this design is the "across time counterbalancing". This means that the different interventions are presented one after the other, with random variations in their order. For example, if two interventions (B & C) are involved, the ATD notation may look like this: A-B-C-C-B-C-B-B-C-B--. Interventions are alternated rapidly, on the same day or at every session.

Data for each independent variable are plotted on the same graph, creating clear and different data trends, one for each intervention. Data points for each intervention are represented by different symbols or colors. The connection of data points forms a clear and distinguishable curve for each variable. Unlike other single subject designs, the ATD does not require stability in data in order to introduce a new condition, because all trends are plotted concurrently.

All interventions are presented an equal number of times until a specific intervention demonstrates a clear superiority over the others. The final phase of the design continues the favorite intervention, terminating with therapeutic data.

Experimental Control

Graphs are analyzed for vertical differences between data trends for each intervention. Experimental control is concluded only if data trends are separated from one another. The larger the gap between the data trends, the more powerful is the experimental control. In case of an overlap between the data trends, no experimental control may be claimed. Data trends may be compared among themselves, with no need for baseline measures. However, comparing several interventions to a no-treatment condition may strengthen its credibility.

The rapid alternation of intervention controls for time and sequencing threats, is strengthening the ATD internal validity. External validity is achieved, as in all SSR designs, by replicating the intervention effect across participants, behaviors and settings.

Advantages

The ATD is an effective way to determine the relative advantage of a certain intervention over others. Although baseline data are recommended, interventions may be compared while skipping the baseline phase. This may be a significant advantage when an immediate intervention is required, or when collecting BASELINE DATA is intrusive or expensive.

Unlike the MTD, all interventions are presented in the same time frame, eliminating sequencing limitations associated with this design. The ATD is flexible and reactive, enabling the early detection, maintenance and follow-up of the more effective intervention.

Limitations

Due to the rapid alternations, a high level of proficiency is required for a reliable presentation of interventions. This highly technical expertise is essential because implementing the ATD is not natural to sport and educational contexts. It is uncommon to apply a few interventions, the same time, in order to attain the same goal.

The numerous alternations may interfere with the maintenance of behavior change in the presence of a certain intervention. The reason is the short exposure to each intervention, which is soon discontinued, to allow presentation of a different one. This problem is addressed in last phase of the ATD, maintaining the most effective treatment. However, relatively weak interventions may not "survive" the alternation period successfully.

Conclusions

This chapter introduced SSR designs that can be used in sport settings. WITHDRAWAL designs study causality by repeatedly producing the effect of the independent variable with the same athlete and on the same target behavior. MULTIPLE BASELINE and its variations evaluate the effect of an intervention by staggering its introduction into three or more baselines data series, across behaviors, participants, or settings. CHANGING CRITERION design evaluates experimental control by shifting the performance standards across time, in a step-by-step manner. COMPARATIVE DESIGNS measure the relative effectiveness of two or more interventions, by introducing them over the same time period.

The products of SSR are defined as "an increased ability to control the phenomenon of interest" (Johnston & Pennypacker, 1993, p. 13). SSR goes beyond the description of a process or the demonstration of correlation. Its main interest is showing functional relationships between measures of the dependent variables (e.g., athlete's motivation) and measures of the independent variable (e.g., motivation training intervention). This empirical/interventionist orientation allows the coach or the sport psychologist to assume accountability over the athlete's / team progress, ruling out the possibility that other extraneous variables were responsible for that change. Strategic and tactical decisions of athletes, coaches, and administrators, based on empirical findings should improve coaching and athletes' performance and add to the sport and exercise sciences accumulating knowledge.

SSR methodology is ideal for sport settings. Studying every athlete in individual sports is unique, requiring specific attention and a well-tailored methodology. Participants in team sports are also characterized by unique specialization. Studying each at a time, should enable the sport and exercise scientist and the professional to assess specific interventions and to recommend the suitable one.

The graphic presentation of the accumulated data may be used for an ongoing formative evaluation. It should be valuable for the coach and for the athlete to observe the data and to analyze performance accordingly, without waiting for the summative evaluation. This is powerful information, having a reactive power in itself.

Although still in its first steps, SSR is welcomed and published in quite a few journals. Let us hope that the use of this methodology in sport and exercise sciences will grow, adding to the body of knowledge in these fields, and to a high level of performance.

References

Baer, D. M. (1977). Reviewer's comment: Just because it's reliable doesn't mean that you use it. *Journal of Applied Behavior Analysis, 10*, 117-119.

Baer, D.M., Wolf, M.M., and Risley, T. R. (1968). Current dimensions of applied behavior analysis. *Journal of Applied Behavior Analysis, 1*, 91-97.

Barlow, D.H., and Hersen, M. (1984). *Single Case Experimental Designs: Strategies for Studying Behavior Change* (2nd ed.). New York: Pergamon Press.

Barlow, D.H., and Hayes, S. C. (1979) Alternating treatments design: One strategy for comparing the effects of two treatments in a single subject. *Journal of Applied Behavior Analysis, 12*, 199-210.

Browning, R. M. (1967). A same – subject design for simultaneous comparison of three reinforcement contingencies. *Behavior Research and Therapy, 5*, 237-243.

Cooper, J.O., Heron, T. E., and Heward, W. L. (1987*). Applied Behavior Analysis*. Columbus, OH: Merill Publishing Company.

Cuvo, A. J. (1979). Multiple-baseline design in instructional research: Pitfalls of measurement and procedural advantages. *American Journal of Mental Deficiency, 84*, 219-228.

Hartmann, D. P., and Hall, R. V. (1976). The changing criterion design. *Journal of Applied Behavior Analysis, 9*, 527-532.

Hersen, M. H., and Barlow, D.H. (1976). *Single Case Experimental Designs: Strategies for Studying Behavior Change*. New York: Pergamon Press.

Heward, W. L. (1978). *The Delayed Multiple Baseline Design*. Paper presented at the Fourth Annual Convention of the Association for Behavior Analysis, Chicasgo.

Horner, R. D., and Baer, D.M. (1978). Multiple-probe technique: A variation on the multiple baseline design. *Journal of Applied Behavior Analysis, 11*, 189-196.

Johnston, J. M., and Pennypacker, H. S. (1993). *Strategies and Tactics of Human Behavioral Research*, Hillsdale, NJ: Lawrence Erlbaum Associates.

Kazdin, A. E. (1982). Single – Case Research Designs. New York: Oxford University Press.

Kratochwill, T. R. (Ed).(1978). *Single Subject Research – Strategies for Evaluating Change*. New York: Academic Press.

Michael, J. (1974). Stratistical inference for individual organism research: Mixed blessing or curse? Journal of *Applied Behavior Analysis, 7*, 647-653.

Parsonson, B. S., and Baer, D. M.(1978) The analysis and presentation of graphic data. In T.R. Kratochwill (Ed.) *Single Subject Research-Strategies for Evaluating Change*. New-York: Academic Press.

Repp, A. C. (1983). *Teaching the Mentally Retarded.* Englewood Cliffs, N. J.: Prentice-Hall, Inc.

Risley, T.R., and Hart, B.M. (1968). Developing correspondence between the non-verbal and verbal behavior of preschool children. *Journal of Applied Behavior Analysis, 1*, 267-281.

Sidman, M. (1960). *Tactics of Scientific Research*. New York: Basic Books.

Skinner, B. F. (1938). *The Behavior of Organisms: An Experimental analysis*. New York: Appleton-Century.

Skinner, B. F. (1953). *Science and Human Behavior*. New York: Macmillan.

Skinner, B. F. (1956). A Case history in scientific method. *American Psychologist*, 11, 221-223

Skinner, B. F. (1969). *Contingencies of Reinforcement: A Theoretical Analysis*. New York: Appleton-Century-Crofts.

Watson, P. J., and Workman, E. A. (1981). The non-concurrent multiple baseline across-individuals design: An extension of the traditional multiple baseline design. *Journal of Behavior Therapy and Experimental Psychiatry, 12,* 257-259.

CHAPTER V: AN INTRODUCTION TO QUALITATIVE RESEARCH

What is qualitative research? After working through chapters devoted to statistical techniques and experimental research methods, you may be tempted to answer, "Research that doesn't involve statistics!" And you would be partly correct. Qualitative research involves the collection of primarily non-numerical data, such as rich descriptions of the research setting or interview transcripts with key participants. But a more important distinction is that qualitative research is *systematic empirical inquiry into meaning* (Shank, 1994). What does this mean exactly and how does it differ from the rest of this book? Qualitative is similar to quantitative research in that it is systematic and empirical. That is, both types of inquiry are carefully planned, executed in an orderly fashion, and open to audit by the scholarly community. Similarly, both depend on the world of experience and the collection of data to answer questions of interest. Qualitative and quantitative research differ, then, in their PURPOSE and FOCUS.

In quantitative inquiry, researchers attempt to understand phenomena by REDUCING their COMPLEXITY into COMPOSITE PARTS and testing predictions about how these parts work. In qualitative inquiry, however, the primary focus is on examination and INQUIRY into MEANING (Shank, 2002). An example may help to illuminate this distinction. One of the variables that has come under investigation as having a possible impact on the sport performance of female athletes is their menstrual cycle. Many studies have been conducted seeking to demonstrate a link between the athlete's performance as measured by indicators such as speed and endurance and where she happens to be in her menstrual cycle. Quantitative methods are appropriate for addressing questions about this possible relation between sport performance and menstruation, but these methods beg the question of what it means to a female athlete to be on her period during competition. Is she distracted by the fear of soiling her white uniform or worried that she may have to run to the bathroom in the middle of a quarter? Is she worried that the judges will see her as "fat" because she's retaining water and feeling bloated? These are questions of meaning that are best addressed through qualitative research.

The purpose of this chapter is to introduce concepts of qualitative research—how it is planned, conducted, and interpreted. The chapter begins with a brief discussion of how to CONCEPTUALIZE and ASK QUESTIONS of a qualitative nature. Then the discussion turns to the three primary means of qualitative data collection—OBSERVATION, INTERVIEWING, and EXAMINING DOCUMENTS. These are put into context of TYPES of QUALITATIVE RESEARCH DESIGNS and the research traditions from which they have sprung. It is important to realize that there are many different forms and traditions of qualitative inquiry. It is a field in its own right, and to become a skilled qualitative researcher requires far more training and experience than can be accomplished with this book alone. Finally, the chapter introduces techniques for DEALING WITH QUALITATIVE DATA and assuring that the research findings of a qualitative study meet scientific standards.

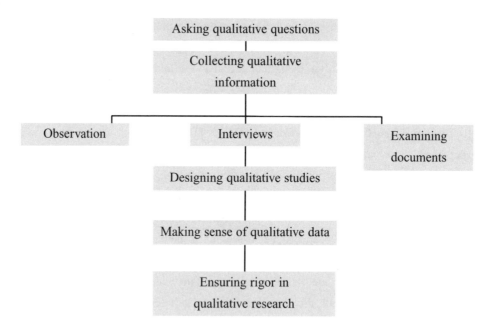

The chapter is structured as follows:

Contents

5.1   ASKING QUALITATIVE QUESTIONS

Because qualitative research is inquiry into meaning, the kinds of questions investigated in qualitative studies tend to focus on what things mean. Although many research questions lend themselves to numerical answers, which has been amply demonstrated in this book so far, questions of meaning typically do not. Patton (2002) considers the choice of qualitative or quantitative methods in research a pragmatic one depending on what you really want to know.

> If you want to know how much people weigh, use a scale. If you want to know if they're obese, measure body fat in relation to height and weight and compare the results to population norms. If you want to know what their weight *means* to them, how it affects them, how they think about it, and what they do about it, you need to ask them questions, find out about their experiences, and hear their stories. (Patton, 2002) (p. 13, emphasis his)

As Patton illustrates, what qualitative researchers usually want to know is something about meaning. Shank (2002, p. 99) puts it this way:

> The prototypical qualitative research question is: What does it mean to be X? Variants include: What does X mean? What does it mean for X to be present? For X to be absent? What do we currently understand X to mean, and in what ways is that current understanding incomplete? What way of understanding X, if brought to light and explored in detail, would change the way we look at or use X in our ordinary lives?

Applying Shank's prototypical question to some aspect of sport or exercise suggests a number of useful and interesting questions that could be the focus of qualitative research. For instance:

1)   What does it mean to be obese?

2)   What does anorexia mean (for the athlete, her family, her team, her coach, society in general)?

3)   What does it mean for female athletes to be on their periods during competition?

4)   What does it mean for female athletes to be amenorrheac (not having periods)?

5) What do we currently understand burnout among coaches to mean, and in what ways is this current understanding incomplete?

6) What way of understanding sexual harassment in the sport context, if brought to light and explored in detail, would change the way we view sexual harassment in any context?

In addition to focusing on meaning, qualitative research questions run the gamut from EXPLORATORY to EXPLANATORY. In some cases, researchers have no clear sense as to what is going in. Prior research results may be contradictory or unclear, or researchers haven't thought to ask about a particular phenomenon before. The impact of menstruation on sport performance may be an example. Some female athletes perform better during their menstrual periods, whereas others perform worse, but even those athletes are not consistent in their performance from one period to the next (Johnson, 2003). Why is this the case? What do these findings mean? An EXPLORATORY study could investigate in depth the experiences of female athletes during their menstrual cycles, thus enhancing our understanding of this phenomenon.

By contrast, the purpose of an EXPLANATORY study is to investigate the possible reasons, or hypothesized causes, for a phenomenon. Burnout among coaches has been studied extensively enough to suggest reasonable explanations for why some coaches appear to be less subject to burnout than others. In-depth studies of these coaches may reveal insights about their coping mechanisms that would enhance understanding of burnout and lead to possible interventions that would help others to cope effectively.

Like research questions that call for quantitative and experimental methods, qualitative research questions determine the research design and the kinds of data to be collected. It is a misconception to think that qualitative researchers go into the field without knowing what they will do when they get there. A good qualitative researcher has a RESEARCH STRATEGY, or general plan, for what actions are required to adequately answer the question of interest. An important difference between qualitative and quantitative researchers, however, is in their ability to make TACTICAL changes during the research process. Qualitative researchers must be skillful at responding to unanticipated circumstances that can quickly change the direction of the research. This will become evident as we discuss the kinds of information typically collected in a qualitative investigation.

5.2 COLLECTING QUALITATIVE INFORMATION

Qualitative information comes from three basic forms of data collection: OBSERVING, INTERVIEWING, and EXAMINING DOCUMENTS. Entire volumes have been written about each one, addressing techniques as well as issues of definition. We attempt here to provide a basic introduction and examples of how such data might be collected in sport and exercise psychology research.

(1) Observation

"Observation is both the most basic and the single trickiest skill for qualitative researchers to master" (Shank, 2002) (p. 19). Consider why this might be so. The most basic acts of living from day to day require us to pay attention to the things around us. For the most part, however, our observation of our surroundings is rather routine. On the drive to work, for instance, we note automatically whether the light at the corner is turning yellow, thus signaling the impending requirement to stop. In qualitative research observation must be deliberate and sustained. It is not automatic and, as a consequence, it is difficult and taxing to do.

Conducting observation takes place most often as part of what qualitative researchers call fieldwork. That is, they spend time in a field setting where they can observe the phenomenon of interest naturalistically. The point of observation is to render a description of what is going on in that setting without unduly influencing what is being studied. This raises the first set of issues that a qualitative researcher must resolve when conducting observation: 1) what should be the focus of the observation, 2) what is the role of the researcher during fieldwork, and 3) how much time should the researcher devote to observation?

1.1   *Focus of Observation*

A common model of observation is reminiscent of the strategy taken by journalists to establish the context for a story (i.e., *who, what, when, where,* etc.). The grand tour OBSERVATION STRATEGY (Spradley, 1980) addresses issues of:

1)	*Space*: what does the setting look like?
2)	*Actors*: who are the people involved?
3)	*Activity*: what are the people doing?
4)	*Object*: what are the physical "props" in the setting?
5)	*Acts*: what are the specific things people are doing in the setting?
6)	*Event*: What related activities make up events?
7)	*Time*: What sequences of acts or events can be observed?
8)	*Goal*: What are the participants trying to accomplish?
9)	*Feelings*: What sorts of emotions are being expressed?

(cited in Shank, 2002, pp. 29-30)

Even with these categories, however, it is often hard to decide how much or how little detail to record or what aspects of the observation deserve the greatest emphasis. Shank (2002) suggests that the beginning researchers first become aware of their own "observational styles." People tend naturally to pay more attention to some aspects of their surroundings than others. He characterized eight OBSERVER TYPES that describe extremes in the approaches that researchers take to observation (see Table 5.1).

The observational style (or styles) with which you feel most comfortable is likely to represent your strength; the others with which you are less comfortable could signify observational skills that you might want to work on.

Table 5.1

Types of Observers in Qualitative Research   Adapted from Shank (2002)

Observer Type	Characteristics	Positive Side	Negative Side
The Embracer	Attempts to take in all details.	Creates rich and textured report that allows reader to "re-experience" the account.	Cannot make decisions as to what to exclude in the account.
The Photographer	Overwhelmingly visual; "observation *is* looking."	Produces a careful visual record.	Tends to miss crucial information coming in other sensory modes.
The Tape Recorder	Drawn to sound and sound patterns, especially speech	Keenly aware of nuances in verbal communication	Tends to miss nonverbal communication, such as mannerisms and facial expressions of the speaker
The Categorizer	Creates and assigns observations to categories as an ongoing process	Categorizing is a useful organizational strategy.	Categorizing can sway observing, rather than the other way around.
The Baseliner	Organizes experiences along a time dimension.	Sensitive to the role of time in the observational process.	May make too much of time in linking events.
The Abstracter	Tries to be as objective as possible.	Likely to see complex, higher order patterns in observational data.	May discard critical information when it's not easily translated into objective accounts.
The Interacter	Observation focuses on people as the object of study.	Reveals important aspects of culture.	Can mss important cues about the setting.
The Reflecter	Sees observation in part as an exercise in self-discovery.	One of the most humane of all observers.	Such a stance can be prone to narcissism, self-absorption instead of self-discovery.

The observer styles shown in Table 5.1 also show the necessity of both a convergent and divergent observational focus. A CONVERGENT FOCUS occurs when various observations seem to CONVERGE on a CENTRAL EVENT MEANING. This happens when the events unfolding before you capture your attention so completely that you fail to notice other things going on at the same time. Sometimes, however, it is important for qualitative researchers to adopt a DIVERGENT OBSERVATIONAL FOCUS so as not to miss apparently PERIPHERAL EVENTS that may in fact be critical to understanding the overall phenomenon. A good example of this occurred in a research study conducted by the second author (Driscoll). She and a group of colleagues were interested in the role of textbooks in the learning process. Their grounding assumption was that certain things must happen during a lesson for students to learn most effectively, and these events can be supplied by the teacher, by the textbook (or other materials), or by the students themselves.

Driscoll et al. conducted a pilot study where they developed an observational protocol surrounding these instructional events, so as to record what they looked like when they occurred in the lesson and how the textbook was involved. For example, the teacher *gained attention* by inflections in her voice, while the textbook achieved this event with diagrams and colored text. Unfortunately, this convergent focus caused the observers to miss many ways in which the teacher and students used the textbook that did not conform to the protocol. Students frequently looked things up in the textbook, using it more as a reference source such as a dictionary than a text. To consider observations like this, Driscoll and her research team had to broaden their focus and view the situation more divergently (Driscoll et al., 1994). To do this, they discarded the observation protocol in favor of taking descriptive notes, and they shifted the focus of observation to the textbook, using the instructional events from the protocol as part of an analytic framework during data analysis.

1.2   *Researcher Role in Observation*

A fundamental difference among observational research strategies in qualitative research concerns the extent to which the researcher is a participant in the setting or is purely an observer. As shown in Figure 5.1, there exists a continuum of participation in the researcher's role from complete observation to complete participation.

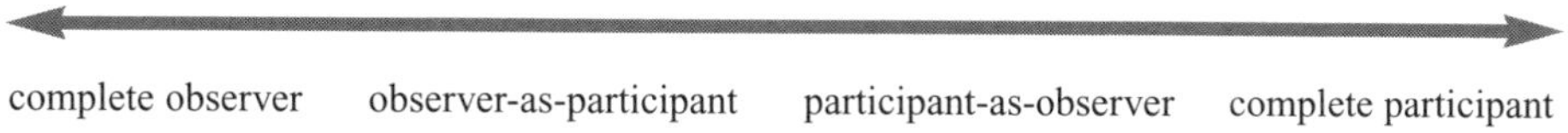

$$\longleftrightarrow$$

complete observer   observer-as-participant   participant-as-observer   complete participant

Figure 5.1   A continuum of observation and participation in qualitative research.

When the researcher is a COMPLETE OBSERVER, he or she adopts an 'ETIC' or outsider perspective. This was true in Dricoll's textbook study, for instance. She and her colleagues observed in a seventh grade science class, where they were clearly outsiders who did not participate in any of the activities that took place in the classroom. In qualitative studies like this, the researcher is not a member of the population under investigation and may have no prior experience with the setting where the study is taking place. An advantage of the researcher-as-complete-observer is the ability to stand apart from what is being studied and make comparisons to other settings. To develop a broad theory about textbook roles, for example, it would be desirable to observe the use of texts in different subject areas, different grade levels, and even different types of schools, such as urban versus rural. The interpretive framework applied to understanding observations when the researcher is a complete observer is imposed by the researcher and stems from his or her interests and values.

By contrast, the researcher who assumes a role of COMPLETE PARTICIPANT is an insider immersed in the field setting and participating fully in the events that are being studied. The research is conducted from an 'EMIC' perspective, which means that the interpretive framework is driven by the interests and values of the participants, of which the researcher is one. As an example, consider a researcher who is interested in the relation of loosely organized groups such as running clubs to the exerciser's persistence in following an exercise regimen. The researcher is a member of such a club and wants to understand how club activities, interactions among club members, and so on might influence how exercisers set goals and carry out exercise programs. An advantage of the researcher-as-complete-participant is the ability to see and understand things from the perspective of the other participants.

Roles in between complete observation and complete participation include OBSERVER-AS-PARTICIPANT and PARTICIPANT-AS-OBSERVER. In many situations, researchers enter a setting as complete observers but gradually become partial participants as the fieldwork progresses. For instance, a researcher may be interested in some aspect of coaching and studies the interactions among a particular coach and her players. In time, the researcher may become a confidante to the girls and take on tasks characteristic of an assistant coach, thus becoming a participant in the setting. However, there is always an expectation that the researcher's time is limited and time-bounded, and so participation is also limited. On the other hand, suppose a researcher is interested in a topic such as the effect of parental involvement in sport by virtue of the fact of having a student-athlete in the family. The researcher enrolls in a special program for parents of athletes to experience it firsthand but gradually withdraws participation and becomes more of an onlooker over time. In both these cases, the researcher attempts to develop an insider's view of the phenomenon of interest but remains aware of being an outsider.

Researcher roles that include some amount of participation can also be collaborative in nature. It may be, for instance, that a coach as well as the researcher is interested in the research question because the coach views the study as a means of improving his or her own practices. When this occurs, the researcher may become a facilitator, collaborator, and teacher in supporting the coach and helping the coach learn from the research findings. Participatory research has a long history and is common in feminist and other critical approaches to inquiry.

1.3   *Duration of Observations*

How much time is important to spend in the field conducting observations? In the anthropological tradition of field research, investigators spend months and sometimes years in the field, living in the culture under observation. Some research in the sport and exercise realm might demand this level of involvement, such as a study examining pre-Olympic training where a sport psychologist is working with a team and the researcher is interested in the effect of a particular intervention on the team's performance. In other cases, observation might be limited to a much shorter time-frame, such as a single competition or a single segment of an educational program. A common guideline for determining how long to observe in a particular setting is SATURATION.

Saturation occurs when the DATA you are collecting STARTS REPEATING itself and you are not learning anything new. You will feel this happening when you begin to anticipate and predict what is going to happen next. Similarly, if you find yourself easily able to categorize everything you are seeing because nothing is unique any longer, than you have probably reached the point of saturation (Shank, 2002).

Patton (2002) says this about how long to observe a program to conduct a good evaluation:

> *My response to students . . . follows the line of thought developed by Abraham Lincoln during of the Douglas-Lincoln debates. In an obvious reference to the difference in stature between Douglas and Lincoln, a heckler asked, "Tell us, Mr. Lincoln, how long do you think a man's legs ought to be?"*
>
> Lincoln replied, *"Long enough to reach the ground."*
>
> Fieldwork should last long enough to get the job done—to answer the research questions being asked and fulfill the purpose of the study.
>
> (p. 275)

Finally, before we leave observation, it is important to consider practical issues such as note-taking, videotaping, and how to minimize the obtrusiveness of observation.

1.4 *Practical Issues of Observation*

One way or another, researchers must keep careful records of their observations. This can be done by means of checklists, time-sampling techniques, taking extensive field notes to describe what is going on in the setting, and videotaping the action.

CHECKLISTS and TIME-SAMPLING reflect an a priori, quantitative orientation because they result in numerical data. That is, the researcher defines in advance exactly what will be observed and that it is the occurrence of an action or event that will be noted. With checklists, the event or action is recorded as having happened and it does not matter whether it occurs more than once during the observation period. In time-sampling, the researcher records the instance of an event or action within each sampled time period. Time periods are generally kept quite short (e.g., a few minutes) and repeated several times during the observation period. The results of both techniques are analyzed for relative frequencies so that the researcher can determine the incidence of various actions or events.

FIELD NOTES, on the other hand, are a means for the researcher to record in extensive detail what he or she observes in the setting under investigation. Researchers develop a personal style for taking field notes, but whatever model they follow they must be sure to distinguish observations from interpretations or opinions. For example, suppose as the researcher you observe an interaction between a coach and a referee in which the coach gets red in the face, raises his voice, and comes face-to-face with the referee. These are all signs that the coach is angry, but you cannot know for sure that is the case because you cannot observe directly what the coach is thinking or feeling. Thus, making a note that "the coach is angry at the referee" would be an interpretation, not an observation. It would be more accurate to note as an observation that "the coach's face is red, he has raised his voice, and he has walked to stand nose-to-nose with the referee." Alongside or below this observation, you could then supply a possible interpretation of these events, such as "the coach appears to be angry with the referee," or, phrased as a question, "is the coach angry? Check with coach later to verify." Figure 5.2 displays two styles for recording field notes in a way that makes it clear what notes are observations and which ones are impressions, or hypotheses about what may be going on.

Sample A

Observations:	Personal Notes:
2:15 p.m. Arrived at practice. Was a little bit late and coach has already started practice matches. There are two mats and coach is standing off to one side where he can see both. Jimi is wrestling Rodney, and Hank is wrestling Marcus. 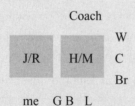	Why has coach matched up Rodney with Jimi? They look like different weight classes to me. Ask coach.
The rest of the team is watching one mat or the other and making comments to each other, although Lenny is standing by himself.	I wonder if something is up with Lenny.

Sample B

2:15 p.m. Arrived at practice. Was a little bit late and coach has already started practice matches. There are two mats and coach is standing off to one side where he can see both. Jimi is wrestling Rodney, and Hank is wrestling Marcus.

Coach

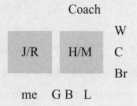

W

J/R   H/M   C

Br

me   G B L

Why has coach matched up Rodney with Jimi? They look like different weight classes to me. Ask coach.

The rest of the team is watching one mat or the other and making comments to each other, although Lenny is standing by himself.

I wonder if something is up with Lenny.

Figure 5.2   Two different styles of recording field notes to distinguish observations from personal impressions.

It is useful in taking field notes to record details about the setting and circumstances, as well as the relative placement of things and people within the setting (see Figure 5.2). It is a common mistake to take the physical setting for granted—e.g., "the match took place at the school"—when schools vary considerably in their physical features, which can have an enormous impact on the activities that take place within them.

Sometimes it is worthwhile to consider videotaping observations. The primary advantage is that the VIDEOTAPE provides a COMPLETE and EXACT RECORD of events that can be viewed repeatedly after the fact. This allows the researcher to go back and analyze nuances that may have been missed during the live action. Videotapes also enable the researcher to examine relations among observations that would be difficult to accomplish otherwise. For instance, a researcher may be interested in understanding the stresses that affect a coach during competition. By monitoring and recording a coach's blood pressure throughout the competition and then matching it up to a videotape of the competition itself, the researcher can begin to see what events in the match appear to precipitate an increase in blood pressure, or stress. Tentative explanations can be corroborated further by asking the coach to view the videotape and reflect on his or her feelings of stress at various points in the match.

Videotaping observations is not without its hazards, however. There is always a danger of equipment failure, so that it pays to have backup equipment such as spare tapes and batteries. Such equipment can also be expensive to purchase or difficult to obtain. Depending on the complexity of the events being observed, it can be difficult to determine where to focus the camera, and whether it should remain at a fixed vantage point or be moved periodically. Finally, video cameras may not record sounds that are relatively far away, or they may record so much background noise that conversation is difficult to follow.

In addition to the potential for technical problems, videotaping can be overly obtrusive to the people being observed, and it will most certainly result in an overwhelming amount of footage to be analyzed. Strategies for analyzing data of this sort are discussed later in the chapter, but the question of the obtrusiveness of observation is an important one to consider. Regardless of how sensitive the researcher is, observation can make people self-conscious and anxious and cause them to behave differently than they would if the researcher were not present. Qualitative researchers must be aware of this possibility and take steps to minimize the obtrusiveness of their observations. Incorporating an acclimation period can help those being observed to become used to the observer's presence before the formal period of observation begins. In addition, the researcher can look for opportunities to collect UNOBTRUSIVE OBSERVATIONS. "Unobtrusive measures are those made without the knowledge of the people being observed and without affecting what is observed" (Patton, 2002, p. 292).

For example, Patton (2002) described "learning logs" as an unobtrusive indicator of a particular program's impact on participants' self-reflection. Participants were given 3-ring-binder logs to record their private reflections, and they brought the logs with them each time they came to a session of the program being examined. The number of pages participants added to their logs was an indicator of the extent to which the logs were being used. So what might constitute unobtrusive observation in the sport and exercise context? The teeth marks on the pencil behind the coach's ear or the number of cups of coffee consumed during practice might be an unobtrusive measure of stress, and the amount of dust or wear shown by gym equipment can be an unobtrusive indicator of its use by exercisers.

(2)   Interviews

It is almost impossible to do good qualitative research without learning how to interview someone.

(Shank, 2002, p. 34).

Observations take the qualitative researcher only so far. We cannot observe everything, and we cannot be sure how people organize the world and attach meaning to things unless we ask them. The purpose of INTERVIEWS, then, is to GAIN INFORMATION from the OTHER PERSON'S PERSPECTIVE, to gather their stories (Patton, 2002). Interviews range from informal and conversational to completely structured and standardized, depending on the focus of the research. We present three types of individual interviews, consider a special type of individual interview plus a type of group interview, and then discuss issues related to practical aspects of interviewing, such as ways to record the data and enhance the interview process. In addition, Chapter 6 includes an extensive section on developing the context and skills for conducting in-depth interviews.

2.1   *The Unstructured Interview*

The most open-ended approach to conducting interviews is the UNSTRUCTURED INTERVIEW (Fontana & Frey, 2000). In this type of interview, there is no predetermined set of questions. Rather, the questions emerge from the field setting, often in the context of conversation between the researcher and those being observed in that setting. The researcher seeks elaboration on or the informant's perceptions about something that was observed. Each interview builds on observations and other interviews that have been conducted previously to expand understanding of the phenomenon under investigation. Consider the examples given earlier about the researcher as participant observer. In the first instance, the researcher who gradually assumes a role similar to an assistant coach will have many informal opportunities to interview both the head coach and the players to learn their perceptions about the aspects of coaching that interest the researcher. Likewise, the researcher who enrolls in the program for parents of athletes may interview other parents as well as the program's leaders in the course of participating in the program. In both cases, the questions asked will be opportunistic based on what is happening at the point of the interview and what the researchers have already learned to that point.

The unstructured interview is the most difficult kind of interview to conduct because it is guided by the interviewee, and the researcher must "go with the flow." The danger in this approach is that the interview may become unfocused and too conversational, so that the researcher fails to gather information pertinent to the research question. Another weakness is the amount of time it may take to gather useful information. The researcher may have to interview the same person several times to make sure that all relevant questions have been answered, or the researcher may have to pose the same question to a variety of different people to grasp the entire picture of what's going on. A third weakness revolves around the time between the interview and the documentation of that interview. Frequently, a significant period of time has elapsed, and the researcher must rely heavily on memory and recall skills. Careful attention should be paid to differentiating between recall and interpretation of the interview.

On the positive side, the flexibility and spontaneity of unstructured interviews allow the researcher to adapt readily to individual differences of the people being interviewed. An advantage of being guided by the interviewee is that this person likely knows more about the topic of interest than the researcher, so as Shank (2002, p. 46) put it, "Why not let that person guide the process then?" Finally, the researcher most likely to use the unstructured interview is engaged and participating in the field setting, and as a consequence of this engagement, is developing a certain amount of rapport with the participants. With rapport come empathy and trust, which may make it easier for people to open up to the researcher and answer questions honestly. It is important to recognize, however, that this also puts a responsibility on the researcher to honor that trust and treat information gained from informants with respect and confidentiality.

2.2   *The Semi-structured Interview*

The SEMI-STRUCTURED INTERVIEW is much easier to conduct than the unstructured interview, making it a better tool for novice researchers. This type of interview consists of a set of QUESTIONS or ISSUES to be EXPLORED with EACH PERSON who is interviewed. The researcher develops an interview guide that contains the topics or subject areas to be explored and elaborated, but then he or she is free to probe a particular area and phrase questions spontaneously. The interview guide serves as a kind of checklist to make sure that all areas of interest either come up naturally in the course of the interview or are specifically raised by the researcher.

As an example, consider a study examining what it means to female athletes when they menstruate during competition. To answer this question requires interviewing them about their experiences, their own feelings about their experiences, and perhaps their perceptions about how others may view them during this time. In semi-structured interviews, the researcher could ask female athletes about these three topics, using an interview guide such as the one shown below.

Interview Guide

Athlete's experience of menstruation during competition
- kind of competition
- circumstances surrounding the event

Athlete's reactions to her experience
- what she thought about this experience
- how she felt about the experience
- what actions she took during the experience
- perceptions about the causes of her reactions (i.e., why she felt and responded the way she did)

Athlete's perceptions of others' reactions
- coach's reactions
- teammates' reactions
- reactions of family

In probing these areas, the researcher could begin by asking the interviewee to describe a particular example where she started her period either immediately before or during competition. This would provide a concrete focal point for exploring the other topics. Although all of the athletes interviewed would eventually speak to all of the issues, they would do so in an individualized manner, depending on their experiences and what in those experiences was most salient to them to report. The guide therefore provides a framework for the semi-structured interview, but it does not constrain it.

An interview guide for semi-structured interviews can be developed in more or less detail. More detail leads to a more systematic and comprehensive collection of data across many different individuals to be interviewed. It can also assure that different interviewers all collect the same data. However, the more detailed and structured the guide becomes, the greater the risk of asking leading questions (Shank, 2002). For instance, asking a question like, "Do you think that being on your period made it more difficult for you to perform well?" presupposes the belief in a link between performance and menstruation. Instead, it is better to ask questions in a more open-ended way, such as "What did you think about when your period started the day before the meet?" You may be surprised at the answer if it isn't consistent with your expectations, but it is more likely to be an honest explanation than if the interviewee were led to telling you what you want to hear.

2.3 The Structured Interview

In a fully STRUCTURED, STANDARDIZED INTERVIEW, the researcher asks the SAME QUESTIONS in the same way in the same order to ALL INTERVIEWEES. The probes are also scripted so as to assure the greatest consistency possible across interviewers and people interviewed. This approach is useful when there are multiple researchers or multiple sites at which the research is being conducted. It can also compensate for a lack of interviewing skills or provide for a highly focused interview when time is a premium for the people being interviewed. Finally, a structured, standardized interview facilitates analysis because responses are easy to find and compare across individual interviews.

An example of a protocol for a structured interview can be found in the appendix. It was developed by Jean Cote to investigate the quantity and type of sport-specific and other practice activities engaged in by elite athletes and how these activities contribute to the development of expert decision-making (Baker et al., 2003). In this research, athletes are interviewed individually for 2-3 hours each. As can be seen by the nature of the questions, many of the answers are easily quantifiable and thus subject to statistical analysis. Because of this characteristic, some qualitative researchers see very little difference between structured interviews and surveys. As Shank (2002, p. 46) commented,

> If I want to ask the same questions, the same way, at the same place in the process, then why wouldn't I use a survey instrument instead? Surveys have the advantage of being easily distributed to lots of people at the same time, and the people can take their time and think about their answers before they write them in. As long as I provide room on my survey for narrative comments, there does not seem to be any reason to do a strictly structured interview instead. In fact, a strictly structured interview is probably most useful as a pilot tool for writing an effective survey instrument.

2.4   *Think-Aloud Interview*

The THINK-ALOUD INTERVIEW is a special type of individual interview aimed at uncovering COGNITIVE PROCESSES that occur WHILE a person is PERFORMING a task (Ericsson & Simon, 1993). In this type of interview, the individual is asked to perform a task such as solving a problem and to "think aloud" while he or she is doing this. The interviewer's role is not to ask particular questions but rather to encourage the person to keep talking and to elaborate on or explain his or her thinking. For instance, suppose a researcher is interested in a coach's decision-making processes regarding game strategy. The coach could be provided with a game scenario and asked to think aloud while devising a strategy to respond to that scenario.

The think-aloud approach has been shown to reveal people's thoughts and feelings while they are performing a task. It provides more accurate and reliable data than asking people to report on their thinking after-the-fact when they would have had time to reflect on and interpret their thoughts and behavior. Retrospective reports typically include people's beliefs and interpretations, not just what they were thinking while in the act of performing. Because most people are not used to thinking aloud, it may take some time and training for them to become comfortable with this approach. Most researchers who use think-aloud interviews begin with a training exercise such as asking the interviewee to recall the 50 states of the U.S. and to talk aloud while doing it. Then a practice problem like the ones to be used for data collection can be provided to accustom the person to the experimental conditions. Finally, the think-aloud interview is audio-taped and analyzed for the cognitive processes it reveals.

2.5   *Focus Group Interview*

To this point, the types of interviews discussed have all pertained to talking with one person at a time. Interviewing a small group of 6—10 people about a specific topic is called a FOCUS GROUP INTERVIEW (Greenbaum, 1997, 2000; Morgan, 1988, 1998; Morgan & Kreuger, 1997). The focus group is useful when PEOPLE are more LIKELY to SHARE EXPERIENCES and arrive at greater AWARENESS of ISSUES by participating in a group. They can listen to what others have to say and perhaps expand or elaborate on their own answers as they consider their views in relation to others. For example, the researcher studying burnout among coaches might bring a small group of Division I coaches together to probe both their experiences of burnout and the ideas they may have for coping or preventive strategies for dealing with burnout.

It is important to remember that the focus group is an interview—not a problem-solving session, not a decision-making group, and not a discussion (Patton, 2002). Therefore, it must be carefully planned and moderated. Focus group interviews are most effective when:

- the group is large enough to provide a diversity of opinion but still small enough to allow everyone to speak and answer every question;
- a limited number of questions is used, and the interview lasts for no longer than 1-2 hours;
- people in the group have similar backgrounds but are strangers to each other; and
- the moderator manages the interview so that it is not dominated by one or two people and that those who are reticent have the opportunity to share their views.

When a focus group interview is conducted with a group of people who already know one another, the researcher must be particularly sensitive to group dynamics. Because participants have prior established relationships, they may respond in ways consistent with those relationships rather than express their true feelings or beliefs.

Focus group interviews can be complex and difficult to manage, so it is a good idea to conduct them in teams of two. One person asks the questions and moderates the interview, while the other takes detailed notes and deals with technical aspects such as tape-recording. If the interview is audio-taped, the researcher should have each person state his or first name or choose a pseudonym by which the person can be recognized. In audio- or video-taping, multidirectional microphones should be used and the equipment tested prior to the interview commencing.

2.6   *Practical Issues Surrounding Interviews*

We have already mentioned the issue of asking leading questions during interviews. The aim of most qualitative research is to minimize the chance of predetermined responses during data collection, which means that INTERVIEW QUESTIONS should be OPEN-ENDED for the most part.

Typical open-ended questions follow a format such as:
How do you feel about . . .?
What do you think about . . .?
What can you tell me about . . .?
What are your perceptions about . . .?

According to Patton (2002), there are six types of questions that qualitative researchers typically ask during interviews. These include

1)   EXPERIENCE and behavior questions—ask about what participants do and how they behave;

2)   OPINION and value questions—ask about participants' opinions and beliefs;

3)   FEELING questions—ask about participants' feelings and emotions;

4)   KNOWLEDGE questions—ask about participants' factual information, i.e., what they know;

5)   SENSORY questions—ask about participants' sensory experiences, such as what they have seen or heard; and

6)   BACKGROUND/demographic questions—ask about participants' characteristics and prior experience, such as age, education, years of experience, and so on (pp. 348-351).

In conducting interviews, qualitative researchers must decide HOW MANY QUESTIONS to ask, HOW LONG the interview should last, and HOW the data should be RECORDED during the interview. There are no hard and fast rules for determining these matters, and the answers depend on the nature of the research and how structured the interview is. For example, unstructured, conversational interviews are likely to take place in the field, making it difficult to tape-record them. By contrast, semi-structured and focus group interviews are likely to take place in a more formal setting, where a tape-recorder would be a relatively unobtrusive means of recording what is said. Likewise, interview times can vary considerably. A researcher may conduct many short, unstructured interviews with a single person or conduct only one, semi-structured interview of greater length with a number of individuals or a group. With experience, the qualitative researcher learns to "read" an interviewee and sense when the interview should be brought to a close. It is often useful to END an INTERVIEW with a question that gives the person the last word, such as "Is there anything you would like to add?" or "What should I have asked you that I didn't think about?"

Regardless of where the interview takes place or whether it is tape-recorded, the researcher should consider TAKING NOTES. In both instances, it is valuable to note body language or other environmental cues that will help during the analysis and interpretation of the interview. Furthermore, when an interview is not tape-recorded, notes are essential to record major points made by the person being interviewed, including direct quotes. As with field notes, the researcher must develop a convention for distinguishing between what the interviewee has actually said and the interpretations made by the researcher about what was said.

Immediately AFTER the INTERVIEW, the researcher should GO OVER his or her NOTES, elaborate on them, and check the tape-recording if one was made. This process enables the researcher to check the quality of the data, make sure that things make sense, and determine areas of ambiguity that might require further follow-up. This is also a period of reflection in which the researcher can think about what is being learned and alter procedures if things are not going in the desired direction.

Finally, it is important to touch briefly on ELECTRONIC INTERVIEWING (Fontana & Frey, 2000). Because of advances in technology, it is now possible to engage in "virtual interviewing," or collecting and archiving information solely through electronic means. This can be done synchronously or asynchronously and has the advantage of being fast, inexpensive (compared to telephone charges for interviews conducted over the phone), and able to target specialized audiences. The disadvantages of electronic interviewing include the inability to read nonverbal behavior or judge the possible impact of personal characteristics, such as age, race, or gender. In addition, it is easier to deceive and claim experiences that are difficult to verify, and this can be true of both the interviewer as well as the interviewee. Clearly, there are trade-offs. "Markheim (1998), in her autoethnography of Internet interviewing, reports that electronic interviews take longer than their traditional counterparts and that responses are more cryptic and less in depth, but the interviewer has more time to phrase follow-up questions or probes properly" (Fontana & Frey, 2000, p. 97).

(3) Examining Documents

Documents can provide a behind-the-scenes view of many aspects to a phenomenon that might not be revealed through observations and interviews (Hodder, 2000). Therefore, it is important for qualitative researchers to negotiate access to DOCUMENTS, RECORDS, and other ARTIFACTS that pertain to the inquiry at hand. Patton (2002) defines documents as including: "Written materials and other documents from organizational, clinical, or program records; memoranda and correspondence; official publications and reports; personal diaries, letters, artistic works, photographs, and memorabilia; and written responses to open-ended surveys. Data consist of excerpts from documents captured in a way that records and preserves context" (p. 4).

Sometimes, qualitative research may focus on documents almost to the exclusion of other forms of data. For instance, a student conducted a research project in Driscoll's qualitative analysis course that investigated the impact of immigration laws in a professional sport context. She was interested in understanding the role that the particular sport played in the disposition of cases, and so she examined the case files of athletes who sought immigration and used their professional sports expertise as the primary reason supporting immigration. The documents in the case files, therefore, served as the primary source of data for the research.

In other instances, documents can supplement information obtained from observations or interviews, often revealing discrepancies between "official" and actual aspects of a program or event. For example, Patton (2002) described a program evaluation he conducted in which he examined 10 years of annual reports and discovered that the mission of the organization had undergone a dramatic change over the years, a phenomenon that had gone unnoticed by program participants. Similarly, Driscoll was involved many years ago in a study of testing programs nationwide. Official documents frequently told one story about a testing program while program personnel told a different story during interviews. It is important to point out that this was not due to some sort of nefarious plot! Rather, it is common for programs to be implemented differently than planned. Furthermore, as personnel come and go, the oral history that gets passed from one person to the next changes slightly.

In the example cited earlier in this chapter concerning the special program for parents of athletes, the researcher might wish to examine documents such as materials given to the parents, program planning documents, or grant applications used to secure funding to support the program. Information gleaned from these sources would help the researcher to put into context things reported during interviews or observations and experiences of things in the program itself.

Finally, documents can reveal things that cannot be observed or which do not come out in interviews. Actions and events that took place before the research began are a good example; they may be recorded in the minutes of meetings and provide an historical picture that is useful for understanding the current state of affairs.

Working with documents as sources of qualitative data requires attention to two important details. First, the researcher must establish a SYSTEM for LABELING and FILING any documents that are collected as part of the research. The system chosen must preserve the integrity of each document, so that copies rather than the originals are used during data analysis. In this way, the researcher may always return to the original document for additional analyses. Second, the researcher must RESPECT the CONFIDENTIALITY of documents, particularly client or patient records. Some documents may be considered part of the public record and therefore able to be used and quoted without breach of confidentiality. This would include, for example, published reports or records legally designated as public. In other cases, steps may be taken to secure permission for the use of documents. For example, the subjects of photographs can be asked to sign a release allowing the photos to be used in a final report or published account of the study. But in some cases, documents may be considered private and not open to public scrutiny, and in these cases, the researcher must be particularly careful to engage proper safeguards to maintain the confidentiality of the information.

5.3 DESIGNING QUALITATIVE STUDIES

To summarize the main points of this chapter so far, qualitative research is inquiry into meaning and involves the collection of data primarily through observations, interviews, and examining documents. Qualitative research is often contrasted with quantitative or experimental inquiry as though both were uni-dimensional, leaving "the impression that there are only two methodological or paradigmatic alternatives" (Patton, 2002, p. 76). However, "when one looks more closely . . . the apparent unity of the qualitative approach vanishes, and one sees considerable diversity. What has been called 'qualitative research' conveys different meanings to different people" (Jacob, 1988, p. 16). The confusion this causes is easy to see in the struggle that many doctoral students experience attempting to label dissertation studies that are qualitative in nature.

Consider the research designs that have been discussed in other chapters of this book. It is relatively straightforward to identify studies that involve factorial, correlational, or single subject designs. However, qualitative inquiry stems from MANY different TRADITIONS of THOUGHT that reflect disciplinary roots in diverse fields such as anthropology, sociology, philosophy, psychology, linguistics, political science, and literary arts. This has yielded a proliferation of terminology and practices to describe the variations of qualitative approaches used in social sciences research, including education (see, for example, Schwandt, 1997). Patton (2002) quotes a letter he received from a graduate student that illustrates this well:

Dear Dr. Patton:

I desperately need your help. I am a graduate student in education, planning to do my dissertation observing classrooms and teachers identified as innovative and effective. . . . I took this idea to one professor, who asked me if I was proposing a phenomenological or grounded theory study. When I asked what the difference was, he said it was my job to find out. . . .Another professor told me that I could do a qualitative study, but that asking about "best practices" meant that I was a positivist not a phenomenologist...

(p. 77)

The confusion can become even greater when one considers the integration of qualitative and quantitative methods into a mixed method design. There are many examples of research in which qualitative information is gathered to elaborate or understand mediating variables in an experimental study. Likewise, it is common for qualitative researchers to collect quantitative information, or to quantify some of the data they collect, in what is otherwise a qualitative design.

The disciplinary base and philosophical orientation of various qualitative approaches certainly influence their application. But a comprehensive review of qualitative research traditions is beyond the scope of this chapter and, indeed, this book. The next chapter delves into some of the philosophical discussions that permeate qualitative inquiry and provides several specific examples of qualitative research in sport psychology that are developed in some detail. Therefore, in this chapter we discuss briefly several of the most common traditions in qualitative research that might be particularly useful for answering questions in the sport and exercise psychology arena. We adopt a pragmatic stance, i.e., that it is less important to force a choice of research design label when conducting qualitative inquiry than it is to find appropriate methods for answering the research question of interest.

(1)   Case Study

One of the most straightforward qualitative research designs is the case study. The CASE STUDY focuses on understanding the HOW and WHY of a PARTICULAR INDIVIDUAL, SITUATION, PROGRAM, or PHENOMENON (Merriam, 1998; Stake, 1995; Yin, 1994). It "turns us away from the typical to the unique" (Shank, 2002, p. 53). That is, the purpose of a case study is to examine and UNDERSTAND the

COMPLEXITIES of a SINGLE CASE, not to generalize from the case to a larger population. The value in a case study comes from the EXTENSIVE DESCRIPTION of the phenomenon under study that can facilitate discovery of new insights or extend the reader's experience.

Let's consider some hypothetical examples that build on examples already discussed in this chapter. First, the researcher interested in the special program for parents of athletes may conduct a case study of a particular program. The purpose of the study would be to understand that program in all its complexities, from how it was conceived and designed to the impacts it may be having on the parents and how the parents interact with their child-athlete. The study could examine how specific characteristics of this program relate to particular results or impacts. In this example, the CASE is defined as the PROGRAM. While there is no intent to generalize to the population of all such programs, what is learned from this case study will nonetheless provide insights that could be useful to other programs. The lessons learned in this situation may help planners make better decisions in another situation.

Alternatively, a researcher interested in the phenomenon of burnout may conduct case studies of individual coaches in the effort to develop a theory explaining burnout. The intent of each case study would be to understand an individual coach's experience. What were the unique antecedents to burnout for each person? How did he or she respond to or cope with the situation? What were the unique influences or contributors to this person's experience? Here, the CASE is defined as the INDIVIDUAL coach, and each case study contributes to the emerging picture of the overall phenomenon of burnout. In this instance, the researcher seeks to identify the salient variables that appear to affect the individual's experience. So, for example, perhaps male coaches respond differently than female coaches, or those with more years of coaching are affected differently than those with fewer years under their belt. In the ideal world, the researcher keeps adding cases until all relevant variables have been identified and investigated.

Again, there is no generalization from case to population, but there is an attempt to generalize from case to theory. It is a subtle difference, but the logic goes something like this. Suppose gender is found to be relevant variable in the experience of burnout. The researcher would *not* conclude that the experience of a particular male or female in the case study is representative of all males or all females in the population of coaches. Rather, the researcher would conclude that male and female coaches generally experience burnout in ways that are different from each other.

Depending on how the case is defined in qualitative case study research, there is more or less emphasis on different forms of data collection. When a program or situation is defined as the case, it is likely that all three forms of data collection—observations, interviews, and examining documents—will be utilized. The researcher may participate extensively in the situation or program under study, or he or she may take the role of an outside observer. By contrast, when an individual is defined as the case, it is likely that interviewing will become the primary means of collecting data. As an example of the latter, Hart (2001) investigated the impact that "coming out" had on the commercial endorsements of lesbian athletes. She conducted extensive interviews with Martina Navratilova and Missy Giove to understand their experiences and relate them to the nature and extent of the commercial endorsements they received. Although interviewing was the primary data collection method in this study, Hart also collected documents such as news releases and advertisements that yielded evidence of the athletes' commercial success and people's reactions to their sexual orientation (Hart, 2001).

(2)   Naturalistic Inquiry

Perhaps the most broadly defined qualitative research design is NATURALISTIC INQUIRY, which means simply to STUDY a PHENOMENON in its REAL-WORLD or NATURAL SETTING (Lincoln & Gruba, 1985). The researcher attempts to DISCERN PATTERNS that tell the story of WHAT IS GOING ON in that setting. In naturalistic inquiry, the researcher makes no attempt to manipulate what goes on in the study setting and puts no constraints on what the outcomes of the research might be. Rather, observation is non-participant in nature, with the researcher taking pains to be as unobtrusive as possible so as not to affect the natural course of events in the field setting. As such, naturalistic inquiry is sometimes referred to as a DISCOVERY-ORIENTED approach to investigation.

The study described earlier in the chapter on the role of textbooks in learning is an example of naturalistic inquiry. The researchers sought to understand what was going on in the classroom—the natural setting—with respect to the role the textbook played in teaching and learning—the phenomenon of interest. They did not attempt to manipulate anything in the study setting, and in fact, had to back away from an early interpretive framework because it was too constraining on the observational outcomes.

It is probably obvious that naturalistic inquiry and case study are not necessarily mutually exclusive. The textbook research was, in fact, both a case study and an example of naturalistic inquiry. The researchers defined the case as the particular eighth grade classroom that they observed, and had they decided to build a theory around the role of textbooks, they would have added cases that investigated variables such as grade level or subject matter. But as seen in the example of Hart's research on lesbian athletes, a case study need not be naturalistic inquiry. The phenomenon of interest in that research was the athletes' experience, not a natural event that could be observed.

In naturalistic inquiry, observation is the primary means of collecting data, although interviews are often used to bring meaning to events that have been observed in the field setting. For instance, participants can be asked why, in their perception, certain observed events occurred as they did. Likewise, documents may be examined to help the researcher derive a more accurate picture of what is going on.

(3)   Ethnography

ETHNOGRAPHY is the STUDY of CULTURE (LeCompte & Preissle, 1993). It comes out of anthropology and is one of the oldest forms of qualitative research. Ethnography is often equated with the term 'FIELDWORK' largely because it involves extensive observation and participation in the field setting. Techniques for conducting ethnography typically include participant observation and informal, conversational interviews (Schensul & LeCompte, 1999). Ethnography is like naturalistic inquiry in its emphasis on research conducted in the natural setting, but whereas naturalistic inquiry may focus on any aspect of the setting, ethnography focuses specifically on culture.

How might ethnography be applied in sport and exercise psychology? To answer this question, consider where the study of culture might provide important insights into sport phenomena. Many subcultures or micro-cultures exist in the world of sport. One might consider, for instance, that each sport—such as figure-skating, gymnastics, or volleyball—has its own culture. Likewise, a particular team, a certain program, even a sport location such as a exercise club can develop its own peculiar CULTURE, or the COLLECTION of BEHAVIOR PATTERNS and BELIEFS that constitute the norm for the people participating on that team, in that program, or belonging to that club. For the ethnographer, then, the intent is to understand how a particular culture operates, how it has evolved, and how it influences the people who participate within it.

Three issues in particular arise when conducting ethnographic studies. These revolve around entry, rapport, and informants. Gaining ENTRY has to do with ACCESS and getting permission to be in the field setting. This can be tricky to negotiate especially when the research question is of a sensitive nature. For example, suppose a researcher is interested in how the culture of professional, male-dominated sports such as football or basketball relates to players' treatment of women. Gaining entry to travel with a team that has players who have faced allegations of sexual assault would not be an easy matter. But it is important to have permission to legitimate one's presence in the setting.

Once in the field setting, the researcher must establish RAPPORT or get the various players in the setting to accept him or her. This can involve a delicate balance between revealing enough about oneself and the research to be accepted and not revealing so much that the research is compromised because people behave differently when the researcher is there than when he or she is not there. Wolcott (1995) referred to the 'darker art' of fieldwork with this wonderful quote from John Leonard: "It took me a long time to recognize that the key to acting is honesty. Once you know how to fake that, you've got it made" (Wolcott, 1995, p.122). The researcher must fake, in at least some small sense, being a member of the culture he or she is studying in order to gain acceptance.

Finally, a major part of conducting ethnography is finding INFORMANTS who can provide an inside look at the culture being studied. These are TRUSTWORTHY INDIVIDUALS who have useful information to impart and who do not have an ulterior motive for their willingness to share information. In the example of studying the culture of a professional sports team, informants might include some of the players themselves, or some of the other people who travel with the team, such as trainers and coaches, who have the opportunity to observe team members in a variety of circumstances.

(4)   Grounded Theory

GROUNDED THEORY is an INDUCTIVE approach to BUILDING THEORY from the ground up (Glaser, 1978; Glaser & Strauss, 1967; Strauss & Corbin, 1998). We have not discussed specifically the role of theory in conducting qualitative research, but most studies are conducted from a theoretical perspective, just as in quantitative research. The qualitative researcher seeks to build on prior knowledge of a phenomenon and is likely to have guiding questions or even tentative hypotheses for which evidence is gathered and examined. However, in grounded theory, a priori assumptions are set aside, and the researcher lets the data guide the growth and development of the theory. In this approach the RESEARCH DESIGN is EMERGENT, with the researcher conducting additional fieldwork as theoretical concepts come out of data analysis and require testing in the field.

Because of its emphasis on the process of generating theory from data, grounded theory can be considered as much an approach to interpretation as an approach to research design (Shank, 2002). Strauss and Corbin (1998) lay out a set of coding procedures known as the CONSTANT COMPARATIVE METHOD that provide a systematic and rigorous means of analyzing data. The researcher begins with a microscopic examination of the data, breaking it down into discrete parts, and comparing it for similarities and differences. Then, the researcher develops categories and subcategories that integrate these discrete parts, with a theory gradually and inductively emerging from this process. As the theory evolves, the researcher may find it necessary to collect additional information to help flesh out a particular aspect and will then return to the field. Thus, in grounded theory there is a strong interplay between data collection and data analysis. "Generating a theory from data means that most hypotheses and concepts not only come from the data, but are systematically worked out in relation to the data during the course of the research. *Generating a theory involves a process of research*" (Glaser & Strauss, 1967, p. 5-6, emphasis theirs).

(5)   Phenomenology

PHENOMENOLOGY stems from an interest in UNDERSTANDING HOW PEOPLE EXPERIENCE the world and how they INTERPRET those EXPERIENCES.

"Phenomenology aims at getting a deeper understanding of the nature or meaning of our everyday experiences" (van Maanen, 1990, p. 9). A question of phenomenology asks: What is the meaning of this phenomenon to the people who have experienced it? "The phenomenon that is the focus of inquiry may be an emotion—loneliness, jealousy, anger. The phenomenon may be a relationship, a marriage, or a job. The phenomenon may be a program, an organization, or a culture" (Patton, 2002, p. 104). According to this approach, the key to understanding the meaning of any of these phenomena comes through describing how people experience them. So, for example, the study posed earlier in the chapter regarding what it means to female athletes to menstruate during competition is consistent with a phenomenological approach. The intent is to understand the women's experiences of this phenomenon.

With respect to research methods, phenomenology is based on the following principles:

- A commitment to the use of qualitative methods;
- A primary focus on the whole experience, rather than on its parts;
- A search for meaning over a search for rules;
- Primary use of first person accounts as main data sources;
- Insisting that accounts of experience are a necessary part of any scientific understanding of any social phenomenon;
- Performing research that is guided by the personal interests and commitments of the researcher;
- The necessity of treating experiences and behavior as integrated parts of a single whole.

(Moustakas, 1994, cited in Shank, 2002, p. 81)

(6)   Critical Theory

The final approach to qualitative research that is discussed in this chapter is critical theory. CRITICAL THEORY "provides a framework—both philosophy and methods—for approaching research and evaluation as FUNDAMENTALLY and EXPLICITLY POLITICAL, and as CHANGE-ORIENTED forms of engagement" (Patton, 2002, p. 131). In other words, critical theorists look to expose ideology, or organized sets of belief that guide social action. Most of the time ideology is implicit and unacknowledged, and the reason to expose it is to raise consciousness or awareness so that corrective actions might be taken. "A critical social theory is concerned in particular with issues of power and justice and the ways that the economy, matters of race, class, and gender, ideologies, discourses, education, religion, and other social institutions and cultural dynamics interact to construct a social system" (Kinchloe & McLaren, 2000, p. 281).

Questions about women's non-participation in sport, for example, often tend to be investigated from the perspective of critical theory, especially if it is suspected that some sort of structural impediment exists to prevent women from participating in a given sport. The intent of the research is then to expose those impediments in the hope that they can be removed and women allowed or encouraged to participate. Feminist research, in which gender is the specific focus of interest, derives from the critical theory tradition and is discussed in detail in the next chapter.

5.4   MAKING SENSE OF QUALITATIVE DATA

At some point, every qualitative researcher wonders, "What am I going to do with all these data?" You may have pages upon pages of field notes or interview transcripts. You may have documents such as program descriptions and published reports. You may have hours of videotapes or photographs taken in the field setting. How do you begin to make sense of it all? Analyzing and interpreting qualitative data is undoubtedly the scariest part of conducting qualitative research. Although doing statistical analysis can be difficult and demanding, there is some comfort in knowing that once you enter the data and click on the analyses you want, the computer will do the rest and produce a report that means the same to all who view it. With qualitative analysis, however, there is no formula to rely on, no standard set of procedures that produce the same result no matter who implements them. Qualitative analysis requires a great deal of skill involving interpretation and judgment that come only with extensive practice.

This chapter cannot turn you into a skilled qualitative data analyst. Rather, it introduces you to basic concepts of qualitative analysis so that you have an idea of how to turn data into findings. It will provide you a sense of where you need to go and how you might get there. For more detailed instruction on technical skills, however, you are encouraged to consult with more comprehensive sources that are mentioned here.

(1)   Organizing the Data

Long before they begin analyzing their data, qualitative researchers face the problem of how to manage and organize it. We mentioned previously in this chapter the need to develop systems for labeling and archiving documents. The same is true for all kinds of data that are collected during a qualitative investigation. The researcher must be able to identify and find relevant pieces of data as the analysis proceeds. A first step to ORGANIZING the DATA is RENDERING RAW NOTES or RECORDINGS into a form that is reproducible and easy to analyze. For instance, handwritten field notes should be typed, and printed transcripts should be produced from audio or video recordings.

Even these apparently simple steps require some decisions on the part of the researcher. Should "er," "uh," "like," "you know," and other such expressions be included in the transcript? How should pauses or word emphases be rendered? There is no right answer to these questions, and much will depend on how important particular expressions or emphases are to understanding the speaker's meaning. For example, suppose a professional player responds to an interview question about sexual harassment with a smirk. This expression probably says as much about the person's opinion as what he actually says out loud, and as a consequence, it would be useful to note the facial expression in the interview transcript. Whatever the decision, the researcher must be consistent in how he or she converts raw data into the form to be used during analysis.

Once produced from raw data, write-ups from field notes and transcripts from interviews must be archived using an organizational scheme that will enable the researcher to identify and locate individual pieces of data easily and quickly. Some researchers find it useful to develop a summary sheet for each observation, interview, or document that identifies salient information about that piece of evidence (Miles & Huberman, 1994). This could include, for instance, when, where, and with whom an interview was conducted or a brief outline of a document's contents. See Figures 5.3 and 5.4 for illustrations of possible data summary forms.

Name of Interviewee: —————————————— Today's Date: ——————————

Date and Time of Interview: ———————————— Written by: ————————————

Location of Interview: ——————————————

Summary of information obtained in this interview:

Observations about the interview (anything salient or interesting that was noted):

Any remaining information or target questions to ask in the next contact with this person:

Figure 5.3   Interview summary form illustration.

Title or description of document: Date Obtained:

Type of document (e.g., published book or article, report, memo, etc.):

Importance of document (e.g., reason for obtaining document, relation of document to research project):

Brief summary of contents:

Researcher observations about document (anything interesting or salient to note):

Figure 5.4   Document summary form illustration.

It is also useful to make a separate copy of data files for use during analysis, keeping the original copies archived. Then if the researcher decides to modify the approach to analysis, it is easy to make a fresh copy and start over without damaging the integrity of the data set.

(2)   Coding for Themes

Perhaps the most central activity in analyzing qualitative data is CODING the DATA for THEMES, or looking for patterns that will help the researcher make sense of the data. This often seems like the most mysterious part of data analysis because many authors provide very little detail about how they actually did this to arrive at the findings they report in published articles. Instead, they make statements like "themes seemed to emerge" from the data. According to Shank (2002), however, "the notion that themes emerge from data is one of the most misunderstood concepts in qualitative research," and he offers this quote to help readers understand what researchers mean when they make that claim:

> Doing qualitative research is not a passive endeavor. Despite current perceptions and students' prayers, theory does not magically emerge from data. Nor is it true that, if one is only patient enough, insight wondrously enlightens the researcher. Rather, data analysis is a process that requires astute questioning, a relentless search for answers, active observation, and accurate recall. It is a process of piecing together important data, of making the invisible obvious, of recognizing the significant from the insignificant, of linking seemingly unrelated facts logically, of fitting categories one with another, and attributing consequences to antecedents. It is a process of conjecture and verification, of correction and modification, of suggestion and defense. It is a creative process of organizing data so that the analytic scheme will appear obvious.
>
> (Morse, 1994, p. 25; cited in Shank, 2002, p. 129)

So, how does one begin to code qualitative data for themes? In grounded theory, as described earlier, the process of coding is purely inductive. The researcher inspects the data, identifies descriptive codes, compares codes to one another, aggregates codes to develop themes, and integrates themes to eventually derive a "picture" or theory of the phenomenon under investigation. As the term INDUCTIVE implies, this process of CODING goes from the SPECIFIC to the GENERAL, where themes take shape based on how codes seem to fit together.

An alternative approach to coding is more DEDUCTIVE in nature. The researcher CREATES a set of PROVISIONAL CODES based on theory, prior observation or related literature. These may stem from the kinds of questions the researcher asked during interviews and would represent what he or she expects to see as important variables in the data. For example, in the study about women athletes' experience of menstruation during competition, the researcher might establish initial coding categories such as:

- Type of sport,
- Athlete's thoughts,
- Athlete's emotions,
- Athlete's actions,
- Athlete's attributions,
- Perceptions about coach's reaction,
- Perceptions about teammates' reactions, and
- Perceptions about family's reactions.

These categories directly parallel the interview guide, which contained the broad topics of interest to be explored with each of the individuals who were interviewed. As such, these coding categories are likely to contain more specific codes within them, for instance, a separate code for each sport that is represented in the sample of athletes interviewed. As codes are applied in the analytic process, the researcher may find it necessary to add new codes or modify existing ones to better capture the essence of the data. Thus, CODING becomes an ITERATIVE PROCESS, where the researcher revisits, and perhaps re-codes, data to be sure that coding is comprehensive and consistent throughout.

In this type of coding process, THEMES BECOME APPARENT as the researcher aggregates codes and looks for relations among them. For example, suppose coding reveals differences among female athletes in their emotional reactions to competing while on their period, with some women reporting much more emotional stress than others. This would become a theme to be explored in terms of what conditions appear to contribute to which sorts of emotional responses. Suppose further that the researcher notices in the interview transcripts that the women who reported extreme emotions also described a great deal of conflict in their families. Family conflict is not a variable contained in the interview guide, but, as an unanticipated factor, it should be coded and examined as a possible theme. Therefore, the researcher would code the instance of family conflict that first caught his or her attention and then reexamine previously coded data to see if any instances of family conflict were missed and how these instances related to reported emotion.

Coding one's data for themes raises a variety of issues, from deciding how to name codes to determining how detailed the analysis should be and when to stop coding. Let's take a brief look at each.

2.1   *Naming Codes*

Miles and Huberman (1994) recommend giving a code a name that is semantically close to the concept that the code is describing. Some researchers employ abbreviations of codes to expedite the coding process, such as FAM CON for 'family conflict', but this requires keeping a meticulous key and it can cause confusion if the abbreviations are used in a report. The researcher should also be clear as to when code names come from the data itself or are the invention of the researcher to describe what is in the data. For instance, suppose one of the athletes interviewed referred to "all the fighting that goes on in my house," which the researcher codes as 'family conflict.' In this case, the code name has been chosen by the researcher. If the researcher had chosen the label 'fighting' to code this excerpt, then the code name is derived directly from the data. The distinction is important because researchers can create code names that are inferential, rather than descriptive, which means that they have already arrived at a particular interpretation of the data.

After choosing a code name, the researcher should define what the code pertains to and describe how to know when an instance of the theme or code appears (Boyatzis, 1998). Considering what would be positive or negative examples of the code is a useful means for determining how broadly it should be applied. For example, suppose 'family conflict' has been identified as a possible theme. Consider whether it should be applied to the following interview excerpts:

A: My baby sister thinks I get all the attention in the family, especially when I'm getting ready for a meet. When she gets whiny and I'm on my period, I feel like I could just explode!

B: There is always so much tension around my house, because my mom and dad aren't getting along too well. So, when my period started the day before our biggest game of the season, it was, like, 'A Perfect Storm'!

Depending on how broadly the concept of family conflict is construed, it might apply to both excerpts. However, from a narrower perspective, excerpt B is probably a better match to the concept than excerpt A.

2.2   *Level of Code Detail*

How detailed should coding be? Should coding be done line by line, sentence by sentence, or paragraph by paragraph? How many levels of codes and subcodes are appropriate? The unit of analysis depends largely on the research question(s), which should be kept prominently displayed during the coding process. Computer programs for qualitative data analysis make it not only possible but easy to code at a very detailed level. However, most researchers apply codes to larger, more meaningful units such as sentences or paragraphs. It is best to keep asking yourself, how does this code help me to answer the research question? If it does not help, then perhaps your coding has become too fine-grained and detailed.

2.3   *Saturation*

The concept of saturation was discussed previously in relation to observation and how long one should remain in the field, and the same concept applies to coding. Saturation in coding occurs when no new codes emerge from the data and the same patterns of codes seem to be appearing as analysis continues. There is a sense that "as you look at more and more data, you start seeing the same old patterns over and over" (Shank, 2002, p. 132). When this occurs, you can be reasonably confident that your code list is complete and it is time to take the next steps in analysis and interpretation.

2.4   *Checking Codes*

Before moving on to the interpretation and explanation of themes that are becoming apparent in the data, it is useful to check the clarity and reliability of a coding scheme by discussing it with someone else. Do the definitions and names of codes make sense to another researcher? Is there agreement with the way the codes have been applied to the data? Eventually, the researcher must be able to show how he or she created codes and used them to analyze the data, so that any reader can understand and follow the process. It is not necessary to have complete agreement on the choice of code names or the definitions of codes. Rather, one must be able to see how the code names and definitions were derived and how they are being used in the data analysis.

For example, either 'fighting' or 'family conflict' could be used as the code name, but whichever is used should be consistently applied to the data with agreement as to what constitutes an instance of it. Likewise, if 'family conflict' is defined narrowly so that only excerpt B above constitutes an example, then there should be agreement that instances such as A do not constitute examples of that theme whereas other instances resembling B are examples.

(3)   Interpreting and Explaining the Data

During the process of coding data, the researcher will have a growing sense of what is important and what things mean. This happens through being immersed in the data and re-reading it many times. But to be systematic about developing interpretations and explanations of the data requires another organizational step. Miles and Huberman (1994) suggest that researchers develop various types of DATA DISPLAYS to help them see patterns and map relations among variables. Doing this makes meanings easier to find. Think of the process sculptors such as Michelangelo follow to reveal what is hidden in a piece of marble; they chip away the irrelevant and unnecessary pieces until a form emerges. When qualitative researchers create data displays, they are doing much the same thing—removing irrelevant pieces of data and arranging the rest so that patterns become apparent and meanings can be derived.

Miles and Huberman provide one of the most comprehensive sources for creating data displays, and we recommend that you consult their guidelines when you are ready to construct your own displays. However, it is useful here to consider the two types of displays that they describe as well as a variety of strategies they recommend for ordering data within a display.

3.1   *Within-Case Displays*

WITHIN-CASE DISPLAYS are used to help sort out relevant variables and events that pertain to a SINGLE CASE, whether the case is defined as an individual or some larger unit such as a program or community. According to Miles and Huberman, the format for displays typically falls into one of two categories—matrices or networks. Matrices are tables and charts with rows and columns, whereas networks consist of nodes or concepts connected by links that are labeled according to the relationships between the nodes. Choosing a particular format and ordering data within it depend upon the research question and what kinds of things are important to illuminate through the display.

A CONCEPTUALLY-ORDERED DISPLAY focuses on RELEVANT CONCEPTS that are important for developing an explanation of a phenomenon. For example, in the study on burnout among coaches, suppose a particular interest of the researcher is to understand whether a coach has coping strategies for particular kinds of problems he or she experiences. Interview data could be coded for problem type and strategies reported and then arrayed for each coach as shown in Figure 5.5. This also shows that the researcher has derived different categories of coping strategies that may be systematically related to the types of problems with which a given coach uses the strategies.

Coach: Sport: Years of Experience: Gender:			
TYPE OF PROBLEM	**COPING STRATEGIES**		
	Sport-specific	**Internal**	**Cultural**
Stress in competition			
School expectations			
Parental pressure			
…			

Figure 5.5   Conceptually-ordered data display illustration.

CONCEPT MAPS are also useful for presenting conceptually-ordered data, especially to show CAUSAL LINKS that are apparent in the data. For example, suppose that a coach used only certain categories of coping strategies in response to certain types of problems. This could be revealed in a concept map such as that shown in Figure 5.6.

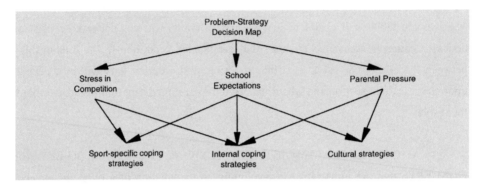

Figure 5.6   A Concept Map Illustrating Conceptually-Ordered Data.

On the other hand, when the chronology of events is important, then a TIME-ORDERED DISPLAY can be used to MAP EVENTS, activities, decisions, critical incidents or other similar sorts of data ALONG a TIME CONTINUUM. For instance, Hart's (2001) study of the two lesbian athletes revealed that two aspects of time had to be considered in understanding each woman's experience. First was the critical incident of when the athlete 'came out' and revealed her sexual orientation. The number and kinds of endorsements that were offered to Martina Navratilova, for example, were quite different after she came out than before. But when this event occurred in terms of year was also important because of societal conditions and mores at the time she came out. Developing a time-ordered display helps to reveal those findings.

Finally, ROLE-ORDERED DISPLAYS are used to ORGANIZE data AROUND PEOPLE and the ROLES they fill within the context or setting that is being studied. For example, in the study of the special program for parents of athletes, the researcher may want to know how the program is being perceived by the different groups of people who are being affected by it—parents, athletes, coaches, the instructor. Each group is likely to find different aspects of the program to be salient or they may have different expectations that are being more or less met. Figure 5.7 shows an example of a possible role-ordered display.

Participant Role	Goals for participation	Salient characteristics	Perceptions about program effects
Parents			
Athletes			
Siblings			
Coaches			
Instructors			

Figure 5.7   Role-ordered display illustration.

3.2   *Cross-Case Displays*

When the focus of an investigation is a LARGER PICTURE that cuts across MANY CASES, then CROSS-CASE DISPLAYS are used to make comparisons and develop broad-based explanations. These can preserve information about individual cases and at the same time integrate information across cases to derive generalizations and theories. For example, in a study investigating stressors experienced by women ice hockey players, Heller, Neil and Bloom (2003) conducted in-depth interviews of 6 players. Although each player constituted a case, the primary interest in the study was to identify higher-order categories of stress (Heller et al., 2003). A simple cross-case display such as the sample shown in Figure 5.8 would help to reveal the types of demands that these ice hockey athletes contended with as a consequence of their participation in a NCAA Division I sport.

Athlete	Higher-order Categories of Stress		
(all names are pseudonyms)	*Educational demands*	*Hockey pressures*	*Relationship issues*
Moira			
Sophie			
Teresa			
Jayne			
Anne-Marie			
Kelly			

Figure 5.8   Illustration of Cross-Case Display Revealing Themes of Stressors Experienced by Women Ice-Hockey Athletes.

Similarly, the CASE-ORDERED META-MATRIX shown in Figure 5.9 is an example of how a great deal of data from multiple cases can be ordered to facilitate making comparisons and contrasts. This matrix could be expanded to include data from all of the coaches who were interviewed as part of the study on burnout. The matrix could also be organized to display data from all of the female coaches followed by all of the male coaches, or according to sport, or according to years of experience.

For instance, years of experience could be categorized as 'inexperienced' (0 to 5 years), 'moderately experienced' (6—15 years), and 'highly experienced' (16 or more years), with the coaches' data then arrayed in those three groups. Which particular order is chosen will depend on what variables are likely to be most related to an explanation of why burnout occurs and the kinds of coping strategies used by coaches to combat it. If gender differences appear to be important, then ordering the matrix by gender will help to reveal what is the nature of these differences.

COACH	DEMOGRAPHICS			TYPE OF PROBLEM	COPING STRATEGIES		
					Sport-specific	Internal	*Cultural*
Taylor (pseudonym)	Yrs Experience:	Gender:	Sport:	– Stress in competition			
				– School expectations			
				– Parental pressure			
				– …			
Patrice	Yrs. Experience:	Gender:	Sport:	–			
				–			
				–			
				–			

Figure 5.9   Case-ordered meta-matrix display illustration.

Like within-case displays, cross-case displays can be time-ordered, conceptually-ordered, or role-ordered. Individual case data can be preserved, as in Figures 5.8 and 5.9, or it can be integrated across cases when it is more important to develop a broad explanation or theory. The burnout study may be a good case in point. It may not be especially important to know that Coach Taylor used particular coping strategies whereas Coach Patrice used other strategies. Rather, it may be that because they are both highly experienced coaches, the strategies they used differ systematically from those used by less experienced coaches.

3.3   *Contents of Data Displays*

When qualitative researchers construct a data display, an important decision they must make is exactly what content to put into the display. Consider the illustrations in Figures 5.5, 5.7, 5.8, and 5.9. Should the researcher put excerpts from the data into each cell of the matrix? Or is it better to insert summaries or descriptions of the data that exemplify the concepts represented in the matrix? Miles and Huberman suggest that both strategies are useful at different points during the analytic process. That is, early in the analysis, the researcher should consider using excerpts from the data to construct a display. So for example, one would include in Figure 5.8 what an athlete actually said during an interview that was coded as an "educational demand" or "hockey pressure."

Using raw data to construct data displays accomplishes two things. First of all, it serves as a check on code definitions and the researcher's choice of code categories to display in the matrix. It is easy for another person to examine a data display and provide feedback as to whether the codes and categories chosen by the researcher seem to fit the data. Second, it keeps the researcher close to the data and provides a source of illustration when the researcher is writing a report on the study. Quoting what people actually said helps make a research report come alive and facilitates a reader's understanding of the participants' experience.

Later in the analysis, constructing displays that summarize data or show relations among codes, as shown in the concept map illustration (Figure 5.6), assist the researcher in generating explanations and making meaning of the data.

3.4   *Making Meaning from Data Displays*

Miles and Huberman (1994) describe a hierarchy of strategies for generating explanations and drawing conclusions from data displays. They suggest beginning with a "squint analysis" (p. 190), which means looking over the display for areas of data that are either dense or sparse. Let's suppose as an example that the display in Figure 5.9

reveals few data entries for the category of cultural coping strategies. Of all the coaches who were interviewed, perhaps only one or two mentioned strategies that were coded as cultural in nature. This would be a significant finding that the researcher would want to explore further. In other words, what unique characteristics did those coaches possess that might offer a plausible explanation for their experience?

Other strategies that Miles and Huberman suggest for making sense of data displays include those in the following list. Along with each strategy is provided a hypothetical example to illustrate how the strategy could be employed in the burnout study. The purpose of these strategies is to query the data so as to derive meaningful findings.

1) CLUSTERING AND COUNTING (e.g., ordering the data by gender and then counting to see how many coping strategies are reported by men versus women coaches. A finding might be that men and women coaches differ in the kinds of coping strategies they use or in the types of problems to which they apply a particular coping strategy);

2) MAKING CONTRASTS AND COMPARISONS (e.g., looking to see if more experienced coaches responded differently from less experienced coaches. A finding might be that years of experience relates to an emphasis on a particular category of coping strategies);

3) SEARCHING FOR VARIABLES (e.g., asking what variables besides gender, years, of experience, and type of sport might contribute to an understanding of burnout among coaches. A finding might be that coaches' experiences differ across Division I vs. Division II or in terms of the athletic conferences in which their teams compete);

4) NOTING RELATIONS AMONG VARIABLES (e.g., deriving a finding that experienced coaches used more personal coping strategies whereas inexperienced coaches used more sport-specific coping strategies);

5) CONSIDERING EXTREME CASES and FOLLOWING UP SURPRISES (e.g., seeing that one coach presented a very different profile concerning burnout and coping strategies than any of the others and considering why this might be so);

6) MAKING IF-THEN TESTS (e.g., asking if gender is related to coping strategies used, then have the female coaches generally been more successful at avoiding or overcoming burnout than the male coaches?);

7) LOOKING FOR NEGATIVE EVIDENCE (e.g., checking to see if the female coaches reported strategies that were always different from the male coaches or whether there might be examples of strategies they used that were the same or similar to those used by men);

8) SEARCHING FOR PLAUSIBLE EXPLANATIONS (e.g., using the data to construct an explanation for why men and women coaches appear to have different coping strategies);

9) FORMULATING LOGICAL CHAINS OF EVIDENCE (e.g., using evidence to build an argument that certain kinds of strategies can help coaches to avoid or overcome burnout); and

10 CREATING THEORETICAL OR CONCEPTUAL MODELS (e.g., creating a theory of burnout).

As researchers use any or all of these strategies to draw conclusions from their data, they must also consider the weight of evidence. Some data are stronger than other data. Firsthand observations, for instance, provide stronger data than that collected from secondhand reports and documents. Likewise, interviews with trusted informants will yield stronger data than those with marginal or untrustworthy informants. Finally, data gathered later in the research process are often stronger than that collected early. This is because the researcher is more experienced and has begun to learn what is important so that observations become sharper and interviews more tailored to the question of interest.

(4) Writing the Research Report

The final step in making sense of qualitative data is writing the research report. Writing is an integral part of qualitative research and, for some, it is an act of inquiry in itself (Richardson, 2000). This means that insights and understanding about a study's findings can emerge from the very process of writing up those findings. Most authors understand this idea, because even when writing from an outline, they may find themselves being taken in unanticipated directions, as though the piece were writing itself. A friend of second author Driscoll recounted an experience of his brother-in-law, who is a playwright, regaling relatives during a family gathering about his latest play. He came to a certain point in the story and simply stopped. When prompted to tell the rest of the story, he replied, "I don't know what happens. I haven't written it yet!"

Writing a qualitative research report is very much like telling a story. There is no fixed format, and the researcher selects, transforms and interprets facts and findings to tell a particular research tale so that it will have intended effects on a certain audience. In the highly influential *Tales of the Field*, van Maanen (1988) distinguished between three "voices" with which ethnographies can be written. The Realist tale is the most traditional style, in that "a single author typically narrates . . . in a dispassionate, third-person voice" (van Maanen, 1988, p. 45). The Realist tale tends to be highly descriptive and attempts to convey the perspective of the participants in the research by using their own words. The researcher is "interpretively omnipotent," which means that he or she has the final say on the selection and interpretation of findings, often appealing to theory to justify claims.

By contrast, van Maanen's (1988) Confessional tale is a highly personalized account of the research. The researcher is frank and open about mistakes or "lucky accidents" that took place in the field and assumes personal responsibility for creating a sense of intimacy with the reader so that the reader will trust the account. Confessional tales tend to be more dramatic than Realist tales, and they usually supplement rather than replace Realist tales.

Finally, the Impressionist tale is an attempt to render the research in such a way as to place the reader "on the scene." The research tale is told in the first person and present tense, and information unfolds in the telling. According to van Maanen, "the audience cannot know in advance what matters will prove instructive, and thus by trying to hang on to the little details of the tale, they experience something akin to what the fieldworker might have experienced during the narrated events" (1988, p. 104). Like Confessional tales, Impressionist tales tend to be dramatic, and they adhere more to literary standards than to scientific ones.

Which voice or stance a researcher adopts in writing a qualitative research report depends a great deal on the audience for the report and the intended impact of the findings. When it is important to convey feelings, then a more dramatic rendition such as the Impressionist tale can reveal the essence of findings more effectively than a Realist rendition. For example, Chin (2003) found that artistic expressions such as poetry and cartoons enabled readers of an evaluation report to better understand the emotional effects of a school reading program on the children it was intended to benefit (Chin, 2003).

Adopting a particular sort of tale also depends on the skill of the writer and the research conventions of his or her particular field. Realist tales are easier to write and more accepted by many research communities. Regardless of the style chosen, however, the qualitative researcher should make clear what perspective he or she is bringing to the research and the report. For example, it is important to let the reader know that the researcher is a former coach who left the sport because of burnout or is a female athlete who stopped menstruating because her body fat got too low. These experiences will clearly influence the researchers' data analysis and interpretation.

5.5 ENSURING RIGOR IN QUALITATIVE RESEARCH

It is likely that the preceding discussion on writing up qualitative research has raised a number of questions in your mind about the scientific rigor of doing qualitative research. If writing the research report is a matter of telling a story, then what assurance is there that the story is accurate, that the researcher "got it right?" Patton (2002) describes a student who became paralyzed in writing a report because he wasn't sure if the patterns he found in the data were true. Patton writes,

> I suggested that he not try to convince himself or others that his findings were true in any absolute sense but, rather, that he had done the best job he could in describing the patterns that appeared to him to be present in the data and that he present those patterns as *his* perspective based on his analysis and interpretation of the data he had collected. Even if he believed that what he eventually produced was Truth, sophisticated people reading the report would know that what he presented was no more than his perspective, and they would judge that perspective by their own commonsense understandings and use the information according to their own needs.

(2002, p. 578)

So what does it mean to do "the best job he could" and how do qualitative researchers assure that they have done the best job possible to collect, analyze, and interpret data? The remainder of this chapter addresses the issue of standards in qualitative research.

Like the diversity among qualitative research traditions, there is little unanimity among the standards that researchers hold for conducting qualitative research. Patton (2002) contrasts five sets of criteria that he argues are based on different paradigms or worldviews. In other words, how one views reality and thinks about the world determines how one approaches research and the criteria by which the quality of research is judged. To illustrate, Patton recalls the classic story of three baseball umpires discussing how they call balls and strikes:

> "I call them as I see them," says the first.
> "I call them as they are," says the second.
> "They ain't nothing until I call them," says the third.
>
> (2002, p. 543)

Consider how those three views line up with the perspectives represented in quantitative as well as qualitative research traditions. For perspectives in the more realist vein, traditional scientific criteria are likely to be emphasized. These include minimizing researcher bias, using rigorous data collection techniques, cross-checking sources during fieldwork, and establishing inter-coder consistency in data analysis. On the other hand, for perspectives that are more interpretivist in nature, artistic or literary criteria are likely to prevail.

For example, the extent to which the research vividly portrays participants' experience and feels authentic will be important. You are encouraged to consult sources such as Miles and Huberman (1994), Patton (2002), and Shank (2002) for a more detailed discussion of a range of criteria used to judge the rigor of qualitative research. For purposes of discussion here, we have attempted to distill a broad range of issues and recommended criteria into a set of guidelines. Following these guidelines will not guarantee that you will make no mistakes in conducting and reporting qualitative research. But following these guidelines will assure a result that you can defend.

(1)   Match Data Collection and Analysis to the Research Question(s)

It is important throughout a qualitative study to know where you are going and to take appropriate steps for getting there. This is not to say that you never change directions or that you stick with a research plan no matter what happens. During many qualitative studies, new questions emerge that the researcher chooses to investigate further, or unexpected findings come out that require additional follow-up in the field. The point is that decisions about what to do—what data to collect, how to gather it, and how to analyze it—are done for good reason, because taking a given step will advance the researcher closer to finding answers to the research question.

A common mistake made by novice researchers is to propose a data collection method based on a belief that "more is better." In addition to interviews, for example, a focus group is planned in which the same questions are to be asked as those probed in the interviews. But if no new data can be anticipated by taking this step, why should the researcher do it? With every means of data collection to be utilized in a study, the researcher should consider how it will help to answer the research question and what unique advantages it provides over other means that could be used instead. If, for example, participants are likely to reveal more or different things that pertain to the research question in a focus group than they would in an interview, then use the focus group.

It should be clear from this guideline how critical it is to begin with a good research question. According to Shank (2002), the single most important source of error in qualitative research is asking a bad question. Bad questions in his view include those that contradict prior knowledge, those that have already been answered, and those that are ambiguous or unclear. Doing your homework and becoming aware of trends in your chosen area of interest will help to avoid asking questions that contradict prior knowledge or have been answered already. Asking clear and unambiguous questions is a matter of practice and feedback from other researchers in the field. If you can articulate how the data you plan to collect, and the trends you might see in that data, relate to your research question, then it is probably clear and unambiguous.

(2) Be Systematic and Tactical

Being systematic and tactical are almost opposing skills. On one hand, it is important to follow a research plan that helps you maintain consistency throughout a research study. Are features of the study design congruent with the research questions? Have you made your procedures clear and explicit so that another researcher could follow in your footsteps? Have you used comparable protocols in collecting data across informants or from different sources? Has your coding been consistent so that there is reasonable agreement that codes have been applied in the same way to different segments of data? These are all questions of research reliability in following procedures that assure similar results over time.

On the other hand, it is just as important in qualitative research to be flexible and capable of making adjustments as the inquiry proceeds. Shank (2002) calls it the sin of rigidity to make a priori decisions from initial assumptions and then relentlessly filter out any other issues that come up. Instead, researchers should be prepared to go in "the direction that ongoing circumstances suggest is actually the most fruitful line of inquiry to pursue" (Shank, 2002, p. 187). Shank uses the analogy to whitewater rafting to explain this point: "The rafter works with the river, allowing it to do most of the work, and yet is always alert and mindful of potential problems and sources of trouble. Occasionally the rafter must paddle furiously to avoid overturning, but if the raft is guided with skill, these exertions can be kept to a minimum. In one sense, the rafter is always in control, but rarely in charge" (pp. 197-188).

(3) Dig Deep Enough

This guideline pertains to the issue of how much is enough in qualitative research—how long to stay in the field, how many cases to include in the study, how many informants to interview, how detailed to code. While saturation is the desired way to make these decisions, practical issues often get in the way. Perhaps the researcher can get access to a field site for only a short time. Or perhaps only a few agree to be interviewed. It may be extremely time consuming and expensive to pursue the breadth in cases or sites that the research would seem to dictate. All of these are threats to the validity of a qualitative study.

To counteract these threats, you should be prepared to take further steps and dig deeper, to follow up rather than ignore issues that arise. In the event that limitations are known from the outset, you may have to decide whether there is likely to be sufficient evidence to justify conducting the inquiry in the first place. Hart's (2001) study of professional lesbian athletes is a good example.

There was a small number of possible informants to begin with, and of those, only two agreed to be interviewed. However, with so little known about the experiences of gay and lesbian athletes, any insights that could be gleaned from these particular two would be valuable and more than outweigh the limitations of the small number. informants.

(4)   Document What You Do

This guideline relates partly to the notion of an audit trail and partly to the importance of making your reasoning clear in linking evidence to conclusions. One way to establish external credibility, especially in high stakes situations, is having an audit performed by a disinterested expert who renders judgment about the quality of data collection and analysis (Patton, 2002).

To do this requires an audit trail of the study's methods and procedures that would permit someone to come along afterward and essentially replicate the study. While audits themselves are comparatively rare, the audit trail has become a standard in reporting qualitative research. Documenting procedures carefully is especially important when the research diverges from its intended course. It is easier to document these changes as they happen than to reconstruct after the fact what must have happened.

Similarly, the logic and reasoning that a researcher followed from evidence to conclusions and interpretations should be transparent. That is, a reader should be able to disagree with an analysis or set of conclusions but understand how one was derived from the other. This is much like critiquing the analysis and results of a quantitative study. The reader may see how a researcher derived findings from an ANOVA but argue that a MANOVA would have been the more appropriate analysis leading to a different result.

(5) Make Biases Explicit

The standard of transparency is key in all aspects of science, and it has to do with the extent to which research can be considered neutral or free of bias. Thus, procedures are undertaken during data collection, analysis, and interpretation to minimize researcher bias and ensure the replicability of the research. Replicability has been addressed in the guideline related to documentation of research procedures. But researcher bias is another matter. From a qualitative perspective, no research is truly objective or neutral because it involves human judgment. Even in experimental and other types of quantitative research, someone decides what questions are most important to investigate, and these decisions can be influenced by political and other non-scientific reasons. For instance, what kind of research and about what sorts of topics will a funding agency be willing to support?

To address the issue of objectivity in qualitative inquiry, researchers make their biases explicit. What role do they play in the research and what background, skills, and beliefs do they bring to the field setting? How do they feel about what they are observing, especially if those feelings are strong? During data collection and analysis, it is important to be self-aware about one's values and beliefs and how these may be affecting what is seen or what may be overlooked. Are you seeing what you want to see or making interpretations that support implicit, and perhaps unacknowledged, assumptions? Or have you amassed corroborating evidence that supports the conclusions you are drawing from your field work and analysis? It is important to be honest about one's perspective, but it is also important to collect and compare data from different perspectives. This brings us to the last guideline, which is to triangulate.

(6) Triangulate

"By combining multiple observers, theories, methods, and data sources, [researchers] can hope to overcome the intrinsic bias that comes from single-methods, single-observer, and single-theory studies" (Denzin, 1989, p. 307). "The logic of triangulation is based on the premise that no single method ever adequately solves the problem of rival explanations" (Patton, 2002, p. 555). Thus, to add confidence to the validity of their findings, qualitative researchers triangulate during both data collection and data analysis.

During data collection, there are three common ways to triangulate—through multiple observers, methods, or data sources. Observers triangulation means checking the consistency of data collected by different observers. It strengthens the credibility of findings to establish that different researchers observed and recorded the same things, as in the textbook study described earlier in this chapter. Methods triangulation means checking the consistency of findings that are generated through different means of data collection. That is, data collected through such means as interviews and documents provide converging evidence about the phenomenon under investigation. For example, in Hart's (2001) study, news stories reporting Martina Navratilova's commercial endorsements can confirm her perception that the amount and type of endorsement changed after she came out. Finally, triangulation of sources refers to checking consistency of data within the same method. To use the same example, data from an interview with Martina's agent could have been triangulated with data obtained directly from her.

Triangulation can occur as well during data analysis and interpretation. Analyst triangulation refers to the use of multiple researchers to analyze and review findings. The extent of agreement lends credibility and strength to the coding scheme that is used and the findings that are generated from it. Lastly, theory triangulation means using multiple theories or perspectives to interpret the data.

While triangulation is most often used to reveal consistencies in the data, which are then presumed more credible by virtue of this consistency, triangulation can reveal discrepant or divergent findings. These do not mean that credibility is weakened necessarily. Rather, discrepant findings can lead to important new insights when a coherent explanation for them can be derived (Mathison, 1988). For example, Hart (2001) found that Martina Navratilova's endorsements changed when she came out, but Missy Giove's did not. These are conflicting results, which could tempt us to conclude that sexual orientation doesn't matter where endorsements are concerned. However, a more plausible explanation that accounts for both results concerns the age of the athletes and when they came out, both in terms of at what point in their respective careers and in what decade. Martina went public later in her career, so that she had much more to lose in endorsements than Missy. Moreover, there were few others at that time to make such an announcement so that public reaction was that much more pronounced.

Triangulation thus offers strategies for reducing bias and strengthening the findings of qualitative research. In whatever form, it "increases credibility and quality by countering the concern (or accusation) that a study's findings are simply an artifact of a single method, a single source, or a single investigator's blinders" (Patton, 2002, p. 563).

Summary

This chapter has focused on the design and conduct of qualitative research. Qualitative data are collected primarily through means of observation, interviews, and examining documents, and a variety of qualitative designs provide different perspectives and strategies for conducting qualitative inquiry. These range from narrowly defined case studies to the study of culture through ethnography. Strategies were presented for aggregating and making sense of qualitative data, and guidelines were suggested to strengthen the quality and rigor of research results. In the next chapter, some of these concepts will be revisited as they appear in specific examples of qualitative inquiry.

References

Baker, J., Cote, J., & Abernethy, B. (2003). Sport-specific practice and the development of expert decision-making in team ball sports. *Journal of Applied Sport Psychology, 15,* 12-25.

Boyatzis, R. E. (1998). *Transforming qualitative information: Thematic analysis and code development.* Thousand Oaks, CA: Sage.

Chin, C. M. (2003). *An investigation into the impact of using poetry and cartoons as alternative representational forms in evaluation reporting.* Unpublished doctoral dissertation. Florida State University. Tallahassee, FL,

Denzin, N.K. (1989). *The research act: A theoretical introduction to sociological methods.* Englewood Cliffs, NJ: Prentice-Hall.

Driscoll, M. P., Moallem, M. et al. (1994). How does the textbook contribute to learning in a middle school science class? *Contemporary Educational Psychology, 19,* 79-100.

Ericsson, K. A., & Simon, H. A. (1993). *Protocol Analysis.* Cambridge: MIT Press.

Fontana, A., & Frey, J. H. (2000). The interview: From structured questions to negotiated text. In N. K. Denzin & Y. S. Lincoln (Eds.) *Handbook of Qualitative Research* (pp. 645-672). Thousand Oaks, CA: Sage.

Glaser, B. G. (1978). *Theoretical sensitivity: Advances in the methodology of grounded theory.* Mill Valley, CA: Sociology Press.

Glaser, B. G., & Strauss, A. (1967). *Discovery of grounded theory: strategies for qualitative research.* Chicago: Aldine.

Greenbaum, T. L. (1997). *The handbook for focus group research.* Thousand Oaks, CA: Sage.

Greenbaum, T. L. (2000). *Moderating focus group: A practical guide for group participation.* Thousand Oaks, CA: Sage.

Hart, K. (2001). *Lesbian professional athletes: What was the cost of coming out?* Unpublished doctoral dissertation Florida State University. Tallahassee, FL,

Heller, T. L., Neil, G. I., et al. (2003). *Sources of stress in NCAA division I women ice hockey players.* Paper presented at the Annual Meeting of the Association for the Advancement of Applied Sport Psychology, Philadelphia, PA.

Hodder, I. (2000). The interpretations of documents and material culture. In N. K. Denzin & Y. S. Lincoln (Eds.) *Handbook of Qualitative Research* (pp. 703-715). Thousand Oaks, CA: Sage.

Jacob, E. (1988). Clarifying qualitative research: A focus on traditions. *Educational Researcher, 17*(1), 16-24.

Johnson, T. (2003). *A foundation for understanding the menstrual cycle.* Unpublished manuscript. Florida State University, Tallahassee, FL.

Kinchloe, J. L., & McLaren, P. (2000). Rethinking critical theory and qualitative research. In N. K. Denzin & Y. S. Lincoln (Eds.) *Handbook of Qualitative Research* (pp. 279-313). Thousand Oaks, CA: Sage.

LeCompte, M. D., & Preissle, J. (1993). *Ethnography and qualitative design in educational research.* San Diego, CA: Academic Press.

Lincoln, Y. S., & Guba, E. G. (1985). *Naturalistic inquiry.* Beverly Hills, CA: Sage.

Mathison, S. (1988). Why triangulate? *Educational Researcher, 17*(2), 13-17.

Merriam, S. B. (1998). *Qualitative research and case study applications in education.* Thousand Oaks, CA: Sage.

Miles, M. B., & Huberman, A. M. (1994). *Qualitative data analysis.* Thousand Oaks, CA: Sage.

Morgan, D. L. (1988). *Focus groups as qualitative research.* Newbury Park, CA: Sage.

Morgan, D. L. (1988). *The focus groups guidebook.* Thousand Oaks, CA: Sage.

Morgan, D. L., & Kreuger, R. A. (1997). *The focus kit.* Thousand Oaks, CA: Sage.

Patton, M. Q. (2002). *Qualitative research & evaluation methods.* Thousand Oaks, CA: Sage Publications.

Richardson, L. (2000). Writing: A method of inquiry. In N. K. Denzin & Y. S. Lincoln (Eds.) *Handbook of Qualitative Research.* Thousand Oaks, CA: Sage.

Schensul, J., & LeCompte, M. D. (1999). *Ethnographer's toolkit.* Walnut Creek, CA : AltaMira Press.

Schwandt, T. A. (1997). *Qualitative inquiry: A dictionary of terms.* Thousand Oaks, CA: Sage.

Schank, G. D. (1994). Shaping qualitative research in educational psychology. *Contemporary Educational Psychology, 19*, 340-359.

Shank, G. D. (2002). *Qualitative research: A personal skills approach.* Upper Saddle River, NJ: Pearson Education, Inc.

Spradley, J. P. (1980). *Participant observation*. New York: Holt, Rinehart and Winston.

Stake, R. E. (1995). *The art of case study research*. Thousand Oaks, CA: Sage.

Strauss, A., & Corbin, J. (1998). *Basics of qualitative research: Techniques and procedures for developing grounded theory.* Thousand Oaks, CA: Sage.

van Maanen, M. (1988). *Tales of field: On writing ethnography*. Chicago: University of Chicago Press.

van Maanen, M. (1990). *Researching lived experience: Human science for an action sensitive pedagogy.* New York: State University of New York.

Wolcott, H. F. (1995). *The art of fieldwork*. Walnut Creek, CA: AltaMira Press.

Yin, R. (1994). *Case study research: Design and methods*. Newbury Park, CA: Sage.

CHAPTER VI: QUALITATIVE RESEARCH IN SPORT PSYCHOLOGY

The previous chapter provided an introduction to the concepts of qualitative research, what it is and how it is conducted. This chapter offers contributions by several authors who are themselves engaged in doing qualitative inquiry. The purpose of the chapter is to afford a glimpse of some of the debate going on among qualitative scholars and to provide specific examples of qualitative inquiry in sport psychology.

It is hoped that these examples will help you to see how the concepts of qualitative inquiry are being applied in sport science research. Because the sections of this chapter are, for the most part, independent of each other, they need not be read and studied at one time. Indeed, it may be more beneficial to read and reflect on the sections one at a time. The structure of the chapter is shown below, followed by a content outline.

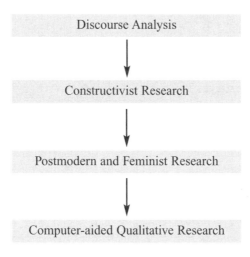

Discourse Analysis

↓

Constructivist Research

↓

Postmodern and Feminist Research

↓

Computer-aided Qualitative Research

Contents

(1)   Discourse Analysis

Mark Rapley

1.1   *Introduction*

Sport is a social drama ... but it is also a cultural drama, and it demonstrates
how a group draws on rituals and symbols as well as language to face a crisis
... as Euripides so well understood, questions of control, power, and supremacy
are relevant, and the language of sport in all its slangy and facetious style offers
us a fascinating window into the very soul of our existence.

(Segrave, 1997, pp. 218-219).

"WHY? 'The judgment was made with the knowledge that the club needs a
coach committed, in the long-term, to Perth, Western Australia. It was as simple
as that. Bernd had not indicated he was prepared to make such a long-term
commitment and I believe he would always be attached to Germany in some
way. There would come a day when Bernd felt the need to return to his
homeland.' —*Nick Tana*"

Mel Moffat in *The West Australian*, 21st February 2000.

On February 16th, 2000 the Chairman and majority shareholder of Perth Glory
Soccer Club, Mr. Nick Tana, precipitated what was described in the media as a major
"crisis" (Moffat, 2000a) for the club by announcing that he was not going to offer coach
Bernd Stange a renewal of his contract. In the following three weeks, even after the story
left the front page[1] of the State's daily newspaper, sports reporting in print and electronic
media in Western Australia, as well as the business and letters pages, were dominated by
the story of Stange's "sacking" (Keddie, 2000) and his eventual reinstatement after a
campaign by Perth Glory supporters against Tana's decision.

An everyday story of everyday soccer (mis) management perhaps? While
obviously a story of intense interest to Perth Glory fans, it might be thought that the
strange story of Stange's "dismissal" and eventual "reinstatement" is surely of serious

---

[1] Moffat (2000c) "Glory days over as Stange dumped", *The West Australian*, 17th february, page 1.

academic interest only to students of journalism, the media or sports management. However, this is not the case: this chapter draws on the coverage of the Stange story in *The West Australian* to illustrate the way in which the serious academic study of (the reporting of) everyday life can offer students in sports and exercise sciences a critical and reflexive perspective on their disciplines, an appreciation of the inevitable and inescapable interplay of "scientific" and "everyday" knowledge, and the place that these knowledge occupy in our culture. This sort of qualitative study also promises to make available a much wider set of understandings about the manner in which our culture organizes knowledge about persons, about their psychological makeup, and, crucially, about the everyday organization of sociality, of the moral life of our culture.

This section outlines the epistemological commitments and methodological stance of discursive psychology and demonstrates the practical application of the approach. While qualitative approaches are not entirely foreign to sports and exercise sciences, quantitative approaches tend to be more common. A brief review of the published literature suggests that Hallinanís (1994, p. 10) plea "that we should not underestimate the sociocultural influence of "doing" sport science," has not been widely heard in the mainstream of the disciplines. However, the literature does contain a small, and extraordinarily theoretically disparate, corpus of "qualitative" papers[2].

In general, qualitative studies have analyzed the place of sport in popular culture, and the reciprocal influences of culture and sport upon each other. Very little work has taken the discursive psychological approach adopted here and asked what these analyses can tell us specifically about the nature of persons, and their moral entitlements, in the particular cultures under study. Where these studies agree, however, is in their understanding of sport as a peculiarly sensitive index of a culture. For example in Lukes' (2000) analysis of sports broadcasting it is suggested that "athletics can be a window to broader cultural issues, but so can the way in which athletic events are transmitted to fans . . . a rising arrogance among sports announcers . . . relate[s] to American culture in general" (p. 78). Similarly, in a study of the prevailing metaphors in the contemporary language of sport, Segrave (1997) draws together an account of the way in which sport

---

[2] See also Miller, 1990; Scambler and Jennings, 1998; Tyler-Eastman & Billings, 1999; MacAloon, 1996.

is routinely talked about in Anglophone cultures (in terms of sex, war, or machinery) with a philosophical critique of culture informed by Nietschean and feminist analyses, to argue that "the language of sport . . . offers us a fascinating window into the very soul of our existence" (p. 219). Likewise, Staurowsky (1998), citing Jansen and Sabo (1994, p. 1), argues that sport metaphors are "crucial rhetorical resources for mobilizing the patriarchal values that construct, mediate, and maintain . . . hegemonic forms of masculinity and femininity.

Published studies' levels of analysis vary from the extremely fine-grained, for example McHoulís (1997) paper on the use of the single utterance "We won" in one specific speech episode, to the more wide-ranging critique of entire genres of sports discourse such as Eskes, Duncan and Miller's 1998) examination of women's "fitness" magazines. Their study of the "discourse of empowerment" in women's fitness texts employs the theoretical framework of critical discourse analysis (see Fairclough, 1993), and draws extensively on the work of Foucault and Marcuse, to identify the manner in which "by co-opting feminist ideals, fitness texts encourage readers to concentrate on their physical selves, specifically physical beauty, not health, at the expense of true physical health and gains in the social arena" (Eskes, Duncan & Miller, 1998, p. 317). At the other end of the analytic spectrum, McHoul's (1997) analysis draws upon the work of Harvey Sacks (1995) and later work in ethnomethodology and conversation analysis (see tenHave, 1999; Psasthas, 1995) to examine the (grammatically impermissible) use of the categorical "*We* won" by the Australian team coach as swimmer Duncan Armstrong won the 200 meter finals at the 1988 Olympic Games. McHoul concludes that this analysis can demonstrate the way in which "the everyday techniques [of sociality] of the sporting arena . . . are, at one and the same time, identical with those used everywhere else in the culture and unique to sport. Sport is neither completely separate from everyday life nor is it quite "ordinary" life as usual" (p. 320). Hughson's (2000) work, on the other hand, draws on temporally extensive ethnographic fieldwork with the Bad Blues Boys, a group of young Australian/Croatian soccer fans from the western suburbs of Sydney, in his analysis of the social reproduction of masculinity as a social and a cultural identity via sports team allegiance.

In contrast to these studies much of the existing sports and exercise science literature takes its subject matter as an *a priori* given. Studies of expert- novice differences in tennis skills, comparative analyses of aggressive play across sports such as ice hockey, and basketball and experimental studies of soccer goalkeepers' reaction times all presuppose sport as an unproblematic aspect of human experience and, moreover, study these fragmentary aspects of sport performance in isolation from the matrix of culture and society. It seems to be clear, however, that if we take the place of sport in everyday life as *the site of analysis*, qualitative research can help us to develop insights into the social organization of sport as an unique human activity and, by virtue of this, a richer appreciation of the social matrix into which sport is embedded.

1.2   *The Epistemological Position and Basic Principles of Discursive Psychology*

Discursive psychology (Edwards & Potter, 1992; Edwards, 1995, 1997; Potter, 1996; Wetherell & Potter, 1992) represents an explicit reworking of the (usually) implicit epistemological commitments of mainstream psychology. If the approach can be described as having a fundamental principle, it might be that, in the most profound sense, *language* "talks the world into being" (Rapley, in press). Perhaps the second most important theoretical principle is that "method" is always and already "theory" in disguise (Edwards, Ashmore & Potter, 1995).

Discursive psychology is explicitly social constructionist in its approach and treats language (be it in the form of talk or text) not as *a medium* for "telementation" (Taylor & Cameron, 1987), or the representation and transmission of thoughts between minds, but rather as **the site** where social objects such as "thoughts," "minds," and "attitudes" are *constructed* and made relevant in the conduct of social action. Talk "does, rather than is" (Rapley, 1995, p.18). The principle of the *epistemological* and *ontological* primacy of language is elegantly stated by Reicher and Hopkins (1996, p. 355):

> Language [is] not simply ... a resource from which underlying cognitive representations can be read off ... instead language (is) a domain in which category definitions are constructed and contested.

Put simply, discursive psychology grants *prior status* to language: without the *prior* existence of language, such "psychological things" as "cognitions" can, quite literally, not sensibly be talked of. Discursive psychology is, as such, anti-cognitivist in approach, viewing opinions, beliefs and attitudes, or in the sports psychology context, constructs such as expertise, judgment and skill, not as *a priori* (cognitive) phenomena which it is the task of psychology to map and to explain, but rather as shared discursive resources upon which members can draw in talk, or which can, and often do, constitute talk's business, in order to achieve locally relevant social actions.

The inspection of members' talk thus offers us the opportunity to study, empirically, the way the mind-world relationship, the nature of persons and their respective (psychological) attributes, are confected, constructed and contested in *actual* social practices. The imposition of our own, prior, categorizations (for example, schemas, causal attributions, self-categorizations) are, unless demonstrably of relevance to the members whose practices we are attempting to describe, analytically unwarranted impositions (Antaki, 1994).

What discursive analyses work towards then are the description and analysis of the prosecution of social action by members, in their terms. Drawing heavily on work in ethnomethodology and conversation analysis (Garfinkel, 1967; Psasthas, 1995; Sacks, 1972, 1995; Schütz, 1962), the task is to elucidate how versions of the social world, the nature of objects within it, and the (moral) standing and entitlements of persons, are achieved, contested and defended in descriptions, or accounts, in the course of social interaction. Edwards (1995, p. 579, emphasis added) suggests that

> Descriptions of persons, things or events are *always* ones that could have been otherwise, such that actually occurring descriptions are *always* contingent, particular and occasioned phenomena.

Accounts of the phenomena which sports and exercise scientists might wish to study are also contingent, particular and occasioned, and are thus open to study as social objects in themselves. It is, of course, also the case that there is no good epistemological case, *a priori*, for according the scholarly accounts or descriptions of sports and exercise scientists in learned journals any greater truth value than those of "ordinary" persons, be they soccer fans, sports journalists or football coaches, and that therefore the accounts offered by *these* members may offer a route to the analysis of the production of our cultures' common knowledge of sporting matters that conventional approaches, to "expertise" for example, cannot provide.

1.3   *The Discursive Psychological Approach: A Summary*

Following Edwards and Potter (1992), discursive psychology has a number of theoretical commitments, which may, otherwise, be describable as "analytic principles."

- Social action is accomplished primarily through language.
- The construction of accounts as *factual*, the management of speakers' *interest* in accounts offered, and the interplay of fact and interest are central to *all* accounts of events, things and persons.
- Attention to the management of speakers' moral *accountability* for actions and accounts of actions is pervasive in all discourse.
- It is not analytically useful to produce descriptions of social action, which rely on psychologized accounts of conduct. Such descriptions merely place the explanatory burden onto the ghost in the machine. The organization and use of such accounts is, however, a legitimate topic for discourse analytic work.
- The production of accounts, or descriptions, as persuasive or "truthful" is accomplished in an orderly, formally describable, manner. In other words, there are a number of identifiable routine conversational devices, "ways of talking" as it were, which are used in talk to achieve social actions.
- These ways of talking are rule-oriented not rule-governed (as indeed is discourse analysis).
- The central purpose of analysis is the examination and description of the mundane, but intuitively non-apparent, construction of everyday life, using materials that are independent of the analyst for their production.

In the remainder of this section I use accounts of the Stange controversy in the Western Australian print media, accounts which satisfy the criterion of *not* having been produced to order, both to demonstrate what discourse analysis is and how it works, and also to illustrate how, in ordinary members' talk, these matters are attended to.

Seeing newspaper pieces as a form of "talk," and talk as *social action* rather than the outward symptom of hidden *cognitions*, I show how speakers' dilemmas of stake, or interest, are managed by the doing of *attributions*, frequently of psychological or cognitive states or traits to others. We will see the way that reports are constructed and displayed as factual by a variety of discursive techniques, and how reports are rhetorically constructed and organized in order to contest, or otherwise to undermine, alternative versions[3].

Throughout, however, it is important to remember a further three key points. Firstly that, following Wittgenstein (1958), there is no standpoint outside of language from which to adjudicate on the "truth" of knowledge claims. That is to say, the discursive approach is resolutely relativist in its stance towards *all* "facts," and is particularly suspicious of claims, which proclaim themselves to be "factual." Secondly, discursive psychology does not aspire to the claims of (statistical) generalizability sought by mainstream psychology, but rather to achieve a rich pragrammatological (McHoul, 1997) account of phenomena of interest. Thirdly, as Reicher and Hopkins (1996, p. 355) have noted, discursive psychology is: "not *a method* in the sense of a mechanical set of rules for processing data . . . rather *it is a general analytic approach* whose precise implementation depends on the particular theoretical issues at hand."

1.4 The "Methodological" Approach of Discursive Psychology

Following from Reicher and Hopkins' (1996) point, it is not possible to specify, in advance, "how to do discourse analysis?" as one might specify "how to do analysis of variance?" Unlike quantitative approaches, which stipulate standardized rules for study design, data collection, statistical analysis, hypothesis testing, and the interpretation of results, the version of discourse analysis presented here has no recipe book[4]. Good discursive analyses are, rather, the product of the practical application of an extensive body of empirical findings, from the perspective of the theoretical position outlined above, to real-world (rather than experimentally contrived) language data.

Discourse analysis is, then, a *way of approaching questions* about the orderly manner in which social action is accomplished, characterized by open-minded intellectual curiosity. If a parallel with quantitative approaches is possible, discourse analysis may be described as being analogous to doing factor analysis with words: it is about taking collections of mundane, everyday utterances, and dissecting out from them

---

[3] There is insufficient space here to provide the level of detail usually presented in discourse analytic studies. See Potter (1996) Wetherell & Potter (1992) and Edwards (1997) for further examples.

[4] Some variants of discourse analysis attempt to offer a methodological formula (see for example, Parker, 1992, Banister, *et al*, 1994). Space precludes discussion of the major theoretical and analytic difficulties with these efforts (see Potter, 1996).

the structures and devices which produce (particular, local) meaning. A "cook-book" listing of steps is both non-feasible and also theoretically incoherent (indeed, recipes themselves are normatively produced *a posteriori*). However, in the broadest terms, discourse analysis may be understood to start from a *general intellectual interest*, perhaps a wondering about how the idea of persons having "expert sporting knowledge" is used in social interaction; through *the collection (and if necessary transcription into text) of a corpus of materials* where such notions are routinely deployed (such as newspaper articles, TV shows, talkback radio, scholarly journal papers, academic textbooks); to a *detailed examination and description* of the use of the discourse of "expertise" in the materials under study, and the uses to which it is put, informed by a wide and detailed reading of the existing (particularly conversation analytic) literature on the devices of everyday conversation management. Discourse analysis is then an analytic orientation and an acquired craft skill, rather than a set of formally teachable technical procedures. In consequence, the best way both to understand what discourse analysis "is," and to develop an appreciation of what it is that discourse analysis "does to" texts, is to study examples of the application of approach. Just such a "worked example" is presented in the next section.

1.5 *"Tana Says it's Time to Move on": A Discursive Analysis of the Print Media and the Bernd Stange Controversy*

As noted in the introduction to this chapter, the ending of Bernd Stange's appointment as Perth Glory's coach caused considerable controversy in Western Australia. The ensuing societal "conversation" (Goldhagen, 1996) in the print media between sports journalists, newspaper editors, their readers, business commentators and the discursively distributed dialogue between Glory fans and the key players in the issue, Bernd Stange and Nick Tana, illustrate several of the key issues raised by discursive psychology. Two of these issues will be dealt with here. Firstly the management of moral accountability in talk by the attribution of "psychological" traits or states to others, and by the rhetorical organization of the talk makes these attributions. Secondly, the management of stake and interest in the production of versions of events. What is analytically at issue here is not why Tana "really" decided to dispense with Stange's services, nor what either party's "real" psychological states, decision-making processes or motivations were. Such matters are, in principle, not knowable. Rather, what is of interest to discursive psychologists is the manner in which such purported social scientific "things" as "motivations," emotion states such as "homesickness" or "attachment," and cognitive skills or attributes such as "judgment" or "expert knowledge of football," are brought to bear in interaction in order to achieve specific social actions.

1.6   *A discourse analysis of the use of cultural knowledge of "psychological" states and the management of moral accountability in newspaper texts*

Since the arrival of "Reaganomics" and "Thatcherism" in the early 1980's, economic and business life have generally been constructed (at least in rhetoric) as essentially "rational" matters. Indeed the discourse of economic rationalism has spread far beyond business to encompass much of social and cultural life (Rapley & Ridgway, 1998) and, arguably, has become part of the stock of commonsense knowledge of our culture. As such one might expect that major decisions about a sports team, such as terminating the appointment of a highly successful, charismatic and popular coach, should be, purely and simply, a rational matter of business management: with decisions informed solely by a cool appraisal of the good of the club. But perhaps matters are not this straightforward. What we see in extract 1, where Glory chairman Nick Tana's account of events is quoted, in what is presented as direct reported speech[5], by the *West Australian*, is the way in which Tana attends to producing *two distinct types* of psychologic in accounting for Stange's departure.

Extract 1: WHY?[6]

1→   "The judgment was made with the knowledge that the club needs a coach

2   committed, in the long-term, to Perth, Western Australia. It was as simple as that.

3→   Bernd had not indicated he was prepared to make such a long-term commitment

4→   and I believe he would always be attached to Germany in some way. There would

5→   come a day when Bernd felt the need to return to his homeland."

Nick Tana

The West Australian, 21st February 2000.

It is of note that Tana appeals (in line 1) to at least two, rational, psychological states of his own (judgment and knowledge) as the grounds for his "simple" decision. Ending Stange's contract is a straightforward business decision based in what is *known*, and is contingent upon and subsequent to ratiocination (*judgment*).

By contrast, however, Stange's psychological state is constructed rather differently: Tana talks (lines 3 - 5) of Stange's lack of "commitment" to Perth, his competing "attachment" to Germany, and his "feel[ing] the need" to return to "his homeland."

Stange's *psychological state* (as opposed, for example, to his qualities as a coach) is thus produced as the primary contribution to Tanaís decision and, notably, Tana's account of Stange's psychological state is entirely couched in what are *emotional*, and hence, in the common-knowledge of Western cultures, non-rational terms. Such a contrasting construction serves to position Tana as the dispassionate business decision-maker, but one who is also solicitous and understanding of Stange's primeval emotional "needs," his putative homesickness and his devotion to his fatherland, and the inevitability of these non-rational, emotional, needs over-riding his "commitment" to the Glory.

It is, further, of interest that the one possibly non-rational psychological state that Tana acknowledges for himself in accounting for his actions, his "belief" that Stange would always be attached to Germany, is promptly qualified by the contention, delivered grammatically as an ineluctable statement of fact, that "there *would* come a day when Bernd felt the need to return to his homeland" (emphasis added).

This deployment of commonsensical understandings of psychological states as warrants for action is also to be seen in Extract 2. Of note here too is the implicit commentary by the journalist, Mel Moffat, on the adequacy of the moral accounting accomplished by Tana in his version of the "split."

---

[5] See Holt (1996) for a discussion of the rhetorical uses of reported speech in everyday conversation and McCarthy & Rapley, forthcoming, for a discussion of the uses of reported speech in Australian print reporting.
[6] All extracts are reproduced *exactly* as printed in the West Australian. Line numbers have been added to facilitate reference in the text.

Extract 2: GLORY SPLIT: Tana says it's time to move on.

1 [...] Tana would not comment on the way the decision was taken.

2→ "It is not a personal issue," said Tana, who escaped most of the drama of the day

3 by spending it at his farm in Manjimup.

4→ "There is no rift between us. All I can say is that in terms of where the club is now

5 — and where it needs to go and what we need to do —I never considered Bernd

6 to be a long-term stay.

7→ "I never asked him about long term. He was given a one-year contract with a one

8→ year option, which was taken up. I have no other reasons for not offering him

9 anything longer.

10 "We set ourselves certain objectives in Bernd's contract. He's achieved those.

11 It's now time to move on.

The West Australian, 17th February, 2000.

Again, in lines 2 and 4, we see Tana discounting (possibly morally disreputable) "personal" motives for the decision and, rather, appealing to both objective, historical, facts (the details of the original contract, lines 7-8), again stressing his ratiocination (consideration of the length of Stange's stay, line 5; the absence of "other reasons," line 8; the rational evaluation of the achievement of objectives, line 10) as warrant for Stange's discontinuation as coach. Tana's production of Stange's departure as the result of a rational, dispassionate, impersonal decision-making process is achieved here then partly by the repeated stress he places on rational *cognition* as the wellspring of action, and also by emphasizing the "needs" of the club (line 5). Indeed, Tana implies (in line 10) that the decision is one consensually or mutually arrived at: it is "we" who set the objectives for Bernd's contract.

Note that here the term "needs" is not, as in the previous extract, to be understood as indexing emotionality and (possible) irrationality, but rather as a synonym for *requirements*[7]. It is a requirement (for the successful future of the club) that Perth Glory "move[s] on." Of course, and again in a drawing upon the common-knowledge of the culture, the notion of "moving on" implies the growth, progress and betterment of the club: the core tropes of the economic rationalist/consumerist discourses within which Tana seeks to locate himself, and, simultaneously, his actions.

What these extracts demonstrate then is that Tana's orientation to the necessity of attending to the issue of *his own rationality* is central to the construction of *events* he seeks to establish. His talk attends to both managing his stake, or interest, in the matter (Potter, 1996) and also to his moral accountability. His talk then functions to establish a *version* of himself as motivated by other than emotional, base or "personal," concerns, and as acting not out of spite, because of a possible "rift" between himself and the coach, but rather out of his concern for the (emotional) needs of Bernd Stange and the (sporting) needs of the Glory. What are supposedly private "psychological" states or processes are here understandable *not* as veridical reports of Tana's interior "cognitive" activity, but rather as public deployments of cultural knowledge of "psychological" states as *rhetorical resources* designed to achieve very particular *social* ends.

But this, it might be argued, is just personal idiosyncrasy, a part of the way that Nick Tana conducts himself in the world, an aspect of his personality? Examination of a range of convergent evidence, however, would suggest that this is not so. That precisely such a moral accounting is a necessary component of everyday sociality, and the terms in which it is normatively to be managed, are already implicit in Moffat's indirect condemnation of Tana's actions in Extract 2. In lines 2-3 we are told, in a break from the reporting of Tana's own voice, and in a detail quite unnecessary to the story, that Tana, accountably, "escaped the drama" and spent the day after the "split" (hiding?) at his farm, and also by ordinary members' contributions to the letters page of the *West Australian*. For example in Extract 3, having established his incumbency in a membership category especially *entitled* to an account (a Perth Glory member), McDermott (2000) directly addresses Tana and explicitly makes the rationality of his actions the issue at stake:

---

[5] The very local contingency of meaning emphasised in discursive psychology is well illustrated here. Other qualitative approaches, such as content analysis, are entirely unable to manage such indexicality.

Extract 3: Please explain.

1   Nick Tana, I am a Perth Glory member and I am not sure whether
           Bernd Stange is

2→   the right man for the job or not. I obviously haven't got the facts, as
           you have, but

3   I do know that the way you have terminated his contract is wrong.
           [...]

4→   Come on Nick, give a rational explanation or be guided by your board
           and extend

5   Stange's contract.

The West Australian, 22nd February 2000.

McDermott constructs an epistemological discontinuity between Tana's psychological state (his knowledge of the facts) and his failure to offer a "rational" (i.e., knowledge-based) account. "Having the facts" (line 2) and giving a "rational explanation" (line 4) are states which, in logic, are necessarily related. However, discursive psychology insists that facticity and rationality are primarily *social* categories with more of a *moral* than an *evidential* or epistemic status, and that the status of utterances or actions with regard to these categories is not determinable *a priori*, but rather is local and contingently worked up. While it may be argued that the letter writer is perhaps less than articulate, or is grammatically challenged, the epistemological discontinuity worked up here, between Tana's purported psychological state and his actions, functions effectively to leave open the inference that his actions are, indeed, irrational (he has all the facts but he has disregarded them) and, as such, not only (doubly) morally wrong but also accountable and in need of rectification.

Connew (2000) similarly trades on membership category incumbency as warrant for demanding that Tana offer a moral account of his reasoning (lines 3-4: "an explanation of why you are dumping a popular and successful coach"). Connew's accusation of ontological gerrymandering (Potter, 1996), that Tana is deliberately, and accountably, offering an incomplete version of events, is strengthened here by a number of rhetorical devices. Connew stresses the number of persons affected by Tana's actions: "you owe *us all* an explanation"; the use of the emotive descriptor "dumping" ("discontinuing," while strictly speaking a more accurate gloss on the contractual details, would have considerably less rhetorical force); citing positive aspects of the un-named Stange's "personality" (he is "popular") and his performance (he is "successful"); and the provision of a three-part list (Jefferson, 1990) of candidate (understandable, reasonable, rational) motives (money, results and conflict) for the decision which Tana himself has not offered.

Extract 4: Why, Mr. Tana?

[...]

1 I am a loyal supporter and season ticket holder who takes an interest in what

2 happens to my team.

3→ Mr. Tana, as chairman, you owe us all an explanation of why you are dumping a

4→ popular and successful coach. If you can't afford him, say so. If he is not getting

5→ results say so. If there is a conflict, say so. At least show a bit of openness and

6 honesty.

7→ Just like any business, the stability and success of a sporting club is built on

8 the quality of its staff. Perth Glory can't afford to alienate its supporters by letting

9 go of its best people. Please explain.

The West Australian, 18th February 2000.

Having constructed Tana's account as duplicitous and dishonest (lines 4-5; line 6), Connew blends (lines 7-9) the tropes Tana himself has deployed as warrant for his actions - see extracts 1 and 2, economic rationalism/ consumerism (Connew : "just like *any business*, the *stability and success* ... is built on the *quality of its staff*": Tana, "we set ourselves certain *objectives* in Bernd's *contract* ... *time to move on*) and loyalty/commitment to the Glory (Connew, the club "can't afford to alienate its *supporters* ... *[Glory's] best people*": Tana : "the club needs a coach *committed, in the long-term, to Perth*, Western Australia"), to turn Tana's account against him. Again, the very local flexibility of description, and the rhetorically organized deployment of culturally commonsensical discourses displayed in these contrasting accounts, notionally of the same set of events, is analytically suggestive. The indexicality of meaning shown here suggests that we must exercise extreme caution in relying upon notions of language which comprehend meaning as lexically or semantically given, as opposed to pragmatically determined. Furthermore the prior indeterminacy of meaning demonstrated throughout these extracts suggests that an uncritical reliance on notions of "discourses" as monolithic and deterministic meaning structures (e.g., Parker, 1992) is unlikely to offer a sufficiently sophisticated theoretical framework within which to analyze the finely crafted use of language to achieve locally contingent social action.

In the final extract such sophisticated management of linguistic resources is displayed in the reflexive deployment of "psychological" (knowledge) attributes, which are here attributed to Tana as *his own* claims to specialist expertise in and knowledge of football, to ironize both his cognitive capacities and also his managerial actions. Bechta's (2000) ironic quotation of Tana in his letter to the editor not only demonstrates the way in which the media afford discursively distributed dialogues (Leudar & Antaki, 1998), but also illustrates the manner in which texts such as these display their continuity with everyday conversation.

Extract 5: Leave our coach.

1   After failing to renew Bernd Stange's contract, Glory chairman and self-appointed

2→   "I know everything there is to know about football person," Nick Tana said: "It's

3   time to move on," (report, 17/2).

4   Well all I can say to Mr. Tana is, yes, the sooner you move on the better. But leave

5   the coach where he is needed and where he has succeeded.

The West Australian, 20th February 2000.

The ironizing of Tana's use of the modernist/consumerist discourse of progress and development invoked in the notion of "moving on" is accomplished by concretizing and personalizing the pro-term (Sacks, 1995) (the suggestion that it is Tana who should "move on"). This deployment once more suggests that some approaches to discourse analysis which explicitly claim a Foucaultian inspiration, particularly approaches which attempt an algorithmic, "cook-book," approach (c.f., Parker, 1992; Banister *et al*, 1994), have been insufficiently attentive to the crucial notion of "mundane or everyday acts of resistance" (McHoul & Grace, 1993, p. 86) in Foucault's analysis of discourse.

The important point that discursive psychology makes here is that "discourses" may most profitably be understood not as *a priori* social scientific things, but as *resources* which are available to members, as repertoires for the production of locally relevant meanings. The task of the analyst then, becomes not the rather tedious and trivial enumeration of a tally of discourses identified, but rather the explication of the way in which social (and sporting) life, what is to count as "true," what is to be allowable as "rational," what may be understood as an aspect of the "psychology" of others, is produced, in and for the moment, by and through the use of language, the local crafting of discursive repertoires and the flexible deployment of rhetorical devices.

Indeed, as Segrave observed, in the quote opening this chapter, if we carefully examine talk of and about sport: "control, power, and supremacy are relevant, and the language of sport....offers us a fascinating window into the very soul of our existence" or, as McHoul put it, it is in language that sport and everyday life leak into each other.

References

Antaki, C. (1994) *Explaining and Arguing: The social organization of accounts.* London: Sage

Banister, P., Burman, E., Parker, I., Taylor, M., & Tindall, C. (1994) *Qualitative Methods in Psychology: A Research Guide.* Buckingham: Open University Press

Bechta, E. (2000) Leave our coach. Letter to the editor. *The West Australian,* 20th February.

Connew, R. (2000) Why, Mr. Tana? Letter to the editor. *The West Australian,* 18th February.

Edwards, D. (1997) *Discourse and Cognition*, London: Sage.

Edwards, D. (1995) Sacks and psychology. *Theory and Psychology, 5,* 579-596

Edwards, D., Ashmore, M., & Potter, J. (1995). Death and Furniture: The rhetoric, politics, and theology of bottom line arguments against relativism. *History of the Human Sciences, 8,* 25-49.

Edwards, D. & Potter, J. (1992) *Discursive Psychology*, London: Sage.

Eskes, T. B., Duncan, M.C. & Miller, E.M. (1998) The discourse of empowerment: Foucault, Marcuse, and women's fitness texts, *Journal of Sport and Social Issues, 22,* 317-344.

Fairclough, N. (1993). Critical Discourse Analysis and the marketisation of public discourse: The universities. *Discourse and Society, 4,* 133-159.

Garfinkel, H. (1967) *Studies in Ethnomethodology*. Englewood Cliffs, NJ: Prentice-Hall

Goldhagen D. J. (1996) *Hitlerís Willing Executioners: Ordinary Germans and the Holocaust.* London, Little, Brown & Co.

Hallinan, C. J. (1994) The presentation of human biological diversity in sport and exercise science textbooks: the example of "race." *Journal of Sport Behavior, 17,* 3 -13

Holt, E. J. (1996). Reporting on talk: The use of direct reported speech in conversation. *Research on Language & Social Interaction, 29,* 219-246.

Hughson, J. (2000) The boys are back in town: Soccer support and the social reproduction of masculinity, *Journal of Sport and Social Issues, 24,* 8-23.

Jansen, S., & Sabo, D. (1994) The sport/war metaphor: Hegemonic masculinity, the Persian Gulf War, and the new world order. *Sociology of Sport Journal, 11,* 1-17.

Jefferson, G. (1990) List construction as a task and resource. In G. Psathas (Ed.) *Interaction Competence.* Lanham, MD, University Press of America.

Keddie, P. (2000) Goodbye to Glory. Letter to the editor. *The West Australian,* 20th February.

Leudar, I., & Antaki, C. (1998) *Using voices of others in Parliamentary argumentation.* Paper presented at the International Pragmatics Association Conference, Reims, France, July.

Lukes, T. J. (2000) I'm not really a doctor, but I play one on TV: Glibness in America. *Journal of Sport and Social Issues,* 24, 78-83.

McCarthy, D., & Rapley, M. (Forthcoming) Making madmen and monsters: The Australian print media and the social construction of Martin Bryant. Manuscript submitted for publication.

McDermott, G. (2000) Please explain. Letter to the Editor, *The West Australian*, 22nd February.

McHoul, A. (1997) On doing "we's": Where sport leaks into everyday life. *Journal of Sport and Social Issues,* 21, 315-320.

McHoul, A., & Grace, W. (1993) *A Foucault Primer: Discourse, power and the subject.* Melbourne, Melbourne University Press.

MacAloon, J. J. (1996) On the structural origins of Olympic individuality. *Research Quarterly for Exercise and Sport,* 67, 136-147.

Miller, T. (1990) Sport, media and masculinity. In D. Rowe & G. Lawrence (Eds.) *Sport and leisure: Trends in Australian popular culture* (pp. 74-95). Sydney: Harcourt, Brace Jovanovitch.

Miller, T. and McHoul, A. (1998) *Popular Culture and Everyday Life.* London: Sage

Moffat, M. (2000a) Glory near crisis as owners fall out. *The West Australian,* 25th February.

Moffat, M. (2000b) Glory split: Tana says it's time to move on. *The West Australian,* 17th February.

Moffat, M. (2000c) Glory days over as Stange dumped. *The West Australian,* 16th February.

Parker, I. (1992) *Discourse Dynamics: Critical analysis for social and individual psychology.* London, Routledge.

Potter, J. (1996) *Representing reality: Discourse, rhetoric and social construction.* London: Sage.

Psathas, G. (1995) *Conversation Analysis: The study of talk-in-interaction.* Thousand Oaks, CA.: Sage.

Rapley, M. (in press) How to do *x* without doing *y*: accomplishing discrimination without "being racist" - doing equity. In M. Augoustinos & K. Reynolds (Eds.) *Us and Them: The psychology of prejudice and racism.* London, Sage.

Rapley, M., & Ridgway, J. (1998) Quality of Life talk and the corporatisation of intellectual disability. *Disability and Society, 13*, 451-471.

Rapley, M. (1995) Black swans: Conversation analysis of quality of life interviews with people with learning disabilities. *Clinical Psychology Forum, 84*, 17-23.

Reicher, S., & Hopkins, N. (1996) Self-category constructions in political rhetoric; an analysis of Thatcherís and Kinnockís speeches concerning the British miner's strike (1984-5). *European Journal of Social Psychology, 26*, 353-371.

Sacks, H. (1972) An initial investigation of the usability of conversation for doing sociology. In D. Sudnow (ed.) *Studies in Social Interaction* (pp. 31-74). New York: Free Press.

Sacks, H. (1995) *Lectures on Conversation, Vols. 1 and 2.* Ed. G. Jefferson; Intro. E.A. Schegloff. Oxford: Blackwell.

Scambler, G., & Jennings, M. (1998) On the periphery of the sex industry: Female combat, male punters, and feminist discourse, *Journal of Sport and Social Issues, 22*, 416-430

Schütz, A. (1962) *Collected Papers Vol. 1: The problem of social reality.* Ed. and intro. M. Natanson. The Hague: Martinus Nijhoff.

Segrave, J. O. (1997) A matter of life and death: Some thoughts on the language of sport, *Journal of Sport and Social Issues, 21*, 211-220.

Staurowsky, E. J. (1998) Critiquing the language of the gender equity debate, *Journal of Sport and Social Issues, 22*, 7-26

Taylor, T. J. & Cameron, D. (1987) *Analysing Conversation: Rules and units in the structure of talk.* Oxford: Pergamon Press.

tenHave, P. (1999) *Doing Conversation Analysis: A practical guide.* London: Sage

Tyler-Eastman, S., & Billings, A.C. (1999) Gender parity in the Olympics, *Journal of Sport and Social Issues*, *23*, 140-170.

Wetherell, M., & Potter, J. (1992) *Mapping the Language of Racism: Discourse and the legitimation of exploitation.* Hemel Hempstead: Harvester Wheatsheaf

Wittgenstein, L. (1958) *Philosophical Investigations.*Oxford: Blackwell.

(2) Constructivist Research: Methodology and Practice

Kathleen Fahy and Karey Harrison

This section, which focuses on constructivist research and the next (which is concerned with critical, postmodern and feminist methodology) are related to each other. These methodologies use qualitative research methods extensively. This section therefore, takes a broad perspective on qualitative research. Qualitative research, it will be shown, is the most appropriate approach when one is studying human feelings, actions and values.

The main aim of this section is to provide the researcher with the knowledge and skills to be able to (a) design and using philosophical arguments, defend qualitative research within sports science (b) design research that maintains consistency between methodology, research design, data collection and data analysis methods (c) conduct in-depth interviews in ways that produce high quality data and (d) select and apply appropriate qualitative data analysis processes carefully matching the chosen technique to the research tradition, the research question and the purpose of the study.

This section includes a significant discussion on philosophy. This is needed because the methodology of constructivism is such a departure from the dominant way of conducting research. The section on the Philosophy of Science, although it may initially appear to be abstract and difficult for beginners, is in fact highly useful to the novice researcher. This is because qualitative researchers are generally operating outside the methodologically accepted framework of traditional science where the philosophical assumptions are generally accepted unquestioned. Researchers need to have the rhetoric to defend their methodological decisions and to situate their arguments within a broad understanding of the arguments that are being discussed in the Philosophy of Science literature.

Notwithstanding the worth of working through the first section of this chapter the reader is invited to skim it initially and move quickly to the main section of the chapter concerning Research Practice Within the Constructivist Framework. It may be that after reading the methodological implications for research practice that the reader will be more interested in returning to the philosophical foundations for these practices.

2.1   *Critique of Positivism*

Positivism in the Bio-Physical Sciences: Essentially the problem created by positivism is that biological, psychological and social sciences have been modeled on what had been prescriptively advocated by positivist philosophers of science as the methodology of the physical sciences (Giddens, 1979). Researchers in the human sciences have often clung to outdated philosophical assumptions that have long been discarded by physical sciences e.g., the Newtonian understanding of the universe has given way to Quantum Physics and Chaos Theory (Gleick, 1987).

The so-called 'scientific method' is based on many positivistic philosophical assumptions which are not normally made explicit. The purpose of this section is to clarify and critique the metaphysical commitments of traditional science concerning facts and theories and the supposed relationship between them so that the problems concerning knowledge claims in logico-empirical science can be made evident. The reason for critiquing these assumptions within the bio-physical sciences first is to show that they are a problem even in these sciences and that many of these discredited assumptions still infect logico-empirical research today; thus this critique is relevant to all researchers in the Sports Sciences even those who will never conduct qualitative research. This section of the chapter also demonstrates that the methodological problems of using logico-empiricism multiply exponentially when inappropriate assumptions are applied to a natural system like human behavior and motivation.

This section uses philosophical concepts and arguments to discuss and critique research methodology and practice. A number of terms are used that are defined in Table 6.1.

Table 6.1

Definitions of terms for research methodology

Where there is general consensus about the meaning of terms only one definition is given but where logico-empiricism differs from newer research frameworks a distinction is made thus: a) = Logico-empirical definition b) = Inclusive definition

Science

a)   'A branch of study which is concerned with a connected body of demonstrated truths or with observed facts systematically classified and more or less colligated by being brought under general laws and which includes trustworthy methods for the discovery of new truths within its domain'. (Flew 1983).

b) The production of knowledge by systematic and verifiable means (Punch, 1994)

Research

a) A systematic, reproducible, process of problem-solving which uses empirical data, reductive processes and logical procedures to generalize from individual events in order to establish general relationship among variables (Thomas & Nelson, 1996)

b) "A scientific process of inquiry that involves purposeful, systematic and rigorous collection, analysis and interpretation of data to gain new knowledge" (Talbot, 1995, p57).

Philosophy

Philosophy speculates on matters as to which there is no definite knowledge. Philosophy appeals to human reason as a way of influencing scholars to a particular position or point of view. There are three main branches of philosophy: Logic, metaphysics and ethics (Russell, 1946)

Metaphysics

Metaphysics is that branch of philosophy which deals with first principles including concepts such as being, essence, knowing, causation etc. Metaphysics has two main sub-branches; ontology and epistemology (Flew, 1983).

Ontology

Ontology is concerned with existence itself. Researchers want to know what exists, what is 'real' as opposed to what is merely appearance or illusion. Ontology is central to research methodology (Crotty, 1998).

Epistemology

Epistemology is the study and theory of knowledge and knowing. It concerns the scope of knowledge and the trustworthiness of knowledge claims (Crotty, 1998). Put more simply, epistemology is about how we 'know' what we claim to know.

a) Rationalists argue that human reason, intrinsic to the mind, is the primary source of knowledge (Flew, 1983).

b)   Empiricists argue that the experiences of the five senses are the primary source of knowledge. Empiricists are also objectivists believing in the objective reality which they seek to observe (Crotty, 1998).

Logico-empiricists attempt to combine both 'objective' reason and sense data as a way of acquiring sure knowledge.

In contrast, qualitative researchers believe that there is neither objective 'reason' nor objective sense 'data', and that the categories and relations of human reason and perception emerge from our engagement with the world (Crotty, 1998).

Concept

A concept is a theoretical idea e.g. 'anaemia' 'aggressiveness'; 'social isolation'; 'masculinity'. The idea of a concept implies deciding what is and what is not part of that concept.

a)   In the logico-empirical framework it is important that concepts are clearly defined so that there is little, or no, room for ambiguity. This is achieved by the researcher or theorist defining their terms such that each concept has a number of properties, which are identified, and they, in turn, are defined. These properties are then operationalized as indicators or variables which can be measured in research. 'Determination' for example is a property of the concept 'aggressiveness' therefore questions can be asked on a survey instrument such that the property (variable) 'determination' can be measured.

b)   An alternative view is that concepts in the social sciences are inherently non-definable and have shades of meaning depending upon the particular speaker and the context. Thus, generally, the researcher does not attempt to define concepts but instead allows the meanings of research participants to emerge.

Theory

a)   A theory is a set of concepts, definitions and propositions that projects a systematic view of phenomena by designating specific interrelationships among concepts for the purposes of describing, explaining, predicting, and/or controlling phenomena (Chinn & Jacobs 1987, p.70).

b)   Theory comprises a creative and rigorous structuring of ideas (or concepts) that projects a tentative, purposeful and systematic view of phenomena (Chinn & Cramer, 1991, p. 73)

Facts and Theories are not 'the Truth':

Logico-Empiricism acts 'as if" Facts are true: Popper: Logico-empiricism is so named because of its belief that truth can be derived through the application of logical theories to empirical facts. This belief is exemplified in Figure 6.1 using a theory from biology to illustrate the relationship between theory and 'facts'. The relation between initial conditions, explanatory theory or covering law, and prediction is seen as equivalent to the logical relationship holding between the premise and warrant of an argument, and its conclusion. The advantage of acting as if facts and theories are parts of an argument, is that logically, if the premise and warrant of a sound argument is true, the truth of the conclusion is guaranteed. In an argument, if the conclusion is false, then either the premise or the warrant must be false. Logico-empiricism treats the 'facts' regarding the initial conditions of an experiment as equivalent to an argument's premise, the hypothesis, law or theory being tested as equivalent to its warrant, and the 'facts' predicted by the outcome of the experiment as equivalent to an argument's conclusion. If this was an accurate reflection of scientific practice, then if what the theory predicts does not happen and we are sure the facts are true, then the theory must be wrong. This is the logical basis of Popper's falsification theory which has been so influential in logico-empirical science but which we are about to deconstruct.

Table 6.2

Mapping the form of scientific explanation onto that of logical argument.

Argument	scientific explanation
Premise: a is x	**initial conditions:** observable event a at (time) t_1
	John (a), an athlete who lives in Sydney (i.e. sea level) has a normal Hemoglobin (Hb) level of 150g/l and no symptoms of anaemia (x)
Warrant: if x then y	**covering law (or theory or hypothesis):** *e.g.. If an athlete with a normal Hb goes to an area of very high altitude (x) then he will develop symptoms typical of anaemia (breathlessness, tiredness). The severity of the symptoms is directly related to the level of altitude (y)*
Conclusion: so, a is y	**Prediction:** observable event b at (time) t_2
	Outcome: *John(a) goes to Mexico City (i.e. high altitude) and develops symptoms that are typical of anaemia even though he has a 'normal' hemoglobin level (y)*

In the next section it will be demonstrated that there are no such things as unproblematic 'facts' and that facts and theories are not separate but inextricably entwined. If it can't reliably be established that 'facts' are true then it follows that 'facts' can't reliably be used to test the truth or falsity of theories either.

Critique: Facts and Theories Inextricably Linked: A common problem for traditional science is that people, including researchers, tend to think of 'facts' as being 'out there'; this understanding of the relationship between facts and theories is represented in Figure 6.1 (below). In scientific research, however, the 'facts' are not 'things out there'. Scientific facts are statements that scientists make that report what they believe to be the case. The 'facts' are a representation of our understanding of the world and are not the world itself. For example, when John has his blood tested for hemoglobin levels, his blood in the test tube is the 'thing out there' it is not the 'fact'. A 'fact' is always a statement of belief about the 'thing out there' in this case the laboratory reports the 'fact' that 'John has Hb 150g/l of whole blood'. Further, the inference that can be taken by knowing this 'fact' is that John does not have anaemia.

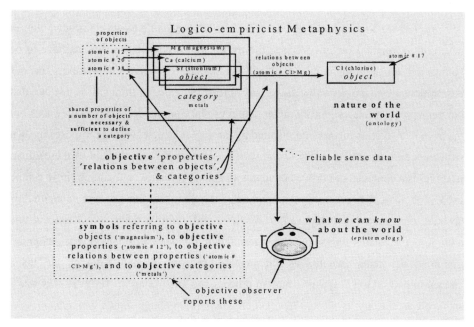

Figure 6.1   This is a representation of logico-empiricist beliefs about the relation between what exists in the world and what we can know about what exists.

Between the 'thing' and the 'fact' are human perceptual processes, laboratory equipment and techniques. Scientists know, on the one hand, that human perception does not correspond to reality, and yet traditional science proceeds as if getting agreement between scientists is sufficient to establish knowledge or 'the truth'. Science's attempts to protect its claims to truth do not go far enough. Having rigorous processes for reliability of measuring tools offers protection against individual biases but ignores problems of perception which are shared by all humans. Perceptual 'distortions' are built into the very structure of our perceptual apparatus. Television, for instance, would not work if what humans 'see' was not different from what 'is there'. To the extent that we understand how our perceptual apparatus works we can guard against known perceptual biases. But we do not, and cannot know all of these perceptual biases. Therefore any 'objectivity' we gain will continue to be relative to our beliefs about the world, particularly our beliefs about how our perceptual apparatus and our brains work. This illustrates one way in which facts are dependent upon theory, in this case the working scientist's understanding of, and attempted compensation for, the way the brain works in perception.

For the logical argument described in Table 6.2 to have explanatory value in describing a method for uncovering 'the truth', logico-empirical scientists have to be committed epistemologically to a correspondence between the symbols in our descriptions of phenomena (the facts) and objectively existing things. It is not just that our perceptual structures modify rather than reproduce or mirror 'things as they are', but the truth of a 'fact' is further complicated by the way in which language imposes its own structures on our understanding of the world. For example, the concept of the element iron (Fe) is a concrete and stable concept with fixed properties so the noun 'iron' can be used in a logical argument unambiguously. By contrast, the concept 'anaemia' is abstract, constructed and imposed on dynamic and multiple bodily processes yet this ambiguity is usually ignored. This means that the statement 'John has anaemia' grammatically treats 'anaemia' as if it was the same kind of noun that 'iron' is. This is an example of taking a dynamic human process and attempting to 'fix' it as if it was a stable physical thing.

The way in which language is used to try to fix essentially dynamic processes causes not only philosophical but also practical difficulties. For example: the properties of 'anaemia' include having a low Hb level, the signs of hypoxia (breathlessness, tiredness, tachycardia) and pallor. In the practice of medicine, however, anaemia is a laboratory diagnosis such that if someone complains of the symptoms of hypoxia but their laboratory report indicates 'normal' Hb then the person is said to be 'not anaemic'. Yet, when athletes moves to high altitude they do experience most of the symptoms of anaemia and the symptoms will not improve until their Hb level increases, sometimes above normal. This is because "normal" Hb levels are based on people living near sea level. Again, unlike 'Iron', which is stable in different times and places on earth, 'Anaemia' is not a stable concept because it has so many properties that can vary and because these properties vary relative to altitude.

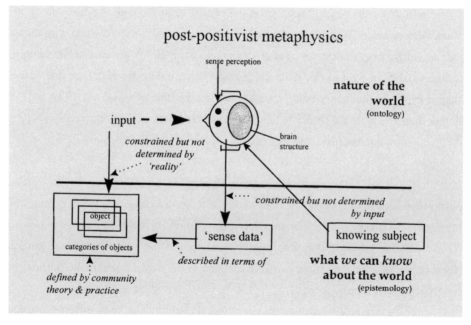

Figure 6.2   This is a representation of post-positivist beliefs about the relation between what exists in the world and what we can know about it.

Whereas statements of fact make reference to specific things, like 'John's symptoms of anaemia', theories and hypothesis refer to classes of things, like 'anaemia as a disease'. To establish the validity of an argument or logic-empirical scientific explanation, scientists must be able to identify specific things, or events, as clear-cut members of a particular class. Category membership needs to be determined by the specific 'fact' fitting the 'theoretical concept' exactly. In the case of John's symptoms of anaemia when he first moves to Mexico, he has some of the features (properties) of the theoretical concept or class 'anaemia as a disease' i.e., breathlessness and tiredness, but not others i.e., 'low' Hb and pallor. Thus there is debate about whether John is 'really' anaemic or whether his anaemia is 'true'. Whereas 'objective categories' have clear-cut membership, so that a specific case either is or is not an example of that category, categories like 'anaemia as a disease' fit the specific case more or less well. The logic of Table 6.2, however, depends on specific cases (as identified in the initial condition and in the outcome) being unambiguously members of the general class mentioned in the hypothesis or covering law.

In this section we have given some examples of the way in which 'facts' are always theory laden. We have shown that since facts are always intertwined with theory then scientific research cannot consist - as positivists claim it does - of comparing or testing theories in light of the evidence, because the evidence (or facts) are themselves shaped by either the theory being tested or some other theory (Giddens, 1979, p.275). Rather than giving up the theory being tested one can always modify the theory shaping the 'facts' in ways that make the incompatible 'data' disappear (Lakatos, 1976).

Goals of Science: Broader than Prediction and Control: Pragmatically, positivist researchers claim to be committed to the uncovering of objective truth and predictive explanatory laws. The above critique, however, draws the whole notion of 'objective truth' into question. The mastery and control over the physical and natural world that predictive laws make possible remains as the primary pragmatic purpose of positivistic scientific research.

Just as the epistemological and ontological commitments of positivistic research have been subject to critique, so too have these pragmatic commitments. The determinism of Newtonian physics, that had initially made the goal of control over the physical and natural world seem feasible, was first brought into question by the developments in quantum mechanics, and more recently developments in the modeling of complex non-deterministic systems. Theorists studying such systems have proven that even if you start with a simple system following simple rules the iteration of rules can result in 'immensely complicated and [inherently] unpredictable consequences' (Waldrop, 1992).

Both natural systems, like forests and human brains, and social systems, like economies, seem to have the properties of sensitive dependence on initial conditions[8] and/or a non-deterministic relation between the causes and effects[9] operating in the system that produce such unpredictability. Although scientists are beginning to develop relatively sophisticated models of such systems, giving us a reasonable degree of confidence in our understanding of the causes operating in particular systems, the success of such models does not enable us to predict with certainty the outcome of any particular intervention in, or modification of the system we are interested in.

In the section above, our aim in deconstructing the philosophical assumptions of logico-empiricism is neither to reject it entirely nor to assume a post-modern position of nihilism. We agree that Logico-empiricism, particularly post-positivism, is still the best way we have of acquiring knowledge in the physical and biological sciences. Our purpose rather has been to illuminate that our faith in the scientific method has been too trusting and too complete. We can no longer see ourselves as Masters of the natural world, who, if we only know enough, will be able to control a clockwork universe. Rather, we are forced to see ourselves as gambling strategists, playing the odds in a world of uncertainty and unpredictability. Even though we can no longer believe that we can have total control, playing the odds intelligently is better than having no knowledge at all. Logico-empirical researchers are called to be conscious of their assumptions, more explicit about their theories and humble about their findings.

Positivism in the Social and Behavioral Sciences:

Facts and Theories are not 'the Truth': In this section we plan to demonstrate how the problems of positivism in the biophysical sciences multiply exponentially when inappropriately applied to the social sciences. In the biological and physical sciences, it sometimes is the case that the properties of a class concept apply universally to members

---

[8] The 'butterfly effect' is a metaphor based on this idea of 'sensitive dependence on initial conditions'. The idea is that small, unmeasurable, differences between initial conditions can produce dramatic differences in final outcome. So, a butterfly flapping its wings in Arizona may create a pattern of turbulence that over a few weeks will change the state of the atmosphere, producing, for instance, a storm in Brisbane that might not otherwise have occurred.

[9] In a forest, for instance, the probability that a seed will germinate 'may increase as the rainfall increases and the sunlight increases and as the abundance of animals that spread the seeds increase', but none of these causal factors guarantee seed germination, it just increases the probability that a particular seed will germinate rather than not. The relation between cause and effect in such cases is **probabilistic** rather than **deterministic**. See Botkin, D. *Discordant Harmonies: A New Ecology for the Twenty-first Century*, Oxford University Press, Oxford, pp.119ff.

of that class. So we can say, for instance, that 'all saltwater is composed of water and sodium chloride' (the class concept being 'saltwater' and the properties being 'sodium and water'). Social and psychological concepts however are complex and rarely observable and measurable in the same way that physical concepts are. This will be discussed in more detail below. Because of the difficulties associated with defining and measuring in the social science the previous logical argument (Table 6.1) cannot be used. In the behavioral and social sciences therefore, overwhelmingly, logico-empiricists rely upon statistical correlations between individual examples of proposed general classes. Logico-empiricists continue to rely on the logic of argument but the mapping of 'argument' is changed to a statistical one. An example of a statistical argument mapped onto scientific explanation is provided in Figure 6.3, which should be compared with Figure 6.1 for similarities and differences.

Table 6.3

Argument Mapping in the Social Sciences

Statistical argument	scientific explanation
Premise: a random of *xs* are examined sample for *y*ness	**initial conditions:** observable event a at (time) t_1 e.g.. *A random sample of female participants in the Olympic games* (x) *are tested for masculinity traits* (y) .
Warrant: most *xs* are *ys*	**covering law (or theory or hypothesis)** e.g., the majority of women who are successful sportswomen (x)will score highly on tests for masculinity (y) The greater their success the higher their rating on masculinity scales (Bem, 1974)
Conclusion: so, most of this sample of *xs* are *ys*	**prediction: observable event b at (time)** t_2 *The majority of women tested will score highly on masculinity traits.* **Outcome:** *The majority of women tested scored highly on masculinity traits even though, when questioned, very few indicated that they felt themselves to be 'masculine' women.*

Using the example above, a brief application of the ideas previously developed will demonstrate the way in which the problems of positivism are amplified in the social sciences.

Problems with Objectivism: Ontologically and epistemologically, logico-empirical researchers are committed to treating people, their thinking, feelings and behavior, as if they were 'objects' 'in the same manner as natural 'objects' (Giddens, 1979, p. 224). So instead of having 'objects' and their 'properties' as the observational data, people and our theoretical concepts about them become the 'facts' to be studied and explained by science. It is obvious that all the problems, which were relevant to facts and theories in the biosciences, apply here too. This way of viewing the social world is represented in Figure 6.3.

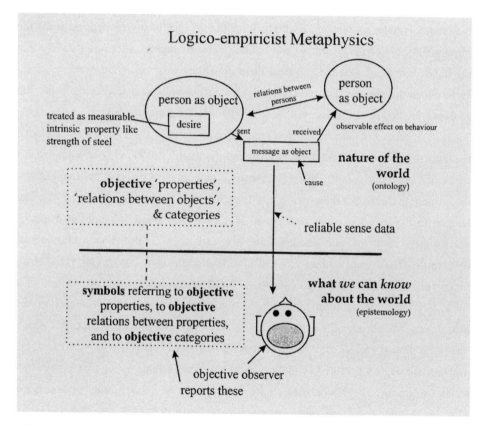

Figure 6.3   A Representation of Logico-Empiricist Beliefs Applied to the Social World.

In the previous section, we demonstrated that a basic premise of logico-empiricism is 'that facts can be used to falsify theories' but this is not a premise that could be supported. This is in part, we demonstrated because 'facts' are really 'statements' of current understanding. By acting as if 'facts' were 'true' we make fundamental errors in research which leads to unacknowledged (and usually unknown) errors in knowledge. In the example of the female athlete (Table 6.3) what 'facts' exist? The theoretical construct of masculinity is not a 'fact' and neither are the various measures of 'determination', 'aggressiveness', etc. that are supposed to be the properties of the class concept 'masculinity'.

In the preceding section, we identified further problems with 'the facts'. In the language of biosciences language people are treated 'as if' they are 'facts' as scientists struggle to be 'objective' as if they are somehow outside the realm of humanity which they share with their subjects. The difficulty with the objectivist view of language is the impossibility of defining, limiting and holding dynamic human processes stable so that the logico-empirical scientist can treat them as if they were objective, stable physical facts. Given the abstract and even more dynamic nature of social science concepts, the problems created by the objectivist view of language are compounded.

Another problem with 'the facts,' as understood in the biosciences, included that human perception is not a direct mirror of the world 'out there'. Although tests of reliability can guard against individual bias (or perceptual problems) by a researcher, they cannot protect against the perceptual bias that we all experience by virtue of being human. In the social sciences it is not so much our perceptual apparatus that lets us down, since most of our concepts are not amenable to direct or technological observation. The corresponding problem for social scientists is conceptual. Our human social constructs, including the concepts of social science theory, are not mirrors of a world 'out there'. In addition, although we have tests to measure the reliability of our instruments, the history of the social sciences is littered with discarded concepts, which were once thought to be true, and we taught to others as 'scientific knowledge'. This problem can be demonstrated by looking at the example in Table 6.3 concerning women athletes who scored highly on masculinity. A high score on a masculinity scale is not a 'fact' but a statement derived from a culturally and historically specific theory. Unlike the bio-physical world where at least there is something real 'out there' a concept like masculinity is entirely a social conceptual construction so that it is even more difficult to describe, observe and measure something like 'masculinity' which does not even exist. Further, even if we acted 'as if' there was something real called masculinity, some of the properties of 'masculinity' i.e., assertiveness, competitiveness and being highly individual are essential for success in competitive sport such that all successful sportswomen are likely to score highly. This is because sportspeople are highly motivated to achieve in sport. High masculinity scores do not mean that someone is 'really' masculine or that they necessarily rate highly on other gender-related traits that are not related to sports. This example shows that if the biosciences have problems with not being able to distinguish 'facts' and 'theories', that problem is much greater in the social sciences.

Finally, we indicated that the advances in understanding in physics acknowledge the impossibility of prediction and control in natural systems. The pragmatics of logico-empiricism concerns the desire to predict and control human behavior. Yet that is not really possible because humans are inner directed, at least to some extent, and live in complex, uncontrollable social environments. This means that logico-empirical social science often risks being seen as either imperialistic and of dubious ethics or so non practical as to be questioned in terms of why bother to do the research at all.

2.2   *Interpretivism and Constructivism: 'Making Meaning of Actions'*

Shared Assumptions: Interpretative and constructivist researchers reject the objectivist view of language (discussed in the section on Positivism in the Social Science). Once the 'object' of our understanding shifts from the physical to the social world, the critique of the nature of language ceases to be merely an epistemological problem and becomes, as well, an ontological problem, i.e., it concerns the existence and nature of the objects we claim to know. Once the objectivist view of language is rejected, interpretative and constructivist theorists have a number of ways of conceiving their ontological commitments. If the argument that language does not have 'objective' meanings is accepted, a minimal modification of the positivist ontology is to shift the meaning of words from being their correspondence to things in the world to its being determined by the intentions of the speaker. Although this is a minimal shift in ontology it transforms the subject of study from a user of objective meanings into a creator of the meanings in their world. Epistemologically, this forces the researcher from the position of observer of behavior, into an interpreter of meanings to which the object of study has privileged access. This is an ontological position that the interpretative research framework adopts.

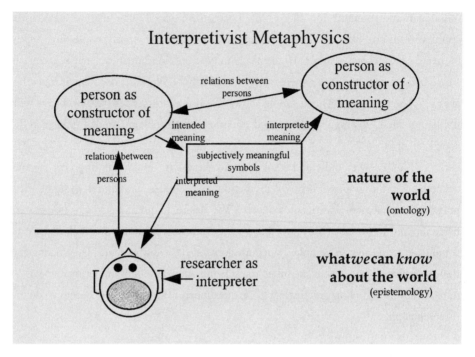

Figure 6.4   Representation of the Object of Study as the Constructor of Meaning
                   Rather than the Meaning User.

As can be seen from Figure 6.4, the researcher, as interpreter cannot be seen as having access to a privileged or 'objective' way of knowing the world they are studying. The interpretative researcher can only gain knowledge of the social world in the same way as the subjects they are studying. What the researcher 'knows' about the world is simply one person's, context dependent, interpretation of their experiences and interactions. Pragmatically, such interpretations may help generate greater understanding between people, but they have no 'objective' status. In addition, because of their context dependence, research findings from interpretative studies cannot be 'generalized' in the way that logico-empirical finding usually are.

An example that illustrates the problem of interpreting intentions and motivations arose from watching and listening to one of our daughters, a pubescent, 12 year old girl, Lauren. She has always avoided sports and found reasons for not participating. Lauren generally does not do well in sport. She is a little uncoordinated which has led to embarrassment and criticism from teammates. It is surprising, therefore, that she would insist on playing after school competitive basketball. She began playing and really loved it. She is not the team's best player but she runs hard and passes well.

As a researcher this was interesting because existing evidence is that at puberty young women were likely to drop out of sport, not want to take it up with vigor and commitment as Lauren was doing. Lauren's apparent desires and intentions conflicted with what you would expect given existing research results. This discrepancy suggests that exploring the motivation of girls like her, and contrasting it with the motivations of girls who have dropped out of sport, could increase our understanding of the factors influencing girls' motivation to stay or leave sport.

If, as in Figure 6.4, persons are the constructors of meaning, and if each person constructs their own meaning, then the only person who can be sure of the meaning intended is the person who constructed it. If the person with the intention is the only one who has direct access to that intention, the only way of answering the question of why some girls, aged 10-14 years, take up new sports whilst other girls drop out of sport, is to ask them. We need to get the girls to tell us what their experiences and feelings have been.

Actions are Meaningful: The interpretative/constructivist researcher focuses on describing behavior which is done with a purpose such that one can ask: what is the point, aim or intent or what was the person trying to do, desiring or meaning? (Fay, 1975). The difference between behavior and action is represented in Figure 6.5.

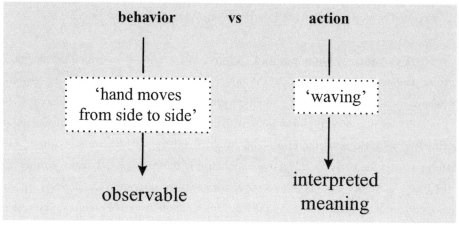

Figure 6.5   Behavior vs. Action

The interpretative/constructivist researcher focuses on action concepts as they attempt to give an account of human experience. Action concepts represent intentional social processes such as negotiating, waving, sharing, waiting, and bribing. Acts such as these cannot be described in behavioral terms but require an interpretation of action that must include reference to the actor's intentions in relation to social rules and shared cultural meanings.

As Giddens points out, behavioral and action descriptions are not equally acceptable alternative descriptions of the same thing, but rather are competing descriptions with conflicting commitments regarding the nature of the reality being described (Giddens, 1979, p. 280). Behavioral descriptions refer only to observable physical motion, and hence people are being described in the same terms as are applicable to inanimate objects.

However, whereas the Law of Momentum says that objects will continue moving with the same velocity in the same direction unless an outside force intervenes, humans, and other animate beings, are self-moving. In other words, the initiation of change in motion (that researchers are mostly interested in) comes not from outside force but from our capacity as agents to move as we will or desire. Behavioral descriptions misdescribe actions by omitting their internationality. 'Brushing the flies away' and 'waving' are both descriptions of intentional actions that happen to have the same behavioral content. One cannot describe an action as an action without interpreting the intention behind the behavior. Interpretation and description are one and the same.

Centrality of Language and Culture: Interpretivists recognize the symbolic nature of language, as opposed to the positivistic treatment of language as 'object'. Researchers in the interpretative framework generally solve the epistemological problem of interpreting the meaningful actions of participants by treating those meanings as culturally specific and therefore shared with others of the same culture. For interpretivists, the person's subjective experience is the primary raw data. 'Reality' or 'the truth' is simply this subjective experience, which, interpretivists believe, can be reported unproblematically through the language which is shared between the researcher and the researcher's audience. In research practice, the researcher's role is to facilitate the participant to tell their experience as fully as possible with a few interruptions as possible. In this framework, 'truth' is best found by an accepting, non-judgmental, open approach which encourages the participant to 'tell it like it is'.

Validating Truth Claims: Within the interpretative framework, researchers attempt to present the emic perspective when reporting research findings. Selecting what to report and writing the research report requires methodological decisions on the part of the researcher. The best interpretative practice honors the methodological position of privileging the participant's experience as the truth by using the participant's own words without researcher interpretation being added. If the researcher wants to make broad statements about how a group of participants experience a particular phenomenon, then, methodologically, this interpretation should be validated by the participants. Because interpretivists take the participant's unmediated 'experience' as the only 'reality', what they can not do is interrogate participants to clarify meanings, or push them to consider ways of interpreting their experience that were not reported without such intervention.

Critique of Subjective Truth: The interpretative idea, that what the participant says they experienced is 'the truth', fails to accommodate the implications of the postpositivist understanding concerning the social nature of language. Contemporary language theory supports a model of language as a feedback loop rather than a 'sender' - 'message'- 'receiver' model which interpretivism allows. In the feedback model of language, what one perceives is shaped by the language, which is available to label that perception. We cannot, for example, share an experience with another, or even describe them to ourselves, if that experience is outside the language available to us in our culture.

Therefore language shapes and determines the content of our subjective experience. From our perspective, this failure to account for the role of language in shaping experience is a methodological fault, which, if not acknowledged or corrected for, reduces the validity of interpretative research. As we show below, constructivism, is a methodological advance on interpretivism? Constructivism shares the methodological aim of interpretivism i.e., gaining understanding from the emic perspective without assuming that what participants say is 'the truth'. In addition, constructivism incorporates the feedback loop model of language.

Differences Between Constructivism and Interpretivism:

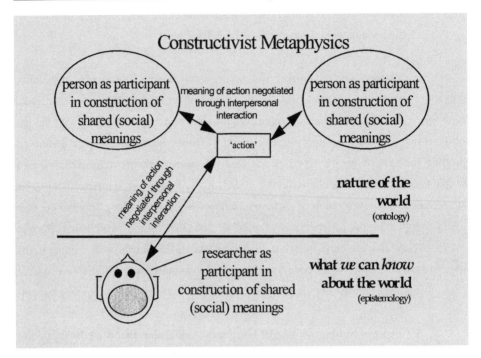

Figure 6.6   A Representation of Constructivist Metaphysical Beliefs

Constructivist and Interpretative researchers share most methodological assumptions. The major difference is that constructivists believe that all 'truth' in terms of human action, is constructed, both individually and jointly. In contrast to the way in which interpretivists treat language and meaning, constructivists treat it as something that must be (and is) intersubjectively negotiated in every interaction.

They do not assume that a person's 'subjective experience' is some form of pre-social 'primary data' as interpretivists do. Constructivist methodology recognize that construction of meaning happens at two levels: the individuals level i.e., the stories we tell ourselves about our experiences, and at the intersubjective level, the stories we tell others.

Since participants' reports of their 'experience' are not primary, it is methodologically appropriate for the constructivist researcher to probe and question the participant. Constructivist researchers, therefore, openly negotiate with participants to determine their meaning and the researcher's understanding. Such negotiating can include leading questions and challenges to the participant to reinterpret their 'experience', because, for constructivists, 'experience' is something that is always mediated by social understandings.

Because constructivists do not treat communication as transparent they cannot assume that the subject of study will (or can) accurately report their motivations or intentions. The relation between researcher and 'object' of study cannot be seen as one of objective observation, but rather must be seen as one of social interaction.

The researcher must therefore be sensitive to the nature of the relationship between themselves and the people they are interviewing, as well as to the factors that might affect that relationship and hence influence what their subjects choose to tell them and choose to conceal or distort. Interpretative and Constructivist researchers both aim to avoid imposing their own framework, beliefs and values on participants.

This ethical imperative is more difficult for constructivist researchers to defend because they engage in the negotiating meaning that increases the opportunities for ideological imposition when compared with interpretivism. When writing up their research, constructivists do not change the words that they negotiated with participants as this would be to negate the meaning that was arrived at through the research process.

2.3 *Comparison of Positivist and Constructivist Methodology*

Before concluding this section of the chapter it may be helpful to compare the methodological assumptions of the two main methodological frameworks which we have been critiquing and contrasting; see Table 6.4 that summarizes and contrasts positivism and constructivism.

Table 6.4

Positivist and Constructivist Methodological Frameworks

Positivist **Epistemological Assumptions:**	**Constructivist** **Epistemological Assumptions:**
a) There is **one, research method** that is applicable to all fields of study. b) **Science progresses by reducing** less basic to more basic science.	a) There **are multiple research methods,** which should be matched to the type of research question asked. b) **Human beings cannot be understood by reducing** them to smaller units of observation. They need to be understood holistically, biographically and within a cultural context.
c) **Science is value-free and objective.** (NB This denies that values drive the researcher in their choice of question, sampling and interpretation of data). d) **Facts and theories can and should be separated**. (NB This involves a denial of both the theory-laden dimensions of observation and the value-laden dimensions of theory). e) **One reality** which is knowable through correct measurement methods. f) **The goal** of science is to discover universal laws that predict the occurrence of events by combining descriptive laws with statements of initial conditions. The ultimate goal of science is control of the natural and social world.	c) **Science is value-laden**. Researchers need to make their values explicit so that readers can make their own judgments about validity. d) **Facts and theories cannot be separated**. Theories tell us what to look for and how to interpret what we observe. e) **Multiple realities** which are individually and socially constructed. f) **The goal** of social science is to understand human action and to enhance harmony between human beings by promoting understanding.
Archetype Method: Theory driven experimental research. Surveys (Fay, 1975). **Validity** Depends upon reliability and predictability. (Validity about human action and motivation is the weakest point of positivistic research because research instruments are often designed by researchers in relation to theory or previous studies but not in relation to the lived experience of the people to be researched).	**Archetype Method:** Interviews. Observation.(Denzin & Lincoln, 1994) **Validity** Validity is enhanced if the theory and explanations are developed in collaboration with at least a sub-sample of the original informants. Validity is enhanced if there is triangulation of methods, inclusion of the perspective of different stakeholders and the generation of alternative theoretical explanations. The weakest point of interpretive/constructivist research is that theory generated in one context may not be transferable (generalizable) to another context.

2.4 *Summary*

This first section has concerned the methodological foundations for research in the social sciences. We have considered positivism, postpositivism, interpretivism and constructivism. It should be clear from the discussion above that for research questions which concern developing an understanding of why subjects behave as the do, then a constructivist framework offers the best approach for producing valid research results and theories. As a way of summarizing what has been discussed above Table 6.4 compares and contrasts the two extremes of the methodological continuum i.e., positivism and constructivism. Both methodological frameworks have their place in research. The logico-empirical approach is best research approach for studying the behavior and predictability in the biological and physical world. The constructivist methodological framework is the right approach when the researcher wants to answer questions about why or how humans act as they do as individuals or groups. This methodological approach is broad, encompassing such research designs as ethnography, participant observation, oral history, personal narrative and case studies. Theory may be generated from constructivist research; such theory is context dependent, descriptive, emotionally evocative and designed to promote understanding between people.

2.5 *Turning Methodology into Methods*

One common error in research design and reporting is the conflation between research method and methodology. Often, only methods are reported but these are described as methodology. This is a flaw in research writing because researchers always have a set of philosophical beliefs that guide their practice as researchers and it is good practice to make this available to the reader so that the reader can evaluate the methodology of the study. If these methodological beliefs are not made explicit then what the researcher actually does in research is often confusing and even contradictory resulting in invalid research. In well-designed qualitative research, including interpretive and constructivist, the selected methodology should be in harmony with the methods chosen for data collection and interpretation.

The Researcher as Data Collection Instrument: Bringing methodology and method together means giving attention to the way in which data will be collected and interpreted. In laboratory research, the scientist has to rely on their understanding of perception and of the way their equipment works to ensure their research methods deliver the most valid data. In qualitative research the researcher has to ensure that their 'instrument' for data collection, i.e. themselves, is a clear and non-distorting instrument. This means developing the skills and attitudes that are most likely to facilitate the participant being able to go deeply within themselves and tell their story to you in a way that is most open, truthful and complete. Social researchers also have to rely on their understanding of the factors motivating people to lie, misrepresent, and manipulate others by what they say to them. Part of being a good researcher is being aware that one's understanding of such factors may be inadequate, and hence to be prepared to modify them in the light of experience. The skills and attitudes of a good qualitative researcher are given below.

Interviewing: Interviewing is the most important skill to develop if one planning to be a qualitative researcher in any research tradition. The section which follows draws on Keats (1988) and Reinharz (1992). A good interviewer is like a good therapist: attentive, accepting, encouraging, interested and non-judgmental. A good interviewer is someone with whom others feel really safe to tell their story. In the early days of interviewing one may find that she/he only gets superficial, condensed data, not full, descriptive, detailed stories. This could be partly due to one's interviewee being not very talkative but it is most likely that the interviewer has not been a skilled and sensitive person.

Prepare the Interviewee: Having a clear research question and knowing why you are interviewing a particular person in relation to the question is critical.

Meet the potential participants before the interview and share with them what your study is about and why you want to interview them. Ensure participants of confidentiality and let them know that there are no right answers that you will not judge them, whatever they say.

Letting the participant know this will help you to get the type of data you want in the form that you want. Give the participants an information sheet (usually part of the research consent form). On the form for the adolescent girls in sport study you might prepare them in advance by writing "I would like you to think about a time or an example when you enjoyed sport and a time or a situation when you did not. I would like you to tell this to me as a story with as much detail as you can recall. I am particularly interested in your feelings and who or what influenced your feelings, before, during and after participating in sport."

Take the Right Amount of Time for the Interview: Individual interviews require approximately 45 to 90 minutes. If the interview takes any less time then the data will not be rich enough. If the interview takes any more time then either you or the participant will become too tired. If necessary schedule a second session. In the case of the adolescent girls; forty-five minutes should be sufficient time.

Skills and Attitudes Most Helpful for Quality In-Depth Interviews:

Develop Trust and Rapport: This involves ensuring confidentiality. Although this was addressed in the information sheet it is important to reinforce it; nothing will cause an interviewee to dry up more quickly than the fear that their vulnerable issues will be exposed to others. Trust and rapport develop best if the researcher is genuinely her or himself. It is important to be a true participant, not a detached distant observer. It helps if you give appropriate self-disclosure but do not overdo this as you do not want to embarrass yourself or the other person. Neither do you want the focus of the interview to turn to you or for the interviewee to feel that they must in some way measure up (or down) to your experience.

If the subjects do not trust the researcher to protect their interests, they are not likely to be willing to reveal sensitive information about themselves. The researchers intention or willingness to protect the subjects' interests does not, however, guarantee their capacity to do so. A researcher being employed by the department of social security, for example, no matter how well they protect the individual identities of their subjects, is developing an understanding of their subjects' motivations that can be used by the department to increase the degree of control they have over these subjects. Because interpretivists do not include in their ontology such structural dynamics of power and interpersonal relations they are not well equipped to reflectively account for such dynamics in their research. We will be exploring these issues more fully in the next chapter.

If the participant perceives that what the researcher wants to know is potentially damaging (for instance, to the reputation of) the subject, they have good reason to hide, misrepresent, or distort their representation of their motivations or actions. Guaranteeing the confidentiality of the information provided is one way of addressing such fears. Sometimes, however, that is not enough. Even if the name of the informant is changed or withheld the details of the case may be such as to uniquely identify that person as the source of the information. In such cases, if reliable information is desired the researcher may have to make a commitment to alter the details they report in their results so as to protect the identity of the informant. It may even be necessary to give the informant the opportunity to vet reports before they are published to give them the confidence that they have the control over outcomes to protect their interests.

Even if the participants trust in the researcher's willingness and capacity to protect their interests, however, there is no guarantee that the subjects are interested in serving the theorizing interests of the researcher. Participants may in fact find it entertaining to provide plausible but false stories about their motivations and actions simply to confound the efforts of a so-called 'expert'. Participants may also misrepresent themselves in order to please or favorably impress the researcher by presenting themselves in a way the subject perceives as worthy. As discussed for Interpretivism, unintentional misrepresentations of self do occur due to participant not really knowing themselves and their own motivation or not being able to articulate their knowing in words that are jointly understandable. For constructivist researchers some degree of probing, suggesting possible interpretations and challenging participants' initial interpretation in order to promote self-awareness and fuller self-expression is warranted.

Besides intentional deception or misrepresentation we know that subjects who do not know what their motivations are tend to confabulate by creating a plausible explanation of their actions. The subject him/herself may not recognize or know that they have done this. In other words such misrepresentations may be entirely unintentional.

Be a Reflective Listener: If you have prepared the interviewee well you should be able to settle into the role of listener and prompter but not say much. As a guide we recommend interviewer talk time not exceed 10% of the interview time. If you find yourself talking too much it is probable that you are nervous or that your interviewee is not saying what you had hoped or that there are silences that are making you uncomfortable. If you become aware of this stop yourself, take a break if necessary and analyze why the interview is not going well. Then take steps to correct it. Maybe you have not prepared the interviewee well enough and she/he is not sure what is wanted, feels psychologically unsafe or is afraid of boring you by saying too much.

Focus on Feelings and Meanings: We gain our best understanding of another when we understand both the feelings that motivate them to action or inaction and the meanings that they make of what happens to and around them. When interviewees are talking about feelings or meanings, these are core issues and should be fully explored. You need to notice when this is occurring in the interview and be prepared to interrupt and probe gently for emotions and understandings. E.g. an adolescent girl in our study may say "When the boys take over the basketball courts at lunch time we just leave." This leaving is an action that is motivated by a feeling so ask about it. You might get a difficult to interpret "I feel bad" kind of response. So again, probe "In what way, are you feeling bad; is it sad, put down, angry or something else"? "Are there other times you feel like this"? What do you normally do with these feelings"? "If you could change the rules about sport at school what rules would you change? Why?" The researcher needs to explore emotions and understandings fully and not leave them as superficial glosses or worse, inferences that the reader of the research will have to make.

Make it OK to Say the 'Unsayable': There are two aspects here: your comfort with hearing the 'unsayable' and the participant's willingness to say it. Your own comfort with hearing painful, shameful, angry or other emotionally charged stories is directly related to your own self-knowledge and self-acceptance. If you find it unacceptable for you to feel angry then you will most likely send indirect cues to the participants that indicate that anger is not something you want to hear. Suppose, for example, that you are interviewing someone who has been sexually abused and that you have been sexually abused but have never dealt with your own abuse. In that situation, it will be impossible for you to hear the participant's story because your own feeling will get in the way. One way to identify if you are finding it uncomfortable to hear the participant's story and that it is you who are stopping them from speaking is for you is to listen to your own interviewing. See if you change direction before the issue is fully explored, this will indicate your discomfort is getting in the way of gaining good quality data. If the participant changes direction before the issue is fully explored this may mean that they are picking up your cues about your discomfort. The way to improve your own comfort in hearing painful or shameful stories is to deal with your own issues. Dealing with your own issues may involve having therapy, writing a reflective journal, being supervised in your practice and having a mentor who has already dealt with their own issue and so can act as a guide.

Even if you are able to hear the difficult or painful things that participants might say, that doesn't mean that they will tell you their stories fully. Sometimes you suspect that the participant want to tell you something but is feeling ashamed. You can address this by saying something like "Someone I was interviewing said" and then add something that is pretty difficult for people generally to say, e.g., "Some girls tell me they stop playing sport because they do not like the boys looking at their bodies or some girls tell me that they do not like sport because they do not like to feel competitive…. Then follow with "is that something you feel?" Although good interviewing has a conversational tone, remember you are still the interviewer and you need to understand what is meant, so paraphrase to check understanding and probe if necessary to get at deeper levels of meaning.

Developing a Constructivist Research Proposal in Sports Science: In describing a constructivist research proposal, an example relevant to sports science has been chosen. The elements of a qualitative research proposal do not have the same level of agreement as is found in logico-empiricism and therefore there is no single method for writing a qualitative research proposal or report (Heath, 1997). The steps involved in writing a constructivist research proposal are set out below.

Steps in Writing the Research Proposal:

Step 1: Identify the Phenomena of Interest or Concern.

Step 2: Review the Literature Related to Research Interest

Step 3: Describe the Significance of the Study

Step 4: Describe the Research Design

    4a: Outline Data Collection Methods and Data Management

    4b: Describe Sampling Techniques

    4c: Address Issues of Gaining Access to the Participants.

    4d: Address Issues of Accessing an Appropriate Research Site

    4e: Outline Data Analysis

Step 5: Describe the Ethical Aspects of the Study

Identify the Phenomena of Interest or Concern: As previously discussed, the area of interest concerns girl's participation in sport and trying to understand why some girls drop out of sport whilst others take it up with vigor and commitment as my daughter Lauren was doing. So, using this example, at this point we can set up a working Research Question: Q. How do girls' feelings and beliefs about sport influence their participation in sport. Notice this is a 'How' question, not the kind of question that can be answered by survey method. It is the kind of question that seems to demand good interviewing. We need to get the girls to tell us what their experiences and feelings have been.

Review the Literature: There is some debate about reviewing the literature before collecting data in qualitative studies. Strauss and Corbin (1990) argue that the researcher should avoid taking on the views and conceptual frameworks of previous research. This argument only makes sense if the positivist assumption that the mind is an empty mirror, which can reflect reality, is accepted. Reading previous research could then be interpreted as a contamination of the data collection vessel. Post-positivist critiques, however, show that we unavoidably bring the cultural assumptions and systems of categorization embedded in our shared language to our research. There is no such thing as a mind which 'reflects reality'. Moreover, no one reaches the stage of undertaking research without already being trained in the preconceptions and assumptions of at least one discipline. Researchers always bring preconceived ideas to their research. The only question is whether those preconceptions are left unexamined, or whether they get exposed to information and ways of looking at the phenomena of interest that could bring such preconceived ideas to consciousness and the possibility of critique. A literature review that ranges widely across both methodological and disciplinary boundaries is one of the best ways of bringing unexpected phenomena and novel ways of looking or thinking about your research topic to your attention. A beginning literature review is an important part of the development of the research proposal.

The purposes of the literature review are to:
a)   examine other qualitative studies of the phenomenon of interest. Are there any? Do you agree with the way the study was done? Could another way of looking

at the phenomena add to our understanding? Is your proposed study needed and if not, what about a variation or development on what has already been found.

b)   examine quantitative studies with particular emphasis on determining how the data collection instrument was developed. What assumptions were made to fit the phenomena into fixed and bounded categories that were susceptible to measurement or counting? Could an in-depth qualitative study provide a new perspective on the aspects of the phenomena taken for granted by quantitative research?

c)   refine the research question in the light of what is already known or as a way to challenge current thinking.

Now, returning to the research question: Why do some girls, aged 10-14, take up sport while other girls of the same age drop out of sport? Let's assume that the literature review found that although much research into girls' participation in sport has been done, this particular question had not been studied. The next step in writing the research proposal is to decide whether the study is worth the time, effort and money that will be needed to answer the question.

State Significance of the Study: In all research it is important to deal with the 'so what' factor of research. In thinking about significance, the researcher needs to answer the question, 'how does the proposed research extend or critique current knowledge'? Another important question is 'who will be interested'? Significance also involves the researcher thinking about potential contributions that their proposed research will make to theory, research, practice and policy? In writing the research proposal, the researcher needs to address as many of these elements of significance as are relevant.

It is useful at this stage to describe what you intend to accomplish scientifically; what will the academic achievement be (e.g. isolating factors to generate hypotheses for quantitative research, identifying concepts and the development of theory, describing phenomena, collecting stories about a phenomena of interest). If you know in the beginning what you hope to achieve then it will make data collection and data analysis so much easier.

Briefly, the scientific contribution in the proposed study would be in terms of isolating factors that girls identify as either inhibiting or facilitating their participation in sport. The practical contribution of the study is in providing information to interested parties. In this case, parents of girls will be interested because health and fitness are cultural values. Adolescent girls lag behind adolescent boys in terms of fitness and parents, generally, would like to know what might motivate and de-motivate their daughters to participate in sport so that they can more effectively nurture their daughters to participate in sport. Schools and teachers will be interested for the same reasons. Teachers and administrators would value understanding what schools currently do that inhibits girls' participation. Teachers and administrators would like to know what could they do differently to enhance girls' involvement.

Describe Research Design:

Data Collection Method and Data Management: When the researcher wants to know what someone else has experienced, or what they think about something, the method of choice is in-depth interviewing. Being a good interviewer is the most important skill to develop if you are planning to be a qualitative researcher in any paradigm. The skills of in-depth interviewing have been previously discussed in this chapter.

A high quality tape recorder will be needed for recording the interviews. Consistent with Australian National Health and Medical Research Council's Guidelines (1994) for the Ethical Conduct of Research the tapes, and subsequent transcriptions, will need to be labeled with a code name and stored by the researcher for a minimum of five years.

The tapes will need to be transcribed. It normally takes a good transcription typist three hours to type one hour of well-recorded interview data. These costs need to be considered in the development of the research proposal. Also issues of confidentiality need to be considered in relation to the transcription typist; this will be discussed below in the section on research ethics.

Describe Sampling: Compared with logico-empiricism, sampling is quite different in qualitative research; this is because the purpose of sampling is different. In logico-empiricism, the aim is to be able to generalize the findings to a population. In constructivist research the aim is to develop a full, multi-faceted, theoretical understanding of the phenomenon of interest. In this example of why some girls drop out of sport and other take it up during adolescence the aim of sampling is to get the best understanding of the girls' perspectives. The sampling method in qualitative research is called *purposive sampling*, because the researcher decides in advance the criteria which will be used to select participants (Holloway, 1997). In the example of pubescent girls' participation in sport, the criteria for selecting participants would be that they are:

i)   female

ii)   aged 10-14 years.

iii)   have taken up sport with enthusiasm after previously not enjoying sport.OR

iv)   have dropped out of sport after previously enjoying it.

v)   girls will be selected from a range of academic abilities.

vi)   girls will be selected from a range of socio-economic backgrounds.

vii)   girls will be selected from a range of racial and ethnic backgrounds.

If including girls from cultures other than the dominant culture makes the research too difficult to conduct this must be reported. Like all good researchers, we should not imply that our findings could be applied outside the population from which it was generated.

It is not possible to predict sample size in advance. This is because sampling continues until data saturation has occurred. Data saturation means that no new data is emerging from new interviews so that further interviews become redundant (Holloway, 1997). In order to be sure that data saturation has been reached and to be able to present as full a theoretical understanding as possible, the researcher specifically searches for disconfirming cases. Disconfirming cases in the example study would be girls who say they desire to play sport but do not and girls who play sport but say they really do not want to.

Gaining Access to the Participants: There is a close relationship between sampling and gaining access to participants. In qualitative research, the main ways to gain access to potential participants, are through known places where you would expect to meet the type of person you would like to participate. For example, if you wanted to study diabetic people's participation in sport you could approach the Diabetic Foundation and ask them to mail out invitations for you or to put an advertisement in their newsletter.

In the example we are using here, approaching schools may seem to be an appropriate first step. However, the type of question and form of interviewing may be seen as somewhat threatening to some headmaster/mistresses and they may not facilitate access for the researcher. Since the girls in the example study are under age the researcher will need parental consent in addition to the consent of the girls. A more direct approach is to go to sporting clubs and approach parents who are watching their girls participate in sport. For the other arm of the study i.e., the girls who have dropped out of sport, then informal networks may be the best way to track these girls down. The ethical implications will be addressed in the section on Research Ethics later in this chapter.

Selecting and Accessing an Appropriate Research Site: Qualitative research is best conducted in a naturalistic setting because it diminishes power differentials between the researcher and the participant and participants are likely to feel more comfortable and therefore are more likely to speak freely (Holloway, 1997; Neuman, 1994; Talbot, 1995).

In considering a site for this study the girls own home may be appropriate, a park or a coffee shop might also be considered. The researcher's home is also a possibility.

Describe Ethical Implications of the Study: The researcher needs to gain ethical approval for the study. The Australian Health Ethics Committee (AHEC) has produced some useful ethical guidelines for qualitative research. These guidelines have been adopted by the National Health and Medical Research Council of Australia and are recommended to beginning qualitative researchers. A brief overview only is presented below.

Many ethical issues in a qualitative study are the same as for a quantitative study. Essentially they are about not harming the participants, obtaining informed consent, ensuring confidentiality and storing the data in a safe place. Because of the in-depth and sensitive nature of the interviews there is a potential to raise issues which are emotionally upsetting to the participant. The researcher needs to have basic counseling skills so that they can manage the immediate situation sensitively. In addition, the researcher needs to have a plan for referral for ongoing counseling if it is required.

In the present study girls aged 10-14 are to be interviewed. This will require parental consent in addition to the girl's consent.

Conduct In-Depth Interviewing: See earlier discussion concerning the skills of in-depth interviewing.

Conduct data analysis: The skills of data analysis are discussed in the section below.

Introduction to Qualitative Data Analysis and Interpretation: Unlike traditional research where all terms are precisely defined and agreed, in qualitative research there is lack of agreement about the meaning of many terms. Often different researchers use different terms to describe the very same activity. In the area of qualitative data analysis the lack of agreed meaning is a particularly difficult problem. This conceptual confusion can make it difficult for students, so in table 6.5 we provide some clarification of terms that will allow you to approach qualitative data analysis and interpretation with a level of confidence.

Table 6.5

Terminology for Qualitative Analysis

Term	Meaning
Emic Perspective	The insiders or native's perspective. The knowledge, experience or perception of the participant (Holloway, 1997, p 53)
Etic Perspective	A framework imposed from the outside. The researcher's words, perspective or world view (Holloway, 1997, p 53).
Analysis	1. Separation of a whole into its constituent elements (opposed to *synthesis*). 2. The process as a method of studying the nature of a thing or of determining its essential features (Macquarie Dictionary, 1998)
Interpretation	1. the act of interpreting; elucidation: the interpretation of nature. 2. an explanation given: e.g.: to put an interpretation on a passage. 3. a construction placed upon something (Macquarie Dictionary, 1998)

Content Analysis	Usually used in document or conversational analysis. Manifest analysis to measure the frequency of the use of pre-determined words or concepts and/or the number of instances of action or interaction. Latent analysis searches for instances of predetermined meanings in data that are not immediately apparent by making inferences and interpretations. Because of the imposed nature of the frameworks of analysis and the emphasis on counting this form of analysis is closely associated with qualitative research within the logico-empirical paradigm (Holloway, 1997, pp 34-35).
Thematic Analysis	Analysis of data to find related categories, concepts or similar meanings within the data (Holloway, 1997, p.152). Unlike content analysis in thematic analysis the researcher has no pre-conceived theoretical framework, the themes emerge inductively as the researcher reads and re-reads the data to find similar factors, patterns or meanings across cases.
Grounded Theory Analysis	This should only be used as part of a grounded theory study (Strauss & Corbin, 1987). Grounded theory involves using the constant comparison method of data analysis; this involves identifying and naming concepts (categories), integrating concepts and their properties and developing a theory, which is grounded in the qualitative data. Grounded theory is used for across case analysis.
Narrative Analysis	This should only be used if the data collected was narrative (or story) data. Narrative analysis takes a number of forms but generally focuses on how people make meanings of their lives organized by the stories that they tell. There is debate about the degree to which the story can been separated from the contextual detail within which it is embedded (Emden, 1998; Manning & Cullum-Swan, 1994). Narrative analysis can be used within and across cases.
Phenomenological Analysis/Interpretation	This matches phenomenological studies where the aim is to understand the meaning of particular phenomena. There are a number of forms of phenomenological data analysis depending upon the school of phenomenology one is working within. Some phenomenologists *analyze* data whereas others only add *interpretive* comment as needed to elucidate meaning (Holloway, 1997, p.p.118-119). Phenomenological analysis is generally used across cases to distil the essence of the phenomena.
Interpretation Using Existing Theory	This etic strategy cannot be used within the interpretive/constructivist paradigm because it violates validity. Using existing theory to interpret qualitative data is a strategy used most commonly by postmodern and feminist researchers: e.g.: an analysis of how power operates using feminist theory. May be used within and across cases.

The Practice of Data Analysis and Interpretation: Qualitative researchers find the analysis and interpretation of data the most conceptually challenging aspect of the research process. The scientific value of the whole project depends upon the rigor and validity of the methods used at this stage of the research process.

Researchers should <u>never</u> collect their data and then begin to worry about how to analyze it. Although the researcher may change his or her mind as the study unfolds it is important to have a clear idea of the form of data analysis at the beginning of the study. At the time of proposal submission the researcher should have described what they intend to accomplish scientifically (e.g. isolating factors to generate hypotheses for quantitative research, identifying concepts and the development of theory, describing phenomena, collecting stories about a phenomena of interest). The research question should be written in such a way that, when it is answered, it will provide the type of qualitative data that will be able to be analyzed and interpreted in the most scientifically beneficial way.

Application to Sports Science Example: Data analysis and interpretation can be better understood by application to the case of adolescent girls and sport. The researcher asks themselves a series of questions to determine the best data analysis/interpretation method for their particular study.

Q. What type of data output is implied by the research question: e.g., factors, concepts, stories, phenomena, patterns of behavior, theory, etc.

The question in this study was: **Q. How do girls' feelings and beliefs about sport influence their participation in sport?** This implies that the data analysis output will be feelings and beliefs which girls identify as enhancing or inhibiting their participation in sport.

Q. Will this need an across case or within case analysis/interpretation?

In our study we will need an across-case analysis to identify feelings and beliefs which are common to a number of girls. This is because the significance of the study has to do with identifying issues that can possibly be modified in teachers, parents and the media in order to enhance girls participation in sport.

Q. To what extent, if any, should the data be separated from the contextual detail?

This question is particularly important in phenomenological and ethnographic studies where isolating bits of data may completely distort the meaning of the data. In other studies, such as the adolescent girls in sport study, isolating factors from the rest of the data that participants provide is the most appropriate strategy.

After the researcher has answered these questions then they are able to decide which data analysis method is best suited to their particular study.

Table 6.6

Terminology for Qualitative Analysis

Term	Meaning	Suitability for Adolescent Girls in Sport Study
Emic Perspective	The insiders or native's perspective. The knowledge, experience or perception of the participant (Holloway, 1997, p. 53)	YES because in interpretive research methodology validity require this.
Etic Perspective	A framework imposed from the outside. The researcher's words, perspective or worldview are used (Holloway, 1997, p. 53).	NO
Analysis	1. Separation of a whole into its constituent elements (opposed to *synthesis*). 2. the process as a method of studying the nature of a thing or of determining its essential features (Macquarie Dictionary, 1998)	YES because need to isolate factors involved in girls' participation in sport
Interpretation	1. the act of interpreting; elucidation: the interpretation of nature. 2. an explanation given: e.g.: to put an interpretation on a passage. 3. a construction placed upon something (Macquarie Dictionary, 1998)	YES because the girls words or meanings may not be self evident to the intended readers of the research.

Content Analysis	Usually used in document or conversational analysis. <u>Manifest analysis</u> to measure the frequency of the use of pre-determined words or concepts and/or the number of instances of action or interaction. <u>Latent analysis</u> searches for instances of predetermined meanings in data that are not immediately apparent by making inferences and interpretations. Because of the imposed nature of the frameworks of analysis and the emphasis on counting this form of analysis is closely associated with qualitative research within the logico-empirical paradigm (Holloway, 1997, p. 34-35).	NO because not compatible with interpretive methodology and the emic perspective.
Thematic Analysis	Analysis of data to find related categories, concepts or similar meanings within the data (Holloway, 1997, p. 152). Unlike content analysis in thematic analysis the researcher has no pre-conceived theoretical framework, the themes emerge inductively as the researcher reads and re-reads the data to find similar factors, patterns or meanings across cases.	YES because this allows the emic perspective to be honored and allows the analytic process to uncover the factors associated with girls' participation in sport.
Grounded Theory Analysis	This should only be used as part of a grounded theory study (Strauss & Corbin, 1987). Grounded theory involves using the <u>constant comparison</u> method of data analysis; this involves identifying and naming concepts (categories), integrating concepts and their properties and developing a theory which is grounded in the qualitative data. Grounded theory is used for across case analysis.	NO this is not a grounded theory study and a theory is not what is required to answer the research question.
Narrative Analysis	This should only be used if the data collected was narrative (or story) data. Narrative analysis takes a number of forms but generally focuses on how the meanings that people make organized by the stories that they tell. There is debate about the degree to which the story can been separated from the contextual detail within which it is embedded (Emden, 1998; Manning & Cullum-Swan, 1994). Narrative analysis can be used within and across cases.	NO because this is not a narrative study; it is not stories that are required to answer the research question.

Phenomenological Analysis/Interpretation	This matches phenomenological studies where the aim is to understand the <u>meaning</u> of particular phenomena. There are a number of forms of phenomenological data analysis depending upon the <u>school of phenomenology</u> one is working within. Some phenomenologists *analyze* data whereas others only add *interpretive* comment as needed to elucidate meaning (Holloway, 1997, p118-119). Phenomenological analysis is generally used across cases to distil the essence of the phenomena.	NO because this study is not concerned with phenomenology or the meaning of the deep inner world of the adolescent girls.
Interpretation Using Existing Theory	This etic strategy cannot be used within the interpretive/constructivist paradigm because it violates validity. Using existing theory to interpret qualitative data is a strategy used most commonly by postmodern and feminist researchers: e.g., an analysis of how power operates using feminist theory. May be used within and across cases.	NO because not needed to answer the research question and not appropriate to the research paradigm.

Example Data Analysis: Here is a section of data that Lauren gave me. We have underlined the sections of text that relate to feelings and beliefs about sports participation. As we collect more interviews we would look for similarities and differences within and across cases. What appears below is the first step in data analysis.

First Step in Data Analysis: Focus on the responses to do with feelings and beliefs, as they are directly relevant to the research question.

KF. Why did you get excited about playing basketball when you do not generally like sport?

LF. I'd played basketball just a little and I tried it and it <u>was really fun</u>.

KF. What other sports are available for girls at your school?

LF. Netball, softball and hockey. We should have girl's soccer but only three girls wanted to play so they had a mixed year 6 and year 7 team. I was the only girl who didn't want to play netball or softball but I had to play it or otherwise I would have been given alternative options.

KF. What does that mean?

LF. It means being mixed in with other kids and doing non-sport. Other kids
assume that if you do options that you were kicked out of a team sport. Options
sport is embarrassing.

KF Why don't you like netball and softball?

LF You can't really get into it and use your aggression. I feel weak when I play
netball but really strong when I play basketball. Netball and softball are girly
sports; there is no real strength; it doesn't get my adrenaline going like
basketball does.

KF. How do boys feel about you playing basketball?

LF The boys in my class made jokes like: "Oh you reckon you can play
basketball"!

KF Like only boys can play basketball?

LF Yeah, I thought they were idiots but it did made me annoyed.

KF Do you think that reaction from boys would stop some girls playing?

LF Oh heck yes. They would feel like they couldn't do it. It would take away
their confidence.

This small section of data was gathered for the purposes of this chapter and we do
not have any additional data to demonstrate how cross-case analysis can proceed. In
analysis where cross-case comparisons are being done one uses the initial research
question to guide analysis and looks for similarities and differences between and across
cases. We will give further examples of data analysis and interpretation in the chapter
concerning Critical, Feminist and Postmodern Research.

2.6 *Conclusion*

In this chapter we have introduced a philosophical critique of logico-
empiricism as a foundation for claiming that logico-empiricism is not the most
appropriate research framework for studying phenomena which have to do with human
actions, feelings, motivations and values. This critique is particularly strong when
logico-empiricism is used to try to understand the feelings, motivations and actions of
people. The section concerning the philosophical foundations for research also discussed
alternative views of science and the epistemological basis for such views. The particular

focus of the chapter has been on research in the Constructivist tradition. We provided the novice researcher with the knowledge and skills to be able to design and use philosophical arguments to defend qualitative research within sports science. This involved describing how to maintain consistency between methodology, research design, data collection and data analysis methods. There was special attention paid to the attitude and skills necessary to conduct in-depth interviews so that high quality data is produced. Finally, a section on qualitative data analysis was included to assist the qualitative researcher, in any research tradition, to be able to select and apply appropriate qualitative data analysis processes.

In the introductory part of this section it was suggested that readers might want to skim the first (epistemological) section and concentrate on the research design and practice sections which followed. If that was your strategy it would be desirable at this point to return to a consideration of the epistemological issues in order to anchor your understanding and enable you to convincingly justify your research practice. This chapter, and the next, are related to each other since they are both about qualitative research, specifically constructivist, critical, postmodern and feminist methodology.

References

Chinn, P.L., & Jacobs, M. (1987). *Theory and Nursing: A Systematic Approach* (2nd ed.). St. Louis: Mosby.

Chinn, P.L., & Kramer, M.K. (1991). *Theory and Nursing: A Systematic Approach* (3rd ed.). St. Louis: Mosby.

Denzin, N.K., & Lincoln, Y.S. (Eds.). (1994). *Handbook of Qualitative Research.* London: Sage Publications.

Emden, C. (1998) Conducting Narrative Analysis. *Collegian, 5,* 34-39.

Fay, B. (1975). *Social Theory and Political Practice.* London: George Allen Unwin.

Feyerabend, P. (!975). *Against Method: An Outline of Anarchistic Theory of Knowledge.* London: N.L.B.

Flew, A. (Ed.). (1983). *A Dictionary of Philosophy*, 2nd ed., London: MacMillan.

Gleick, J. (1987). *Chaos.* London: Cardinal.

Giddens, A. (1979) Postpositivism and it critics. In Bottomore, T. & Nisbett, R. (Eds.), *A History of Sociological Analysis* (pp. 237-86). London: Heinemann.

Harré, R. (1981). The positivist-empiricist approach and its alternatives. In Reason, P. & Rowan, J. (eds.). *Human Inquiry: A Sourcebook of New Paradigm Research.* Chichester: John Wiley and Sons.

Holloway, W. (1997). *Basic Concepts for Qualitative Research.* Oxford: Blackwell.

Keats, D. (1988). *Skilled Interviewing* (2nd. ed.). Hawthorn: ACER.

Kuhn, T.S. (1970). *The Structure of Scientific Revolutions.* Chicago: Chicago University Press.

Lakatos, W., & Musgrave, A. (Eds.). (1970). *Criticism and the Growth of Knowledge*, Cambridge: Macquarie Dictionary (1998) Available from Macquarie Net [online] http://macgate.dict. mq.edu.au. Accessed March, 1999.

National Health and Medical Research Council (1994) Ethical Aspects of Qualitative Methods in Health Research. AGPS. Canberra.

Neuman, W. (1994). *Social Research Methods: Qualitative and Quantitative Approaches.* (2nd ed.). Boston: Allyn & Bacon.

Popper, K. (1959). *The Logic of Scientific Discovery.* London: Hutchinson.

Reinharz, S. (1992). *Feminist Methods in Social Research.* New York: Oxford University Press.

Russell, B. (1946) *History of Western Philosophy.* London: George Allen Unwin.

Strauss, A., & Corbin, J. (1990). *Basics of Qualitative Research: Grounded Theory Procedures and Techniques.* Newbury Park: Sage.

Talbot, L. A. (1995). *Principles and Practice of Nursing Research.* London: Mosby.

(3) Postmodern and Feminist Qualitative Research: Methodology, Methods and Practice

Karey Harrison and Kathleen Fahy

Women's participation in sport is a feminist issue deserving of research and theory development. On a number of objective measures women are disadvantaged relative to men with respect to sports participation (Plaisted, 1995). From school and community sports through to Olympic and professional sports females participate at a lower rate than males. Whether we look at facilities, finance, or media coverage, the resources available to female athletes are less than those available to male athletes. Despite these disadvantages, however, the female 21% of Australian Olympic teams from 1948 to 1992 won Australia 39% of its medals (Australian Sports Commission, 1992). Women are overcoming obstacles to put in outstanding performances but their achievements are not being recognized or encouraged to the same extent as men's.

Women's athletic abilities are being neglected at a far greater rate than those of males, so that, even apart from the issue of equity, resources redirected towards female athletes have the potential for producing a far greater return than increasing the already inequitable proportion of resources available to males. Given the relative discouragement of female participation in sports the pool of unrecognized and unrealized female talent is likely to be far greater than for males. To the extent that mainstream sports psychology research marginalizes gender issues it tends to contribute to the maintenance of existing inequities rather than to their removal. Identifying and altering the factors that discourage women and direct resources away from them has the greatest potential for increasing sports performance. Feminist research is explicitly oriented towards identifying, understanding and changing social factors that sustain women's subordinate status.

There are many forms of feminist research and a large number of feminist research methods (see Reinharz, 1992 in particular). In all forms of feminist research, feminist theory provides a theoretical framework that guides the entire research process, from the choice of research question through to the way the research report is written. This chapter focuses on feminist qualitative research methods but it should be clear that feminists also conduct quantitative research, but without taking on all the methodological assumptions of logico-empiricism. In this chapter we will firstly review the historical development of feminism, with particular emphasis on the similarities and differences between liberal, radical, and neo-Marxist feminisms. We will compare feminist epistemological commitments with those of gender blind methodological approaches. This discussion incorporates an overview of linguistic and Marxist forms of structuralism as a way of situating post-structuralism, particularly feminist responses to post-structuralism and (neo-Marxist) critical theory. Because of its praxis orientation, we argue, feminist research has been able to link post-structural and critical ideas into a methodological framework that resolves many of the acknowledged difficulties with both of these approaches to research practice. The methodological and epistemological advances made by feminist theory makes this chapter, and feminist theory more generally, a useful resource for researchers whether or not gender is the primary focus of their interest.

As in the previous chapter section a research proposal format is used to apply feminist methodology to a particular research question in sports science: *"What needs to happen so that young women, who want to, will use the skate parks"?* In this chapter section we have chosen to focus upon post-modern feminist qualitative research methodology. Before describing in some detail how a Feminist Praxis Study might proceed, we briefly discuss some of the difficulties that feminist researchers experience with logico-empirical methodological assumption, particularly claims to be non-biased, value neutral and objective. In contrast, we outline some research values that have broad agreement with feminist research circles. The praxis research design draws upon action research design. The qualitative research method of participant observation is described and discussed as it applies to the chosen research question and design.

3.1   *Historical Overview of Feminism*

Although feminism includes a belief that women are systematically disadvantaged relative to men, such a belief, by itself, is not enough to make someone a feminist. Feminism is not simply a theoretical belief system, it is primarily a movement to change society in ways that remove the disadvantages women face. All feminists are committed to act in ways that facilitate such change. Feminists differ, however, about the causes of women being systematically disadvantaged relative to men and hence about which 'facts' need to be examined to expose this disadvantage. Feminists also differ about what the appropriate remedies or strategies for change might be.

Feminists are part of broader movements of men and women who are committed to social change. Contemporary feminists can be distinguished from one another in terms of their political or theoretical association with either liberal, radical, or (neo) Marxist visions of a non-discriminatory society. The terms, of feminists' association with these traditions are not the same as that of non-feminists. The dominant versions of the theoretical and political traditions, that feminists have drawn upon, marginalize issues of gender, the very category that is central to feminist theorizing. Feminists who wish to use mainstream theoretical ideas have had to confront the theoretical difficulties of accommodating gender as the central category while simultaneously retaining the main ideas of the masculine version of the tradition. This has meant that feminist versions of liberal, radical and neo-Marxist theory have had to relate to male-written theory in terms of critique and discernment, rather than total acceptance.

First wave feminism was part of the broader liberal (and to a lesser extent socialist) tradition and developed out of women's reflection on their participation in the struggle to extend the vote to (propertied) black men and unpropertied white men. Despite the fact that some of the suffragettes had links to the socialist movement, they were generally privileged middle class white women who asked themselves why they shouldn't fight for the vote for themselves, rather than expend their energy fighting for the vote for excluded men. The aim of first wave feminists was primarily equality with males in terms of women's right to vote.

Second wave feminism had three relatively distinct faces: liberal, (e.g. Betty Friedan) radical (e.g. Mary Daly) and socialist (e.g. Mary O'Brien). Middle class liberal feminism re-emerged because of women's disenchantment with the post war ideology of women's supposed domestic bliss. The achievement of the vote had not prevented the exclusion of women from many areas of public participation, particularly employment. Liberal women, with their focus on 'equality' began to fight against the prejudices that justified their exclusion from work, and for removal of the legal barriers that prevented their full and equal participation in the workforce. Many women involved in the 'revolutionary' counter culture movement of the 60's began to resent their being allocated the typing and coffee making while the movement's men planned revolution. The failure of the women's attempts to have female liberation included as a central plank in male-dominated liberation movement's agenda led to the separatist focus on female oppression as the primary form of oppression by the newly defined radical feminists. In addition the revisionist efforts of Marxist and anarchist feminists rewrote and reinterpreted the corpus of working class movement theorists in an attempt to get class recognized as just one amongst a range of systemic sources of oppression that included sex and race. Second wave feminists came together, however, in their focus on consciousness raising and the idea that the personal is political as tools for achieving social change.

In the present era, women struggle with the consequences of the partial success of second wave feminist reforms. Liberal feminism and, to a lesser extent, socialist feminism are manifestations of humanism which is the dominant Western philosophy. Humanism is expressed in our social institutions (politics, law, medicine, mass-media, schools, science and technology). Humanism is articulated as cultural ideology in all aspects of the lives of Westerners, so much so that it seems 'right' and 'natural' to believe humanistic assumption. Humanistic values (some of which are contested, to some degree in Socialist theory) include individual separateness and autonomy, an integrated and non-conflicted sense of self' (essentialism) and individual human rights and the superiority of detached rationality. The resulting (liberal) humanist subject turns out not to be a universal 'human'; rather, the image is of one particular, culturally constituted form of human subjectivity: the young, strong, white, elite and male (Johnson, 1994). The humanist subject, the relatively autonomous man (sic) creating his own destiny, (including playing sports) has been purchased at the price of increasing the oppression of women (Pateman, 1988). Only by women assuming all responsibility for child-care, elder care and home care have men be able to be free of their relational responsibilities and therefore able to follow their self-actualizing path. This idealized subject functions as a standard against which diverse lives can be assessed to see if they 'measure up'. This has had negative consequences for women and non-elite men because he, or she, who is not like this idealized subject is judged inferior to and in need of the 'guidance', 'normalization' and 'protection' from dominant, white males.

Humanism has come under increasing criticism both from postmodernists and feminists. Post-modern critiques include the idea that valuing autonomy and individual rights comes at the price of devaluing the rights of other family members, the community, other animals, and the environment. Humanistic values underpinning logico-empirical science and, as we discussed in the previous chapter, these assumptions have been profoundly challenged because they privilege reason over emotions and ethics. This privileging of reason has meant that decisions about how we treat each other and the natural world have been studied and enacted without reference to emotions, values or relational attachments. Along with many others, feminists argue that the way in which science has been rationalized and decontextualized has been to the detriment of our society and our planet. Importantly feminists reject this mind-emotion split because when logico-empiricism eliminates emotions as a way of knowing, an important way in which women 'know' is invalidated.

First and second wave feminists participated in humanism, but particularly for liberal feminists, instead of the privileged white male as their subject, they substituted the privileged white female. Many women have felt disenfranchised by these feminist theorists' commitments to a particular image of the liberated subject. Like the male humanistic subject, the feminist subject, the liberated woman, acted as a criterion against which other women judged themselves or were judged by others. Before postmodernism emerged, socialist feminists were criticizing liberal feminists because only privileged women could expect to be able to afford the financial costs of liberation i.e. paying others to perform caring functions. Many women have complained that their lives were distorted or ignored by these early feminist writers. For example, women who wanted to care for their families felt disparaged and alienated. Lesbian women felt excluded by the heterosexist assumptions that underpinned the idealized liberated woman living in equality with a male partner and co-parent. Women of color, who often feel even more oppressed because of their race than they are because of their sex, have complained of being subsumed by early white feminist theorists who are blind to the oppressiveness of both racism and colonialism (Hill-Collins, 1990).

Third wave feminism is the response of feminism to postmodern critiques of liberal humanist commitments. Feminists have had difficulty, however, with the post structural critiques of essentialism which also challenge radical and (neo) Marxist feminists. Post-structural theory argues that the integrated, humanist subject is a myth and that subjectivity and identity are irrevocably split such that subjects are in fact comprised of multiple subject-positions and identities (or sub-personalities). Radical and neo-Marxist versions of feminism are essentialist to the extent that they rely on sex, class, or race identity (all essentialist notions) as a basis for causal explanation or collective action.

Third wave radical feminists (e.g. Liz Stanley and Sue Wise) have tended to identify themselves as 'post-structuralist feminists' (e.g. Luce Irigary, Julia Kristeva) while third wave (neo) Marxist feminists relate to the post-Marxism of critical theory (e.g. Patti Lather) rather than to earlier versions of neo-Marxism. In contrast to the mainstream versions of post-structuralism and critical theory, which have tended to face off one another as opponents, feminist appropriations of these traditions, we are arguing, have made the epistemological and ontological commitments of post-structural feminists and critical feminists almost identical.

For the purposes of exposition, we are emphasizing the differences between the focus of interest of liberal, radical, and (neo) Marxist feminists. Rather than treating each one of these political categories as a fixed and static box (or 'object') with definite boundaries whose members share a fixed set of defining beliefs and values, however, we are treating them as dynamic discourses whose participants develop and change their views through their interactions and disagreements. While we do not identify these theoretico-political traditions in terms of defining beliefs and values, common preoccupations and themes can be identified as linking their discussions.

To simplify the complexity of these discourses, we are emphasizing liberal feminists' focus on **legal and political *rights***, radical feminists' on **sexual and reproductive *identity***, and (neo) Marxist feminists' on **economic *exploitation***. Figure 6.7 is our attempt to capture certain relational aspects of these discourses. For our purposes this is a useful representation, but it shouldn't be reified as a mirror of 'the way the world really is'.

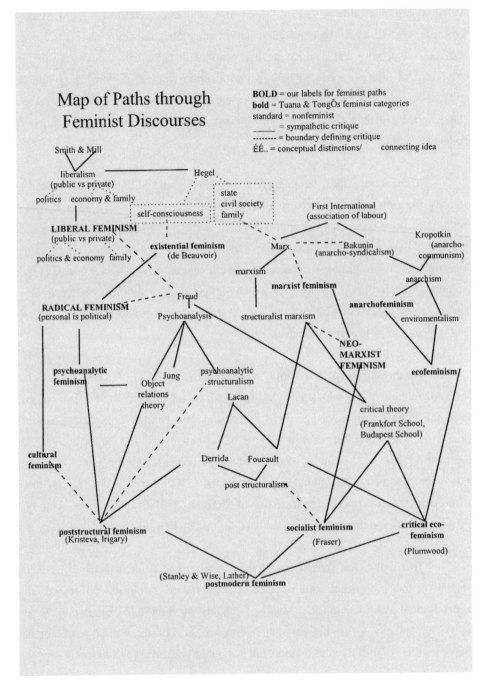

Map of Paths through Feminist Discourses

BOLD = our labels for feminist paths
bold = Tuana & TongÕs feminist categories
standard = nonfeminist
_____ = sympathetic critique
-------- = boundary defining critique
ÉÉ.. = conceptual distinctions/   connecting idea

Smith & Mill

liberalism
(public vs private)

Hegel

politics   economy & family

state
civil society
family

self-consciousness

First International
(association of labour)

LIBERAL FEMINISM
(public vs private)

existential feminism
(de Beauvoir)

Marx

Bakunin
(anarcho-syndicalism)

Kropotkin
(anarcho-communism)

politics & economy family

marxism

marxist feminism

anarchism

RADICAL FEMINISM
(personal is political)

Freud

Psychoanalysis

structuralist marxism

anarchofeminism

enviromentalism

psychoanalytic feminism

Jung

Object relations theory

psychoanalytic structuralism

Lacan

NEO-MARXIST FEMINISM

ecofeminism

critical theory
(Frankfort School, Budapest School)

cultural feminism

Derrida   Foucault

post structuralism

poststructural feminism
(Kristeva, Irigary)

socialist feminism
(Fraser)

critical eco-feminism
(Plumwood)

(Stanley & Wise, Lather)
postmodern feminism

Figure 6.7   Map of paths through feminist discourses.

As postmodernists, we have to be aware that our representations are just as contingent, partial and 'interested' as everyone else's. Mapping discursive paths, rather than positing fixed categories is consistent with postmodern critiques of objective and universal categories. We choose to emphasize the **path** or branches on an evolutionary tree **connecting** traditions of debate within each category we name, rather than the various steps or **direction changes** along the way.

Our pathways contrast with Tong's (1989) and Tuana & Tong's (1995), who, while acknowledging the difficulties generated by doing so, create separate categories to cope with persisting shifts in position and focus. Figure 6.7 shows how their set of categories maps onto our discursive path. Although the diagram is complex, it is actually a simplification and partial representation of a complicated social reality. To read Figure 6.7 we suggest you pick a starting point at the top, such as de Beauvoir and existential feminism, and follow a line connecting it to other developments down to the bottom. Whereas Tong and Tuana separate them, we show that their categories of **radical**, psychoanalytic, cultural, and post-structural feminists are on a common path or discursive thread, while anarchist, Marxist, **neo-Marxist**, socialist, and critical feminists are on parallel paths with a common source in the labor movement. The paths we have distinguished reflect who 'talks' with or against whom, more than a commonality of ideas. With post-structural and critical feminism these hitherto largely separate paths reconnect.

3.2   *Feminist Theory and Sports Psychology*

Objective Individualism: Early research into sex differences in sports psychology assumed that the significant differences, in both physical performance and psychological characteristics, believed to exist between males and females were biologically based (see Plaisted, 1995, p.43, and Gill, 1992, p.144 for overview). This approach to sex differences is consistent with the epistemological and ontological commitments represented in Figure 6.9 in the previous chapter that is a representation of logico-empiricist beliefs applied to the social world. Figure 6.8 above elaborates on some of the ontological commitments concerning the nature of the person and society associated with logico-empiricism, while reducing information about epistemological commitments. For the purposes we are considering it in this chapter, we have relabeled these commitments 'objective **individualism**' because the focus is on the individual (rather than the society) and on the objective observable properties of individuals (rather than on their subjective experiences). Methodologically, the sort of thing believed to exist in the world has a great impact on the way researchers study it. Objective individualism treats bio-physiology as an objective, intrinsic, and independent essence which determines the functioning of the mind and hence of behavior.

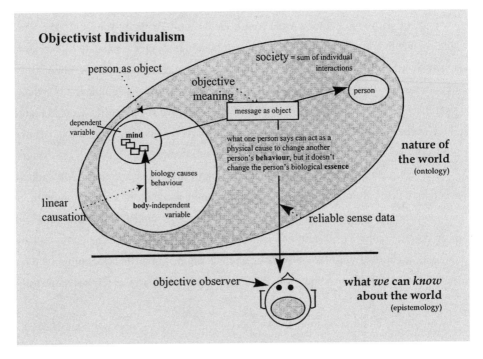

Figure 6.8   Epistemological and ontological commitments common to liberalism and to biological determinist psychology.

Society is seen as the sum of the interactions of such independently constituted individuals. In other words, the individual is seen as the independent variable and society as the dependent variable. With this view one believes that the way society is structured and functions is determined by human nature and therefore cannot and should not be changed.

Liberalism in general shares these ontological commitments with logico-empiricism, and politically they have the effect of legitimating the status quo that has negative effects for women. Portraying 'muscularity' and 'aggression' as an inevitable physiological and psychological properties of males, and 'softness' and 'nurturance' as inevitable physiological and psychological properties of females naturalizes traditional sex role stereotypes, reinforcing mainstream liberal tendencies to essentialize characteristics which, feminists argue, are social constructs that benefit men and disadvantage women. Liberal feminists challenge the notion that the differential participation of females and males in sports and other physically demanding activities is biologically determined. They argue that from an early age, whether natural, chosen or imposed, girls' lesser participation in sport amplifies the **apparent** difference between the physical capacities of men and women with the consequence of reinforcing the stereotypes that support such social constructs. The evidence indicates that men and women who train their bodies are more like one another than they are like the men and women who don't train (See Plaisted, 1995, p.44, and Gill, 1992, p.144, for references to the literature which substantiates this claim). Liberal feminists argue that until females are subjected from birth to the same regimes of physical activity and training, as males are, it won't be possible to disentangle whether physiological or social factors are producing the differences in physical performance between males and females. Even apparent physiological factors like testosterone levels, which are used to provide biological explanations for differences between men and women, turn out to be much more dependent on, and responsive to, environmental or contextual factors than previously recognized. (Money, 1988, quoted in Greer, 1999, p156)

Objective Structuralism: Liberal feminists successfully critiqued biologically oriented research into 'sex' differences which motivated the shift from discussions, within sports psychology, of 'sex' as a biological construct to discussions of 'gender' as a social construct. Research into role socialization, role conflict, and role orientation marks this development in sports psychology research. While research into role conflict and female participation in sport has confirmed the existence of such stereotypical roles. These results go a significant way towards explaining women's relative non-participation in sports and are consistent with feminist arguments that such role stereotypes dissuade many girls and women from participating in sports. What is more difficult for feminists to explain is that only a small proportion of female athletes reported experiencing the role conflict predicted (see Plaisted, 1995, p.546-7 for a detailed discussion of this research). The fact that most female athletes do not experience role conflict, however, makes the concept of role stereotypes of less use for understanding the performance of those who are already athletes.

To understand both the explanatory successes and the limitations of this research into role socialization and stereotypes, it is necessary to understand the shift in ontological commitments it represents. Whereas objectivist individualism sees the individual as independent variable and society as dependent variable, role research reverses this so that society is seen as the independent causal variable and the individual as a dependent variable constructed in accordance with social prescriptions. Figure 6.9 represents such (social) **structuralist** ontological commitments. The structuralist approach (which was first developed by the liberal, Talcott Parsons in the 1950s) retains the view (from Figure 6.8) that the individual can be researched and understood objectively. Objectivist individualism claimed that the behavior of individuals is determined by biology whereas structuralism saw individual behavior as determined by **objective** functional requirements of the social system.

While Figure 6.9 appears complex, it is in fact a simplification of a more complex social reality. For instance, given the likely institutional locations of readers of this chapter, the absence of educational, research, and sporting institutions could be seen as a serious omission. However, for the purposes of understanding the structural basis of the social roles examined in role research Figure 6.9, while as simple as we could get it, is complicated enough. It is not too difficult to elaborate on Figure 6.9 to include sports institutions. Sports psychology has not addressed the issue, however, except indirectly in terms of its impact on things like gender differentiated resource allocation or eating disorders in athletes (see Plaisted, 1995). Like politics and paid employment, sport is a gendered activity. Competitive participation in sports develops traits associated with 'masculinity' and affirms masculine identity. For example, sports develop skills such as speed, endurance, strength, and aggression, quick reflexes and teamwork that are required by hunters and warriors or soldiers. These traits are at odds with stereotypical notions of 'femininity'. Men who participate in competitive sports enhance their identification with socially prescribed notions of 'masculinity'. Women's participation in competitive sports is bought at the expense of conflict with socially prescribed notions of 'femininity'.

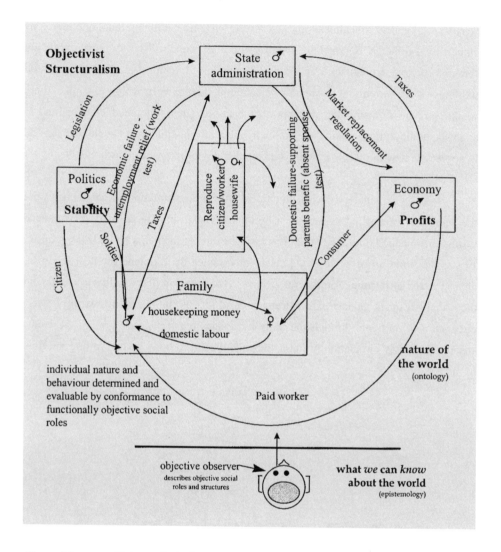

Figure 6.9   Epistemological and ontological commitments held (with some minor variations) by social determinists, such as liberal feminists, structural functionalists, linguistic structuralists, neo-Marxist structuralists, and dichotomous role definition and socialization theories in psychology.

Structural Functionalism vs. Conflict Structuralism: Figure 6.9 is based on Fraser's gendered inflection of Habermas' analysis of society in terms of the systems stabilizing functions of the state (Fraser, 1989,). What Fraser's analysis shows is that stereotypical gender role allocations also serve a systems stabilizing function ignored by Habermas. Although Figure 6.9 is useful for understanding the systems stabilizing function of stereotypical sex roles, it is too complex to demonstrate the strengths and weaknesses of **functional** systems explanations. Figure 6.10 helps elucidate these weaknesses by exposing the metaphorical basis of such functional explanations to analysis. It allows us to readily see both why the major institutions of society work, and to appreciate how the whole system is affected if any of its institutions break down.

As an explanatory device, functionalism works by treating society as if it were the same sort of unified system as a biological organism. Figure 6.10 shows social institutions mapped onto the human body as an example of such a biological organism. Just as the **function** of white blood cells, for instance, is to defend the host organism against attack by invading foreign organisms, so the **function** of the military is to defend the social organism against external attack. And just as the heart ensures the orderly circulation of nutrients through the body by controlling the blood flow, so the banks ensure the orderly circulation of goods through the social body by controlling the flow of money.

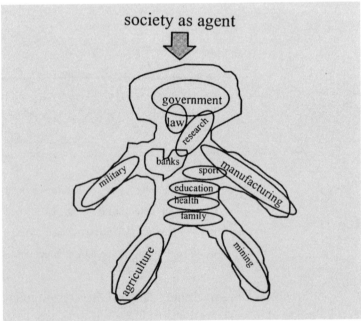

Figure 6.10   Functionalism: society mapped onto organism.

While functional explanations can be extremely powerful, they do have their limitations. Moving our attention from systems as wholes to the parts that constitute them can best see these limitations. While white blood cells can be said to have a purpose, that purpose is defined by the functional integrity of the organism of which it is a part. While we can speak, anthropomorphically, as if white blood cells intend their actions, in fact white blood cells have no consciousness and cannot strictly be said to 'intend' anything. Functional 'purposes' of body parts and intentional 'goals' of (self) conscious human agents are not the same. While both are directed towards some end, for body cells, those ends are externally imposed and regulated, whereas for people, individual intentions and goals are internally derived. The difference between body parts and social parts is clearer if, rather than describing society as if it were a body, as functionalism does, we anthropomorphize and describe body parts as if they were human individuals. From this perspective, we could say that the interest of the white blood cells in their own survival is subordinated to the interests of the body as a whole. Now white blood cells do not, in fact, have a personal interest in survival, but human individuals do. As individuals we care not just about the survival of the society as a whole, but also about our individual survival and prosperity.

To the extent that our survival and prosperity depends on the survival and prospering of society then risking ourselves to protect our society is also a way of protecting ourselves. However, although total systems breakdown may be bad for everyone, existing systems constraints on the extraction and distribution of resources may serve the interests of some parts of society at the expense of other parts. In other words, while asking about the fairness of white blood cells sacrificing themselves so the body can survive may be absurd, asking about the fairness of women being denied the opportunity of developing the individual talents and capacities to ensure they fulfill their functionally required reproductive role is not absurd. Similarly, Marxists ask about the systems constraints on the equity of the exchanges between workers and employers and between developing and advanced industrial economies.

By drawing an analogy between human societies and biological organisms, Parsons (1951) suggested that specific features of human societies can be explained in terms of the role or **function** they play in securing the survival of the society as a whole, rather than in terms of the benefit such features provide for constitutive parts of the society. Social structure can constrain people to act in ways that are systems supporting but individually deleterious. Whereas structural functionalist explanations, like Parsons, focus on systems supporting consensus and cooperation, structural **conflict** theories like Marxism focus on the conflict between the interests of structurally defined parts of the social system. Because they are both objective structuralist forms of explanation, however, both structural functionalist and structural conflict theorists (implicitly) refer to some sorts of systems model as represented in Figure 6.9. For instance, the flow of wages to workers, and the products of their labor to capital, in the working of the economy, can be looked at from either a functional or a conflict perspective. From a functionalist perspective this exchange serves to ensure maintenance of the market systems functions of production and distribution of goods. From a conflict perspective, however, the same exchange is described as maintaining the functional extraction of surplus monetary value from the sweat of labor and transferring that monetary value to the control of capitalists. Both theoretical perspectives see the exchange as systems supporting but one perspective values it positively, while the other, emphasizing the lack of reciprocity and equity in the exchange, sees supporting the present system negatively. Both functional and conflict **structuralists** are social determinists. That is, they both see society as the independent causal variable and the individual as a dependent variable constructed in accordance with social prescriptions.

Structural functionalism focuses on the systems supporting aspects of social structures, where, Marxism, and its contemporary manifestation, critical theory, sees capitalist economic structures as intrinsically flawed. Much like a steel beam with a crack in it, Marx argued those intrinsic features of the social system would itself lead to its collapse. As long as individuals are seen as merely 'dependent variables' they can't be treated, independently of structural dynamics, as agents for social change. From within (social) structuralist forms of explanation individuals are denied independent agency. If individuals were able to act as agents free to secure their own 'interest' or personal advantage, those in a position of structural disadvantage could be expected to resist attempts to exercise power at their expense. In support of structuralist forms of explanation, and against individualist ones, individuals commonly act in systems supporting ways, whether or not such acts are to their personal disadvantage. Habermas (a contemporary critical theorist) argues that normative structures legitimating the right of those in structurally privileged positions to exercise power secure the compliance of structurally disadvantaged groups (Habermas, 1976). It is here, at the level of individual consciousness-raising and collective action that feminism seeks to have one of its' major impacts.

Research into the effects of role stereotypes on sports participation demonstrates the power of such normative structures. Feminists have argued that maximizing the differences and minimizing or disregarding similarities between males and females, as the dichotomous construction of 'masculinity' and 'femininity' does (Plumwood, 1993) serves both to legitimate male privilege and to bolster a process of male identity formation that is dependent on their differentiating themselves from females which, in turn, bolsters the current system. Minimal physiological and psychological differences are exaggerated and enforced by accepted social practice, and, when that is not sufficient to obtain conformance to social stereotypes, power is used to exclude or sanctions are imposed on deviating individuals.

Venus Williams' recent attempt to enter a male tennis tournament represents an example of the way in which those in structurally privileged positions can use those normative structures to legitimate their power to maintain elite male control of sport. Does a woman wanting to enter male-only sport mean that if she were accepted then gender distinctions would be removed entirely so that all sport would then be unified across sex lines? Is it possible that some women may choose to enter 'open' competition and still retain women's separate sport? These are the kinds of questions that feminists are considering when challenging gender differences in sport participation.

Postmodern Intersubjectivist Ontologies: Although individuals, and structurally defined classes of individuals, commonly act in systems supporting ways, they do not always do so. Ontologically, objectivist individualism which focuses on biological imperatives (discussed above) lacks mechanism for explaining individuals who don't conform to expected behaviors or how it happens that individuals sacrifice themselves for a larger entity. Likewise, both forms of objectivist structuralism lack a theoretical mechanism for explaining individual resistance to structural imperatives.

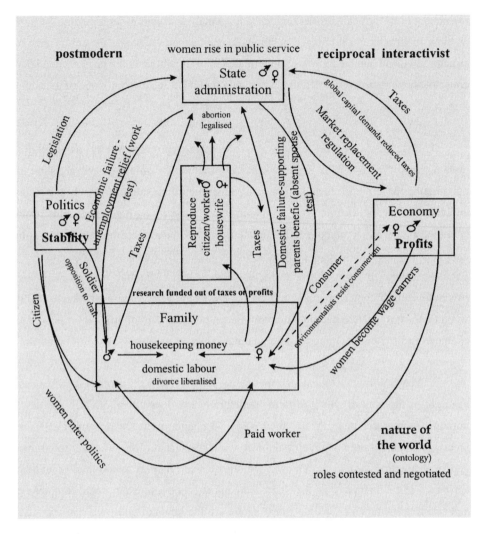

Figure 6.11   Postmodern, contextually situated, multi-dimensional interactive causation.

Refer again to Figure 6.9 which shows how stereotypical gender roles play systems supporting functions as part of a system of supporting structures. While the social structures represented in Figure 6.9 may have been an adequate representation of empirical social reality in the 1950's, however, it is hardly adequate as a representation of current social practice. Figure 6.11 is an attempt to modify Figure 6.9 in ways that better reflect current (postmodern) social practices. It is hard to represent these changes as systems stabilizing, however, because, on the one hand, transformations in information technology have undermined nation states' capacity to control monetary flows in and out of national boundaries. This has had the effect of shifting the power balance away from the state towards the interests of global capital. On the other hand, the collective organization and resistance of women has led to the transformation of rules and institutions in ways that reduce the degree to which the power balance is in men's favor.

Ontologically, these social changes draw attention to the effect that just as sex roles are not determined by biology, neither are gender roles determined by social structures. Individual psychology and behavior cannot be represented simply as a dependent variable of either biology or of social stereotypes. Of the social theorists represented in Figure 6.7, only the post-structuralists, critical theorists and the feminists have attempted to account for the interdependency of social structure and the individual subject. Figure 6.11 represents the shift from objectivist to postmodern ways of understanding categorization. Objectively definable categories lend themselves to quantitative analysis. In order to be able to count the frequency of phenomenon it has to be possible to identify a particular instance as an example of those phenomenon. Necessary and sufficient conditions of category membership guarantee this can be done. Neither sex nor gender, however, turns out to be objectively definable categories. If gender roles are understood to be 'objective' social constructs then it makes sense to ask subjects 'do you experience role conflict', so that the researcher can count the subjects that do experience such conflict. Once gender roles are seen as part of a complex and dynamic social process, in which both individual and group expectations are negotiated and fought over, undermined or transformed by changing circumstances, gender roles can no longer be treated as 'things' with fixed properties.

Sports psychology has accommodated post-modern critiques of both individualism and structuralism by attempting to design research which recognizes that behavior, both generally and with specific reference to gender linked behaviors, as multiply determined by biological, psychological, socio-historical factors. In addition, situationally context dependent factors interact with the other factors in ways that are interactive rather than independent (Plaisted, 1995, Gill, 1992).

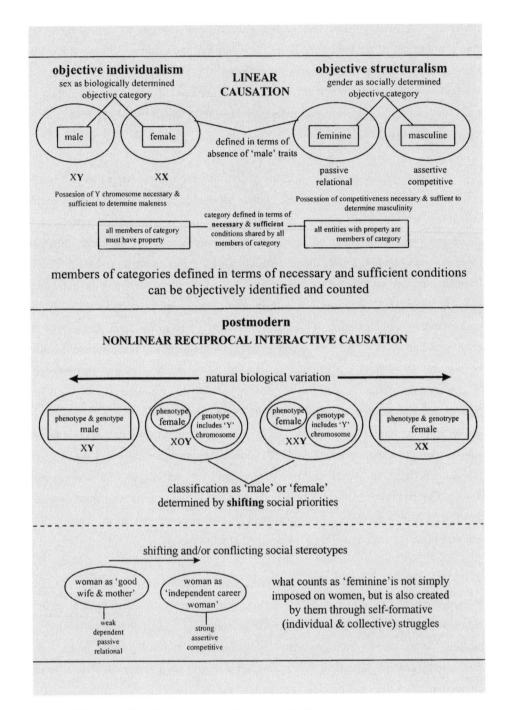

Figure 6.12   Objectivist and postmodern categorization.

Even if a postmodern researcher wants to count, they must first undertake qualitative research in order to establish what it is they are counting. Individual or focus group interviews can be set up in which participants are asked questions such as 'how do parents/ teachers/ trainers/ friends/ boyfriend/ husband/ children think you should act/ be?' ' How do you think you should act/ be?' These could be followed up by questions exploring conflicting expectations. In the section below we demonstrate how participant observation can be used to supplement subjects self-understandings with records and analysis of role negotiation in process.

Such non-linear dynamic systems are poorly modeled by logico-empirical methods that rely on the manipulation of independent variables. While chaos theory and probabilistic computer modeling have had explanatory success for physical systems, qualitative approaches are more appropriate when part of the dynamic system being studied is the interactive constitution of meaning engaged in the very process of carrying out research. The researcher does not stand outside of the process of social transformation, as independent observer. Rather, in asking research participants to reflect on their social context, and by challenging participants' initial self-understandings by casting doubt on their taken for granted life world, researchers are actively engaged in a transformative process. By being self-reflective and accepting responsibility for their part in social change, researchers can embrace research designs that promote libratory change. Evasion and denial of this role, however, is as likely to reinforce coercive and restrictive social practices as it is to expand the participants' capacities to develop their potential.

In the next section we apply the ideas that have been developed here to show how feminist research can be designed to be methodologically rigorous and yet take account of the complexities of the world as postmodernists see it.

3.3   *Feminist Research: Advancing the Interests of Women*

Feminism, as a political movement, is grounded in theory that in turn is grounded in the embodied experiences of women. The relationship between feminist theory and feminist practice is dialectical; theory helps illuminate the ways in which women are oppressed and it helps women to see the ways in which their own actions are implicated in their oppression. Bringing more consciousness to the way in which oppression operates, and how it might be more effectively challenged, allows women to theorize the ways in which they may achieve their own liberation (Fine, 1992, Fonow & Cook, 1991, Harding, 1987,, Lather, 1991, Reinharz, 1992, and Stanley & Wise, 1993). Feminist research links experience to theory in a way that can be used politically to further the interests of women.

Feminists generally feel alienated from logico-empirical research because, as previously discussed, it is based on the humanistic dream that we can, by the use of reason alone arrive at knowledge which means ignoring our passions, our unconscious drives and our history. Logico-empiricists purport to believe that adherence to the 'rules' of logico-empiricism can lead to knowledge which is non-political, universally true, and equally valuable to all people regardless of culture, race or class. An important way in which logico-empirical researchers present their knowledge claims is by writing in the third person which grammatically detaches the claim to know from a particular person, thus giving the claim an impersonal, objective, non-emotional force (Hodge & Kress, 1993). This appearance serves to disguise the fact that the reliability of the claim actually depends on the authority and integrity of a specific speaker, with limited knowledge and particular situated interests, biases and limitations.

Feminists argue that all research is grounded in values and serves political purposes; for logico-empiricists the purposes are usually those of the powerful, white male elite (e.g. governments, professional fraternities and multinational organizations). The fact that the logico-empiricist researcher's values and political commitments are not made explicit does not mean, feminists argue, that their values have no influence. Rather, by not knowing or not acknowledging their own values the researcher's values are profoundly affecting the research question, design, methods and interpretation of results in ways that the reader of the researcher cannot determine. Feminists believe that better research is conducted when the researcher is conscious of, and makes explicit their own values, beliefs and political commitments. Rather than trying to hide the contextual, value-laden limits of our knowledge claims by writing in the 'universal' third person, feminist researchers signify their subject position as value driven researcher by writing in the **first** person. Grammatically, a first person knowledge claim announces to the reader that they must judge for themselves the writer's reliability, honesty and authority (Hodge & Kress, 1993). When values are made explicit the consumers of research can make informed judgments about the effect that the researchers values has had on the validity of the research (Alcoff, 1995, Lather, 1991, Reinharz, 1992, Stanley & Wise, 1993).

On the other hand, the belief that **all** values, beliefs, commitments, and interests **can be made conscious** itself reflects the humanistic dream in the power of reason. Given the feminist critique of this we cannot expect to succeed in being conscious of, or making explicit, all our commitments. Rather, value explicitness is seen as a never to be fully achieved goal that must be sought by continual critical self-reflexivity. For instance, we (the authors of this chapter) must always be on guard for the ways in which our relatively privileged position as white academics may place our interests (in publication and the pursuit of 'knowledge') in opposition to the interests of less privileged women and men who may purchase this book and rely upon our authority.

Feminist Research Praxis: Feminist praxis research formalizes women's consciousness raising. Consciousness-raising usually involves small groups of women studying their daily lives in order to try to understand and change them. In the section below we will apply feminist praxis methodology to sports science by developing an outline of a research proposal using a modification of the framework that was used in the last chapter. Where we have made a modification this will be shown in ***bold italics.***

As discussed in the previous chapter, the elements of a qualitative feminist research proposal do not have the same level of agreement as is found in logico-empiricism. This means that there is no single method for writing a qualitative research proposal or report. We present, below, one way in which a feminist proposal this could be developed and defended. This time the example chosen concerns young women's use of public space for sports activities.

Use a Feminist Framework throughout the Research: The feminist framework for this study is postmodern feminism. Some core values and political commitments of that framework are set out in Table 6.7 As previously discussed, in writing a feminist research proposal it is necessary to state one's values.

Table 6.7

Values Guiding Feminist Postmodern Qualitative Research Practice

1.	Research focuses on women's embodied experiences
2.	The diversity of women's experiences is valued (e.g. race, class, age, disability, sexuality).
3.	The researcher's experience is included where relevant.
4.	The researcher's values and beliefs are made explicit in the research proposal and report.
5.	The use of 'I' and 'We' is appropriate when referring to self or self in collective with other women, and when referring to contextually situated knowledge claims.
6.	The relationship between the researcher and the researched is one of partnership in knowledge construction.
7.	The researcher demonstrates reflexivity and increasing consciousness.
8.	The research participants participate in reflection and interpretation of data.
9-	Theory and knowledge arising from the research has an activist feminist intent.

Identify the Phenomena of Interest or Concern: In our town there are a number of skateboard ramps that are used almost exclusively by boys. The same is true of the sports ovals. For the purposes of this example let us accept the following scenario. Helen, a community worker, at The Young Women's Center, has had discussions with five young women who expressed concern that there are very few places for them to just 'hang out' with others in ways that promote healthy activity. The young women expressed the belief that if they want to be physically active then they have many less choices than boys do. Helen was concerned that young women are much less physically active than young men that may in turn be linked to apathy, depression, smoking and drug use. Helen has a friend, Jackie, who was about to embark on an honors research degree. Jackie was 21 years old and studying Sports Psychology. After meeting the young women, Jackie agreed to take on the project with Helen and the five young women, all agreeing to participate in the research and trying to work out how to get young women, who express a desire to participate in skateboarding, to actually use the skateboarding parks.

The initial research question then is

"What needs to happen so that young women who want to, will use the skate parks"?

The young women from the women's center are educationally and socially disadvantaged; four out of the five in the study group are separated from their family of origin. The intersection of social class and the psychology of sports achievement are as neglected as research into the influence of racial, ethnic, and cultural factors, to the extent that Plaisted (1995) fails to even mention the need for it. Given that certain sports have long been recognized as appropriate avenues for working class (male) achievement, it can't be assumed that low class status and limited educational achievement is necessarily disadvantageous with respect to female sports participation. Consistent with postmodern emphases on differentiation, empirical investigation would be required to determine whether the role expectations of working and lower class girls presented lesser or greater obstacles to sports participation than for middle and upper class girls.

Social institutions like the city councils, schools, Churches, families, and media place much greater emphasis on, recognition of, and provision of resources for boy's access to sport and recreation spaces (Plaisted, 1995, p.41; Dempsey, 1992, esp. pp. 64ff.). A number of psychological responses open to the young women are conceivable in relation to this state of affairs. The girls at the young women's center could accept and defend these social practices as 'natural' and appropriate. They could object but feel powerless to do anything to change things. Or, they could resist, identifying opportunities and strategies for initiating social change. A concomitant feature of being a socially and educationally disadvantaged young woman is alcohol and drug use and a sense of apathy and lack of ambition (Testa, 1992). Such behaviors and attitudes can be considered (particularly from the perspective of middle class achievement oriented academics) to be self-destructive. Habermas (1976) argues, however, that these attitudes and behaviors can also be seen as a form of passive resistance in a context of social powerlessness. For social classes who perceive no opportunities for legitimate achievement and social rewards, illegitimate pleasures taken from a society which offers them little seem better than no pleasure in life at all. Clegg (1989) points out that perceptions of powerlessness can arise out of either ignorance of potential strategies or allies, or from a realistic assessment that organized resistance will cost more in the circumstances than will be gained or is available to give to the struggle (pp. 221-2). The researcher needs to realistically assess the resources available to themselves and to the research participants. The researcher also needs to assess whether the participants have a stake in powerlessness - the participants can avoid self-blame for non-achievement if they are facing overwhelming social odds. This is an important ethical consideration because if the researcher puts forward a strategy for achieving change in the participants' circumstances, and that strategy fails, the researcher will be contributing to the entrenchment of the participants' feelings of powerlessness rather than to their empowerment. A researcher that has personal experience in successfully organizing for social change, and resources in the form of knowledge and contacts in potential allies that makes the outcome of action likely to be successful, may be in a position to transform the participants understanding of their situation so that they are capable of acting successfully on their own behalf.

State Significance of the Study: How to address the significance of a particular study was addressed in the previous chapter and is also relevant here. This study is local and contextual but has the advantage of being able to access the personal, detailed stories and experiences of young women as they attempt to use male dominated sports space. This local, context-dependent knowledge is useful for confirming critiquing and/or extending abstract theory that has been generated primarily by academics who are well removed from the daily world of these young women. This study has the potential to isolate, in fine detail, the factors that are inhibiting young women's participation in a sport that is male dominated. The practical contribution of the study is in carefully studying and theorizing about attempts to change current practice regarding the use of public sport space. This practically useful knowledge will be of broad interest to feminists who are concerned about girls' participation in sport. Other interested parties include sports administrators, coaches, teachers and parents who all have some level of concern about girls' lesser participation in sports, the gendered nature of sports and ways in which girls' participation in all forms of sport may be better facilitated.

Review the Literature: In the previous chapter section concerning Constructivist research, the review of literature in a qualitative study was discussed and is relevant here. In summary, we argued there that it is important to conduct at least a beginning literature review at the research proposal stage. A feminist study, in a sense, is research 'against the grain' in that it takes a critical approach and looks for different ways of conceptualizing a particular research problem. The previous recommendation, that the literature review needs to range widely across theoretical, methodological and disciplinary boundaries, is a useful strategy for unsettling previous ways of conceptualizing the research problem and of finding novel ways of looking or thinking about the research topic.

It is particularly important to review feminist theoretical literature on the subordination of women and women's participation in their own subordination so that any practical strategies are informed by feminist theory. The literature review should begin with the research in sports psychology that discusses the many ways in which women are disadvantaged relative to men with respect to sports participation (see Plaisted, 1995). However, given postmodern recognition of the interdependency of psychological and social factors, it is important to extend your initial literature review to include feminist social research into gender and identity formation, and social theories concerning resource distribution and legitimization processes.

Describe Research Design: The proposed research design is that of Feminist Praxis. The notion of changing practice while researching it comes from critical social theory, particularly Marx and Habermas. Praxis methodology is a loosely structured research process which has the effect of guiding the researcher to first make explicit, and then critique and modify, the informal theories which are guiding both the researcher's and the participants' practices, both public and private.

Praxis means developing increasing consciousness during practice and reflecting upon practice in order to draw out the learning. In practice our actions are guided by what we think or, put another way, by our theories of what is going on, and what we predict will happen, in a given situation. Our informal theories, however, are often based on incorrect assumptions and are usually not well founded on either theory or experience. The aim of increasing our consciousness, through praxis, is to be able to contribute to changing both the oppressive social structures that limit our actions and our own relations to these structures. The aim is to improve our actions to better serve our own interests and the interests of women as a group.

Praxis research has become a major methodology for feminist researchers because it gives a philosophical foundation to the feminist principle that 'the personal is political.' This means that the everyday experiences of individual women, including the experiences of the researcher, are a legitimate focus for research (Reinharz, 1992; Lather, 1991 and Stanley and Wise, 1993). The essential elements for praxis then are action, reflection, theorizing, and changed action at an individual and institutional level. Praxis research therefore, is conceptualized as an on-going spiral of practice, self-reflection, scholarly inquiry and theorizing which leads to changed practice, further reflection, scholarly inquiry and theorizing about practice.

Practice: Praxis is a political notion that has the aim that practitioners will become increasingly conscious about their practice in the world in order to change both their own practice, and collectively with others, contribute to changing the world. In mainstream, conservative, thinking there is a division between the personal and the political such that the personal realm of practice is said to be 'not public' and therefore and therefore not political and not worthy of either research or theory.

The notion of 'praxis' challenges this division claiming that all human actions are political and need to be researched and theorized. Feminists, for example, have been quite effective in bringing 'private' practices, like wife bashing and date rape, firstly to women's consciousness and later to public consciousness. The result of feminist praxis has been institutional change in the way schools, the police, hospitals and the churches now conceptualize and respond to these abusive practices.

Praxis researchers are involved in:
- challenging their own ways of understanding social practices (like the use of public sport space) and examining the cultural ideals and imperatives that impels these;
- sensitively challenging the beginning understandings that the young women participants have of why sports spaces work the way they do (see section below on the centrality of relationships)
- critiquing accepted theory and research;
- challenging existing power relations and the organizational structures that support them.

To practice as a researcher in this sense, is to problematize the taken for granted way that culture creates and maintains separate spheres for men's and women's sports and to challenge these ingrained practices. Praxis research calls forth courage, endurance and creativity in the researcher and the participants.

Centrality of Relationships: The relationship between researcher and participant is of paramount importance in praxis research. There are two reasons for this: firstly, the quality of the information gathered in any qualitative study depends upon how well the researcher can come to know the participants in deeply personal ways. Secondly, attempting to facilitate the empowerment of another person, in this case the young women requires intimate and trusting relationships to develop, usually over an extended period of time.

Praxis research challenges the researcher to be aware of their own needs and what they are prepared to offer within each relationship. There are no predetermined boundaries between researcher and participant; these have to be articulated and negotiated. The researcher must essentially 'be themselves' in relationship and not hide behind the role of the researcher. The form of the relationship between the researcher and each participant will therefore be different.

It is in the researcher's interest to develop intimate relationships with each of the participants. Without intimacy a researcher cannot develop understanding of her/his participants. Intimacy allows knowledge of each participant to grow and over time they will share something of their life history, current relationships and activities as well as their hopes and desires. Intimacy is not a 'one way street'; Anne Oakley (1974) wrote that there is "no intimacy without reciprocity." Reciprocity involves negotiating all aspects of the relationships to foster a level of equality between the researcher and the participant. Reciprocity involves a true human-to-human encounter with all the emotionality that this implies. Procedures that foster reciprocity include that:

- interviews are interactive
- there is appropriate self-disclosure on the part of the researcher
- a number of interviews are conducted over time.
- the participants are in control of the information that the researcher uses.

- theoretical ideas that emerge have their meanings negotiated with participants.
- the researcher behaves in such a way that research participants are at all times free of coercion and able to choose their own action or inaction in a particular situation.

Reflection: Critical self-reflection is at the heart of critical science. Habermas (1971) writes that the history of the species is a self-formative process based on the emancipatory power of critical self-reflection. Self-reflection provides a way of "rendering both problematic and provisional our most firmly held assumptions and, nevertheless, acting in the world, taking a stand" (Lather 1991, p29). For Habermas, self-reflection is linked to an understanding of psychoanalysis and the therapeutic relationship. "Self-reflection can be conceived as the internalization of the therapeutic discourse" (Habermas 1971, p28). In the analyst-analysand relationship, the therapeutic dialogue is based on the analyst helping the analysand see the ways in which their previous understandings were based on self-deceptions. Within the relationship the analysand comes to realize that this self-deception has prevented their achievement of personal freedom (Habermas 1971). The researcher will use critical self-reflection to reconsider their own experiences with sport and sport spaces and more generally their experiences with 'male' and 'female' spaces and what happens when women encroach on 'men's space'. As the data collection stage of the research progresses the actions of the researcher and the participants will produce incidents which require reflection in order to explicate understanding.

The process of reflection involves one reliving the experience and firstly focuses on the emotional content (Schon, 1983). Strong emotional responses are the keys to unlocking the learning inherent in the situation. In this sense, emotions function as a research instrument. For instance, when reflecting on an experience of not being able to prevent young women participants from experiencing rejection and humiliation at the skateboard park the researcher may need to acknowledge, accept and express feelings of guilt, remorse and powerlessness. This emotional expression, at least to some extent, will be needed before she can move on to focus on the boys' behavior that in retrospect could have been predicted. She will also need to consider the lack of preparation of the girls that meant that they attempted integration into a male sport space prior to being really ready to deal with negative responses that they encountered. If, as logico-empiricists would have it, the researcher is closed off to her emotions then she will not be able to learn from this experience and her theoretical understanding will be impoverished

Reflection also involves critical conversations between the researcher and the participants and also with colleagues and friends. During and after these conversations both parties develop a better understanding of the phenomenon of the study and the way in which one's own actions contribute to processes of oppression. Sharing transcripts of interviews and discussing their meanings with participants can enhance participant self-reflection. Theoretical ideas that emerge from the study should be discussed and negotiated together with participants (Lather 1991). By these processes the researcher and the participants are able to see the situation from the perspective of all the key players and can work out what actions best serve their own interests and values and are most likely to be effective. For the researcher, reflective journaling and having a critical mentor are useful ways for deepening the self-reflective process and for developing an expanded and critical awareness of one's own world and the world as experienced by others.

Scholarly Inquiry: Scholarly inquiry proceeds at two levels during praxis research; it is both specific and general. In its specific sense a focused literature review is useful when the researcher is confronted with practice issues that are still problematic after self-reflection and joint-reflection. Trans-disciplinary books and journals may help the researcher clarify what actions they should take now, or plan to take in similar situations in the future.

As discussed in the section on literature review, during the research process the general level of scholarly inquiry proceeds simultaneously with practice, reflection and theorizing as each element of the research process informs and gives direction to each of the others.

Theorizing: As discussed in the section on 'reflection', theorizing is anchored in the reflected upon experiences of both the research participants and the researcher. Theory, for the praxis researcher, means "quasi-causal" accounts of the way in which social structures and relations give rise to particular actions, specifically relations of domination and submission (Habermas, 1971). The explanations are "quasi-causal" rather than causal because people, unlike things, are not directly governed by conditions external to themselves (Fay 1975). Theory evolving out of praxis research is interactive with what has previously been written. The new Theory arising out of praxis research should provide guidelines for bringing about changes to the way in which sports spaces are used both from the perspective of women and from the perspective of social institutions which fund and control sport space.

Describe Sampling: As for constructivist research the aim of sampling is to develop a full, multi-faceted, theoretical understanding of the phenomenon of interest thus purposive sampling is used. In this example what would need to change before girl's who wanted to actually use the skate parks along with the boys.

The criteria for selecting research participants would be that they are:

i)   female

ii)   aged 13-21 years.

iii)   Initiated a discussion about her desire to skateboard at the park (so no possibility of coercion).

iv)   Having participants from a range of educational, economic and ethnic background would be valued but cannot be ensured because of the risk of subtle coercion.

Like all good researchers, feminists are careful to document the demographic details of the sample and not imply that our findings could be applied outside the population from which it was generated.

Gaining Access to the Participants: There is a close relationship between sampling and gaining access to participants; in this case, the participants are all clients of the Young Women's Center. Jackie has a good start in doing this particular study because she was approached by Helen and is quite likely to get the support of the management committee to research at the Young Women's Center.

Selecting and Accessing an Appropriate Research Site: The participant observation will occur primarily at the Young Women's Center but also at the skateboard park which is public space and easy to access. Using participant observation as a method of data collection is discussed in the section concerning collection of data.

Jackie, the researcher is young and can behave in ways that help her blend in with other young women who sit and watch their boyfriends skateboard. As previously discussed, interviews are best conducted in a naturalistic setting because it diminishes power differentials and because participants are likely to feel more comfortable. The Young Women's Center, a park or the young women's homes, are appropriate venues for interviewing.

Describe Ethical Implications of the Study: In the section 'Identify the Phenomena' we discussed the ethical implications of the researcher suggesting to disadvantaged young women that change is possible when it may not be. This issue would need to be addressed in any proposal to go before an ethics committee. Ethical aspects of qualitative studies were discussed in the previous chapter; therefore, a brief overview only is presented below.

Many ethical issues in a qualitative study are the same as for a quantitative study. Essentially they are about not harming the participants, obtaining informed consent, ensuring confidentiality and storing the data in a safe place. Because of the in-depth and sensitive nature of the interviews there is a potential to raise issues which are emotionally upsetting to the participant. The researcher needs to have basic counseling skills so that they can manage the immediate situation sensitively. In addition, the researcher needs to have a plan for referral for ongoing counseling if it is required.

In the present study the ethical aspects of conducting research at the Skateboard Park will need to be considered. It creates less ethical concern for an ethics committee if the researcher is open about what she is doing at the Skate Park. If the researcher believes that declaring herself to be researching will interfere with the validity of the study then she will have to mount a careful defense for conducting covert research if she wants to gain ethical approval for the study.

Conduct Data-Collection: See previous chapter concerning the skills of in-depth interviewing in constructivist research and integrate in-depth interviewing within the praxis research spiral as discussed above.

Participant Observation: Participant observation is also frequently referred to as fieldwork. The study we are describing is not a full fieldwork study such as an anthropologist might do with people of a different culture or subculture and yet there are so many similarities that the praxis researcher would need to be informed by the knowledge, attitudes and skills of experienced fieldworkers. The reader who is interested in reading an extensive description and discussion of participant observation is referred to Bogdan and Taylor, (1999). The following notes are based on feminist methodology and modifications of Bogdan and Taylor's work on participant observation.

Fieldwork involves learning how to deal with each of the following issues:

1. *Entering the field.* The section from the previous chapter concerning the Researcher as Data Collection Instrument is relevant here and many of the skills of establishing relationships for interviewing also transfer to the setting where you are observing and asking more casual questions. When the researcher enters a new area, or field, she is more likely to be accepted by being relatively unobtrusive and establishing easy communication with the people from whom she wants to learn. Don't rush the entering the field stage; collecting data is secondary to getting to know the setting and the people and allowing the people to get to know you as a person.

2. *Negotiating your role.* For the present study, Jackie will have to negotiate a role for herself at the Young Women's Center. She will need to decide whether she will participate at the skateboard park or leave that to the young women. If she goes to observe, Jackie will need to think about how she will explain herself at the Skateboard Park. Jackie will also need to think through how she and the young women participants will deal with each other while at the skateboard park.

   Because researchers generally take notes it is important to think about the impact that may have on the actors in a situation. It is not wise to use as tape recorder, ask lots of questions or write notes otherwise you will disturb the 'natural' environment and end up researching the effects of your intervention in the field rather than what occurs when the participants feel at ease. It is generally recommended to save field-note writing until immediately after an observation session.

3. *Building relationships.* One of the easiest ways to build relationships is to find out what you share with those that you are interested in studying. This may mean spending social time with the young women and doing things together. In addition to what was written in the previous section, about the centrality of the relationships with participants, it is helpful to consider how the researcher might build relationships at the skate park with the young men. For both the young men and women, it is helpful in building relationships if the researcher is young, dresses in ways that match their ways, talks like they talk and knows about the kind of music they like. Relationships work best when they are reciprocal, so by helping out when you can, it is more likely that you will be able to get the information that you want. If you want to be liked and accepted it helps to be helpful, but don't go overboard. With the young women this may mean being a driver, baby-sitter, book lender, letter-writer and a shoulder to cry on.

4. *Participate if appropriate.* If the researcher is able to skateboard then that would be a bonus and should help with getting the guys to open up and accept them. If the researcher can't participate in skateboarding directly, then talking with the girlfriends who go to watch may be an appropriate strategy. It is also good to participate in social activities like nights out as a way of getting to really know the informants and understanding the particular subculture, including the norms about male and female roles. Be on guard about offering too much and the risk of getting 'off the research track' or being exploited by informants. The researcher needs to balance the desire to 'fit in' and be accepted with the need to be authentic. Although it is really important for the researcher to understand the perspectives of the young women and the young men it is also important not to lose your identity and your own beliefs in the process. In the final research account you will need to be able to present all perspectives in such a way that the reader of the research can discern whom is speaking; in postmodern parlance, this is referred to as a multi-vocal account.

5. *Deal with difficulties as they arise.* "Fieldwork is characterized by all the elements of human drama found in social life: conflict, hostility, rivalry, seduction, racial tension and jealousy" (Taylor & Bogdan, 1999, p. 55). The researcher is advised to think about the potential difficulties and prepare both

herself and the young women in advance of approaching the Skateboard Park. That the researcher and the young women will be treated as sexual objects is predictable. It would be wise, therefore, to do some role-playing beforehand to work out strategies for coping with 'friendly' and not so 'friendly' sexual advances, as well as how to respond to sexist and offensive behavior. Some young men may react in a hostile way to the researcher or the participants and this too needs to be thought through. If it seems like a significant threat then doing covert research may be able to be defended ethically. If the researcher decides to let the young men know that she is conducting research, it is best to be vague about it so that they don't become so self-conscious about their behavior that they actually change it for the benefit of the researcher (the Hawthorn effect).

6. ***Plan interventions later in the study.*** The first phase of the fieldwork is gaining admission and acceptance. The second phase is gaining information about how the skateboard park culture works, just as it is. As the fieldwork is being conducted as part of a praxis study the researcher and participants will need to intervene to change the status quo in order to observe what happens and to make more explicit the power that is operating to maintain the status quo.

7. ***Keep notes, develop theory and ask specific questions unobtrusively.*** The need to take unobtrusive notes has already been mentioned. As this is a praxis study the researcher keeps reading and writing throughout the data collection phase of the study. This will allow you and the young women to refine your knowledge and increase your consciousness. Ask questions that evolve out of your developing theoretical hypothesizing so that you can refine and develop your understanding. There is no substitute for careful observation and thinking, so avoid asking vague, annoying questions. Specifically, do not ask lots of questions as some kind of 'fishing expedition' hoping that something useful will emerge

When entering the scene be aware that you will need to recall what you observed and heard. Pay attention to those things that seem relevant to the research question and avoid getting sidetracked on interesting but irrelevant issues. It is useful to take photos, maybe when no one is there but this will act as a map and will be a valuable aid in recalling action. Write your notes using pseudonyms. It helps to recall what you heard if you note key words and phrases. Leave the setting as soon as you have observed as much as you can remember; it is useful to keep a tape recorder in the car (but do avoid being seen using it). When writing notes keep them descriptive and emic: write what you heard or saw, not a summary of what you heard or saw. Use single quotation marks when you can recall words fairly closely. Use double quotation marks when you can recall exact words.

Conduct Data Analysis/Interpretation: Data analysis in qualitative research generally was discussed in the previous chapter on constructivism and these ideas are relevant here. It is common in postmodern research reports to present a multi-theoretical and multi-perspectival account (Lather, 1991). This means firstly, that extant postmodern theory may be used to illuminate understanding. For instance Michael Foucault's theory of power may be used to explain the multiple intersecting ways in which power operates to exclude women from sport participation and feminist theories about corporeality may be used concurrently to explain women's relationship and experience of embodiment. A multi-perspectival account means representing all the key stakeholders' perspectives in the research account. In the study under discussion this would mean being able to represent the male perspective as well as the perspective of the young women. Having separate chapters generally does this. It is not possible, without actually conducting the study to show how data analysis or interpretation would actually proceed in the particular case.

3.4   *Conclusion*

In this chapter section we firstly outlined a history of the development of feminist thought and showed its' relationship to mainstream liberalism, socialism and more recently, postmodernism. The discussion then focused on feminist theory as it applies to sports science, particularly concerns about whether the apparent gender difference in sport participation and sporting prowess is the result of biology or society, or the interaction of both. We introduced and critiqued the notion of 'objective individualism' which means the belief that the person can be viewed as an object whose behavior has biological causes. This led to critiquing the notion of 'objective structuralism' which also sees the individual as an object but this time their behavior is understood as determined by social structures and processes. We discussed two versions of structuralism: functionalist (which sees the status quo as 'good') and conflict structuralism (which sees the status quo as inequitable and needing to change). These varying positions were then subjected to feminist and postmodern critique which goes some way to explaining how individuals can act in ways that are against their own best interests or in ways that are system destabilizing. Feminist postmodern researchers embrace non-linear, interactive causation and accept that neither sex nor genders are objective categories. These ontological commitments have profound implications for postmodern feminist research. We used the example of Feminist Praxis research design and participant observation method to demonstrate one way in which postmodern feminist research of rigor and integrity can be conducted.

References

Alcoff, L. (1995). Cultural Feminism Versus Post-Structuralism: The Identity Crisis in Feminist Theory. In L.Tuana, & R. Tong. (Eds.), *Feminism and Philosophy: Essential Readings in Theory, Reinterpretation and Application.* Bolder Colo.: Westview Press.

Australian Sports Commission (1992). *Australian Sports Directory.* Canberra. Australian Sports Commission.

Bodgan, S. & Taylor, R. (1999). *Introduction to Qualitative Methods* (3rd Ed.). New York: John Wiley.

Clegg, S. (1989). *Frameworks of Power.* London: Sage Publications.

Dempsey, K. (1992). *A Man's Town: Inequality Between Women and Men in Rural Australia.* Melbourne : Oxford University Press.

Fahy, K. (1996). Praxis Methodology: Action Research Without a Group. *Contemporary Nurse.* 5, 54-58.

Fay, B. (1975). *Social Theory and political practice.* London: George Allen Unwin.

Fine, M. (1992*). Disruptive Voices: The Possibilities of Feminist Research.* Ann Arbor: University of Michigan Press.

Fonow, M. M., & J. A. Cook, (Eds.). (1991) *Beyond Methodology: Feminism as Lived Research.* Bloomington: Indiana University Press.

Fraser, N. (1989). What's critical about critical theory? The case of Habermas and gender'. In Fraser, N. *Unruly Practices: Power, Discourse and Gender in Contemporary Social Theory*, University of, Minneapolis: Minnesota Press.

Gill, D. (1992). 'Gender and Sport'. In T. Horn. (Ed.), *Advances in Sport Psychology.* Champaign, IL: Human Kinetics Publishing.

Greer, G. (1999). *The Whole Women.* London: Doubleday.

Habermas, J. (1971). *Knowledge and Human Interest.* Boston: Beacon Press.

Habermas, J. (1976). Problems of Legitimation in Late Capitalism. In P. Connerton (Ed.), *Critical Sociology.* New York: Penguin Books.

Harding, S. (1986). *The Science Question in Feminism.* Ithaca: Cornell University Press.

Hill Collins, P. (1990). *Black Feminist Thought: Knowledge, Consciousness, and the Politics of Empowerment.* Boston: Unwin Hyman.

Hodge, R., & Kress, G. (1993). *Language as Ideology.* (2nd Ed.). London: Routledge.

Johnson P. (1994). *Feminism as Radical Humanism*. St. Leonards, NSW: Allen and Unwin.

Lather, P. (1991). *Getting Smart, Feminist Research and Pedagogy With/in the Postmodern*. New York: Routledge.

Lewin, K. (1952). Group decision and social change. In Swanson G E, Newcomb T M & Hartley E L (Eds.), *Readings in Social Psychology*. New York: Henry Holt.

Money, J. (1988). Commentary: Current Status of Sex Research. *Journal of Psychology and Human Sexuality*. *1*, 5-15.

Oakley, A. (1974). *Women's Work, the Housewife Past and Present*. New York: Pantheon Books.

Parsons, T. (1951). *The Social System*. New York. Free Press.

Pateman, C. (1988). *The Sexual Contract*. Cambridge: Polity Press.

Plaisted, V. (1995). Gender and Sport. In T. Morris, & J. Summers. *Sport Psychology: Theory, Application and Issues*. Brisbane: John Wiley and Sons.

Plumwood, V. (1993). *Feminism and the Mastery of Nature*. London: Routledge.

Reinharz, S. (1992). *Feminist Methods in Social Research*. New York: Oxford University Press.

Schon, D. A. (1983). *The Reflective Practitioner*. New York: Basic Books.

Stanley, L., & Wise, S. (1993). *Breaking Out Again: Feminist Ontology and Epistemology*. (2nd Ed.). London: Routledge.

Testa, M. F. (1992). Introduction. In M. K. Rosenheim & M. F. Testa. (Eds.), *Early Parenthood and Coming of Age in the 1990's*. New Brunswick, NJ: Rutgers University.

Tong, R. (1989). *Feminist Thought: A Comprehensive Introduction*. London: Allen & Unwin.

Tuana, L., & Tong, R. (Eds.) (1995). *Feminism and Philosophy: Essential Readings in Theory, Reinterpretation and Application*. Bolder Colo.: Westview Press.

(4)   Computer Aided Qualitative Research: A NUD*IST 4 Approach
Andrea Lamont-Mills

Over the past 10 years there has been a rapid growth in the development and use of computer programs to assist qualitative data analysis. Computer programs are being widely used by qualitative researchers to perform a variety of analytical tasks, from simple editing functions through to complex theory development (Miles & Huberman, 1994). Computer programs that assist qualitative data analysis can be broadly grouped into five categories based on the analytical functions of the programs. These categories listed in increasing levels of sophistication are text retrievers, textbase managers, code-and-retrieve programs, code-based theory-builders, and conceptual network-builders[10].

Text retrievers search and retrieve words, phrases, and other string characters. For example search and retrieve all instances of the word *feminine* across each interview text file. In most text retrieval programs the raw data is not entered into the program but stands outside of the program where it is searched by the program. Textbase managers organize the raw data within the textbase manager program. These programs store the raw data and systematically sorts the database into meaningful subsets for comparison and contrast by the researcher. For instance search and retrieve all instances of the word *feminine* across male responses and then across female responses. Code-and-retrieve programs are an advance on the previous two categories in that they enable the researcher to retrieve and code the data. That is lines, sentences or paragraphs can be coded on the basis of keywords. For example search and retrieve all instances for keywords *feminine, girly girl, girl stuff, wearing make-up*, and label all located items with the code feminine.

Code-based theory-builders not only retrieve-and-code but also assist the researcher to develop and test theory. Here categories can be developed from the assigned codes, memo's written and linked to these codes and categories, hypotheses that

---

[10] See Weitzman & Miles (1995) for a comprehensive overview and evaluation of each grouping and commonly used programs within each grouping.

have been induced from the data can be formulated and tested. For example search and retrieve all instances for keywords *feminine, girly girl, girl stuff, wearing make-up*, and label all located items with the code feminine. In subsequent analysis the code feminine is grouped with the code masculine into the category "gender stereotypes."

Further analysis of the gender stereotypes category could results in this being subsumed under the higher order theme "gender." The development and defining qualities of the two codes and the two categories are reported in a memo within the program that is attached to the category "gender stereotypes." The resulting data appears to suggest that male athletes construct gender stereotypes differently than female athletes. This hypothesis can be tested via a search-retrieve-and-comparison of male and female responses. The last category is conceptual network-builders. These programs use semantically meaningful networks to build and test theory. The researcher's thinking and conceptualization of the data is represented graphically in these programs.

The aim of this chapter section is to demonstrate the logic underpinning one particular code-based theory-builder, NUD*IST 4 (Qualitative Solutions and Research Pty Ltd, 1999–QSR). NUD*IST stands for Non-numerical Unstructured Data Indexing Searching and Theorizing. The choice to discuss NUD*IST 4 is driven by the author's familiarity with the program. The author has used NUD*IST 4 in Doctoral dissertation studies and extracts from this research will be used to illustrate the points made during this chapter. The section will begin with a brief discussion regarding computer-aided analysis in qualitative research. A brief outline of what this section will not cover will then be presented. The main body of the section illustrates the formal logic and flexibility of the NUD*IST 4 program by contrasting the two interlocking data systems associated with the program, the documents system and the index system. The section concludes with some limitations of the NUD*IST 4 program.

4.1   *A Word of Warning—Computers and Qualitative Data Analysis*

The phrase "computer assisted qualitative data analysis" is somewhat of a misnomer in that qualitative analysis computer programs do not follow the same analytical principles as quantitative analysis programs (e.g., SPSS, SAS, BMDP, etc.). This is an important point for the reader to understand. Those readers who are familiar with quantitative analysis programs understand that after raw data is entered into a program such as SPSS, the researcher proceeds with a particular analysis of interest and then the program analyses the data.

Quantitative analytical programs compute the variance in the data and then determine whether this variance is of some importance. That is, whether there are differences in the variance between groups, between pre and post treatment conditions, and so forth. Quantitative data analysis programs tell the researcher whether the measured variance is important or of some value based on probability levels, effect size, and power.

For example one is able to say with 95% confidence that men and women do not differ in their responses to the PAQ because the F value was not significant at $p=.05$. Probability levels, effects size, power and so forth are well-established parameters or standards of importance in quantitative statistics[11]. These parameters are used to determine whether what was measured or the changes that occurred are a true reflection of the research question.

Computer programs for qualitative analysis, and in particular code-based theory-builders, do not analyze the data in the same manner as quantitative programs. Instead qualitative programs **assist** analysis by making information more accessible to the researcher. They **do not** perform the analysis itself. Qualitative programs can systematically and logically organize the data, and this organization may lead to the highlighting of an area of potential importance for the researcher, but it will not tell the researcher whether this is important or of some value. Qualitative programs potentially enhance the researcher's thinking about complex data by logically and systematically structuring and storing information in ways that facilitate the discovery and exploration of meaning in unstructured data.

Here the use of the word potentially is a deliberate choice by the author. Qualitative analysis programs only potentially enhance the researcher's thinking and

---

[11] The author notes the current debate between significance levels and effect size. See Smithson (1999) for a review of this debate.

conceptualization of the data. The programs are only as good as the researchers using them as is true of quantitative programs. The qualitative researcher still needs to engage in reflexivity, critical thinking about the data, rigorous methodological practices, and so forth. Qualitative computer programs may make the data more manageable but they **do not** automatically make sense of the data, they **do not** automatically make the research more rigorous, and thus more methodologically sound.

4.2   *What this Section Will Not Cover*

This section is not a users' guide to the NUD*IST 4 program nor will it go into any detailed technical description of the program. For those readers interested in these aspects the QSR web site http://www.qsr.com.au/ and the User guide (QSR, 1997) that accompanies NUD*IST 4 are the best places to find this information.

This section will not debate the advantages of the NUD*IST 4 program over other qualitative data analysis computer programs. For this the reader is directed to the Weitzman and Miles (1995) book. This section focuses on the logical structure of the NUD*IST 4 program and how this structure can potentially enhance analysis.

4.3   *NUD*IST 4: The Logic and the Structure*

As mentioned previously NUD*IST 4 is a code-based theory-builder program that stores, searches, retrieves, codes, and aids in the analysis of qualitative data. The program allows the researcher to manage and explore the data in two interlocking systems, the documents system and the index system. The **documents system** is the holding system for the raw data. Raw data or documents can be explored and coded within this system. By doing so the documents are linked to codes or categories that reside in the index system.

The **index system** is therefore where the codes, categories or themes are organized. Note that NUD*IST 4 refers to nodes not codes. Nodes contain the coded data as well as the researcher's thinking about the data as a memo attached to the node. These nodes can be explored and further coding done on them. By doing this, nodes are linked to the documents that reside in the documents system (see Figure 6.13 the documents system and index system as they appear in NUD*IST 4.).

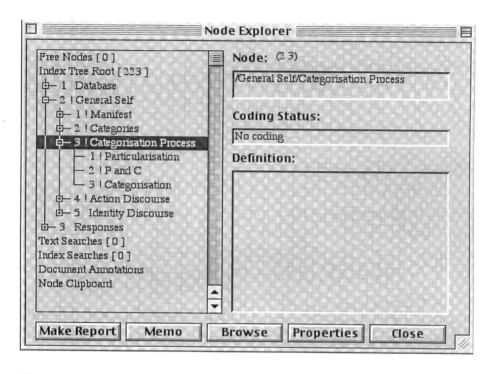

Figure 6.13   Index and documents systems in NUD*IST 4, the construction of gender and gender identity in elite Australian sport research project.

The Document System: How to Manage Mountains of Data: The documents system allows the researcher to collect and organize the raw data (e.g., interview transcripts), study and explore the raw data, develop ideas about it, edit and annotate the raw data, make notes and memos about raw data, and search and retrieve words, phrases from the raw data. It is the researcher's entry point to all the raw data in the research project. For example, in the author's research the 75 transcribed interviews conducted with elite athletes and coaches are held in the documents system. The documents system allows the researcher to work on the raw data, code it, and think about the raw data. Exploration organizes the documents first, nodes second. The advantage of the documents system is that it codes, retrieves, and browses raw data more thoroughly, more rigorously, and faster than can be done manually. Thus repetitious, factual, and descriptive coding can be efficiently handled by the documents system.

As previously mentioned, coding results are not stored in the documents system. They are stored in the index system. Through interlocking with the index system exploration and interpretation of the data becomes a continuous process. Coding that is both inductive (codes that emerge from the data) and a-priori (codes that are imposed on the data) can be efficiently handled in this system.

Different researchers can use the documents system in various ways. The researcher can work predominantly with the documents system where individual documents can be explored, and the text contained in each document coded with the results of each code being placed in the index system. Therefore the researcher works on the raw data within the documents system. Working in this way however limits the researcher to basic word or phrase searches on the documents. This is analogous to working with different colored highlighter pens when coding the original transcript.

The Index System: Thinking about Mountains of Data: Other researchers, including myself, prefer to work primarily within the index system, and treat the documents system as a raw data storage area. There is an initial search, code, and retrieval within the documents system for factual data. The results of this search are placed at the database node in the index system (see Figure 6.14 for an example of a database node). This approach requires some forethought by the researcher as to what should be included in the database node. This is determined by the research question and the background and interests of the researcher. A node in NUDI*ST 4 may be set up so that it has two or more sub nodes or children that sit under the one node. Remember that nodes hold all the researchers thinking about the node and can hold lower order concepts within the one node. To illustrate I have set up a database node that separates the raw data into a *sex* node, which has two children nodes or sub nodes—"males" and "females." A *status* node with two children nodes—"coaches" and "athletes" and so forth. That is, all the male interviews are stored within the database child node "male," and all the coaches interviews are stored within the database child node "coaches." I also set up a separate responses node that contains the responses to each question in the interview[12].

---

12 Note that this could have been included under the database node.

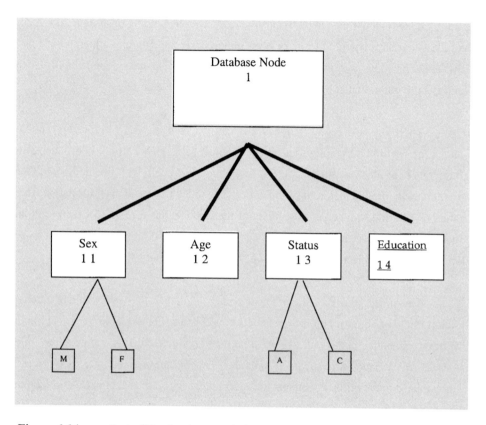

Figure 6.14   Part of the database node in gender and gender identity project. Sex and status children displayed (M=male 1 1 1, F=female 1 2 1, A=athlete 1 3 1, C=coach 1 3 2). The numbers refer position that the node and children of the node have in the research projects overall index tree.

All the responses to question one are contained in the child of this node. Coding can then be done within the index system by searching and retrieving raw data that has been stored at one of the branches of the database node or the response node.

The index system forces the researcher to think about relationships between nodes or concepts and is often thought of as the thinking system. It manages ideas and exploration of the ideas that emerge from coding. Exploration organizes codes first and documents second. It stores and locates codes, categories, higher order concepts, and associated ideas all within a node. It aids the researcher by helping to structure the codes and ideas that have emerged from, or been imposed, on the data into a hierarchical tree structure. The index system takes a top down approach to data organization, which contrasts the traditionalist bottom up approach to qualitative coding.

There are two types of nodes that can be used in NUD*IST 4. Free nodes contain information pertaining to a specific subject (e.g., physical free node - contains all references to physical attributes). The researcher may begin with free nodes and then structure them into the hierarchical index tree. The index tree contains information from numerous sub nodes in separate sections of the tree (Figure 6.15 is an example of an index tree). The index tree allows for categories, themes, and higher order themes to be developed and organized, and thus relationships to be represented.

The index tree is a hierarchical coding structure that helps the researcher develop thinking about relationships between categories. For example, in my research one of the index tree nodes is *Categorization* (see Figure 6.15) and contains three child nodes: *Particularization, Particularization and Categorization*, and *Categorization*. All coding related to the differing categorization strategies is contained at the *Categorization* child node, all coding related to differing particularization strategies is contained at the *Particularization* child node, and so forth. *Particularization, Particularization and Categorization*, and *Categorization* are all examples of the categorization process (Billig, 1996) and thus are organized within the *Categorization* node.

Inductive and a-priori types of analysis are possible in the index system. I have used both an inductive coding scheme within a discursive psychological theoretical framework[13] and an a-priori coding scheme where the items from the Personal Attributes Questionnaire (Spence & Helmreich, 1978) have been imposed upon the raw data.

---

[13] It is beyond the scope of this chapter to discuss the theoretical framework used by the author. For an overview of discursive psychology the reader is directed to the book by Potter and Wetherell (1987) Discourse and social psychology.

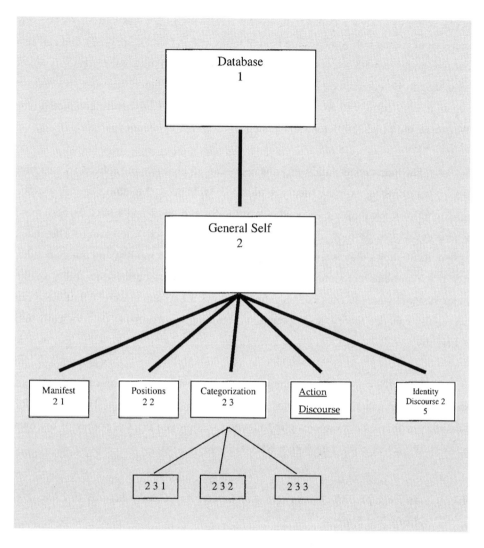

Figure 6.15   Part of the index tree in gender and gender identity project. General self branch including Categorization sub branch and children is displayed (2 3 1 = Particularization, 2 3 2 = Categorization and Particularization, 2 3 3 = Categorization). The numbers refer position that the node and children of the node have in the research projects overall index tree.

As mentioned in the documents system section, results of text searchers within the documents system are held in the index system, in the text searchers area (see Figure

6.13). These can become nodes in their own right within the index system. Conversely searches of coding held at nodes are held in index search (see Figure 6.13), and can also become nodes as with the text searches. The index system allows for greater types of searching to be conducted. Boolean searches such as collation searches, contextual, negation, restriction, and tree-structured can be easily and efficiently conducted (see Weitzman and Miles, 1995 for a discussion of each type of search operator).

The index system allows for the researcher to logically and coherently structure his or her thinking so that theory building is enhanced. Memoing allows for the researcher to track thinking associated with nodes and child nodes such as how these where developed, defined, decided upon, and other related information. The index system itself allows the researcher to quickly and easily edit, modify, and build an index tree that represents emerging relationships amongst nodes. Further the ability of the index system to use searches as data sources, allows for system closure. All of these can potentially enhance theory development and building by organizing data logically and coherently.

Both, the documents system and the index system, have a logical and coherent structure for organizing, managing, and thinking about the data. Both allow for flexibility within their structure. The following section is a brief overview of my own research project as it is set up within NUD*IST 4.

4.4 *An Example: The Construction of Gender and Gender Identity in Elite Australian Sport*

Figure 6.1 shows the documents system and index system as they appear in the particular research project in NUD*IST 4. This research is exploring how gender and gender identity is constructed in elite Australian sport using a discursive social psychological framework. Of interest is how elite sportsmen and elite sportswomen do being male and female, and what it means to be male and female in elite Australian sport. The data pertains only to question 1 - "If you were to describe yourself as a person to another person how would you do this?" In the index system there are 223 nodes in total. These nodes have inductively and deductively arisen from the data as discussed earlier.

Thirty seven elite Australian athletes and 38 elite Australian coaches were interviewed using a semi-structured format. Each transcribed interview, that is the raw data, is stored within the document system in NUD*IST 4. Thus Raw Data 1 holds the transcribed interview from participant 1 and so on. Each document also has attached to it a memo. I set up a memo for each transcribed interview that holds field notes associated with each interview.

I work predominantly within the index system. The database node was the first section of the research project that was set up (see Figure 6.14). All basic demographic information was organized as a child node[14] All the participants' responses to question 1 were put into the *response* node in the child node question 1. This allowed me to search just the responses to question 1 both inductively and a-priori.

Work was carried out by browsing the question 1 child node in the index system and applying codes. Also engagement in a manifest code of the data took place. Here content codes were allowed to emerge from the data. These content codes became free nodes in the first instance. After numerous passes through the data it was felt that some free nodes appeared to be related to a common theme. Participants described themselves in reference to social or vocation roles—*etic* free node, and also with reference to informal or culturally specific roles—*emic* free nodes. It was felt that the underlying theme associated with these two free codes was reference to a role. Hence the two free codes were re-organized under a newly created *role* node in the manifest node section of the index tree. It was also felt that some nodes were being discussed in particular relationships with other nodes. I hypothesized that when participants described themselves in terms of attributes, traits, behaviors they often used roles to exemplify these traits, attributes, and/or behaviors. For example " I think I'm very understanding, like when I'm with my kids I really listen to what they're saying." Hence a Boolean collation search was conducted. I used a similar strategy with the discursive coding. Thus it can be seen how theory building can be aided by the logical structure of NUD*IST 4.

---

[14] The author could have subdivided the data differently, so that under sex the breakdown was female athlete, female coach, male athlete, and male coach. However this would not have enabled the author to the compare athletes to coaches responses as a whole or female to male responses as a whole. The former division is more flexible in terms of greater search breakdown.

4.5   *Some Limitations of NUD*IST 4*

NUD*IST 4 is a logically structured program that coherently organizes qualitative data in a manner that facilitates the researchers' thinking about the data. Its logical structure helps the researcher make sense of the data. There are some limitations with the program, which are primarily technical in nature, such as the inability to switch between text units of a line to text units of a paragraph. One of the most detracting features of the program is that it is not able to graphically represent relationships between concepts. However NUD*IST 4 can be linked to the Decision Explorer program (Banxia Software Ltd, 1999) to counter this problem. QSR has developed a program that accounts for NUD*IST 4's shortcomings NVivo. NVivo is a PC only program. An overview of NVivo **http://www.qsr.com.au/** can be found at the website.

This section has provided the reader with a brief overview of the inherent logic subsumed within NUD*IST 4. What stands NUD*IST 4 apart from other programs and a manual approach to qualitative data analysis is this logical, coherent, and flexible nature of this framework. However like all programs be these qualitative or quantitative, NUD*IST 4 will only be as good as the researcher who uses it.

Acknowledgments: The author would like to thank Steve Christensen for his helpful comments on an earlier draft of this chapter.

References

Decision Explorer (Version 3.1) [Computer software]. (1999). Glasgow, Scotland: Banxia Software Ltd

Billig, M. (1996). *Arguing and thinking: A rhetorical approach to social psychology* (2nd ed.). Cambridge: Cambridge University Press

Miles, M. B., & Huberman, A. M. (1994). *Qualitative data analysis: An expanded sourcebook* (2nd ed.). Beverley, Hills, CA: SAGE

NUD*IST (Version 4, Macintosh build 1038). [Computer software]. (1999). Melbourne, Australia: Qualitative Solutions and Research Pty Ltd

Potter, J., & Wetherell, M. (1987). *Discourse and social psychology: Beyond attitudes and behavior.* London: SAGE Publications

Qualitative Solutions and Research Pty Ltd, (1997). *QSR NUD*IST 4: User guide.* Melbourne, Australia: Qualitative Solutions and Research Pty Ltd.

Smithson, M. J. (1999). *Statistics with confidence.* London: SAGE Publications

Spence, J. T., & Helmreich, R. L. (1978). *Masculinity and femininity.* Austin, TX: University of Texas Press.

Weitzman, E. A., & Miles, M. B. (1995). *A software sourcebook: Computer programs for qualitative data analysis.* London: SAGE Publications

APPENDIX

Table 1

Normal Curve Areas

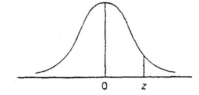

z	.00	.01	.02	.03	.04	.05	.06	.07	.08	.09
0.0	.0000	.0040	.0080	.0120	.0160	.0199	.0239	.0279	.0319	.0359
0.1	.0398	.0438	.0478	.0517	.0557	.0596	.0636	.0675	.0714	.0753
0.2	.0793	.0832	.0871	.0910	.0948	.0987	.1026	.1064	.1103	.1141
0.3	.1179	.1217	.1255	.1293	.1331	.1368	.1406	.1443	.1480	.1517
0.4	.1554	.1591	.1628	.1664	.1700	.1736	.1772	.1808	.1844	.1879
0.5	.1915	.1950	.1985	.2019	.2054	.2088	.2123	.2157	.2190	.2224
0.6	.2257	.2291	.2324	.2357	.2389	.2422	.2454	.2486	.2517	.2549
0.7	.2580	.2611	.2642	.2673	.2704	.2734	.2764	.2794	.2823	.2852
0.8	.2881	.2910	.2939	.2967	.2995	.3023	.3051	.3078	.3106	.3133
0.9	.3159	.3186	.3212	.3238	.3264	.3289	.3315	.3340	.3365	.3389
1.0	.3413	.3438	.3461	.3485	.3508	.3531	.3554	.3577	.3599	.3621
1.1	.3643	.3665	.3686	.3708	.3729	.3749	.3770	.3790	.3810	.3830
1.2	.3849	.3869	.3888	.3907	.3925	.3944	.3962	.3980	.3997	.4015
1.3	.4032	.4049	.4066	.4082	.4099	.4115	.4131	.4147	.4162	.4177
1.4	.4192	.4207	.4222	.4236	.4251	.4265	.4279	.4292	.4306	.4319
1.5	.4332	.4345	.4357	.4370	.4382	.4394	.4406	.4418	.4429	.4441
1.6	.4452	.4463	.4474	.4484	.4495	.4505	.4515	.4525	.4535	.4545
1.7	.4554	.4564	.4573	.4582	.4591	.4599	.4608	.4616	.4625	.4633
1.8	.4641	.4649	.4656	.4664	.4671	.4678	.4686	.4693	.4699	.4706
1.9	.4713	.4719	.4726	.4732	.4738	.4744	.4750	.4756	.4761	.4767
2.0	.4772	.4778	.4783	.4788	.4793	.4798	.4803	.4808	.4812	.4817
2.1	.4821	.4826	.4830	.4834	.4838	.4842	.4846	.4850	.4854	.4857
2.2	.4861	.4864	.4868	.4871	.4875	.4878	.4881	.4884	.4887	.4890
2.3	.4893	.4896	.4898	.4901	.4904	.4906	.4909	.4911	.4913	.4916
2.4	.4918	.4920	.4922	.4925	.4927	.4929	.4931	.4932	.4934	.4936
2.5	.4938	.4940	.4941	.4943	.4945	.4946	.4948	.4949	.4951	.4952
2.6	.4953	.4955	.4956	.4957	.4959	.4960	.4961	.4962	.4963	.4964
2.7	.4965	.4966	.4967	.4968	.4969	.4970	.4971	.4972	.4973	.4974
2.8	.4974	.4975	.4976	.4977	.4977	.4978	.4979	.4979	.4980	.4981
2.9	.4981	.4982	.4982	.4983	.4984	.4984	.4985	.4985	.4986	.4986
3.0	.4987	.4987	.4987	.4988	.4988	.4989	.4989	.4989	.4990	.4990

Table 2

Critical Values of t

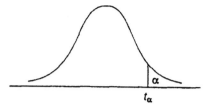

Degrees of Freedom	$t_{.100}$	$t_{.050}$	$t_{.025}$	$t_{.010}$	$t_{.005}$
1	3.078	6.314	12.706	31.821	63.657
2	1.886	2.920	4.303	6.965	9.925
3	1.638	2.353	3.182	4.541	5.841
4	1.533	2.132	2.776	3.747	4.604
5	1.476	2.015	2.571	3.365	4.032
6	1.440	1.943	2.447	3.143	3.707
7	1.415	1.895	2.365	2.998	3.499
8	1.397	1.860	2.306	2.896	3.355
9	1.383	1.833	2.262	2.821	3.250
10	1.372	1.812	2.228	2.764	3.169
11	1.363	1.796	2.201	2.718	3.106
12	1.356	1.782	2.179	2.681	3.055
13	1.350	1.771	2.160	2.650	3.012
14	1.345	1.761	2.145	2.624	2.977
15	1.341	1.753	2.131	2.602	2.947
16	1.337	1.746	2.120	2.583	2.921
17	1.333	1.740	2.110	2.567	2.898
18	1.330	1.734	2.101	2.552	2.878
19	1.328	1.729	2.093	2.539	2.861
20	1.325	1.725	2.086	2.528	2.845
21	1.323	1.721	2.080	2.518	2.831
22	1.321	1.717	2.074	2.508	2.819
23	1.319	1.714	2.069	2.500	2.807
24	1.318	1.711	2.064	2.492	2.797
25	1.316	1.708	2.060	2.485	2.787
26	1.315	1.706	2.056	2.479	2.779
27	1.314	1.703	2.052	2.473	2.771
28	1.313	1.701	2.048	2.467	2.763
29	1.311	1.699	2.045	2.462	2.756
∞	1.282	1.645	1.960	2.326	2.576

Source: From M. Merrington, 'Table of Percentage Points of the t-Distribution, *Biometrika* 32 (1941): 300. Reproduced by permission of the *Biometrika* Trustees.

Table 3

Critical Values of x^2

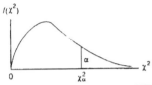

Degrees of Freedom	$\chi^2_{.995}$	$\chi^2_{.990}$	$\chi^2_{.975}$	$\chi^2_{.950}$	$\chi^2_{.900}$	$\chi^2_{.100}$	$\chi^2_{.050}$	$\chi^2_{.025}$	$\chi^2_{.010}$	$\chi^2_{.005}$
1	0.0000393	0.0001571	0.0009821	0.0039321	0.0157908	2.70554	3.84146	5.02389	6.63490	7.8794
2	0.0100251	0.0201007	0.0506356	0.102587	0.210720	4.60517	5.99147	7.37776	9.21034	10.596(
3	0.0717212	0.114832	0.215795	0.351846	0.584375	6.25139	7.81473	9.34840	11.3449	12.8381
4	0.206990	0.297110	0.484419	0.710721	1.063623	7.77944	9.48773	11.1433	13.2767	14.860:
5	0.411740	0.554300	0.831211	1.145476	1.61031	9.23635	11.0705	12.8325	15.0863	16.749(
6	0.675727	0.872085	1.237347	1.63539	2.20413	10.6446	12.5916	14.4494	16.8119	18.547(
7	0.989265	1.239043	1.68987	2.16735	2.83311	12.0170	14.0671	16.0128	18.4753	20.277:
8	1.344419	1.646482	2.17973	2.73264	3.48954	13.3616	15.5073	17.5346	20.0902	21.955(
9	1.734926	2.087912	2.70039	3.32511	4.16816	14.6837	16.9190	19.0228	21.6660	23.589.
10	2.15585	2.55821	3.24697	3.94030	4.86518	15.9871	18.3070	20.4831	23.2093	25.188:
11	2.60321	3.05347	3.81575	4.57481	5.57779	17.2750	19.6751	21.9200	24.7250	26.7565
12	3.07382	3.57056	4.40379	5.22603	6.30380	18.5494	21.0261	23.3367	26.2170	28.299:
13	3.56503	4.10691	5.00874	5.89186	7.04150	19.8119	22.3621	24.7356	27.6883	29.819-
14	4.07468	4.66043	5.62872	6.57063	7.78953	21.0642	23.6848	26.1190	29.1413	31.319:
15	4.60094	5.22935	6.26214	7.26094	8.54675	22.3072	24.9958	27.4884	30.5779	32.801:
16	5.14224	5.81221	6.90766	7.96164	9.31223	23.5418	26.2962	28.8454	31.9999	34.267:
17	5.69724	6.40776	7.56418	8.67176	10.0852	24.7690	27.5871	30.1910	33.4087	35.718:
18	6.26481	7.01491	8.23075	9.39046	10.8649	25.9894	28.8693	31.5264	34.8053	37.156-
19	6.84398	7.63273	8.90655	10.1170	11.6509	27.2036	30.1435	32.8523	36.1908	38.582:
20	7.43386	8.26040	9.59083	10.8508	12.4426	28.4120	31.4104	34.1696	37.5662	39.9968
21	8.03366	8.89720	10.28293	11.5913	13.2396	29.6151	32.6705	35.4789	38.9321	41.401(
22	8.64272	9.54249	10.9823	12.3380	14.0415	30.8133	33.9244	36.7807	40.2894	42.795(
23	9.26042	10.19567	11.6885	13.0905	14.8479	32.0069	35.1725	38.0757	41.6384	44.181:
24	9.88623	10.8564	12.4011	13.8484	15.6587	33.1963	36.4151	39.3641	42.9798	45.558:
25	10.5197	11.5240	13.1197	14.6114	16.4734	34.3816	37.6525	40.6465	44.3141	46.9278
26	11.1603	12.1981	13.8439	15.3791	17.2919	35.5631	38.8852	41.9232	45.6417	48.2899
27	11.8076	12.8786	14.5733	16.1513	18.1138	36.7412	40.1133	43.1944	46.9630	49.644!
28	12.4613	13.5648	15.3079	16.9279	18.9392	37.9159	41.3372	44.4607	48.2782	50.993:
29	13.1211	14.2565	16.0471	17.7083	19.7677	39.0875	42.5569	45.7222	49.5879	52.335(
30	13.7867	14.9535	16.7908	18.4926	20.5992	40.2560	43.7729	46.9792	50.8922	53.672(
40	20.7065	22.1643	24.4331	26.5093	29.0505	51.8050	55.7585	59.3417	63.6907	66.765!
50	27.9907	29.7067	32.3574	34.7642	37.6886	63.1671	67.5048	71.4202	76.1539	79.490(
60	35.5346	37.4848	40.4817	43.1879	46.4589	74.3970	79.0819	83.2976	88.3794	91.951:
70	43.2752	45.4418	48.7576	51.7393	55.3290	85.5271	90.5312	95.0231	100.425	104.215
80	51.1720	53.5400	57.1532	60.3915	64.2778	96.5782	101.879	106.629	112.329	116.321
90	59.1963	61.7541	65.6466	69.1260	73.2912	107.565	113.145	118.136	124.116	128.299
100	67.3276	70.0648	74.2219	77.9295	82.3581	118.498	124.342	129.561	135.807	140.169

Table 4

Percentage Points of the F Distributions, α =.10

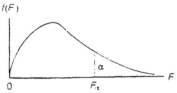

	v_1	Numerator Degrees of Freedom								
v_2		1	2	3	4	5	6	7	8	9
	1	39.86	49.50	53.59	55.83	57.24	58.20	58.91	59.44	59.86
	2	8.53	9.00	9.16	9.24	9.29	9.33	9.35	9.37	9.38
	3	5.54	5.46	5.39	5.34	5.31	5.28	5.27	5.25	5.24
	4	4.54	4.32	4.19	4.11	4.05	4.01	3.98	3.95	3.94
	5	4.06	3.78	3.62	3.52	3.45	3.40	3.37	3.34	3.32
	6	3.78	3.46	3.29	3.18	3.11	3.05	3.01	2.98	2.96
	7	3.59	3.26	3.07	2.96	2.88	2.83	2.78	2.75	2.72
	8	3.46	3.11	2.92	2.81	2.73	2.67	2.62	2.59	2.56
	9	3.36	3.01	2.81	2.69	2.61	2.55	2.51	2.47	2.44
	10	3.29	2.92	2.73	2.61	2.52	2.46	2.41	2.38	2.35
	11	3.23	2.86	2.66	2.54	2.45	2.39	2.34	2.30	2.27
	12	3.18	2.81	2.61	2.48	2.39	2.33	2.28	2.24	2.21
	13	3.14	2.76	2.56	2.43	2.35	2.28	2.23	2.20	2.16
	14	3.10	2.73	2.52	2.39	2.31	2.24	2.19	2.15	2.12
	15	3.07	2.70	2.49	2.36	2.27	2.21	2.16	2.12	2.09
	16	3.05	2.67	2.46	2.33	2.24	2.18	2.13	2.09	2.06
	17	3.03	2.64	2.44	2.31	2.22	2.15	2.10	2.06	2.03
	18	3.01	2.62	2.42	2.29	2.20	2.13	2.08	2.04	2.00
	19	2.99	2.61	2.40	2.27	2.18	2.11	2.06	2.02	1.98
	20	2.97	2.59	2.38	2.25	2.16	2.09	2.04	2.00	1.96
	21	2.96	2.57	2.36	2.23	2.14	2.08	2.02	1.98	1.95
	22	2.95	2.56	2.35	2.22	2.13	2.06	2.01	1.97	1.93
	23	2.94	2.55	2.34	2.21	2.11	2.05	1.99	1.95	1.92
	24	2.93	2.54	2.33	2.19	2.10	2.04	1.98	1.94	1.91
	25	2.92	2.53	2.32	2.18	2.09	2.02	1.97	1.93	1.89
	26	2.91	2.52	2.31	2.17	2.08	2.01	1.96	1.92	1.88
	27	2.90	2.51	2.30	2.17	2.07	2.00	1.95	1.91	1.87
	28	2.89	2.50	2.29	2.16	2.06	2.00	1.94	1.90	1.87
	29	2.89	2.50	2.28	2.15	2.06	1.99	1.93	1.89	1.86
	30	2.88	2.49	2.28	2.14	2.05	1.98	1.93	1.88	1.85
	40	2.84	2.44	2.23	2.09	2.00	1.93	1.87	1.83	1.79
	60	2.79	2.39	2.18	2.04	1.95	1.87	1.82	1.77	1.74
	120	2.75	2.35	2.13	1.99	1.90	1.82	1.77	1.72	1.68
	∞	2.71	2.30	2.08	1.94	1.85	1.77	1.72	1.67	1.63

Denominator Degrees of Freedom

SOURCE: From M. Merrington and C. M. Thompson, "Tables of Percentage Points of the Inverted Beta (F)-Distribution," *Biometrika 33 (1943):* 73-88. Reproduced by permission of the *Biometrika* Trustees.

Table 4

Continued

v_2	|	**10**	**12**	**15**	**20**	**24**	**30**	**40**	**60**	**120**	**∞**
	|				**Numerator Degrees of Freedom**						
1	|	60.19	60.71	61.22	61.74	62.00	62.26	62.53	62.79	63.06	63.33
2	|	9.39	9.41	9.42	9.44	9.45	9.46	9.47	9.47	9.48	9.49
3	|	5.23	5.22	5.20	5.18	5.18	5.17	5.16	5.15	5.14	5.13
4	|	3.92	3.90	3.87	3.84	3.83	3.82	3.80	3.79	3.78	3.76
5	|	3.30	3.27	3.24	3.21	3.19	3.17	3.16	3.14	3.12	3.10
6	|	2.94	2.90	2.87	2.84	2.82	2.80	2.78	2.76	2.74	2.72
7	|	2.70	2.67	2.63	2.59	2.58	2.56	2.54	2.51	2.49	2.47
8	|	2.54	2.50	2.46	2.42	2.40	2.38	2.36	2.34	2.32	2.29
9	|	2.42	2.38	2.34	2.30	2.28	2.25	2.23	2.21	2.18	2.16
10	|	2.32	2.28	2.24	2.20	2.18	2.16	2.13	2.11	2.08	2.06
11	|	2.25	2.21	2.17	2.12	2.10	2.08	2.05	2.03	2.00	1.97
12	|	2.19	2.15	2.10	2.06	2.04	2.01	1.99	1.96	1.93	1.90
13	|	2.14	2.10	2.05	2.01	1.98	1.96	1.93	1.90	1.88	1.85
14	|	2.10	2.05	2.01	1.96	1.94	1.91	1.89	1.86	1.83	1.80
15	|	2.06	2.02	1.97	1.92	1.90	1.87	1.85	1.82	1.79	1.76
16	|	2.03	1.99	1.94	1.89	1.87	1.84	1.81	1.78	1.75	1.72
17	|	2.00	1.96	1.91	1.86	1.84	1.81	1.78	1.75	1.72	1.69
18	|	1.98	1.93	1.89	1.84	1.81	1.78	1.75	1.72	1.69	1.66
19	|	1.96	1.91	1.86	1.81	1.79	1.76	1.73	1.70	1.67	1.63
20	|	1.94	1.89	1.84	1.79	1.77	1.74	1.71	1.68	1.64	1.61
21	|	1.92	1.87	1.83	1.78	1.75	1.72	1.69	1.66	1.62	1.59
22	|	1.90	1.86	1.81	1.76	1.73	1.70	1.67	1.64	1.60	1.57
23	|	1.89	1.84	1.80	1.74	1.72	1.69	1.66	1.62	1.59	1.55
24	|	1.88	1.83	1.78	1.73	1.70	1.67	1.64	1.61	1.57	1.53
25	|	1.87	1.82	1.77	1.72	1.69	1.66	1.63	1.59	1.56	1.52
26	|	1.86	1.81	1.76	1.71	1.68	1.65	1.61	1.58	1.54	1.50
27	|	1.85	1.80	1.75	1.70	1.67	1.64	1.60	1.57	1.53	1.49
28	|	1.84	1.79	1.74	1.69	1.66	1.63	1.59	1.56	1.52	1.48
29	|	1.83	1.78	1.73	1.68	1.65	1.62	1.58	1.55	1.51	1.47
30	|	1.82	1.77	1.72	1.67	1.64	1.61	1.57	1.54	1.50	1.46
40	|	1.76	1.71	1.66	1.61	1.57	1.54	1.51	1.47	1.42	1.38
60	|	1.71	1.66	1.60	1.54	1.51	1.48	1.44	1.40	1.35	1.29
120	|	1.65	1.60	1.55	1.48	1.45	1.41	1.37	1.32	1.26	1.19
∞	|	1.60	1.55	1.49	1.42	1.38	1.34	1.30	1.24	1.17	1.00

v_1

Denominator Degrees of Freedom

Table 5

Percentage Points of the F Distributions, α =.05

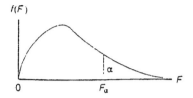

v_2	Numerator Degrees of Freedom								
	1	2	3	4	5	6	7	8	9
1	161.4	199.5	215.7	224.6	230.2	234.0	236.8	238.9	240.5
2	18.51	19.00	19.16	19.25	19.30	19.33	19.35	19.37	19.38
3	10.13	9.55	9.28	9.12	9.01	8.94	8.89	8.85	8.81
4	7.71	6.94	6.59	6.39	6.26	6.16	6.09	6.04	6.00
5	6.61	5.79	5.41	5.19	5.05	4.95	4.88	4.82	4.77
6	5.99	5.14	4.76	4.53	4.39	4.28	4.21	4.15	4.10
7	5.59	4.74	4.35	4.12	3.97	3.87	3.79	3.73	3.68
8	5.32	4.46	4.07	3.84	3.69	3.58	3.50	3.44	3.39
9	5.12	4.26	3.86	3.63	3.48	3.37	3.29	3.23	3.18
10	4.96	4.10	3.71	3.48	3.33	3.22	3.14	3.07	3.02
11	4.84	3.98	3.59	3.36	3.20	3.09	3.01	2.95	2.90
12	4.75	3.89	3.49	3.26	3.11	3.00	2.91	2.85	2.80
13	4.67	3.81	3.41	3.18	3.03	2.92	2.83	2.77	2.71
14	4.60	3.74	3.34	3.11	2.96	2.85	2.76	2.70	2.65
15	4.54	3.68	3.29	3.06	2.90	2.79	2.71	2.64	2.59
16	4.49	3.63	3.24	3.01	2.85	2.74	2.66	2.59	2.54
17	4.45	3.59	3.20	2.96	2.81	2.70	2.61	2.55	2.49
18	4.41	3.55	3.16	2.93	2.77	2.66	2.58	2.51	2.46
19	4.38	3.52	3.13	2.90	2.74	2.63	2.54	2.48	2.42
20	4.35	3.49	3.10	2.87	2.71	2.60	2.51	2.45	2.39
21	4.32	3.47	3.07	2.84	2.68	2.57	2.49	2.42	2.37
22	4.30	3.44	3.05	2.82	2.66	2.55	2.46	2.40	2.34
23	4.28	3.42	3.03	2.80	2.64	2.53	2.44	2.37	2.32
24	4.26	3.40	3.01	2.78	2.62	2.51	2.42	2.36	2.30
25	4.24	3.39	2.99	2.76	2.60	2.49	2.40	2.34	2.28
26	4.23	3.37	2.98	2.74	2.59	2.47	2.39	2.32	2.27
27	4.21	3.35	2.96	2.73	2.57	2.46	2.37	2.31	2.25
28	4.20	3.34	2.95	2.71	2.56	2.45	2.36	2.29	2.24
29	4.18	3.33	2.93	2.70	2.55	2.43	2.35	2.28	2.22
30	4.17	3.32	2.92	2.69	2.53	2.42	2.33	2.27	2.21
40	4.08	3.23	2.84	2.61	2.45	2.34	2.25	2.18	2.12
60	4.00	3.15	2.76	2.53	2.37	2.25	2.17	2.10	2.04
120	3.92	3.07	2.68	2.45	2.29	2.17	2.09	2.02	1.96
∞	3.84	3.00	2.60	2.37	2.21	2.10	2.01	1.94	1.88

(Denominator Degrees of Freedom)

SOURCE: From M. Merrington and C. M. Thompson, "Tables of Percentage Points of the Inverted Beta (F)-Distribution," *Biometrika* 33 (1943): 73-88. Reproduced by permission of the Biometrika Trustees.

Table 5

Continued

	v_1	Numerator Degrees of Freedom									
v_2		10	12	15	20	24	30	40	60	120	∞
	1	241.9	243.9	245.9	248.0	249.1	250.1	251.1	252.2	253.3	254.3
	2	19.40	19.41	19.43	19.45	19.45	19.46	19.47	19.48	19.49	19.50
	3	8.79	8.74	8.70	8.66	8.64	8.62	8.59	8.57	8.55	8.53
	4	5.96	5.91	5.86	5.80	5.77	5.75	5.72	5.69	5.66	5.63
	5	4.74	4.68	4.62	4.56	4.53	4.50	4.46	4.43	4.40	4.36
	6	4.06	4.00	3.94	3.87	3.84	3.81	3.77	3.74	3.70	3.67
	7	3.64	3.57	3.51	3.44	3.41	3.38	3.34	3.30	3.27	3.23
	8	3.35	3.28	3.22	3.15	3.12	3.08	3.04	3.01	2.97	2.93
	9	3.14	3.07	3.01	2.94	2.90	2.86	2.83	2.79	2.75	2.71
	10	2.98	2.91	2.85	2.77	2.74	2.70	2.66	2.62	2.58	2.54
	11	2.85	2.79	2.72	2.65	2.61	2.57	2.53	2.49	2.45	2.40
	12	2.75	2.69	2.62	2.54	2.51	2.47	2.43	2.38	2.34	2.30
	13	2.67	2.60	2.53	2.46	2.42	2.38	2.34	2.30	2.25	2.21
	14	2.60	2.53	2.46	2.39	2.35	2.31	2.27	2.22	2.18	2.13
	15	2.54	2.48	2.40	2.33	2.29	2.25	2.20	2.16	2.11	2.07
	16	2.49	2.42	2.35	2.28	2.24	2.19	2.15	2.11	2.06	2.01
	17	2.45	2.38	2.31	2.23	2.19	2.15	2.10	2.06	2.01	1.96
	18	2.41	2.34	2.27	2.19	2.15	2.11	2.06	2.02	1.97	1.92
	19	2.38	2.31	2.23	2.16	2.11	2.07	2.03	1.98	1.93	1.88
	20	2.35	2.28	2.20	2.12	2.08	2.04	1.99	1.95	1.90	1.84
	21	2.32	2.25	2.18	2.10	2.05	2.01	1.96	1.92	1.87	1.81
	22	2.30	2.23	2.15	2.07	2.03	1.98	1.94	1.89	1.84	1.78
	23	2.27	2.20	2.13	2.05	2.01	1.96	1.91	1.86	1.81	1.76
	24	2.25	2.18	2.11	2.03	1.98	1.94	1.89	1.84	1.79	1.73
	25	2.24	2.16	2.09	2.01	1.96	1.92	1.87	1.82	1.77	1.71
	26	2.22	2.15	2.07	1.99	1.95	1.90	1.85	1.80	1.75	1.69
	27	2.20	2.13	2.06	1.97	1.93	1.88	1.84	1.79	1.73	1.67
	28	2.19	2.12	2.04	1.96	1.91	1.87	1.82	1.77	1.71	1.65
	29	2.18	2.10	2.03	1.94	1.90	1.85	1.81	1.75	1.70	1.64
	30	2.16	2.09	2.01	1.93	1.89	1.84	1.79	1.74	1.68	1.62
	40	2.08	2.00	1.92	1.84	1.79	1.74	1.69	1.64	1.58	1.51
	60	1.99	1.92	1.84	1.75	1.70	1.65	1.59	1.53	1.47	1.39
	120	1.91	1.83	1.75	1.66	1.61	1.55	1.50	1.43	1.35	1.25
	∞	1.83	1.75	1.67	1.57	1.52	1.46	1.39	1.32	1.22	1.00

Denominator Degrees of Freedom

Table 6

Percentage Points of the F Distributions, α =.025

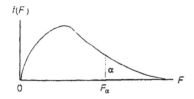

v_2	Numerator Degrees of Freedom								
v_1	1	2	3	4	5	6	7	8	9
1	647.8	799.5	864.2	899.6	921.8	937.1	948.2	956.7	963.3
2	38.51	39.00	39.17	39.25	39.30	39.33	39.36	39.37	39.39
3	17.44	16.04	15.44	15.10	14.88	14.73	14.62	14.54	14.47
4	12.22	10.65	9.98	9.60	9.36	9.20	9.07	8.98	8.90
5	10.01	8.43	7.76	7.39	7.15	6.98	6.85	6.76	6.68
6	8.81	7.26	6.60	6.23	5.99	5.82	5.70	5.60	5.52
7	8.07	6.54	5.89	5.52	5.29	5.12	4.99	4.90	4.82
8	7.57	6.06	5.42	5.05	4.82	4.65	4.53	4.43	4.36
9	7.21	5.71	5.08	4.72	4.48	4.32	4.20	4.10	4.03
10	6.94	5.46	4.83	4.47	4.24	4.07	3.95	3.85	3.78
11	6.72	5.26	4.63	4.28	4.04	3.88	3.76	3.66	3.59
12	6.55	5.10	4.47	4.12	3.89	3.73	3.61	3.51	3.44
13	6.41	4.97	4.35	4.00	3.77	3.60	3.48	3.39	3.31
14	6.30	4.86	4.24	3.89	3.66	3.50	3.38	3.29	3.21
15	6.20	4.77	4.15	3.80	3.58	3.41	3.29	3.20	3.12
16	6.12	4.69	4.08	3.73	3.50	3.34	3.22	3.12	3.05
17	6.04	4.62	4.01	3.66	3.44	3.28	3.16	3.06	2.98
18	5.98	4.56	3.95	3.61	3.38	3.22	3.10	3.01	2.93
19	5.92	4.51	3.90	3.56	3.33	3.17	3.05	2.96	2.88
20	5.87	4.46	3.86	3.51	3.29	3.13	3.01	2.91	2.84
21	5.83	4.42	3.82	3.48	3.25	3.09	2.97	2.87	2.80
22	5.79	4.38	3.78	3.44	3.22	3.05	2.93	2.84	2.76
23	5.75	4.35	3.75	3.41	3.18	3.02	2.90	2.81	2.73
24	5.72	4.32	3.72	3.38	3.15	2.99	2.87	2.78	2.70
25	5.69	4.29	3.69	3.35	3.13	2.97	2.85	2.75	2.68
26	5.66	4.27	3.67	3.33	3.10	2.94	2.82	2.73	2.65
27	5.63	4.24	3.65	3.31	3.08	2.92	2.80	2.71	2.63
28	5.61	4.22	3.63	3.29	3.06	2.90	2.78	2.69	2.61
29	5.59	4.20	3.61	3.27	3.04	2.88	2.76	2.67	2.59
30	5.57	4.18	3.59	3.25	3.03	2.87	2.75	2.65	2.57
40	5.42	4.05	3.46	3.13	2.90	2.74	2.62	2.53	2.45
60	5.29	3.93	3.34	3.01	2.79	2.63	2.51	2.41	2.33
120	5.15	3.80	3.23	2.89	2.67	2.52	2.39	2.30	2.22
∞	5.02	3.69	3.12	2.79	2.57	2.41	2.29	2.19	2.11

Denominator Degrees of Freedom

Table 6

Continued

v_2 \ v_1	Numerator Degrees of Freedom									
	10	12	15	20	24	30	40	60	120	∞
1	968.6	976.7	984.9	993.1	997.2	1001	1006	1010	1014	1018
2	39.40	39.41	39.43	39.45	39.46	39.46	39.47	39.48	39.49	39.50
3	14.42	14.34	14.25	14.17	14.12	14.08	14.04	13.99	13.95	13.90
4	8.84	8.75	8.66	8.56	8.51	8.46	8.41	8.36	8.31	8.26
5	6.62	6.52	6.43	6.33	6.28	6.23	6.18	6.12	6.07	6.02
6	5.46	5.37	5.27	5.17	5.12	5.07	5.01	4.96	4.90	4.85
7	4.76	4.67	4.57	4.47	4.42	4.36	4.31	4.25	4.20	4.14
8	4.30	4.20	4.10	4.00	3.95	3.89	3.84	3.78	3.73	3.67
9	3.96	3.87	3.77	3.67	3.61	3.56	3.51	3.45	3.39	3.33
10	3.72	3.62	3.52	3.42	3.37	3.31	3.26	3.20	3.14	3.08
11	3.53	3.43	3.33	3.23	3.17	3.12	3.06	3.00	2.94	2.88
12	3.37	3.28	3.18	3.07	3.02	2.96	2.91	2.85	2.79	2.72
13	3.25	3.15	3.05	2.95	2.89	2.84	2.78	2.72	2.66	2.60
14	3.15	3.05	2.95	2.84	2.79	2.73	2.67	2.61	2.55	2.49
15	3.06	2.96	2.86	2.76	2.70	2.64	2.59	2.52	2.46	2.40
16	2.99	2.89	2.79	2.68	2.63	2.57	2.51	2.45	2.38	2.32
17	2.92	2.82	2.72	2.62	2.56	2.50	2.44	2.38	2.32	2.25
18	2.87	2.77	2.67	2.56	2.50	2.44	2.38	2.32	2.26	2.19
19	2.82	2.72	2.62	2.51	2.45	2.39	2.33	2.27	2.20	2.13
20	2.77	2.68	2.57	2.46	2.41	2.35	2.29	2.22	2.16	2.09
21	2.73	2.64	2.53	2.42	2.37	2.31	2.25	2.18	2.11	2.04
22	2.70	2.60	2.50	2.39	2.33	2.27	2.21	2.14	2.08	2.00
23	2.67	2.57	2.47	2.36	2.30	2.24	2.18	2.11	2.04	1.97
24	2.64	2.54	2.44	2.33	2.27	2.21	2.15	2.08	2.01	1.94
25	2.61	2.51	2.41	2.30	2.24	2.18	2.12	2.05	1.98	1.91
26	2.59	2.49	2.39	2.28	2.22	2.16	2.09	2.03	1.95	1.88
27	2.57	2.47	2.36	2.25	2.19	2.13	2.07	2.00	1.93	1.85
28	2.55	2.45	2.34	2.23	2.17	2.11	2.05	1.98	1.91	1.83
29	2.53	2.43	2.32	2.21	2.15	2.09	2.03	1.96	1.89	1.81
30	2.51	2.41	2.31	2.20	2.14	2.07	2.01	1.94	1.87	1.79
40	2.39	2.29	2.18	2.07	2.01	1.94	1.88	1.80	1.72	1.64
60	2.27	2.17	2.06	1.94	1.88	1.82	1.74	1.67	1.58	1.48
120	2.16	2.05	1.94	1.82	1.76	1.69	1.61	1.53	1.43	1.31
∞	2.05	1.94	1.83	1.71	1.64	1.57	1.48	1.39	1.27	1.00

Denominator Degrees of Freedom

Table 7

Percentage Points of the F Distributions, $\alpha = .01$

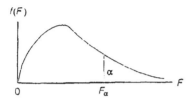

v_1	Numerator Degrees of Freedom								
v_2	1	2	3	4	5	6	7	8	9
1	4,052	4,999.5	5,403	5,625	5,764	5,859	5,928	5,982	6,022
2	98.50	99.00	99.17	99.25	99.30	99.33	99.36	99.37	99.39
3	34.12	30.82	29.46	28.71	28.24	27.91	27.67	27.49	27.35
4	21.20	18.00	16.69	15.98	15.52	15.21	14.98	14.80	14.66
5	16.26	13.27	12.06	11.39	10.97	10.67	10.46	10.29	10.16
6	13.75	10.92	9.78	9.15	8.75	8.47	8.26	8.10	7.98
7	12.25	9.55	8.45	7.85	7.46	7.19	6.99	6.84	6.72
8	11.26	8.65	7.59	7.01	6.63	6.37	6.18	6.03	5.91
9	10.56	8.02	6.99	6.42	6.06	5.80	5.61	5.47	5.35
10	10.04	7.56	6.55	5.99	5.64	5.39	5.20	5.06	4.94
11	9.65	7.21	6.22	5.67	5.32	5.07	4.89	4.74	4.63
12	9.33	6.93	5.95	5.41	5.06	4.82	4.64	4.50	4.39
13	9.07	6.70	5.74	5.21	4.86	4.62	4.44	4.30	4.19
14	8.86	6.51	5.56	5.04	4.69	4.46	4.28	4.14	4.03
15	8.68	6.36	5.42	4.89	4.56	4.32	4.14	4.00	3.89
16	8.53	6.23	5.29	4.77	4.44	4.20	4.03	3.89	3.78
17	8.40	6.11	5.18	4.67	4.34	4.10	3.93	3.79	3.68
18	8.29	6.01	5.09	4.58	4.25	4.01	3.84	3.71	3.60
19	8.18	5.93	5.01	4.50	4.17	3.94	3.77	3.63	3.52
20	8.10	5.85	4.94	4.43	4.10	3.87	3.70	3.56	3.46
21	8.02	5.78	4.87	4.37	4.04	3.81	3.64	3.51	3.40
22	7.95	5.72	4.82	4.31	3.99	3.76	3.59	3.45	3.35
23	7.88	5.66	4.76	4.26	3.94	3.71	3.54	3.41	3.30
24	7.82	5.61	4.72	4.22	3.90	3.67	3.50	3.36	3.26
25	7.77	5.57	4.68	4.18	3.85	3.63	3.46	3.32	3.22
26	7.72	5.53	4.64	4.14	3.82	3.59	3.42	3.29	3.18
27	7.68	5.49	4.60	4.11	3.78	3.56	3.39	3.26	3.15
28	7.64	5.45	4.57	4.07	3.75	3.53	3.36	3.23	3.12
29	7.60	5.42	4.54	4.04	3.73	3.50	3.33	3.20	3.09
30	7.56	5.39	4.51	4.02	3.70	3.47	3.30	3.17	3.07
40	7.31	5.18	4.31	3.83	3.51	3.29	3.12	2.99	2.89
60	7.08	4.98	4.13	3.65	3.34	3.12	2.95	2.82	2.72
120	6.85	4.79	3.95	3.48	3.17	2.96	2.79	2.66	2.56
∞	6.63	4.61	3.78	3.32	3.02	2.80	2.64	2.51	2.41

Denominator Degrees of Freedom (row label v_2)

Table 7

Continued

v_2 \ v_1	Numerator Degrees of Freedom									
	10	12	15	20	24	30	40	60	120	∞
1	6,056	6,106	6,157	6,209	6,235	6,261	6,287	6,313	6,339	6,366
2	99.40	99.42	99.43	99.45	99.46	99.47	99.47	99.48	99.49	99.50
3	27.23	27.05	26.87	26.69	26.60	26.50	26.41	26.32	26.22	26.13
4	14.55	14.37	14.20	14.02	13.93	13.84	13.75	13.65	13.56	13.46
5	10.05	9.89	9.72	9.55	9.47	9.38	9.29	9.20	9.11	9.02
6	7.87	7.72	7.56	7.40	7.31	7.23	7.14	7.06	6.97	6.88
7	6.62	6.47	6.31	6.16	6.07	5.99	5.91	5.82	5.74	5.65
8	5.81	5.67	5.52	5.36	5.28	5.20	5.12	5.03	4.95	4.86
9	5.26	5.11	4.96	4.81	4.73	4.65	4.57	4.48	4.40	4.31
10	4.85	4.71	4.56	4.41	4.33	4.25	4.17	4.08	4.00	3.91
11	4.54	4.40	4.25	4.10	4.02	3.94	3.86	3.78	3.69	3.60
12	4.30	4.16	4.01	3.86	3.78	3.70	3.62	3.54	3.45	3.36
13	4.10	3.96	3.82	3.66	3.59	3.51	3.43	3.34	3.25	3.17
14	3.94	3.80	3.66	3.51	3.43	3.35	3.27	3.18	3.09	3.00
15	3.80	3.67	3.52	3.37	3.29	3.21	3.13	3.05	2.96	2.87
16	3.69	3.55	3.41	3.26	3.18	3.10	3.02	2.93	2.84	2.75
17	3.59	3.46	3.31	3.16	3.08	3.00	2.92	2.83	2.75	2.65
18	3.51	3.37	3.23	3.08	3.00	2.92	2.84	2.75	2.66	2.57
19	3.43	3.30	3.15	3.00	2.92	2.84	2.76	2.67	2.58	2.49
20	3.37	3.23	3.09	2.94	2.86	2.78	2.69	2.61	2.52	2.42
21	3.31	3.17	3.03	2.88	2.80	2.72	2.64	2.55	2.46	2.36
22	3.26	3.12	2.98	2.83	2.75	2.67	2.58	2.50	2.40	2.31
23	3.21	3.07	2.93	2.78	2.70	2.62	2.54	2.45	2.35	2.26
24	3.17	3.03	2.89	2.74	2.66	2.58	2.49	2.40	2.31	2.21
25	3.13	2.99	2.85	2.70	2.62	2.54	2.45	2.36	2.27	2.17
26	3.09	2.96	2.81	2.66	2.58	2.50	2.42	2.33	2.23	2.13
27	3.06	2.93	2.78	2.63	2.55	2.47	2.38	2.29	2.20	2.10
28	3.03	2.90	2.75	2.60	2.52	2.44	2.35	2.26	2.17	2.06
29	3.00	2.87	2.73	2.57	2.49	2.41	2.33	2.23	2.14	2.03
30	2.98	2.84	2.70	2.55	2.47	2.39	2.30	2.21	2.11	2.01
40	2.80	2.66	2.52	2.37	2.29	2.20	2.11	2.02	1.92	1.80
60	2.63	2.50	2.35	2.20	2.12	2.03	1.94	1.84	1.73	1.60
120	2.47	2.34	2.19	2.03	1.95	1.86	1.76	1.66	1.53	1.38
∞	2.32	2.18	2.04	1.88	1.79	1.70	1.59	1.47	1.32	1.00

Denominator Degrees of Freedom

Table 8

Critical Values of the Wilcoxon Rank Sum Test for Indepedent Samples

Test statistic is $T = T_A$. where T_A is the rank sum of the sample with the smaller sample size.
(a) $\alpha = .025$ one-tailed; $\alpha = .05$ two-tailed

n_2 \ n_1	3 T_L	3 T_U	4 T_L	4 T_U	5 T_L	5 T_U	6 T_L	6 T_U	7 T_L	7 T_U	8 T_L	8 T_U	9 T_L	9 T_U	10 T_L	10 T_U
3	5	16														
4	6	18	11	25												
5	6	21	12	28	18	37										
6	7	23	12	32	19	41	26	52								
7	7	26	13	35	20	45	28	56	37	68						
8	8	28	14	38	21	49	29	61	39	73	49	87				
9	8	31	15	41	22	53	31	65	41	78	51	93	63	108		
10	9	33	16	44	24	56	32	70	43	83	54	98	66	114	79	131

(b) $\alpha = .05$ one-tailed; $\alpha = .10$ two-tailed

n_2 \ n_1	3 T_L	3 T_U	4 T_L	4 T_U	5 T_L	5 T_U	6 T_L	6 T_U	7 T_L	7 T_U	8 T_L	8 T_U	9 T_L	9 T_U	10 T_L	10 T_U
3	6	15														
4	7	17	12	24												
5	7	20	13	27	19	36										
6	8	22	14	30	20	40	28	50								
7	9	24	15	33	22	43	30	54	39	66						
8	9	27	16	36	24	46	32	58	41	71	52	84				
9	10	29	17	39	25	50	33	63	43	76	54	90	66	105		
10	11	31	18	42	26	54	35	67	46	80	57	95	69	111	83	127

SOURCE: From F. Wilcoxon and R. A. Wilcox, "Some Rapid Approximate Statistical Procedures" (1964), p. 28. Reproduced with the permission of American Cyanamid Company.

Table 69

Critical Values of T_l in the Wilcoxon Signed Rank Sum Test for the Matched Pairs Experiment

n	$P(T \le T_L) = .05$	.025	.01	.005	n	$P(T \le T_L) = .05$	.025	.01	.005
	T_L	T_L	T_L	T_L		T_L	T_L	T_L	T_L
5	1	—	—	—	28	130	117	102	92
6	2	1	—	—	29	141	127	111	100
7	4	2	0	—	30	152	137	120	109
8	6	4	2	0	31	163	148	130	118
9	8	6	3	2	32	175	159	141	128
10	11	8	5	3	33	188	171	151	138
11	14	11	7	5	34	201	183	162	149
12	17	14	10	7	35	214	195	174	160
13	21	17	13	10	36	228	208	186	171
14	26	21	16	13	37	242	222	198	183
15	30	25	20	16	38	256	235	211	195
16	36	30	24	19	39	271	250	224	208
17	41	35	28	23	40	287	264	238	221
18	47	40	33	28	41	303	279	252	234
19	54	46	38	32	42	319	295	267	248
20	60	52	43	37	43	336	311	281	262
21	68	59	49	43	44	353	327	297	277
22	75	66	56	49	45	371	344	313	292
23	83	73	62	55	46	389	361	329	307
24	92	81	69	61	47	408	379	345	323
25	101	90	77	68	48	427	397	362	339
26	110	98	85	76	49	446	415	380	356
27	120	107	93	84	50	466	434	398	373

SOURCE: From F. Wilcoxon and R. A. Wilcox, "Some Rapid Approximate Statistical Procedures" (1964), p. 28. Reproduced with the permission of American Cyanamid Company.

Table 10

Critical Values of the

Kolmogorov-Smirnov Test

Sample Size n	Significance Level α				
	.20	.10	.05	.02	.01
1	.900	.950	.975	.990	.995
2	.684	.776	.842	.900	.929
3	.565	.636	.708	.785	.829
4	.493	.565	.624	.689	.734
5	.447	.509	.563	.627	.669
6	.410	.468	.519	.577	.617
7	.381	.436	.483	.538	.576
8	.358	.410	.454	.507	.542
9	.339	.387	.430	.480	.513
10	.323	.369	.409	.457	.489
11	.308	.352	.391	.437	.468
12	.296	.338	.375	.419	.449
13	.285	.325	.361	.404	.432
14	.275	.314	.349	.390	.418
15	.266	.304	.338	.377	.404
16	.258	.295	.327	.366	.392
17	.250	.286	.318	.355	.381
18	.244	.279	.309	.346	.371
19	.237	.271	.301	.337	.361
20	.232	.265	.294	.329	.352
21	.226	.259	.287	.321	.344
22	.221	.253	.281	.314	.337
23	.216	.247	.275	.307	.330
24	.212	.242	.269	.301	.323
25	.208	.238	.264	.295	.317
26	.204	.233	.259	.290	.311
27	.200	.229	.254	.284	.305
28	.197	.225	.250	.279	.300
29	.193	.221	.246	.275	.295
30	.190	.218	.242	.270	.290
31	.187	.214	.238	.266	.285
32	.184	.211	.234	.262	.281
33	.182	.208	.231	.258	.277
34	.179	.205	.227	.254	.273
35	.177	.202	.224	.251	.269
36	.174	.199	.221	.247	.265
37	.172	.196	.218	.244	.262
38	.170	.194	.215	.241	.258
39	.168	.191	.213	.238	.255
40	.165	.189	.210	.235	.252
Over 40	$\dfrac{1.07}{\sqrt{n}}$	$\dfrac{1.22}{\sqrt{n}}$	$\dfrac{1.36}{\sqrt{n}}$	$\dfrac{1.52}{\sqrt{n}}$	$\dfrac{1.63}{\sqrt{n}}$

SOURCE: From L. H. Miller, "Tables of Percentage Points of the Kolmogorov Statistics," *Journal of the American Statistical Association* 51 (1956): 111–21. As adapted by Conover, *Practical Nonparametric Statistics* (New York: John Wiley, 1971), p. 397. Reprinted by permission of John Wiley & Sons, Inc., and the American Statistical Association.

Table 11

Critical Values of the Spearman Rank Correlation Coefficient

The α values correspond to a one-tail test of H_0: $\rho_s = 0$. The value should be doubled for two-tail tests.

n	$\alpha = .05$	$\alpha = .025$	$\alpha = .01$	$\alpha = .005$
5	.900	—	—	—
6	.829	.886	.943	—
7	.714	.786	.893	—
8	.643	.738	.833	.881
9	.600	.683	.783	.833
10	.564	.648	.745	.794
11	.523	.623	.736	.818
12	.497	.591	.703	.780
13	.475	.566	.673	.745
14	.457	.545	.646	.716
15	.441	.525	.623	.689
16	.425	.507	.601	.666
17	.412	.490	.582	.645
18	.399	.476	.564	.625
19	.388	.462	.549	.608
20	.377	.450	.534	.591
21	.368	.438	.521	.576
22	.359	.428	.508	.562
23	.351	.418	.496	.549
24	.343	.409	.485	.537
25	.336	.400	.475	.526
26	.329	.392	.465	.515
27	.323	.385	.456	.505
28	.317	.377	.448	.496
29	.311	.370	.440	.487
30	.305	.364	.432	.478

SOURCE: From E. G. Olds, "Distribution of Sums of Squares of Rank Differences for Small Samples," *Annals of Mathematical Statistics* 9 (1938). Reproduced with the permission of the Institute of Mathematical Statistics.

Table 12

Random Numbers

Row	1	2	3	4	5	6	7	8	9	10	11	12	13	14
1	13284	16834	74151	92027	24670	36665	00770	22878	02179	51602	07270	76517	97275	45960
2	21224	00370	30420	03883	96648	89428	41583	17564	27395	63904	41548	49197	82277	24120
3	99052	47887	81085	64933	66279	80432	65793	83287	34142	13241	30590	97760	35848	91983
4	00199	50993	98603	38452	87890	94624	69721	57484	67501	77638	44331	11257	71131	11059
5	60578	06483	28733	37867	07936	98710	98539	27186	31237	80612	44488	97819	70401	95419
6	91240	18312	17441	01929	18163	69201	31211	54288	39296	37318	65724	90401	79017	62077
7	97458	14229	12063	59611	32249	90466	33216	19358	02591	54263	88449	01912	07436	50813
8	35249	38646	34475	72417	60514	69257	12489	51924	86871	92446	36607	11458	30440	52639
9	38980	46600	11759	11900	46743	27860	77940	39298	97838	95145	32378	68038	89351	37005
10	10750	52745	38749	87365	58959	53731	89295	59062	39404	13198	59960	70408	29812	83126
11	36247	27850	73958	20673	37800	63835	71051	84724	52492	22342	78071	17456	96104	18327
12	70994	66986	99744	72438	01174	42159	11392	20724	54322	36923	70009	23233	65438	59685
13	99638	94702	11463	18148	81386	80431	90628	52506	02016	85151	88598	47821	00265	82525
14	72055	15774	43857	99805	10419	76939	25993	03544	21560	83471	43989	90770	22965	44247
15	24038	65541	85788	55835	38835	59399	13790	35112	01324	39520	76210	22467	83275	32286
16	74976	14631	35908	28221	39470	91548	12854	30166	09073	75887	36782	00268	97121	57676
17	35553	71628	70189	26436	63407	91178	90348	55359	80392	41012	36270	77786	89578	21059
18	35676	12797	51434	82976	42010	26344	92920	92155	58807	54644	58581	95331	78629	73344
19	74815	67523	72985	23183	02446	63594	98924	20633	58842	85961	07648	70164	34994	67662
20	45246	88048	65173	50989	91060	89894	36063	32819	68559	99221	49475	50558	34698	71800
21	76509	47069	86378	41797	11910	49672	88575	97966	32466	10083	54728	81972	58975	30761
22	19689	90332	04315	21358	97248	11188	39062	63312	52496	07349	79178	33692	57352	72862
23	42751	35318	97513	61537	54955	08159	00337	80778	27507	95478	21252	12746	37554	97775
24	11946	22681	45045	13964	57517	59419	58045	44067	58716	58840	45557	96345	33271	53464
25	96518	48688	20996	11090	48396	57177	83867	86464	14342	21545	46717	72364	86954	55580

Column

Table 12
Continues

26	35726	58643	76869	84622	39098	36083	72505	92265	23107	60278	05822	46760	44294	07672
27	39737	42750	48968	70536	84864	64952	38404	94317	65402	13589	01055	79044	19308	83623
28	97025	66492	56177	04049	80312	48028	26408	43591	75528	65341	49044	95495	81256	53214
29	62814	08075	09788	56350	76787	51591	54509	49295	85830	59860	30883	89660	96142	18354
30	25578	22950	15227	83291	41737	79599	96191	71845	86899	70694	24290	01551	80092	82118
31	68763	69576	88991	49662	46704	63362	56625	00481	73323	91427	15264	06969	57048	54149
32	17900	00813	64361	60725	88974	61005	99709	30666	26451	11528	44323	34778	60342	60388
33	71944	60227	63551	71109	05624	43836	58254	26160	32116	63403	35404	57146	10909	07346
34	54684	93691	85132	64399	29182	44324	14491	55226	78793	34107	30374	48429	51376	09559
35	25946	27623	11258	65204	52832	50880	22273	05554	99521	73791	85744	29276	70326	60251
36	01353	39318	44961	44972	91766	90262	56073	06606	51826	18893	83448	31915	97764	75091
37	99083	88191	27662	99113	57174	35571	99884	13951	71057	53961	61448	74909	07322	80960
38	52021	45406	37945	75234	24327	86978	22644	87779	23753	99926	63898	54886	18051	96314
39	78755	47744	43776	83098	03225	14281	83637	55984	13300	52212	58781	14905	46502	04472
40	25282	69106	59180	16257	22810	43609	12224	25643	89884	31149	85423	32581	34374	70873
41	11959	94202	02743	86847	79725	51811	12998	76844	05320	54236	53891	70226	38632	84776
42	11644	13792	98190	01424	30078	28197	55583	05197	47714	68440	22016	79204	06862	94451
43	06307	97912	68110	59812	95448	43244	31262	88880	13040	16458	43813	89416	42482	33939
44	76285	75714	89585	99296	52640	46518	55486	90754	88932	19937	57119	23251	55619	23679
45	55322	07589	39600	60866	63007	20007	66819	84164	61131	81429	60676	42807	78286	29015
46	78017	90928	90220	92503	83375	26986	74399	30885	88567	29169	72816	53357	15428	86932
47	44768	43342	20696	26331	43140	69744	82928	24988	94237	46138	77426	39039	55596	12655
48	25100	19336	14605	86603	51680	97678	24261	02464	86563	74812	60069	71674	15478	47642
49	83612	46623	62876	85197	07824	91392	58317	37726	84628	42221	10268	20692	15699	29167
50	41347	81666	82961	60413	71020	83658	02415	33322	66036	98712	46795	16308	28413	05417

Source: Abridged from W. H. Beyer, ed., *CRC Standard Mathematical Tables*, 26th ed. (Boca Raton: CRC Press, 1981). Reproduced by permission of the publisher. Copyright CRC Press, Inc., Boca Raton, Florida.

Kathleen Fahy

Dr Kathleen Fahy is Dean of Nursing and Midwifery at Newcastle University, Australia. She is professor of midwifery with practicing rights at the John Hunter Hospital. Kathleen was a member of a Ministerial Inquiry into neonatal deaths at The King Edward Memorial Hospital in Western Australia. She led the design and conducts the clinical file review for the Inquiry using qualitative methods. Kathleen holds a degree in Nursing, a Master of Education and a PhD in Sociology.

Kathleen's research and scholarship is within a postmodern, feminist framework and is concerned with issues of women's access to physically, psychologically, and culturally safe and satisfying childbearing experiences. Her papers have appeared in nursing, midwifery and health journals including the international journal Health, Nursing Inquiry and Nursing Practice. Kathleen is a member of the Editorial Board of the Australian Journal of Midwifery and the New Zealand Journal of Midwifery.

Karey Harrison

Dr. Karey Harrison has been lecturing in Communication Studies at the University of South Queensland since 1992. Prior to that she lectured in philosophy for five years at various institutions in the United States, including two years as a Mellon Fellow at Rice University in Houston, Texas where she taught teaching philosophy of science, philosophy of psychology, philosophy of mind, and feminist and critical theory. Her research into the ways in which metaphors frame scientific, political, economic, and ethical discourses has proven to be a useful tool to substantiate and develop feminist critiques of disciplinary and theoretical biases. This approach underpins her analysis of epistemological and methodological frameworks in this volume. In 2001 she was an invited speaker at the International Association for Feminist Economics (IAFFE) Conference in Oslo, and in 2002 was an invited speaker at the Agent Modeling and Cross-Disciplinary Discourse Conference in Las Cruces.

Ronit Hanegby

Dr. Ronit Hanegby received her PhD in Educational Administration from Tel-Aviv University in 1998 and at the same time founded Eastat Ltd. She taught in the school of education at Tel Aviv University and Zinman College for Sport Physical

Education. Since 2000 Dr. Hanegby is serving as a partner and scientific director of several Israeli and international companies. Dr. Hanegby specializes in the applications of advanced statistical methodologies in organizations. Her academic interests are mainly in knowledge based management, applications of Structural Equation Modeling and Multilevel analysis and data-mining. Eastat Ltd. is involved in developing solutions to financial institutions, Automotive Industry, and online companies using predictive modeling algorithms.

David Kaplan

Dr Kaplan received his Ph.D. in education from UCLA in 1987, and is currently Professor in the School of Education and (by courtesy) the Department of Psychology at the University of Delaware. Dr. Kaplan's research interests are in the development and application of statistical models to problems in educational evaluation and policy analysis. Mainly he has published on statistical issues in latent variable modeling - including structural equation modeling, factor analysis and latent growth curve modeling. His current program of research concerns the development of dynamic continuous and categorical latent variable models for studying the diffusion of educational innovations. He has been a consultant to the U.S Department of Education and the Organization for Economic Cooperation and Development (OECD). Dr. Kaplan's research has been supported by the National Science Foundation, the National Institutes of Health, the U.S. Department of Education, and the Spencer Foundation. During the 2001-2002 academic years, Dr Kaplan was the Jeanne Griffiths Fellow at the National Center for Education Statistics.

Eitan Eldar

Dr. Eitan Eldar is a graduate of the Zinman College of Physical Education and Sport Sciences at the Wingate Institute, Israel, and completed his doctoral studies at Ohio State University in the area of Teacher Education and Applied Behavior Analysis. Today he heads the School of Education and the Applied Behavior Analysis Program at the Zinman College. He is the chairman of IABA - the Israeli Applied Behavior Analysis Association and Vice President of AIESEP - The International Association for Physical Education in Higher Education. In addition to Dr. Eldar's experience as a physical education teacher and team handball coach, he has served as a behavior analyst for various soccer and basketball teams as well as for Israel's national basketball team. He developed the Behavior Rehabilitation through Sport Model, through which students acquire self-control and cooperation skills. He teaches pedagogy, applied behavior analysis, and single subject research methods at Zinman College and at Haifa University, Israel. Dr. Eldar is a staunch proponent of single subject research methodology as an appropriate and effective empirical and clinical tool in the fields of sport, education, and teacher education. For two decades he has trained students and clinicians in this area, as well as conducting a variety of studies based on this methodology.

Gretchen Kluter Ghent

Gretchen Ghent is a Librarian Emeritus at the University of Calgary, having taken early retirement after serving 25 years from staff librarian to in her last position as Head of the Sciences/Professions Area in the University of Calgary Library. A founding member and currently the Chair of the North American Sport Library Network, she also is Vice-President for North America and Publications Officer for the International Association for Sports Information and a member of the Editorial Board of the International Council for Sport Science and Physical Education. Her website, Scholarly Sport Sites: a Subject Directory was created in 1999 to assist IASI, NASLIN and the academic community with links to important resources for sport sciences research. She was the main editor and a contributor to the ICSSPE publication, Perspectives, Vol. 4, Sport and Information Technology (2002) and contributes regularly to ICSSPE's Bulletin. She is currently the editor of NASLINE, the e-newsletter of the North American Sport Library Network and the IASI Newsletter.

Andrea Lamont-Mills

Dr. Andrea Lamont-Mills is a lecturer in the Department of Psychology, University of Southern Queensland, Toowoomba, Australia. Dr. Lamont-Mills teaches in the undergraduate Psychology program in Research Methods and Sport Psychology. She is particularly interested in how discursive practices (language) influence how we think, feel, and behave. Thus working from a discursive psychological position, her current research interests are in understanding how injury pain is discursively negotiated in the athlete-physiotherapist interaction and understanding how exercise behavior is discursively accounted for in everyday conversations.

Mark Rapley

Mark Rapley is a Professor of Human and Community Studies, School of International and Community Studies, at Edith Cowan University, Western Australia. His research primarily focuses on developing a discursive psychological understanding of the doing of power in everyday interaction. This work, which draws on the sociology of scientific knowledge, ethnomethodology and Wittgensteinian ordinary language philosophy to respecify social psychology, has examined the management of racism in political and everyday talk, the production of disability as a social identity and the subordination of the client in psychotherapy. He lives in Fremantle with Susan, Tom, and Ella.

Perspectives, Volume 4
Gretchen Ghent, Darlene Kluka & Denise Jones (eds.)

Sport and Information Technology

This collection of articles in this special issue of Perspectives reflects a part of the wide range of sport information.

It includes articles on the delivery of audiovisual information to coaches, the use of the internet and websites to find information as well as the functions and the evolution of the sport documentation centre.

192 pages
31 figures, 5 tables
Paperback, 5^3/4" x 8^1/4"
ISBN 1-84126-086-X
£ 14.95 UK/$ 19.95 US
$ 29.95 CDN/€ 20.90

Perspectives offers:

The thorough dissemination of sport science information to all interested organisations and institutions, and the application of sport science results to practical areas of sport. In each volume of Perspectives, expert contributions from several different sport science disciplines address relevant physical education and sport science themes.

Reinhard Stelter & Kirsten Kaya Roessler

New Approaches to Sport and Exercise Psychology

The book is a collection of the keynote addresses of the 11th European Congress of Sport Psychology in Copenhagen, July 2003. It includes three additional articles, one from the president of the congress, Reinhard Stelter, one from the winner of the Young Researchers award, and one from the new president of FEPSAC. The book is an important contribution to the future development of sport.

192 pages
5 photos, 15 illustrations
Paperback, 6^1/2" x 9^1/4"
ISBN: 1-84126-149-1
£ 14.95 UK/$ 19.95 US
$ 29.95 CDN/€ 18.90

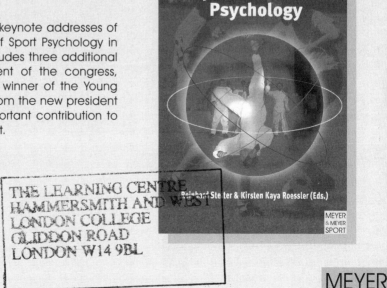

MEYER & MEYER Sport | sales@m-m-sports.com | www.m-m-sports.com

MEYER & MEYER SPORT